# Iconic Books and Texts

# Iconic Books and Texts

Edited by
James W. Watts

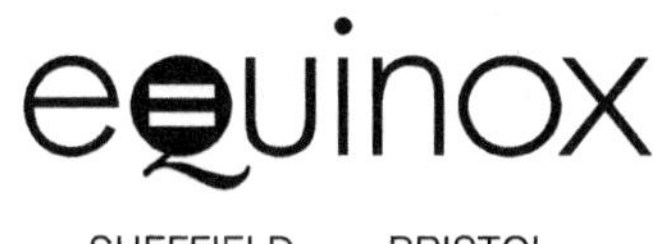

SHEFFIELD UK BRISTOL CT

Published by Equinox Publishing Ltd.

UK: Office 415, The Workstation, 15 Paternoster Row, Sheffield, S1 2BX
USA: ISD, 70 Enterprise Drive, Bristol, CT 06010

www.equinoxpub.com

First published in Volume 2.2-3 and Volume 6.1-3 of the journal *Postscripts*.


First published in book form 2013.
Paperback edition published 2015.



ISBN 978-1-78179-254-4 (paperback)

**British Library Cataloguing-in-Publication Data**

A catalogue record for this book is available from the British Library.

**Library of Congress Cataloging-in-Publication Data**

Iconic books and texts / edited by James W. Watts.
p. cm.
Proceedings of 3 symposiums held 2007-2010.
Includes bibliographical references and index.
ISBN 978-1-78179-254-4 (pb)
1. Sacred books--Congresses. 2. Books--Religious aspects--Congresses. I. Watts, James W. (James Washington), 1960-
BL71.I36 2012
208'.2--dc23

2011033512

Edited and Typeset by Queenston Publishing, Hamilton Canada.

Printed and bound in the UK.

# Contents

*Contributors*

Introduction 1
*James W. Watts*

**I. Categorizing Iconic Books**

1. The Three Dimensions of Scriptures 9
*James W. Watts*

2. "Winged Words": Scriptures and Classics as Iconic Texts 33
*William A. Graham*

3. Talking about "Iconic Books" in the Terminology of Book History 47
*Deirdre C. Stam*

**II. Images and Texts**

4. The Iconic Book: The Image of the Bible in Early Christian Rituals 63
*Dorina Miller Parmenter*

5. Images to be Read and Words to be Seen: The Iconic Role of the Early Medieval Book 93
*Michelle P. Brown*

6. Looking at Words: The Iconicity of the Page 119
*S. Brent Plate*

7. Between the Textual and the Visual: Borderlines of Late Antique Book Iconicity 135
*Zeev Elitzur*

8. It Is What It Is (Or Is It?): Further Reflections on the Buddhist Representation of Manuscripts 151
*Jacob Kinnard*

9. The Tell-Tale Iconic Book 165
*M. Patrick Graham*

**III. Materials and Markets**

10. *Muṣḥaf* and the Material Boundaries of the Qur'an 189
*Natalia K. Suit*

11. The End of the Word as We Know It: The Cultural Iconicity of the Bible in the Twilight of Print Culture 207
*Timothy Beal*

12. Iconic Books from Below: The Christian Bible and the Discourse of Duct Tape 225
*Dorina Miller Parmenter*

13. Be-Witching Scripture: The *Book of Shadows* as Scripture within Wicca/Neopagan Witchcraft 239
*Shawn Loner*

**IV. Book Rituals**

14. Engaging with the Guru: Sikh Beliefs and Practices of Guru Granth Sahib 261
*Kristina Myrvold*

15. A Birthday Party for a Sacred Text: The Gita Jayanti and the Embodiment of God as the Book and the Book as God 283
*Joanne Punzo Waghorne*

16. Possession and Repetition: Ways in which Korean Lay Buddhists Appropriate Scriptures 299
*Yohan Yoo*

17. The Bible in British Folklore 315
*Brian Malley*

**V. Power and Scholarship**

18. The Pride and Prejudice of the Western World: Canonic Memory, Great Books and Archive Fever 347
*Karl Ivan Solibakke*

19. Indigenous "Texts" of Inhabiting the Land: George Washington's Wampum Belt and the Canandaigua Treaty 361
*Philip P. Arnold*

20. The Gospels as Imperialized Sites of Memory in Late Ancient Christianity 373
*Jason T. Larson*

21. Possessing the Iconic Book: Ben Sira as Case Study 389
*Claudia V. Camp*

22. Ancient Iconic Texts and Scholarly Expertise 407
*James W. Watts*

*Acknowledgements* 419
*Author Index* 421
*Subject Index* 429

# Contributors

Philip P. Arnold is Associate Professor of Religion at Syracuse University in Syracuse, New York and Founding Director of the Skänoñh—Great Law of Peace Center.

Timothy Beal is the Florence Harkness Professor of Religion at Case Western Reserve University in Cleveland, Ohio

Michelle P. Brown is Professor of Medieval Manuscript Studies at the School of Advanced Study, University of London

Claudia V. Camp is Weatherly Professor of Religion at Texas Christian University in Fort Worth, Texas

Zeev Elitzur is head of the Humanities Department at the Israel Center for Excellence through Education in Jerusalem

M. Patrick Graham is Margaret A. Pitts Professor of Theological Bibliography and Librarian at Candler School of Theology, Emory University in Atlanta, Georgia

William A. Graham is Murray A. Albertson Professor of Middle Eastern Studies at Harvard University in Cambridge, Massachusetts

Jacob Kinnard is Associate Professor of Comparative Religious Thought at the Iliff School of Theology in Denver, Colorado

Jason T. Larson is Instructor in Religion and Philosophy at The Hotchkiss School in Lakeville, Connecticut

Shawn Loner is a Ph.D. student in Religion and Graduate Assistant in the Graduate School at Syracuse University in Syracuse, New York

Brian Malley is a Lecturer in the Department of Psychology at the University of Michigan in Ann Arbor

Kristina Myrvold is Assistant Professor of Religious Studies at Linnaeus University in Sweden

Dorina Miller Parmenter is Assistant Professor of Religious Studies at Spalding University in Louisville, Kentucky

S. Brent Plate is Visiting Associate Professor of Religious Studies at Hamilton College in Clinton, New York

Karl Ivan Solibakke is Assistant Research Professor in German at Syracuse University in Syracuse, New York

Deirdre C. Stam is Associate Professor at the Palmer School of Library and Information Science at Long Island University in New York

Natalia K. Suit is a Ph.D. student in Anthropology at the University of North Carolina Chapel Hill

Joanne Punzo Waghorne is Professor of Religion at Syracuse University in Syracuse, New York

James W. Watts is Professor of Religion at Syracuse University in Syracuse, New York

Yohan Yoo is Associate Professor of Religious Studies at Seoul National University in Korea

# Introduction

James W. Watts

In 2001, I taught a graduate seminar for the first time on "the idea of scripture." It covered the canonization, reception, and interpretive traditions of the scriptures of Judaism, Christianity and Islam. Half-way through the semester, one student pointed out that the course syllabus omitted any readings or discussion about the forms and functions of the physical books of scripture. When I tried to fill out the course bibliography with readings on this topic, I discovered to my great surprise a large gap in scholarship. There are, of course, extensive bibliographies on the manuscript traditions of religious texts and, to a lesser extent, on their histories of print publication. But aside from some seminal essays on the form and function of material scriptures in specific cultures and periods (Gregory Schopen on early Mahayana Buddhism, Martin Marty on American culture, Karel van der Toorn on early Judaism), I found very few discussions of the symbolism and social power of books, and even less comparative analysis of this phenomenon across cultures and history.

That student, Dorina Miller Parmenter, and I set out to collect a pictorial and digital database of books and other texts whose forms or images carry significant cultural symbolism and/or which are used as props in ritual performances of various kinds. We did not limit the collection to religious scriptures, but instead tried to include every kind of book or text that carried such "iconic" cultural force. As the scope of our database expanded, its contents revealed implications for understanding phenomena as diverse as the marketing of e-books, radical Islamic uses of media images, the relationship between image and text in Buddhism, the role of religion in U.S. law, the distinctive nature of library architecture, and the historical influence of scriptural religions.

It also became clear that we needed help in understanding the phenomenon in its diverse cultural and historical contexts and in considering how they could legitimately be compared. That need was addressed by a series of three symposia held at Syracuse University in 2007 and 2010 and at Hamilton College in 2009. These symposia brought together scholars (see list below) specializing in diverse cultures and historical periods, including ancient Christianity, medieval Indian Buddhism, medieval insular book production, comparative religions, art history, globalization and religion, contemporary American iconography, Sikh traditions, Native American cultures, Muslim traditions, media studies, ancient Near Eastern cultures, cognitive psychology, Hindu traditions, Jewish culture, histories of the book, and library studies. At the first two symposia, participants were asked simply to share some material pertaining to iconic books and texts. The wide-ranging discussions that followed compared and contrasted various text practices and also experimented with possible theoretical formulations of the phenomenon. Panelists were then asked to write formal papers that were circulated and discussed at the last symposium. After further revisions in light of all three symposia, those papers were published in a thematic issue of the journal, *Postscripts* (vol. 6, 2010) that appeared in 2012. Together with four articles on iconic books from an earlier issue of *Postscripts* (vol. 2.2–3, 2006, published in 2008), they are presented here to make them more accessible to a wider audience.

One persistent strand in the discussions of all three symposia involved terminology: what should the subject that elicited our common interest be called? Dori Parmenter and I debated that issue when first embarking on this project. After considering and rejecting possibilities such as "idol," "fetish," and "talisman," we settled on the adjective "iconic" to describe the form and social function of these books and texts. Though each of the other terms have long and useful histories of critical development in several fields of scholarship, they also carry pejorative connotations that would hinder the project more than help it. The term "icon" also carries a very long history of polemical as well as critical analysis. However, the issues that swirl around it seem more likely to provoke further insight and reflection, as Vincent Wimbush argued in the first symposium, even if the term itself is ultimately inadequate to cover the range of phenomena under discussion.

As it turned out, however, Parmenter (see Chapter 4 below) does employ theories of icons developed by Greek iconophiles during the medieval Byzantine iconoclastic controversies to theorize the nature of the Christian Bible as precisely an "icon" in this strict sense. I build on her work to characterize the "iconic" dimension of books and texts as one of three dimensions in which texts may be ritualized (the others are the performative and semantic dimensions; see Chapter 1 below). Some of our interlocutors who accept, at least in broad strokes, the direction of our theorizing nevertheless still protested that the term "iconic" carries too many Christian implications to be suitable to the texts of other religions and cultures. Our discussions, however, failed to produce a term more acceptable to the group as a whole. Nevertheless, most participants do feel that there is an important and understudied phenomenon that links our research together. Therefore, the volume carries the title, "Iconic Books and Texts," even if many would prefer a different label, or none at all. (Adam Shear in a personal communication suggested calling it simply "the third dimension.")

A second persistent topic of methodological reflection in the symposia involved the problem of cross-cultural comparison. The participants were very aware of the strong and well-founded criticisms in, especially, the fields of religious studies and anthropology against facile comparative studies. They were nevertheless drawn to the symposia out of recognition of an understudied phenomenon, or set of similar phenomena, involving iconic books and texts in various cultures and time periods. The symposia discussions did not produce methodological agreement on how to do such comparisons, but did demonstrate the illuminating effect of juxtaposing diverse cultural materials along with their ritual, social and political contexts.

In accord with this impulse, the papers in this volume have been arranged under broad themes rather than by culture or time period. The groupings do not do justice to their contents, since every piece addresses most of the other themes as well as the one under which it appears. Other topical arrangements would certainly be possible. By placing them under these headings, I hope to reproduce for readers the stimulating experience of alternating amazement and recognition that the seminar and symposia discussions provided to their participants. The headings also serve to put readers on notice that the study of iconic books and texts has wide-ranging intellectual, religious, social, economic and political implications.

The first section contains essays that address the central problem of how to differentiate and classify iconic texts from other kinds of texts. In the first chapter, I argue that texts function in three dimensions—iconic, performative, and semantic—and that scriptures are regularly ritualized in all three. William Graham (Chapter 2) provides a cross-cultural typology that distinguishes religious and cultural classics from scriptures, though they all exhibit features of iconicity. Deirdre Stam (Chapter 3) introduces some standard categories and vocabulary from the antique book trade and book history that can be used to specify exactly what features of a text give it iconic status.

The visual appearance of books and texts fuels much of the interest in textual iconicity. The second section therefore contains those essays that give particular attention to the imagery of texts. Dorina Parmenter (Chapter 4) argues that the medieval iconophiles' insight that icons and scripture are functionally equivalent applies to Bibles in most periods of Christian history. Michelle Brown (Chapter 5) paints a vivid portrait of book culture in the early Middle Ages from the Sinai peninsula to Ireland to show how Gospels books were given iconic status and in turn established the iconicity of the codex book form. Brent Plate (Chapter 6) analyzes the visible forms of words in examples ranging from modern popular typography to European Christian print culture to Islamic calligraphy to show that written words function iconically to produce a form of "religious seeing." Zeev Elitzur (Chapter 7) argues that the iconicity of scripture was developed in two different directions in antiquity: Jewish interpreters increasingly focused on the iconic sign while

Christians increasingly celebrated the iconic image of the book. Jacob Kinnard (Chapter 8) wonders if images of books in medieval Buddhist art represent the use of real books or are rather polemical statements about the role books should play in devotion. Patrick Graham (Chapter 9) catalogs the purposes for which books were displayed in sixteenth-century European printed images of themes related to biblical interpretation.

Despite all the attention to how books look, an iconic book remains a physical object that can be handled, bought and sold. The third section contains essays that assess the impact of iconicity on how people behave with and in the presence of books, how they market them, and how marketing as scripture shapes the books themselves. Natalia Suit (Chapter 10) summarizes her field research in Cairo, Egypt, on customs for the proper handling of copies of Qur'ans. Timothy Beal (Chapter 11) wonders if the ever-increasing plurality of forms in which publishers market Bibles may be undermining the cultural idea of this scripture's unity and consistency. Dorina Miller Parmenter (Chapter 12) studies the contemporary backlash against commercial Bibles represented by people treasuring and taping together tattered scriptures rather than replacing them with new ones. Shawn Loner (Chapter 13) demonstrates that iconic form preceded contents in the twentieth-century evolution of the Wiccan Book of Shadows.

It is through ritualization that books become iconic. The essays in the fourth section focus particular attention on the ritual treatment of scriptures. Kristina Myrvold (Chapter 14) summarizes how Sikh rituals embody the belief that the scripture functions as a living guru. Joanne Punzo Waghorne (Chapter 15) describes a birthday party for the Bhagavad Gita, a recent ritual innovation that is gaining popularity among Hindus in Singapore. Yohan Yoo (Chapter 16) collects examples of how Korean Buddhists attempt to gain merit by possessing sutras and repeating their message, often adapting internet technology to this end. Brian Malley (Chapter 17) assesses the practices and conflicts involved in manipulating scriptures in British folklore.

People ritualize books and texts in order to legitimize or challenge power relationships. The essays in the last section address especially the social power mediated by iconic books and texts. Karl Solibakke (Chapter 18) charts the ideological concerns motivating the curriculum and publication of the "Great Books" series in twentieth-century America. Philip Arnold (Chapter 19) describes the use and abuse of wampum in eighteenth-century treaties between Native American peoples and the U.S. federal government. Jason Larson (Chapter 20) explains the development of Christian scriptures, and especially Gospels, in the second-through-fifth-century context of imperial Roman textuality. Claudia Camp (Chapter 21) exposes the gendered ideology of scribal power in the third-century BCE book by Jesus ben Sira. And in the last chapter, I categorize four forms of ancient Near Eastern iconic textuality to demonstrate how the iconic dimension continues to this day to empower non-scholars while experts dominate the semantic dimension of textual interpretation.

Projects in collaborative scholarship such as this become possible only through the support of many individuals and institutions. I deeply appreciate the work and generous spirit of all the authors represented in these pages and the many other people who contributed to this project by participating in the discussions of the seminars and symposia. The three symposia were made possible by generous financial underwriting from the Ray Smith Symposium of the College of Arts and Sciences at Syracuse University, from the Gladys Krieble Delmas Foundation, and from Hamilton College, through the active support of Deans Catherine Newton, George Langford, and Joseph Urgo, and of David Stam and Brent Plate. Elizabeth Castelli made possible the original publication of these essays in special issues of *Postscripts*, and Janet Joyce willingly agreed to their republication by Equinox in this volume. Wendy DeBoer prepared the indices. My heartfelt thanks to all.

Panelists at the Iconic Books Symposia in 2007, 2009, and 2010:

Philip Arnold (2007, 2009, 2010)
Timothy Beal (2009, 2010)
Michelle Brown (2007)
Claudia Camp (2010)
Zeev Elitzur (2009, 2010)
Lisa Gitelman (2009)
M. Patrick Graham (2009, 2010)
William Graham (2010)
Tazim Kassam (2007, 2009)
Jacob Kinnard (2007, 2010)
Jason Larson (2009, 2010)
Brian Malley (2007, 2010)
Gurinder Singh Mann (2009)
David Morgan (2007)
Kristina Myrvold (2009, 2010)
Dorina Miller Parmenter (2007, 2009, 2010)
Laurie Patton (2010)
S. Brent Plate (2009, 2010)
Claudia Rapp (2007, 2010)
Deepak Sarma (2007)
Karl Solibakke (2010)
Deirdre Stam (2010)
Natalia K. Suit (2010)
Joanne Punzo Waghorne (2009, 2010)
James Watts (2007, 2009, 2010)
Vincent Wimbush (2007, 2010)
Yohan Yoo (2009, 2010)

## References

Marty, Martin. 1982. "America's Iconic Book." In *Humanizing America's Iconic Book*, edited by Gene M. Tucker and Douglas A. Knight, 1–23. Chico, CA: Scholars Press.

Schopen, Gregory. 1975. "The Phrase 'sa prthivipradesas caityabhuto bhavet' in the Vajracchediku: Notes on the Cult of the Book in Mahayana." *Indo-Iranian Journal* 17: 147–181. http://dx.doi.org/10.1163/000000075790079574

Toorn, Karel van der. 1997. "The Iconic Book: Analogies Between the Babylonian Cult of Images and the Veneration of the Torah." In *The Image and the Book: Iconic Cults, Aniconism and the Rise of Book Religion in Israel and the Ancient Near East*, edited by K. van der Toorn, 229–248. Leuven: Peeters.

# I

# Categorizing Iconic Books

# 1

# The Three Dimensions of Scriptures

James W. Watts

*This essay proposes a new model for understanding the ways that scriptures function. Several big media stories of recent years, such as those surrounding controversies over Ten Commandments monuments in U.S. courthouses and Qur'ans desecrated at Guantánamo Bay, involve the iconic function of scriptures. Yet contemporary scholarship on Jewish, Christian, or Muslim scriptures is ill-prepared to interpret these events because it has focused almost all its efforts on textual interpretation. Even the increased attention to the performative function of scripture by Wilfred Cantwell Smith and his students does not provide resources for understanding the iconic roles of scriptures. This essay addresses the gap by theorizing the nature of scriptures as a function of their ritualization in three dimensions—semantic, performative, and iconic. The model provides a means for conceptualizing how traditions ritualize scriptures and how they claim and negotiate social power through this process.*

## The three dimensions of scriptures

The use and abuse of scriptures figured prominently in news stories of recent years (2003–2005). Courts and politicians in the United States led intense public debates over whether to display monuments of the Ten Commandments in public buildings. Tens of thousands of Muslims marched in streets around the world to protest news that American interrogators desecrated Qur'ans at the prison in Guantánamo Bay, Cuba. These events and the media coverage that they generated demonstrate that Muslim, Christian, and Jewish scriptures remain potent symbols in popular culture.

These controversies do not involve the interpretation of the meaning of these scriptures, nor even how they are to be learned or obeyed. They focus rather on the physical display and manipulation of scriptures. It is therefore not scriptures as texts or even as verbal performances that are at issue, but rather scriptures as physical symbols of religions, cultures, and ideas, that is, scriptures as icons.

Scholarship on religion and scriptures is ill-prepared to discuss and evaluate these developments. Modern research has focused on other aspects of the phenomenon of scripture. Scholars have devoted the vast majority of their time and publications to explaining the origins and meaning of scriptural texts. Thus, to take biblical studies as an example, modern research has focused on describing the process by which the Bible was composed and the original meaning intended by its authors. Biblical scholars have also given considerable attention to the process by which the Bible became scripture. Such studies of canonization, however, still concentrate on the Bible's semantic form and contents, that is, on questions of when particular books became part of the Jewish and Christian scriptures and under what circumstances.

Some time ago, Wilfred Cantwell Smith, a historian of religion, criticized biblical scholars for their preoccupation with origins, which he described as studying the Bible before it was Bible. He called for more historical and comparative studies of how the Bible *functions* as scripture (W. C. Smith 1971). In recent decades, many biblical scholars have in fact given more attention to the history of the Bible's interpretation. Some have even elevated subsequent meanings of biblical texts to the same level of importance as its original meaning to its authors. That begins to answer the challenge, but W. C. Smith envisioned an approach focused on more than just the history of interpretation. He advocated study of the Bible's religious functions and effects in comparison with the scriptures of other religious traditions.

It was left to some of Smith's own students to develop that approach. William Graham (1987), most prominently, argued that traditional scholarship on scriptures has ignored their *performative* function. He pointed out that the most characteristic uses of scriptures in various religious traditions and cultures have to do with their reading, recitation, and memorization rather than with their interpretation. Graham argued that such textual performances are just as important as exegesis, often more important, for understanding the cultural significance of scriptures.

Graham's study of performance was not comprehensive enough, however, to describe all the cultural functions of scriptures, or even all of their performative functions. His survey of the ways that texts are performed through reading, recitation, and memorization omitted or downplayed practices of performing the *contents* of scriptures. These take many forms, ranging from artistic depictions of scenes from scriptural narratives to the enactment of scriptural stories in dramas and, more recently, movies. Artistic and dramatic performances of scriptural contents have played prominent roles in Hindu and Christian cultures, among many others.[1] In fact, it is without doubt

1. Barbara A. Holdredge (2003, 144–146) presented an account of scripture in the W. C. Smith/ William Graham tradition that recognizes the cultural importance for African Americans of performances of scriptural contents, as well as scripture's iconic role. Nevertheless, like almost all other interpreters, she found the most legitimate and legitimizing uses of scripture

the dominant mode of scriptural performance in modern Christianity and has been reinforced by the media revolution of the twentieth century. The changes wrought by new technology, however, are not as innovative as might be imagined. Late nineteenth- and early twentieth-century culture, at least in America, was already infused with imaginary recreations of biblical landscapes and the extravagant staging of biblical epics (Long 2003).

Graham's omission of this aspect of scriptural performance led him to misrepresent the last five centuries of Christian history. He argued that, whereas previously most people's knowledge of scripture would have come through aural reception and oral recitation and memorization, such modes of oral performance have more recently been displaced by textual interpretation. That may have been true in some Protestant sub-cultures in some periods, but Graham's exclusive focus on performances of the words of texts obscured the fact that contemporary Christian culture remains infused and informed by scriptural performances. Anecdotal evidence suggests that most Christians' knowledge of the Bible is mediated by movies, music, and art as much as by reading the text for themselves. Dramatic and artistic performances of scriptural contents as well as public readings and musical performances of scriptural texts remain primary modes by which scripture influences people. If one included these more creative forms of scriptural performance alongside textual recitation, comparative and historical accounts of the use of scriptural performances would present a more balanced assessment of contemporary culture.

Even with such an augmentation of the kinds of performances included in the study of scriptures as advocated by Smith and Graham, however, we are still in no better position to explain news about protests over desecrations of the Qur'an or court battles over Ten Commandments monuments. These conflicts concern neither scriptural interpretation nor performance. Something is still missing in the scholarship on scriptures, namely research on its iconicity. *Scriptures are icons.* They are not just texts to be interpreted and performed. They are material objects that convey religious significance by their production, display, and ritual manipulation.

Martin Marty (1982) called attention twenty-five years ago to the Bible's role as "America's Iconic Book." He argued that, more than its contents, the book itself has become a dominant symbol in the nation's mental "carapace." Other scholars have noted the iconic function of scriptures in various periods and cultures. Karel van der Toorn (1997) pointed out that, in ancient Judaism, Torah scrolls functioned ritually in the same manner as divine images did in Babylonian religions. Rather than being the aniconic religion of modern scholars' imaginations, he argued that Judaism simply focused iconic attention on the scrolls themselves. Jacob Kinnard (1999, 2002) has documented

to involve the interpretation of their words: "It was the *content* of the Bible—not simply its status as a sacred object—that captivated the imagination of the slaves, catalyzing their devotion, nurturing their hopes, inspiring their visions, and fuelling their rhetoric" (147).

book veneration in medieval Indian Buddhism. Its practice by the Buddhist Nichiren sect, Soka Gakkai, in contemporary Japan is well known. Michelle Brown (2003) described the devotional function of Christian manuscript illustration in medieval England. A survey of African-Americans' use of the Bible documented the book's widespread iconic use in addition to its contents being a source for interpretation (Shopshire, Mukenge, Erickson, and Baer 2003). Until now, however, there has been no comparative historical research that gathers these diverse studies into a more comprehensive analysis of the nature and function of iconic books.

Dorina Miller Parmenter is now engaged in research to construct a broader theoretical understanding of iconic books (see Chapter 4, below). Starting with scripture's ritual manipulation and display in Christian traditions, she describes the parallel between Eastern Orthodox Christians' use of images of saints (icons) and scriptures. Both icons and scriptures are handled in rituals and displayed prominently, both receive veneration, both are believed to mediate divine presence. She is also studying the history of myths of heavenly books—divine documents in heaven that determine human destinies and prescribe religious practices. Such myths have their origins as early as the Babylonian and Egyptian cultures of the second millennium BCE and remain pervasive in the modern era. Parmenter argues therefore that, like Orthodox icons, iconic scriptures are not only potent religious symbols. They are also believed to participate in a heavenly exemplar of which they are the earthly manifestations.

This research lays the basis for a better understanding of the scriptures in our news headlines. Clearly, iconic scriptures remain powerful motivators in contemporary cultures. New research into iconic books as a trans-cultural, trans-historical phenomenon should shed interesting light on current developments. The iconic aspect of scriptures, however, also needs to be understood in relation to scriptures' other religious and cultural functions. It is therefore time to develop an explanatory model of scriptures with the capacity to include all of their aspects and effects.

The history of comparative studies of scriptures cautions us that this enterprise can easily become a tool for inter-religious polemic and supercessionism, rather than for inter-cultural understanding. For example, the traditional Muslim recognition of the three "religions of the book" (Judaism and Christianity, in addition to Islam) creates a polemical hierarchy of religions that is a typical strategy in all three Western traditions. The idea of scripture has been used from antiquity as a religious yard-stick to measure the distance of other cultures from the epitome of divine "truth" in the Torah, the New Testament, or the Qur'an (Graham 1987, 47). Early attempts to provide more balanced comparisons between religious traditions nevertheless tended to export the Western model. Thus Max Müller's massive series of books introducing nineteenth-century Europeans to "eastern" traditions presented them under the title, *The Sacred Books of the East*, to raise their status by analogy with Christian scriptures. Even W. C. Smith's comparative efforts to explore the functions of scriptures produced an evolutionary hierarchy of cultural development, with the Qur'an at the pinnacle: "The Islamic instance represents the notion par excellence of Scripture as a religious phenomenon," he argued, and though the processes of scriptural development continue a thousand years later in the Adi Granth of the Sikhs and in the nineteenth-century Book of Mormon, Smith maintained that "none of these instances carry our development any further" (1989, 31, 32). Graham repeated these sentiments (1987, 52–53) and also reflected a distaste for popular iconic uses of scriptures: "Certain forms of Jewish and Christian treatment of their scriptures involve not only reverence for the physical text but even magical or quasi-magical uses of it that can only be termed bibliolatry," and he went on to cite examples in many religious traditions (1987, 61, 196 nn. 17–18). Historical judgments thus easily reinforce the traditional self-congratulations of Western "scriptural" traditions. Theorizing about the nature of scriptures frequently falls prey to self-serving value judgments and colonial exploitation.

It is therefore understandable that many scholars suspect not only the methods but also the motives behind any comparative model of scriptures. Why compare the use of scriptures in different traditions at all when doing so runs such dangers? Why not study each community's use of scriptures separately and only in the context of its own religious and cultural practices?

The importance of cultural context for understanding the functions of scriptures certainly cannot be overstated. As Graham has emphasized, "scripture" is a relational concept that can only be understood in its relationship to a specific group: "The significant 'scriptural' characteristics of a text belong not only to the text itself but also to its role in a community and in individual lives" (1987, 5–6). The long history of textual studies within the Western religious traditions also shows, however, the limitations of a single-culture approach, as W. C. Smith pointed out. A major value of comparative study is that it can bring to attention aspects of a religion that have been ignored, or consciously suppressed, by traditional scholarship. The fact that our deep traditions of scholarship on scriptures are nonplussed, not by newly discovered cultures or practices, but rather by scriptural practices in the heart of contemporary Western religious traditions such as those mentioned at the beginning of this essay, illustrates the need for a broader, comparative study of the nature and functions of scriptures.

I believe that functional models of scriptures can be developed that address this need in a responsible and even-handed manner. The purpose of any such model should be to understand better those religious traditions that are self-consciously "scriptural" and to evaluate their claims about the role of scripture within their own tradition against historical and comparative evidence both within that tradition and outside it. In order to minimize the very real dangers that attend this enterprise, a successful model of scriptures should meet three criteria. First, it should provide several non-disparaging bases or scales for comparison within and between traditions to avoid the reduction of scriptural phenomena to a single dichotomous scale easily susceptible to polemical manipulation. Second, it should also be capable of accommodating the full range of religious expressions and uses of scriptures and resist the temptation to focus on textual interpretation just because that is easier for scholarship to understand.[2] Third, it should be able to explain in a non-hierarchical manner the relationship and distinction between scriptures and other, non-scriptural, writings and between scriptures and other, unwritten, religious traditions.

## Three dimensions

To meet these criteria, I propose a three-dimensional model of scriptures to explain their cultural functions and religious significance. The religious adoption and use of scriptures should be understood as a form of ritual. Religious communities ritualize scriptures along three different dimensions: a semantic dimension, a performative dimension, and an iconic dimension.

By describing these aspects as *dimensions*, I mean that all three forms of ritualization are intrinsic to scriptures and necessary to their nature and function. Scriptures have all three dimensions, but different religious groups and individuals ritualize the three dimensions to different degrees. The model thus provides a conceptual grid for comparing the ways that religious traditions regard and use their scriptures.

By describing the dimensions in terms of *ritualization*, the model explains the similarities and differences between scriptures and other books and writings. All books and writings exhibit semantic, performative, and iconic dimensions at least to an incipient degree. Some secular texts (such as national constitutions and theatrical scripts) are also typically ritualized along one or two of their dimensions. What distinguishes scriptures, however, is that their religious communities ritualize all three dimensions.

In what follows, I will elaborate on these claims by describing each of the three dimensions of scriptures, then exploring the processes by which each dimension is ritualized before analyzing the claims to power made by ritualizing them.

2. Graham noted that understanding scriptures requires taking the affective aspects of religious life into account: "seeing, hearing, and touching... A sacred text can be read laboriously in silent study, chanted or sung in unthinking repetition, copied or illuminated in loving devotion, imaginatively depicted in art or drama, solemnly processed in ritual pagentry, or devoutly touched in hope of luck and blessing. In each instance, in very diverse and not always predictable but still very real ways, such contact with scripture can elicit in reader, hearer, onlooker, or worshiper diverse responses: a surge of joy or sorrow; a feeling of belonging or even of alienation; a sense of guidance or consolation (or the want of either); or a feeling of intimacy with or awesome distance from the divine. These kinds of religious response are important to an adequate understanding of what it means to encounter a text as scripture. Such aspects are difficult, perhaps finally impossible, for the scholar to get at in any systematic way, but to ignore them entirely is to omit a substantial portion of their reality" (1987, 6–7). He narrowed the focus of his own book, however, to analyzing only the performative function of scriptural texts.

The *semantic dimension* of scriptures has to do with the meaning of what is written, and thus includes all aspects of interpretation and commentary as well as appeals to the text's contents in preaching and other forms of persuasive rhetoric. This dimension has always received most if not all of the attention of scholars, for the very good reason that religious traditions themselves place great emphasis on scholarly expertise in scriptural interpretation. Most religious communities with written scriptures encourage many of their devotees to gain expertise in their interpretation, not only for personal devotion but also as a means for directing community behavior and for adjudicating conflicts. Insofar as the text is understood to be divine communication, its interpretation becomes a form of divination, usually the preferred if not the only legitimate means for determining the divine will. Religious leadership therefore depends, to a degree that varies from one tradition to another, on exegetical mastery of semantic meaning.

The *performative dimension* of scriptures has to do with the performance of what is written. As already mentioned, scriptural performances come in two major modes: performance of the words of scriptures and performance of the contents of scriptures. Performance of scriptural *words* includes many ritualized forms of public and private reading, as well as the memorization and recitation of texts. Often the words are sung in musical genres ranging from highly prescribed chants through choral oratorios to congregational hymns. Artistic displays of scriptural quotations, such as monumental calligraphy and inscriptions, should also be included under the category of performances of scriptural words, though these artistic examples have iconic aspects as well.

Performance of scriptural *contents* includes dramatizations of various sorts, including simple tableaus, street performances, staged dramas, and cinema. Artistic illustrations of scenes from scriptures also belong in this category. The two modes of performance often work in tandem to expose devotees to their tradition's scriptures. They hear the text read and sung, and also see it enacted in drama and art. Nevertheless, religious leaders are more likely to dictate precisely how scriptural words are to be recited than they are to control dramatic performances and artistic illustrations. Thus the first mode of performance tends to be regulated by religious traditions more than the second. As a result, drama and art often express creative appropriations of scriptures beyond the control of religious authorities.[3]

3. To give just two examples: the depictions of the story of the binding of Isaac (the *Akedah*, Gen 22) in Jewish and Christian artwork developed independently and often at variance with the exegetical traditions, and have therefore often been criticized as incorrect (see Kessler 2004, 173–174). A contemporary example has been provided by Monica Jyotsna Melanchthon (2005), who noted that Dalit women in India use biblical role-playing and storytelling to "enable women to release themselves from androcentric interpretive processes... This process of acting out the text empowers Dalit women, whom society has trained not to act or to act in certain predefined ways."

The *iconic dimension* of scriptures finds expression in the physical form, ritual manipulation, and artistic representation of scriptures. Scriptures often take special forms that distinguish them physically from other books: e.g. hand-written and "clothed" Torah scrolls, jewel-encrusted gospel books, leather-bound Bibles, bark sutras with lacquered covers, illustrated Sanskrit scrolls, and so on. They are often displayed prominently on podiums or tables, hung on walls, or else hidden within special cases that call attention to them while simultaneously protecting them or even hiding them from casual view (e.g. synagogue arks). The Sikh scripture, the Adi Granth, must be given its own room if it is kept in a private house—a way of simultaneously hiding and displaying the sacred text. The text of scriptures may be presented with distinctive typographies (e.g. red-letter Bibles) or elaborate calligraphy (e.g. many Qur'ans), or illustrated with expensive hand-drawn illuminations. When copies of scriptures look too much like other books, their owners often find ways to give them a distinctive form (such as Bible covers in leather or with distinctive decorations). In these ways and many others, scriptures are often distinguished physically from other books.

Scriptures are also often treated differently from other books. They are carried in religious processions, displayed to congregations, and venerated through bowing and kissing. Many traditions have rules governing how scriptures should be treated, such as requiring that they never have other books placed on top of them or that a person be in a state of ritual purity before touching them. They are also manipulated in political ceremonies— displayed or touched as part of oath ceremonies and waved in political rallies and protests. Of course, what can be venerated can also be desecrated, so books of scriptures are defiled and destroyed as a means of attacking the religious traditions they represent.

The distinctive forms and uses of scriptures make them potent symbols in representational art. Saints and deities hold sacred texts in the artworks of many religious traditions. The artistic association of a deity with scripture legitimizes the scripture as authentic, and the association of a human with recognized scripture legitimizes the person's spiritual status. In recent (nineteenth- and twentieth-century) art, scriptures and other books have increasingly been depicted alone to represent various religious traditions or truth in general. Thus in the physical forms they take, in their ritual uses, and in their symbolic representations, scriptures function as icons.[4]

4. Graham recognized the iconic function of scriptures, but subsumed it under its textual function to preserve a dichotomy between textual and performative uses. He thus contrasted the moderns' conception of a "holy book" with the oral/aural scripture that was once the "primary and pervasive mode of contact with the Word" (1987, 46). Graham identified the effects of textual and iconic modes in mutual opposition to performative ones: "Even when the Bible remains a powerful symbol of revelation and guidance according to its spirit rather than its letter, it is today much more easily conceived of as a documentary text than a voice of inspired utterance. It is more likely to occupy a visible and symbolic place such as the ark of the syna-

## Ritualizing books

My thesis is that scriptures are produced by ritualizing their three dimensions—semantic, performative, and iconic—but these three dimensions are not unique to scriptures. All books and other texts participate in them. The use of any written document invokes the three dimensions at an incipient level. Most users of ordinary books, however, ignore the three dimensions of these writings as trivial.

Reading any book or other writing involves interpreting its meaning if it is to be understood. Understanding texts requires using their semantic dimension. That process of interpretation, however, usually occurs automatically and receives little attention when, for example, reading a newspaper or e-mail—or this essay, for that matter. Only when one becomes aware of one's lack of understanding does the process of interpretation receive attention, and then only until the problem is resolved.

The same thing can be said of the performative dimension of books and other writings. Writing is a visual code that must be translated into spoken or mental language. Any kind of reading is a kind of performance: it requires readers to translate visual letter forms into words, at least in their own minds. Again, this process usually occurs automatically unless one becomes aware of difficulties, such as when the typeface or hand-writing is obscure. Otherwise, the performative dimension of books and other writings remains an unremarkable feature of the reading process.

Before one can interpret a text's meaning, one must translate visual shapes into words, and that requires recognizing this physical object as a text. The text's physical shape, whether in the codex form of modern books or as a scroll or as a letter in an envelope, represents to viewers the possibility of reading its contents. The iconic dimension of books and other writings represents at its most basic level an invitation to viewers to "read me." This too is a trivial pre-

gogue or a church altar, lecter, or home bookshelf than it is to occupy the time of the faithful in sustained reading, recitation, memorization, and study. The authority of Torah or Bible is as likely to stem from its status as a fixed, tangible, and visible book as from its theological status as word of God" (47). Textual modes of scriptural study, while legitimate in and of themselves, "limit our ability as scholars to grasp the functional roles of scripture in other historical contexts" (47). Though he described the iconic function of holy texts, Graham argued that mass production has made scriptures like any other book. "The cheap and easy availability of myriad versions of the Jewish and Christian scriptures has done much to reduce the special quality of the physical text as an object of reverence and devotion in and of itself. Scripture's presence as a bound volume in a living-room book-case, a church pew, or a hotel-room drawer may conceivably encourage Bible reading, but it also reinforces the primary image of scripture as but another printed book... Consequently, we have some difficulty empathizing with persons for whom a copy of a sacred text was or is a seldom and wonderful thing, perhaps a magical and awesome thing, to be handled with solicitude and to which the proper response is reverential deference or even worshipful veneration" (46). I maintain, on the contrary, that the ubiquity of these bound volumes show that iconic veneration remains very high. Complaining that the ubiquity of Bibles diminishes their reverential quality is like complaining that the mass production of icons reduces their spiritual effectiveness. Graham's value judgments became clear when he criticized fundamentalism for "objectifying Holy Writ" (46–47).

requisite to any act of reading. These physical shapes, however, also receive various other symbolic associations, such as of education, learning, and truth. As a result, books *per se* play iconic roles in very many cultures.

Though these three dimensions play intrinsic roles in the use of all books and other writings, they are easily ignored when their use is unproblematic. Drawing attention to them emphasizes seemingly trivial aspects of normal reading practices. By contrast, the ways in which religious traditions use scriptures draw attention to each of the three dimensions, giving spiritual importance to what is otherwise trivial.

Jonathan Z. Smith (1987b) noted that this is precisely the function of ritual. Building upon observations by Sigmund Freud and Claude Lévi-Strauss, he argued that ritual calls attention to and makes intentional the ordinary practices of everyday life. "Ritual relies for its power on the fact that it is concerned with quite ordinary activities placed within an extraordinary setting, that what it describes and displays is, in principle, possible for every occurrence of these acts" (J. Z. Smith, 1987a, 109). Thus ritual turns everyday routines such as washing oneself, entering and leaving a room, and eating meals into deeply meaningful practices by focusing attention on them, formalizing them and, often, by prescribing precisely how they get done (similarly Bell 1992, 74, 92; for a broad survey of "ritual-like" activities under the categories of formalism, traditionalism, invariance, rule-governance, sacral symbolism, and performance, see Bell 1997, 138–169).

Applying J. Z. Smith's definition of ritual to the three dimensions of scriptures illuminates the relationship between normal books and scriptures. Scriptures are books or writings whose use in all three dimensions has been ritualized. The otherwise trivial practices involved in reading a book are, in the case of scriptures, given sustained attention. Semantic interpretation is ritualized by commentary and preaching.[5] Reading and dramatization both become ritual performances. The book's physical form is decorated, manipulated in public and private rituals, and highlighted in artistic representations. In each case, special attention is given to otherwise routine acts of reading. Thus religious traditions maintain the status of their scriptures by ritualizing

5. Many scholars, in particular, are likely to resist the notion that textual interpretation should be considered a form of ritual. But J. Z. Smith's definition of ritual as detailed attention to ordinary activities describes rather well the practices of academic interpretation. Scholarly exegesis tends to be rule-bound and requires explicit location within particular traditions of interpretation, and its expression in conference papers and journal articles tends to take the form of highly formalized performances—all characteristic features of ritualized activities as described by Bell. Despite these points, discomfort at imposing the label "ritual" on scholarship will likely continue because Western culture carries a deep-seated suspicion of ritual as empty and meaningless behavior. The burden of ritual theorists over the last three decades, including Smith, Bell, and many others, has been to counter this bias and insist that rituals not only convey deep and important significance to their participants, but also that human culture is saturated with ritualized behaviors. So by saying that scholarly exegesis in general, and scriptural exegesis in particular, is a ritual activity, I do not mean in any way to disparage its significance.

normal features of books and other writings.

Of course, other kinds of texts may also be ritualized in one way or another. Nations ritualize the semantic dimension of their laws and constitutions by giving their interpretation prolonged attention through court decisions and legal commentaries, and their iconic dimension through public display and reproduction (Watts 2004). Nor is the ritualization of these dimensions limited to physical texts. Non-textual symbols and oral textual traditions may also be ritualized in similar ways. Oral epics are performed ritually in many cultures, both by recitation and by dramatization. They may also be subject to ongoing interpretive scrutiny that ritualizes their semantic as well as their performative dimensions. Oral epics, however, have no iconic dimension because they are not physical objects. Non-textual symbols, such as a cross or a flag, are subject to ritual manipulation and display (iconic dimension). They lack a semantic dimension, of course, but they also have no performative dimension because they do not encode language. (The origins of writing in pictographs illustrates the vexed problem of distinguishing precisely the boundary between pictorial representation and writing, but this is not an issue that I can engage here.) Therefore it is not primarily their semantic dimension that distinguishes scriptures from oral traditions and visual symbols. Scriptures differ from oral traditions because they are physical objects and so can be ritualized as icons. They differ from non-textual visual symbols because their words can both be interpreted and performed in highly ritualized ways. Scriptures can unite epic and totem in one and the same thing.

Only a book or other form of writing can be ritualized in all three of these dimensions. That distinguishes scriptures from other kinds of religious symbols and traditions. It does not, however, distinguish scriptures from other books and texts, which as I have noted may be ritualized as well. The *more* a book or text is ritualized in *all three* dimensions, however, the more likely it is to be regarded as a scripture. Thus the functional identification of scriptures depends not on a difference in kind from other books and writings, but on the *degree* to which a particular book or writing is ritualized as text *and* as performance *and* as icon.

## Dimensional variations

Religious traditions that utilize scriptures ritualize their three dimensions to different extents. They sometimes emphasize different dimensions in ritualizing different books. For example, though one can find tendencies towards ritualizing all three dimensions of the various scriptures in Hindu traditions, they usually ritualize the performative dimension more than the others. Recitation of the Vedic hymns from memory is so privileged that it has given rise to the belief that the fundamental characteristic of these scriptures is pure sound. This observation led Graham to state that "the unique Hindu case offers the one unassailable example of a highly developed scriptural tradition in which the importance of the oral word has been so central as to dominate and largely even to exclude the written word altogether over most of its long history" (1987, 66). Other Hindu scriptures, however, such as the Ramayana, tend to be performed through dramatic portrayals, sometimes lasting for days or weeks on end. This contrast in performative modes is formalized in Hindu thought by classifying scriptures into two categories: *shruti* "what is heard" (the Vedas and other Sanskrit traditions) and *smriti* "what is remembered" (myths, epics, and laws, often in vernacular languages). Since mastery of the Sanskrit Vedas has traditionally been monopolized by male Brahmins, other Hindus have especially used and celebrated the vernacular epics as their scriptures, though also employing priests who know the Vedas when they need them for special ceremonies. Popular performances of the Ramayana have been so influential that not just marginalized groups but also various political powers have appropriated their social influence.[6]

Jewish tradition provides more examples of how the three dimensions can be ritualized in different ways for separate books. The elaborate rules that govern the creation, handling, and storage of a Torah scroll emphasize its iconic dimension, while great stress is also placed on proper performance of the text in public Torah readings. The textual authority of Talmudic and Midrashic interpretation, however, has often overshadowed that of the Torah, and the prayer book (*Siddur*) has often been almost as important for oral performance as the scroll of the Torah, though the kinds of performances they receive differ markedly from each other.

Muslims tends to ritualize all three dimensions of the Qur'an. The semantic dimension receives great emphasis through interpretation and commentary, though many interpreters of Muslim practice argue that oral performance of the words of the Qur'an by recitation eclipses all other uses in importance.[7] Elaborate calligraphy of the Qur'an's text and monumental displays of its codex form, however, also elevate its iconic dimension, as do purity rules for handling it. The protests over its desecration in 2005 show how one dimension of a scripture may occasionally receive greater emphasis than usual for circumstantial reasons.

6. For a historical summary and analysis of the power dynamics involved in the distinction between *shruti* and *smriti*, see Holdrege 2003, 147–51. The contents of the two categories of Hindu scriptures suggest that the kinds of performance given a particular scripture may, to some extent, be directed by the dominant genre of its contents. This observation applies not only to Hindu traditions: narrative genres (e.g. the Ramayana, the Gospels) tend to evoke dramatic performances and artistic portrayals of their contents, while hymnic and hortatory genres (the Vedas, the Adi Granth, the Qur'an, much of the Torah) are more likely to find expression in performances of their words through recitation, memorization, calligraphy and the like.

7. Thus Daniel A. Madigan asserted that "Islam is also characterized by an almost entirely oral approach to its scripture. One finds no physical book at the center of Muslim worship; nothing at all reminiscent of the crowned Torah or the embellished lectionary. On the contrary, the simple ritual and the recitation of the Qur'an that forms part of it are carried out from memory" (2001, 3). See also W. C. Smith 1989, 32–35 and Graham 1987, 88–115.

Sikh tradition ritualizes all three dimensions of the Adi Grandh to a very high degree. Temples serve as shrines to the scripture, which is treated with the utmost respect and veneration. Recitations of its words are a prominent feature of Sikh ceremonies, which occasionally include non-stop readings of the whole text over two days. Yet consultation of the meaning of particular scriptures also plays a key role in providing spiritual direction to individuals and communities.

Protestant Christians are famous for emphasizing the meaning of scripture, that is, proper interpretation of the Bible's contents. Conflicts with liberals over biblical interpretation and theology led to the development of Christian fundamentalism in the early twentieth century. Christians of all denominations continue to ritualize the Bible's semantic dimension through preaching, teaching (in churches and universities), scholarship, and a vast enterprise of popular and academic publishing. They also invest heavily, however, in ritualizing the Bible's performative dimension, most obviously in the ever-changing forms of Christian vocal music—much of it containing biblical texts as well as themes. As already mentioned, dramatic performances of various kinds also feature prominently in contemporary Christian culture and frequently evoke public controversies over the interpretive authenticity of particular films (such as surrounded the release of *The Last Temptation of Christ* in 1988 and *The Passion of the Christ* in 2004). Despite Protestantism's aniconic heritage that tends to obscure the iconic dimension from their awareness, evangelicals also ritualize the Bible's iconicity in many ways. Worshippers carry Bibles to church and often in secular settings as well. In their hands, Bibles function as badges of Christian identity, a visual role enhanced by special book covers that distinguish the scripture from secular books. Ministers carry Bibles as symbols of religious authority, especially in portraits. Gifts of Bibles mark rites of passage such as baptisms, confirmations, and weddings. In recent years, evangelicals have become increasingly vocal in objecting to any public slights to the Bible's iconic status in secular society.

These brief descriptions of scriptures in various traditions are very broad and superficial, for ritualizations of scripture within any religious tradition vary dramatically in kind and degree from time to time and place to place. Controversies over the proper use of scriptures often distinguish rival sects in doctrine and practice. Take Buddhism, for example: the training of Buddhist monks usually emphasizes rigorous study of scriptures to understand their meaning, thus ritualizing their semantic dimension. Yet lay people often sponsor recitations and publications as a means of attaining merit, thus ritualizing the performative dimension. Several sects in various periods have made one or another sutra the object of ritual veneration, thus ritualizing its iconic dimension. On the other hand, Zen schools typically downplay the significance of scriptures in any dimension. Thus the explanatory value of recognizing the three dimensions of scriptures does not depend on them being ritualized to the same degree in all times and places: they are not. It rather helps explain the religious tendency towards ritualizing scriptures in all three dimensions. It also provides a means for explaining the social effects of doing so.

## The powers of scriptures

Publicly ritualizing each dimension of scripture exerts different kinds of public power. Private ritualization produces various kinds of effects as well. So I conclude with some preliminary observations about the effects of ritualizing the three dimensions of scriptures on social position, on the persuasiveness of scriptures and their handlers, and on inner-religious conflict.

Ritualizing the semantic dimension of scriptures in public usually produces a claim to social *authority.* In disputes over doctrine or practice, the meaning of this or that scriptural text is cited to claim divine support for one or another position. Textual interpretation is used to justify opposing positions, and is also employed to arbitrate solutions. Those who, by persuasive skill or institutional position, wield the greatest exegetical influence in determining which text should apply to this situation and how it should be understood thereby gain authority to direct the community's beliefs and practices. As a result, in traditions with written scriptures, most internal controversy has an exegetical component. Communities privilege the ritualized interpretation of their scriptures' semantic dimension as the arena in which conflicts should be aired and settled. Hence the high premium placed by scriptural traditions on scholarly mastery of textual interpretation.

Ritualizing the performative dimension of scripture exhibits and conveys a sense of *inspiration.* Though claims for divine inspiration of scriptures are common, it is in their performance that they have an inspiring effect on an audience and, often, the performers themselves. Inspirational performances in public may involve recitation or dramatic display, or lavish artistic reproduction of either the texts (calligraphy) or contents (illustration) or both. Those who claim interpretive authority often display performative mastery as well. Preaching, though based in textual interpretation and its authority, becomes inspiring to the degree that it also performs the text, often through a virtuosic recital of a string of textual quotations and allusions. In this way, inspiring performances are regularly used to buttress interpretive authority. But non-clerical actors and artists frequently present performances of the contents of scriptures that inspire audiences quite apart from, or even in conflict with, the concerns of institutionally authorized interpreters.

Ritualizing the iconic dimension of scripture serves purposes of *legitimation.* Elaborate decorations of scriptures and ritual manipulations of them legitimate religious ceremonies and institutions. Thus, for example, Gospel books and Bibles are paraded in church processions and placed in prominent positions on altars and pulpits to represent visually the legitimate source of the community's practices and beliefs. In portraiture, scriptures in the hands of rabbis, priests, monks, sages, ministers, imams, politicians, street protestors, and soldiers all attempt to legitimate the person in that position or role. The most elaborate forms and ritual uses of iconic books are often created and displayed to legitimate the powers of governments (kings, courts, legislatures, and presidents). The legitimation conveyed by scriptures is most apparent in oath ceremonies by which public officials take office through the mediation of a book of scripture. Public monuments of the Qur'an or the Ten Commandments also evoke the image of scripture to legitimize the state. Conversely, those same monuments use the state's power, money, and influence to legitimate particular religious traditions, as do priceless jeweled bindings and elaborate calligraphies lavished on state-sponsored copies of scriptures. The display and manipulation of scriptures therefore legitimizes persons and institutions by ritually connecting them with a central symbol of the religious tradition.[8]

The terms "authority," "inspiration," and "legitimacy" are, of course, inexact and their connotations overlap, especially when used to describe scriptures. My purpose in distinguishing them here is not to claim strictly demarcated functions for ritualizing the three dimensions of scriptures, but only to indicate that ritualizing the different dimensions does exert different kinds of effects. Clearly, ritualizing all three dimensions reinforces each dimension's effects with those of the others to enhance the persuasive appeal of scriptures and their handlers.

## Persuasive scriptures

The persuasive function of scriptures is another neglected topic in scholarship. Despite widespread devotional claims to the decisive influence of one or another scripture on many people's beliefs and practices, academic study of scriptures has focused on their literary forms, historical development, and doctrinal influence rather than on their rhetorical impact. In part, this omission may be due to the fact that many scriptures appear anything but persuasive to a casual reader. Their language is often difficult and archaic, even in vernacular translation; their literary forms can be hard for moderns to understand; and their contents frequently outrage modern sensibilities. To readers outside the religious communities that treasure a particular scripture, that scripture often appears anything but persuasive. The claims of devotees that

8. Roy A. Rappaport's theory of religion emphasized the *indexical* function of rituals to demonstrate the participants' acceptance of the religious tradition, which he called the *canon*. He noted that objects manipulated in ritual may index the performer, such as offerings, or may represent the canon, such as ancient temples and churches that demonstrate the endurance of the liturgical order. Some items, such as the crowns of kings, "seem to be intermediate ... Such objects are themselves parts of the canonical order, but their manipulation is in part self-referential" (1999, 145). The iconic ritualization of scriptures provides another example of objects that reference both the "canonical order" (literally, in this case) as well as indexing those who hold, touch and read them in a self-referential manner.

they find their scriptures enormously persuasive need to be taken seriously, however, all the more so if outsiders find the claim puzzling. What accounts for the persuasiveness of these texts? Can recognizing the three dimensions of scriptures help us understand how scriptures exert persuasive influence?

Persuasion is the traditional subject of the study of rhetoric. Therefore, noting the persuasive effects of ritualizing scriptures suggests looking to rhetoric for some analytical tools for understanding these effects. As it happens, there is an ancient model of persuasion that matches the three dimensions of scriptures described here very well. Rhetorical theory has since Aristotle (*Rhetoric* II.1.1–30) recognized three different circumstances that affect the persuasiveness of speeches: the persuasiveness of the arguments—*logos*; the credibility of the speaker—*ethos*; and the feelings of the audience—*pathos*. Various strategies can be used to enhance a speech's effectiveness in each of these three modes. A speech must communicate a carefully reasoned argument clearly for it to be convincing (*logos*), and for this purpose Aristotle developed the enthymemic or rhetorical proof. The argument will be more appealing, however, if the speech evokes, for example, the audience's sympathy towards a victim or outrage against injustice or fear of foreign attack (*pathos*). Yet a carefully reasoned speech that appeals to the audience's emotions may still fail to be persuasive if the speaker lacks credibility. Therefore, speakers must buttress their *ethos* by presenting an appealing demeanor, by behaving in an appropriate and attractive manner, and, if possible, by carrying with them a reputation for honesty and trustworthiness. In Aristotle's words, they must demonstrate "good sense, good moral character, and goodwill" (*Rhetoric* II.1.9).

Though scriptures are not public speakers, ritualizing each of the three dimensions of scriptures enhances their persuasiveness in one of these three rhetorical modes as well. Ritualizing the semantic dimension through detailed interpretation and commentary emphasizes the special importance of these words and their possible meanings. Much of the burden of commentary and preaching is to show that the archaic language and antiquated ideas contained in many scriptures in fact do address contemporary concerns with realistic and appropriate ideas, instructions, and models for behavior. The infinite elaboration of the interpretive tradition that encourages more and ever larger commentaries by growing numbers of specialists trained in esoteric cultures and long-extinct languages further enhances the worth of scriptures. They give the impression that only texts of extreme value could possibly be worth the time and expense of such elaborate scholarly enterprises. The great religious authority credited to scriptures reflects long traditions of such enhancements of their *logos*.

Ritualizing the performative dimension through recitations, dramatic enactments, and the like prompts feelings of inspiration in those who hear and see them, and often in the performers as well. Through long exposure and communal reinforcement, people associate feelings of inspiration with the sound of a scripture's words, with the melodies with which its lines are sung, with the sight of its most famous verses, and with the dramatic and artistic portrayals of its stories. Ritualizing the *pathos* of scriptures in these ways promotes the idea that scriptures not only inspire but are themselves the products of uniquely divine kinds of inspiration. Doctrines of scriptural inspiration develop from such emotional experiences and tend to grow in strength over time and in the uniqueness they ascribe to scriptures.

Just as speakers portray themselves to an audience as trustworthy by their dress and behavior, ritualizing the iconic dimension of scriptures through their decoration, ritual manipulation, and display demonstrates visually their *ethos* as scripture. The expense of lavish decorations portrays the great worth of the books. The scriptures' ritual display calls attention to them as objects to be respected and obeyed. Their ritual veneration presents them as material manifestations of divinity. All of these practices serve to legitimize the scriptures and, by derivation, those people connected in some way to them. Thus scriptures' iconic status enhances their own *ethos* and by association grants legitimacy to those in contact with them.

The rhetorical effect of ritualizing the three dimensions of scriptures is therefore to buttress claims for their persuasiveness. Devotees of various scriptural traditions commonly attest to the persuasive power of their scriptures. They like to tell stories of immaculate conversions, in which people adopted their religion only because of reading its scriptures. Belief in the persuasive power of particular scriptures have therefore prompted movements to expose as many people as possible to them by, for example, placing Bibles in hotel rooms and broadcasting Qur'anic recitations on radio and television.

It may seem odd to suggest that a book can be described by categories developed for public speakers. Yet ritual emphasis on the *logos*, *pathos*, and *ethos* of scriptures has the effect of giving them personas more like people than like books (see George Heyman 2006, 209–225). For example, devotees describe receiving comfort from the physical presence of the scriptures and from the sounds of their words just as one might be comforted by the presence and conversation of a friend. Nor is this tendency to personify the scriptures restricted to private devotions. In a number of religious traditions, personification of scriptures has been formally expressed by close identification between the scriptures and the prophet who revealed them (e.g. Moses and the Torah, Mohammad and the Qur'an). Christians went further: the opening chapter of the Gospel of John equates the *logos* of God metaphysically with Jesus Christ. As a result, it is common for Christians to describe both Christ and the Bible as "the Word of God." Some Buddhist traditions venerate the wisdom (*prajña*) that leads to enlightenment in the physical form of a book. The scriptures used for this purpose all employ the term *Prajñāpāramitā* ("wisdom perfected") as part of their titles. Medieval Mahāyāna sculptures often depicted *Prajñāpāramitā* as a goddess (Kinnard 1999, 114–175). Though most interpreters have considered *Prajñāpāramitā* a real mother goddess, Kinnard argued that the sculptures reflect a more metaphorical understanding of wisdom as the "mother," that is, source, of enlightenment (1999, 127–130). Thus, the feeling of being persuaded by the scriptures has generated the sense that they are more than just texts. Their ritualization produces personal effects that lead to their identification with human prophets or supernatural personalities.

Scriptures, however, do not keep their persuasive effects all to themselves. They share their ritualized enhancements of *logos*, *ethos*, and *pathos* with those who have special status as their interpreters, guardians, and performers. Religious leaders, scholars, and politicians find their own persuasive abilities enhanced from association with scriptures. Their words gain more authority by sharing the scriptural *logos*, their public performances become more inspiring by invoking scriptures' *pathos*, and the legitimacy of their positions of leadership is reinforced by the visible presence of scriptures' iconic *ethos*.

## Conflicts over scriptures

Ritualizing the three different dimensions of scriptures provides religious communities with a large repertoire of strategies for responding to internal and external challenges. For example, historical study of the Bible has for two centuries challenged scripture's traditional interpretation in Judaism and Christianity. Yet the Bible's religious status within these traditions seems largely unaffected, much to the amazement of many observers. Recognizing the roles of all three dimensions of Jewish and Christian scriptures permits a more complete and complex understanding of these modern developments. The debates over historical criticism's claims remain restricted to the Bible's semantic dimension, which is the traditional forum for controversies over scriptural authority and meaning. In fact, sustained public arguments over the meaning and interpretation of scripture are themselves ritualized behaviors in J. Z. Smith's sense of ritual—calling attention to every detail of textual interpretation. The very vehemence of these debates and the media publicity about them ironically reinforces the impression of the Bible's importance and authority even as they challenge various traditional understandings of it. (On the role of biblical scholarship in maintaining the cultural status of the Bible, see Schüssler Fiorenza 1999 and Wimbush 2003.)

At the same time, ritualizations of other dimensions of the Bible continue and have even increased over the last two centuries, unaffected by the controversy. Increased liturgical use of scriptures (in Reform Judaism including greater performance of the Hebrew text), campaigns to encourage memorization of key portions, and Hollywood movie enactments of biblical stories reinforce its performative ability to inspire. Even in the academy, some philosophers, theologians, and cultural critics have begun advocating a return to ostensibly more authentic practices of scriptural performance, influenced in part by the works of W. C. Smith and Graham. Thus Paul Griffiths (1999) excoriated the modern academy for "consumerist" practices of reading and wished for a return to the meditative uses of scriptures by medieval monastics, the *lectio divina*; Wesley Kort (1996) argued for retrieving the sixteenth-century Reformers' use of scripture as a lens by which to view the rest of life; Catherine Pickstock (1998) maintained that medieval reading practices offer the only solution to the quandaries of post-modern epistemology; and Shlomo Bidderman (1995) argued that the idea of scripture should itself function as a primary category of philosophical reflection. Diana Walsh Pasulka (2006) demonstrates that the programs of Griffiths, Kort, and Pickstock represent a nostalgic attempt to retrieve a lost heritage. Given the usual tendency of religious orthodoxies to exert control over verbal performance, it is not surprising that this nostalgic appeal for pre-modern reading practices has reinforced conservative trends in several fields. At the same time, mass-marketing of inexpensive Bibles and media-savvy evangelistic campaigns have made the Protestant Bible one of the most recognizable religious symbols of Western culture. These developments have reinforced the legitimacy of this iconic scripture and also its public power to legitimate those who hold it. They shift the emphasis from its problematic semantic dimension to the Bible's performative and iconic dimensions. This illustrates how public ritualization of all three dimensions of scriptures makes them resilient to controversies about any one dimension.

Individual people also ritualize the dimensions of scriptures as part of their devotional practice, as do small communities. Such private or communal uses gain power by ritualizing scriptures as well, but the effects differ in kind and degree from the effects of more public ritualizations. Scriptural texts are widely used for personal divination through methods ranging from contextual interpretation to random selection. Frequently, they are searched for esoteric meanings unknown to others. Such secret knowledge can convey personal advantage (spiritually or temporally) and can also be marketed for economic gain (e.g. Michael Droznin's *The Bible Code*, which was listed on the New York Times bestseller list for thirteen weeks in 1997). As to the performative dimension, individuals frequently memorize scripture for personal spiritual benefit. Scriptural texts may also be recited as proverbs for rhetorical advantage or as spells for achieving instrumental results. The iconic dimension is manifestly ritualized when people display physical scriptures or parts of scriptures in their homes, carry them as amulets, or manipulate them to gain blessings or merit for individuals and families. In these and other ways, personal religious practice ritualizes the three dimensions of scriptures in many cultures.

Religious authorities often discourage some private uses of scriptures while trying to control others. On the other hand, private use frequently circumvents, even challenges, the public ritualization of scriptures. These disputes can express conflicts between entrenched social elites and dissident individuals, minority religious groups, or other dis-empowered population groups.

Thus the iconic use of scriptures by individuals and minority groups can pose challenges to the larger religious and secular cultures. For example, many non-Muslims in both Africa and India carry and manipulate scraps of Qur'ans as protective amulets (for Africa, see Goody 1971; Gomez 2003, 509; information for India comes from personal communication with my colleague Ann Gold). Such talismanic uses challenge the religious boundaries maintained by religious and academic authorities alike. Black Hebrew Israelites preaching on New York City streets sometimes wear Bibles strapped to their waists like swords wielded in opposition to a corrupt society (research by Marshall Mitchell, summarized in Love 2003). In this case, the iconic books present an intentional challenge to the majority population of American society. Individuals and minority groups of various kinds can also employ the other dimensions of scriptures for self-empowerment in distinctive ways that clash with more broadly normative uses and applications. I have only hinted here at the ways that these practices and conflicts negotiate various kinds of social power by ritualizing the three dimensions of scriptures. They deserve to be explored in far greater detail to understand better the power transactions carried out through the ritualization of scriptures.

## Exception: Relic books

Examination of the iconic dimension of books and other writings draws attention to a category of texts that break the pattern described here. Though highly venerated iconic texts, they are not ritualized either in the semantic or the performative dimensions. I term such texts "relic books." Relic books are writings that are valued for being the *specific* objects that they are; they are in theory not reproducible. Examples would include most books on prominent display in museums: such as the earliest known copies of the Bible and the Qur'an, Gutenberg Bibles, Shakespeare's first folio and any valuable first edition, the autographs of the Declaration of Independence and U.S. Constitution, and so forth. These objects are rare, if not oneof-a-kind, and are not reproducible, at least in theory. The effect of reproduction on the status of iconic books was observed by J. Z. Smith, who commented:

> Beyond this ordinary sense of the mythology of "sacred book," there is a second sense of sacrality that has yet to be studied fully; namely the sacred book as a sacred object, one that is always manufactured and all but infinitely reproducible, and, therefore, one to which there is almost never attached a claim of being "original." Some of these reproductions become themselves the subjects of narratives, as is the case, for example, of the Lindisfarne Gospels, the Stonyhurst Gospel and the cult of St. Cuthbert. (1998, 298)

The difference between the reproducible sacred objects of Smith's first sentence and the irreproducible gospels of his second needs to be emphasized and analyzed. Icons are less appropriate models for how the latter books function than are relics: both icons and relics are believed to mediate sacred influence, but the value of icons is that they are reproducible, whereas the value of relics derives precisely from the fact that they are unique. (Of course, because the demand for relics always outstrips the supply, the [re-]production of relics has long been the subject of scandal.)

Considered from the perspective of the three dimensions of scriptures, one can say that the iconic dimension of relic texts has grown so large as to eclipse the other two dimensions. Virtually no one worries about how to interpret a relic like a Gutenberg Bible, nor are relic books actually read (performed) very much, because they share their semantic and performative dimensions with other (non-relic) copies of the same texts. Relic books are valued for their iconic dimension alone. Thus their authority is not invoked to settle disputes over doctrine nor do people look to them for help in achieving performative inspiration. Instead, their chief function is legitimation. Unlike scriptures in general, relic books do not convey legitimacy to their owners, except in the form of prestige at being the owner of a famous object. (That prestige can be considerable and monetarily valuable. As a result, collectors often treat relic books like the relics of saints. Just as the bodies of dead saints are separated into small pieces to produce the maximum number of relics which are then displayed in elaborate, often framed, reliquaries, book sellers often tear apart relic books to maximize profits by selling their pages individually to collectors, who frame them like artwork for public display.) Instead of providing authority or inspiration, relic books rather legitimize the textual tradition itself. Their antiquity and/or rarity confirms the legitimacy of the reproduced texts, and this is how they are chiefly used. Scholars consult relic books to authenticate details of the text, while public viewings of them serve to legitimate the prestige that the reproducible iconic text enjoys.

The Dead Sea Scrolls provide an illuminating example of the distinctive treatment accorded relic books, because modern culture treats some of these ancient texts as relics while using others primarily for interpretive purposes. These manuscripts dating from the third to the first centuries BCE were discovered in the mid-twentieth century CE. One-quarter of them contain texts of the Hebrew Bible, the earliest biblical texts now in existence. They have been the object of intense scholarly comparison with younger biblical manuscripts in order to legitimize and correct the biblical text. The other three-quarters of the scrolls contain non-biblical and previously unknown compositions. They also have received intense scrutiny as important sources for the history and religion of Judaism in the last centuries BCE. Thus interest has focused on interpretation of the semantic dimension of the non-biblical scrolls, while the biblical scrolls function as relic books to legitimize the biblical text. The distinction is confirmed by the display of the scrolls in the aptly named "Shrine of the Book" at the Israel Museum in Jerusalem: a biblical scroll (Isaiah) receives pride of place in the central display. The dominance of its iconic dimension for both scholars and the public confirms its status as a relic book.

Relic books should therefore be considered the exception that proves the rule. Though they are themselves not subject to semantic and performative ritualization, they owe their exceptional iconicity to the fact that other, non-relic, reproductions of the same text are ritualized in all three dimensions. When particular books are readily available for semantic, performative, and iconic ritualization, a few special exemplars can be set aside to serve purely iconic purposes as relic books.

## Conclusion

This essay can only begin to unpack the implications of the three-dimensional model for understanding the phenomenon of scriptures. It is, of course, only a model. The reality of religious practices and beliefs in the myriad of human communities that use scriptures will always exceed the ability of any single conceptual tool to reduce it to a few principles. I advance this model not to preclude other ways of analyzing the nature and functions of scriptures, but simply as one useful means for understanding the impact of scriptures on historical and contemporary affairs.

The power dynamics surrounding scriptures influence the politics and cultures, and of course the religious practices, of very many societies in the twenty-first century. To take only my two original examples, many people wonder why the treatment of an inexpensive, mass-produced book in a military prison should prompt such outrage when the prisoners themselves live under great duress. Many also wonder why American politics and media can get fixated on the appropriate placement of a granite monument containing scriptural texts when so many more pressing issues seem to demand resolution. By appreciating how the iconic dimension of scriptures conveys legitimacy, we can better understand the religious passions and social forces aroused by such incidents.

I believe that the three-dimensional model of scriptures proposed here illuminates the nature of peoples' stakes in these incidents, and in many other situations involving the semantic, performative, and iconic uses of scriptures. Further studies of the three dimensions of scriptures are required to explore and define the extent and limits of this model's application.

## References

Bell, Catherine. 1992. *Ritual Theory and Ritual Practice.* Oxford: Oxford University Press.

———. 1997. *Ritual: Perspectives and Dimensions.* Oxford: Oxford University Press.

Bidderman, Shlomo. 1995. *Scripture and Knowledge: An Essay on Religious Epistemology.* Leiden: Brill.

Brown, Michelle. 2003. *The Lindisfarne Gospels: Society, Spirituality and the Scribe.* London: British Library.

Gomez, Michael A. 2003. "The Preacher-Kings: W. E. B. Du Bois Revisited." In

*African Americans and the Bible: Sacred Texts and Social Textures,* edited by Vincent L. Wimbush, 501–513. New York: Continuum.

Goody, Jack. 1971. "The Impact of Islamic Writing on the Oral Cultures of West Africa." *Cahiers d'études africaines* 11: 455–466.

Graham, William A. 1987. *Beyond the Written Word: Oral Aspects of Scripture in the History of Religion.* Cambridge: Cambridge University Press.

Griffiths, Paul J. 1999. *Religious Reading: The Place of Reading in the Practice of Religion.* Oxford: Oxford University Press.

Heyman, George. 2006. "Canon Law and the Canon of Scripture." *Postscripts* 2(2-3): 209–225.

Holdrege, Barbara A. 2003. "Beyond the Guild: Liberating Biblical Studies." In Wimbush 2003, 138–159.

Kessler, Edward. 2004. *Bound By the Bible: Jews, Christians and the Sacrifice of Isaac.* Cambridge: Cambridge University Press.

Kinnard, Jacob N. 1999. *Imaging Wisdom: Seeing and Knowing in the Art of Indian Buddhism.* Richmond: Curzon.

———. 2002. "On Buddhist 'Bibliolaters': Representing and Worshiping the Book in Medieval Indian Buddhism." *The Eastern Buddhist* 34(2): 94–116.

Kort, Wesley. 1996. *Take, Read: Scripture, Textuality and Cultural Practice.* College Park, PA: Pennsylvania State University Press.

Long, Burke. 2003. *Imagining the Holy Land: Maps, Models and Fantasy Travels.* Bloomington, IN: Indiana University Press.

Love, Velma. 2003. "The Bible and Contemporary African American Culture I." In *African Americans and the Bible: Sacred Texts and Social Textures,* edited by Vincent L. Wimbush, 49–65. New York: Continuum.

Madigan, Daniel A. 2001. *The Qur'an's Self Image: Writing and Authority in Islam's Scripture.* Princeton, NJ: Princeton University Press.

Marty, Martin. 1982. "America's Iconic Book." In *Humanizing America's Iconic Book,* edited by Gene M. Tucker and Douglas A. Knight, 1–23. Chico, CA: Scholars Press.

Melanchthon, Monica Jyotsna. 2005. "Dalits, Bible, and Method." *SBLForum,* December 2005. www.sbl-site.org/Article.aspx?ArticleId=459. Accessed August 2006.

Pasulka, Diana Walsh. 2006. "Pre-Modern Scriptures in Postmodern Times: The Philosophical Movement to Revive Traditional Reading Practices." *Postscripts* 2(2-3): 293–315.

Pickstock, Catherine. 1998. *After Writing: The Liturgical Consummation of Philosophy.* Oxford: Blackwell.

Rappaport, Roy A. 1999. *Ritual and Religion in the Making of Humanity.* Cambridge: Cambridge University Press.

Schüssler Fiorenza, Elisabeth. 1999. *Rhetoric and Ethic: The Politics of Biblical Studies.* Minneapolis, MN: Augsburg Fortress.

Shopshire, James M., Ida Rousseau Mukenge, Victoria Erickson, and Hans A. Baer.

2003. "The Bible and Contemporary African American Culture II: Report on a Preliminary Ethnographic Project." In *African Americans and the Bible: Sacred Texts and Social Textures,* edited by Vincent L. Wimbush, 66–80. New York: Continuum.

Smith, Jonathan Z. 1987a. *To Take Place: Toward Theory in Ritual.* Chicago, IL: University of Chicago Press.

———. 1987b. "The Domestication of Sacrifice." In *Violent Origins,* edited by Robert G. Hamerton-Kelly, 191–235. Palo Alto, CA: Stanford University Press.

———. 1998. "Canons, Catalogues and Classics." In *Canonization and Decanonization,* edited by A. van der Kooij and K. van der Toorn, 295–311. Leiden: Brill.

Smith, Wilfred Cantwell. 1971. "The Study of Religion and the Study of the Bible." *Journal of the American Academy of Religion* 39: 131–40; reprinted in *Rethinking Scripture: Essays from a Comparative Perspective,* edited by Miriam Levering, 18–28. Albany, NY: State University of New York Press, 1989.

———. 1989. "Scripture as Form and Concept: Their Emergence for the Western World." In *Rethinking Scripture: Essays from a Comparative Perspective,* edited by Miriam Levering, 29–57. Albany: State University of New York Press.

Toorn, Karel van der. 1997. "The Iconic Book: Analogies between the Babylonian Cult of Images and the Veneration of the Torah." In *The Image and the Book: Iconic Cults, Aniconism and the Rise of Book Religion in Israel and the Ancient Near East,* edited by Karel van der Toorn, 229–248. Leuven: Peeters.

Watts, James W. 2004. "Ten Commandments Monuments and the Rivalry of Iconic Texts." *Journal of Religion & Society* 6. http://moses.creighton.edu/JRS/2004/2004-13.html.

Wimbush, Vincent L. 2003. "Introduction: Reading Darkness, Reading Scriptures." In *African Americans and the Bible: Sacred Texts and Social Textures,* edited by Vincent L. Wimbush, 7–22. New York: Continuum.

———. ed. 2003. *African Americans and the Bible: Sacred Texts and Social Textures.* New York: Continuum.

# 2

# "Winged Words": Scriptures and Classics as Iconic Texts

William A. Graham

*We consider first some difficulties of facilely differentiating "religious" from "cultural" phenomena, and similarly "scriptures" from ("religious" or "cultural") "classics." Texts in the latter three categories can be identified by their "iconic" status within a given tradition or context, but only on the basis of their social function, not by their form or content. We then consider how it may be possible to study "scriptural" texts constructively in shared discourse with scholars of differing religious backgrounds. Such a common discourse would be facilitated by a heuristic model of scripture as a text extending functionally in two directions, towards the human through interpretation and towards an Absolute or Transcendent ontologically (allowing it to participate in or mediate something of the Absolute to contingent human beings). Finally, we consider whether this model is applicable to "classics" as well as "scriptures" and conclude that on balance it is not. The model thus confirms one of the differences between classics and scriptures.*

For a number of years, I taught an undergraduate course entitled "Scriptures and Classics," which was offered explicitly as a topical introduction to the history of religion. The particular topic was thus not the sole focus, but rather meant to serve as a fruitful point of entry into the rich, complicated world of diverse religious traditions, and religious history, thought, and practice more generally. Why this choice of topic makes sense, when a straight "scriptures" course might seem more logical, is something that I often thought about, especially since the "classics" I used were not all unambiguously "religious" in character (even though all reflected religious thought and usage in their respective cultural contexts).

I will return to this question, but first a bit of "back-story" to explain why I start by referring to this course. I came rather late to the study of religion, and specifically the history of religion, as an academic enterprise, without work in religion before I began doctoral studies. I had instead devoted myself to Western history and comparative literature involving Greek, Latin, French, and German. Once engaged in doctoral study, after spending some time with Sanskrit and Indian studies before finally landing in Arabic and Islamic studies, I inevitably brought to the wider historical and comparative study of religion my own background in the Western classics, both ancient and European. As a result, I often puzzled about but never sorted out satisfactorily for myself exactly where the line between the cultural and the religious, the philosophical and the theological, can be drawn. Literature in particular presented, in my estimation, an arena in which the religious intersected, if not permeated, other types of human meaning-making that we usually label "literature," "poetry," "philosophy," or the like. The traditional literary "classics" of east and west seemed to me, however, to include both overtly religious texts and also texts that one would not identify as "religious" but which have been culturally and imaginatively formative and generative—texts that are truly *iconic* in the sense of being among the highest achievements of their particular linguistic, ethnic, regional, national, or cultural traditions, and thus emblematic of those traditions—and as such also influenced by, and important to, one or more religious traditions of their respective cultures as well.

Such important literary works that are defining expressions, or what I would call "icons," of a given culture, but neither scriptures nor even overtly religious texts, I would distinguish for our purposes as "cultural classics" to separate them from non-scriptural "religious classics." I consider "cultural classics" to include the Homeric epics, the great Greek tragedies, *The Aeneid, Don Quixote,* Shakespeare, *The 1001 Nights*, Kalidasa's *Shakuntala*, the Chinese *Dream of the Red Chamber,* or Lady Murasaki's*Tale of the Genji.* By contrast, I would suggest as "religious classics" works such as Augustine's *Confessions*, Dante's *Divine Comedy*, Teresa of Ávila's *Interior Castle,* Maimonides' *Guide for the Perplexed,* Halevi's *Kuzari*, Ghazali's *Revivification of the Religious Sciences,* Rumi's *Mathnawi,* Valmiki's *Ramayana,* Ramanuja's *Sri [Brahma Sutra] Bhasya,* the Japanese *Kojiki,* and Dogen's "vernacular" [*Kana*] *Shobogenzo.* One could argue about some of these, and there are also texts that are difficult to locate firmly in only one of these two categories: the various medieval Arthurian Grail romances, Milton's *Paradise Lost,* Goethe's *Faust*, the Sanskrit epics of the *Mahabharata* and *Ramayana,* or the eighth-century Japanese *Nihon Shoki* are examples. Certainly there is much religion behind and inside each of these, but are they really significantly "religious" in intent and content? Most perplexing are some of the famous Chinese "four books and five classics" (*shu* and *jing*), for example the *Mengzi,* which some scholars would call "cultural" or "philosophical," others "religious," and still others even "scriptural." So these two categories are decidedly only provisional or heuristic ones to put alongside "scripture" *per se.*

I use *icon* here simply to mean major religiously or culturally charged objects, including books—objects with symbolic, signifying capacity and observable power and/or authority in their respective contexts: objects that are culturally or religiously meaningful for anyone who sees them as *emblem-*

*atic* of something larger, whether something religious, philosophical, or "cultural." Any classic, religious or not, like any scripture, carries a surplus of meaningful signification, symbolism, or affective power that is important, even crucial, to those for whom it is in some sense "classic." In other words, I use "iconic" to designate a book (or anything else) that carries significant cultural and/or religious, and consequently intellectual and/or spiritual, meaning. I want to leave it at this, without hairsplitting as to what is religiously versus culturally significant, or whether anything of human significance can be "*merely* cultural" or "*merely* religious."

This question as to where religion stops and culture begins in literature or any other creative work in the history of civilization was very much at the back of my mind when I began teaching "Scriptures and Classics" in the 1980s. From the outset, I included works that were "classics," but not unambiguously "religious" "classics" in a given culture, and for the most part not "scriptural" in any usual sense. Thus, in addition to scriptures such as the Enuma Elish, Torah, New Testament, Qur'an, Veda, Upanishads, Gita, Buddhist Sutras, Guru Granth Sahib, or the like, I treated the *Analects of Confucius* and the Taoist *Zhuangzi*, about the designation of which as "classic" or "scripture" we could argue, but I also mixed in *Gilgamesh*, the *Aeneid*, Basho's *Narrow Road to Oku*, and *Black Elk Speaks*. We could as easily have read Teresa's *Interior Castle* or *The Divine Comedy* or varied mystical classics of Jewish, Islamic, Christian, or Buddhist tradition; or literary classics such as Ovid's *Metamorphoses*, Sophocles' *Antigone*, the *Mahabharata, Don Quixote*, or *The Brothers Karamazov*. I was not interested in the classification of the texts so much as reading texts that have functioned, we might say, "iconically," whether as scriptures in religious faith and practice or as "religious" or "cultural" literary classics that either present religious issues or simply reflect powerfully the checkered role of religion in human affairs.

The major reason I juxtaposed overtly non-scriptural, "cultural classics" such as *Gilgamesh* or Basho's *Narrow Road* with scriptural texts such as the Vedas, the Lotus Sūtra, or the Bible, was that I wanted my students to find it difficult (and often problematic), as I do, to delineate too sharply where the "religious" and the "cultural" part ways, both in our own Western traditions, where we generally think it is clear how they divide, and much more in other traditions that have traditionally not tried to distinguish religion from culture or even religious from secular. The distinctions among great cultural texts we term "classics," great religious texts we also dub "classics," and the special type of religious texts we identify as "scripture" are similarly not rigid or absolute. Indeed, we apply all three categories only on the basis of the divergent histories of their respective uses and functions, not their content or form. Thus it is finally what I am calling the *iconic* character of all the texts that I chose for the course, not their specific category among different *kinds* of iconic books, which, along with their interest for the history of religion, qualified them.

I cite this course experience because it was the context in which I came to consider the question of the distinctions that we apply to iconic books in order to clarify either what makes one a scripture and another a "religious" classic, or what shows us in a "classic" where the religious leaves off and the cultural or even the secular begins. (Here, please note that I am bracketing altogether the question of great religious texts that might be termed "secondary" but still function *de facto* as "scriptures"—the Mishna, the Hadith, the Bhagavad Gita, or the Ramcarita Manasa, for example.) Ultimately I decided that while it is very useful in the study of religion to understand the important phenomenon of texts that have functioned historically as "scripture," it is less useful to worry too much about whether even some foundational texts—the *Analects, Laozi,* and *Zhuangzi* being notable examples—be called "classics" or "scriptures" (in these cases it is my judgment that they have been both). Nor is it of great consequence whether we distinguish non-scriptural, "religious" classics too sharply from "classic" literary or philosophical texts that may have minimal overt religious content but major moral and philosophical import. "Classic" is a category even more difficult to generalize about and to make satisfactorily precise than is "scripture." Broadly speaking, however, such a classification comes down (as with scripture) to its *iconic* functions in a given society and tradition. Just as I have argued elsewhere that no text is inherently "scriptural" in its content or origin but becomes so only in its reception and function, neither is any text inherently "classical" because of form or content, but instead only so because of its *Wirkungsgeschichte* as a defining, *iconic* text in a given cultural and literary tradition. I would argue that a "classic" of a given tradition can only be distinguished on the one hand from a scriptural text by (i) the latter's ritual, devotional, and liturgical functions and (ii) uniquely sacred and authoritative status, and on the other hand from literary texts of lesser cultural importance by the clearly *iconic* power of its cultural status and function. It of course achieves its status as "classic" because of its inherent quality and universality of content, but it can be recognized as classic only by the status accorded it over time by generations of readers or listeners who find it uniquely important and treat it in iconic fashion in their cultural context.

Here James Watts' elegant suggestion (Chapter 1 above) is a helpful one. He argues there that we should see scripture as a text that is "ritualized along three different dimensions": the semantic, performative, and iconic. This is useful in that we may agree that while scriptures generally exhibit all three dimensions, most classics lack at least one of them—usually the performative, in my estimation. This tallies with my own judgment that Siegfried Morenz and Johannes Leipold got it right over a half-century ago when they identified ritual and especially liturgical functions as particularly indicative of scriptural books (at least in Mediterranean and Near Eastern traditions). I would add the ascription of ultimate theological or religious authority to the liturgical/devotional function as characteristic of scriptures, but either way, texts that we term "classics," even "religious classics," but *not* "scriptures," usually lack most performative functions that scriptures exhibit, apart from their typical semantic and iconic role as texts to be memorized, repeated, and alluded to in much the same way that scriptural texts are.

I have distinguished these text categories and terminology at such length because I think it salutary in studying religion to try to see the gray areas as well as the possibly black-and-white ones in our scholarly as well as everyday usages. Questions of such categories and their terminology are implicit and sometimes explicit in several of the papers prepared for this symposium—in particular the contribution of Karl Solibakke, but also those of others as well. I do not want, however, to debate issues such as the cultural roles of the Vulgate, Luther, or King James Bible versus those of the *Aeneid* in Western Christian culture down to the twentieth century, or the question of the *Bhagavad Gita* as part of the *Mahabharata* epic and the appropriate classification of both in light of the Vedas, Upanishads, or Puranas. Rather, I want to focus on, first, some particular reflections about iconic *scriptural* texts that I hope will prove more fruitful and suggestive, before closing with some thoughts and questions about iconic "*classic*" texts in the light of these reflections.

Specifically, I want to consider two questions: First, how can we best think about, or conceptualize, the functionality of iconic scriptural texts in such a way that we as scholars can deal with them adequately in today's religiously and culturally plural academy? Second, can any answers to this question about scriptures also be applied to those other iconic texts that are not scriptures but "religious" or "cultural" classics?

First, regarding "scriptures": I have puzzled a long time about how to think and talk most usefully about a scriptural book in a scholarly context where participating scholars (as well as any listeners or readers) are variously adherents of the tradition in which the text is seen as scripture and adherents of other traditions who do not view the text as "scripture" at all (indeed who may view wholly different texts, or no texts at all, as "scripture"). In other words, how might scholars representing both *emic* and *etic* approaches to a given scriptural text fruitfully speak about and study that text in the same hermeneutic locus? This is not easy: many persons, scholars or not, have great difficulty with any attempt to contextualize historically and to analyze their own scripture, let alone with historical or literary criticism of its inception, redaction, and fixation. In considering this problem, I wrote a short German *Festschrift* article nearly twenty years ago that contained the seed of an idea that I have developed in more recent years in two further English lectures, one of which is available in print and the other scheduled for publication (Graham 1994, [2012]). In what follows I draw on these earlier efforts to present what I hope to be relevant considerations for this symposium regarding both scriptural and classic "iconic books."

Briefly put, regarding the question as to how a scriptural text might be studied and discussed by a circle of scholars, some of whom consider the text "scripture" and some of whom do not, my solution has been to conceive of scripture heuristically as involving a text that can be seen in its religious function as opening out or extending in two opposite directions, one the human, worldly, or mundane extension and the other the supramundane or transcendent extension. The first, mundane (*diesseitige*) extension is the interpretive engagement with the text by human interpreters who consider it scripture—those to whom it presents itself as a uniquely sacred and authoritative text preserved in writing, print, memorization, chanted repetition, artistic rendering, or the like. In my original German article I argued that this dimension of scripture is characterized by what I termed *Deutungsnotwendigkeit* "interpretive necessity"—every scripture is *necessarily* always being interpreted, in how it is read, recited, illustrated, glossed, handled, or otherwise engaged. The second, and opposite, extension of any scripture involves its linkage to or participation in a transcendent, divine, or otherwise veridical dimension—for the faithful, this is the transmundane (*jenseitige*) connection of their sacred text to some Absolute, be it Truth, Knowledge, God, the Transcendent, or Ultimate Reality. This extension, in my original nomenclature, involves a *Bedeutungsüberschuß*, "a surplus of meaning," an awareness on the part of the faithful that any text perceived as scripture is always more than merely its words and text; it always extends beyond human capacities for understanding it into an ontologically different dimension of reality, truth, and meaning—what a religious person might call the Divine, Transcendent, or Ultimate dimension, which is what he or she sees as crucial to making the text *scripture*.

My chosen terminology here is not meant to be theological but rather descriptive and functional: I am arguing that when we observe how scripture is dealt with *emically* by the faithful of a given religious tradition, what appears is a text that extends in two, diametrically opposed, directions: one towards the faithful (which I now term *the interpretive* extension), and one (which I now term the *ontological* extension) toward the Divine, the Transcendent, God, Truth, or the Ultimate—whatever is perceived by the faithful as the source of their scripture and/or the ultimate, veridical Reality that that scripture mediates to those that "have ears to hear" or "eyes to see."

This is not a complex or particularly startling observation, but heuristically, making it explicit when speaking of scripture opens up possibilities for productive exchange among scholars who themselves differ sharply in their religious and philosophical allegiances—and specifically in their notions about the status of *das Jenseitige*, the transcendent dimension of reality. Whether from an *emic* or *etic* standpoint, scriptures can be considered phenomenologically iconic texts with a special power to mediate, in particular historical contexts, between the mundane, human world and the transmundane, ideal, or normative Reality that *homo religiosus* everywhere has understood to transcend in some absolute way this contingent, material world of sense-perception. That Ultimate Reality may be conceptualized as God or the gods, Truth or Beauty, Changelessness or

Eternality, the Dharma or the Dao, Wisdom or the Good, Order or Reason, the Universal or the Absolute. However conceived, it is always whatever is whole and perfect over against the contingent and limited human condition. Whether this deeper, more abiding Reality is conceived concretely or abstractly, "scriptures" are those texts that religious communities have considered to be its prime mediators. To make this clearer, let me offer examples for each of the two extensions of scripture that I am suggesting are primary to its role in mediating trans-temporal reality in the temporal world.

With regard to the interpretive extension, it is a truism, but an important one, that scripture cannot *exist* without constant interpretation. Here I want to repeat a point I have made above and elsewhere (Graham 1986): scripturality is a *functional*, *relational* quality of a text, not a formal, absolute one. A text only becomes scripture when a community of faith deems it uniquely sacred and authoritative *and uses it as such*, and the interpretive extension of a scriptural text into the minds and lives of the faithful is a defining scriptural function. Simply to read or hear a text or to treat it iconically as scripture is already to engage in interpretation. Scripture is always being extended in the meaning-making of the faithful, always becoming something more than its concrete text alone. Post-modern literary criticism has made this point less radical than it might have been thirty years ago; but it is the case that every text, and none more so than a book of scripture, is at every moment being interpreted by any reader in the light of his or her comprehension, experience, context, faith, and tradition. Just as there is no one physical form of a text that defines it as "scripture," neither is there one "literal" or "true" meaning of a scriptural text, however much every literalist orthodoxy wants to insist that there is. The interpretive extension of scripture, when we conceive of it relationally instead of absolutely, means that scripture could not function as scripture—that is, as holy and authoritative—without the implicit and explicit interpretation that occurs in the very act of treating it as scripture rather than as merely another text. In a real sense, there is no "*sola scriptura,*" even for the first Protestant reformers, since anyone who takes a scriptural text as sole authority already in doing so stands both in an interpretive tradition and in a discrete historical context and cannot escape reading the scriptural word through that tradition and out of that context. In a real sense, the scripture vs. tradition tension that has produced so much polemic in Christian sectarianism and in academic scholarship, is a false dichotomy; scripture is always read in dialogue with whatever cumulative tradition the reader stands in, however novel his or her reading may be, and conversely, tradition is always informed by past and present scriptural readings, both individual and collective.

A telling example of interpretive extension is found in the Jewish notion of the "oral Torah" (*Torah she be-'al peh*), which encompasses the Mishna, Talmud, and Midrash. This is the vast body of discussion and commentary of the rabbis, built up over centuries, on the meanings of the written Torah (*Torah she bi-ktab*). Historically, this oral Torah has carried the same authority for Jews as the written Torah. The Oral Torah is held to have been revealed already to Moses at Sinai alongside the written: whatever interpretations the rabbis have been able to tease out of the written Torah were already given by God at Sinai for the guidance of His people. Here the division between scripture and tradition is no longer clear—and in considerable degree no longer meaningful: functionally, neither exists without the other, and both are ontologically and theologically Torah, God's revealed Law. At Sinai, God saw not only to the revelation of His Law, but also to its exegesis. The written Torah without the interpreting tradition of rabbinic learning is unthinkable. "Love of Torah" is the heart of rabbinic Judaism, determining every other aspect of the tradition, and fundamentally it means unceasing Torah interpretation.

One striking example from Islamic tradition is also noteworthy. While Muhammad was living, he was the effective interpreter of the individual *qur'ans* that were being revealed through him as God's messenger. After his death, the community could only rely on transmitted traditions of his verbal utterances and his observed example to assist them in interpreting the Word of God. One admonition ascribed to him and preserved in the text of an hadith says, "The *Sunnah* [tradition] is judge over the Qur'an, not the Qur'an over the *Sunnah*" (Al-Dārimī 1966, 3). Authentic or not, this saying expresses the inevitable interpretation that mediates (and thus determines) scriptural meaning among the faithful in any tradition.

The Hindu and Buddhist traditions also provide clear examples of scripture's "interpretive extension." In the Hindu case, it has been historically almost unthinkable for anyone to read a sacred text independently of a qualified teacher, a guru who stands in a long line of teachers (the *guruparampara*). Thomas Coburn puts it well in noting that in India, "written documents, unvivified by personal relationship, are meaningless" (Coburn 1989). Meaning is developed and maintained here in a teaching tradition based on interpreting texts. In the related Buddhist case, texts that can be called scriptures have been in a constant process of expansion over the centuries as new texts attach themselves to older ones and claim to be equally the *Buddhavacana*, or "Word of the Buddha" preserved in tradition, voiced by Buddhas in every age, or rediscovered long after the last historical Buddha's death. These texts clearly expand as well as expound the meaning of the oldest sacred texts, and in this way the so-called "Buddhist Canon" of the *Tripitaka* ("Three Baskets"), has been largely built up through the addition of later interpretive texts. This has been especially visible in the Mahayana, where one sees the tendency to identify a single text, for example the Lotus Sutra, as the holiest of scriptures and the key to interpreting all other scriptures. Sometimes even purely commentarial texts like the *Abhidharma* books are reckoned as scripture: one sūtra (the *Adhyāshaya-samcodana*) goes so far as to say that "anything that is well said is a word of the Buddha" (cited from Shantideva's *Shiksa Samuccaya* and from the *Anguttara*

*Nikaya* by McDermott 1984, 29, and Griffiths 1994, 50). This blurs completely the line between scriptural word and interpretive word in a kind of infinite interpretive extension of the basic *Buddhavacana*.

We could multiply examples, but the point would be the same: scripture as a relational reality rather than a literary genre is always being interpreted by being used; it never stands alone, apart from its interpretation. This is both its dynamic quality and its endless potential relevance to any situation at any time, any place.

When we turn from this interpretive extension to my postulated second and contrasting ontological extension of scripture in the understanding of the faithful, in addition to describing this veridical extension as ontological, we might also identify this dimension of scripture as its "transcendent valence" over against the "exegetical valence" of the interpretive extension. "Ontological extension" or "transcendent valence" is a term meant to reflect the fact that a scriptural text is for the faithful never *merely* a text. In scriptural piety, the tangible text of scripture has rarely if ever been seen as its essence or deepest reality; it is what the text communicates or mediates that ultimately counts. There is an observable tendency in every tradition for a scriptural text to partake of the transcendent reality it is perceived to reveal, represent, or mediate. Whether we are talking about Torah, which is for faithful Jews something far greater than the biblical text; or the Guru Granth Sahib, which for Sikhs is far more than its words or venerated physical form; or the Veda, which for Hindus is the Eternal Wisdom, the cosmic *Śabda*, or "Sound" at the heart of creation and reality—in each case we are speaking about a scripture that shares in, or even is itself, The Divine or Ultimate Reality. One recurring aspect of the treatment of a text as holy and authoritative, as bearing ultimate truth, is that for the faithful the text rapidly comes to participate in, and thus to mediate or even embody, transcendence in the mundane, contingent world where it is encountered. Scripturally oriented mystics may understand and express this best (witness the personification of Torah in kabbalistic thought, which holds, as Holdrege [1987, 219] describes it, that "Torah is not simply a book to be studied; it is a living aspect of God with which one can enter into divine communion"). For any person of faith, however, this phenomenon is functionally an expression of the ontological extension of the holy Word into Transcendence (or of Transcendence into the holy Word), and it is this that ultimately gives that Word its unique authority and sacrality as scripture.

In the Islamic case, this is most vivid in the Muslim understanding of the Qur'an as God's verbatim Speech, which can best be understood in Christian terms by saying that the Qur'an is the Divine Logos equivalent in Christian faith not to the Bible, but to the Christ (thus likening Qur'an recitation to the Eucharist). Muslims recognized early on the danger for their theocentrism of calling the Word of God in the Qur'an an eternal Divine attribute, but the fact that this was a point of contention at all indicates how much the Qur'an as God's

Speech participates in the Divine, even if it is theologically understood as the created Word rather than an eternal attribute of the One God. I find great intuitive truth regarding the transcendent tendency in Muslim experience of the Qur'an in Clifford Geertz's comment that in reciting the Qur'an, the Muslim "chants not words about God but of Him, and indeed, as those words are His essence, chants God himself" (Geertz 1976, 1490).

Even in the Christian case, the sense for many Christians of the Bible as God's Word makes the Scriptures not only a testimony to the Christ but a medium of contact with God in Christ. At the heart of the book tradition, Luther himself testifies to this in statements such as this: "...God is especially concerned with the revelation and recognition of his Son; throughout the entire Scripture, Old and New Testaments, *everything is directed to the Son*" [*Luthers Werke* 54:88]. Often he speaks of the Holy Spirit as the mediating force in the Scriptures, calling them, for instance, "the Holy Spirit's own special book, writ and word" (*des heiligen Geists eigen, sonderlich Buch, Schrifft und Wort* [*Luthers Werke* 54: 474]). The Christian earns the name "Christian" only through his faith, which Luther explicitly identifies as *auditum verbi Dei,* "hearing the Word of God" (Hirsch and Rückert 1929, 250; cf. *Luthers Werke* 37: 512–513). Scripture is not only the linguistic center of Christian life; it is finally also the medium of intimacy with God Himself, through His Word, theologically understood as the *Logos* of the Christ, mediated in the *logos* of the Bible.

If we consider Hindu traditions, we find in their treatment of the Veda many traits similar to Jewish attitudes toward the Torah, above all the idea that Veda—holy Knowledge or Wisdom—already existed before Creation and continues to exist eternally. What is striking is the repeated claim that "Veda" is much more than a body of texts. Thus we read in *Rg Veda* X.164.39: "The hymns [of the Veda] exist in the immortal [realm] *(Aksara),* beyond the universe *(Vyoman)* where all the gods live. Whoever knows not that immortal [realm], how could the hymns help him? You, who do know it, are grounded in Eternity." In the *Taittiriya Brahmana*, the "three Vedas" (i.e. *Rg*, *Sama*, and *Yajur*) are described as "threefold Wisdom" (*traya veda*), which is often understood in later texts as a manifestation of the Veda as primordial Being, equivalent to Brahman or an aspect thereof. Still later, in the Puranas, we find that Veda is made an equal to, or even identified with, Brahman or Visnu or Śiva—namely Supreme Reality. The transcendent character of the Veda can also be glimpsed in the unforgettable answer of an eighteenth-century Brahmin to a European visitor who asked him about "the vedic books": *Vedam est, quidquid ad religionem pertinet, vedam no sunt libri,* "Veda is that which pertains to religion; books are not Veda" (Zachariae 1921, 160). In other words, Veda transcends its earthly linguistic vehicle.

To say that a biblical or qur'anic word is "God's Word" is to say that in this Word the faithful have the possibility of encountering God. In an analogous way, in Buddhist tradition, the Mahayana in particular, we find frequently the attempt to identify Sacred Scripture with the Holy Teaching or eternal Dharma that it embodies, and also with both the Buddha himself and the Ultimate Realization of release from rebirth—Nirvana. This is evident in the Lotus Sūtra, which says of itself: "[Among other scriptures,] ... this scripture is the first. / If there is anyone who can hold it, / then he holds the Buddha-body" (trans. from Chinese by Hurwitz 1976, 193; cf. trans. from Sanskrit by Kern 1884, 21: 242). Here "Buddha-body" is the *Dharmakaya*, or eternal form of the Buddha in Mahayana philosophy. *Dharma* refers both to the Buddha's Teaching, which is what Scriptures transmit, and also to the eternal Truth underlying all Reality, which is the goal of the *Dharma* as Teaching. The *Dharmakaya* is associated with the latter. Here Scripture becomes not just a text, but Ultimate Truth itself. Mahayana commentators have also clearly linked Scripture, Dharma (as Teaching or Path), the Buddha-Nature, and Reality. With respect to the "*Prajñaparamita*, or Perfection of Wisdom," which is also the name of a genre of scripture, Dignāgā says, for example,

> Here Scripture is the Truth, the Book, and the path to Truth; all are referred to by the same term and interpenetrate. Scripture extends to encompass the Ultimate. the perfection of Wisdom [*Prajñāpāramitā*] is nondual knowledge; it is also the [Buddha (*Tathagata*)] and [the goal] to be attained. The word also refers to the book and the path, since [the book and the path] have this [*Prajñāpāramitā*] as their meaning and their goal (*Prajñāpāramitā jñānam advayam sā tathāgatah / sādhyā tādarthyayogena tācchabdyam granthamārgayoh*: text in Tucci 1947, 56; trans. Eckel 1992, 99–100).

Similarly, the famous exegete, Vasubandhu, in his *Abhidharmakośa* 4.32, says that "The Master's true Dharma is twofold: it is scripture (*āgama*) and understanding (*adhigama*)" (trans. Eckel 1992, 100). In his commentary, he explains that *āgama* refers to both the three segments of the Buddhist canon (Sutras, Vinaya, Abhidharma) and the understanding of the Path—the way to Enlightenment. These cases show that the Perfection of Wisdom is at once the Truth/Dharma, the Buddha, the scripture, and the path to Truth; all interpenetrate as dimensions of the same ultimate reality. Scripture partakes of the Buddha nature, the Ultimate itself, of which the tangible scriptural word is only one manifestation.

If we can accept the dual scriptural extension I have described, at least as a heuristic model for thinking functionally about scripture, let us turn finally back to our other category of iconic books, namely "classics," religious or cultural. Can we apply this model of dual extension to "classic" as well as "scriptural" texts? When I originally began to think about this essay, I thought that the model might also work for "classics," since they also have an inextricable interpretive extension and are so culturally powerful and meaningful as texts that they too might be seen as mediating some larger realm of truth. On further reflection, however, I have come to believe that classics *do not* present the same kind of ontological extension that the faithful perceive in their scripture, even though the interpretive extension of each is obviously comparable in many ways. I do think that when we consider books that have functioned as scripture for any religious community, we find that these texts carry a mediating force derived from their perceived participation in transcendence—to varying degrees and in varying ways, from tradition to tradition, to be sure. On the other hand, even religious, let alone "cultural" classics, as much as they are beloved and deeply influential in a given context and tradition, do not carry the same quality of ontological *difference* or explicit *participation* in transcendence that a scriptural text typically does (and when they do, they function effectively as scriptures for some subset of the faithful). There seems to me a difference of category here, even though a classic text, whether primarily religious or cultural in character, can exercise great power in the lives of its readers, just as can a scripture.

If I had to fall back on the classic terms of history-of-religions scholarship, I would say that a scripture is always in some sense—in my model, in its ontological extension, obviously—what Gerardus van der Leeuw described as a *kratophany,* or manifestation of power, or what Mircea Eliade called an *hierophany,* or manifestation of the holy. I do not think that even the greatest classics of various cultures and traditions could easily be characterized by either term.

I have come, however, to appreciate the application of the term "iconic" to *both* "scriptures" *and* "classics." Perhaps we could agree on that adjective as at least one that binds these two categories of text together. *Iconic texts* carry special power in both religious and cultural traditions. Often the same iconic text can be a scripture or a religious classic for many members of a given culture and also a cultural classic for many others in the same cultural world who nevertheless do not revere it as scripture. The King James Bible in the Anglophone world and the *Luther Bibel* in the Germanic world have been iconic classics culturally in literature, rhetoric, politics, and art even as they have been iconic scriptures in their respective Protestant-Christian religious traditions. The conundrum of whether to translate the single Chinese term *jing* as "classic" in the case of the so-called "Confucian" text-traditions of Han and post-Han scholars and as "scripture" in the case of the foundational Daoist texts and Buddhist sûtras is both a reminder of the difficulty of cross-cultural translation and also a warning against too-rigid use of categories such as "classic" and "scripture" altogether. Still, the notion of translating *jing* in both cases as "iconic book(s)" is an attractive one that might bracket the issue of "scripture" versus "classic" and even "religious" versus "cultural" while still recognizing the shared power and religio-cultural significance of both kinds of texts. I do not offer it as a solution I am ready to go to the mat for, but I do find it suggestive and worth pursuing further.

The iconic texts we call scriptures as well as those we call classics might both have one quality in common that we can agree on, if only as a gloss on the "iconic books" of our title. That is the quality encapsulated poetically in the famous Homeric phrase of my title tonight: *epea pteroenta,* "winged words."

I use this to designate not only speech that flies from the speaker's or reciter's or reader's mouth to the ears of listeners (or from the page to the eyes of solitary readers), but also speech of which the words, phrases, tropes, or sentences have so impressed themselves on our language and thought that they are imbedded in our unconscious as well as conscious vocabulary. In other words, not only are they preeminent sources of citation and reference in public and private discourse; they also contain words often spoken or cited that lie so deeply imbedded in a given cultural vocabulary that many who use them are not even aware they are drawn from Bible, Homer, Laozi, Ramayana, Gita, Lotus Sutra, Qur'an, Dante, Shakespeare, Basho, Goethe, Montaigne, Melville, or the like. These words belong to the ages largely because of the profundity, historical importance, literary magnificence, persuasive power, sometimes perceived sacrality, and always *iconicity* of the texts from which they have taken flight again and again and soared into the collective consciousness and vocabulary of generation after generation. I suggest that scriptures and classics, as iconic books, are preeminently those texts that we might characterize alike as presenting *winged words.*

## References


Al-Dārimī. 1386/1966. *Kitāb al-Sunan*, ed. 'Abdallāh al-Madanī. 2 vols. Cairo.

Coburn, Thomas. 1989. "'Scripture' in India: Towards a Typology of the Word in Hindu Life," in *Rethinking Scripture: Essays from a Comparative Perspective*, edited by Miriam Levering, 102–128. Albany: State University of New York Press.

Eckel, Malcolm David. 1992. *To See the Buddha: A Philosopher's Quest for the Meaning of Emptiness.* San Francisco, CA: Harper Collins.

Geertz, Clifford. 1976. "Art as a Cultural System." *Modern Language Notes* 91: 1473–1499. http://dx.doi.org/10.2307/2907147

Graham, William A. 1986. "Scripture." In *The Encyclopedia of Religion*, edited by Mircea Eliade *et al.*, 13: 133–145. New York: Macmillan.

———. 1994. "Das Schriftprinzip in vergleichender Sicht." In *Gott ist Schön und Er Liebt die Schönheit/God is Beautiful and He Loves Beauty, Festschrift für Annemarie Schimmel*, edited by Alma Giese and J. Christoph Bürgel, 209–226. Berlin: Peter Lang.

———. 2011. "On the Concept and Functions of Scripture." In *Sacred Texts and Print Culture: The Case of Qur'ān and Bible of the Orthodox Churches During the 18th and 19th Century*, edited by Nadia al-Bagdadi and Mushirul Hasan, forthcoming. Budapest: Central European University Press.

Griffiths, Paul J. 1994. *On Being Buddha.* Albany: State University of New York Press.

Hirsch, E. and H. Rückert, eds. 1929. *Luthers Vorlesung über den Hebräerbrief nach der vatikanischen Handschrift*. Berlin: Walter de Gruyter.

Holdrege, Barbara A. 1987. "Veda and Torah: The Ontological Status of Scripture in the Hindu and Judaic Tradition," Ph.D. dissertation, Harvard University.

Hurwitz, Leon, trans. 1976. *Scripture of the Lotus Blossom of the Fine Dharma*. New York: Columbia University Press.

Kern, H. 1884. "Saddharma-Pundarīka or The Lotus of the True Law." Vol. 21 of *Sacred Books of the East*, edited by F. Max Müller. Reprinted New York: Dover, 1963.

Leipold, Johannes and Siegfried Morenz. 1953. *Heilige Schriften: Betrachtungen zur Religionsgeschichte der antiken Mittelmeerwelt*. Leipzig: Harrassowitz.

Luther, Martin. 1883–. *D. Martin Luthers Werke. Kritische Gesamtausgabe.* Weimar: H. Böhlau.

McDermott, James P. 1984. "Scripture as the Word of the Buddha." *Numen* 31(1): 22–39. http://dx.doi.org/10.1163/156852784X00086

Tucci, G. 1947. "*Prajñāpāramitāpindārtha* of Dignāga." *Journal of the Royal Asiatic Society* 1: 53–75.

Zachariae, Theodor. 1921. *Goettingische gelehrte Anzeigen* (*Königliche Gesellschaft der Wissenschaften*).

# 3

# Talking about "Iconic Books" in the Terminology of Book History

Deirdre C. Stam

*"The book" in its many guises today provides fertile ground for the study of the multiple disciplines and professions in which it has played a central part. Long recognized as a significant carrier of text, the book has lately been seen also as an example of material culture. A consideration of the book's physical properties and uses can provide new insights into the practices and unarticulated beliefs of a cultural community. Here we consider the potential of "the book" for insights into the study of religion. The focus is on "iconic" books, a subset of books that seems intuitively recognizable as a genre but is variously understood by the writers of the essays in this collection. It is not only the nature of iconicity that begs for definition here, but also, more specifically, the aspects of "the book" that cause it to be recognized as iconic. Does its iconicity spring, for example, from the beauty of the copy? The primacy of the edition and the printing? The provenance of the object? As "the book" gains attention, the subject cries out for specific, stable, shared terminology to allow meaningful discussion of its elements across disciplines and fields. Such terminology can be found in the field of book history, a discipline rooted in the world of Gutenberg that continues to flourish in the internet age. This paper discusses terminology. It explores various approaches to defining "iconic," it traces the evolution of the terminology of book history, and it presents a sample of particularly pertinent terms from that discipline to clarify future discussions of aspects of an "iconic book."*

## Defining "Iconic"

The term "iconic" is used promiscuously these days. The related noun, in its literal sense, can be applied to a wide range of entities, including an aspect of the ancient Egyptian hieroglyphic writing system that uses pictorial symbols or "icons" to represent concepts related to those images. The term also can refer to the traditional Greek Orthodox illustration technique used for paintings that become objects of veneration; the religious images depicted with this technique are, of course, usually referred to as "icons." In its adjectival form, the term "iconic" is often used in a metaphorical sense; that is, the term can be applied to objects that enjoy a kind of veneration equivalent in emotive power to that accorded to the "icons"of the Greek Orthodox church. In semiotic theory derived from the nineteenth-century philosopher C. S. Peirce, "icons" are signs that physically resemble their referents, therefore distinguishing them from "symbols" and "indices," which do not.

In contemporary popular culture as seen on the internet, the term "iconic" has been applied to Sophia Loren, Airstream trailers, comic book super-heroes, the old British phone box, Mother Teresa, the Obama campaign t-shirt, Michael Jackson, the World Trade Center, the spectacular movie-flop Cleopatra, and the thin-crusted New York Pizza. Some of these applications relate to literature, but not necessarily the physical book that is the focus of our concern here. These uses remind us of how widely the term is applied in everyday life.

Jonathan Meades (2009) claims that the term is "the adjective of the age"—an icon in itself. He finds extra-logical, and even negative, aspects of the "overused" concept: it is "cosily religiose, softly spiritual...and an expression of humankind's perennial bent towards aggrandizement." In a comment to his essay (which appears beneath these remarks on the same web page), however, Vanessa Hobbs takes a more rigorous approach, claiming that an "iconic" object fulfills three conditions: it is "the first, the best, the most famous or, indeed, the only one of its kind;" it imprints itself indelibly on our minds; and "it embodies specific 'values' and thus speaks to us... in a very clear voice" (Hobbs 2009). Hobbs's comment, in its satisfying logic, amounts to a reasonable working definition for our purposes.

## What is an "iconic" book?

Common modern usage, again drawn from cyberspace, indicates that these "books" are considered "iconic": John Updike's *Rabbit* tetralogy, Irma Rombauer's *Joy of Cooking*, the *Twilight* series of vampire fantasy novels for young adults by Stephenie Meyer, the 120-foot-long scroll-typescript of Jack Kerouac's *On the Road*, Thomas Jefferson's copy of the *Koran*, and Adolf Hitler's *Mein Kampf*. All of these literary entities have the power to summon up a particular cultural milieu, often of a popular kind, relating to a specific time and place. It sometimes happens that a book becomes an icon *out* of its own time, like the *Koran* from Jefferson's library, which has more iconic power today, when Jefferson himself is almost worshipped in some quarters, than it did in its own place and time of manufacture. References to these "iconic books" are immediately recognized by a large segment of their contemporary cultures and in some cases by later cultural contexts. The books embody a concentrated concept, and they call forth strong emotional responses including excitement, inspiration, amusement, and even repulsion. They are thus iconic by Hobbs's definition.

The "iconic power" of a book, however, can be derived from different aspects of books. In the literary examples we have considered thus far, iconic power arose variously from the *contents* of the text (as in *Mein Kampf*), or from the startling *physical form* of the object (as in Kerouac's scroll-form typescript), or from the *association* with a famous person (as in the case of Jefferson's *Koran*, although the text too has an independent claim to iconicity in this example). Other possibilities exist. In order to communicate accurately about the *aspects* of books that contribute to their iconic status, we need a precise set of terms to differentiate among various loci of iconic power. We need to be able to answer unambiguously the question, "Just exactly what qualities of a book make it iconic?"

In describing the common characteristics of "iconic books," James Watts emphasizes their special treatment and notes that these books, in contrast to other books known to a culture, are accorded an emotive reaction by users, admirers, and worshippers. He observes that "Iconic books are texts revered as objects of power rather than just as words of instruction, information, or insight. In religious and secular rituals around the globe, people carry, show, wave, touch and kiss books and other texts, as well as read them" (The Iconic Books Blog). Most of Watts's examples are religious books, but not all aspects of every religious book are iconic; that is, not all aspects elicit public recognition and emotive reaction. Only certain aspects of these books—for example, edition or copy—are accorded this kind of attention. The aspect responsible for "iconicity" thus varies from case to case. The iconic element of specific religious books might involve its aesthetic qualities, one's personal association with it, memories associated with it, and the like. These vary from person to person; in describing our reactions to particular iconic books, some of us might refer to positive emotions of reverence, inspiration, and delight while others might dwell on the negative emotions of fear, anxiety, and even loathing.

Given the variety of our reactions to religious books, we need a consistent vocabulary to distinguish the *aspects* of a religious or literary work that are popularly valued, that is, the aspects that are iconic. What is the determining factor? Is it the contents of the text? Or is it its history as a physical artifact? Or perhaps it is its printing history?

The antiquarian book trade provides such a vocabulary which is available from various sources. The "Bible" of rare book terminology, especially appropriate for the early printed book, is John Carter's *ABC for Book Collectors*, first published in 1952 and now in its eighth edition, which includes brief discussions of terms and their meanings as well as considerable lore about the world of books and book scholarship. A more succinct listing of book-related terms, though focusing to some degree on modern books, is a sixteen-page glossary at the back of Allen Ahearn's *Book Collecting: A Comprehensive Guide*. Yet another, rather terse "dictionary" can be found on the website of the Antiquarian Booksellers' Association of America. Michelle Brown's *Understanding Illuminated Manuscripts: A Guide to Technical Terms* discusses descriptive terms for illuminated manuscripts. Rare Book Schools provide training in the language of descriptive bibliography for professionals of various kinds; the largest is at the University of Virginia which sponsors week-long summer courses.

## A discursive glossary of terms from book history

What follows is a sample of terms that are used, or should be used, in discussions of "iconic books." The list moves from the general to the more specific. Examples of books are drawn primarily from traditional Christian literature.

### *Book*

We have thus far used the word "book" to mean a variety of things: a title, a copy, a format, a volume, an edition, a structure, and a text. All of these meanings for the word "book" are acceptable in every-day speech. The term is useful for referring broadly to an object that records an idea in coded form. While the word "book" is used legitimately in both popular language and in scholarly work in other fields, the word is not actually a technical term in descriptive bibliography. Its usage is too broad and too inconsistent for purposes of precise communication. Since "the book" is properly considered a broad concept, and not a specific thing, and the term should not, among scholars, be used to mean any one particular form of recorded information.

In everyday language, people who use "book" typically have in mind a text that has been printed mechanically on sheets of paper that were later folded and bound together on one of their sides into a form that is convenient to hold, to read, and transport. The technical name for this physical format is a "codex." In everyday speech, the term "book" can actually refer to other formats besides the codex such as a scroll, a structure of attached and inscribed leaves from a bush or tree, a microfiche [card], a "Google Book" file available through the internet, or even the free-standing "Kindle [book]" which processes and displays electronic files. Given the variety of its meanings, it is best to avoid the word "book" altogether in technical discussions of physical entities.

### *Work*

Another problematic term for book historians, a "work" can mean something so general as the product of mental labor, such as a poem or story, or even a musical composition. An idea becomes a "work" when it is given form. A literary "work" might be recorded in written language or alternately it might be transmitted in consistent form by oral tradition. Before it is recorded on some physical medium, it does not necessarily have a physical form at all. Stories of the Christian Bible, for example, are works; known variations in their forms are seemingly countless and the forms keep evolving. Works become "texts" when they are given written (or fixed) form, such as being printed in a specific edition. Like "book," the term "work" is best avoided in technical discussions of the physical book. The term does, however, have a useful place in textual editing, or in general discussions of intellectual history and tradition.

### *Text*

A text is a specific manifestation of an author's recorded words. A "text" is more "fixed" than a "work." In a literary text, chosen words are related to one another according to a specific syntax and a consistent manner. In the purest case, a "text" remains constant whatever the manner of publication. Such consistency is, of course, more of an ideal than a reality.

The term has slightly different meanings in different communities. To readers, the term "text" can refer to the words on the page in contrast to the decorations or footnotes. To the typesetter, "text" can also mean the written document from which he is setting type; it can also refer to the resultant words on the printed page. In Christian religious services, the term "text" is often used to denote the verse or passage chosen from Christian literary tradition as the subject of a sermon, or in support of a doctrine (Webster's 1943). In all these cases, the concept of fixity underlies the term "text." Having recognized the potential for alterations in a text that can occur among various printings and versions, numerous religious denominations have attempted to "fix" biblical and other religious texts throughout the years by authorizing one particular textual form or version to be consistent with their beliefs and history.

### *Manuscript*

Manuscripts are hand-written texts. Although all manuscript "books" (be they codices or scrolls) are unique, and many are considered to be works of art, not all are iconic. To be considered so, they must be widely recognized and they must elicit an emotional response. A few pages of a legal text from the year 1200, for example, might yield major insights for a legal scholar, but the manuscript itself, by virtue of its contents or age alone, might not reach "iconic" status.

Among the brightest stars in this firmament of manuscript icons are the *Book of Kells* and the *Très Riches Heures du Duc de Berry*. While both these examples are recognized as accomplished artistic works in codex form, the reasons for their iconic status are explained in large part by reception theory. That is, their iconicity derives to a large degree from their significance to both medieval and modern culture. Nationalism could be a large part of the explanation. These icons are sometimes interpreted in our time as representing localized manifestations of distinct artistic styles and literary genres that demonstrate the genius inherent to a particular place and a particular culture. (See further Brown in this volume.)

### *Codex*

This Latin term was originally used for hinged pairs of waxed, wooden writing tablets. It came to designate a collection of sheets of papyrus or parchment stitched up the middle and written on both sides. Thus each sheet with a single fold could produce four written pages.

The modern popularity of the *codex* is closely tied to the development of Christianity. By the first century BCE, Roman notebooks, made from leaves of parchment, were used for rough copy, first drafts, and notes. This convenient form was initially used largely for commercial copies of classical literature. Christians probably adopted this parchment manual format for the Scriptures used in their liturgy because a codex is easier to handle than a scroll and because one can fit more text on comparable supporting material for a codex, which has two sides of text, than for a scroll, which has only one. The "new technology" of the codex thus made the production of a book cheaper since it saved on parchment, an expensive material to produce or purchase. By the early second century, virtually all Christian Scripture was reproduced in codex form (for more detailed discussion of the codex's development in iconic form by ancient Christianity, see Larson in this volume). In traditional Christian pictorial iconography, for this reason, the Hebrew prophets are represented with scrolls and the Evangelists with codices (see further Brown in this volume).

### *Volume*

Technically, one volume is a single codex. A specific literary text from a single edition, before the standardization of printing and binding in about 1800, might have been bound into one volume for one customer or into several volumes for another customer. Similarly, two separate texts might be bound together in one volume. When referring to a single text representing one work that is bound into many related volumes, one should use the term "title," or "multi-volume text," rather than simply the singular term "volume." The term "volume" should not, in any case, be used synonymously with "work."

### *Edition and printing*

A single "edition" includes the copies of a book or other printed material which originate from the same printing plates or setting of type. If 500 copies of a book, for example, are printed on October 5, and 300 copies are printed from the same substantially unchanged plates on December 10 of the same year, all 800 copies are part of the same edition.

The term "printing" describes all of the copies of a book or other printed material which originate from the same press run or from the same plates or setting of type *without significant changes and at one time*. In the example given for "Edition" above, the 500 copies would be the first printing and the 300 copies comprise the second printing. It sometimes happens that very minor changes, such as the correcting of spelling errors, are made between printings, or even in the course of a single print run. These minor changes do not warrant the designation of a new printing.

In collecting circles, there is a fetish for the first appearance of a work. The greatest enthusiasm is accorded the original manuscript. Next in importance, in the ordinary course of thing, is the "first edition, first printing." There is also great enthusiasm for primacy of other kinds: the first appearance of a work in a particular place, a particular feature such as illustrations, or a specific language. A prime example of a "double first" is John Eliot's "Indian Bible," printed between 1660 and 1663. It was the first Bible printed in America and the first in a native American language, in this case in a dialect of the Algonquin people.

### *Binding*

Of all that might be said about binding, the most useful facts for book historians concern technological history and publishing practice. Very early in the history of printed books, printed sheets were often sold as a unit in unbound form. Bindings, usually leather in some form, were usually created uniquely for individual copies of an edition. These bindings were designed and executed by independent craftsmen for specific owners. (All manuscript codices were, and are, seen as unique, and their bindings are correspondingly unique.) When fairly large editions—in the thousands—became possible in the early 1800s because of advances in hand-set printing technology, all of the copies of one edition/one printing were typically issued with uniform, inexpensive, paper-covered boards (or bindings); these covers might be removed and the volumes rebound for particular buyers. With the adoption of machine typesetting and printing in the nineteenth century, very large editions became the norm, and all copies of one edition/one printing were typically issued with decorative covers, rendered in coverings of cardboard or cloth rather than leather, mimicking the look of decorated leather bindings. After about 1830 or so, all copies of one commercial edition usually had virtually identical bindings. In short, for codices printed prior to the twentieth century, one cannot assume that all copies of an edition (or a printing within an edition) were both printed and bound at one time and in one place; nor can one assume that all copies of one edition/one printing would look, or even essentially be, substantially alike. Scholars are used to seeing copies of the *Nuremberg Chronicle* of 1493 (Schedel), for example, with unique bindings, but they expect, and indeed find, most copies of the single-volume *Oxford Lectern Bible* of 1935 designed by Bruce Rogers to be commercially bound in black leather with minimal gold lettering (*The Holy Bible* 1935).

### *Provenance*

Provenance, or, as the English prefer, "provenience," traces a book's previous ownership. The provenance of a copy may be clearly marked by the owner's name, arms, bookplate, or other evidence in the book itself; it may also be less clearly indicated by press-marks from his/her library; or it may have to be pieced together from outside sources such as auction records or booksellers' catalogues.

### *Association copy*

Often closely tied to provenance, this term is applied to a copy which once belonged to, or was annotated by the author, a copy which once belonged to someone connected with the author or someone of interest in his own right, a copy which was used by a famous person, or, perhaps most interestingly, a copy which belonged to someone peculiarly associated with its contents. The term "association copy" might be used, by extension, to mean any book owned by a famous person, although this is too casual a use of the term. Indications of a meaningful connection between book and well-known person require establishing some point of real contact other than the simple fact of possession.

An example of a copy whose value derived largely from association would be the "Washington Bible" used for the swearing-in ceremonies of U.S. Presidents George Washington, Warren Harding, Dwight Eisenhower, and George H. W. Bush at their inaugurations (Bible 1767). While the Bible text or the edition of the book used here might generally be considered "iconic" on account of its content, in fact it is in this case the association with the U.S. Presidents that gives this codex its claim to elevated iconic status. Extensive documentation exists to substantiate the claim to iconicity on this account.

### *Errata*

The history of significant mistakes in the printing of the Christian Bible has been the cause of great interest among readers, collectors, and book dealers over the years. The more egregious errors have made all copies with such mistakes the source of strong emotional reactions including glee, bemusement, horror, and even rage. An example of an iconic book whose renown comes from a type-setting error is the "Wicked Bible"of 1631 , known also as the "Adulterous Bible" or the "Sinners' Bible" (Holy Bible 1660–1663). In the first edition/first printing, the seventh commandment was rendered initially as: "Thou shalt commit adultery." The printers were fined for their significant and presumably accidental omission of the negative, and most copies were withdrawn immediately. The eleven surviving copies of this icon of biblical error are today a curiosity that is accorded more notoriety than respect.

## The development of antiquarian book terminology

Among the first standardized listing of books, with physical characteristics noted, were the catalogues of the well-known, international Frankfurt Book Fairs. The first examples known are from the mid-1500s, just a century after Gutenberg's printing innovations. These catalogues responded to a need in the book trade to advertise available titles to potential purchasers and to provide a means for ordering from publishers. Early printing was a commercial venture and the vocabulary for describing their publications was an essential tool for the trade.

That trade involved manufacturing a product that would stimulate the buyer to part with significant sums of money for the satisfaction of ownership. Here, iconicity enters the picture. In his catalogue, the publisher and/or the dealer needed to make a case for both the technical excellence and the emotional appeal of his product. These two aspects of his wares—their physical properties and their iconic elements–were not at all antithetical. In fact, they were entirely complementary in the eyes of the book dealer. He needed an agreed upon vocabulary in order to make his claim of value convincing.

Let us look more closely at the relationship of iconicity and commercial value as these concepts apply to the book. I once heard an unusually philosophical accountant explain that "a budget is a metaphor for the values of an institution." Similarly, the market value of cultural artifacts, including books, is at least a gross indication of the emotive value placed on them at a given time by their society. (Here, we readily admit to a Western situation and bias where capitalism reigns supreme.) Included in antiquarian book dealers' catalogues are both prices and extensive descriptions that attempt to justify the usually elevated prices. The descriptive data supplied about each book in such catalogues can be considered an indication to the book sellers of what *aspects* of a book are known to be valued by the contemporary society. Furthermore, they quantify the degree of value ascribed to these artifacts.

Over the past five centuries of book production, a vast network of people engaged in the antiquarian book trade has developed standards, or at least guidelines, to describe and "price" antiquarian books, religious texts prominent among them. This network of book dealers has been and still is highly motivated, primarily by commercial concerns, to develop and refine a method for describing books in consistent and unambiguous ways. Judging from catalogue descriptions, criteria for "iconicity" or cultural value have changed very little in the West over the past five centuries since the emergence of printing and of the attendant book trade. For example, among the elements that we recognize as constituting iconicity, antiquarians, even today, especially value the first appearance of a work, its authorship, and its connection to famous owners.

The terminology of book sellers used to describe the elements of a valuable book has also remained relatively stable over the past 400 years or so. Their very precise definitions that have international acceptance are used not only in the book trade itself and by its institutional and private customers, but also by scholars of the book whose investigations often focus on the physical manifestations of texts, iconic or otherwise. This terminology is, to a large degree, shared by dealer, customer, and scholar alike. This precision therefore makes these terms useful for clear communication among those who are interested in analyzing and describing why a society values one book above another, and, more specifically, what aspect of the book causes it to be raised to iconic status.

We add here a caveat about pricing and "value." One does not *always* find that antiquarian dealers' prices are an indication of scholarly evaluation, popular evaluation, or even owners' evaluation. Supply and demand, as well as elements of iconicity, enter into pricing decisions. Let us consider some examples. Sometimes a book, a Bible for example, is considered "iconic" and highly valued by at least a small circle of admirers mainly on account of the attributes of a unique *copy*. Nineteenth-century family Bibles, for example, are regarded as significant legacies by descendants of a family that prizes its copy not primarily for its textual content but mainly for its association with beloved forebears and significant family events. It might carry notations of births and deaths over many years. A copy of such a Bible may well have had a hefty "cover price" when new. The copy is unique by reasons of association and is therefore rare, but the demand currently is extremely low and the market value today would be correspondingly very low, likely far lower by any standard than its original price. In other words, supply is adequate to the demand and thus the market value is negligible. In a contrasting example, a ubiquitous book of low original market value (or even supplied free to the reader by its publisher) can nonetheless be considered "iconic" because of its unique and telling *distribution mode*, among other qualities. Despite the recognition and respect the book enjoys in contemporary society, it may still have little market value. An example is the *Holy Bible* distributed by the Gideons International, a published text regarded fondly by many lonely travelers from a timely encounter with a copy in a bleak hotel room. In this case, it is the *mode of distribution* that makes the publication iconic, though not valuable in a monetary sense (see Beal in this volume). All editions, and all printings, of the Bible bearing the Gideon identification share the designation of iconicity among those with affecting memories of their first encounter. The "Gideon Bible" has crept into popular culture so fully that no less an icon than Marilyn Monroe sings about this book in the movie *Gentlemen Prefer Blonds*. As she leaves her boyfriend for a road trip, she attempts to reassure him of her intention to remain faithful by crooning:

> *I'll be in my room alone,*
> *Every post-meridian.*
> *And I'll be with my diary and*
> *That book by Mr. Gideon.*

The set of terms developed by the book trade and its partners is alive and well in our time. Many contemporary scholarly projects in book history, frequently internet-based, attest to the utility of this vocabulary. Examples of such scholarly projects include the *Incunabula Short Title Catalogue* [ISTC], which is an electronic bibliographic database maintained by the British Library, and the *English Short-Title Catalog* [ESTC], a collaborative library project consisting of a "vast database designed to include a bibliographic record, with holdings, of every surviving copy of letterpress produced in Great Britain or any of its dependencies, in any language, worldwide, from 1473–1800." A related example is *Early English Books Online* [EEBO], consisting largely of ESTC metadata and full digital facsimiles derived from the Early English Books microfilm collection. An example of a more analytical and focused work issued in paper is Owen Gingerich's *An Annotated Census of Copernicus' 'De Revolutionibus,'* the original work by Copernicus having been published in Nuremberg, 1543, and in Basel, 1566. As for projects that deal with religious literature more specifically, an online example would be the *Gutenberg Bible Census*, a scholarly tool being compiled by Clausen Books.

### Twentieth-century refinement of the vocabulary of book history

The technical vocabulary of the book trade and the library prospers today in the inter-disciplinary field of "book history." The past few decades have seen book history techniques and terminology, such as analytical bibliography, creep into other various fields as well, from history to law to scripture studies. The consciousness, and consequent study, of how ideas represented in specific physical forms have been circulated in disciplines and in society more broadly have come to be labeled "book history" or, more recently, "print culture" (even though some documents of closely related interest are actually in manuscript form).

Modern book history developed out of the positivism prevalent in British academia after World War II, which led to the development of "bibliographical description," a discipline that concerns itself in its purest form with the physical properties, consistently described, of printed books. Prominent works in this vein in its early years were Fredson Bowers's *Principles of Bibliographical Description,* 1949; W. W. Greg's investigations of printed English drama before the Restoration, 1939-1959; Ronald B. McKerrow's *An Introduction to Bibliography for Literary Students* of 1928; and Philip Gaskell's *New Introduction to Bibliography*, 1972, which includes much information on manufacturing processes prior to 1900. Some of this early work, known as "descriptive bibliography," is dry as dust to read as narrative, but its development of a scientifically inspired, specific vocabulary is enormously useful today to anyone—scholar or collector—who is trying to differentiate among "bookish" artifacts that seem to be similar at first glance.

After an historical interlude of literary theory in the last half of the twentieth century, largely derived from French scholarship focusing on understanding the socially negotiated construction of meaning in texts, book history developed a synthesis of approaches. In the 1980s, Donald McKenzie advocated *both* the close examination of the physical object *and* the exploration of its societal context in order to understand the "book's" production and, ultimately, its reception into contemporary society. More recently, Robert Darnton and Anthony Grafton have emerged as eloquent spokesmen for this integrated approach. Today, the most active work in book history seems to involve exploring reading practices as indicators of what various reading communities thought and understood about what they read. Most book historians today would agree with Marshall McLuhan, writing in the 1960s, that the medium—the physical book in this case—is at least a very large part of the message. McLuhan's contention could, with a little stretching, be considered a justification for the descriptive and analytical aspects of book history.

### Why learn this language to describe the all-familiar "book"?

The advancement of scholarship in the field of book history, widely defined, depends upon reasonable consistency in language and meaning among those participating in its intellectual conversations. Book history, an emerging interdisciplinary field, cannot depend upon the unity of a traditional discipline to provide a language understandable to all of its participants. Those who toil in these multi-varietal vineyards need to agree on a meta-language to describe the fine points of their evidentiary base which is comprised of manuscripts and printed publications. Scholars from all fields, religion among them, interested in iconic books who wish to draw upon the work of book historians and engage them in exploratory conversations will need to understand the technical language of book history which has endured since the sixteenth century, and which is enjoying a renaissance in our own time.

Scholars wishing to draw from the long tradition of book knowledge and to participate in current conversations about the history of the book, including the conception of the iconic book specifically, would do well to become familiar with the technical language of this subfield. It is not, after all, an altogether foreign language to many historians of religion and other humanistic scholars, but it is one that was put aside for many years as attention turned to other aspects of this broad field. There is strong evidence today—some contained in the papers of this collection—that this "language" can yield insights of current interest to many whose knowledge traditions have come to them through "the book."

### References

Ahearn, Allen. 1989. *Book Collecting: A Comprehensive Guide*. New York: Putnam, 1989.

Antiquarian Booksellers' Association of America. "Glossary" and "Learn about Rare Books." http://hq.abaa.org/books/antiquarian/abaapages/glossary Accessed 18 March 2011.

Bible. 1767. London: Printed by Mark Baskett. [Known as the "Washington Bible" and used on occasion for presidential inaugurations since that of George Washington; owned by the Masonic St. John's Lodge No. 1].

Bowers, Fredson. 1949. *Principles of Bibliographical Description.* Princeton, NJ: Princeton University Press.

Brown, Michelle P. 1994. *Understanding Illuminated Manuscripts: A Guide to Technical Terms.* Malibu, CA and London: J. Paul Getty Museum and the British Library.

Carter, John, and Nicholas Barker. 2004. *ABC for Book Collectors*, 8th ed. New Castle, DE: Oak Knoll Press; London: British Library, [Note: John Carter was sole author of the previous 7 editions.] This work is online at http://www.ilab.org/eng/documentation/29-abc_for_book_collectors.html [Note underscoring between title words. Accessed 18 March 2011.

Clausen Books; Gutenberg Bible Census. www.clausenbooks.com/gutenbergcensus.htm Accessed 18 March 2011.

Darnton, Robert. 1979. *The Business of Enlightenment: A Publishing History of the Encyclopédie, 1775–1800*. Cambridge, MA: Harvard University Press.

Early English Books Online. http://eebo.chadwyck.com Accessed 18 March 2011. [Note: EEBO is a subscription service, available through many research libraries.]

Eliot, John [translator]. 1660–1663. *The Holy Bible...Translated into the Indian Language...* Cambridge, MA: Samuel Green and Marmaduke Johnson.

English Short-Title Catalog (1473–1800). http://estc.ucr.edu Accessed 18 March 2011.

Gaskell, Philip. 1972. *A New Introduction to Bibliography.* Oxford: Oxford University Press.

Gingerich, Owen. 2002. *An Annotated Census of Copernicus'* De Revolutionibus. Leiden: Brill.

Grafton, Anthony. 1997. *Commerce with the Classics: Ancient Books and Renaissance Readers.* Ann Arbor: University of Michigan Press.

———. 2008. *Codex in Crisis.* New York: The Crumpled Press.

Greg, W. W. 1951. *A Bibliography of the English Printed Drama to the Restoration.* London: Printed for the Bibliographical Society at the University Press, Oxford.

Hitler, Adolph. 1925. *Mein Kampf.* Munich: Franz Eher.

Hobbs, Vanessa. 2009. Comment following "Iconic: The Adjective of the Age." The Economist: More Intelligent Life, Spring. http://moreintelligentlife.com/story/cover-whats-iconic-and-whats-not Accessed March 18, 2012.

*Holy Bible.* 1631. [*"The Wicked Bible" or "The Adulterous Bible" or "The Sinners' Bible."*] London: Robert Barker and Martin Lucas [Royal Printers].

*The Holy Bible.* 1935. Appointed to be Read in Churches. Oxford: Oxford University Press. [Known as the "Oxford Lectern Bible."]

The Iconic Books Blog. http://iconicbooks.blogspot.com/ Accessed 18 March 2011.

*Koran.* [*Alcoran of Mohammed.* Translated by George Sale.] 1734. London: Hawes, Clarke, Collins and Wilcox.

McKenzie, Donald. 1986. *Bibliography and the Sociology of Texts: The Panizzi Lectures.* London: The British Library.

McKerrow, Ronald B. 1927. *An Introduction to Bibliography for Literary Students.* Oxford: Clarendon Press.

Meades, Jonathan. 2009. "Iconic: The Adjective of the Age." *The Economist: More Intelligent Life*, Spring. http://moreintelligentlife.com/story/cover-whats-iconic-and-whats-not

Meyer, Stephanie. 2005. *Twilight.* New York: Little, Brown. Also in the series: *New Moon* (2006), *Eclipse* (2007), and *Breaking Dawn* (2008).

National Heritage Museum: George Washington's Inaugural Bible. http://nationalheritagemuseum.typepad.com/library_and_archives/2009/01/george-washingtons-inaugural-bible.html Accessed 18 March 2011.
Rare Book School [located at the University of Virginia]. http://www.rarebookschool.org/ Accessed 18 March 2011.
Rombauer, Irma von Starkloff; Marion Rombauer Becker; and Ginnie Hofmann. c. 1951. *The Joy of Cooking*. Indianapolis: Bobbs-Merrill Co.
Schedel, Hartmann. 1493. *Liber Chronicarum*. Nuremberg: Anton Koberger. [Printed without title page; known in English as *The Nuremberg Chronicle*.]
Updike, John. 1995. *Rabbit Angstrom: a tetraology*. New York: Knopf. Contains these works: *Rabbit, Run* (1960), *Rabbit Redux* (1971), *Rabbit Is Rich* (1981), *Rabbit At Rest* (1990), and *Rabbit Remembered* (2001).
*Webster's Collegiate Dictionary*. 1943. Springfield, MA: G. & C. Merriam Company.

# II

# Images and Texts

# 4

# The Iconic Book: The Image of the Bible in Early Christian Rituals

Dorina Miller Parmenter

*To elucidate some of the origins of what Martin Marty has called "America's Iconic Book," this essay analyzes early Christian rituals in which the Bible functions as an icon, that is, as a material object that invokes the presence of the divine. After an introductory discussion of icons, it shows that early Christian communal rituals of Gospel procession and display as well as popular and private ritual uses of scripture as a miracle-working object parallel the uses and functions of Orthodox portrait icons while circumventing issues of idolatry. Examples come from a survey of early Christian liturgies, conciliar and legal records, the physical appearance of Bibles and Gospel books, the representations of books in art, and written arguments from the iconoclastic controversies of the eighth and ninth centuries.*

> Salute the cross, and take the Gospel in your hands. Place it on your eyes and on your heart. Stand on your feet in front of the cross, without sitting down, and after every chapter you have read, place the Gospel on the cushion and prostrate yourself before it up to ten times.... Thanks to this external adoration which you give to God, you will conceive in your heart the internal adoration and the effect of divine grace which a human tongue cannot describe.
>
> (Philoxenos of Mabbug, cited in Rapp 2007, 198; see Graffin 1961, 463–464 for original)

## Introduction: The Bible as an icon

I first became aware of the iconicity of the Bible from an iconoclastic religion professor when I attended a small, midwestern Christian college. One day, while reminiscing with a group of students over how scandalous he was, someone recounted the story of how this teacher had dropped a Bible on the classroom floor and nonchalantly stood on it as he continued with his lecture. Upon hearing of this incident, everyone gasped, including me. After considering my own surprise and shock, which I am sure was the effect he intended to produce,

I began to think that the professor's gesture was totally cool and continued to repeat the story to others. Now, after hearing similar tales from many other religion students and teachers, it seems to me that this classroom phenomenon is either a widespread academic myth or a well-used heuristic device. Either way, the visceral response that the iconoclastic gesture elicits reveals deeply ingrained attitudes within Christian culture about the Bible as an icon.

This attitude was articulated by the prominent historian of American religions, Martin Marty, in his centennial address to the Society of Biblical Literature in 1980. Commenting on Americans' reluctance to embrace or even acknowledge biblical criticism, Marty claims that Protestant-infused America is far from aniconic, that is, lacking in religious images. Instead, the Bible is a ubiquitous image that is taken for granted and whose status remains largely untouched by the conclusions of historical research, as in President Grover Cleveland's famous statement that "[t]he Bible is good enough for me, just the old book under which I was brought up" (Parker 1911, 382, in Marty 1982, 3). Marty argues that the image of the Bible provides a "carapace," or a "protective covering, the sort of cocoon that individuals, subcultures, and in their own way societies need for the structuring of experience" (Marty 1982, 6). He continues:

> [t]he Bible, in American history and in much of present-day culture, provided and provides as an object a basic element in the carapace of images, and its presumed contents, that for which one would consult if one did consult it, remove the "just happening" dimension from human existence.
>
> (Marty 1982, 6–7; see also 16)

At the most basic level, the Bible is an iconic book in this way: it is an immediately recognizable symbol with connotations of admiration or veneration that has both social and psychological import (Wharton 2003, 4).[1]

But lost in this common modern perception that an icon is an untouchable sacred symbol is the history of icons that takes seriously their ritual aspect, particularly as revealed by the history and uses of Orthodox Christian portrait icons. My claim is that the Christian Bible is an icon not only because of the status accorded to its textual contents, but also because of the familiarity generated and sustained by its use as a ritual object. This function is generally denied or ignored because of the tradition of anti-ritualism in Protestant Christianity that denigrates many revered material objects as "idols." This tradition strips icons of their materiality in order to make images purely ref-

1. The next edition of the *Oxford English Dictionary* will include a new addition under the definition for "icon": "A person or thing regarded as a representative symbol, esp. of a culture or movement; a person, institution, etc. considered worthy of admiration or respect. Freq. with modifying word." *Oxford English Dictionary Online*, draft additions 2001, dictionary.oed.com, s.v. "icon." In contemporary American culture, most people are familiar with symbolic icons in the sense of "pop culture icons" such as Oprah, Superman, and Elvis (the top three American pop culture icons, according to VH1 television and *People* magazine; see "200 Greatest Pop Culture Icons List: The Folks that Have Impacted American Society," *Newsweek*, October 27, 2003).

erential or symbolic. But despite these aniconic and iconoclastic ideals, the Bible remains one of the few legitimate religious images and manipulable objects in modern Protestantism. Present yet highly unremarkable, the Bible is prominently displayed in churches on pulpits, altars, banners, and stained-glass windows. The Bible is ritually engaged in many church processionals, including wedding and funeral processions, but also in the more mundane individual ritual of walking into church with a Bible in one's hand or tucked under one's arm. These practices show that the Bible is more than an object for one's private gaze. It is also an image for social display and physical manipulation that contributes to community cohesion.

The academic study of religion, particularly the study of Christianity, has usually overlooked the Bible as a ritual object. *Religionswissenschaft*, growing from its Protestant and philological roots in the ideas of F. Max Müller and others, has privileged words, concepts, or beliefs recorded in texts as the content of "religion," and belittled actions and objects as "magical" or "primitive" in comparison. Thus the use of sacred writings has been a sign of "advancement" in civilization and religion; conversely, "less advanced" religions have been depicted as centered around objects and actions rather than reading texts. A related element in this hierarchy is that advanced religions orient towards an abstract god, while less advanced religions orient towards the material world (Bianchi 1995). Since these perspectives can and have been used to justify the superiority of particular religions or cultures over others, both academically and politically, examining scripture as an object and not just a text can reveal the roles of and relationships between texts, rituals, and myths in religious studies. I am concerned more specifically with the hegemony of Protestant Christianity in religious studies and in modern colonialism. The latent attitude of superiority that creates the hierarchical binaries of text versus ritual and abstract versus material not only belittles those religions and cultures labeled "less advanced," but overlooks the ritual and material aspects of (Protestant) Christianity itself.

Similarly, theories of the nature of Orthodox Christian icons emphasize how a material image signifies an abstract reality, much like the signifying function of language. One should "read" an icon in ways analogous to how one reads a text (Stuart 1975, 25–27). Reverence properly belongs to what is signified, thus circumventing charges of idolatry. What is frequently down-played but still present in icon theory is the value of the material world and the necessity for humans to engage it ritually to get closer to the divine.

In order to emphasize material aspects that are often disregarded in both the study of icons and the study of scripture, this essay will focus on the early uses and contexts of the Christian Bible as a ritual object. As scholars mine historical texts, we understandably focus on what the text is "saying." But when reading texts (as well as other historical evidence such as pictorial images, architecture, and liturgical objects), we can also keep an eye on material and ritual concerns. The assumption of the ritual theorist is that cultures construct value in multifaceted ways that involve all parts of the human being rather than just the individual and inner feelings, cognitions, or beliefs that are usually associated with texts. Collective and external actions generate meaning by engaging the body and the senses, thereby connecting us with communities and their histories, and with objects in our world (usually associated with ritual). This is not to say that rituals cannot be private, individual, innovative, or textual, as the second part of this essay makes clear. But if a ritual action does not somehow express or coincide with shared cultural meanings and assumptions about value, if it is too removed from the economies of one's own society, it is no longer considered ritual but marginalized as "neurotic" or "fetishistic" (Pietz 1985, 1987, 1988).

The book has functioned as one of the most powerful tools in Christian history. Undoubtedly the preeminent Western book, the Christian Bible, has influenced more people than any other book in world history. But the foundations and legitimizations for actions, morals, and beliefs that Christians derive from this book are not only about the messages gleaned from the text, but also involve the power and authority that have been accorded to the Bible as a sacred object that can be ritually engaged. My thesis is that the Bible, as both text and physical entity, has been and continues to function as an icon—an image that mediates between the material and spiritual world and thus is a portable locus of religious power.

## The form and function of icons

Before surveying Bible rituals, I want to specify what I mean by the category "icon." (These definitions and explanations derive from the Christian tradition but are similar to the perceptions of icons in the ancient Near East; see Toorn 1997.) The ancient Greek understanding of *eikon* as "a figure, image, likeness" (Liddell and Scott) is very broad and not always useful when delineating terms, but this definition does contrast with that for "symbol." *Symbolon* is "a sign or mark to infer a thing by" (Liddell and Scott) where the relationship between the symbol and its referent is arbitrary and must be learned. "Figure," "image," and "likeness" each refer to a direct relationship based on similarity between what is seen and what is represented in the icon; there is a "natural," rather than conventional, connection between the image and the original to which it relates.

As Christians articulated various positions on the legitimacy, role, and function of images in the iconoclastic controversies of the eighth and ninth centuries, they defined the religious icon more precisely. An icon is first of all an image on a material substrate; it is an object that shows something. That is, an icon is not a mental image; it is the image made possible by its existence through the material. According to Byzantine icon theory, an icon is a secondary visual depiction that represents a primary prototype or model, a divine original. As one sees the material image with the eyes, one is shown something that cannot be seen (Stuart 1975, 27–31). Thus the controversy over icons not only concerned the relationship between the representation and what was represented, but also the relationship between the visual, tactile world and the invisible, immaterial world of the divine. Supporters of icons generally followed a Neoplatonic-Christian worldview and did not advocate a strict dualism between body and spirit, the visible and the invisible, or materiality and immateriality. They instead visualized a hierarchy between these and other polarities. While the spiritual referent is consistently primary (or higher) in the iconic relationship, the materiality of the image is still essential. An icon that is immediately present and physical makes the invocation of higher realities possible—the icon acts as a mediator. As Peter Brown has eloquently described it, "The icon was a hole in the dyke separating the visible world from the divine, and through this hole there oozed precious driblets from the great sea of God's mercy: icons were active" (P. Brown 1973, 7).

Therefore, what I mean by "icon" involves not only an issue of visuality, but also one of materiality. The debates over icons and images in the Byzantine churches as well as during the Reformations of the sixteenth century concern the legitimacy of material, earthly objects being used to facilitate a relationship with immaterial, divine beings. How one perceives an icon depends on one's perception of the status of the material world and the efficacy of human practice in facilitating a relationship with the divine world. That is, the issue of icons is an issue of ritual.[2]

## Part One: Early Christian communal book rituals

In "The Question of the Book: Religion as Texture," David Miller articulates underlying images associated with texts and books through an etymological analysis. He writes:

> [p]erhaps there is resident within our notion of "text" a picture, an image, a way of imagining the authority and power of books, a perspective. And perhaps this unconscious perspective may be discovered by mining the meanings of our linguistic ways of speaking and thinking about books, by digging for the picture which lays deep within the soil of our language, by descending into the imagery which captivates our understanding all the more by our not knowing its presence or whereabouts. (D. Miller 1987, 54)

Just as Miller explores our possible unconscious perceptions in the vicissitudes of words about books, I would like to point out the image of the Book that emerges in an examination of various early Christian rituals. It is my contention that the image of the Bible carried over from these ritual contexts, and

2. Divergent perspectives on icons and rituals (i.e. the status of human objects, practices, and capabilities in relation to one's theology) are further elucidated in Jonathan Z. Smith's distinction between "locative" and "utopian" religions. See in particular his essays in *Map is not Territory* (1978).

supported by Christian myths of the Book (which I will explore in a separate study), generates an unconscious perspective that contributes to the iconic status of the Bible. Part One of this survey will focus on rituals of Gospel procession and display in early Christian communities. I will examine how Bibles were brought into a congregation, where they were put for viewing, and why these actions took place. (Here "Bible" refers to any biblical text or group of texts, which in Christian tradition is generally in a codex form, but not exclusively the pandect Bible that binds the Old and New Testaments together in one volume. The objects used in these rituals were usually codices of the four canonical Gospels [see Humfress 2007, 149–158].) Part Two will examine more popular and private (that is, less regulated) ritual uses of scripture as a miracle-working object, akin to manipulations of wonder-working relics.

## Early Christian ceremonies with the book

Scholars do not know much about the rituals of early Christians. The letters of Paul, the Acts of the Apostles, and other early Christian literature indicate that in the first century Christians gathered in the homes of the wealthier Christians in the community (Phil 2; Col 4:15; 1 Cor 16:19; cf. Rom 16:5). There is no archaeological evidence that specific places for Christian worship were built until the third century; the house-church at Dura in Syria is the earliest archaeological example (Lowden 1997, 17–25). It is likely that the earliest Christians modeled their gatherings after synagogue practices, so the focus was on scripture reading, religious instruction, prayer, singing, and the sharing of food and funds (1 Cor 11:17–33; 16:1; cf. Pliny, *Letters* 10.98–99, trans. Firth 1900, in MacMullen and Lane 1990, 164–66). In the middle of second century, Justin Martyr writes in his first *Apology:*

> on the day called Sunday, all who live in cities or in the country gather together to one place, and the memoirs of the apostles or the writings of the prophets are read, as long as time permits; then, when the reader has ceased, the president verbally instructs, and exhorts to the imitation of these good things. Then we all rise together and pray, and...when our prayer is ended, bread and wine and water are brought, and the president in like manner offers prayers and thanksgivings, according to his ability, and the people assent, saying Amen; and there is a distribution to each, and a participation of that over which thanks have been given, and to those who are absent a portion is sent by the deacons.
> (*1 Apol.* 67, in *ANF*, vol. 1, 186)

There is literary evidence for the Christian office of "reader" in the early third century from Hippolytus, who tells us that "the reader is appointed by the bishop's giving him the book" (*Apostolic Tradition* I.12, in Easton 1934, 40), but it seems the task of reading to the congregation was absorbed into the higher orders by the fourth century, when communicating scripture became more about authoritative interpretation than merely the ability to read (Gamble 1995, 221–223). Isidore of Pelusium reports from the fifth century that the bishop reads the Gospels, but only after he "removes the stole that signals his role as the representative of Christ in order to show that 'the Lord himself is present' " (Rapp 2007, 197, citing Isadore, *Ep*. 1.136 [*PG* 78:272D]; for a contemporary example, see Dilasser 1999, 134).

After Constantine gave public legitimacy to Christian worship in the fourth century, we find evidence of further ceremonial surrounding the Gospel book. Egeria's *Travels* (ca. 380 CE) describes the Sunday service at Constantine's Church of the Holy Sepulchre in Jerusalem, where the bishop processes with the Gospel book and incense before the Gospel is read:

> After... three psalms and prayers they [the clergy] take censers into the cave of the Anastasis, so that the whole Anastasis basilica is filled with the smell. Then the bishop, standing inside the screen, takes the Gospel book and goes to the door, where he himself reads the account of the Lord's resurrection. At the beginning of the reading the whole assembly groans and laments at all that the Lord underwent for us, and the way they weep would move even the hardest heart to tears.
>
> (Egeria, *Travels* 24.8–24.11, trans. Wilkinson 1971, 123–27; see also Dix 1945, 426–429; Petrucci 1995, 23–24)

Perhaps to justify why Christians used a pagan custom of lighting lamps and carrying candles at religious festivities (so Dix 1945, 416–18), Jerome interprets the lighting of candles at Gospel readings as symbolic at many levels, the highest of which is the light representing the Word.

> Throughout the whole Eastern Church...whenever the Gospel is to be read the candles are lighted, although the dawn may be reddening the sky, not of course to scatter the darkness, but by way of evidencing our joy. And accordingly the virgins in the Gospel always have their lamps lighted [Matt 25:1]. And the Apostles are told to have their loins girded, and their lamps burning in their hands [Luke 12:35]. And of John Baptist we read, "He was the lamp that burneth and shineth" [John 5:35] so that, under the figure of corporeal light, that light is represented of which we read in the Psalter, "Thy word is a lamp unto my feet, O Lord, and a light unto my paths" [Ps. 119:105].
>
> (*Against Vigilantius* 7, in *NPNF*, ser. 2, vol. 6, 420; cf. John 1:1–9)[3]

### The development of the liturgy

As Christian liturgical spaces and practices were increasingly demarcated, it became standard for the Gospel to be processed through the congregation before it was read. From liturgical writings and also from the design of many of the extant Gospel bindings from this period, it seems that the Gospel was

3. These ritual elements of incense and lights were common to processions of various sorts in the Greco-Roman world, including funerals and imperial marches, with various significations like the giving of honor, sacrificial offering, and blessing; see Dix 1945, 416–430. By the fourth century, Christians would not have much contact with Jewish ritual; there is little evidence that Gospel processions are modeled on Torah processions, but instead seem to be more like pagan funerary, cultic, and imperial processions; see Broek 1979.

raised above the head of the deacon, priest, or bishop during the procession as a gesture of respect, and also to allow the Gospel to be seen, touched, and/or kissed by the most people. In the sixth century, Paul the Silentiary writes that the Gospel was carried within reach of the lay faithful:

> Now for these fence walls [of the solea, between the sanctuary and the ambo] they have not placed lofty slabs, but they are as high up as the navel of a man standing by them; and here the priest (lit., the "gospel man") as he holds the golden Gospel passes along, and the surging crowd strive to touch the sacred book with their lips and hands, while moving waves of people break around. (*Descr. ambonis*, lines 244–251 [ed. Bekker 1837, 56], in Mathews 1971, 124–125)

Art historian John Lowden has argued that, unlike the Byzantine iconography of processions such as the mosaic of Justinian and his court at San Vitale, where the emperor is the focal point and the sacred objects are depicted carried low so the men's faces can be seen, and unlike most contemporary Gospel-raisings where the codex is either carried closed or open with the text out, the iconography of early Christian luxury bindings themselves indicates that they were processed with the codex open and the covers displayed out, so the binding acted as a diptych. One such diptych, panels now at the Metropolitan Museum of Art in New York, illustrates two evangelists in procession with a large cross, each carrying a Gospel with the covers visible to spectators, showing "self-referential images of the book on the book." Lowden suggests, "[p]erhaps they are processing toward us bearing Christ himself. As the cross is an image of Christ, so is the gospel book. As the evangelists bear Christ, so does the person who carries this book in procession" (Lowden 2007, 28, and fig. 5).

By the fifth century we begin to have both visual and textual references to Gospels displayed on altars during the liturgy. Our best images come from the mosaics of the Orthodox Baptistery of Ravenna, which depict four altars that serve as pedestals for one of each of the four Gospels. Similar iconography can be seen at the Rotunda of St. George in Thessaloniki and the Church of the Nativity in Bethlehem. Between the sixth and the ninth centuries, when relics were removed from martyr's tombs and enshrined beneath altars, the initial part of the liturgy that involves the entrance of the Gospels was understood as a funeral procession, with the altar representing Christ's tomb (Bogdanović 2002, 13). Comparison of three pyxides from the sixth century clearly shows this interpretation iconographically: the imagery of a visit to the tomb under a tabernacle-like canopy on one pyxis becomes translated on the others into a visit to a canopied altar that holds a Gospel book (St. Clair 1979).

Perhaps more common than the association of the altar with the tomb is the altar with a throne. There were literal thrones in Byzantine and Roman churches—for the bishop and the emperor, if present—but the first enthroned in the liturgical procession was the Gospel when it was placed on the altar. Germanus of Constantinople described this act as Christ enthroned as "the ruler of all, [presiding] in the midst of his apostles" (*Historia ecclesiastica* 7,

13 [*PG* 98:384–453], in Mathews 1971, 150). The fact that the book precedes both the entrance and the seating of all other participants in the procession "gives it precedence of rank," according to Thomas Mathews, since "the place of honor in Byzantine processional order is the first place" (1971, 142). The Christ/codex on a liturgical throne/altar can be seen on a door panel of St. Sophia's in Constantinople (Walter 1970, fig. 114) and in a miniature from the canons of the Second Council of Nicaea (Paris suppl. gr. 1085, f. 107v., in Walter 1970, fig. 28; see also 235–239).

The book on the altar, liturgically and iconographically conflated with tomb, shrine, offering-site, and throne, ritually activates the space for the reenactment of Christ's death, resurrection, and rule in the next part of the liturgy that includes the Gospel reading and the Eucharist. According to St. Germain of Paris, as the book is moved from the altar to the ambo to be read, "thus emerges the procession of the holy Gospels or the power of Christ triumphant over death" (*Exposition brevis antiquiae liturgiae gallicanae* [*PL* 72:91], in Petrucci 1995, 24) and the Word of the "Living Christ" is read (Dilasser 1999, 134).

### Rituals of the book in conciliar and judicial settings

This ritual of enthroning Gospels so that Christ might preside "in the midst of his apostles" also took place at ecumenical councils, presumably beginning with the First Council of Nicaea in 325, but well attested in the Council of Ephesus of 431 and in subsequent councils (Walter 1970, 147; Humfress 2007, 151). The Council of Ephesus convened "with the holy gospels lying on the throne in the middle and showing Christ himself present among us" (Council of Ephesus [Mansi, *Sacrorum conciliorum* 4, 1237C], in Rapp 2007, 197). The monk Besa makes the most of this practice of enthroning Gospels at councils in his heroic tale of his Apa Shenoute of Atripe. In his hyperbolic account, Shenoute bests "the impious Nestorius" at the center chair:

> When [the council participants in Ephesus] went into the church to set out the seats and sit down, they set out in the middle of the assembly another seat and placed upon it the four holy gospels. When the impious Nestorius came in with a great display of pride and shamelessness, he then picked up the four holy gospels, placed them on the ground, and sat down in the chair. When my father Apa Shenoute saw what Nestorius had done, he leaped quickly to his feet in righteous anger in the midst of our holy fathers, seized the gospels, picked them up from the ground, and struck the impious Nestorius on his chest, saying: "Do you want the Son of God to sit on the ground while you sit on the chair?"

When Nestorius questioned Shenoute's authority at the synod, Shenoute replied, "I am he whom God wished to come here in order to rebuke you for your iniquities and reveal the errors of your impiety!" And as befits a heretic, claims Besa, "At that very moment, [Nestorius] fell off his chair to the ground, and in the midst of the synod of our fathers, he was possessed by the devil" (Besa 1983, 78–79).

The tradition of the enthronement of the Gospels/Christ at ecumenical councils is preserved in the twelfth-century illumination of the Manuscript of Gregory of Nazianzus, where the Council of Constantinople (381) is depicted with the Gospels in the most prominent and honorable position (Ainalov 1961, fig. 100). Similar iconography is used for an illustration of the First Council of Nicaea (325) in a sixteenth-century painting (Walter 1970, fig. 46; cf. fig. 44), and both portrayals follow the common pattern of Christ enthroned among his apostles, such as the fourth-century apse mosaic of St. Pudenziana in Rome (Mathews 1993, fig. 71; see 92–114).

On the basis of this idea that Christ sanctioned the outcome of a dispute if the Gospels were present, the Justinian Code of 530 stipulates that courtroom proceedings would only be legal after the Christian scriptures had been "placed before the judicial seat, and remain[ed] there, not only during the beginning, but also throughout the entire examination, until the very end, and the promulgation of the final decision" (*Codex Justinianus* 3.1.14.1, in Humfress 2007, 148). If any party of the dispute were absent, the Justinian Code provides that "the case should proceed without any impediment, for as soon as the Holy Scriptures are brought forward, the absence of the litigant is supplied by the presence of God" (*CJ* 3.1.13.4). Caroline Humfress has noted that the Gospels in the room were not used as reference books on proper Christian law or behavior; the "letter of the law" was Roman. Humfress concludes that:

> In Justinianic courtrooms, however, it was enough to have copies of the gospel texts on display during legal processes and to rely upon them in procedural contexts, such as the swearing of oaths. Justinian thus harnessed the power and identity of the quintessential Christian books, without the need to actually open those texts in order to consult their words during every legal process. What was important to Justinian was that the Christian God should be literally called in to the courtroom, should be spiritually "present," and the gospel books functioned as the avenue of invocation. The placing of gospel books within Justinianic courtrooms thus ensured that the place of judgment and the legal participants were animated by the Holy Spirit, but the cases themselves were still judged according to the letter of "Roman" law. (Humfress 2007, 158)

In addition to the ritual act of bringing the Gospel and thus the legitimizing presence of Christ/God to the entire legal procedure, individuals involved in the case were to "be sworn with their hands upon the Holy Gospels," sometimes stipulated as the same "copy of the Gospels that has already been placed before the judge in the tribunal" (*CJ* 3.1.14.4 [530] and 2.58[59].2pr [531]; see Humfress 2007, 150). Participants thus engaged a multifaceted tradition of legitimation, validation, and judgment by the book. The idea that there exists a heavenly writing that aids creation, records destinies, and confers power on those who access or possess it is articulated on ancient clay tablets from Mesopotamia. Judaism, Christianity, and Islam retain the same myth pattern with the image of a heavenly book or books, referenced for creation, revealed to humans, and consulted for judgment. I will pursue the origins and Christian development of this myth of the book in a separate study.

The New Testament incorporates the person of Christ into the imagery of judgment by the book in the poetry of the Gospel of John and more graphically in the apocalyptic visions in the Revelation of John. In these texts, Christ is the first and last Word, instrumental in creation, and finally enthroned in judgment (John 1; Rev 1:8; 21:6; 22:13). In Revelation 4–5, John has a vision of God on a throne who offers the scroll with seven seals, which no one can open but the slaughtered lamb that is Christ. After the seals are opened, Christ sits on a white throne and opens the books of judgment and the book of life to determine the fates of the dead (Rev 20:11–15). In the Heavenly Jerusalem,

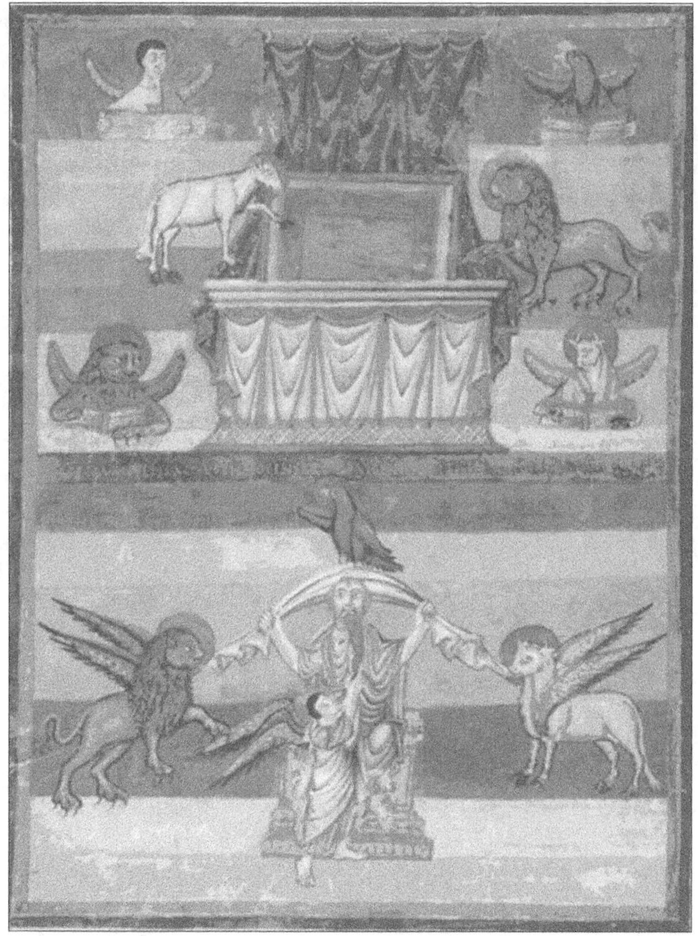

Figure 1. Frontispiece for the Revelation of John, the Grandval Bible, British Library Add. Ms. 10546, f. 449fr. (British Library, London, England). 

John sees the "throne of God and of the Lamb" where God will be worshipped in eternal light (Rev 22:3–5). Another early Christian text, *The Gospel of Truth*, draws these images together clearly:

> In their hearts appeared the living book of the living, which is written in the father's thought and intellect.... [A]nd no one had been able to take it up, inasmuch as it was ordained that whoever should take it up would be put to death. Nothing would have been able to appear among those who believed in salvation, had not that book come forward.
>
> Therefore the merciful and faithful Jesus became patient and accepted the sufferings even unto taking up that book: inasmuch as he knew that his death would mean life for many.... Jesus appeared, wrapped himself in that document, was nailed to a piece of wood, and published the father's edict upon the cross. (*Gospel of Truth* III. 19.34–20.27 [Malinine *et al.*, 1956, 1961], in Layton 1987, 255]

These symbols for Christ as Word, Book, Lamb, Judge, and Ruler are conflated in mosaic images like the scroll and cross enthroned on the Triumphal Arch of S. Maria Maggiore and the altar with lamb, cross, and scroll at S. Prassede in Rome. A similar image is found with a scroll and dove enthroned at S. Prisca at Capua Vetere (Baranov 2002, after Grabar 1968, 115; see also Walter 1970, 235–39). Illuminated frontispieces for the Revelation of John from the Grandval Bible (British Library Add. Ms. 10546, f. 449fr.) and the First Bible of Charles the Bald (Bibliothèque nationale Ms. lat. 1, fol. 415v, in Kessler 2000, color plate VII) show a codex on an throne/altar with other symbols of apocalypse

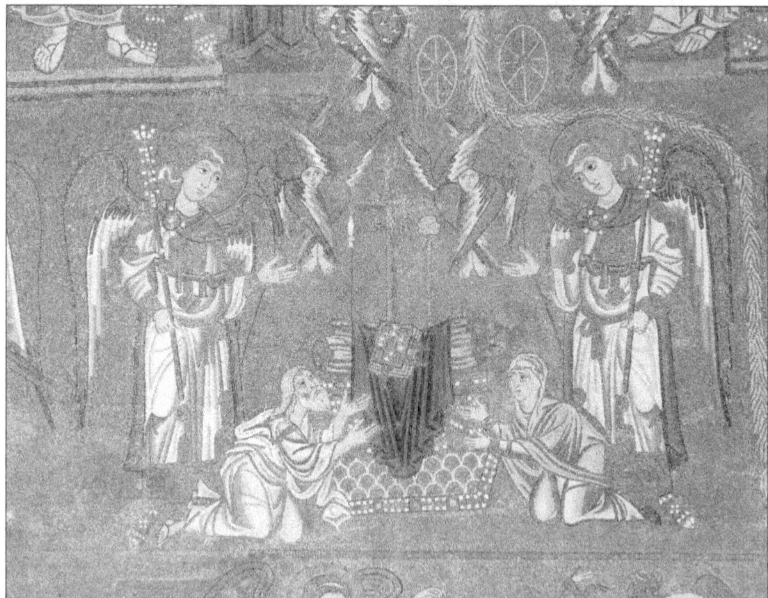

Figure 2. detail from the Last Judgment, S. Maria Assunta, Torcello, Italy (CameraphotoArte, Venice / Art Resource, NY).

and judgment from Revelation. Iconographic parallels to the bottom register of each picture tie the spoken revelations of the Old Testament to the visual and material revelation of the Word (here, the Book) in the New Testament (Kessler 2006).

Another grand mosaic, the Resurrection register of the Last Judgment wall of S. Maria Assunta in Torcello, unites the beginning (Genesis) and the end (Revelation) of the book, as Adam and Eve kneel in supplication before a codex enthroned (see Brandon 1967, 119).

Again, I would like to distinguish between symbols and icons: to the observer of these two-dimensional mosaics, the book, throne, cross, lamb, and so on, operate as symbols of Christ. There is no intrinsic relationship between the signifier and what is signified; one has to know the code established through Christian myths of Christ as the divine Logos, the Word that dwelled with God in heaven and became accessible to humans, appearing in the flesh (John 1:1–14), dying on the cross as a sacrificial lamb, opening the books of judgment, and ruling over the faithful. In the mosaic from Torcello, we see this symbolic code operating effectively: instead of the human form of Christ seated on the throne, he is here represented as the heavenly Book itself: the eternal divine Word and also the Book of Life. Between this two-dimensional symbolic imagery of the book and the invisible heavenly Book, however, there is the iconic book that can be engaged through ritual. This is the *object* that invokes the heavenly Book: the Word of God. The iconic book is the ritual mediator between the human actors and the divine presence that they seek.

## The Bible and iconoclasm

Between the sixth and the ninth centuries, when the liturgy was solidified and elucidated by Patriarchs like Germanus of Constantinople, the iconoclastic controversy was also brewing. Even though material practices surrounding icons were the principal issue in the debates, iconoclasts approved the Bible as an object for worship. The elevation of the text apparently made its materiality innocuous. Many supporters of icons noted the inconsistency of this position that sustained and supported the Bible as a ritual object while other images of Christ were rejected. Iconophile John of Damascus wrote against the iconoclasts, "Why do you worship the book and spit upon the picture?" (*Against Constantius* 3 [*PG* 95:316], in Pelikan 1974, 131) as did Nicephorus, "[E]ither accept these [icons], or get rid of those [Gospels]" (*Refutation* 1.37 [*PG* 100:292] in Pelikan 1974, 131). They argued that between the words of the Gospels and the pictures of the icons the image of Christ was the same, and while both media were human-made, they were necessary for theological knowledge and worship of God (Pelikan 1974, 125, 133). In the anti-iconoclastic Decree of the Second Council of Nicaea (787), icons were validated on a par with the cross and the Gospels as important items for religious worship, "[f]or the honour which is paid to the image passes on to that which the image represents, and he who reveres the image reveres in it the subject represented" (*NPNF* ser. 2, vol. 14, 550). This idea was reaffirmed in the pronouncement of the synod of 869: "The holy images of our Lord Jesus Christ shall be honored in like manner as the Gospel-book" (*Canons of the Fourth Council of Constantinople* 3 [Mansi, *Sacrorum conciliorum* 16:400], trans. Schroeder 1937).

Peter Brown and other historians consider the sixth century to be the end of antiquity and the beginning of the Middle Ages because of a shift from complex spiritual ideas, represented by the holy man and his literary products, to the "hardening of boundaries" and "inner rigidity" represented by a veneration of holy things, including books and icons (P. Brown 1971, 172–183). This conclusion is confirmed by Armando Petrucci, who has examined the iconography of Christian books in Western mosaics and sarcophagi from the fourth to the eighth century. Petrucci divides the iconography into two distinct styles and periods. The first period, from the fourth to the sixth century, is fairly consistent in its depiction of books that are open with text to be read, often held in the hands of Christ, apostles, evangelists, or saints. Petrucci detects a shift in the iconography of the Christian book in the sixth century to portraits with a closed, jeweled Gospel book or Bible, an iconographic pattern that is firmly in place by the eighth century and continues into the medieval period. He concludes that "the book itself had gradually been transformed from an instrument of writing and reading, to be used and thus open, into an object of adoration and a jewel-box of mysteries, not to be used directly and thus closed" (Petrucci 1995, 29).

## Rituals of the book: Theory and practice

Theoretical justifications for the use of portrait icons and other sacred icons like the Christian Bible or Gospels consistently focus on the process of mediation: while the material is essential for the manifestation of the divine, this medium also creates an important difference. That is, the image that one can see through the material substrate is not the divine form itself because pure form is unmediated and therefore invisible. Theoretically, in the iconic relationship, the prototype is necessarily primary and the visible image secondary; thus, any adoration given to the image is intended for the divine original and not the individual manifestation.

But in practice, the theoretical process of mediation is taken for granted. One interacts with what is sensible and accessible, and therefore the representative icon is treated as though it were the represented itself. As mentioned above, Peter Brown relates the "rise" of the use of icons in the sixth century to a "decline" of accessibility to holy men and their relics: people's "search for a face" (1973, 15) led to the use of portrait icons which were considered relics, or remnants, of a holy person's life on earth. Like the healings and other miracles once provided by the holy person ("a living icon") who could channel and intercede with God's power,

> the icon merely filled a gap left by the physical absence of the holy man, whether this was due to distance or death. The same mechanisms that had focused on the figure of the holy man (who was often as silent or as far removed above the beholder, as would have been the case with St. Symeon Stylites, as was any icon) could be brought to bear on the icon: they could even be heightened by the capacity of the silent portrait of the dead to take an even heavier charge of urgency and idealization without answering back.
>
> (P. Brown 1973, 12–13)

Iconoclasts could accept the theoretical justification of icons (that some material objects could represent the divine), but they limited acceptable holy objects to those that had been consecrated by the Church (the Eucharist and the basilica) or had been given directly by God (the sign of the cross given to Constantine and the Eucharist given by Christ at the Last Supper) (P. Brown 1973, 5; in a larger study, I will show that myths of the Bible claimed that the heavenly book was given directly to humans by God). According to iconoclasts, "[i]cons could not be holy because they had received no consecration from above," that is, from God or from the Church, "[t]hey had received only an illegitimate consecration from below" through the stories of their origin and powers (1973, 6; see also Belting 1994, 4–6 on "legends of veracity"). According to Peter Brown, the issue of the iconoclastic debates was not how images worked, but which images were considered holy. As we have seen, some non-figurative icons remained acceptable in most Christian liturgies despite regional variations: Christ was believed to be present in the ritual of the Eucharist and the rituals of procession and enthronement of the Gospels. But private iconic rituals with either portrait icons or Gospel books were not controllable by the Church. It is the popular and more private uses of iconic scripture that reveal the attitudes that Christians have toward the power of their holy books. From the perspective of Church authorities, these attitudes could be (and were) perceived to be "superstitious" pagan holdouts, based on a misunderstanding of the relationship between the human and the divine. But the religious practices of ordinary Christians outside of liturgical rituals reveal attitudes that also underlie official Church practices involving the veneration of the book. Thus, the boundary between sanctioned communal rituals and popular practices is heuristic and fluid rather than argumentative (Broek 1979). This was particularly the case in the British Isles, where Rome (and Constantinople even less) had little direct control over "official" Church rituals such as, for example, the procession of the relics of St. Columba in making appeals for rain (see below).

## Part Two: Early Christian popular book rituals

Sanctioned liturgical rituals that employed the Gospels or Bible as a functional icon operated in dialogue with several cultural assumptions about the contagious power of holy objects connected to holy people, including their written products. Just as a relic's beneficial effect was brought about by its physical contact with a holy person, that power further entered other areas of proximity to the relic. Thus the reliquary, the altar over the reliquary, the chapel that housed the altar, the church that contained the chapel, and the city where the church was built all became sacred ritual sites to the pilgrim who believed in the object's power (Drogin 1989, 32–33). Pilgrims came to these places and touched particular objects associated with the relic with a desire for protection from future harm or for the cure of immediate wounds.

A similar attitude toward the effective power of language and writing was prevalent in cultures where few were literate and those who were usually held positions of status and influence. The manipulation of written language can and still does have great effect on others. Combined with widespread myths that explain how writing originates with the gods and then is given to humans for their use (while the gods still control the books that record cosmic fates), the use of books with sacred status, such as the Gospels or the Bible, not to mention other sacred texts like the Torah and the Qur'an, is doubly potent. As with blessings from other holy sources, the ritual manipulation of Christian scriptures, either in whole or in part, was believed by many to bestow protection and healing from present or future suffering.

Church leaders accepted and/or encouraged this use of the Bible to different degrees, which are closely related to their acceptance of the possibility that objects could function as icons. If there were no mistake that the ritual with the physical copy of the book and/or scriptural text was tapping God's miraculous power, there was little problem. But when it seemed that people were focused on the materials themselves and not their spiritual referent, then clergy often condemned manipulating the Bible for purposes other than textual edification or redirected practitioners to the effective power of the spirit rather than the desired effects of material manipulation.

## The power of writing in the Western tradition

Like the myths of many cultures, Western mythologies tell of the divine origins of language. In ancient Egypt, Thoth was the god of wisdom, the inventor of writing, and the bearer and bestower of secret knowledge that was sought by learned scribes, priests, and princes (Lesko 1987). Thoth was associated with Hermes in the Greek tradition, who was the inventor of the alphabet as well as a trickster and spellbinder. Plato's *Phaedrus* tells the story of Thoth/Hermes who gives the king of Egypt the gift of writing, "a drug [*pharmakon*] for memory and wisdom" (274e, in Nichols 1998, 85), a charm or spell that is a dangerous potion (see P. C. Miller 1986, 488–492). Plato's acknowledgment of the paradox of writing—that it bears the power to create and destroy—lies behind most Western associations of writing with "magic" and molds a tradition of philosophical and religious commentary "about the powers that supervise our ex nihilo creation of discourse for altering reality" (Covino 1994, 5). Covino uses this association of writing and "spelling," seen in the medieval meaning of the word "grammar" as general learning, including magic and astrology, to point out the powerful qualities of all language. Language has the power to influence the course of events either by spellbinding, which limits experience, or by expanding the creative possibilities for human action (1994, 9, 21). Evidence of magical writing from the Hellenistic period includes inscribed gems, curse tablets, spells written on papyrus or metal, magic handbooks, and written hymns (Betz 1987, 93), all of which demonstrate the compulsive force of language (P. C. Miller 1986, 494) and the power given to the written word in the Greco-Roman imagination. This power inherent in words makes books all the more authoritative, as Jack Goody has observed: "To the extent that spells and other attempts to control the course of events are dependent upon the magic of the words, to this extent they tend to give way to the worship of the book" (1977, 149–150). Adding to this sacred aura of writing was the perception that writing (i.e. hieroglyphics, the "speech of the gods") revealed the divine or was the image of the god itself. Marc Drogin explains this relationship between divine speech and presence:

> A proper noun, when it described or named a god, *was* the god and not merely a symbolic equivalent. Similarly, his words did more than represent him; they *were* him, to such an extent that when a god was carried in a religious procession, it was his words and not necessarily a statue of him that was carried.
> (1989, 34)

## The Bible as a popular Christian icon: Private Gospel rituals

Christianity was the first religious and intellectual tradition of the West to implement the codex book form, used consistently by Christians after the fourth century. While Christianity retained the Jewish esteem for texts, the smaller and less expensive codex form encouraged and fostered a reliance on the written word. According to Harry Gamble, though the average early Christian was probably not literate, his or her religious community was organized around books, "read aloud in worship, interpreted in preaching and catechesis, cited in apologetical debates, deployed in intramural theological disputes, and perused for personal edification" (1995, 141). This new relationship to books and writing was accompanied by veneration for and manipulation of Christian texts. Gamble points out that "in a society in which few could read, texts were esoteric objects to many, and if spoken words were powerful, so were inscribed words, for they had the advantage of duration and secrecy" (1995, 237).

If Christians possessed a Bible or Gospel book, they therefore had a potent tool. They had a traditional repository of power—a book of divine writing—that not only provided the narrative of God's revelation in Christ, but effectively acted as a representative of Christ himself. Just as rituals of the book brought legitimacy to communal events such as worship services, councils, and legal hearings, private book rituals harnessed the same power for protection and healing from potentially destructive forces. Stories abound of Gospels putting out fires, being untouched by fire or water, and providing the antidote to snakebite or cures of other illnesses (Drogin 1989, 75–77; Rapp 2007, 199).

The Church Fathers were ambivalent about private Gospel rituals in much the same way that some iconoclasts were wary of ritual icons. In theory, God did manifest his power through holy objects, but the likelihood that popular practices would promote "misunderstandings" of how sacred objects and images work by focusing on the representation rather than on what it represented held the potential for idolatry. Iconoclasts could prohibit figurative sacred images altogether to help people resist their idolatrous temptations, but the use of the Bible could not be prohibited.

Augustine and John Chrysostom each refer to the use of the Gospels as apotropaic devices, not to ban the practices, but to spurn practitioners to focus on the spiritual effect and meaning of the text instead of using biblical charms and amulets. For example, Augustine is frequently cited as attesting to the practice of placing the Gospels under one's head to relieve a headache. But his attitude toward the practice is sarcastic and mournful:

> When thy head aches, we praise thee if thou placest the gospel at thy head, instead of having recourse to an amulet. For so far has human weakness proceeded, and so lamentable is the estate of those who have recourse to amulets, that we rejoice when we see a man who is upon his bed, and tossed about with fevers and pains, placing his hope on nothing else than that the gospel lies at his head; not because it is done for this purpose, but because the gospel is preferred to amulets. If, then, it is placed at the head to allay the pain of the head, is it not placed at the heart to heal it from sin? Let it be done then. Let what be done? Let it be placed at the heart, let the heart be healed.
>
> (*Tractates on John* 7.12, in *NPNF*, ser. 1, vol. 7, 52)

Similarly, John Chrysostom bemoans the fact that many Christians have:

> draughts and dice, but books nowhere, except among a few. And even these few have the same dispositions as the many; for they tie up their books, and keep them always put away in cases, and all their care is for the fineness of the parchments, and the beauty of the letters, not for reading them.... For if the devil will not dare to approach a house where a Gospel is lying, much less will any evil spirit, or any sinful nature, ever touch or enter a soul which bears about with it such sentiments as it contains.
>
> (*Homily on John* 32.3, in *NPNF*, ser. 1, vol. 14, 114)

Chrysostom also attests to the practice of hanging Gospels by one's bed; in combination with placing alms in a bedside coffer, "you have a defense against the devil...and the night will not be troubled with fantasies" (*Homilies on First Cor.* 43.7, in *NPNF*, ser. 1, vol. 12, 262).

Some scriptural charms have survived the centuries, such as the amulet of the Letter of Agbar to Jesus (*Oxyrhynchus Papyri* vol. 65 no. 4469, trans. Maltomini

1998, 122–129) and miniature codices created to serve as amulets (Haines-Eitzen 2005). The textual and material evidence thus shows that many Christians made amulets out of scriptures, despite criticism from Church leaders:

> Dost thou not see how women and little children suspend Gospels from their necks as a powerful amulet, and carry them about in all places wherever they go [?] Thus do thou write the commands of the Gospel and its laws upon thy mind. Here there is no need of gold or property, or of buying a book; but of the will only, and the affections of the soul awakened, and the Gospel will be thy surer guardian, carrying it as thou wilt then do, not outside, but treasured up within; yea, in the soul's secret chambers.
>
> (John Chrysostom, *Homily on the Statues* 19.14, in *NPNF*, ser. 1, vol. 9, 470)

Similar attestation to the popular use and official condemnation of scriptural amulets is found in the canons of the Synod of Laodicea (360):

> They who are of the priesthood, or of the clergy, shall not be magicians, enchanters, mathematicians, or astrologers; nor shall they make what are called amulets, which are chains for their own souls. And those who wear such, we command to be cast out of the Church.
>
> (*Canons of the Synod of Laodicea* 36, in *NPNF*, ser. 2, vol. 14, 151)

By the seventh and eighth centuries, other conciliar decrees prohibited corrupting the Bible in any way, "unless to be sure it has been rendered useless either by bookworms, or by water, or in some other way. He who henceforth shall be observed to do such a thing shall be cut off [excommunicated] for one year" (*Canons of the Council in Trullo* 68, in *NPNF*, ser. 2, vol. 14, 396). These prohibitions testify to the popular practices of using pieces of vellum from the Bible for protective amulets, incense wrappers, and healing charms. Bits of the Bible were used as ritual objects because they were believed to be divine writing with effective powers.

## Relic books in the British Isles

The most poignant examples of Christian scriptures functioning as icons come from the fusion of Roman Christian traditions with Celtic and Anglo Saxon culture in the British Isles between the sixth and ninth centuries. With a small infrastructure to support these missionary outposts and a great demand for liturgical and devotional books, insular scribe-priests like Columba (521–597), Cuthbert (634–687), and Bede (673–735) were, according to Michelle P. Brown, "preaching with the pen in the scribal desert," not only through commentaries, sermons, and letters, like the continental scholar-priests, but by supporting the copying and transmission of the Gospels (2003, 395–398). These elaborately illuminated manuscripts were created as a form of meditative practice on the scriptures, revealing the scribe's (or the scribe working in tribute to a saint's) intense devotion to the Word. The products of this activity were intended to be enshrined as vehicles of divine power and as a "revelatory

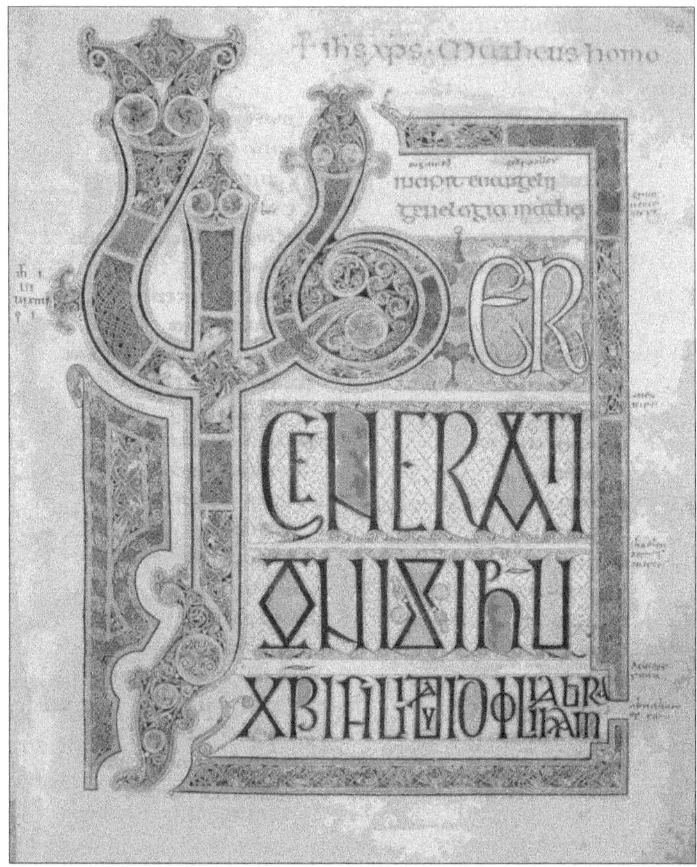

Figure 3 Saint Matthew's Gospel from the Lindisfarne Gospels, Cotton Nero D.IV, f. 27 (British Library, London, England). 

glimpse of the vision of God to come" (2003, 77). In other words, the intricate insular illuminations, such as the Lindisfarne Gospels (710–725), that today are displayed in museums and libraries and published in color plates for the detailed examination of spectators, were not created for the contemplation of the viewer, but of the scribe.

The scribe's or saint's access to God through his word and image then became a part the object of the book itself: it was a relic of the saint's intercessory power. According to Michelle P. Brown, these Gospels were "designed primarily for display in a cult context," in a book-shrine of precious metals and jewels, and were only occasionally, if at all, removed for liturgical performance (2003, 69, 193).

Some enshrined texts from this period clearly played more utilitarian roles prior to the creation of their last resting place. According to Harry Miller, if a simple text had been copied or used by a saint, the guardians of the relics in the British Isles "saw no benefit in taking the book apart and rebinding it in a fancy cover, as might be done in other countries; they preferred in general to leave the book just as the saint used it and instead create a magnificent shrine to house it" (H. Miller 1996). One of the most famous Irish book-shrines is the Cathach (battle) reliquary believed to contain a controversial copy of the Psalms penned by St. Columba around 560. Tradition holds that Columba copied Finnian of Moville's psalter without his permission, thus devaluing the book and prompting Finnian to present the crime to King Diarmait. The king ruled in favor of Finnian, stating "to every book belongs its son-book as to every cow her calf," and a war over Columba's psalter began (Fowler 1894, lxii). For centuries after Columba's victory, the manuscript was carried into battle in the Cathach shrine, on the breast of one of the O'Donnell family, conferred with guarding the relic. One *Life* of St. Columba claims, "if carried three times to the right around the army...going into battle, it was certain that they would return victorious" (Raftery 1941, 51). This book was used for its protective powers associated with the saint (and the saint's proximity to God); it was not intended to be read (Stokes 1972, 76; H. Miller 1996; see Drogin 1989, 130–131).

Another example of an insular book-shrine, the eighth-century Lough Kinale, was designed in such a way that it could not be opened without destroying the wood and metal housing, much like a ceramic piggy-bank. In 1986, its remains were found in pieces and the book missing, but its carrying-strap indicates that it was carried on a circuit of a saint's relics and/or into battle (H. Miller 1996). Michelle P. Brown writes that the design of the Lough Kinale implies "that the knowledge that it contained a sacred book was enough to ensure its efficacy," just as a relic book buried with a saint in his coffin would have continued to fulfill its sacred function even though the text was not accessible to pilgrims at his shrine (2003, 69, 209).

Insular hagiographies do not hesitate to laud the special powers of the books connected with the scribal saints. For a culture continually threatened by its surroundings, one of the most important qualities of a sacred text was its immunity to water damage. Adamnan's *Life of St. Columba* relates a story of a youth who fell from his horse into a river and was under the water for twenty days:

> When he fell he had a number of books packed up in a leathern satchel under his arm; and so, when he was found after the above-mentioned number of days, he still had the satchel of books pressed between his arm and side. When the body was brought out to the dry ground, and the satchel opened, it was found to contain, among the volumes of other books, which were not only injured, but even rotten, a volume written by the sacred fingers of St. Columba; and it was as dry and wholly uninjured as if it had been enclosed in a desk.
>
> (Adamnan, *Life of St. Columba* II.VIII [Reeves 1874]; cf. Fowler 1894, 63)

Adamnan immediately follows this with "another miracle in similar circumstances." Upon opening the rotten satchel of another drowned boy, Columba's manuscript was "uninjured, and as clean and dry as if it had...never fallen into the water." Adamnan continues that "we have ascertained, as undoubted truth, from those who were well informed in the matter, that the like things happened in several places with regard to books written by the hands of St. Columba namely, that the books could suffer no injury from being immersed in water" (Adamnan, *Life of St. Columba* II.IX [Reeves 1874]; cf. Drogin 1989, 66–67; Fowler 1894, 63).

With such power over the elements, manuscripts could aid in other miracles as well. One seventeenth-century story of the *Book of Durrow*, a seventh-century Irish manuscript, claims that "the Ignorant man that had the [*Book of Durrow*] in his Custody, when sickness came upon cattle, for their Remedy putt water on the booke & suffered it to rest there a while & saw alsoe cattle return to their former or pristine state & the book to receave no loss" (Drogin 1989, 74–75).

Attempts at achieving a miracle by the book were not limited to "ignorant men." Adamnan writes that the relics of Columba saved the island of Iona from drought when they were used analogously to Hebrew processions of the Ark of the Covenant in the wilderness:

> We [the monks of Iona]...took counsel together, and resolved that some of the senior members of the community should walk round a newly ploughed and sowed field, taking with them the white tunic of St. Columba, and some books written in his own hand, that they should raise in the air, and shake three times the tunic which the saint wore at the hour of his death; and that they then should open the books and read them on the little hill of the angels.... When these directions had been executed in the manner prescribed, then, strange to relate, the sky, which during the preceding months of March and April had been cloudless, was suddenly covered with dense vapours that arose from the sea with extraordinary rapidity; copious rain fell day and night, and the parched earth being sufficiently moistened, produced its fruits in good season, and yielded the same year a most abundant harvest. And thus the invocation of the very name of the blessed man, by the exhibition of his tunic and books, obtained seasonable relief at the same time for many places and much people.
>
> (Adamnan, *Life of St. Columba* II.XLV [Reeves 1874]; cf. Fowler 1894, 103–104; see also O'Reilly 1997, 90–93)

## Miracles by the book

Book miracles appear most frequently in texts that intend to persuade or demonstrate to the reader the holiness of the saints associated with the book, either by their scribal creations or by their extraordinary piety (that is, their incorporation of the book). This is also the case in early Christian hagiographies on the continent, such as the *Life of Melania the Younger*, and instructions to scribal monks, such as Cassiodorus' *Institutiones* (Rapp 2007, 211–212). But in many cases the spiritual state of the employer of the book and/or the scribal provenance of the manuscript are not relevant to the efficacy of the book miracle; instead, the book itself produces the effect by virtue of being an instrument of the power of God and the legitimacy of Christianity. For example, one early hagiographical story tells of a traveling monk who exorcised a demon and restored the health of a young girl when he produced a small book of the Gospels from his bag. This miracle, which parallels many of the exorcisms and healings of Jesus, does not depend on the holiness of the monk, as is made clear by the rest of the story. Overcome by guilt, the monk with the book admitted that he had stolen the precious object (John Moschus, *Pratum spirituale* 8 [Mioni 1951, 90–91], in Rapp 2007, 199).

Seeing or being in the presence of a biblical codex, even without reading the text, is often depicted as sufficient for encouragement or conversion. Epiphanius of Salamis opined in the fourth century that "[t]he acquisition of Christian books is necessary for those who can use them. For the mere sight of these books renders us less inclined to sin, and incites us to believe more firmly in righteousness" (*Apophthegmata* 8 [*PG* 65:165 A], trans. Ward 1981, 58, in Rapp 2007, 197). One was more fully immersed in the presence of the Word of God if the book were open. In the sixth century, John of Ephesus wrote that one of his monastic teachers, Apa Abbi, spent much of his days gazing at an open Gospel, without turning a page, while both his head and the book were covered with his cloak. When Apa Abbi was available to dispense advice to the other monks, he would only speak when the book was open before him (Brooks 1923–25, 1: 214–217; Rapp 2007, 198).

The most famous example of conversion by the book is probably that of Augustine, who follows the pattern of scriptural conversion established by the *Life of St. Anthony*. There are differences in the accounts: the supposedly illiterate Anthony hears his command to asceticism (from the Gospel of Matthew) when passing by a church, while the foreshadowing and climax of Augustine's conversion involves the visual and tactile experiences of a man of letters. After hearing the aural command to "pick up and read" the book of the Apostle on the table, Augustine writes that "I interpreted it solely as a divine command to me to open the book and read the first chapter I might find" to "put on the Lord Jesus Christ and make no provision for the flesh in its lusts," referring to Rom 13:13–14 (Augustine, *Confessions* VIII.xii [29], trans. Chadwick 1998, 153). This practice of *sortes biblicae*, following the tradition of *sortes Homericae* and *sortes Vergilianae*, involved the ritual yet random consultation of texts for personal directive or to predict the future. Bibliomancy was practiced throughout the Christian West despite its condemnation in 829 (Manguel 1996, 209–211; MacMullen 1997, 41; Drogin 1989, 80), and continues in some Christian practices today (Malley 2004).

The idea that the Book detects truth and lies provides the basis for taking an oath on a sacred book, a ritual that used to be performed in secular American courtrooms and still continues in the ritual of taking an oath of office. The assumption is that speaking in front of the Word of God will prompt the truth, and if that is not the case, either state-sponsored or divine punishment will befall the liar in the future. Early Christian texts often describe the physical tortures of heretics and sinners: one punishment for swearing falsely on the scriptures landed on a murderous sister in the ninth century. When the body of Cwenthryth's infant brother, whom she had killed, was lauded a martyr by the crowds, the fratricidess looked up from her psalter and claimed, "He is indeed God's martyr, as truly as my eyes are resting on this psalter!" Immediately after she spoke, "her two eyes were torn from her head and fell plop on the open book, where you can still see the marks of her blood to this day" (Gerard of Wales 1978; Drogin 1989, 79).

These last examples of punishment "by the book" return us to the dialectic relationship between the spiritual quality of the person who engages the book, the book as an embodiment of Christ's perfect spiritual state, and the book as an instrument of divine power and judgment. Christian myths (contained in the Bible itself) explain that through the Word one accesses the divine creative power that is present "in the beginning," operative in the present, and in control of future judgment. Small wonder then that Christians of every kind tried to access the divine power in the Bible in whatever way they could.

## The image of the word: Book and icon

> Should we not conceive of his corporeal appearance on the board as of the divinely engraved Gospels? For nowhere has He [Christ] said to engrave the "concise Word" (Is 10: 23, cf. Rom 9: 28). However, it is being engraved from the [time] of the Apostles until now. And what in this case is engraved by paper and ink, is in the same way engraved in the case of the icon by varied pigments, or whatever other materials that happen [to be used].
>
> (Theodore the Studite, *Refutations of the Iconoclasts* 1:10 [*PG* 99:340D], cited in Baranov 2002)

During the Iconoclastic Controversies, many supporters of icons constructed their apologies by appealing to images of Christ that were acceptable to iconoclasts, such as the liturgical book of the Gospels, and then drawing parallels to the same image in different media, such as painted icons, as does Theodore the Studite (759–826) in the above passage. What is important to these appeals is the ability of matter to reveal the divine, rather than the specificities of the revelation itself. That is, these iconophiles are not arguing for the correctness of what is seen—of the accuracy of representation—but the possibility of a relationship with the divine mediated by the material world. Thus John of Damascus (ca. 675–ca. 749) attempts to demonstrate that iconoclasts have functional icons as well:

> You want to say that "I do not venerate things made-by-hands" and you do not know what you say or what you venerate. Tell me, is not the Church made-by-hands, and the Cross, and the Gospel, and the table of preparation, and the rest

of the vessels of the Church?
(John of Damascus, *Against Constantinus* II.73 [*PG* 95:326B] cited by Baranov 2002)

Iconophiles were appealing to the accepted use of the Christian books of scripture to legitimize icons. In many ways, I am making the reverse claim: the iconophiles' justifications for how icons function as mediators of the divine presence can help scholars today understand the veneration that has been shown to the Christian Bible in diverse, yet often unconscious, ways throughout Christian history. This reverence for the Bible as both text (Word) and object (Book) can be found in rituals that treat the book as if it were the divine presence itself and in myths that offer imagery of powerful divine books made available to humans. These rituals and myths linger in contemporary Christian attitudes, ideas, and practices: most overtly in formal liturgical rituals such as Gospel processions, but also in low-church Protestant displays of the Bible. The latter may be less formalized than the former, but they nevertheless manipulate the same image of the divine presence made possible through the medium of the book.

## References

Adamnan. 1874. *Life of Saint Columba, Founder of Hy*, edited by William Reeves. Edinburgh: Edmonston & Douglas.

———. 1894. *Adamnani Vita S. Columbae*, translated and edited by J. T. Fowler. Oxford: Clarendon Press.

Ainalov, D. V. 1961. *The Hellenistic Origins of Byzantine Art.* New Brunswick, NJ: Rutgers University Press.

Augustine. 1886–1889. *Tractates on John.* In *Nicene and Post-Nicene Fathers*, 1st series, edited by Philip Schaff, vol. 7, 7–452. Edinburgh: T. & T. Clark. Reprinted, Grand Rapids, MI: Eerdmans, 1989.

———. 1998. *Confessions.* Translated by Henry Chadwick. Oxford: Oxford University Press.

Baranov, B. 2002. "The Theology of Early Iconoclasm as found in St. John of Damascus' Apologies." Христианский Восток (*Khristianskii Vostok*) 4(10): 23–55. www.nsu.ru/classics/Baranov/earlyiconoclasm.htm. Accessed July 2012.

Belting, Hans. 1994. *Likeness and Presence: A History of the Image before the Era of Art*, translated by Edmund Jephcott. Chicago, IL: University of Chicago Press.

Besa. 1983. *The Life of Shenoute.* Translated by David N. Bell. Cistercian Studies 73. Kalamazoo, MI: Cistercian Publications.

Betz, Hans Dieter. 1987. "Magic in Greco-Roman Antiquity." In *The Encyclopedia of Religion*, edited by Mircea Eliade, vol. 9, 93–97. New York: Macmillan.

Bianchi, Ugo. 1995. "History of Religions." In *The Encyclopedia of Religion*, edited by Mircea Eliade, vol. 6, 399–408. New York: Simon & Schuster Macmillan.

Bogdanović, Jelena. 2002. "The Proclamation of the New Covenant: The Pre-Iconoclastic Altar Ciboria in Rome and Constantinople." *Athanor* 20: 7–19.

Brandon, S. G. F. 1967. *The Judgment of the Dead: The Idea of Life after Death in the Major Religions.* New York: Scribners.

Broek, R. van den. 1979. "Popular Religious Practices and Ecclesiastical Policies in the Early Church." In *Official and Popular Religion: Analysis of a Theme for Religious Studies*, edited by Pieter Hendrik Vrijhof and Jacques Waardenburg, 11–54. The Hague: Mouton.

Brooks, E. W. 1923–1925. *Lives of the Eastern Saints.* Syriac texts edited and translated in 3 vols. Paris: Firmin-Didot. Reprinted, Turnhout: Brepols, 1974.

Brown, Michelle P. 2003. *The Lindisfarne Gospels: Society, Spirituality, and the Scribe.* London: British Library.

———. 1971. *The World of Antiquity.* New York: W. W. Norton.

———. 1973. "A Dark-Age Crisis: Aspects of the Iconoclastic Controversy." *English Historical Review* 88 (346): 1–34. doi:10.1093/ehr/LXXXVIII.CCCXLVI.1

*Canons of the Council of Ephesus.* 1759–1798. In Mansi 1903–1927, vol. 4, 1237.

*Canons of the Council of Trullo (Quinisext Council).* 1890–1900. In *Nicene and Post-Nicene Fathers*, 2d series, edited by Philip Schaff and Henry Wace, vol. 14, 355–408. Edinburgh: T. & T. Clark. Reprinted, Grand Rapids, MI: Eerdmans, 1989.

*Canons of the Fourth Council of Constantinople.* 1759–1798. In Mansi 1903–1927, vol. 16, 400.

*Canons of the Synod of Laodicea.* 1890–1900. In *Nicene and Post-Nicene Fathers*, 2d series, edited by Philip Schaff and Henry Wace, vol. 14, 123–160. Edinburgh: T. & T. Clark. Reprinted, Grand Rapids, MI: Eerdmans, 1989.

*Codex Justinianus.* 1877. In *Corpus Juris Civilis*, vol. 2, edited by P. Krueger and T. Mommsen. Berlin: Weidmann.

Covino, William A. 1994. *Magic, Rhetoric, and Literacy: An Eccentric History of the Composing Imagination.* Albany: State University of New York Press.

*Decree of the Second Council of Nicaea* 1890–1900. In *Nicene and Post-Nicene Fathers*, 2d series, edited by Philip Schaff and Henry Wace, vol. 14, 549–554. Edinburgh: T. & T. Clark. Reprinted, Grand Rapids, MI: Eerdmans, 1989.

Dilasser, Maurice. 1999. *Symbols of the Church*, translated by Mary Cabrini Durkin, Madeleine Beaumont, and Caroline Morson. Collegeville, MN: Liturgical Press.

Dix, Gregory. 1945. *The Shape of the Liturgy.* Westminster: Dacre Press.

Drogin, Marc. 1989. *Biblioclasm: The Mythical Origins, Magic Powers, and Perishability of the Written Word.* Savage, MD: Rowman & Littlefield.

Egeria. 1971. *Egeria and Her Travels*, translated by John Wilkinson. London: SPCK.

Fowler, J. T., ed. 1894. *Adamnani Vita S. Columbae.* Oxford: Clarendon Press.

Gamble, Harry Y. 1995. *Books and Readers in the Early Church.* New Haven, CT: Yale University Press.

Gerard of Wales. 1978. *The Journey through Wales and the Description of Wales.* Translated by Lewis Thorpe. New York: Penguin.

St. Germain of Paris. 1844–1865. *Expositio brevis antiquiae liturgiae gallicanae.* In *Patrologia cursus completus, series latina*, edited by J. P. Migne, vol. 72, 89–94. Paris: Garnier. [1878 ed.]

Germanus of Constantinople. 1857–1866. *Historia ecclesiastica*. In *Patrologia cursus completus, series graeca*, edited by J. P. Migne, vol. 98, 384–453. Paris: Garnier. Reprinted, Turnhout: Brepols, 1967.

Goody, Jack. 1977. *The Domestication of the Savage Mind*. Cambridge: Cambridge University Press.

Grabar, André. 1968. *Christian Iconography: A Study of Its Origins*, translated by Terry Grabar. Princeton, NJ: Princeton University Press.

Graffin, Pierre. 1961. "La lettere de Philoxène de Mabboug à un supérieur de monastère sur la vie monastique." *L'orient syrien* 6: 455–486.

Haines-Eitzen, Kim. 2005. "Miniature Books and Rituals of Private Reading in Late Antiquity." Paper presented at the American Academy of Religion Annual Meeting, Philadelphia, Pennsylvania, November.

Hippolytus. 1934. *Apostolic Tradition*, translated by Burton Scott Easton. Cambridge: Cambridge University Press. Reprinted, Ann Arbor, MI: Archon Books, 1962.

Humfress, Caroline. 2007. "Judging By the Book: Christian Codices and Late Antique Legal Culture." In Klingshirn and Safran 2007, 141–158.

Isidore of Pelusium. 1857–1866. *Epistles*. In *Patrologia cursus completus, series graeca*, edited by J. P. Migne, vol. 78, 177–1646. Paris: Garnier. Reprinted, Turnhout: Brepols, 1967.

Jerome. *Against Vigilantius*. 1890–1900. In *Nicene and Post-Nicene Fathers*, 2d series, edited by Philip Schaff and Henry Wace, vol. 6, 417–423. Edinburgh: T. & T. Clark. Reprinted, Grand Rapids, MI: Eerdmans, 1989.

John of Damascus. 1857–1866. *Against Constantinus Cabalinus on the Images*. In *Patrologia cursus completus, series graeca*, edited by J. P. Migne, vol. 95, 310–343. Paris: Garnier. Reprinted, Turnhout: Brepols, 1967.

John Chrysostom. 1886–1889. *Homilies on First Corinthians*. In *Nicene and Post-Nicene Fathers*, 1st series, edited by Philip Schaff, vol. 12, 258–262. Edinburgh: T. & T. Clark. Reprinted, Grand Rapids, MI: Eerdmans, 1989.

———. 1886–1889. *Homily on John*. In *Nicene and Post-Nicene Fathers*, , 1st series, edited by Philip Schaff, vol. 14, 1–334. Edinburgh: T. & T. Clark. Reprinted, Grand Rapids, MI: Eerdmans, 1989.

———. 1886–1889. *Homily on the Statues*. In *Nicene and Post-Nicene Fathers*, 1st series, edited by Philip Schaff, vol. 9, 315–489. Edinburgh: T. & T. Clark. Reprinted, Grand Rapids, MI: Eerdmans, 1989.

Justin Martyr. 1868–1873. *First Apology* In *ANF*, vol. 1, 159–193.

Kessler, Herbert L. 2006. "The Book as Icon." In *In the Beginning: Bibles Before the Year 1000*, edited by Michelle P. Brown, 77–103. Washington, DC: Smithsonian Institution.

———. 2000. *Spiritual Seeing: Picturing God's Invisibility in Medieval Art*. Philadelphia: University of Pennsylvania Press.

Klingshirn, William E., and Linda Safran, eds. 2007. *The Early Christian Book*. Washington: Catholic University of America Press.

Layton, Bentley. 1987. *The Gnostic Scriptures*. New York: Doubleday.

Lesko, Leonard H. 1987. "Thoth." In *The Encyclopedia of Religion*, edited by Mircea Eliade, vol. 14, 493. New York: Macmillan.

Liddell, Henry George, and Robert Scott. *Greek–English Lexicon*, abridged ed. Oxford: Oxford University Press, 1997.

Lowden, John. 1997. *Early Christian and Byzantine Art.* New York: Phaidon.

———. 2007. "The Word Made Visible: The Exterior of the Early Christian Book as Visual Argument." In Klingshirn and Safran 2007, 13–47.

MacMullen, Ramsay. 1997. *Christianity and Paganism in the Fourth to Eighth Centuries.* New Haven, CT: Yale University Press.

———, and Eugene Lane, eds. 1990. *Paganism and Christianity 100–425 CE: A Sourcebook.* Minneapolis, MN: Augsburg Fortress.

Malinine, M. *et al.*, eds. 1956. *Gospel of Truth [Evangelium Veritatis]: Codex Jung f. VIIIv-XVIv, f. XIXr-XXIIr*. Zürich: Rascher.

———. 1961. *Gospel of Truth [Evangelium Veritatis]: Codex Jung f. XVIIr-F. XVIIIv.* Zürich and Stuttgart: Rascher.

Malley, Brian. 2004. *How the Bible Works: An Anthropological Study of Evangelical Biblicism*. New York: Altamira Press.

Maltomini, F., ed. and trans. 1998. "Letter of Abgar to Jesus." In *The Oxyrhynchs Papyri,* edited by M. W. Haslam, A. Jones, F. Maltomini, and M. L. West, vol. 65, no. 4469, 122–129. London: British Academy.

Manguel, Alberto. 1996. *A History of Reading.* New York: Viking.

Mansi, J. D., ed. 1759–1798. *Sacrorum conciliorum nova et amplissima collectio.* 31 vols. Florence and Venice. Reprinted, Paris: H. Welter, 1903–1927.

Marty, Martin. 1982. "America's Iconic Book." In *Humanizing America's Iconic Book: Society of Biblical Literature Centennial Addresses 1980*, edited by Gene M. Tucker and Douglas A. Knight, 1–23. Chico, CA: Scholars Press.

Mathews, Thomas. 1971. *The Early Churches of Constantinople: Architecture and Liturgy.* University Park, PA: Pennsylvania State University Press.

———. 1993. *The Clash of Gods: A Reinterpretation of Early Christian Art.* Princeton, NJ: Princeton University Press.

Migne, J. P., ed. 1844–1865. *Patrologia cursus completus, series latina* (= *PL*). 221 vols. Paris: Garnier. [1878 ed.]

———. 1857–1866. *Patrologia cursus completus, series graeca* (= *PG*). Series 1 and Series 2. 161 vols. Paris: Garnier. Reprinted, Turnhout: Brepols, 1967.

Miller, David L. 1987. "The Question of the Book: Religion as Texture." *Semeia* 40: 53–64.

Miller, Harry. 1996. "Cumdachs and Polaires: Medieval Irish Book Shrines and Book Satchels." http://groups.yahoo.com/group/celt-archive/message/2664. Accessed September 2012.

Miller, Patricia Cox. 1986. "In Praise of Nonsense." In *Classical Mediterranean Spirituality: Egyptian, Greek, Roman*, edited by A. H. Armstrong, 481–505. New York: Crossroads.

Mioni, Elpidio. 1951. "Il Pratum Spirituale di Giovanni Mosco. Testi inediti del cod. Marc. gr. II, 21." *Orientalia Christiana Periodica* 17: 61–94.

Nicephorus of Constantinople. 1857–66. *Refutation.* In *Patrologia cursus completus, series graeca*, edited by J. P. Migne, vol. 100, 202–534. Paris: Garnier. Reprinted, Turnhout: Brepols, 1967.

O'Reilly, Jennifer. 1997. "Reading the Scriptures in the Life of Columba." In *Studies in the Cult of Saint Columba*, edited by Cormac Bourke, 80–106. Dublin: Four Courts Press.

Parker, George F. 1911. *Recollections of Grover Cleveland.* New York: Century Company.

Paul the Silentiary. 1837. *Descriptio ecclesiae sanctae Sophiae et ambonis*, edited by Immanuel Bekker. Bonn.

Pelikan, Jaroslav. 1974. *The Christian Tradition: A History of the Development of Doctrine.* Vol. 2, *The Spirit of Eastern Christendom (600–1700).* Chicago, IL: University of Chicago Press.

Petrucci, Armando. 1995. "The Christian Conception of the Book in the Sixth and Seventh Centuries." In *Writers and Readers in Medieval Italy*, edited and translated by Charles M. Radding, 19–42. New Haven, CT: Yale University Press.

Pietz, William. 1985. "The Problem of the Fetish I." *Res: Anthropology and Aesthetics* 9 (Spring): 5–17.

———. 1987. "The Problem of the Fetish II: The Origin of the Fetish." *Res* 13 (Spring): 23–45.

———. 1988. "The Problem of the Fetish IIIa: Bosman's Guinea and the Enlightenment Theory of Fetishism." *Res* 16 (Autumn): 105–123.

Plato. 1998. *Phaedrus*, translated by James H. Nichols, Jr. Ithaca, NY: Cornell University Press.

Pliny. 1900. *Letters*, translated by J. B. Firth. London: W. Scott.

Raftery, Joseph. 1941. *Christian Art in Ancient Ireland*, vol. 2. Dublin: Stationary Office of Ireland.

Rapp, Claudia. 2007. "Holy Texts, Holy Men and Holy Scribes: Aspects of Scriptural Holiness in Late Antiquity." In Klingshirn and Safran 2007, 194–222.

Reeves, William, ed. 1874. *Life of Saint Columba, Founder of Hy. Written by Adamnan, Ninth Abbot of that Monastery*. Edinburgh: Edmonston & Douglas. www.fordham.edu/halsall/basis/columba-e.asp. Accessed July 2012.

Roberts, Alexander, and James Donaldson, eds. 1868–1873. *Ante-Nicene Fathers* (= *ANF*). 10 vols. Edinburgh: T. & T. Clark. Reprinted, Grand Rapids, MI: Eerdmans, 1993.

Schaff, Philip, ed. 1886–1889. *Nicene and Post-Nicene Fathers* (= *NPNF*). First Series. 14 vols. Edinburgh: T. & T. Clark. Reprinted, Grand Rapids, MI: Eerdmans, 1989.

———, and Henry Wace, eds. 1890–1900. *Nicene and Post-Nicene Fathers* (= *NPNF*). Second Series. 14 vols. Edinburgh: T. & T. Clark. Reprinted, Grand Rapids, MI: Eerdmans, 1989.

Schroeder, H. J. 1937. *Disciplinary Decrees of the General Councils: Text, Translation, and Commentary.* St. Louis: B. Herder. http://www.fordham.edu/halsall/basis/const4.asp. Accessed September 2012.

Smith, Jonathan Z. 1978. *Map is not Territory*. Chicago, IL: University of Chicago Press.

St. Clair, Archer. 1979. "The Visit to the Tomb: Narrative Liturgy on Three Early Christian Pyxides." *Gesta* 18(1): 127–35. doi:10.2307/766798

Stokes, Margaret. 1972. *Early Christian Art in Ireland*. First published 1887, rev. G. N. Count Plunkett, 1911. Freeport, NY: Books for Libraries Press.

Stuart, John. 1975. *Ikons*. London: Faber.

Theodore the Studite. 1857–1866. *Refutations of the Iconoclasts*. In *Patrologia cursus completus, series graeca*, edited by J. P. Migne, vol. 99, 328–436. Paris: Garnier. Reprinted, Turnhout: Brepols, 1967.

Toorn, Karel van der. 1997. "The Iconic Book: Analogies Between the Babylonian Cult of Images and the Veneration of the Torah." In *The Image and the Book: Iconic Cults, Aniconism, and the Rise of Book Religion in Israel and the Ancient Near East*, edited by Karel van der Toorn, 229–248. Louven: Peeters.

Walter, Christopher. 1970. *L'Iconographie des conciles dans la tradition byzantine*. Paris: Institut français d'études byzantines.

Ward, Benedicta, ed. and trans. 1981. *The Sayings of the Desert Fathers: The Alphabetical Collection*, rev. ed. London and Oxford: Mowbray.

Wharton, Annabel. 2003. "Icon, Idol, Totem and Fetish." In *Icon and Word: The Power of Images in Byzantium*, edited by Antony Eastmond and Liz James, 3–11. Aldershot: Ashgate.

# 5

# Images to be Read and Words to be Seen: The Iconic Role of the Early Medieval Book

Michelle P. Brown

*How did the codex take on iconic status? This paper surveys the history of the early medieval book, especially the transmission of religious texts in the codex format, in order to understand how the material form of the book itself came to take on religious significance.*

In 2007, Prospero's Bookstore in Kansas City burnt its old stock—as performance artwork and also as a wake-up call to the public who would not read these unloved books (Prospero's Bookstore 2007). This was a powerful symbol of the commodification of books as stuff. Why should people want them all, when not everything published is worth reading? And yet the codex has assumed a role as a cultural icon which inclines us to value it for what it represents, evoking in us a natural abhorrence of book burnings which we associate with oppression. In the epic Hollywood film *Cleopatra*, a fiery young Elizabeth Taylor in the title role upbraids Rex Harrison's Julius Caesar regarding the burning of the great library of Alexandria, as a casualty of war, crying that it is one thing for Rome to destroy or seize people and lands, but that it has no right to destroy even one human thought. Has she hit upon something profoundly and simply instinctual here; that the book, in whatever codicological form, is the physical embodiment of human intellect—the cerebral equivalent of the "soul"?

To pursue the perceptions of this popular medium further, in the film *The Day After Tomorrow* (2004), a post-apocalyptic survival romp, the protagonists take refuge in the Metropolitan Museum in New York, where, in order to keep warm, they burn books. This act of iconoclasm is intended to shock: book burnings serving as a paradigm for the collapse of society. The electronic heirs of the codex are discarded as being of no material value in the fight for physical survival—in itself a metaphor for the current reification of the book in its study as a cultural artefact. The desperate, degenerate party cannot, however, bring themselves to consign one particular book to the flames: a Gutenberg Bible. The book thus serves as the ultimate icon of civilization.

It is indicative that it should be this particular book. It is in the codex form that has prevailed for two millennia and which, despite premature predictions of its demise, is likely to remain with us in a mixed economy of communication for some time to come. It stands at the cusp between the painstaking craftsmanship and individuality of the manuscript tradition and the potential mass-availability of the printed word. And it is the repository of the sacred text of one of the peoples of the Word.

## Book production in the early Middle Ages

How did the book come to assume this iconic significance? In addressing this question, it will be useful to briefly consider some aspects of the dissemination of scripture in the aftermath of the Roman Empire.

With the fragmentation of the Empire in the early fifth century, urban classical civilization was transformed into a new network of power-bases and intellectual centers. Some towns continued to trade, becoming bishoprics or royal seats. They were joined by rural manors, princely citadels, and monasteries, which proliferated throughout the Middle East and Europe. Literacy contracted among the general populace but book production—no longer undertaken by secular scribes and publishers—was perpetuated and carried beyond the old Empire's frontiers by the Church.

From the time that the codex and Christianity achieved social acceptability during the fourth century, books were no longer just a cheap alternative favored by a persecuted underclass but rather the honored receptacles of sacred text for a powerful established religion. Grander parchment books, such as Codex Sinaiticus (consisting of several portions now in the Monastery of St. Catherine on Mount Sinai, and in London, St. Petersburg, and Leipzig), Codex Vaticanus (Vatican, Biblioteca Apostolica, MS Vat. Or. 1209) and Codex Alexandrinus (London, British Library, Royal MSS 1.D.v-viii.) —the earliest complete Christian Bibles now extant—were made in response to the need for imposing volumes of Scripture for prestigious churches. Such buildings proliferated from the time that the first Christian emperor, Constantine, commissioned scriptural volumes from Eusebius of Caesarea for his foundations in Constantinople in 332 and his mother, Helena, established pilgrimage churches at the holy sites of the Middle East (Roberts and Skeat 1983).

Early Christian copies of scripture were undecorated, but, during the fifth and sixth centuries, images began to be applied to biblical books, with great picture cycles illustrating books such as the Byzantine Cotton and Vienna Genesis (Vienna, Österreichische Nationalbibliothek, Cod. Theol. Gr. 31) tomes and the Syriac Rabbula Gospels (Florence, Biblioteca Medicea-Laurenziana, MS Plut. I.56; Weitzmann 1977; Pächt 1986; Nordenfalk 1988; de Hamel 1986; Alexander 1992). Pictures had not found favor with classical bibliophiles, but Italian publishers now even illustrated old literary favorites by Virgil, Terence, and Homer (Weitzmann 1977; Wright 1993). The use of opulent materials, with gold and silver scriptures on purple pages, also imparted imperial stature to the grandest Byzantine, Syriac, and Italian tomes, such as the sixth-century Italian Codex Brixianus (Brescia, Biblioteca Civica Queriniana) and the Golden Canon Tables (London, British Library, Add. MSS 5111–2) made in Constantinople around 600.

Books made in early medieval Britain and Ireland were particularly responsive to such trends. The full-page figurative scenes of the Rabbula Gospels, made at the Syrian monastery of Beth Zagba in 586, find rare western responses in the crucifixion miniature of the Durham Gospels (Durham Cathedral Library, MS A.ii.17), and the Temptation, Arrest, and Virgin and Child miniatures of the Book of Kells (Dublin, Trinity College Library, MS 58), both probably made in monasteries associated with the mission of St Columba, the former around 700 and the latter around 800. The Stockholm Codex Aureus (Stockholm, Royal Library, MS A.135), made in Kent in the mid-eighth century, features display script dripping with gold and purple pages inscribed with gold and white script, recalling Byzantine purple volumes. The various peoples and kingdoms that emerged from the maelstrom of the Roman Empire's demise also contributed their own distinctive forms of ornament to manuscript illumination, producing intricate decorated initials formed of interlace, spiral-work, and animal forms. Copies of sacred text produced in the second half of the first millennium would be very different in appearance and character from the simple, disposable pamphlets used by early Christian communities; they became not only the vehicles of Christian teaching but potent symbols of local identity and of emerging powers.

In the Middle East and North Africa, book production increasingly became centered in remote monasteries. These Christian communities escaped persecution and tax hikes by following the lead of Saint Anthony, who had retreated to the eastern Egyptian desert in the late third century. In Caesarea, Armenia, Syria, Coptic Egypt, Nubia, and Ethiopia, monastic scriptoria developed distinctive styles of codicology (the ways in which books are put together), script, and illumination (Badawy 1978; Gabra 1993; Nersessian 2001). Some important monastic libraries survive, notably that at Saint Catherine's on Mount Sinai and Deir el-Suriani ("the monastery of the Syrians") in the Egyptian Wadi Natrun, where additional caches of long-lost manuscripts have recently been found in forgotten corners. Their contents graphically portray the varied cultural influences that impacted these remote outposts.

Christian bibliographic traditions in such areas, like those of Hebrew scribes, weathered the Islamic conquest of the eastern and southern Mediterranean from the seventh century onwards (Avrin 1991; Déroche and Richard 1997). Although little survives from before the ninth century, Islamic book production was underway in the eighth. Muslim scribes, like their Jewish counterparts, did not use figural imagery in scripture for fear of idolatry, but evolved their own sacred calligraphy and decoration for the glorification of the Word.

In Europe, book production became firmly established in the centuries between the retraction of the Roman Empire's frontiers in the early fifth century and the Viking raids, which commenced in 793 with the sack of the Holy Island of Lindisfarne, sending shock-waves throughout Europe—a period often inappropriately termed "the Dark Ages," but one that was illuminated by its manuscript culture. One of the major achievements of the age was the construction of northern European successor states, underpinned by the Christian zeal of the newly converted and a re-emerging stability of administration and social structure based upon effective collaboration between Church and State. Crucial in this was the dissemination and reception of Christian scripture, with its emphasis upon law, social reform, and teaching by example. The great bibles, psalters, and gospel books of this age stand as its enduring monument.

## The art of the book

The pagan Celts and Germans of northern Europe had developed proto-writing systems of their own, *ogam* and *runes*, in response to Roman script. But they used them only for short commemorative or talismanic purposes, preferring to cultivate the memory and a finely tuned oral literacy (Ong 1981; Page 1995; Brown 1998). They embraced written literacy along with Christianity and, despite the challenges of learning to write Latin as a foreign language, made major contributions to book production. They evolved their own distinctive scripts and written languages, introduced word separation and systematic punctuation (the latter was also introduced into Hebrew texts in the same period; see Parkes 1992), promoted decoration to help navigate the text, and integrated their indigenous styles of art and poetry. Due largely to their enthusiastic espousal of its potential, the codex assumed much of its distinctive appearance and apparatus.

In Rome itself, the Church, arts, and learning were given a tremendous boost under Pope Gregory the Great (died 604). This great missionary, intent upon reviving Rome's Western Empire in Christian guise, was a gifted theologian whose writings helped shape the Western Church. Books from Gregory's Rome feature elegant uncial script and initials decorated with crosses and fish. The Saint Augustine Gospels (Cambridge, Corpus Christi College, MS 286, on which the Anglican archbishops of Canterbury still take their oaths), feature a classical author portrait and vignettes, resembling "cartoon-strip" scenes, from the life of Christ.

Another force in the conversion of the English was Ireland, operating through monasteries such as Iona and Lindisfarne, founded by the Irish Saint Columba and his followers. Ireland had received Christianity during the fifth century, when Palladius was sent from Rome (431) as bishop to those who already believed and Saint Patrick launched his mission from the Romano-British Church (Brown 2006). Irish scribes developed decorated initials, formal half-uncial hands for scripture and calligraphic minuscule scripts for less formal works. They, followed by their English neighbors, also introduced spaces between words and systematic punctuation to clarify legibility and meaning. These developments were stimulated by Gregory, Isidore of Seville, and Bede, all of whom promoted silent reading to facilitate meditation and comprehension rather than just the more classical emphasis upon reading out loud to foster oratory and rhetoric (Parkes 1992, 2000).

The Anglo-Saxons further developed the range of scripts used, under renewed Roman influence. The power of writing was reinforced by the iconic nature of the book in a religious context. Secular rulers were quick to perceive the value of this new medium and enlisted the support of the Church in penning law-codes, charters, and genealogies to help establish secure states (Kelly 1990; Brown 2011).

Insular missionaries evangelized the courts and countryside of their islands and continental Europe through extensive monastic federations. Monasticism achieved tremendous popularity among them starting around 500 through the influence of the Eastern desert fathers (the early founders of the monastic tradition in the Near East, such as Saints Anthony, Pachomius and Basil) which was thought to have been transmitted via Italy, Spain and Gaul. Their inspirational preaching of the Christian message could lead seasoned warriors to embrace pacifism and kings to free slaves and radically transform society, often at risk of assassination. The role models provided by such energized, charismatic, ascetic individuals—publicly acclaimed as saints during their lifetimes—set new levels of social and spiritual aspiration. Some of the most beautiful medieval gospel books were used as the focal points of their shrines and symbolized the processes of integration and transmission that characterized the transition from the antique to the medieval period.

## Language and identity

The Bible and the codex had initially taken shape within the world of late Greco-Roman Antiquity, within an empire that stretched from Syria to Scotland and within which Greek and Latin were the literary languages and Christianity had become the state religion. The world in which they would be developed was that of the early Middle Ages, within which individual nations began to emerge with their own languages, cultures, and religious traditions—orthodox Christian, heretical, and pagan—all influencing the ways in which bible and book were perceived and produced. Many of these states were, in turn, subsumed within bigger territories as the concept of "empire" continued to beguile and to haunt ambitious leaders who sought to bind together the diverse peoples under their rule, using faith as part of that process. The "sacred languages"—Hebrew, Greek and Latin—and the rise of local vernacular languages such as English and Irish which were amongst the earliest western vernaculars, played an important part in this process and again served to link East and far West in a parallel approach to the significance of local languages.

In the Christian Orient, tension between "official" written languages and those spoken locally was not the issue that it was to become in the West. Christ's teachings probably originally circulated orally in the vernacular Aramaic (the Aramaic language used by Christ was recalled by the survival of a genre known as the *Targum*, an interpretative reading of the Hebrew Bible into Aramaic), even if the gospels were later written in the literary Greek language of the eastern Mediterranean. There was no apparent concern about the appropriateness of communicating belief in regional languages. The Armenian Church employed Armenian; the Syriac Church employed Syriac; the Coptic Church employed Coptic, the Ethiopic Church employed Ethiopic (especially literary northern Ethiopic, Ge'ez); the Nubian Church employed Old Nubian and Coptic; and so forth (Brown 2006a).

The popularity of early written vernaculars owed much to the desire among groups for cultural definition and distinction (religious and ethnic), especially in the face of differences in belief which were characterized by the early church councils as heretical, notable Monophysitism which was favored by the Western Syriac, Coptic, Nubian and Ethiopic Churches. In short, centralized authorities tend to promote the use of a single unifying language, while those affirming local or group identity often use language as a means of signaling independent traditions and histories. The stylistic appearance of a book could therefore render it a powerful visual icon of group identity (Brown 2005, 2006a, 2011).

In the seventh century, another important power emerged on the international scene. The Prophet Muhammad began preaching in Mecca around 610. By 641, his followers had come to dominate much of the Middle East and were rapidly expanding around the eastern and southern Mediterranean. The toleration of religious and ethnic minorities by the Caliphate and its recognition of local religious leaders as community representatives further promoted the development of self-contained regional Churches with inextricably interwoven ethnic cultures and traditions of faith, many of which survive still and periodically explode into conflict amidst the pressures and competition of our often less-tolerant age. The earliest Qur'ans to have survived, dating mainly from the ninth century onwards, are modest in appearance, but as the practice of paying honor to the Word by illuminating it and using graphic symbols as aids to its correction recitation grew, the traditional repertoires of ornament of the Judaic and Christian Orient were brought into service. Thus a Qur'an copied in Morocco in 1568 (London, British Library, Or. MS 1405), the Judaic Lisbon Bible, made in Portugal in the late fifteenth century, and the Lindisfarne Gospels (London, British Library, Cotton MS Nero D.iv; see Figure 1), probably conceived and made by Bishop Eadfrith of Lindisfarne on Holy Island in northern England around 710–720, all share features such as carpet pages, derived originally from sixth- and seventh-century Coptic models (Brown 2003, 2010).

At the monastery of St Catherine's in Sinai, a seemingly remote location but situated on important trade routes, the remains of its medieval library bear witness to the assimilation of incoming groups of Arabic-speaking monks brought up in Islamic territories stretching from Syria to Egypt, from Georgia and Macedonia, and even from western Europe—Gregory the Great himself even lamented that he could not retire there. The physical appearance of the books made there or imported reflect this mix and respond to it, with, for example, Christian Scriptures written in parallel columns of Greek and Arabic (Brown 2006a).

Positions became more entrenched during the Crusades of the late eleventh to late thirteenth centuries as Western forces sought to gain control of the holy places. Closer contact with the Churches of the East served only to deepen their estrangement. Northern armies despoiled the heart of Byzantium in 1204. Finally, in 1453, Constantinople, the Christian city founded by Constantine in 330 as a bridgehead between Occident and Orient, fell to the Turks; the unfortunate and artificial rupture of the world into East and West was complete.

## The incarnate word as icon

This was far from being the case during the early Middle Ages, during which the codex assumed its developed form and its iconic significance.

The decorated incipit to St John's Gospel in the Lindisfarne Gospels (London, B.L., Cotton MS Nero D.iv, f.211r), reminds us immediately of the underlying basis of the medieval approach to sacred text by elevating to due prominence the opening words of what Bede described as "the little Gospel that treats of the things that work of love": "In the beginning was the Word, and the Word was with God, and the Word was God" (John 1:1). Logos, the Word, was the very embodiment of the Creator, revealed to Creation through the incarnation, death and resurrection of Christ and through the abiding physical manifestation of the Gospelbook that contained his teachings, itself incarnated through the combination of divine inspiration, the quickening of human labor and the materials—animal, plant and mineral—of Creation. That book became, literally, the Word made flesh, or rather, the Word made word (Brown 2000, 2003, 2010).

Hebrew scribes had adopted the practice of according particular veneration to the *nomina sacra*, the sacred names by which the Lord was known, by writing them in abbreviated form, as sacred symbols. Christians extended this practice to their early copies of scripture, the *chi-rho* (the first letters of "Christus" in Greek) becoming a particularly potent early Christian device. When the *chi-rhos* in books such as the Lindisfarne Gospels (f.18r) and the St Chad Gospels (Lichfield Cathedral Library, MS 1) explode across the page, they become icons in their own right and may perhaps have helped to allay concerns over iconoclasm at a time when the problem of idolatry was actively discussed in Judaic, Islamic, and Christian circles. The dilemma resurfaced throughout the early Middle Ages and was hotly debated in the West. Nonetheless, early medieval

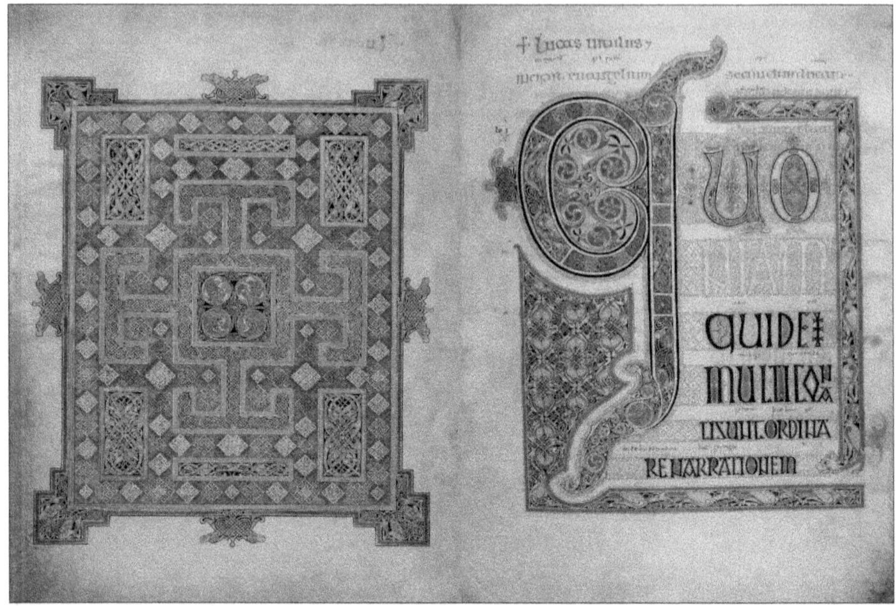

Figure 1. The Lindisfarne Gospels, Luke cross-carpet-page and incipit page. Lindisfarne, Northumbria, c.715-720. London, British Library, Cotton MS Nero D.iv, ff.138v-139r.

copies of Christian scripture are amongst the most beautiful examples of the illuminator's art, their precious contents often enshrined within similarly precious covers—an acknowledgement of their symbolic power at a time when, at the height of eastern iconoclasm, only the Cross and the Book were acceptable visual symbols of faith and the spatial foci of veneration and of gatherings for worship.

Byzantium, ever concerned to contain the schisms that endangered its hegemony, led the way in the debate. Byzantine book production had flourished during the Early Christian period, readily embracing imagery (although little now survives), but hit an all-time low during the Iconoclast Controversy (720s to 787). Imagery was largely outlawed, with only the book and the cross being considered acceptable public manifestations of belief and art. With the Council of Nicaea (787) and the accession of Empress Irene (797-802) images were reinstated and, despite an iconoclastic resurgence in 814-843, book production was stepped up again within the Byzantine Empire (Kitzinger 1975; Buckton 1994; Lowden 1997; Safran 1998).

The fear of idolatry, enshrined in the second commandment, was bequeathed by Judaism to the other monotheistic religions of the Word. From its inception, Islam fostered the use of sacred calligraphy in a religious context to avoid such dangers. In the early Christian Church, images had already assumed an iconic status as focuses of veneration, which, as John of Damascus indicates, might be misinterpreted as the objects of worship (Brown 1998, 2011). Yet, even during the state-sponsored iconoclasm in eighth-century Byzantium under Leo the Isaurian, certain symbols could be used as an alternative to figural representation. Thus the Cross and the Book became acceptable symbols of orthodox Christianity and can be seen occupying the throne and the altar in the fifth-century Orthodox Baptistry in Ravenna. In the 720s, the iconoclast party erected a tablet above the great gate of the imperial palace, recording the substitution of a Cross for the figure of Christ, which read (Ayerst and Fisher 1977, 102):

> *The emperor Leo and his son Constantine*
> *Thought it dishonour to the Christ divine*
> *That on the very palace gate he stood,*
> *A lifeless, speechless efigy of wood.*
> *Thus what the Book forbids they did replace*
> *With the believer's blessed sign of grace.*

The Council of Nicaea of 787, supporting attempts by the Empress Irene to restore images, likewise stated that (Ayerst and Fisher 1977, 103):

> We therefore follow the pious customs of antiquity and pay these icons the honour of incense and lights just as we do the holy gospels and the venerable and life-giving cross.

Byzantine mosaics from Ravenna to Daphni depict treasure bindings and the bejeweled, sealed book. On the fifth-century chancel arch mosaic of Sta Maria Maggiore, that book is enthroned alongside the *Crux Gemmata* and symbolises the divine Wisdom, which is Christ, as a hidden mystery concealed beneath the letter of Scripture (see 1 Corinthians 1.24 and 2.6–7; O'Reilly 2001). Thus the practice of portraying the Godhead by means of abstract or symbolic substitution was reinforced within the Christian tradition from an early date. The *Crux Gemmata* ("jeweled Cross") and the Gospelbook serve as the embodiment of Christ in the mosaics of Ravenna, they are encountered enshrined with Christ's faithful minister, St. Cuthbert, and they combine in an electrifying symbiosis the magnificent diptychs of cross-carpet page and decorated incipit in the Lindisfarne Gospels (see Figure 1), made in his honor. Here, I would suggest, the crosses and adorned words embody the Godhead and we are presented with the physical embodiment of Logos.

Secular authorities were quick to avail themselves of such potent symbolism. Constantine stressed that his authority was based upon the sign of the cross, in the name of which he triumphed at the Milvian Bridge. The mosaics portraying the Emperor Justinian and his entourage at San Vitale, Ravenna feature a shield (the shield of faith) bearing a *chi-rho*-headed cross and a Gospelbook in a jewelled cover. Christ of the Last Judgement is likewise depicted at Sant' Apollinare in Classe, and elsewhere, holding the Book. The

Church was quick to represent the advantages of such tools to the aspirational dynasties encountered in North-Western Europe and a major achievement credited to St Augustine following his conversion of King Ethelbert of Kent and his court was the committal of the ruler's law code to the safe-keeping of writing (Rochester, Cathedral Library, MS A.35, now in Kent Record Office, Maidstone; Webster and Brown 1997, pp. 219–220; transl. Whitelock 1979, no. 29). Augustine is even said, by Bede, to have devised written Old English for this purpose—or rather, to have transliterated it into written Roman characters, supplemented by a few runic symbols such as thorn, eth, and wyn (Bede, *Historia Ecclesiastica*, II.5; Whitelock 1979, 664; Colgrave and. Mynors 1969). A newly converted Anglo-Saxon ruler thereby sought to associate himself with Christian culture, and the ultimate Judge, and to use writing to bolster his role as an heir to the authority of his late Roman precursors.

Such developments are likely to have been indebted to heightened perceptions of the authority of the written word in the context of conversion and liturgy. The earliest extant Anglo-Saxon charters are written not in variants of the late Roman cursive secretary, as seen on the Continent, but in stately, high-grade uncials of the sort usually reserved for religious texts (see, for example, B. L., Cotton MS Augustus II. 2 and II.29; Webster and Backhouse 1991, nos. 27 and 28; Webster and Brown 1997, 220–221). In 735, Boniface sent a letter from the Germanic mission-fields to Abbess Eadburh of Minster-in-Thanet in Kent requesting that she have written for him a copy of the Petrine Epistles penned in gold (which he sent her for the purpose as it was such a valuable commodity) to impress the natives (Whitelock 1979, no. 172). To the Celtic and Germanic peoples of North-western Europe with their sophisticated oral societies, their abstract and symbolic art, their love of words and their proto-literate writing systems (ogham and runes) geared for commemorative and talismanic purposes, the book presented itself as the new symbol of ultimate, divine authority (Brown 2011). What could be more natural than that they should seek to adorn it with the ornamental repertoires which for centuries had conveyed signals of wealth, status, and power through the visible consumption of resource embodied in the metalworker's art (Webster and Brown 1997, 211–212, 232–233, 240).

In Byzantium, honor had been paid to the Word of God by writing it in letters of gold and silver upon purple-stained parchment, but in Insular books the word assumes iconic status, the sacred incipits and monograms of its Gospel books growing to occupy the entire page as vehicles of *contemplatio* intimately combining word and image. The modest initials of sixth- and seventh-century Italy and of Merovingian Gaul, with their crosses, birds and fishes, do not begin to approach the level of adornment accorded to the Word in an Insular context (Brown forthcoming). Nor is it surprising that the historiated, or story-telling, initial should have made its first known appearance in Insular books: the Vespasian Psalter, a Kentish work of around 730, and the St Petersburg

Bede, written at Wearmouth / Jarrow around 746 (B. L., Cotton MS Vespasian A.i and St Petersburg, Public Library, Cod. Q.v.I.18; Alexander, nos 29 and 19; Wright 1967). What more intimate visual symbiosis of text and image could there be, and what greater mutual validation? The intimacy extends in far subtler ways throughout insular Christian images, revealing a level of intertextuality founded upon a wealth of Scriptural and exegetical sources and multivalent levels of "reading" from which our sophisticated electronic age might well learn.

The freedom to explore such relationships in the West was to some extent established by Pope Gregory the Great, although debate concerning the role and acceptability of images continued, especially in the Carolingian orbit. Around 600, Gregory wrote to Bishop Serenus of Marseilles, censuring his destruction of images on the basis that:

> It is one thing to adore a picture, another to learn what is to be adored through the history told by the picture. What Scripture presents to readers, a picture presents to the gaze of the unlearned. For in it even the ignorant see what they ought to follow, in it the illiterate read.
>
> (Ayerst and Fisher 1977, 101–102)[1]

The Carolingian stance on imagery, in which scholars such as Alcuin of York participated, was conflicted. They used it to emphasize the interdependence of Church and State, the emperor combining the symbolic roles of king and priest, but they remained troubled by idolatry. The Carolingian response to the Council of Nicaea took the form of the *Libri Carolini* by Theodulf of Orléans, in which the primacy of the word was asserted over images, which were permitted but deemed to possess no inherent holiness or iconic value (Diebold 2000, 100–101, 117–118). Copies of scripture produced from this time until *c.*810 (when the Lorsch Gospels artists once more dared depict Christ in Majesty) are noticeably devoid of pictures of the divine, preferring illustrations of biblical narratives or evangelist portraits. This of course made way, conveniently, for the development of royal iconography (Mütherich and Gaehde 1976; Deshman 1980, 385–417; Dutton and Kessler 1997).

## The ascetic artist-scribe

From the very beginnings, the codex or book form, first popularized by its use for containing Christian scripture, was itself a sacred space—a tabernacle of the Word and a place for the enshrinement and contemplation of ideals. This space could be inhabited both by the maker and the viewer. For those who dedicated their lives to God's service, to be entrusted with the transmission of his Word as preachers and as scribes was a high calling indeed. In a letter to Bishop Acca of Hexham concerning his commentary on Luke, Bede wrote "I have subjected myself to that burden of work in which, as in innumerable bonds of monastic

1. For a discussion of this see Chazelle 1990, 138–153; Brown 2011.

servitude which I shall pass over, I was myself at once dictator, notary, and scribe" (Hurst 1960, prol. 93–115; Stansbury 1999, 72). This revealing passage shows that he regarded such work as an act of *opus dei,* and that he differentiated between the functions of author, secretary, and scriptural transmitter—an evangelist with the pen.

The influential sixth-century monastic founder Cassiodorus, in his *Institutiones,* said that each word written was "a wound on Satan's body," assigning the scribe the role of *miles Christi* (soldier of Christ). In the same work he says that the Spirit continues to work in those who translate, expand or humbly copy Scripture, just as in the biblical authors who were first inspired to write them. Scripture lends the scribal analogy to the Lord himself (see Jer. 31:33; Heb. 10:16; Ps. 44/45:1–2). Cassiodorus also advocated (in the *Institutiones* and his *Commentary* on Psalm 44/45.1–2) that the scribe could preach with the hand and "unleash tongues with the fingers," imitating the action of the Lord who wrote the Law with his all-powerful finger (Cassiodorus, *De Institutione Divinarum Litterarum*, ch. 30; Corpus Christianorum, Series Latina 96*;* Migne 1847, cols 1144–1145; O'Reilly 2001; Brown 2003, ch. 5, 2010). Bede pursued this theme in relation to Ezra the Scribe, who fulfilled the Law by restoring its destroyed books, dictating them from memory and thereby opening his mouth to interpret Scripture and teach others. He is depicted in the Codex Amiatinus (see Figure 2), one of three massive single volume Bibles commissioned by Ceolfrith, who was abbot of Bede's home twin monastery of Monkwearmouth ' Jarrow before he took this one with him as a papal gift when he left England to retire to Rome in 716. Ceolfrith died in Burgundy and never made it back to Rome, but his book did, becoming the ambassador for the English nation, proclaiming its catholic orthodoxy and announcing that the apostolic age had come to fruition with the islands on the edge of the known world reflecting back to the historic centre that they could be more Roman than the Romans. Indeed, Ceolfrith's name having been replaced in the dedication inscription by that of an Italian saint, the book was not recognized as the work of English hands rather than Italo-Byzantines until the 1880s; so Mediterranean is it in its styles of script, art, and text. It is also the best early representative of Jerome's Vulgate translation of the Bible into the "vulgar" language of the day, Latin. This was the most erudite edition of Christian scripture that the world could produce at this time, undertaken by a team led by Bede, the greatest scholar of the age, nurtured by a nation that had only received Christianity and full literacy a century earlier and drawing upon one of the greatest and newest libraries of the age. The scribal figure depicted in the Codex Amiatinus does not only represent Ezra, but also Cassiodorus (whose own nine-volume biblical edition is alluded to in the illumination by the books in the armarium which are actually labeled on the spines as the works of successive biblical editors, such as Origen and Augustine), and Bede and his scribal brethren themselves, for he is everyone who receives and disseminates scripture—an open invitation to all to participate. The act of writing is therefore presented as an essential act for the preacher-teacher-scribe (O'Reilly 2001).

Such exhortations may have influenced the production of the Lindisfarne Gospels (see Figure 1), for this remarkable book is the work of a single artist-scribe (Brown, 2010). Some modern scribes estimate that at least two years of full-time work in optimum conditions would be required to make it (I have spoken to a number of contemporary scribes on this matter, including some of the team currently working with Donald Jackson on a complete hand-produced Bible for the Benedictine monastery of St John's in Collegeville, Minnesota). Contemporary Ethiopian scribes in the South Gondar region, employing much the same methods and materials as when Christianity became their state religion during the fourth century, can write an undecorated religious codex of some 400 leaves in around eight to twelve months. They write for two or three hours per day amidst agricultural and church duties, simply resting the leaves on their knees as they squat on the ground to write (Mellors and Parsons 2002). Undertaking such an heroic feat of patience alongside the monastic duties of the Divine Office (celebrated eight times each day and night), prayer, study, and manual labor, suggests that making the Lindisfarne Gospels may have taken closer to five years, depending on how much exemption was granted from other duties, such as that accorded to anchorites. If, as seems likely, Bishop Eadfrith of Lindisfarne (698–721) both conceived the vision for its gospel book and physically made it himself, his responsibility for the largest dioceses in Britain would have made such work additionally challenging and difficult to focus upon. Some of it was probably undertaken on "Cuddy's Isle," a windswept tidal islet in the bay beside the monastery on Holy Island, where, for the seasons of Lent and Advent, the bishop retired on retreat—a watery wilderness in which the hermit was emptied out, to be filled with the Spirit and the energy to recommit.

Such solitary eremitic scribal labor may have been a distinctive "Celtic" approach to work as living prayer (Brown 2000, 2003, 2010). For whereas the copying of other texts was the cenobitic work of the scriptorium, transmitting Scripture was entrusted only to the senior members of the community. Within the Columban tradition, Saints Canice and Columba were acclaimed as hero-scribes (Brown 2000, 2003, 2010; Gameson 2001), for, in copying the Gospels, the scribe became an evangelist in turn and, by study, contemplation and meditation upon the text (*ruminatio, contemplatio* and *meditatio*), might actually glimpse the divine (*revelatio*). This accorded with the patristic concept of the "inner library" in which each believer became a library of the divine Word, a sacred responsibility which the Irish sage Cummian referred to as "entering the Sanctuary of God" by studying and transmitting scripture (Walsh and Ó Cróinín 1988, 15–18, 57–59; O'Reilly 2001). Books became the vessels from which the believer's inner ark was filled—enablers of direct Christian action, channels of the Spirit, and gateways to revelation. Such books are portals

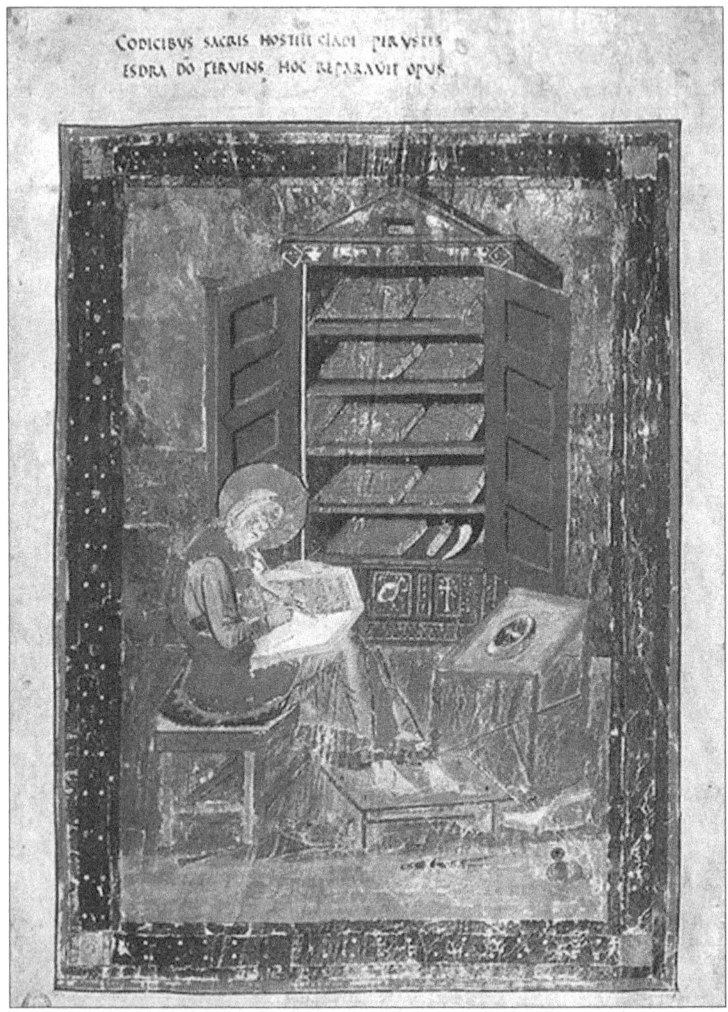

Figure 2. The Codex Amiatinus, Ezra miniature, from one of the Ceolfrith Bibles, made at the Northumbrian twin monasteries of Wearmouth / Jarrow, before 716. Florence, Biblioteca Medicea -Laurenziana, MS Amiatino 1, f. Vr.

of prayer. Just as St. Cuthbert struggled with his demons on the rock of his Inner Farne hermitage on behalf of all, so the bishop-monk who produced the Lindisfarne Gospels as Cuthbert's cult-book undertook an heroic feat of patience and of spiritual and physical endurance, part of the apostolic mission of bringing the Word of God to the furthest reaches of the known world, enshrining it there within the new Temple of the Word—the Book.

As with many other aspects of Celtic eremitic monasticism inherited from the East, the communities producing such books may have practiced the semi-eremitic *lavras* of the Syro-Palestinian monastic tradition, where monks came together for communal worship but lived separately as quasi-anchorites. The gospel book became the scribal desert. Via the "desert" islands of Britain and Ireland, influences from the cradle of the biblical tradition in the Middle East were transmitted to the West alongside the latinised, imperial influences of Rome and a pre-Christian appreciation of nature as what St Columba termed "a second scripture," in which we can perceive God.

## The influence of Christology and Mariology

The Church politics of the East, like its spirituality, also reverberated in the wild West. Early Church Councils spent much time debating the nature of Christ and the question of how he embodied the reconciliation of the human and the divine. The crucial Council of Chalcedon (451), however, pronounced that Christ possessed two natures, human and divine, which co-existed but were not confused. The Egyptians objected, championing the Monophysite belief that he possessed only one nature, which caused a breach between the Orthodox and Monophysite (West Syriac or Jacobite, Coptic and Ethiopic) Churches (Déroche and Richard 1997). The Council of Hatfield was convened in England in 679 to prepare the way for the Sixth Oecumenical Council held in Constantinople in 681, which was called to resolve the monothelete crisis which had divided the Church in the East and West and which had led to the martyrdom of Pope Martin 1 and his adviser, Maximus Confessor, in 655. The Council proclaimed that in Christ the divine and human wills were coherently united and that as Christ was incorruptible he never conflicted with the divine will. It was stressed that this incorruptibility lay in his conception, without corruption, from the Virgin Mary by the Holy Spirit.

It is, accordingly, from the 650s that we find the cult of the Virgin, and the veneration of the Cross and the Book as the embodiment of Logos, developing in Rome (from earlier eastern roots) and influencing its liturgy and art. They also rapidly become major themes in British and Irish (or Insular—of the islands) culture, whether introduced via Rome or directly from the East. This made the subject of the Virgin and her relationship to Christ a particular source of interest and may have shaped early medieval responses to depictions of the Virgin and Child. The Copts were keen to stress the maternal relationship and their approach seems to have influenced that of Insular artists, who were amongst the earliest in the West to illustrate the Virgin, with the Christ-child on her knee. Such images appear on the coffin of St Cuthbert, around 700, and in the Book of Kells, around 800, and were probably derived from Coptic adaptations of the iconography from ancient Egyptian effigies of Isis and Horus. When the Copts moved into the ancient pharaonic temples, they did not stop to redecorate but instead reinterpreted many of the images they found there.

## The effect of iconoclastic controversies

The balancing of approaches, from the temporal territories of East and West, was undertaken in the Insular gospel books with remarkable sensitivity. Their conflation of cultural references reflected the counterpoint of the exegetical writings of figures such as Gregory the Great and Bede. Unity and the avoidance of schism were major considerations, apparent in the careful balancing of iconic and aniconic features at a time when iconoclasm was rife. In the Lindisfarne Gospels, its evangelist miniatures sit like framed icons on the page, set against polished pink grounds intended to recall encaustic icons painted with wax. They portray aspects of Christ's nature obliquely through their symbolism—the evangelist symbols providing a visual exegesis upon aspects of the nature of Christ: Matthew, the man of the incarnation; Mark, the lion of kingship and resurrection; Luke, the calf or bull, the sacrificial offering; and John, the eagle of the second coming, who (like the visionary, John) soars directly to the throne of God for inspiration.

Theological controversy also had a bearing on how Eadfrith chose to depict the evangelists in relation to time and space. Two of the Lindisfarne Gospels' evangelists are bearded and aging; two are youthful and immortal. This is not, as some art historians have suggested, simply a response to the availability of different models—the former from Byzantium and the latter from Rome—but a subtle means of highlighting the complementary nature of the human and perishable and the divine and eternal, brought together in the unity of the Gospels in the one book and in Christ himself. The two "beardies" are Matthew and Luke, who, with their symbols, represent the humanity of Christ and are aging and mortal; Mark and John, who signify his divinity, are eternally young. Like their Byzantine counterparts, these Insular evangelists dwell within the abstract, timeless space of the icon, whether on painted or gilded grounds.

How had this iconic tradition developed? During late Antiquity, Jews and Christians both tended to eschew statuary, owing to its particular associations with the brazen images worshipped by the Israelites and condemned by Moses and also because of its extensive use in the cults of pagan Graeco-Roman deities. Other images were less obviously contentious, however, and the use of icons (Greek *eikōn*) by some Christians can be traced back as far as the second century. Some early panel paintings survive depicting saints and even Christ, based upon images of pagan heroes whose status was signaled by the triumphal halo or nimbus, a ring of light framing the head (with painted panels of nimbed military deities surviving from Egypt and Syria). During the fourth century, Eusebius wrote disapprovingly of them: "I have examined images of his apostles Paul and Peter, and indeed of Christ himself, preserved in colour paintings; which is understandable, since the ancients used to honour saviours freely in this way following their pagan custom" (*Historia Ecclesiastica*, 7.18.4) and "these are excluded from churches all over the world" (Eusebius, letter to Constantina, sister of Constantine). He confiscated a painting of Christ and

St Paul, depicted as philosophers, which a woman brought to him—although he did not destroy it, but kept it in his own home, probably recognizing that it was not images themselves that represented an idolatrous threat, but the way in which people regarded them during their prayers; was the icon the subject or the object of devotion? Public pagan cult figures tended to take the form of statues, whilst domestic deities and the ancestors and emperors (the *lauraton*) venerated in the home were often painted. Despite the misgivings of the Church Fathers, Christians continued to feel the need for images as a focus for contemplation and the icon was destined to play a major role in the development of Christian devotional art, especially within the Orthodox Churches.

The icon became most potent and characteristic form of Byzantine Christian artistic expression. Images in books or other media are sometimes given this epithet, indicating their function as devotional images, but the term refers primarily to panel paintings, whether small, portable, and domestic or large patronal icons (depicting the saints to whom they were dedicated) in major churches. The role of the icon is a distinctly religious one. The act of "writing" (rather than painting) an icon is in itself an act of prayer in which a direct channel of communication is opened between the sacred or saintly persons depicted and those who contemplate their images, enabling the subject to act as intermediary and intercessor between God and supplicant, heaven and earth, whether in the form of a compassionate Virgin and Child, a stern prophet, an ascetic saint or an archangel charged with the weighing of souls—another Coptic borrowing from ancient Egyptian art.

The transmission of such sacred iconic images was, like that of sacred text, considered to be achieved through the interaction of divine inspiration, the agency of the Spirit, and the contemplative work of the transmitter. Certain famous icons depicting Christ (bearded, in Byzantine fashion, rather than in youthful unbearded early Christian Hellenistic guise) were thought to have appeared miraculously (*acheiropoietos*), rather than by human hands, whilst some were attributed to St Luke, who was said to have painted the likeness of the Mother of God (*Theotokos*) from life. It therefore became extremely important that subsequent copies should preserve these images as faithfully as possible, instilling a powerful conservatism into the iconic tradition.

Icons were usually designed so that they could be displayed on liturgical screens, on stands, as diptychs or triptychs, or carried in liturgical processions, much like their counterparts—the great illuminated copies of scripture. The initial low chancel screen gave way to the Middle Period *templon* barrier and then to the Late Byzantine *iconostasis*—a full sanctuary screen separating the Holy of holies from the congregation and carrying an established scheme of icons forming a symbolic cosmos.

Perhaps the ultimate proof, if any were needed, that books of sacred text could be viewed as actual icons themselves at this period, is one of a group of sculptures carved at the Anglo-Saxon monastery of Breedon-on-the-hill in

Leicestershire around 800 (Figure 3). Forming part of what may originally have been a stone iconostasis screen, in the Byzantine tradition, are an arcaded frieze of apostles and a bust of the Virgin, her head veiled and her right hand pointing to the precious charge she holds in her left arm. This is the venerable pose of the Virgin depicted as Hodegetria, the Indicator of the Way, gesturing to the infant Christ—except here he is depicted not as a child, but as a book: Logos, God of all time and by whom all things were made. In the tradition of the Orthodox churches icons were often paid heightened honor by encasing them in silver repoussé mounts which also served to raise parts of the design, such as haloes, giving a three-dimensional effect: that is anticipated here by the depth of the carving. An early example of this can be seen on a fourteenth-century double-sided processional icon, carried on a pole, from Ochrid, whose Virgin has been given the title Saviour of Souls. The Breedon Saviour of Souls points to the book, to Logos and to his revelation through scripture, as the way to salvation (Brown, 2011).

Some of the earliest and most powerful icons to have survived from the Early Period are preserved at the monastery of St Catherine on Mount Sinai. They include a striking sixth-century encaustic icon of St Peter and a sixth- to seventh-century Ascension resembling that in the Syriac Rabbula Gospels. Another particularly fine collection of icons and manuscripts preserved in situ is that on Mount Athos in Greece. Some of the finest icons from the Middle Period were made in Constantinople itself. Following the Latin conquest of that city in 1204 and the consequent dismembering of the Byzantine Empire, the impetus passed to other production centres, such as Crete which became a Venetian colony (Regno di Candia) from 1210 to 1669. The island became one of a number of areas of fruitful Italo-Byzantine economic and cultural interaction, where Constantinopolitan and Italian stylistic influences merged. Icons might be commissioned "alla maniera greca" or "alla maniera italiana / latina," according to style and iconography, by members of the Orthodox or Catholic Churches, often interchangeably. Cretan icon writers had an unusual tendency to sign their work, as a result of which it is possible to chart the existence of some 150 of them in the capital, Candia (modern Heraklion) by the sixteenth century. The anonymity of the icon writer gave way to the identity of the artist, in accordance with Italian trends, identifying for us painters such as the Ritzos family, Angelos, and Andreas Pavias during the fifteenth century and, in the sixteenth, Domenikos Theotokopoulos - better known as "El Greco"—who once more transmitted the mystical and spiritual essence of the iconic tradition to western art.

## Enshrining the book

An eastern Mediterranean appreciation of the iconic status of the book as an object of veneration was also transmitted to the West through the practice of enshrining sacred texts within treasure bindings. Ivories or bejeweled metalwork plates attached to wooden binding boards are found on Byzantine, Coptic, Armenian, Irish, Anglo-Saxon, Carolingian, and Ottonian books (important treasure bindings include the Lindau Gospels, New York, Morgan Library and Museum, MSM 1, and the Codex Aureus of Charles the Bald, Munich, Bayerische Staatsbibliothek, Clm 14000). In Coptic Egypt and Ireland metalwork shrines (Old Irish cumdach) were also made (Ó Floinn 1994). The earliest surviving example of what may be part of a book shrine forms part of the Coptic Treasure of Archbishop Abraham of Harmonthis (Cairo, Coptic Museum) around 600, whilst the modifications made to the original fifth-century binding of the Freer Gospels in seventh-century Egypt included not only painting the wooden boards with encaustic wax images of the evangelists—turning the book into an actual icon and object of prayer—but the addition of a metal fitting that effectively locked the covers and enshrined the text, literally, within them (Brown, 2006a, no. 28). The evangelist miniatures of the Lindisfarne Gospels sit framed, like eastern icons, upon the page, their backgrounds of a thick pink paint polished to emulate the encaustic icon technique. The designs on some early Coptic bindings resemble the decoration of their cross-carpet pages, the sacrality of their texts reinforced by the sacred symbols that introduced them and adorned their protective covers (Brown 2010). A late eighth-century Irish metalwork book-shrine, the Lough Kinale Shrine, also carries a design resembling the Lindisfarne Gospels' carpet pages. It too contained a book and was designed not to be opened (Kelly 1994). Later in the Middle Ages, an early Psalter written in Ireland, and long thought to be that written by St Columba's own hand and occasioned charges of plagiarism that led him to leave Ireland on *peregrinatio*—voluntary exile for Christ—gained its name, the Cathach of Columcille, from the fact that its hereditary keepers carried it, enshrined, before them into battle to ensure divine favor, as their Armenian precursors were wont to do and recalling the Byzantine practice of bearing the *palladium*, an icon of the Virgin, before their imperial hosts. The scriptural book itself had become one of the most powerful of intercessory icons (Brown 2010).

Another telling instance of Eastern Mediterranean influence being transmitted to the West is again related to books and is encountered on the earliest extant Western binding, that of the Saint Cuthbert Gospel, a little copy of John's Gospel found alongside the body of Saint Cuthbert within his coffin (formerly known as the Stonyhurst Gospel, Society of Jesus, now B.L., Loan MS 74; Brown 1969; van Regemorter 1992). This was made in Wearmouth–Jarrow in the 690s and employed not the Western but the "Coptic" binding technique, the mastery of this complex technique providing tangible evidence of communication between these far-flung regions. The Saint Cuthbert Gospel was found inside the saint's coffin in 1104 and had probably been placed there in 698 when his relics were translated to the new shrine beside the High Altar at Lindisfarne. The shrine takes the unusual form of wooden coffin (known as a theca, or box, like the bibliotheca for storing books) to emphasize the corporeal presence of the saint within, whose body had not decayed—a visible sign of sanctity. The invisible presence of the book inside the coffin—like those in metalwork shrines—was evidently of powerful significance.

The Cuthbert Gospel seems to have been contained within a leather or linen pouch or satchel, recalling the tooled leather satchel of fifteenth-century date which contained the Book of Armagh (now preserved at Trinity College, Dublin; Ryan 1983, no 86; Marner 2001; Tudor 1989, 460; Ryan 1983, no 86; Marner 2001; Tudor 1989, 460). Such satchels are often mentioned in Irish literature as containing books or relics, such as that which Adomnán tells us contained a hymnal written by Columba's hand which was lost in a river for several months, after which the book-cum-relic was found incorrupt (Ryan 1983, 50). Later, in the twelfth century, the Cuthbert Gospel was hung, as a special honor, around the necks of visiting dignitaries (Tudor 1989, 460). That such practices existed earlier is demonstrated by Alcuin's condemnation, addressed to the Archbishop of Canterbury, of the popular practice of wearing saints' bones and Gospel texts, presumably for their protective, talismanic merits (Marner 2001). The wearing of sacred texts is an ancient practice, manifest for example in the Judaic wearing of phylacteries (Deuteronomy 6.8). The Gospel of St John was considered particularly efficacious in Christian circles. John of Salisbury claimed that St Cuthbert cured a man by laying a copy of John's Gospel on him and during the Middle Ages its incipit, "In the beginning was the Word, and the Word was with God, and the Word was God,"

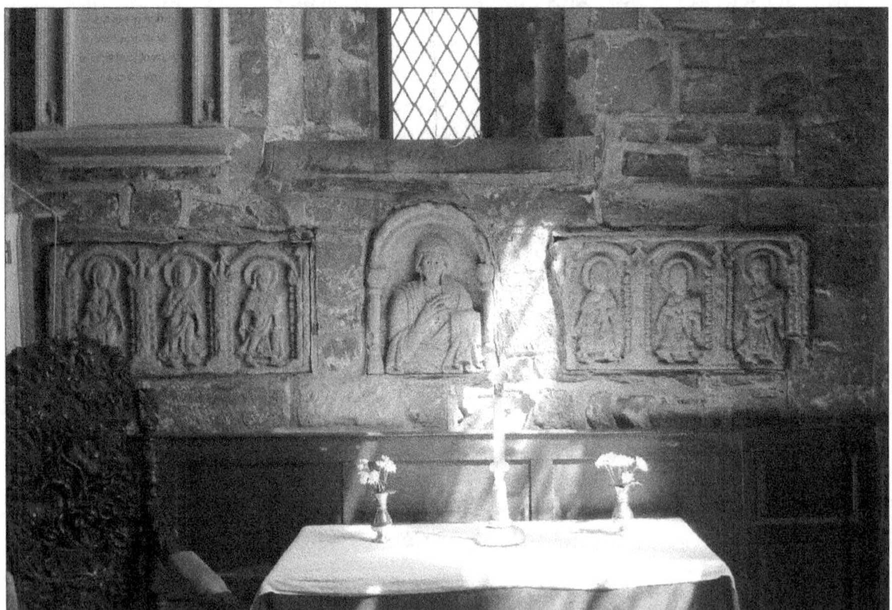

Figure 3. Stone iconostasis screen, ca. 800 C.E., in Breedon-on-the-hill, Leicestershire. Photo by Michelle P. Brown.

was often worn around the neck to as a protective charm (Marner 2001). St Augustine even records the belief that these words could cure headaches (Migne 1844–1864, 87, cols 527–529). Yet the special import of this non-synoptic Gospel extended beyond the merely apotropaic. St John is symbolised by the eagle, an identification discussed by commentators such as Augustine, Gregory and Bede, for his spirit flies directly to the throne of God for inspiration. The "disciple whom Jesus loved" evoked a special proximity to the person of Christ and an insight into the divine will. Its lections featured at key points in the liturgy, including the masses for the sick and dying. It would thus have lent itself particularly well for pastoral work in the field, perhaps explaining why it sometimes circulated as a separate volume. It was the text which Cuthbert and his master, Boisil, studied together in the last week of the latter's life, for it contained "the simple things of 'the faith that works by love'" (Gal. 5:6). It was also an apt focus for meditation for one about to leave this life, and Bede likewise chose to devote his last days to the task of translating it into the vernacular, that its benefits might be more widely enjoyed. In addition to books attracting such attention as potent relics, scribes themselves might also be imbued with miraculous powers. This is not surprising when they happened to be saintly figures such as Columba, but the ninth-century poem *De Abbatibus*, by Aethelwulf, which refers to a daughter-house of Lindisfarne, records that the relics of the accomplished Irish scribe, Ultan, were also wonder-working (Aethelwulf, *De Abbatibus*, ch. 8; Campbell 1967, 20–23; Brown 1989, 157). Speculation has abounded as to where Ultan was based and whether any surviving works might be attributable to him, but he is perhaps of greater value as a literary topos, attesting to the concept of the saintly scribe.

Leslie Brubaker has suggested that relics fulfilled a similar role in the West to that of sacred images in the East. She writes that "Intercession, for the Byzantines, was a primary function of the sacred image: the image channelled prayers to God, and God's goodwill back to the individual or community. The needs of western Christians for intercession and protection—for access, in short, to divine power—were channelled into relics of saints rather than images of them" (Brown 2011; Brubaker 1995, 11). The illuminated Insular Scriptural manuscript could perform such a function in both forms, as icon and as relic.

An earlier case of scripture included in a burial is the earliest surviving complete Coptic psalter (Cairo, Coptic Museum, MS Lib. 6614; Gabra 1993). Around 400 it was lovingly placed open as a pillow beneath the head of an adolescent girl in a humble cemetery at Al-Mudil, 40 kilometers northeast of Oxyrhynchus. An ancient analogy, for both, might be the Egyptian practice of interring the Book of the Dead with the deceased to aid their passage into the afterlife. The small bone peg, shaped like the ancient Egyptian key of life, that was used to unlock the Coptic psalter in question reinforces this con-

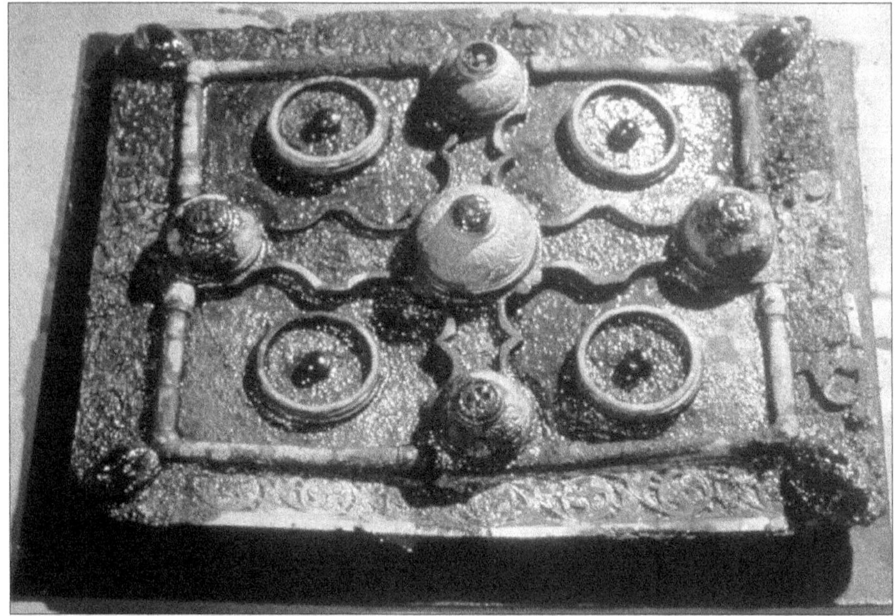

Figure 4. Lough Kinale Book Shrine, Irish, eighth century. National Museum of Ireland.

nection. Perhaps also relevant is the fact that in Ethiopia a short text known as the *Lefafa Sedq* "Bandlet of Righteousness" is still often carried by people throughout their lives, read at their funeral and buried with them. The incorruptibility of Cuthbert's body finds its closest analogies within the emerging contemporary cults of eastern saints, such as St Bishoi in the Wadi Natroun, whose body, clad in thick layers of vestments, can still be prodded by the faithful in order to assure themselves that he is still with them—physically as well as spiritually.

## Conclusion

The books of the Judaic and Christian Bibles had first begun to circulate in the Middle East as informal scrolls and pamphlets. That was a far cry from the way approaches to the sacred nature of scripture developed between 500 and 1000 C.E. In this period, Jews developed the custom of using genizahs, sealed rooms within which even flawed copies of Judaic scripture were carefully stored prior to ritual destruction in honor of their sacred contents. At the same time, Christians enacted and validated the most solemn and binding of legal rituals upon splendid illuminated biblical codices. From the ninth century onwards, many important copies of the Gospels (such as the St Chad Gospels which contains the earliest post-Roman documents freeing slaves entered in its margins) became books of the high altar, displayed there as icons of faith for liturgical, legal, and cultic purposes.

The Lough Kinale Book Shrine (Figure 4) embodies the iconic status that had been acquired by the book during the early Middle Ages as a result of developing perceptions of its significance and authority in both East and West. It was tossed into an Irish lake during the ninth century when a disappointed Viking raider found that it only contained an old book (Kelly 1994). This marked the beginning of a challenge to the iconic status of sacred texts. It may have come initially from "outsiders" who did not belong to any of the Abrahamic religions and did not respect their scriptures, but it would escalate in the late Middle Ages with the increasing demands of believers to have access to the Bible in their own languages so that they could read and interpret it themselves, and with the advent of printing and the mass-production of affordable bibles that today are considered virtually disposable.

At the dawn of the modern era, then, the Bible was once more the unpretentious working manual of ordinary Christian communities, just as it had begun in the Middle East. In the interim, eastern influence transmitted to the West by a number of routes had revolutionized society's perceptions of the role and appearance of the book. It endures still as one of our greatest cultural icons as we enter an electronic age, taking e-books from the virtual shelves of "information commons" (as we seem now to be terming the cage of the muses, or library) as we seek new cognitive and codicological forms for preserving the icon of our collective memory.

## References


Aethelwulf, *De Abbatibus*, ed. and trans. *Alistair Campbell*. 1967. Oxford: Clarendon Press.

Avrin, Leila. 1991. *Scribes, Script and Books*. London and Chicago, IL: British Library and University of Chicago Press.

Alexander, Jonathan J. G. 1992. *Medieval Illuminators and Their Methods of Work*. New Haven, CT: Yale University Press.

Ayerst, David and A. S. T. Fisher. 1977. *Records of Christianity* II. Oxford: Blackwell.

Badawy, Alexander. 1978. *Coptic Art and Archaeology*. Cambridge, MA: MIT Press.

Brown, Michelle P. 1998. *The British Library Guide to Writing and Scripts*. 2nd ed. London and Toronto: British Library and University of Toronto Press.

———. 2000. "'In the beginning was the Word': Books and Faith in the Age of Bede." *The Jarrow Lecture 2000*. Newcastle-upon-Tyne: Jarrow Lectures.

———. 2003. *The Lindisfarne Gospels: Society, Spirituality and the Scribe*. London and Toronto: British Library Publications and University of Toronto Press.

———. 2005. "The Tower of Babel: The Architecture of the Early Western Written Vernaculars." In *Omnia Disce. Medieval Studies in Memory of Leonard Boyle, O.P.*, edited by Ann J. Duggan, Joan Greatrex and Brenda Bolton, 109-128. Ashgate: Aldershot.

———. 2006. *How Christianity Came to Britain and Ireland*. Oxford: Lion Hudson.

———, ed. 2006a. *In the Beginning: Bibles Before the Year 1000*, exhibition catalog,

Freer and Sackler Museum, Smithsonian Institution. Washington, DC: Smithsonian Institute.

———. 2010. *The Lindisfarne Gospels and the Early Medieval World.* London and Chicago, IL: British Library and University of Chicago Press.

———. 2011. *The Book and the Transformation of Britain, c.550-1050.* The Sandars Lectures in Bibliography, 2009. London and Chicago, IL: British Library and University of Chicago Press.

———. 2012. "Insular Script: Display Scripts." In *The History of the Book in Britain,* I, edited by R. G. Gameson. Cambridge: Cambridge University Press.

Brown, T. Julian *et al.*, ed. 1969. *The Stonyhurst Gospel of St John.* Oxford: Roxburghe Club.

Brubaker, Leslie. 1995. "The Sacred Image." In *The Sacred Image, East and West,* Illinois Byzantine Studies 4, edited by Robert G. Ousterhout and Leslie Brubaker, 1–24. Urbana, IL: University of Illinois.

Buckton, David, ed. 1994. *Byzantium. Treasures of Byzantine Art and Culture.* London: British Museum Press.

Cassiodorus, *De Institutione Divinarum Litterarum*, ch. 30; see *Magni Aurelii,* Corpus Christianorum, Series Latina 96*;* Migne, Jacques. P. 1847. *Patrologiae Cursus Completus* 70: cols 1144–1145.

Chazelle, Celia. 1990. "Pictures, Books and the Illiterate: Pope Gregory I's Letters to Serenus of Marseilles." *Word and Image* 6(2): 138–153.

Colgrave, Bertram and Roger A. B. Mynors, ed. and trans.1969. *Bede's Ecclesiastical History of the English People*, Oxford Medieval Texts. Oxford: Oxford University Press.

de Hamel, Christopher. 1986. *A History of Illuminated Manuscripts.* Oxford: Phaidon.

Déroche, François and Francis Richard. 1997. *Scribes et manuscrits du Moyen-Orient.* Paris: Bibliothèque Nationale de France.

Deshman, Robert. 1980. "The Exalted Servant: The Ruler Theology of the Prayerbook of Charles the Bald." *Viator* 11: 385–417.

Diebold, William. 2000. *Word and Image: A History of Early Medieval Art.* Boulder, CO: Westview Press.

Dutton, Paul and Herbert Kessler. 1997. *The Poetry and Painting of the First Bible of Charles the Bald.* Ann Arbor, MI: University of Michigan Press.

Gabra, Gawdat. 1993. *Cairo: The Coptic Museum and Old Churches.* Cairo: Longman.

Gameson, Richard G. 2001. "The Scribe Speaks? Colophons in Early English Manuscripts." *H. M. Chadwick Memorial Lectures* 12.

Hurst, David, ed. 1960. *Bede, Expositio in Lucam*, Corpus Christianorum, Series Latina 120: prol. 93–115. Turnhout: Brepols.

Kelly, Eamonn P. 1994. "The Lough Kinale Shrine: the Implications for the Manuscripts." In *The Book of Kells. Proceedings of a Conference at Trinity College Dublin, 6–9 September 1992,* edited by Felicity O'Mahony, 280–289. Aldershot: Ashgate.

Kelly, Susan. 1990. "Anglo-Saxon Lay Society and the Written Word." In *The Uses of Literacy in Early Mediaeval Europe*, edited by Rosamond McKitterick, 36–62.

Cambridge: Cambridge University Press.
Kitzinger, Ernst. 1975. *The Place of Book Illumination in Byzantine Art*. Princeton, NJ: Princeton University Press.
Lowden, John. 1997. *Early Christian and Byzantine Art*. London: Phaidon.
Marner, Dominic. 2001. *St Cuthbert, His Life and Cult in Medieval Durham*. London: British Library.
Mellors, John and Ann Parsons. 2002. *Ethiopian Bookmaking* and *Scribes of South Gondar*. London: New Cross Books.
Migne, Jacques P. 1844–1864. *Patrologiae Cursus Completus*, 221 vols. Paris.
Mütherich, Florentine and Joachim Gaehde. 1976. *Carolingian Painting*. London: Chatto and Windus.
Nersessian, Vrej. 2001. *Treasures from the Ark: 1700 Years of Armenian Christian Art*. London: British Library.
Nordenfalk, Carl. 1988. *Early Medieval Book Illumination*. New York: Rizzoli.
Ó Floinn, Raghnall. 1994. *Irish Shrines and Reliquaries of the Middle Ages*. Dublin: Country House and NMI.
Ong, Walter J. 1981. *Orality and Literacy: The Technologizing of the Word*. London: Methuen.
O'Reilly, Jennifer, 2001. "The Library of Scripture: Views from the Vivarium and Wearmouth-Jarrow." In *New Offerings, Ancient Treasures. Essays in Medieval Art for George Henderson*, edited by Paul Binski and William G. Noel. Stroud: Alan Sutton.
Pächt, Otto. 1986. *Book Illumination in the Middle Ages: An Introduction*. London: Harvey Miller.
Page, Ray I. 1995. *Runes and Runic Inscriptions*. Woodbridge: Boydell and Brewer.
Parkes, Malcolm B. 1992. *Pause and Effect: An Introduction to the History of Punctuation in the West*. Aldershot: Scolar Press.
———. 2000. "*Rædan, areccan, smeagan*: How the Anglo-Saxons Read." *Anglo-Saxon England* 26: 1–22.
Prospero's Bookstore, 2007, http://www.prosperosbookstore.com/full_content.php?article_id=777&full=yes&pbr=1 Accessed 26 January 2011].
Roberts, Colin H. and T. C. Skeat. 1983 (reptd). *The Birth of the Codex*. Oxford: Oxford University Press.
Ryan, Michael, ed. 1983. *Treasures of Ireland. Irish Art, 3000 B.C.-1500 A.D.* Dublin: NMI.
Safran, Linda, ed. 1998. *Heaven on Earth: Art and the Church in Byzantium*. University Park, PA: Pennsylvania State University Press.
Stansbury, Mark. 1999. "Early Medieval Biblical Commentaries, Their Writers and Readers." In *Frühmittelalterliche Studien, Herausgegeben von H. Keller und C. Meier*, edited by K. Hauck, 50–82. Berlin: Walter de Gruyter.
Tudor, Victoria. 1989. "The Cult of St Cuthbert in the Twelfth Century: The Evidence of Reginald of Durham." In *St Cuthbert, His Cult and His Community to AD 1200*, edited by Gerald Bonner *et al.*, 447–468. Woodbridge: Boydell and Brewer.

van Regemorter, Berthe. 1992. *Binding Structures in the Middle Ages*, translated by Jane Greenfield. Brussels: Bibliotheca Wittockiana; London: Maggs Bros.

Walsh, Maura and Dáibhí Ó Cróinín, eds. 1988. *Cummian's Letter De Controversia Paschale*. Toronto: Pontifical Institute of Mediaeval Studies.

Webster, Leslie and Janet M. Backhouse, eds. 1991. *The Making of England: Anglo-Saxon Art and Culture AD 600–900*. London: British Museum Press.

——— and Michelle P. Brown, eds. 1997. *The Transformation of the Roman World*. London: British Museum Press.

Weitzmann, Kurt. 1977. *Late Antique and Early Christian Book Illumination*. London: Chatto and Windus.

Whitelock, Dorothy. 1979. *English Historical Documents* I, rev. ed. London: Eyre and Spottiswoods.

Wright, David H. 1967. *The Vespasian Psalter*, Early English Manuscipts in Facsimile 14. Copenhagen: Rosenkilde and Bagger.

———. 1993. *The Vatican Virgil*. Berkeley: University of California Press.

6

# Looking at Words: The Iconicity of the Page

S. Brent Plate

*Regardless of their semantic meaning, words exist in and through their material, mediated forms. By extension, sacred texts themselves are material forms and engaged in two primary ways: through the ears and eyes. This paper focuses on the visible forms of words that can stir emotional and even sacred responses in the eyes of their beholders. Thus words can be said to function iconically, affecting a mutually engaging form of "religious seeing." The way words appear to their readers will change the reader's interaction, devotion, and interpretation. Examples range from modern popular typography to European Christian print culture to Islamic calligraphy. Weaving through the argument are two key dialectics: the relation of words and images, and the relation of the seen and the unseen.*

In his commencement address to Kenyon College in 2005, David Foster Wallace tells the parable of two young fish swimming along, talking to each other. An older fish swims past and says, "Good morning boys. How's the water?" The two fish swim on in silence for a while until the one turns to the other and says, "What the hell is water?" The point Wallace makes is that we are all like those young fish: we all live and breathe in an atmosphere that is so pervasive we seldom take notice of it, though part of living a compassionate life is to live with an awareness of the things closest to us (Wallace 2009).

The point of this paper is not quite so noble as Wallace's. Instead, I borrow the fish parable to suggest that printed and scripted words are the water of scriptural studies. When studying scripture, we read, interpret, compare, define, and/or translate words, but seldom recognize the water in which we are swimming: the style of the printed or scripted words and the layout of the pages on which the words appear.

My argument here is twofold. First, regardless of their semantic meaning, words exist in and through their mediated forms and do not exist apart from their materiality. By extension, sacred texts themselves are material forms and engaged in two primary ways: through the ears and eyes. They are also often touched. The Johannine literature has already said as much: "The Word" is "seen," "heard," "touched with our hands" (1 John 1:1). While the ways words are felt and heard are equally important, the focus herein will be on printed and scripted words and the ways these become visual images.

Second, I point toward some of the ways that the visible forms of words have stirred emotional and even sacred responses in the eyes of their beholders. Thus, words can be said to function iconically, affecting a mutually engaging form of "religious seeing," or a "sacred gaze" (see Plate 2002; Morgan 2005). In this way too, interpretation itself is altered by the visual form that words take. The way words appear to their readers will change the reader's interaction, devotion, and interpretation. My examples range from modern popular typography to European Christian print culture to Islamic calligraphy, with a few other examples mixed in. Weaving through the argument are two key dialectics: the relation of words and images, and the relation of the seen and the unseen.[1]

## Words and images

Much has been written and discussed on the relations between words and images—how they compete with, conform to, and contrast with each other. Some works oversimplify a hostile relation, pitting *The Alphabet Versus the Goddess: The Conflict between Word and Image* (Shlain 1998) or *The Rise of the Image, The Fall of the Word* (Stephens 1998). Other projects aim to chart the various relations, such as the journal *Word & Image*, or the artistic collective "Art & Language," as they draw out Michel Foucault's oft-quoted line: "the relation of language to painting is an infinite relation" (Foucault 1970, 9). Meanwhile, visual studies scholars such as W.J.T. Mitchell, Mieke Bal, Norman Bryson, and James Elkins supply a strong set of examples for the ways words and images have interacted through cultural histories (See Mitchell 1994, 2005; Bal 1991, Bryson 1983, Elkins 2001; a good overview is given in Miller 2008).

Within religious histories, there are many examples of visual images serving as the basis of verbal stories. Sacred texts, as other contributions in this volume suggest, are often accompanied by images that not only illustrate but simultaneously interpret the verbal text. There are also suggestions that the visual illustrations can be looked at as the verbal text is ignored, as Christopher de Hamel points out, "Anyone can take delight in turning the pages of a Book of Hours, for example, even without reading the text" (de Hamel 2001, 13). Elsewhere, images become sacred texts, for example with stained glass in Christian churches or the Japanese Buddhist use of *etoki* (Raguin 2003; Kaminishi 2006). Each of these pictured stories was used to spread the doctrines and mythologies of their traditions to non-literate people.

1. Some of the ideas and passages found here also appear in my article "Words," in *Material Religion* 7.1 (2011): 156–162.

The present project is somewhat different than each of those, as it suggests how the word-image opposition is a false distinction in certain circumstances. What is of interest here are the ways in which *a word is an image*. In writing and print, words are visual images that are looked at. An examination of printed and scripted words reveals the visual depths of verbal language, and the ways in which words become iconic.

## Words unseen

The 2008 U.S. presidential campaign pitted candidate against candidate, but also font against font: John McCain's team choose a font designed in the 1950s, Hilary Clinton's team choose from a font family originally designed in the eighteenth century, while Obama's campaign rode in on the most contemporary font, Gotham, created in 2000 by Jonathan Hoefler and Tobias Frere-Jones. It was originally designed for *GQ* magazine.[2] Did this make a difference in the results? It's impossible to gauge. Did people notice? Yes and no. Typeface often sends a message while simultaneously erasing itself. Hoefler and Frere-Jones say about creating typefaces, "If we've done our jobs right, [people] have never noticed our typefaces."[3]

Intriguing here is the way modern typography works to become invisible, a trick not of smoke and mirrors but of strokes and serifs. The most successful and influential typefaces designed in the modern age have grown out of rationalizing processes based on proportions between individual characters, vertical and horizontal relations, and contrasts between thick and thin strokes, including the hairline serifs that quickly move the eye horizontally across the page. The aim was, and continues to be, to speed up the mechanical visual aspects of reading so that the reader no longer feels himself or herself to be reading words. The materiality of the words seems to disappear though it is only through their material form that knowledge is communicated, interpretation can occur, and devotional readings of texts can take place.

In light of modern typographic design, the word-image dichotomy can be seen as a corollary to mind-body dualism, in which the invisible, interior term is praised, just as the material, external form is diminished. Words, seen in this light, become silent, individual, immediate (i.e., "without media"), of the spirit; images are exterior, opaque, available to a collective, carnal. This is bound up with modern reading practices, but those reading practices are themselves fostered by the production, distribution, and design of books (see Fischer 2004; Saenger 1997). Modern typography thus helps foster a sense that words are more spiritual than images. But of course that's a trick of the eye.

2. See a brief history of Gotham at: http://www.typography.com/fonts/font_history.php?historyItemID=1&productLineID=100008

3. The radio show, "To the Best of Our Knowledge," interviewed Hoefler and Frere-Jones. Aired 1 November 2009. Online at http://www.wpr.org/book/091101b.cfm, accessed 1 September 2010.

## Words seen

### *Script*

In other times and places it has been the very visibility of words and their characters that have worked magic, for instance in mythical depictions of runes and in alchemical and Kabbalistic writings. In many cases, the individual characters that comprise words become prominent. Words are the molecular form of atomistic characters, whether in Western alphabets or Chinese writing. Scripted language has long facilitated visual experiences by allowing viewers to engage the physical reality of the characters. This is quite unlike modernism's attempt to erase its signifiers. As Johanna Drucker notes of the creating of the great Chi-Ro page in the Book of Kells: "Such practices bespeak a faith in visuality which escapes the need for textual reference: the image of the letter functions in its own right to communicate effectively" (1995, 108). In such cases, religious responses are produced through the opacity of the visual words and their characters.

The emphasis on the visually opaque word is perhaps most apparent in calligraphic traditions, particularly in China, Japan, and across the Islamic world. Calligraphy triggers visceral, emotional responses before and beyond the intellectual capturing of verbal signification. Discussing the "Intermediary of Writing," art historian Oleg Grabar quotes from a classic source to show the power of Chinese calligraphy: "A well-written character … to the perceiving mind it is a dynamic experience" (1992, 58). Such crucial experiences between imaged characters and perceiving mind-bodies likewise form the glue of religious encounters with words of God.

Islam, with its mostly aniconic bias, developed a strong tradition of calligraphy in which the material, written word is a means of access to the direct revelation itself. While the term Qur'an literally means "recitation," and is thus primarily oral, it is also "taught by the pen," according to the Surat al-Qalam ("The Pen"; Qur'an 68:1). Islamic calligraphers throughout history have sought to embody the very words of Allah in graphically appropriate form, which includes, variously: their inscription in gold ink, the use of lapis lazuli as the source for blue framing surrounding the Quranic verses, the accompaniment by arabesque and geometric patterns, and the continued use of parchment after paper was accessible to the Islamic world through its connections with paper's origination in China. Each of these aspects pays homage to the value of the word itself, in visible form. Ultimately, the Word of God in Islam transcends the bounds of the book (*mushaf*), appearing on jewelry, pottery, epigraphy, wall hangings, mosaics, textiles, and coins, among other media (see entries in Suleman 2007; see also Suit in this volume). The words of the Qur'an have even been believed to "sanctify, politicize, beautify, or bestow talismanic properties on objects and buildings" (Suleman 2007, 16). Among the non-Muslim Nafana in Ghana, for example, a kind of soup is made from a tonic that washes slates with Quranic verses on it. The liquid is captured and used, sometimes drunk, as a holy water for protection.

Though architecture, metalwork, pottery, and weaving are all prominent in the visual arts of Islam, it is calligraphy that takes a central position in the Islamic art of the world. In so doing, calligraphy offers an important understanding of the relation between words and images, and of revelation more broadly. As Seyyed Hossein Nasr explains:

> ...calligraphy provides the external dress for the Word of God in the visible world but this art remains wedded to the world of the spirit, for according to the traditional Islamic saying, "Calligraphy is the geometry of the Spirit." The letters, words, and verses of the Qur'an are not just elements of a written language but beings and personalities for which the calligraphic form is the physical and visual vessel. (Nasr 1987, 18)

Such language is strikingly similar to the incarnational language of Christianity, brought out in passages like 1 John 1:1–2:

> We declare to you what was from the beginning, what we have heard, what we have seen with our eyes, what we have looked at and touched with our hands, concerning the word of life—this life was revealed, and we have seen it and testify to it, and declare to you the eternal life that was with the Father and was revealed to us.

The Word of God in Christianity and Islam is fundamentally embodied, and while its spiritual dimensions are not to be ignored, the material realities of the Word of God are just as significant. As embodied revelation, these traditions both point toward the sensual human body as the primary conduit for receiving revelation. We see, hear, and touch the Word.

To go one step further toward dissolving the word-image split, the practice of calligraphy does not necessarily emphasize legibility. Martin Lings points out how.

> It is a wide-spread practice in Islam to gaze intently at Quranic inscriptions so as to extract a blessing from them, or in other words so that through the windows of sight the soul may be penetrated by the Divine radiance of the "signs of God," as the verses are called. Questions as to how far the object is legible and how far the subject is literate would be considered irrelevant to the validity and to the efficacy of this sacrament." (Lings 1976, 16)

So, besides spanning the difference between the oral and the written, calligraphy can be seen to span the opposition between the verbal and the visual. As Qadi Ahmad stated in a sixteenth-century treatise on calligraphy and painting that is still often referred to today: "If someone, whether he can read or not, sees good writing, he likes to enjoy the sight of it."

Contemporary artists in the Islamic world have recognized the power of the tradition of calligraphy, and incorporate it into their own work to create images out of Arabic characters (see Turgut 2007; Ali 1997). While there are many examples of this, I highlight the work of Shahzia Sikander, who was raised in a Muslim home in Pakistan and moved to the United States sometime after finishing art school in Lahore. In an interview for PBS's "Art 21" program, she states that as a child she would read the Qur'an, but

> with no particular understanding, because I was a child, and I could read Arabic but I couldn't understand it. And the memory of it is this amazing visual memory where the beauty of the written word supersedes everything else. The meaning is there, but it's not just the meaning. It's the ability of the written text to take you to that other level.

This is reflected perhaps most clearly in paintings like *Riding the Written* from 1992 (Figure 1), in which images of galloping horses merge into calligraphed words.

### *Print*

Throughout sacred scripture traditions, there has been a continual oscillation between the iconic and semantic uses of texts. In the Christian tradition, even with the advent of print, the shift from iconic to semantic use of words took some time. In the incunable period, for instance, Paul Saenger suggests there is little indication that the earliest printed bibles were frequently read, as evidenced by lack of marginalia or wear and tear of the pages. Instead, they were "frequently luxuriously illuminated by hand, to enhance their primary function as palpable icons of God's revealed word" (Saenger 1999, 32). Of course, there are examples of both types of uses throughout history, and every book and every context will give a different view. My point here is to indicate how the words, and the overall page layout of books, printed or scripted, is a visual image itself, regardless of illumination or illustration.

The art of typography has furthermore attempted to reproduce worldviews. Once the printing press had revolutionized so much, and literacy rates rapidly ascended, type designers worked on creating appropriate fonts. The eighteenth century, for example, saw the rise of rationalist fonts that eventually replaced the earlier humanist ones. Briefly, humanist types retain something of a connection to script, with serifs on only the top or bottom, and a slanted orientation that mimics the strokes of a handheld pen. Rationalist types are oriented vertically with bilateral serifs, making it more distinct from handwriting and increasingly relying on proportionality to make reading easier for great populations of people. Several typographers working in the eighteenth century were chiefly responsible for the turn to rationalist type that contemporary printed European languages now all rely upon for their news, scholarly endeavors, and devotion. Among them are Giambattista Bodoni in Italy, the Fourniers and Didots in France, and William Caslon and John Baskerville in England.

Baskerville's mid-eighteenth-century typeface particularly brings the art of type firmly together with the Enlightenment philosophy of the time. Baskerville designed his typeface in Birmingham, England, and was commis-

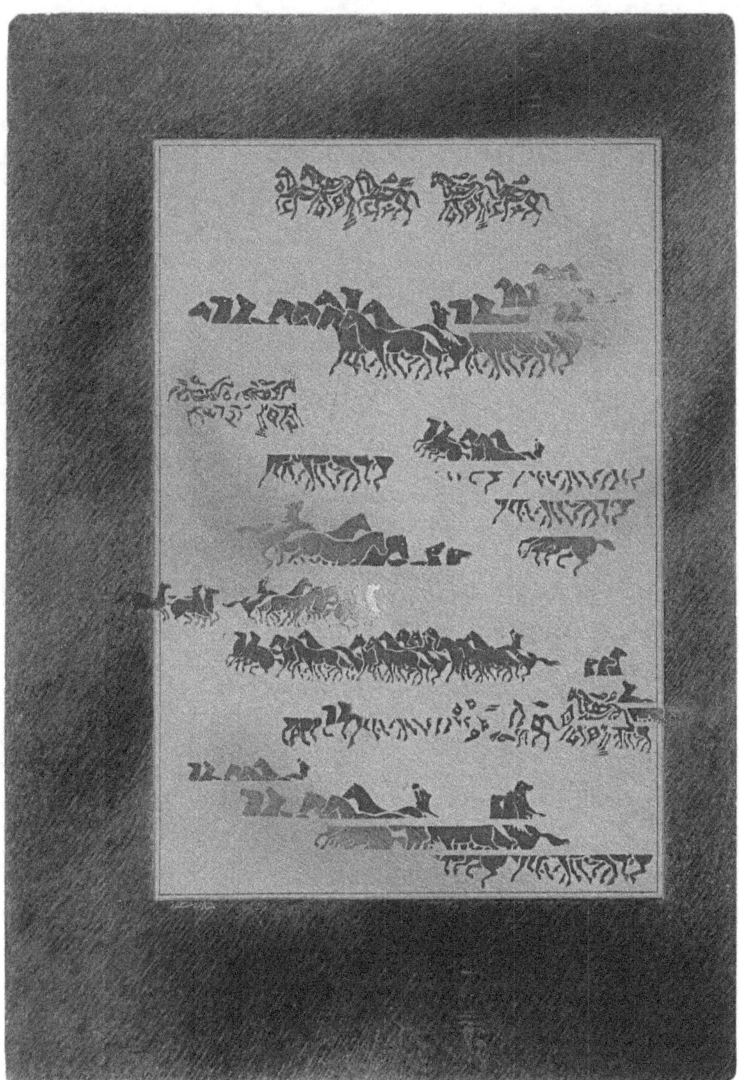

Figure 1. Shahzia Sikander, "Riding the Written," 1992 Screen print. Reprinted by permission. Courtesy of Sikkema Jenkins & Co. New York and Shahzia Sikander.

sioned by the University of Cambridge to produce a Bible, which appeared in 1763 (Figure 2). Gothic scripts were the dominant type for bibles such as the first printings of the 1611 King James Bible. Like certain Arabic calligraphic styles, they worked to wrap an aura around themselves, even to create distance between the text and the reader, letting the reader know how sacred it is. Baskerville's response was to create a perfectly legible and readable text.[4]

4. "Legibility" and "readability" are not identical. Legibility has to do with the ability to recognize the graphic appearance of particular characters or words. Just because individual charac-

Contemporary typographer and critic Robert Bringhurst suggests Baskerville's is "the epitome of Neoclassicism and eighteenth-century rationalism in type" (Bringhurst 2005, 16) because it aimed at "bringing out the spirit of eighteenth-century rationalism inherent in his letters" (Bringhurst and Chappell 1999, 164). (Note the similarities and differences between this project, and, say, Thomas Jefferson's approach to a "rational bible" just a few decades later.)

Visually speaking, words are seen more often than is realized, and it is in seeing printed or written words in a carefully designed layout that religious experiences can occur. In the preface to *A Short History of the Printed Word*, typographer Warren Chappel opines:

> Experience has convinced me that calligraphy and printing have satisfied some of the deepest human needs, intellectually and aesthetically. A page of printed type is one of the most abstract pieces of communication I can imagine. Symbols of the most ancient origin can be put together in ways that stimulate the eye, through pattern, and the mind, through thought.
>
> (Chappell and Bringhurst 1999, xii).

Whether talismanic or technological, visible or seemingly invisible, words have existed through religious cultures as objects that are experienced before and beyond their semantic meanings.

## The affect of the word seen

Gary Hustwit's 2007 film *Helvetica* tells a story of this ubiquitous, eponymous typeface and those who love it and hate it (Figure 3). In an interview, the graphic designer Neville Brody speaks to the power of typeface to affect the viewer:

> The way something is presented will define the way you react to it. So, you can take the same message and present it in three different typefaces.... The immediate emotional response to that will be different, and the choice of typeface is the prime weapon...of communication.

The film's argument becomes most intriguing in conversation with columnist and advertising critic Leslie Savan. Impassioned, she declares, "Helvetica has the perfect balance of push and pull... Helvetica is saying to us, 'Don't worry. Any of the problems you are having, or problems in the world ... all those problems aren't going to spill over. They'll all be contained, and, in fact, maybe they don't even exist'." One wonders, is Savan talking theology or typography here?

But, then again, is this all just an art for the initiated? Some get it and some don't. Does it matter what typeface and design is used for sacred texts? The following section takes a brief account of some effects that print has on the human consciousness and attitudes of those who look at the words on a page. I begin with

ters are legible does not necessarily make the text readable. Readability depends on typeface, size, kerning and spacing in general.

THE

FIRST EPISTLE GENERAL

OF

# J O H N.

After Anno DOMINI 90.

CHAP. I.

1 *He deſcribeth the perſon of Chriſt, in whom we have eternal life, by a communion with God: 5 to which we muſt adjoin holineſs of life, to teſtify the truth of that our communion and profeſſion of faith, as alſo to aſſure us of the forgiveneſs of our ſins by Chriſt's death.*

THAT [a] which was from the beginning, which we have heard, which we have ſeen with our eyes, [b] which we have looked upon, and [c] our hands have handled of the Word of life;

2 (For the life [d] was manifeſted, and we have ſeen *it*, and bear witneſs, [e] and ſhew unto you that eternal life [f] which was with the Father, and was manifeſted unto us;)

3 That which we have ſeen and heard, declare we unto you, that ye alſo may have fellowſhip with us: and truly our fellowſhip *is* with the Father, [g] and with his Son Jeſus Chriſt.

4 And theſe things write we unto you, [h] that your joy may be full.

5 ¶ [i] This then is the meſſage which we have heard of him, and declare unto you, that [k] God is light, and in him is no darkneſs at all.

6 [l] If we ſay that we have fellowſhip with him, and walk in darkneſs, we lie, and do not the truth:

7 But if we walk in the light, as he is in the light, we have fellowſhip one with another, and [m] the blood of Jeſus Chriſt his Son cleanſeth us from all ſin.

8 [n] If we ſay that we have not ſin, we deceive ourſelves, [o] and the truth is not in us.

9 [p] If we confeſs our ſins, he is faithful and juſt to forgive us *our* ſins, and to cleanſe us from all unrighteouſneſs.

10 If we ſay that we have not ſinned, we make him a liar, and his word is not in us.

CHAP. II.

1 *He comforteth them againſt the ſins of infirmity. 3 Rightly to know God, is to keep his commandments, 9 to love our brethren, 15 and not to love the world. 18 We muſt beware of ſeducers: 20 from whoſe deceits the godly are ſafe preſerved by perſeverance in faith and holineſs of life.*

MY little children, theſe things write I unto you, that ye ſin not. And if any man ſin, [a] we have an advocate with the Father, Jeſus Chriſt the righteous:

2 And [b] he is the propitiation for our ſins: and not for our's only, but [c] alſo for *the ſins of* the whole world.

After Anno DOMINI 90.

3 And hereby we do know that we know him, if we keep his commandments.

4 [d] He that ſaith, I know him, and keepeth not his commandments, [e] is a liar, and the truth is not in him.

5 But [f] whoſo keepeth his word, [g] in him verily is the love of God perfected: [h] hereby know we that we are in him.

6 [i] He that ſaith he abideth in him, [k] ought himſelf alſo ſo to walk even as he walked.

7 ¶ Brethren, [l] I write no new commandment unto you, but an old commandment [m] which ye had from the beginning: the old commandment is the word which ye have heard from the beginning.

8 Again, [n] a new commandment I write unto you, which thing is true in him and in you: [o] becauſe the darkneſs is paſt, and [p] the true light now ſhineth.

9 [q] He that ſaith he is in the light, and hateth his brother, is in darkneſs even until now.

10 [r] He that loveth his brother abideth in the light, and [s] there is none [*] occaſion of ſtumbling in him.

11 But he that hateth his brother is in darkneſs, and [t] walketh in darkneſs, and knoweth not whither he goeth, becauſe that darkneſs hath blinded his eyes.

12 ¶ I write unto you, little children, becauſe [v] your ſins are forgiven you for his name's ſake.

13 I write unto you, fathers, becauſe ye have known him *that is* from the beginning. I write unto you, young men, becauſe ye have overcome the wicked one. I write unto you, little children, becauſe ye have known the Father.

14 I have written unto you, fathers, becauſe ye have known him *that is* from the beginning. I have written unto you, young men, becauſe [x] ye are ſtrong, and the word of God abideth in you, and ye have overcome the wicked one.

15 ¶ Love not the world, neither the things *that are* in the world. [y] If any man love the world, the love of the Father is not in him.

16 For all that *is* in the world, the luſt of the fleſh, [z] and the luſt of the eyes, and the pride of life, is not of the Father, but is of the world.

17 And [a] the world paſſeth away, and the luſt

[a] John 1. 1. [b] John 1. 14. 2 Pet. 1. 16. ch. 4. 14. [c] Luke 24. 39. John 20. 27. [d] 1 Tim. 3. 16. [e] ch. 5. 20. [f] John 1. 1, 2. [g] 1 Cor. 1. 9. ch. 2. 24. [h] John 15. 11. 2 John 12. [i] ch. 3. 11. [k] John 1. 9. & 8. 12. & 9. 5. & 12. 35, 36. [l] ch. 2. 4. [m] 1 Cor. 6. 11. Heb. 9. 14. 1 Pet. 1. 19. Rev. 1. 5. [n] 1 Kings 8. 46. 2 Chron. 6. 36. Prov. 20. 9. Eccleſ. 7. 20. Jam. 3. 2. [o] ch. 2. 4. [p] Pſal. 32. 5. Prov. 28. 13. [a] Rom. 8. 34. 1 Tim. 2. 5. Heb. 7. 25. & 9. 24. [b] Rom. 3. 25. 2 Cor. 5. 18. ch. 4. 10. [c] John. 4. 42. ch. 4. 14. [d] ch. 1. 6. & 4. 20. [e] ch. 1. 8. [f] John 14. 21, 23. [g] ch. 4. 12. [h] ch. 4. 13. [i] John 15. 4. [k] Matth. 11. 29. John 13. 15. 1 Pet. 2. 21. [l] 2 John 5. [m] ch. 3. 11. 2 John 5. [n] John 13. 34. [o] Rom. 13. 12. 1 Theſſ. 5. 5, 8. [p] John 1. 9. & 8. 12. [q] 1 Cor. 13. 2. 2 Pet. 1. 9. ch. 3. 14, 15. [r] ch. 3. 14. [s] 2 Pet. 1. 10. [*] Gr. *ſcandal.* [t] John 12. 35. [v] Luke 24. 47. Acts 4. 12. & 13. 38. [x] Epheſ. 6. 10. [y] Matth. 6. 24. Jam. 4. 4. [z] Eccleſ. 5. 11. [a] 1 Cor. 7. 31. Jam. 1. 10.

Figure 2. Baskerville Bible. English. Authorized Version. 1763. From Hamilton College, Rare Books collection. Photo by Marianita Peaslee.

three examples of modern media events and the impact of typeface choices.[5]

First, let's return to brand "Obama." Whether or not Obama's branding choice had a measurable impact on voting citizens, the choice of Gotham type-

5. Alex Poole has a nice webpage that outlines some of the issues of legibility and readability and shows the various ways people have argued for use of one typeface over another. See http://alexpoole.info/which-are-more-legible-serif-or-sans-serif-typefaces, accessed 20 January 2011.

face carried meanings that coincided with and promoted Obama's semantic message. Writing in the *New York Times*, design critic Alice Rawsthorn (2008) stated of the use of Gotham: "A glance at the lettering on the 'Change' banners at Obama's rallies conveys a potent, if unspoken, combination of contemporary sophistication (a nod to his suits) with nostalgia for America's past and a sense of duty." Visceral power stays hidden in typeface, even as a message is carried through.

Likewise, the novelist Nicholson Baker reviewed the Kindle 2 reading tablet in the *New Yorker*. Among his many complaints, he makes the point (that could use further experimental proof) that passages of writing meant to be humorous were simply not funny on the machines. He says he read a passage from Robert Benchley's *Love Conquers All* on the Kindle and didn't laugh at a point he had remembered laughing when he had read a print version earlier. So, he went and got a print copy, reread the passage there, and then laughed. Back to the Kindle: no laughter. He rereads it then on his iPod Touch and laughs again. Baker chalks up the difference to both the lack of contrast with the Kindle screen (too much grey on grey, and not a pure black on white), as well as the typeface used on the reading tablet, Monotype Caecilia. He concludes: "Monotype Caecilia was grim and Calvinist; it had a way of reducing everything to arbitrary heaps of words" (Baker 2009). However unintended by Baker, the fact that "Calvinist" becomes an adjective for a dulled, negative emotion evoked by a typeface begins to suggest something further about the interrelations of type and theology.

Finally, consider the uproar that occurred when the Swedish furniture giant Ikea changed their font. In 2009, their catalog print was switched from the elegant, modern Futura typeface (customized for Ikea and known as "IKEA sans") to the Microsoft-created, internet-friendly Verdana. Futura was created by the German type designer Paul Renner in the 1920s, and meant to evoke efficiency through basic geometric proportions and crisp clean lines: a good rationalist font nicely matched by IKEA's design philosophy. IKEA gave up this archetypal twentieth century design for Verdana, a font that promises to be for the Internet age of the twenty-first century what Futura was for the age of mechanical reproduction in the twentieth. Reactions to IKEA's shift were widespread. *Time* magazine reported several tweeted and blogged responses:

> "Ikea, stop the Verdana madness!" pleaded Tokyo's Oliver Reichenstein on Twitter. "Words can't describe my disgust," spat Ben Cristensen of Melbourne. … On Aug. 26, Romanian design consultant Marius Ursache started an online petition to get Ikea to change its mind. That night, Verdana was already a trending topic on Twitter, drawing more tweets than even Ted Kennedy.
>
> (Abend 2009)

Collectively, these examples, and many others beside, push beyond anecdotal evidence. Each of these design choices, and scores of others every day, are made by groups and corporations that spend millions of dollars researching precisely the ways visual triggers relate to behavioral choices. Choices of style,

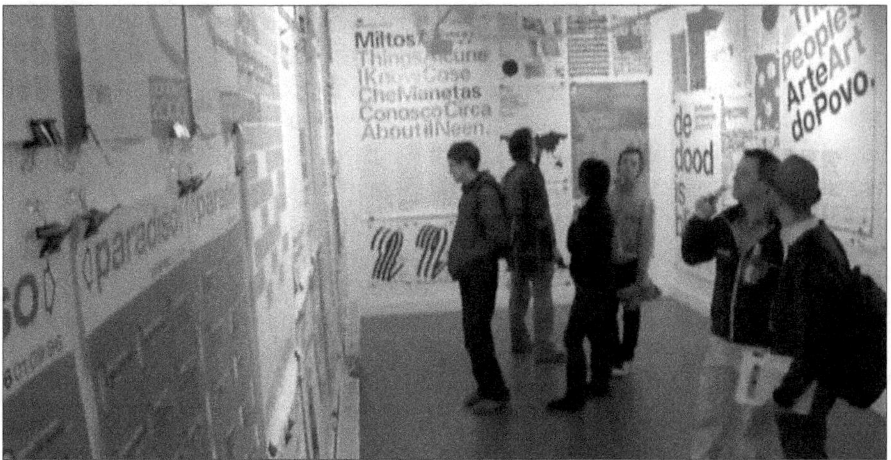


Figure 3. Screen shot from *Helvetica*, directed by Gary Hustwit, 2007.

font, color, lines, and form are intentional choices for the creators of advertisements, as they are for book printers and page designers. Those of us interested in the iconic dimensions of sacred texts can learn from the visual design processes of popular culture.

## Type and design, interpretation and ideology

Typefaces and word designs are visual creations, and do not stand in simple opposition to the pictorial images on a page. Book designers have created pages and fonts for ease of reading, whether silent reading or oral recitation. Visual design processes impact engagement with a text, well before readers grasp its semantic meanings. These choices ultimately have an impact on the ways interpretation and cognitive interactions with texts might occur, and how these serve both ideology and theology.

Paul Saenger's *The Spaces Between Words* (1997) has ably shown us how the long European Christian shift from *scriptura continua* to script with spaces and punctuation between words enabled the cognitive and cultural shift from oral recitation to silent reading. "Word separation, by altering the neurophysiological process of reading, simplified the act of reading, enabling both the medieval and modern reader to receive silently and simultaneously the text and encoded information that facilitates both comprehension and oral performance" (Saenger 13). The change in visible script layout on the page also allowed new forms of written texts, including personal prayer books and bound selections from the canonical Christian scriptures, such as the gospels alone. Along with bookbinding and papermaking technologies, the visual layout of words on a page had profound religious and cultural implications. Roger Chartier extends the importance of silent reading by noting the ways "it made possible a more personal form of piety, a more private devotion, a relation with the sacred not subject to the discipline and mediation of the Church" (Chartier 2006, 165). The long slide from orality to literacy is also a shift from hearing to vision, and from communities to individuals. The sensorium is restructured, leaving deep religious implications.

In the modern book page, highly readable rationalist typefaces are merged with perfectly justified margins that make little rectangles of all the pages. Walter Ong suggests of the medium of the printed book that, "Print encourages a sense of closure, a sense that what is found in a text has been finalized, has reached a state of completion" (Ong 1982, 132). This sense of closure is a visual sense, especially provoked by the technology of type: "Typographic control typically impresses more by its tidiness and inevitability: the lines perfectly regular, all justified on the right side, everything coming out even visually" (Ong 1982, 122). As these visual processes occur, a sense of inevitability is produced. The text is closed, sealed off, complete unto itself. Such printing techniques may have fostered the rise of Christian fundamentalist approaches to the scriptures, though that would be the focus of another study.

At the start of the slim volume *Graphic Design and Bible Reading*, E.R. Wendland and J.P. Louw (1993, 1) consider that "One of the most important, but least utilized, 'helps' for the reader of a printed text, whether the Bible or any other, is the very format in which it appears. It is a vital component of the medium which helps comprise the overall message that is communicated." Somewhere between a "how-to" manual and a semiotic analysis of Bible printing, the authors provide one of the few attempts to theorize on modern bible printing and its effects on interpreting. They note, for instance, how the common printing of many King James Versions gives precedence to individual verses by starting each verse with a new line, e.g.,

> 3 And God said, Let there be light: and there was light.
> 4 And God saw the light, that it was good: and God divided the light from the darkness.
> 5 And God called the light Day, and the darkness he called Night. And the evening and the morning were the first day.

The authors consider how such layout "can also lead to proof-text theology whereby a single verse is utilized as a text 'on its own' without due consideration to the context" (Wendland and Louw, 10). Obviously such design does not necessitate such readings, but the point made is clearly seen in this layout.

Modern scripture printing, including Bible design, is linked with ideological and theological concerns, as already intimated. I offer one final example for this section. In 2003, Zondervan publishers released the "Spirit of the Reformation Study Bible" (NIV translation). Included therein were doctrines of the Reformed tradition (Heidelberg Catechism, Westminster Confession, et al.). Along with its inclusion of historical/theological treatises, the publishers also choose to set the text in single column, something unusual in an overall history of bound bibles, but not uncommon among sixteenth-century reformation bibles, such as Luther's "September" testament of 1522. Zondervan's publication followed the success of Nelson publisher's New Geneva Study Bible of 1995, which was renamed the "Reformation Study Bible" in 1998. Each of these popular publications harken back to the immensely popular 1560 Geneva Bible, which itself was unique in its use of Roman rather than Gothic type, and was the first bible to include numbered verses. Thus, "it was easy to read, use, and comprehend. Church and church-going were changed forever" (Olmert 1992, 48).[6] By rethinking and restyling the page layout, font, and columns, modern publishers like Zondervan and Nelson contribute to the ongoing style of theology itself. To be "authentic" means the visual presentation must have a certain way about it.

## Conclusion

I have attempted to make two key points in this paper. First, words are images, and the so-called word-image split ignores the visuality of script, typeface, and layout. Second, emotional interaction with and cognitive interpretation of printed and scripted words are affected by the visual design of the text. There can then be no clear-cut distinction between the semantic dimensions of texts and the iconic and performative dimensions. The rationality of semantics is not separable from the experiential visual appearance of words. Words, understood as visual, aural, and even tangible objects, are not just texts to be interpreted. Instead, as James Watts has noted, scriptures "are material objects that convey religious significance by their production, display, and ritual manipulation" (Watts, this volume, Chapter 1, 11).

Words become sacred regardless of people making semantic meaning from them. From this perspective, we can begin to evaluate words for their iconic value. Words on a page have been understood to return the gaze of the onlooker, offering a blessing, and even posing an invitation to the biblical scholar in a new way: *tolle vide*.

## References

Abend, Lisa. 2009. "The Font War: Ikea Fans Fume over Verdana." *Time*, August 28. Online at: http://www.time.com/time/business/article/0,8599,1919127,00.html#ixzz1BnIOieeD, accessed 15 January 2011.

Ali, Wijdan. 1997. *Modern Islamic Art: Development and Continuity*. Gainesville: University of Florida Press.

art:21. *Art in the Twenty-First Century*. 2001. PBS Home Video.

6. While researching online for this paper, I found scores of theologically conservative websites that reviewed new bible versions. They very often include reviews of the binding, page thickness, dimensions, whether it had ribbon markers, etc. J. Mark Bertrand has some fascinating thoughts about the design of bibles on his site "Bible Design Blog," at http://www.bibledesignblog.com/. My hunch is that theologically conservative readers are actually more interested in the materiality of the bible than are liberals, though it would take a larger study to determine to what extent this is true.

Baker, Nicholson. 2009. "A New Page: Can the Kindle really improve on the book?" *The New Yorker*, August 3. Online at: http://www.newyorker.com/reporting/2009/08/03/090803fa_fact_baker#ixzz1BnAaU15S accessed 15 January 2011.

Bal, Mieke. 1991. *Reading 'Rembrandt': Beyond the Word-Image Opposition*. Cambridge: Cambridge University Press.

Bringhurst, Robert. 2005. *The Elements of Typographic Style*, version 3.1. Point Roberts, WA: Hartley and Marks Publishers.

———. and Warren Chappell. 1999. *A Short History of the Printed Word*. 2nd ed. Point Roberts, WA: Hartley and Marks Publishers.

Bryson, Norman. 1993. *Word and Image: French Painting of the Ancien Régime*. Cambridge: Cambridge University Press.

Chartier, Roger. 2006 [1989]. "The Practical Impact of Writing." *The Book History Reader*, 2nd ed., edited by David Finkelstein and Alistair McCleery, 157–181. London: Routledge.

De Hamel, Christopher. 2001. *The British Library Guide to Manuscript Illumination: History and Techniques*. Toronto: University of Toronto Press.

Drucker, Johanna. 1995. *The Alphabetic Labyrinth: The Letters in History and Imagination*. London: Thames and Hudson.

Elkins, James. 2001. *The Domain of Images*. Ithaca, NY: Cornell University Press.

Fischer, Steven Roger. 2001. *A History of Writing*. London: Reaktion Books.

———. 2003. *A History of Reading*. London: Reaktion Books.

Foucault, Michel. 1970. *The Order of Things*. Translated by Alan Sheridan. New York: Random House.

Grabar, Oleg. 1992. *Mediation of Ornament*. Princeton, NJ: Princeton University Press.

Hustwit, Gary, director. 2007. *Helvetica*. Veer Production.

Kaminishi, Ikumi. 2006. *Explaining Pictures: Buddhist Propaganda and Etoki Storytelling in Japan*. Honolulu: University of Hawaii Press.

Lings, Martin. 1976. *The Quranic Art of Calligraphy and Illumination*. London: World of Islam Festival Trust.

Miller, David L. 2008. "Legende-Image: The Word/Image Problem." In *Varieties of Mythic Experience: Essays on Religion, Psyche and Culture*, edited by Dennis Patrick Slattery and Glen Slater, 231–247. Einsiedeln: Daimon Verlag.

Mitchell, W.J.T. 1994. *Picture Theory: Essays on Verbal and Visual Representation*. Chicago, IL: University of Chicago Press.

———. 2005. *What Do Pictures Want? The Lives and Loves of Images*. Chicago, IL: University of Chicago Press.

Morgan, David. 2005. *The Sacred Gaze*. Berkeley: University of California Press.

Nasr, Seyyed Hossein. 1987. *Islamic Art and Spirituality*. Albany: State University of New York Press.

Olmert, Michael. 1992. *The Smithsonian Book of Books*. Washington, DC: Smithsonian.

Ong, Walter. 1982. *Orality and Literacy*. London: Routledge.

Plate, S. Brent, ed. 2002. *Religion, Art, and Visual Culture: A Cross-Cultural Reader*. New

York: Palgrave Macmillan.
Raguin, Virginia Chieffo. 2003. *Stained Glass: From Its Origins to the Present*. New York: Abrams.
Rawsthorn, Alice. 2008. "Brand Obama, a leader in the image war." *New York Times*, 4 April. Online at http://www.nytimes.com/2008/04/04/arts/04iht-design7.html, accessed 13 September 2010.
Saenger, Paul. 1997. *Space Between Words: The Origins of Silent Reading*. Stanford, CA: Stanford University Press.
———. 1999. "Impact of the Early Printed Page on the Reading of the Bible." In *The Bible as Book: The First Printed Editions*, edited by Paul Saenger and Kimberly van Kampen, 31–51. London: British Library and Oak Knoll Press.
Shlain, Leonard. 1998. *The Alphabet Versus the Goddess: The Conflict between Word and Image*. New York: Viking.
Singer-Vine, Jeremy. 2009. "Ikea's Font as Cheap as its Furniture." *Slate.com*, online at http://slatest.slate.com/id/2226581/entry/4 , accessed 2 September 2009.
Stephens, Mitchell. 1998. *The Rise of the Image, The Fall of the Word*. New York: Oxford University Press.
Suleman, Fahmida. 2007. "Introduction." In *Word of God, Art of Man: The Qur'an and its Creative Expressions*, edited by Fahmida Suleman, 1–26. Oxford: Oxford University Press.
Turgut, Ayse. 2007. "Sacred Calligraphy in Contemporary Art." In *Word of God, Art of Man: The Qur'an and its Creative Expressions*, edited by Fahmida Suleman, 219–226. Oxford: Oxford University Press.
Wallace, David Foster. 2009. *This Is Water: Some Thoughts, Delivered on a Significant Occasion, about Living a Compassionate Life*. New York: Little, Brown and Company.
Wendland, Ernst R. and J. P. Louw. 1993. *Graphic Design and Bible Reading: Exploratory Studies in the Typographical Representation of the Text of Scripture in Translation*. Cape Town: Bible Society of South Africa.

# 7

# Between the Textual and the Visual: Borderlines of Late Antique Book Iconicity

Zeev Elitzur

*A book is not a regular object. Like other objects, it can be perceived by the sense of sight. Unlike other objects, the visual form of the book subordinates itself to the linguistic sphere. Thus we tend to overlook the outer appearance of books in favor of their contents. In other words we tend to read books as opposed to viewing them. The iconic dimension of the book appears where this assertion fails—that is, when people notice (or even emphasize) the visual form of books. This paper develops this observation in the context of late antique Judaism and Christianity. It describes two modes of crossing the boundaries between the book as an object of reading and the book as an object of viewing. In both traditions, the iconic dimension of the book bypasses the textual level and highlights the visual level. In the Jewish world, the transition is between the textual perception of the written sign and the visual perception thereof. In other words, it is between two alternative modes of perceiving the written sign. This is exemplified by several instances of "Visual Midrash"—a midrash that is based on graphical data. In the Christian world, the transition is between the textual function of the book and its subordination to the hegemony of the visual image—an historical process beginning with the Pauline visual encounter with Christ and culminating with the triumph of the image in eighth century Byzantium.*

At the beginning of his *Guide of Medieval Illuminated Manuscripts,* Christopher de Hamel quotes a character from Bernard Shaw's play *Saint Joan* (de Hamel 2001, 9). The character is a nobleman serving in the English army during the 100 Years War, and while "turning over the leaves of an illuminated book of hours," he says:

> Now this is what I call workmanship. There is nothing on earth more exquisite than a bonny book, with well-placed columns of rich black writing in beautiful borders, and illuminated pictures cunningly inset. But nowadays, instead of looking at books, people read them. A book might as well be one of those orders for bacon and bran that you are scribbling.
>
> (Shaw 1924, 111)

Future generations may view this Bernard Shaw character as the historical precursor of the Iconic Books Project. His view of books is indeed iconic—why should one read a book instead of appreciating its visual form? Later on, we shall dwell on the distinction between the iconic details that are mentioned by this visionary—the "rich black writing" on the one hand and the "illuminated pictures" on the other. But let us begin with the main functional distinction between reading a book and viewing it.

Indeed nowadays (at least while there are still books around) people tend to read books and not to look at them.[1] This tendency was increased by the book's becoming a mass-produced industrial commodity, on the one hand, and the development of mass literacy, on the other. But, in fact, the duality of looking vs. reading is an inherent quality of every book—by definition, I daresay (see Plate's essay in this issue). The purpose of this paper is to discuss some late antique examples of the boundaries between a book's textual aspect—that is the "read" aspect—and its visual aspect—the "looked at" aspect.

The observation made by the character in Bernard Shaw's play highlights the fact that a book is not a regular object. The "object-ness" of a book tends to be overshadowed by the information encoded in the written signs enclosed in the book. In order to illustrate this idea, let us imagine a book—Dostoyevsky's *Crime and Punishment*, for instance. How do we imagine *Crime and Punishment*? Do we visualize the outer form of the material book on the cover of which the words "Crime and Punishment" are written? Or do we rather think of the story of Raskolnikov, the neurotic murderer? I would guess the answer is clear—we focus on the story, which is signified in the written signs written in the book rather than the outward appearance of the book, including those very signs. Let us picture, then, Auguste Rodin's *The Thinker*. I would guess that whoever knows the sculpture visualizes the distinct manner in which its head rests on its hand, rather than the statue's meaning. This observation does not depend on the difference between Peircian iconic signs and symbolic signs.[2] It still holds fast when we imagine, say, a stop sign, which is, like a book, an object that contains symbolic signs.[3] I assume that what we see before our eyes is the written word "stop" on the traffic sign and not the action it signifies.

The phenomenon of books being conceptually identified with their content rather than with their material manifestation is ultimately reducible to the fact that they are read rather than looked at. What this means is that the written surface of the book is phenomenologically different from other seen objects.

1. A major exception is what James Watts terms "relic books"—see Watts, Chapter 1, this volume, 28–30.

2. On the notions of iconic and symbolic signs see Sebeok 1994, 17–38.

3. It is interesting to note however that in Israel, unlike most (or all?) other countries, the stop sign does not show the word "stop" or its equivalent in Hebrew, but rather depicts an outward facing open palm. See http://en.wikipedia.org/wiki/Stop_sign (accessed 16 January 2011).

In his *Course in General Linguistics* Ferdinand de Saussure says:

> A language and its written form constitute two separate systems of signs. The sole reason for the existence of the latter is to represent the former. The object of study in linguistics is not a combination of the written word and the spoken word. The spoken word alone constitutes that object.
>
> (Saussure 1983, 24–25)

The distinction between reading a book and viewing it is closely connected to this theoretical observation. Writing, according to Saussure, constitutes a separate sign system from language, but it is totally subordinate to language. The written surface of the book is, so to speak, an "extraterritorial" domain of the linguistic sign system. When we read a book, the written sign's visual dimension is transparent; and thus the book's "visual outlay" becomes a textual outlay. This illustrates the subordination of writing to language. We are concerned, however, with phenomena that stem from the separateness of writing from language. The object of study in this paper, unlike linguistics, is the point where the written sign exemplifies this separateness by liberating the visual outlay from its textual tyrant.

The textualization of the visual outlay explains the tendency to reduce holy books in Religious Studies to what James Watts calls the semantic dimension.[4] Our concern with the iconic dimension does not of course rule out the importance of the semantic dimension. This importance suggests that exploring the boundaries between the iconic and the semantic dimensions is a worthwhile endeavor. These borderlines may be defined and analyzed from different perspectives. In this paper, our starting point will be the aforementioned phenomenon—the textualization of a book's visual outlay. Human cognition tends to **read** the written signs rather than **look** at them, and this tendency creates a phenomenological gap between the part of the book which is read, and the part which is looked at.[5] The "looked at" parts may, as in the example of the *Saint Joan* Nobleman, be pictures—if the book contains pictures. They may also be other extra-textual visual signs. In these cases, the boundary between the textual and the visual aspects is a line which can be demarcated within the book's visual outlay. A different case is when the writing itself becomes an element that is looked at—its visual quality redeemed, so to speak. This may be achieved by a special portrayal of some of the letters—a common enough custom in medieval manuscripts (see for instance Conley 1996, 51; Lanhamp 2006, 111). The visual aspect of the written letters may also assert itself mentally because of external reasons. When the book's iconic dimension is strength-

4. See Watts, Chapter 1, this volume. For the sake of clarity I am omitting here the performative dimension—which is a fellow traveler of the semantic dimension in the argument presented in this paper. For a classical analysis of the performative dimension, see Graham 1987.

5. Reading is a very complex mental activity, based on the recognition of certain visual signs as written characters, that is as visual signs connected to the linguistic sphere. Letter recognition and word recognition are central foci of modern cognitive science—see Palmer 1999, 453–462; Lupker 2005.

ened, we may notice a process in which it "conquers" the textualized visual outlay of the book and brings new life to the visuality of the written sign—the visual outlay reemerges from the textual outlay. Returning to the example given above—we then witness the book becoming a stop sign.

Henceforth, we shall deal mainly with the last type of visual resurgence—the raising of visual attention to the written sign in the Jewish world of Late Antiquity, as attested by rabbinic sources (Neah 1995, 2008). After we have seen a few examples of this process, we shall compare it in general terms with a separate iconization process that took place in Late Antiquity—the development of the concept of the book as (visual) icon in the Byzantine Christian world.

The process by which the textual outlay of a religious book acquires a visual dimension is closely linked to the development of a Halakhic field containing regulations as to how a (holy) book should be manufactured and written.[6] Since by their very nature these regulations refer to visual aspects of the book, they stimulate an increased visual awareness in the field of midrashic exegesis. This in turn influences an enhanced attention to visual minutiae in the regulations themselves. In this paper, there is not enough space to give examples of the regulations, so we shall limit ourselves to a few examples of visual elements that infiltrate midrashic exegesis.

The first example we shall examine is an excerpt from a Tannaitic Midrash (which is from the earlier phase of the rabbinic period—containing sources roughly from the second century until the mid-third century). This is an extraordinary example, as there is no other example of "visual midrash" in Tannaitic sources that I know of.[7] The Tannaitic midrashim are based on regular linguistic data. Let us take a look, therefore, at the following pericope from the *Mekhilta deRabbi Yishmael*, based on the words "Jethro... heard" in Exodus 18:1:

> Another interpretation: *Now Jethro...Heard*. Originally they called him merely Jether, as it is said: "and Moses went and returned to Jether his father in law" (Ex. 4.18). After he had performed good deeds, they added one more letter to his name so that he was called Jethro.
>
> You find this also in the case of Abraham, whom they originally called merely Abram. And when he performed good deeds they added one letter more, and he was called Abraham.
>
> You find this also in the case of Sarah. Originally they called her merely Sarai. But when she performed good deeds, they added to her name by putting in a larger letter so that she was called Sarah.

6. For a similar observation, see Naeh 2008. This historical development is a complex issue I intend to deal with elsewhere. Suffice it to mention that these regulations do not appear in any Tannaitic compilation, but only in the (Amoraic) Talmudim—see *Bavli Menachot* 29a–37b; *Bava Batra* 13b–14b; *Yerushalmi Megila* 71b–72a.

7. See however *Tosefta Sanhedrin* 4, 7, which displays an awareness of the shape of the Hebrew letters as part of a discussion on the change from the ancient Hebrew Script to the modern Jewish one.

And so you also find it in the case of Joshua, whom they originally called merely Hoshea. And when he performed good deeds, they added one more letter to his name so that he was called Joshua, as it is said, "and Moses called Hoshea the son of Nun Joshua" (Num. 13.16).

And there are others from whose names they took off one letter. You can learn this from the case of Ephron, whose name was originally written in the full manner—"Ephron" [including the mater lectionis *vav*]. After he had taken the money from our father Abraham, they took off one letter from his name and he was called merely "Ephrn", as it is said: "and Abraham weighed to Ephrn" (Gen. 23.16) [without the mater lectionis *vav*]

And you see it also in the case of Jonadab whom they originally called Jehonadab. But after he had come to act as he did, they took off one letter from his name so that he was called merely Jonadab (*Mekhilta deRabbi Yishmael*, Amalek, 1).[8]

Here, the Midrash deals with name changes of biblical figures. In the Bible, only three of the changes are mentioned explicitly—the changes in the names of Abraham, Sarah and Joshua. Thus we read of Abraham: "No longer shall your name be Abram, but your name shall be Abraham" (Gen 17.5; for Sarah, see 17:15; for Joshua, Num. 13:16). As to the other names—Jethro, Ephron and Jonadab—no change is mentioned explicitly. The midrash is based on the fact that the same names are written differently in different places.

Not all the changes of biblical names mentioned in this midrash have a clear meaning: it is unclear what the significance of the change from Abram to Abraham is or of Jether to Jethro, and so on. In these two instances, the written change is also a phonetical change as there is a change in the way the name is pronounced. Therefore, we cannot be sure if the Midrash is referring to the graphical change or to the phonetical change. Regarding, however, two of the other names on the midrashic list, it is clear that the interpretation of the addition or subtraction to the name has to do with the visual graphic addition. In the instance of Sarai changing to Sarah, the Midrash addresses explicitly the size of the letter "he"—"a larger letter" replacing the smaller "yod" in the name as the interpretative factor here.[9] This is where the midrash departs from the pronunciation of the name and addresses the visual aspect of the written word. In the case of Ephron, it is even clearer because the change cannot be rendered in English as the difference between the two forms of the name have to do with the presence or absence of the mater lectionis *vav*. This has no bearing on the pronunciation of the name and is therefore a purely visual observation of the Midrash.

We are witnessing here an ancient, and rather mild, example of what I refer to as "Visual Midrash." It is significant because it is also the oldest example

8. Based on Lauterbach 1961, 164–166. I altered the translation slightly in a few instances.

9. The word "larger" is not attested by all the manuscripts—see Horowitz and Rabin 1931, 189. Even if it is a later variant, however, this does not alter the basic argument I am making here. As in the case of "Ephron," the visual focus is clear.

that I know of what is known in Hebrew as "*midrash khaserot viyeterot*" ("a midrash of deficiency and fullness"), that is, a midrash based on the absence or presence of *matres lectionis* in the spelling of a given word (and thus on the "defective" or "full" spelling). In general, Semitic writing systems denote only consonants. In Hebrew, a partial (and optional) system of signifying vowels uses the Hebrew letters *yod* and *vav*, which in this case are called *matres lectionis*. Their use has always been optional. Many words, therefore, can be written in a "defective" manner without *matres lectionis*, or in a "full" manner with *matres lectionis*. A system was developed over time in which each word in the Bible was determined to be defective or full. This system (part of the Masorah) only emerged fully in the early Middle Ages. In Amoraic sources (that is the later phase of rabbinic sources beginning in the mid-third century), however, we already find an awareness of full and defective spelling, and the use thereof in exegesis. Thus for instance in the following Amoraic Midrash:

> R. Ze'era said in the name of R. Hanina : When the world was created, only the orb of the sun was intended to give light—as the defective spelling of the word "lights" (*m'rt* as compared to *m'orot*) in Gen. 1.14 indicates. Why, then, was the moon created? Because the Holy One foresaw that the nations of the earth were to arise and worship heavenly luminaries as deities and so he said: if the nations of the earth are to worship luminaries as deities, let them at least divide their worship between a sun and a moon.
>
> (*Pesikta deRav Kahana*, Hahodesh, 1).[10]

The midrash here arrives at the conclusion that only the sun was created in order to give light, because the word *meorot* (lights) is written with defective spelling. Two things ought to be emphasized. First (again), there is no difference in the pronunciation of the word according to the manner of its spelling—both ways are legitimate and they **sound** the same. Secondly—the Hebrew word "meorot" is unequivocally in the plural. Therefore, we see here an interpretation, which relies only on the manner of spelling, that is on purely visual grounds, although it does not agree with the linguistic sense of the word. In other words, this midrash detaches the written sign from the usual supremacy of spoken language over it.

Scores of similar midrashim occur in Amoraic compilations and in the Jerusalem and Babylonian talmudim, and they reflect the rise of the visual dimension of the written sign.[11] We should notice, however, that the boundary between the textual and the visual is not crossed only from the textual to the visual, but also in the other direction: the defective spelling of the word "meorot" determines the way the text is understood—"only the orb of the sun

10. Braude and Kapstein 1975, 91.

11. The consequences of this should not, however, be overstated—these instances of visual Midrash are still in the overwhelming minority compared to the regular linguistic midrash. They attest, therefore, to the rise of the iconic dimension, but not at the expense of the semantic dimension—see Watts, Chapter 1, this volume.

was intended to give light." This crossing back and forth between the textual and the visual aspects reappears in other examples. One of the most interesting is the following:

> R. Abbau said, with regards to [the verse "And I will make your name great" (Gen. 12.2), on which the comment is that it is done by adding a 'he' to Abram's name, at Gen. 15.5]. So what is written is not "Look now at the heaven" [*hashamaim*], but "Look now *to* the heaven" (Gen. 15.5) [*hashamaimah*], thus adding a 'he' at the end of the word. The meaning is, "with this additional 'he', I created the world. Now lo, I am going to add it to your name [calling you not Abram but Abraham], so you will also be fruitful and multiply. (*Genesis Rabbah*, 39)[12]

The midrash removes the letter "he" from the word *hashamaimah* (to the heaven). A visual element is separated from the textual domain and thus influences the way the text is understood. But in this instance, it is not only a visual interpretation, but also the visual element itself. According to the midrash, Abraham is supposed to look up and see before his eyes the very letter that has been removed from the text. The letter 'he,' therefore, has a double role here—it is the last letter of the word *hashamaimah* in the textual outlay of the book, but it also penetrates the meaning of the text as a new element in the midrash-manipulated narrative—as something that Abraham, himself, sees before his eyes.

The intrusion of a purely visual element into the level of textual meaning is the most striking crossing of boundaries we have seen so far—as if the text looks at itself from without. This is also a double-crossing of the line as the letter is shorn of its textual function in the first place and then returned to the textual meaning in the second. There are, however, also instances in rabbinic sources in which the border between the textual and the visual aspects is crossed only once with no turning back:

> R. Ashi said, I have observed that scribes who are most punctilious add a vertical stroke to the roof of the letter "heth"... They add a vertical stroke to the roof of the letter "heth," signifying thereby that He lives in the heights of the world. (*Bavli Menachot* 30a)[13]

We notice here a midrashic exposition of the outer form of the letter "heth." The way the upper part of the letter is portrayed is connected to the spatial relation between the word and the heavenly abode in which God lives (the word *hay* "living" in Hebrew starts with the same letter— "heth"). In contradistinction to the previous examples we have seen, there is no textual context interpreted here. We move directly from the outer form of the letter to the outer signification. This is the last phase of visual Midrash—in which the border between the textual and the visual is crossed but it is no longer crossed in the opposite direction.

12. Neusner 1985, vol. II, 70.
13. Online Soncino Talmud—http://www.halakhah.com/pdf/kodoshim/Menachoth.pdf, 112.

This last phase in Visual Midrash—the midrash based on a single letter—is important in terms of the book's iconic dimension. The immediate context of this Talmudic pericope is the manner in which scribes write the letter "heth," and it is part of a larger tract of Talmud devoted to Hilkhot Sefer Torah—the regulations of preparing and writing a Torah scroll.[14] The letter "heth" is removed from the semantic dimension of the book and creates a bridge between two aspects of the iconic book—the scribal regulations, on the one hand, and visual Midrash, on the other. From an historical perspective, however, the emphasis on the writing itself has also led to a certain change in emphasis from the holy book to the holy writing. If a Hebrew letter is inherently holy, then everything written in Hebrew becomes holy. This is the source of the custom, attested since the early Middle Ages, of putting every document written in Hebrew in a *Genizah* (see for instance Schleicher 2010).

To summarize, the development of regulations pertaining to the way books are manufactured and written is connected to a new visual awareness that permeates the textual boundaries of the written signs. This awareness is manifested in the presence of Visual Midrash in Amoraic sources—that is to say, Midrash that is based on the visual aspect of the written sign. This is a prime example of the iconic dimension in the holy book. We have seen several examples of such a midrash, and mentioned its connection with *Halakha*. This "visual turn" in the attitude towards the holy book may also be witnessed in a famous midrash discussing the Torah as a heavenly book, which was used as a prototype in the creation of the world:

> *In the beginning, God created.* ... the Torah speaks, "I was the work-plan of the Holy One, blessed be He." In the accepted practice of the world, when a mortal king builds a palace he does not build it out of his own head, but he follows a work-plan. And [the one who supplies] the work plan does not build it out of his own head, but he has designs and diagrams, so as to know how to situate the rooms and the doorways. **Thus the Holy One blessed be He, looked at the Torah when He created the world.** So the Torah stated, "By means of 'the beginning' [that is to say, the Torah] did God create..." (Gen. 1.1). and word for "beginning" refers only to the Torah, as Scripture says, "The Lord made me as the beginning of His way" (Prov. 8.22). (Genesis Rabbah, 1)[15]

The point I would like to make here is about the way the Torah is used by God in His capacity as demiurge. The Torah is not read; it is looked at. This reflects its visual dimension, which is also reflected in the midrashim based on the look of the earthly book reviewed above. This source connects the visual quality of the Torah to its function as what Moshe Idel (2002, 26–44) calls "world-absorbing"—because the Torah functions here as a prototype for the creation of the

14. See *Bavli Menachot* 29a–37b.

15. Based on Neusner 1985, vol. I, 1. I made a few alterations—the chief of which is substituting "looked at the Torah" for Neusner's "consulted the Torah." My alteration is the direct correlative of the Hebrew "hibit."

world. There are other sources, however, that portray the holy book as a representation of God (see below). It is in this context that I wish to compare the crossing of the boundaries between textual and visual in the rabbinic world with a parallel crossing of the boundaries in the Byzantine Christian world.

In the rabbinic sources, the boundary between the textual and the visual is the boundary between the written sign used as a vehicle for language and the written sign as an independent visual agent. An alternative boundary between the textual and the visual, which we know from the Christian world, is the one between the book and the picture.

Wilfred Cantwell Smith (1999, 46, 110) has asserted that in Christianity the figure of Christ, as a religious focus, substitutes for the role of the holy book in Judaism and Islam. At face value this is an exaggeration, since Christianity is also a religion of the book. It is, however, a fruitful assertion if we take it to attribute a tension between the figure of Christ and the book rather than a substitution (see Parmenter 2009, 91–113). The tension between the figure of Christ and the concept of the book is connected to the tension between textuality and visuality. I believe that the roots of this tension may be found in the epistles of Paul and an historical line can be drawn between these roots and the full-blown tension between the book and the image in the iconoclastic controversy of the eighth century. I shall attempt to sketch the general contours of this historical line.

A prominent feature of Paul's thought is his use of clear-cut distinctions between opposites. The main Pauline distinction is the one between Flesh and Spirit (Dunn 1998, 65–68, 477–482). A close counterpart is the one between Letter and Spirit. This last duality is mentioned in Romans 7:6, 2:29, but the main Pauline source that plays on the dichotomy between the written sign and the spirit is 2 Corinthians 3.[16] In this chapter, Paul mounts a veritable offensive against the written medium.

The chapter opens with a reflective mention of the weakness of the written medium Paul himself is using:

> Are we beginning to commend ourselves again? Surely, we do not need, as some do, letters of recommendation to you or from you, do we? You yourselves are our letter, written on our hearts, to be known and read by all. (2 Cor 3.1–2)

In the first two verses, Paul uses the ancient trope of the heart's precedence over outer things - the written medium in this instance (alluding to Ezek 36:26–27 and Jer 31:33; see Barnett, 1997, 168). In the next verse, Paul begins his more general criticism of writing and the written Torah in particular:

> and you show that you are a letter of Christ, prepared by us, written not with

16. For a survey of the main interpretations of the letter-spirit distinction see Barnett 1997, 176 footnote 30. These interpretations pertain to the meaning of the distinction, and in particular to its implication on the general question of Paul's attitude towards the Torah. I am concerned with a different question, and in a sense the opposite one—what does Paul's use of this metaphor tell us about his attitude towards the written sign?

> ink but with the Spirit of the living God, not on tablets of stone but on tablets of human hearts...
>
> ...who has made us competent to be ministers of a new covenant, not of letter but of spirit; for the letter kills, but the Spirit gives life.
>
> (2 Cor 3:3, 3:6)

The "ministry" of the new covenant is the ministry of heart and spirit, in contradistinction to the old covenant, which is characterized by tablets of stone and lines of ink (see Barnett 1997, 160, especially note 6). The stone tablets are of course a central symbol of the old covenant, the covenant of Sinai, being the object which Moses brought down from the mountain. Here they appear as an inert and external object, manifesting the need for the written sign in the old covenant because of its inferiority vis-à-vis its new counterpart (Barnett 1997, 169–71). The old covenant was a covenant of the written word, whereas the new one is a covenant of spirit. But why is there a dichotomy between the written sign and the spirit? Not only because the spirit gives life, but also because the letter kills. That is to say, Paul not only asserts the potency of the spirit, he also asserts the incompetence of the written sign (Dunn 1998, 149). Claiming the letter is dead is equivalent to claiming it has lost its textual potency and has become an inert visual entity. In contradistinction to the midrashic sources surveyed above, the written sign does not become a signifying visual element here, but rather a visual element without meaning.

Then Paul begins one of his interesting midrashic expositions, an interpretation of Exodus 34:28–29 (Barnett 1997, 178 note 3). The Pauline midrash opens again with a comparison between the glory of the new covenant and the glory of the old one:

> Now if the Ministry of Death, chiseled in letters on stone tablets, came in glory so that the people of Israel could not gaze at Moses' face because of the glory of his face, a glory now set aside, how much more will the ministry of the Spirit come in glory? (2 Cor 3:7–8)

Again, we find here the distinction between the dead written sign, which characterizes the old covenant, and the spirit, which characterizes the new covenant. Paul assumes that the glory of Moses's face reflects the glory of the writing. This puts him in exegetical straits, as it contradicts his negative attitude towards the written sign.[17] He attempts to resolve them a few verses later:

> Unlike Moses, who put a veil over his face to keep the people of Israel from gazing at the end of the glory that was set aside. But their minds were hardened. Indeed, to this very day, when they hear the reading of the old covenant, that same veil is still there, since only in Christ is it set aside. Indeed, to this very day whenever Moses is read, a veil lies over their minds. (2 Cor 3:13–15)

17. See Barnett 1997, 178–179, who phrases this "paradox" as pertaining to the old covenant vs. the new one, and does not address the implications on the written sign.

Moses puts a veil on his face because of the emanation from the writing.[18] The original function of the veil is to conceal the writing, which hints at the final truth about the same writing, that is, its death. In verses 14–15, Paul draws this veil from within the biblical narrative and places it outside the level of textual meaning. The veil on Moses's face becomes the veil on the face of the reader. The written sign appears in this source twice—both within the level of the textual meaning and without. The "inner" writing is the one on the stone tablets mentioned in verse 7. The "outer" writing is the one on the Torah scroll—the Book of Moses mentioned in verse 15. The Pauline midrash takes an element from within the text and uses it to reflect on the very act of reading a text. This is the exact opposite of the exegetical move that we have seen in the above rabbinical Midrash, which secludes an element from the written text—a single letter—and throws it into the level of textual meaning. In the rabbinical Midrash, the visual written sign is the visual alternative to the textual function of writing. But according to Paul, the written sign is dead. The visual alternative to the textual function of writing is therefore the visual image of Christ:

> but when one turns to the Lord, the veil is removed. Now the Lord is the Spirit, and where the Spirit of the Lord is, there is freedom. And all of us, with unveiled faces, seeing the glory of the Lord as though reflected in a mirror, are being transformed into the same image from one degree of glory to another; for this comes from the Lord, the Spirit. (2 Cor 3:16–18)

It is important to note that Paul does not present here the alternative to the dead letter as a correct interpretation of the written sign qua text (although he devotes considerable efforts, here and elsewhere, to interpretation). Writing is dead, and the spirit is the alternative to the dead letter. But receiving the spirit has to do with a direct visual experience of Christ.[19]

In later Christian generations, the new covenant becomes itself a book—in which Paul's epistle is incorporated. Then the Pauline distinction between the written sign and seeing the image of Christ becomes a duality between the written medium and the pictorial medium. This duality is detectable in the rise of the cult of icons beside the prominence of the holy book beginning in the fourth century (Kitzinger 1954), and reaches a high point in the iconoclastic controversy of eighth-century Byzantium (Parmenter 2009, 27).

The common origin of the holy Jewish book and the holy Christian book is not infrequently mentioned (see for instance Evans 1970, 232). It is less common to point to the parallel development of the iconic dimension of the holy books of Judaism and Christianity in Late Antiquity. Claudia Rapp has written

18. This is Paul's own interpretation of the Exodus text. The text does not connect explicitly between the shining of Moses' face and the tablets. See above.

19. For the optical nature of the encounter described in verse 18, see Barnett 1997, 205–206 (particularly the discussion in footnote 38). It is a reasonable conjecture to connect the description of visual encounter here with Paul's own experience on the road to Damascus—see Barnett 1997, 184, 186–87, 198.

that in the fourth century, "we witness the culmination of a long process of Christian appreciation of the Scriptures and the consolidation of the character of Christianity as a 'Religion of the Book'" (Rapp 1991, 129; also Parmenter 2009, 105–109, and Larson in this issue; for connections between Late Ancient Christian and Jewish perceptions of holy books, see Rapp 1991, 147). Several attributes of the iconic dimension of the Jewish book are also traceable to approximately the same era (Rapp 2007; Parmenter 2009, 53–55). This is not the place to go into these attributes in depth. Suffice it to mention what I see as the parallel development of the custom of taking an oath on the holy book, and the similar ceremonies of carrying the holy book in ritual.[20]

We are not concerned here with all the aspects of the iconic book, but rather with the boundaries between the textual and the visual aspects. In terms of the themes we have discussed so far, we find that the visual aspect in the Jewish world manifests itself in an emphasis on the visual sign, whereas in the (eastern) Christian world the books become subordinate to the visual image. In the examples discussed by Claudia Rapp, the book already functions as an icon—that is to say the book represents Christ (Rapp 2007, 196–200; see also Humfress 2007). The later development of the Christian book, however, is more closely connected to the cult of icons, which also developed in the centuries leading up to Byzantine iconoclasm. The attack on the legitimacy of the icons left the book as the main legitimate religious medium. When the iconophiles counterattacked, they tended to describe books in terms of images—as we can see in the following words of John of Damascus:

> The sixth kind of image is to arouse the memory of past events... This kind of image is twofold: **through words written in books—for letters depict the word**, as God engraves the Law on tablets and ordered the lives of men beloved of God to be recorded—and through things seen by the sense of sight, as when he ordered the jar and the rod to be placed in the ark as an eternal memorial, and commanded the names of the tribes to be engraved on the stones of the ephod, but also that the twelve stones should be carried from the Jordan as a figure of the priests... who carried the ark and of the cutting off of the water.
> (*Third Treatise on the Divine Images*, 23)[21]

These words short-circuit the semiotic move made by Paul in 2 Corinthians 3, who replaced the dead written sign with the visual image of Christ. At the beginning of this paper, we observed the phenomenon in which the book is conceptually connected to its content. A basic tenet of Christian interpretation is that the true meaning of the text enclosed in the holy books is the figure of Christ. But in the words of John of Damascus, we witness a more radical move in

20. There is not enough space here to deal with these phenomena in suitable length, and I plan to do so elsewhere. For the Jewish practice of taking an oath on the holy book, see Cohen 1945. Cohen asserts that the Jewish custom preceded the similar Christian one. I believe however that they should be seen as parallel developments. For the Jewish ceremonies of carrying the torah scroll, see Langer 1998. For the Christian ones, see Parmenter 2009, 50–53.

21. John of Damascus 2003, 99–100.

which the narrative function of the book is replaced by the pictorial function of the image, and the concept of the image replaces the textual concept of meaning. In the language of the character from Bernard Shaw's play, the book is now perceived as something you **see** Christ in and not something in which you read about Christ. When the book itself is conceptualized as an image of Christ, the boundary between the textual and the visual aspects is again crossed. But the boundary in this instance is that between the book and the image.

There is a clear similarity between the new visual perception of the book in Judaism and Christianity. This similarity is manifest in the comparison between the following sources, both probably from the eighth century:

> It certainly happens frequently that at times when we do not have the Lord's Passion in mind we may see the image of His crucifixion and, being thus reminded of His saving Passion, fall down and worship. But it is not the material which we worship, but that which is represented; **just as we do not worship the material of the Gospel or that of the cross, but that which they typify.** (John of Damascus, *The Orthodox Faith*, 89)[22]

> Immediately he rolls the Torah scroll to the breadth of three columns and lifts it and shows the face of its writing to the people standing to his right and to his left, **for all men and women are beholden to see the writing and prostrate themselves** and say "This is the Torah that Moses has put before the People of Israel." (Minor tractate *Soferim* 14, 8)[23]

In both sources, the book becomes an object to be worshipped.[24] In both sources, the book is something you look at. In the Christian source, however, the iconicity is that of the image[25] whereas in the Jewish source it is an iconicity of the written sign. In the words of John of Damascus, the book is perceived as if it were a visual image of Christ. We have already noted the midrash in which the Torah is perceived as a prototypical image of the world. The following is another midrashic pericope, in which the written signs of the book are perceived as a representation of God. This is achieved by equating the portrayal of the beloved in Song of Songs 5:10–11 with these written signs:

> *His head is as the most fine gold.* "His head" is the Torah, as it says "The Lord made me as the beginning of His way" (Prov. 8.22)... "Most fine gold": this refers to the words of the Torah of which it says, "More to be desired are they than gold,

22. John of Damascus 1958, 372 (with slight alterations from Chase's translation).

23. My translation. For an explicit connection between this ceremony and the conception of the Torah as a representation of God, see Idel 2002, 73. For a functionally similar Christian monastic custom see Rapp 2007, 198.

24. The similarity between books and images as objects of worship was reiterated in the proceedings of the iconophile councils of 787 and 869—see Parmenter 2009, 28; 58–60.

25. A clearer exposition of this view can be found in a contemporary introduction to Orthodox Christianity: "Orthodoxy regards the Bible as a verbal icon of Christ, the Seventh Council laying down that the Holy Icons and the Book of the Gospels should be venerated in the same way. In every church, the Gospel Book has a place of honour on the altar; it is carried in procession at the Liturgy and at Matins on Sundays and feasts; the faithful kiss it and prostrate themselves before it. Such is the respect shown in the Orthodox Church for the Word of God" (Ware 1963, 209–210).

yea, than much fine gold" (Ps. 19.11). **"His locks are curled": this refers to the rule lines [in the Scroll]. "And black as raven": this refers to the letters.** (Song of Songs Rabbah, 5)[26]

To conclude, we have described two modes of crossing the boundaries between the book as an object of reading and the book as an object of viewing. In the rabbinic world, the transition is between the textual function of the written sign and its visual manifestation. In the Christian world, the transition is between the textual function of the book and its subordination to the hegemony of the visual image. In both worlds, the iconic dimension of the book bypasses the textual level (or, in Wattsian terms, the semantic dimension of the book) and highlights the visual level. In the Jewish world, however, the transition is between the textual perception of the written sign and the visual perception thereof. In other words, it is between two alternative modes of perceiving the written sign. In the Christian world, the transition follows Paul in 2 Corinthians—the true interpretation of the text connects it to the figure of Christ, but the direct perception of Christ is a visual one, and therefore the book itself is perceived as a visual icon.

## References


Barnett, Paul W. 1997. *The Second Epistle to the Corinthians.* Grand Rapids, MI: Eerdmans.

Braude, William G., and Israel J. Kapstein. 1975. *Pesikta Derab Kahana.* Philadelphia, PA: Jewish Publication Society of America.

Cohen, Boaz. 1945. "The Testimonial Oath: A Study in the Reciprocal Relations of Jewish and Roman Law in Medieval Europe." *Historia Judaica* 7: 51–74.

Conley, Tom. 1996. "The Wit of the Letter: Holbein's Lacan." In *Vision in Context: Historical and Contemporary Perspectives on Sight*, edited by Teresa Brennan and Martin Jay, 45–52. London: Routledge.

Dunn, James D. G. 1998. *The Theology of Paul the Apostle.* Grand Rapids, MI: Eerdmans.

Evans, Craig F. 1970. "The New Testament in the Making." In *The Cambridge History of the Bible*, edited by Craig F. Evans and Peter R. Akroyd, vol. I, 232–283. Cambridge: Cambridge University Press.

Graham, William A. 1987. *Beyond the Written Word.* Cambridge: Cambridge University Press.

Hamel, Christopher de. 2001. *The British Library Guide to Manuscript Illumination*, London: The British Library.

Horowitz, Haim S., and Yisrael A. Rabin. 1931. *Mekhilta deRabbi Yishmael.* Frankfurt (Hebrew).

Humfress, Caroline. 2007. "Judging by the Book: Christian Codices and Late Antique Legal Culture." In *The Early Christian Book*, edited by William E. Klingshirn and Linda Safran, 141–158. Washington, DC: Catholic University Press.

Idel, Moshe. 2002. *Absorbing Perfections: Kabbalah and Interpretation.* New Haven, CT: Yale University Press.


26. Simon 1939, 239.

John of Damascus. 1958. *Writings.* Translated by Frederic H. Chase. Washington, DC: Catholic University Press.

———. 2003. *Three Treatises on the Divine Images*, translated by Andrew Crestwood Louth. New York: St. Vladimir's Seminary Press.

Kitzinger, Ernest. 1954. "The Cult of Images in the Age before Iconoclasm." *Dumbarton Oaks Papers* 8: 83–150. http://dx.doi.org/10.2307/1291064

Langer, Ruth. 1998. "From Study of Scripture to a Reenactment of Sinai: the Emergence of the Synagogue Torah Service." *Worship* 72: 43–67.

Lanhamp, Richard A. 2006. *The Economics of Attention: Style and Substance in the Age of Information.* Chicago, IL: University of Chicago Press.

Lauterbach , Jacob Z. 1961. *Mekilta de-Rabbi Ishmael: A Critical Edition on the Basis of the Manuscripts and Early Editions with an English Translation, Introduction, and Notes*, vol. 2. Philadelphia, PA: The Jewish Publication Society of America.

Lupker, Stephen J. 2005. "Visual Word Recognition: Theories and Findings." In *The Science of Reading: A Handbook*, edited by Margaret J. Snowling, and Charles Hulme, 39–60. Malden, MA: Blackwell. http://dx.doi.org/10.1002/9780470757642.ch3

Naeh, Shlomo. 1995. "E'in Em Lamasoret, o' Hai'm Darshu Hatannai'm et Ketiv Hatorah Shelo Kikeria'to Hamekubelet." *Tarbiz* 61: 401–448 (Hebrew).

———. 2008. "A'l Ketav Hatorah Bedivrei Haza'l (A)—Hamasoret al Hahlafat Haketav Biyedei Ezra." *Leshoneinu* 70: 125–143 (Hebrew).

Neusner, Jacob. 1985. *Genesis Rabbah.* Providence, RI: Brown University Press.

Palmer, Stephen E. 1999. *Vision Science: Photons to Phenomenology*. Cambridge, MA: MIT Press.

Parmenter, Dorina. 2009. *The Iconic Book: The Image of the Christian Bible in Myth and Ritual.* PhD dissertation, Syracuse University.

Rapp, Claudia. 1991. "Christians and their Manuscripts in the Greek East during the Fourth Century." In *Scritture, libri e testi nelle aree provinciali di Bisanzio*, edited by Guglielmo Cavallo, 127–148. Spoleto.

———. 2007. "Holy Texts, Holy Men and Holy Scribes: Aspects of Scriptural Holiness in Late Antiquity." In *The Early Christian Book*, edited by William E. Klingshirn and Linda Safran, 194–222. Washington, DC: Catholic University Press.

Saussure, Ferdinand de. 1983. *Course in General Linguistics.* Translated by R. Harris. London: Duckworth.

Schleicher, Marianne. 2010. "Accounts of a Dying Scroll: On Jewish Handling of Sacred Texts in Need of Restoration or Disposal." In *The Death of Sacred Texts: Ritual Disposal and Renovation of Texts in World Religions*, edited by Kristina Myrvold, 11–29. London: Ashgate.

Sebeok, Thomas A. 1994. *Signs: An Introduction to Semiotics.* Toronto: University of Toronto Press.

Shaw, George Bernard. 1924. *Saint Joan.* London: Constable and Co.

Simon, Maurice. 1939. *Midrash Rabbah*, vol. 9. London: Soncino Press.

Smith, Wilfred Cantwell. 1999. *What is Scripture? A Comparative Approach.* Minneapolis, MN: Fortress Press.
Ware, Timothy. 1963. *The Orthodox Church*. London: Harmondswoth.

# 8

# It Is What It Is (Or Is It?): Further Reflections on the Buddhist Representation of Manuscripts

Jacob Kinnard

*Books are a common motif in the art of medieval Indian Buddhism. The questions addressed in this paper are: What are these Buddhist images of books? What are they images of? Or, more to the point, are they images of anything at all? This paper suggests that such images are like sculptural snapshots. These are not images not to be worshipped—although the main goddesses or bodhisattvas presented in the images were certainly objects of veneration—but they are images of worship. As such, they may be evidence of this worship, but they may also be rhetorical or polemical statements about the importance of the book in the Buddhist communities that produced them.*

> How do images accrue values that seem so out of proportion to their real importance? (W. J. T. Mitchell 2005, 76)

> What it is not is a redundancy.... Instead, it is a deliberate tautology (the Greek tauto means "the same") designed to define itself by repetition of itself. Because it needs a name, let's call it a "tautophrase." Often accompanied by a shrug, it is used to deflect inquiry with panache. (Safire 2006)

Sometime around the first century of the common era, the scholar monks who founded the upstart Buddhist movements that eventually came to be known as the Mahāyāna were faced with a significant dilemma: they had new ideas, new interpretations of the Buddha's teachings, and they articulated these in what must have been understood, at least by some in this milieu, as new texts. At the time, new texts had no status in the Buddhist world; indeed, "new" would have essentially been understood as "heretical." In order to legitimate these ideas and interpretations, therefore, they had to freight them with doctrinal authority. "Doctrinal" in this early Buddhist milieu, however, was defined as that which was *buddhavacana*, literally the Buddha's own speech; the process of canon formation which would eventually fix those texts that were truly the Buddha's own speech was well under way, and these new texts were clearly not part of the discussion. So, what to do?

One way these monks created a sense of legitimacy was to argue that these were not new texts at all; rather, these were the doctrines and ideas that the

Buddha himself had withheld while he was on earth because he felt his followers were not yet ready for such powerful ideas. Thus these scholar monks argued that not only were these not new texts—they were just recently discovered—but also that they were better than the so-called older texts. Indeed, these texts were said to be so powerful that "heaps and heaps" of *puṇya*—salvifically efficacious merit—could be generated simply by copying them, by worshipping them, even by just looking at them.[1] Indeed, the books were understood to be equivalent to the Buddha himself; they not only contained his wisdom, but were also said to be the very source of that wisdom.

Although others had noted this attention to books in Mahāyāna Buddhism before (Bagchi 1967), Gregory Schopen was perhaps the first scholar to deem this emphasis on texts the "cult of the book" in Buddhism. Schopen produced a series of articles, beginning in the late 1970s, that radically altered the landscape of Buddhist studies. He called into question what he later called the "Protestant presuppositions" of Western scholars of Buddhism, who had for over a century been constituting their subject as a "pure" textual religious tradition—really not a "religion" at all, but a rational philosophy—devoid of ritual and superstition, a kind of Eastern version of Protestant Christianity (Schopen 1975, 1987, 1988, 1990). This simply was not the case, Schopen argued; Buddhists, including Buddhist monks, were very much involved in the physicality of ritual and worship. Some of Schopen's work has focused on the exaltation and, presumably, the worship of the book in the early Mahāyāna and the shift of the object of worship from the Buddha's relics to the book.

This cult of the book lies at the very heart of the emergence of the Mahāyāna. One important issue—we might even call it a crisis of legitimacy—that the scholar-monks who gave rise to the Mahāyāna faced was the fact that they did not possess the physical relics of the Buddha, which were central to the earliest Buddhist communities. The Buddha's relics were treated as not just physical objects, but were thought (at least by some) to embody the Buddha himself: "[T]he relic in early Buddhist India was thought of as an actual living presence" and was "characterized by — full of — exactly the same spiritual forces and faculties that characterize, in fact constitute and animate, the living Buddha" (Schopen 1987, 203; 1990, 181–217). These early Mahāyāna schools shifted the focus of ritual practice in Buddhism away from relics by elevating the text so that it not only rivaled the Buddha's relics, but surpassed them in value: "[T]he merit derived from the cult of the book is always expressed in terms of its comparative superiority to that derived from the *stūpa*/relic cult" (Schopen 1975, 168–169). A great deal of cultural capital was thus connected to written texts in the early Mahāyāna (McMahan 1998, 2002; Drewes 2007).

1. I am reminded here of the books written by faculty members encased at the entrances of academic departments. These books are clearly not meant to be read by those who enter—the cases are invariably locked—but simply to be regarded with a kind of awe, to be worshipped!

This was no small matter for, as Schopen has pointed out, the redactors of these texts "were attempting to introduce a radical innovation in the face of an established cult of central importance," and thus "had to contend at every step with the historical priority and dominance of the *stūpa*/relic cult of early Buddhism in the milieu in which it was attempting to establish itself" (Schopen 1975, 168–169). In such key texts as the *Lotus Sūtra* and various *Perfection of Wisdom* texts, the book is held up as the physical object par excellence, better, even, than the Buddha's bodily remains: "Further, where this perfection of wisdom has been written down in a book, and has been put up and worshipped, where it has been taken up, etc., there men and ghosts can do no harm..." (*Aṣṭasāhasrikāprajñāpāramitā* 1960, 85). In this and many other passages, the book—specifically these "new" books—is celebrated as the source of the Buddha's wisdom, and is, therefore, superior to the relics: "It is for this reason that the person who would copy and worship the perfection of wisdom would beget the greater merit [than worshipping the Buddha's relics]. For, in doing so, he would worship the cognition of the all-knowing" (Conze 1973, 104–106).

Aside from these various verbal exultations of the book as a physical object to be worshipped, there is no evidence that people really worshipped books in the early Mahāyāna milieu. Ironically enough, scholars such as Schopen—who himself wanted to move beyond the constitution of Buddhism as a purely textual object—have had to rely on the textual record to make the case that such "cults" actually existed, that people actually did what the texts said. Some scholars have called into question Schopen's conclusion that these texts describe actual practices on the ground, arguing instead that all of this is just rhetoric: "What seems more likely is that they are simply hyperbolical assertions of the sacrality of the sūtra and those who memorize it" (Drewes 2007, 124).

It is impossible to say whether or not early Mahāyāna monks and laypeople actually did what the texts suggest—that is, venerated books. All we have as evidence is what the texts themselves say should be done. Indeed, until Schopen most scholars had simply assumed that all of this book-worship talk was just that, talk—polemically charged rhetoric intended to raise the status of these new schools. Representations of books did not actually begin to appear in the art of the Mahāyāna for hundreds of years; images of books as iconographic signifiers began to appear by about the eighth century (Kinnard 1999), but it is not until the tenth century that we see images depicting the worship of the book (Kinnard 2002). As much as these late images may seem like "solid" evidence for the existence of actual book cult practices, however, though a millennium after the texts first describe such "practices," it is also important to remember that images, just as much as texts, do not always tell us what we want to know. They are in fact mute as to their on-the-ground significance. As Giulio Carlo Argan has reminded us, "It is always the scholar alone who speaks in the presence of the work of art, and his entire problem consists in deciding what kind of talking he should do" (Argan 1980, 20).

So the questions I wish to address here are really quite simple: what are these images? what are they images of? or, more to the point, are they images *of* anything at all? Elsewhere I have suggested that these images are images of people venerating books, and that as such they represent solid evidence that there was an actual cult of the book, with ritual practices centered on the book, in medieval Indian Buddhism. Such images were both injunctions to worship and therefore have what I have called a "ritually mimetic function," as well as actual records of worship (Kinnard 2002, 2008; Huntington 1990). I argued that they should be taken as definite proof that Mahāyāna Buddhists did indeed do what the texts suggest—worship books. But I think I have underestimated what we might call, for lack of a better term, the *imageness* of these images. After all, the books represented in Buddhist art are not books at all—they are images of books. But is it the "images" part of that iteration which is most important, or the "of books"?

## The living image

> The theologians, the real intellectuals, were too embarrassed by the power of images to acknowledge it. (Freedberg 1989, 396)
>
> That is, that the image is the real embodiment of the deity. It is not just a device for the focusing of human vision, but is charged with the presence of the god. (Eck 1989, 45)

My main concern here is Buddhist images of people venerating books, such as we see in the detail at the bottom of a Tāra image from medieval Orissa (Figure 1). It will be helpful first to very briefly ground this discussion in the Indian Hindu and Buddhist understanding of religiously significant images. The theology that informs the basic understanding of images in India—and here I refer to indigenous Indian traditions, not those, such as Islam, that arrive from elsewhere—is quite different than that which informs Western understanding of images (though these general statements necessarily oversimplify the complex, contextual understandings of images in both the West and India).

The Hindu image is not an image of a goddess or god at all: it is not a representation, a signifier, but it is the goddess, it is the embodiment of the divine. Thus when one sees an image in a ritual context, one is not really seeing an image at all—or at least not in the agreed upon sense of what an image is in the West, that is, a representation—but rather one is seeing the god or goddess itself. Although there may be a surface similarity to some early Christian understandings of icons, Bonaventure's understanding of the image as a kind of lens through which god can be perceived, say, or Dionysus the Areopagite's conception of the visible image as a means to contemplate the divine (Kinnard 1999, 33–35; Marion 1991), an image in the Hindu context is not a lens or a conduit, but is the deity itself (Eck 1989; Waghorne, Cutler, and Narayana 1985). The image here is similar to the wafer in the mass in that, through transubstantiation, it is no longer a wafer but it is the body of Christ, and thus not a symbol of something at all.

The understanding of images in the Buddhist context is a bit more complicated because there is a deep ambiguity surrounding images in Buddhism. Put simply, on the one hand an image can serve as a reminder of the departed Buddha, and thus a tool in contemplating and cultivating his qualities. On the other hand, an image is an impermanent object, and an image of the Buddha is not the Buddha, and thus there is a danger—paralleling the essential danger that informs Western notions of idolatry—of mistakenly treating the physical object as the person represented. For a very long time, scholars in the West maintained on the basis of certain textual data that early Buddhism was, like Protestant Christianity, an aniconic tradition, that the Buddha himself had prohibited worshipping images of him (they tended to ignore those texts in which the Buddha permitted certain kinds of images).

This understanding of images—what came to be known as the "aniconic thesis," based on a highly influential article written by the French scholar Alfred Foucher—is, if not contradicted, at least complicated by other kinds of data, some of which is textual, some sculptural (Foucher 1917). First, images from a fairly early period in Buddhism were regarded as relics, along with the corporeal remains of the Buddha and various objects with which he came into contact. Not surprisingly, early Buddhists had a complex understanding of such images. On the one hand, they were very much "images of"—objects that were intended to serve as reminders of the long-gone Buddha. There is also substantial evidence, however, to indicate that images were also not just "images of." They were in some contexts like the physical remains of the Buddha, regarded as being imbued with the very presence of the dead teacher himself.

## Prajñāpāramitā as the book embodied

> Prajñāpāramitā is a lovely yellow. In her left hand, she holds the *Prajñāpāramitā* book on a lotus; her two principle hands display the *dharmacakramudrā*. — *Niṣpannayogāvalī* (1962, 65).

I will return to the images of books being worshipped in a moment, but I want first to consider a rather different kind of image of the book, an image that, although it features iconic representations of physical books, is rather more complex than just a representation of a book (Figure 2). This is the semi-goddess Prajñāpāramitā, the embodiment of the Perfection of Wisdom texts, the root texts of the Mahāyāna schools; she is the mother of the Buddha, the "source" of his wisdom. Iconographically this is a fairly simple image, but theologically—if we can use that term to apply to the Buddhist context—this image is extremely complex, although the iconography and the theology here are very much intertwined.

One of things that makes this such a complex image is that the deity here is depicted precisely as one would expect the Buddha himself to be depicted. She is seated crossed-legged displaying the *dharmacakrapravartanamudrā*, literally

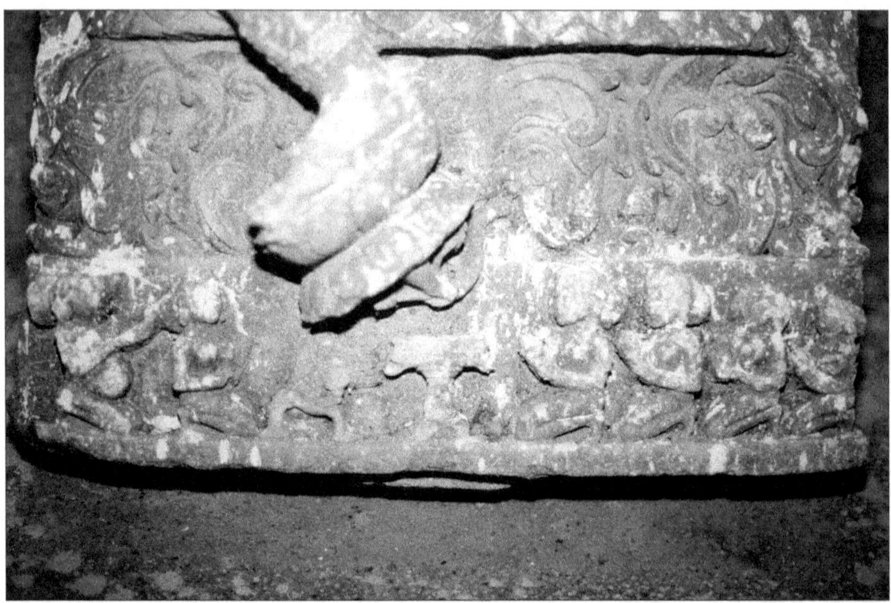

Figure 1. Detail, stone Tārā, 10th century Orissa, Orissa State Museum; photo by the author.

the gesture of the turning of the wheel of dharma, the teaching gesture that is iconographically associated with the Buddha's first sermon. There is more, though; at the bottom of the stele are three small figures that, although easy to miss, are extremely significant: two kneeling people with a deer between them. The Buddha delivered his first sermon to his disciples in the Deer Park at Sārnāth, and, from an early period, images of the first sermon include both his initial disciples and a deer.

It is of course impossible to know the precise intent of the artisans who made this image—or the monks who may have overseen its construction, or the patrons who commissioned it, or, for that matter, those who beheld it in situ—but one thing that seems to be visually suggested here is that the goddess, the embodiment of the Mahāyāna's root texts, replaces, or displaces, the Buddha himself. This is consistent with the theological rhetoric of the Mahāyāna's root texts—the Perfection of Wisdom genre—which hold that these texts in a sense supplant the Buddha's initial teachings because they are the source, the mother, in fact, of his knowledge. There are two lotuses located just above each of her shoulders in this image, on top of which two books—the *Prajñāpāramitā*, of course—further signify the link between the goddess and the text.

This is an image *of* Prajñāpāramitā, certainly, a representation of the goddess, but given what I have said about the devotional and theological context of images in India, the preposition is problematic: this also *is* the goddess.

But she is not just the goddess, she also embodies the book and the contents of the book, that is, *prajñā*, the wisdom that leads directly to enlightenment. The image, then, does not signify; indeed, it is not an image at all, it is the goddess. In other words, to worship this image, or the goddess that is the image, is also to worship the book; and as we have already seen in the early Mahāyāna textual context, the book is so powerful that it is enough to worship or just see it (or her). This image is the goddess, who is the book, which contains the wisdom that is the source of the Buddha himself. Indeed, to worship Prajñāpāramitā is to worship the Buddha: "Therefore, Blessed One, when a pūja is done to Prajñāpāramitā, it is a pūja to the venerable past, present, and future Buddhas" (*Aṣṭasāhasrikāprajñāpāramitā*, 18). The physical book, the contents of that book, and the deity who embodies both all coalesce here. This image, then, does not signify at all. It is what it is.

## Images of books being worshipped: Images of what?

> There is nothing outside of the text. (Derrida 1974, 158)
>
> The story of objects asserting themselves as things, then, is the story of how the thing really names less an object than a particular subject-object relation. (Brown 2001, 4)

As I noted at the outset, my purpose in setting out to write this essay was to engage in what Jonathan Z. Smith has frequently said is one of the primary tasks of the scholar—defamiliarization—that is, making the familiar strange and in the process reexamining what we think we already know (Smith 1982, xiii). Specifically, as I have reflected on the sculptural representations of people worshipping books in the art of medieval Indian Buddhism, I have wondered if I have not, in my earlier writings, been rather too sanguine that such images are proof of what people actually did on the ground. Archaeological evidence, after all, can tell us things about what people actually did that texts cannot, and such images are, certainly, archaeological evidence. By this logic, the texts, in saying that one should set up and worship the book, are really engaged in polemics, in rhetoric that is intended to add legitimacy to their new movement. The images produced hundreds of years later which depict people worshiping books, however, are not just rhetoric, not just words, but are solid evidence—carved in stone, no less—that such practices actually were practiced.

Really? Why should an image, carved in stone or caste in bronze, be any more reflective of the "real" practices of "real" people on the ground than what is expressed verbally in a text? Why are these images not rhetoric, too, only visual rhetoric, evidence not of actual practices but of ideology and polemical positioning? In an earlier article on the cult of the book, I drew attention to a particular iteration of this cult that appears in and around Bodhgayā sometime around the tenth century: the inclusion of the book in

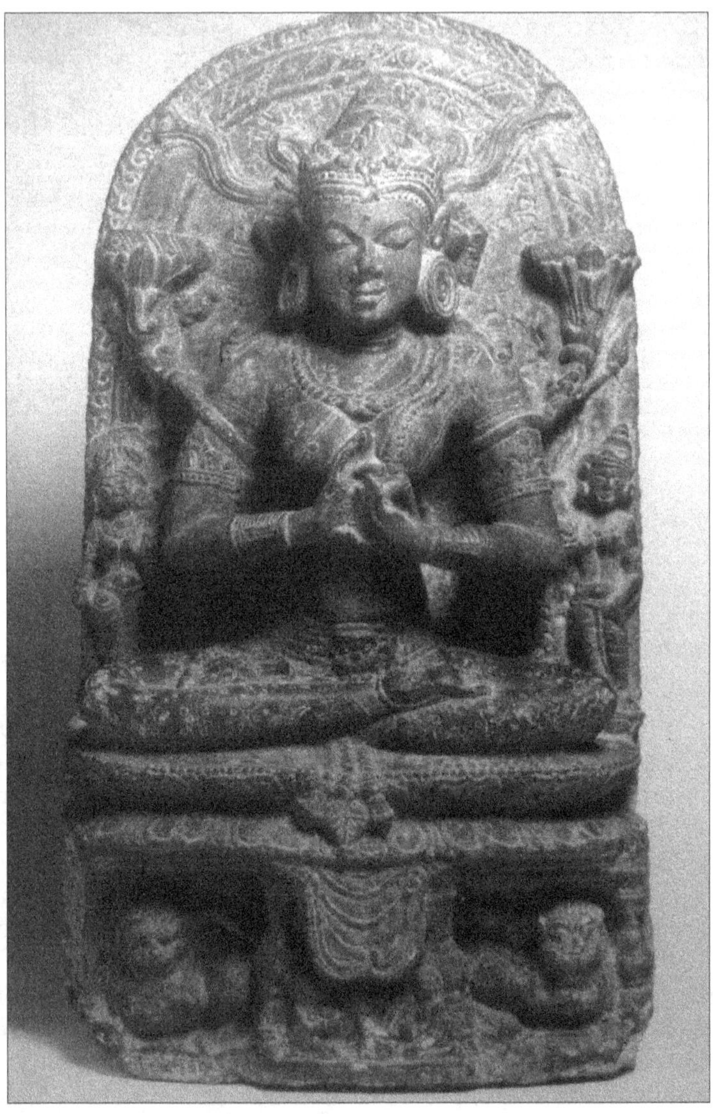

Figure 2. Stone Prajñāpāramitā, 9th century Bihar, Avery Brundage Collection; photo courtesy of the Museum of Asian Art, San Francisco)

the royal image of the *saptaratna*, the seven jewels, that, in some texts, are said to be the legitimizing symbols of the righteous Buddhist king. This sort of image (Figure 3), in my view, is clearly polemical and, as I argued in that earlier article, a powerful bit of visual rhetoric: "As a set, the seven jewels project the image of the perfectly balanced rule, with the proper relationship between *dharma* and *artha*, reason and power" (Kinnard 2002, 107). This is expressed textually in a variety of places, in the Pāli canon and in later texts such as the *Sutra of Golden Light*, and serves as a kind of monastic reminder to the king that he must rule with force at times, but must also be informed by the basic principles of Buddhism. He must, in short, be a Dharmarāja, both protecting (and supporting) Buddhism and ruling according to its ethical tenets of compassion and non-violence.

The inclusion of the book in this set is, as I have said, a late development, and I argued that it comes at a particular point when the cult of the book is in full swing, and when Buddhist monks are particularly concerned—due, in part, to the rise of devotional Hinduism in northern India—to insure the continued support of the king:

> Thus, I am suggesting that the particular agents responsible for the construction of such images (monks, laypeople, royal functionaries) - were engaged in their own polemic, and visually "invoked" the book, not so much to advance a position about the proper "container" of Buddhist doctrine—the *Perfection of Wisdom* texts—nor about the proper object of ritual veneration—the book—but to make a point about the proper Buddhist king: from the monastic point of view, such images would serve to project the need for royal support and protection of the religion; from the laity's point of view, such images would project the need for desired balance between religion and the polity; and, finally, from a royal point of view, such images would promote the basic ideology of the *dharmacakravartin* by "advertising" the king's possession of the most precious of all jewels, the book. Images of the *saptaratna* with the book then might well have functioned as multivalent billboards; at a time when Buddhism was struggling to remain vital in northern India, monks may have made such images to "advertise" the need for the king to continue to support of the monasteries, or, the king may have intended such images to "advertise" his involvement in the life of the monastery. (Kinnard 2002, 113)

Clearly, then, these images signify. What is more, the books depicted in these images are not really books at all, but images of books—the preposition is very much necessary. They are symbols of the entire Buddhist tradition. Hence my earlier remark about the "imageness" of these images.

This is all well and good. But what about those other books from this milieu, those images of books that are sculpturally depicted as set up on platforms and worshipped? Can we really say that these images are any more indicative of actual practices than the verbal exultations of the book contained in the texts? I am not so sanguine. Indeed, I think it is important that these are images of books, not books, and as such they are intended to convey something: the importance of the book, the idea—as expressed in the *Prajñāpāramitā* and other early Mahāyāna texts—that the book is a superior object of worship, better than the relics and better, even than the Buddha himself, because the book contains the *prajñā* that makes the Buddha the Buddha. In other words, these images signify.

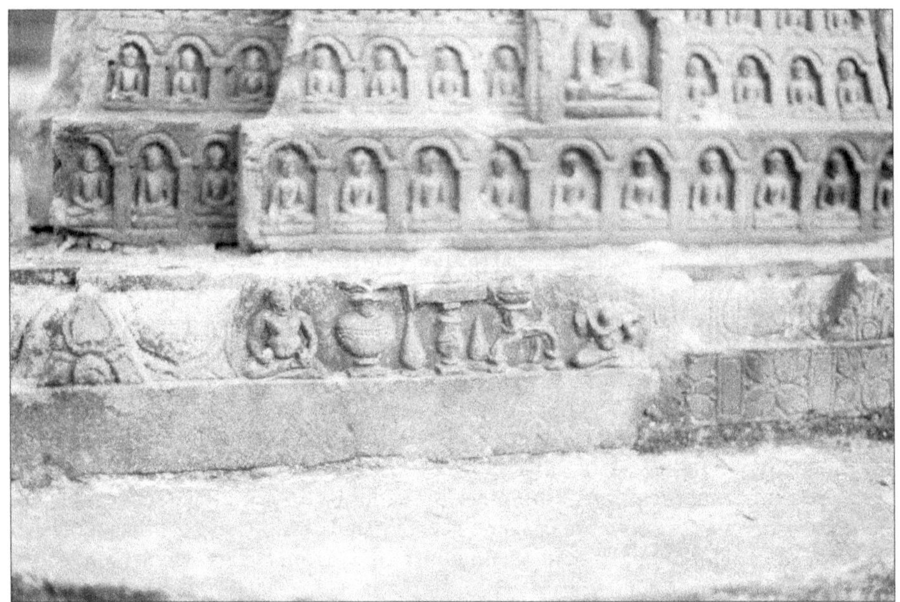

Figure 3. Stone lintel, 10th century, Bodhgayā. Photo by the author.

At the start of this essay, I quoted W.J.T. Mitchell, from his provocative, "The Surplus Value of Images." He goes on: "But perhaps the most interesting consequence of seeing images as living things is that the question of their value (understood as vitality) is played out in a social context. We need to ponder that we don't just evaluate images; images introduce new forms of value into the world, contesting our criteria, forcing us to change our minds" (Mitchell 2005, 93). It may be stating the obvious here, but the representations of the books that I have been discussing are not just the products of a particular ideological position—the early Mahāyāna attempts to legitimize their movements, say—but are also agents in the production of new meanings and new understandings.

Did medieval Indian Buddhists really worship books, and if they did, what sort of ritual action was this? We cannot know. What we do know, however, is that Buddhists represented books in their images, and, further, represented people worshipping books in their sculpture. These images were intended to signify something—the importance of the text as a physical object, the importance of the content of the text, the power of the book as embodied in (or by) the goddess. Gadamer remarked that the work of art "says something about the original" (Gadamer 1975, 124). Indeed, but what? There is, to invoke Ricoeur, a surplus of meaning here, this much seems clear. Let me return to the image of *Prajñāpāramitā* that, as I noted, is several things at once: goddess, book, contents of the book. Ricoeur points out that "for one who participates in the symbolic signification there really are not two significations," or, in this case, more than two, "but rather a single movement, which transfers him from one level to the other and which assimilates him to the second signification by means of, or through, the literal one" (Ricoeur 1976, 75). This is useful, but perhaps too linear. If the primary symbol is the book—which is both a symbol and not a symbol at all, but itself the "original"—then the secondary symbol, the image of the book, is dependent on and constituted by the book. I must say that I have reservations about introducing "symbol language" here at all, but Ricoeur's basic point is relevant nonetheless. I think, though, that we could add fluidity to Ricoeur's discussion, for the way in which the two "comment" on one another must be dialectical, not so much a movement from one to the other, but a discursive movement back and forth; as Appadurai has pointed out, "it is the things-in-motion that illuminate their human and social context" (Appadurai 1988, 5).

We know very little, in fact, about the actual context, the on-the-ground situatedness of these images. We know, certainly, that texts were freighted with a good deal of cultural capital, but we do not, in the end, know how texts—physical books, that is—actually were situated in a human or a social context. That said, though, we can still ask: what is an image of a book in this Buddhist context? It is not a book, but a comment on the book's content, its power—the wisdom, *prajñā* that is articulated in its verses. The image of the book draws attention to this power: it is so powerful, the book, that it is enough to see it, to worship it. But there is more because the image of the book can also be, itself, an object of veneration, and thus not an image at all but also not a book, either. These are, as Mitchell, drawing on Bill Brown, would say, "special things" (2005, 193); in Brown's words, they "hover over the threshold between the nameable and unnameable, the figurable and the unfigurable, the indentifiable and unidentifiable: Dr. Seuss's Thing one and Thing Two" (Brown 2001, 5).

In a paper I presented at the first Iconic Books symposium, I raised the question of whether or not these Buddhist books could be understood as icons, a term that is not, of course, part of the Indian lexicon. I did not have an answer then, and I do not really have an answer now. Or, rather, I do not have a single answer. Of course these are icons, if we take the word in its broadest sense; but, that said, they are at times also not icons, as my discussion of *Prajñāpāramitā* demonstrates: the image is the goddess embodied, not a window through which to see her and not a representation of her. Mitchell, in discussing the totem/fetish/idol triad in the West, points out that the distinction between these three objects is slippery and shifting, and can only be "apprehended through a *sounding* of the image, an inquiry into what it says and does, what ritual and myths circulate around it" (Mitchell 2005, 189). Representations of books in Buddhism, and books themselves—witness the ritual procession of the *Prajñāpāramitā* book by the king in contemporary Nepal (Lewis 2000)—are thus always contextually situated; they are objects—things—that are used, whether that use is reading, writing, venerating, parading, representing.

In some contexts, representations of books function as symbols of the Buddha's or some boddhisattva's or some goddess's ability to bestow wisdom to his or her devotees; in others, though, we cannot even call such objects representations because in their ritual contexts they are beings, living embodiments of wisdom. And in still other contexts, as I have elsewhere noted, such images of books seem to function as ritual injunctions, as visual clues for how to treat the book. In some of these instances, the book is a book, in others not. Mitchell (2005, 196) puts it nicely when he says that objects, images, fetishes, idols—all of those "special things"—are "condensed world pictures, synecdoches of social totalities ranging from bodies to families to tribes to nations to monotheistic notions of metaphysical universality." The surplus of meanings attached to books in Buddhist art may not be quite so grand, but certainly Mitchell's point is well taken: these various "books" meant a lot to the Buddhists who thought about and crafted and venerated them, "a lot" both in terms of value and in terms of the variety of meaning attached to them.

There are really two sorts of images of books here. The first is an image of the book embodied that is to be worshipped in its ritual context. This appears in the Prajñāpāramitā image and others from the medieval period of other bodhisattvas and goddesses associated with wisdom (Mañjuśrī, Tārā, Cundā). We do not know much about the specifics of that image's context, such as where it was located or how it was worshipped or by whom, but it seems entirely likely that such images were, indeed, the objects of ritual veneration. The second sort of image is the many images of books set up on pedestals and worshipped. These are images not to be worshipped—although certainly the main goddess or bodhisattva presented in the stelae were objects of veneration—but images of worship. As such, as I have suggested, they can be seen as evidence of this worship (my earlier conclusion that real Buddhists really did worship real books), as well as (part of my argument here) rhetorical or polemical statements about the importance of the book. In this latter sense, the visual rhetoric is really an extension or compliment to the first-century textual rhetoric about the supremacy of the *Perfection of Wisdom* texts.

It strikes me, though, that there is one final aspect that needs to be considered: never do we encounter an image of just a book, simply a representation of a book by itself, presented as an object for veneration. There are images of books embodied, books being held by bodhisattvas and goddesses, images of people venerating books, but never just a book to be venerated. Although this evidentiary lacuna might seem insignificant, I believe that it is not. There were, after all, physical books that could have been venerated and the same cannot be said of bodhisattvas and goddesses, the beliefs of many Buddhists aside; their images were necessary to make them available for worship (think of John of Damascus here), to make them visible.

Thus there would have been no need to create a sculptural image of a book to be venerated, when one could simply put the book—the "real book"—up on the altar, or on a pedestal, and worship it. This suggests, then, that the images of Buddhists doing precisely that can, and perhaps should, be understood as visual records of this sort of worship. They are like sculptural snapshots. They are not objects to be worshipped, but records of worship, and, like a snapshot or any other record, they can function mimetically as well, as a visual "suggestion" of what to do on the ground. A photo of people marching in protest of a war, say, is certainly a record of that activity; depending on the context, it can also serve as a rhetorical or polemical comment, an endorsement with the (implicit) function of suggesting that others do the same or conversely an indictment (again, depending on the context). As Brown reminds us, these are special things.

## Acknowledgements

I would like to thank all of those who participated in the three Iconic Books Symposia for their insights and for the very lively comparative discussions on the broad topic of the representation and veneration of books. I would also like to thank Ted Vial, Tink Tinker, and Edward Antonio for their careful readings of earlier drafts of this essay and for their insightful critiques.

## References

Appadurai, Arjun. 1988. *The Social Life of Things: Commodities in Cultural Perspective*. Cambridge: Cambridge University Press.

*Aṣṭasāhasrikāprajñāpāramitā*. 1960. Edited by P.L. Vaidya. Buddhist Sanskrit Texts 4. Dharbhanga: Mithila Institute.

Argan, Giulio Carlo. 1980. "Ideology and Iconology." In *The Language of Images*, edited by W.J.T. Mitchell, 15–23. Chicago. IL: University of Chicago Press.

Bagchi, Sitansusekhar S. 1967. *Suvarṇaprabhāsasūtra*. Dharbhanga: Mithila Institute of Post-Graduate Studies and Research in Sanskrity Learning.

Brown, Bill. 2001. "Thing Theory." *Critical Inquiry* 28: 1–16. http://dx.doi.org/10.1086/449030

Conze, Edward. 1973. *The Perfection of Wisdom in Eight Thousand Lines and its Verse Summary*. Bolinas: Four Seasons.

Derrida, Jacques. 1974. *Of Grammatology*. Translated by Gayatri Chakravorty Spivak. Baltimore, MD: Johns Hopkins Press.

Drewes, David. 2007. "Revisiting the Phrase '*sa pṛthivīpradeśaś caityabhūto bhavet*' and the Mahāyāna Cult of the Book." *Indo-Iranian Journal* 50: 101–143. http://dx.doi.org/10.1163/000000007790085815

Eck, Diana. 1989. *Darsan: Seeing the Divine Image in India*. New York: Columbia University Press.

Foucher, Alfred. 1917. "The Beginnings of Buddhist Art." In *The Beginnings of Buddhist Art and Other Essays in Indian and Central-Asian Archaeology*, 1–29. Paris: Paul Geutherner.

Freedberg, David. 1989. *The Power of Images: Studies in the History and Theory of Response*. Chicago, IL: University of Chicago Press.

Gadamer, Hans-Georg. 1975. *Truth and Method.* New York: Seabury Press.

Huntington, Susan L. 1990. "Early Buddhist Art and the Theory of Aniconism." *Art Journal* 49: 401–408. http://dx.doi.org/10.2307/777142

Kinnard, Jacob N. 1999. *Imaging Wisdom: Seeing and Knowing in the Art of Indian Buddhism.* London: Routledge.

———. 2002. "On Buddhist 'Biblioters': Representing and Worshiping the Book in Medieval Indian Buddhism." *The Eastern Buddhist* 34: 94–116.

———. 2008. "Amaravati as Lens: Envisioning Buddhism in the Ruins of the Great Stupa." In *Buddhism in the Krishna River Valley of Andhra*, edited by Sree Padma and Tony Barber, 81–103. Albany: State University of New York Press.

Lewis, Todd. 2000. *Narratives and Rituals of Newar Buddhism.* Albany: State University of New York Press.

Marion, Jean Luc. 1991. *God Without Being.* Translated by Thomas Carlson. Chicago, IL: University of Chicago Press.

McMahan, David. 1998. "Orality, Writing, and Authority in South Asian Buddhism: Visionary Literature and the Struggle for Legitimacy in the Mahāyāna." *History of Religions* 37: 249–274. http://dx.doi.org/10.1086/463504

———. 2002. *Empty Vision: Metaphor and Visionary Imagery in Mahayana Buddhism.* London: Routledge.

Mitchell, W.J.T. 2005. *What Do Pictures Want: The Lives and Loves of Images.* Chicago: University of Chicago Press.

*Niṣpannayogāvalī.* 1962. Edited by B. Bhattacharyya. Gaekwad's Oriental Series 59. Baroda: Oriental Institute.

Ricoeur, Paul. 1976. *Interpretation Theory: Discourse and the Surplus of Meaning.* Abilene: Texas Christian University Press.

Safire, William. 2006. "It is What is Is." *New York Times.* March 5.

Schopen, Gregory. 1975. "The Phrase 'sa pṛthivīpradeśaś caityabhūto bhavet' in the Vajracchedikaa: Notes on the Cult of the Book in the Mahāyāna." *Indo-Iranian Journal* 27: 147–181. http://dx.doi.org/10.1007/BF00221011

———. 1987. "Burial '*Ad Sanctos*' and the Physical Presence of the Buddha in Early Indian Buddhism: A Study in the Archaeology of Religions." *Religion* 17: 193–225. http://dx.doi.org/10.1016/0048-721X(87)90116-3

———. 1988. "On the Buddha and His Bones: The Conception of a Relic in the Inscriptions of Nāgārjunikoṇḍa." *Journal of the American Oriental Society* 108: 527–537. http://dx.doi.org/10.2307/603142

———. 1990. "Archaeology and the Protestant Presuppositions in the Study of Indian Buddhism." *History of Religions* 31: 1–23. http://dx.doi.org/10.1086/463253

Smith, Jonathan Z. 1982. *Imagining Religion: From Babylon to Jonestown.* Chicago, IL: University of Chicago Press.

Waghorne, Joanne, Norman Cutler, and Vasudha Narayana, eds. 1985. *Gods of Flesh/Gods of Stone.* New York: Columbia University Press.

# 9

# The Tell-Tale Iconic Book

M. Patrick Graham

*This study draws on the images from sixteenth-century publications in the Digital Image Archive to explore how books are used in printed images related to biblical interpretation. The investigation finds that images of books are used: (1) to indicate authorship of biblical works; (2) to defend the orthodoxy of later writers; (3) to affirm the learning, piety, and social standing of certain writers, saints, and other figures from antiquity; (4) to contend that the message and ministries of certain biblical figures were based on Scripture; and (5) to link antiquity with the Early Modern period.*

## Introduction

While one may define "iconic book" as "a text revered primarily as an object of power rather than just as words of instruction, information, or insight" (Iconic Book Symposium 2010), this study is concerned with *images* of books—rather than with literary texts or physical books themselves—and how they may have represented something beyond an ordinary physical object. Was the image of a book intended to convey a virtue such as piety, a practice such as reading or writing, or something more profound about a person, publication, or circumstance? Such questions will drive this experimental effort to understand how images of books were used in a particular collection of sixteenth-century book illustrations in order to guide the interpretation of Scripture and reflection on the Christian faith.

This study draws on the corpus of images from sixteenth-century publications available in the Digital Image Archive, a database of more than 40,000 images from printed materials that are held in the Special Collections of the Pitts Theology Library (Candler School of Theology, Emory University). Since the collection of publications from which these images were drawn is only a fraction of what was produced in the sixteenth century, the study can only be regarded as based on a sampling of a much larger corpus. In addition, since most of these materials were issued by Christian authors and presses, they reflect the assumptions, prejudices, and concerns of those responsible for them. Among the most obvious examples of this are the portrayals of Jews and Judaism in the illustrations. There was less concern to understand or portray Judaism fairly than to show Jews as opponents of Jesus and the Christian church. This is a lamentable but indisputable fact of the period.

The woodcuts and engravings that comprise the Digital Image Archive have been indexed by Scripture text and been assigned keywords to facilitate natural language searching (as opposed to the use of a controlled vocabulary for searching). While "book" has been applied as a keyword to most illustrations in which a book appears, this has not always been done, either because of oversight or because of the relatively insignificant role of the book in the image. A search of the Archive for images with the keyword "book" yields about 1,000 hits, half of which derive from the sixteenth century. Those that did not illustrate texts or persons from the Christian Bible were excluded, and the rest were placed in three groups treated in the three sections of this essay below: (1) title-page borders, (2) portraits of biblical authors (in the sense of persons whom Christian tradition credits with the authorship of biblical books), and (3) biblical texts or figures.

Given the substantial number of images to be reviewed, what follows is not an exhaustive study of each image or its artist and engraver. Rather, it is an initial, exploratory attempt to identify significant images, note some of the ways that books are used in the images, and then offer some commentary on this usage. Often, this commentary is quite tentative and so subject to revision after further analysis. In addition, the narrative has made no attempt to deal with exegetical complexities of biblical texts, nor has any attempt been made to point out all the points at which the illustrations are anachronistic or otherwise depart from the historical realities of antiquity.

Finally, a word about citation schema is in order. The Digital Image Archive is available online at http://www.pitts.emory.edu/dia/woodcuts.htm . When a search is executed, the Archive supplies a list of images in chronological order of the publication date of the work in which each image appears. The list supplies the call number of the source publication (typically, the year of publication and the first four letters of the author or title of the work) and the image title for the woodcut or engraving captured. When an image is selected for viewing its JPG or PDF image, its URL (e.g., http://www.pitts.emory.edu/woodcuts/1527BiblB/00009629.jpg) includes four parts: (1) the common address portion for all images (http://www.pitts.emory.edu/woodcuts/), (2) the call number (1527BiblB), (3) the eight-digit, unique image identifier (00009629), and (4) the image format extension (either .jpg or .pdf). In order to conveniently and precisely identify the image and facilitate its retrieval, therefore, references to images will include only the call number and image identifier. Consequently, any of these (call number + image identifier) can be added to the common address portion, along with the format extension, in order to construct a URL that should retrieve the image.

## Title-page borders

In some instances, a publication will have a title-page border that provides decoration for and an introduction to the work. The border may be related to the publication (but is often unrelated), or it may provide a larger overview of Scripture or the Christian faith and so be only remotely relevant to the work that it introduces. Such borders may have been commissioned by the printer or publisher for a particular work but subsequently reused for many other books or pamphlets. What follows is a series, presented largely chronologically, of title borders that include, typically, the Evangelists and a variety of other figures from Scripture or the Christian church.

### *Biblical authors and their interpreters*

In 1515 Matthias Schürer, a printer in Strasbourg, issued a volume of Erasmus' essays on Christian topics (*Lucubrationes*) that emphasized the life and example of Jesus. Its title-page border (1515Eras/00001481) featured David, Isaiah, Paul, and John across the panel at the head; Jerome and Ambrose on the left flank; Augustine and Gregory I on the right; and then a decorative panel at the base. An attribute is usually included for each of the eight figures, and the Latin names are supplied below each portrait. Only the Christian figures are given halos. Two men (Jerome and Pope Gregory I) are shown with books. It is usually (but not always) the case that a book shown with a figure is a tribute to what the person wrote, not to what the person read. In the case of Jerome (appearing with the cardinal's hat), the reference is likely to his translation of the Latin Vulgate, while Pope Gregory I (or Gregory the Great, shown with the papal triple tiara) is remembered as an especially prolific author (Cross 2005, 710–711).

Advancing this design theme of using heroes of the Christian Bible and church, one year later in Basel, Adam Petri used the design of Hans Holbein the Younger for the title page of Ambrose's collected works (*Omnia opera ...* ; June/August 1516; Hieronymus 1984, 200–201; see Figure 1) and for several subsequent publications as well (Hollstein 1988, 14: 157–158). In July 1520, he issued *R.P. Doct. Martini Lutherii Augustiniani theologi Synceri lucubrationum*, the first volume of a projected two-volume collection of Luther's more important works (1520Luth/00001744). The border, executed on a single block of wood, features the symbols of the four New Testament gospels in canonical order on the corners (angel/Matthew, lion/Mark, ox/Luke, and eagle/John), the Apostles Peter and Paul at the top and bottom with their attributes, and the four Latin Doctors of the church along the edges with hats that identify their ecclesial offices (Gregory I, Jerome, Ambrose, and Augustine). Both persons and symbols of the Gospels are given halos, and the figures are arranged in an aesthetically pleasing way: some books open, others closed; all the books of the Evangelists and Fathers are finished, except for one that is being written or annotated; and the figures are looking at one another in various ways, although one gestures, perhaps as a preacher. The writings of the Church

Fathers were especially important to define the doctrines and practices of the church, and so to cite their support for a theological position or interpretation of Scripture lent credibility to one's position. The imagery of this title border was powerful and would have exerted a strong appeal to Catholics and Protestants alike. With the symbols of the four Gospels anchoring the corners, the two leading apostles occupying dominant positions at the head and base, and four Western Fathers filling in the sides, the fence or border for the new work was complete. The impact was to indeed "frame" or assert a context for the new work that it introduced and affirm its orthodoxy—all at a time when Luther's books were being burned and many were speaking out against him (Marty 2004, 53–67). The great reformer is designated, "Reverend Father Doctor" (R.P.Doct.) and "Augustinian," and so presented as an orthodox Catholic cleric. While he had been ordered by Pope Leo X to recant on June 15, 1520, it would not be until January 1521 that he was excommunicated. In this design, all the figures, except for Peter and Paul, are shown with books, and so, just as the books of these ancient Christian writers developed and defined the Christian faith, now Luther instructs the church and must be heard.

The Holbein design was roughly copied: executed less expensively on four blocks of wood, and used by Silvan Otmar in Augsburg (1521LuthC/00001873), where his compositor on at least one occasion reversed the top and bottom panels (1523LuthHHHH/00002931), not an uncommon error among printers of this day. Otmar printed many Lutheran publications and so continued to use the Holbein design for these (Cole 1984, 336). Another Augsburg printer, Jörg Nadler, produced a much cruder variant of the Holbein woodcut with less detail and a central space for text that broke into the lower panel (1522KarlE/00014696), and other printers produced their own versions (e.g., Nickel Schmidt [1526Mens/00003462] and Joseph Klug [1539LuthD/00005515]).

In the Holbein design, the books symbolize authorship of literary works, and in one instance (Ambrose or Augustine; it is difficult to distinguish the two) the figure is writing in the book. The rest of the books are either closed, already opened, or in the process of being opened. The variety of distribution is done effectively to suggest the range of ways that books were written, handled, carried, opened, and so forth—in short, the story of the book and the church: a community that composed, read, and cared for the products of this new technology. This represents a giant step forward from the 1515 woodcut used by Schürer, and the poor copies of Holbein's work make it impossible to find in them the artistry of the block used by Petri.

From a few years later is a design after Hans Holbein the Younger but cut by Hans Lutzelburger and used by Adam Petri, which introduces the Basel *December Testament* (the folio edition of Luther's *September Testament*, 1522BiblC/00010607; Hollstein 1988, 14A: 68–69; Hieronymus 1984, 409-411; see Figure 2; another variant of this was created for Adam Petri's octavo for-

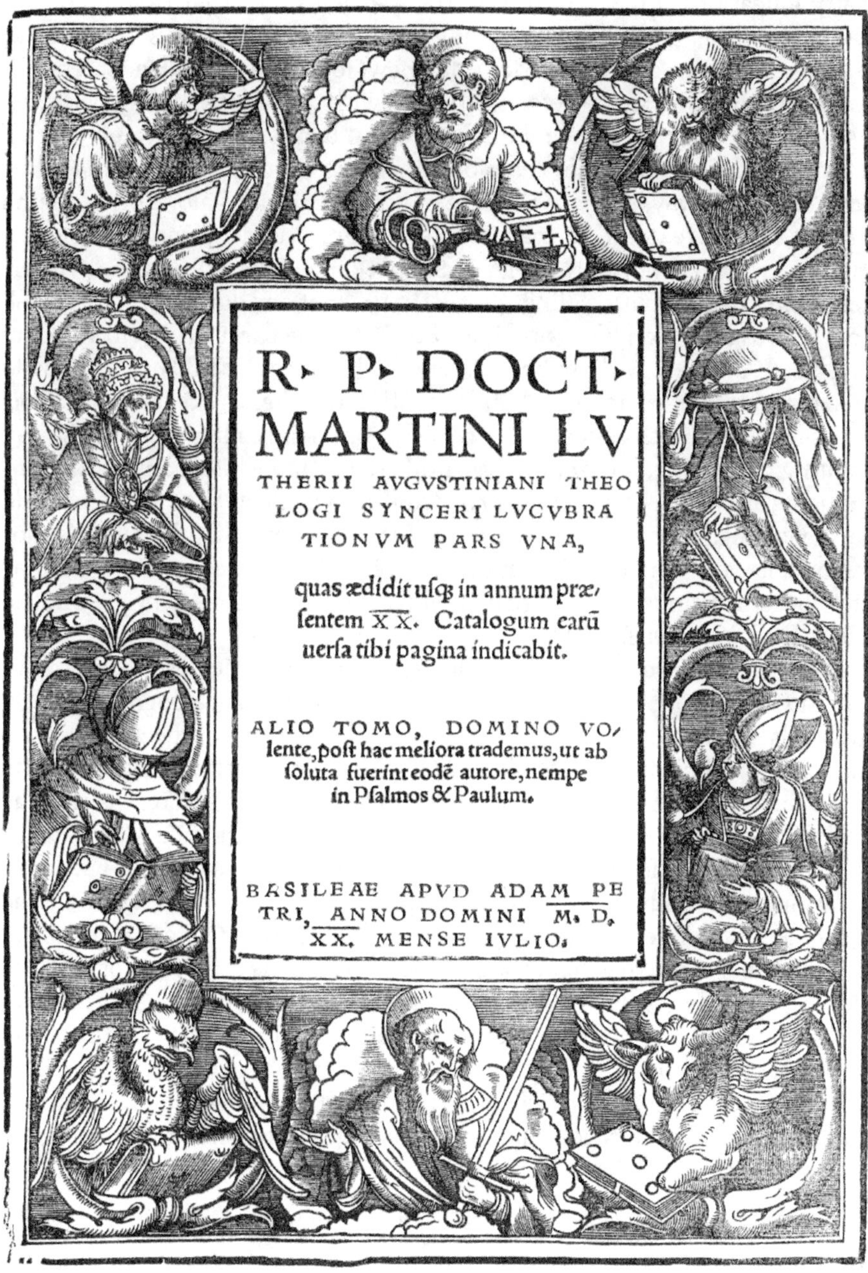
R· P· DOCT·
MARTINI LV
THERII AVGVSTINIANI THEO
LOGI SYNCERI LVCVBRA
TIONVM PARS VNA,

quas ædidit uſq; in annum præ/
ſentem XX. Catalogum earũ
uerſa tibi pagina indicabit.

ALIO TOMO, DOMINO VO/
lente, poſt hac meliora trademus, ut ab
ſoluta fuerint eodē autore, nempe
in Pſalmos & Paulum.

BASILEAE APVD ADAM PE
TRI, ANNO DOMINI M. D.
XX. MENSE IVLIO.

Figure 1. Title page border from Martin Luther, *Synceri Lucubrationum* (Basel: Adam Petri, 1520). Courtesy of Pitts Theology Library, Candler School of Theology, Emory University.

mat publications, 1523MelaD/00003002). As with the other Holbein design, symbols for the four New Testament gospels are in the corners, though they are presented in a different order (Matthew, John, Luke, and Mark). The two apostles are on the flanks (Peter on the left) with their respective symbols, and a seashell or scallop—the symbol of Christian baptism—is delicately worked into the background. While the biblical writers remain, the Church Fathers have dropped away, perhaps because of design priorities alone or to emphasize the biblical text, rather than its interpreters. The city arms of Basel are at the head with the motto INCLYTA BASILEA (Renown Basel), and the printer's device, featuring a putto riding a lion, is at the foot and dated 1523. All six biblical figures are given halos and have books (in the earlier Holbein woodcut, Peter and Paul were without books), two of which are closed. The two apostles hold their attributes in the left hand (as with the earlier woodcut) but the book in the right, and both concentrate intensely on their reading. Both design and printing of the title border are beautifully done, and while many of the same elements are retained from the earlier Holbein woodcut, the 1522 title border has been elegantly recast in order to introduce appropriately Luther's most important work, the translation of the Greek New Testament into German. The border continued to be used by Adam Petri and his son Heinrich for other works (Hollstein 1988, 14A: 69).

John Eck published sermons on the Ten Commandments, printed in folio at Ingolstadt by Georg Krapff in 1539, that used a bold design roughly similar to Holbein's earlier work (1539Eck/00005506). The symbols of the gospels are at the corners (John, Matthew, Mark, and Luke), and on the left are Peter and Saint Willibald (an eighth-century bishop of Eichstätt, Bavaria), and on the right are Paul and Pope Victor II (r. 1055–1057, from Bavaria), with the Madonna and Child at the base. The two apostles seem to be engaged in vigorous debate or are preaching (especially appropriate for a volume of sermons), and while neither has a book, Pope Victor and the symbols of the Gospels do. God as Pantokrator is at the head. While the import of the whole affirms the orthodoxy of Eck's sermons, it is unclear why Willibald and Victor II are included. The former died in Eichstätt, and the latter had been a candidate for the bishopric of Eichstätt, before becoming pope. Since the university at Ingolstadt, where Eck taught, was within the bishopric of Eichstätt, it may be that the Willibald and Victor II are shown on the title page to appeal to their ecclesial authority or prestige for Eck's sermons.

### *The story of scripture as context*

In 1543, Jean Driedo, professor at the University of Louvain, issued a volume on Scripture and tradition (1543Drie/00009515) that was introduced with an elaborate title border featuring a vision of the future reign of God and the saints at the head and eight other figures on the sides: Matthew, Mark, Gregory I, Augustine/Ambrose on the left, and Luke, John, Jerome, Augustine/Ambrose

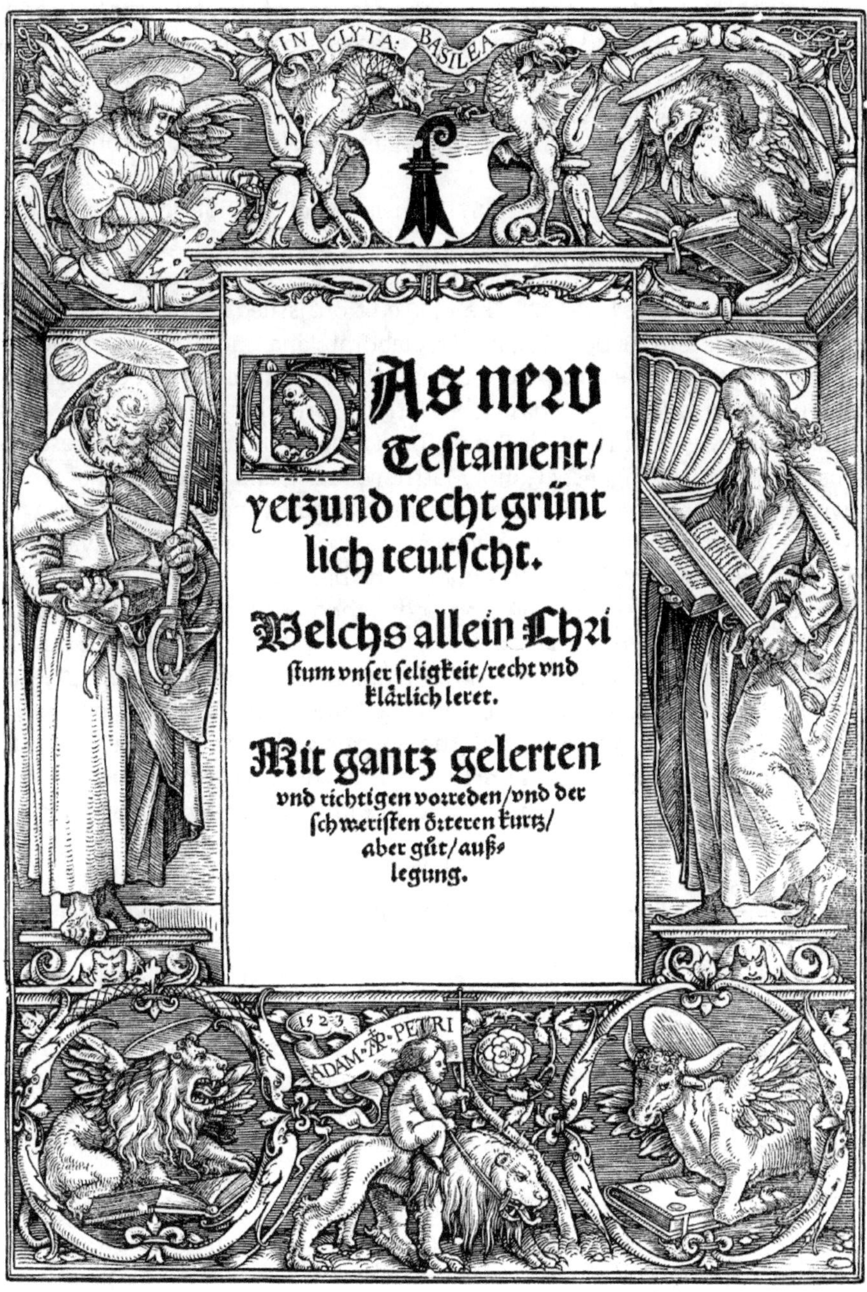


Figure 2. Title page border from the Basel *December Testament* (Basel: Adam Petri, 1522). Courtesy of Pitts Theology Library, Candler School of Theology, Emory University.

on the right. At the base is the scene of the creation of Eve. All eight figures on the sides have books, and the scene as a whole affirms the reign of God from the beginning of creation until its end and the instruction of God's messengers in between, including the current publication. The same border was used for the publication of the sermons of Polyganus (Cologne: Jaspar Von Gennep, 1564; 1564Poly/00001280).

Johann Dietenberger's (1475–1537) translation of the Bible into German was first issued in 1534 and went through fifty-eight editions to become the premiere Catholic Bible in the German language for two centuries (Brown 1996, 1: 484; Wedewer 1967, 147–197). The 1550 edition, issued at Cologne by Johann Quentel (1550BiblA/00001320), has an elaborate and finely detailed title border with several scenes from Scripture at the head (the Garden of Eden and the crucifixion of Jesus) and base (the Nativity, preaching of John the Baptist, baptism of Jesus, and the Last Supper), and along the edge are representations of the four Evangelists (John, Matthew, Mark, and Luke), each of whom is writing his gospel in a book. Neither the Evangelists nor the creatures with them have halos, but it appears that each creature is speaking to an Evangelist and so imparting revelation. The panel at the head distinguishes between the Old and New Testaments by showing God extend the Mosaic tablets toward a scene from the Garden of Eden on the left, but on the right God holds out the eucharistic elements to a scene of the crucifixion of Jesus and an image of Jesus' disciples bearing their own crosses, as they follow him. All that is below this panel concerns the story of Jesus in the Gospels and so affirms that Scripture is essentially the story of Jesus Christ and that those who composed the narratives about the life and teachings of Jesus did so under divine inspiration.

### *Summary*

In this sampling of title-page borders, books are often shown in the hands of the authors of biblical books (or, in the case of the Gospels, with their symbols) or in the hands of the Church Fathers or other ecclesial officials. The books serve as icons of biblical authorship and are part of the complex presentation of their inspiration. Furthermore, they serve as icons of orthodoxy and affirm that the books they introduce are congruent with the historic Christian faith and part of the larger framework of God's creative and redemptive work and instruction of humanity.

## Portraits of Biblical authors

It is relatively common in sixteenth-century illustrations to show the supposed authors of the New Testament with books. In the section that follows, the four Evangelists will be treated, as well as Peter, Paul, and various other figures from Scripture.

*The evangelist Matthew*

Matthew is regularly shown with a halo and seated at a desk, writing his gospel with an angel nearby. A book and the builder's square became his attributes in art (e.g., 1521CathA/00016284). In some instances the angel holds a book for Matthew to view as he writes his gospel (1515Bibl/00018449). Elsewhere, the angel holds an inkwell, suggesting divine assistance with the composition, (1521CathA/00016192) or makes the sign of blessing to indicate divine approval (1522Bibl1-2/00030250). The Basel *December Testament* also shows the angel with inkwell, and with his left index finger raised in instruction, he points to the nativity scene overhead, as Matthew looks intently at him and writes his gospel (1522BiblC/00010605). A variant of this arrangement in the first edition of the Dietenberger Bible shows Matthew seated on a stool near a desk, writing a book in his lap but looking over his shoulder at an angel, who instructs him, though turned half away (1534Bibl/00000472). As is the case elsewhere, when the writer is turned away from his writing surface, the divine aspect of the composition is clear. A 1558 Latin Bible from Lyon (1558BiblC/00011838) shows Matthew in typical fashion—writing his gospel at a desk with halo and angel nearby. In this case, though, other books are adjacent but are not being used by the Evangelist, and the angel is holding up the volume for Matthew's writing. The position of the book seems a bit awkward, but the arrangement may be intended to indicate divine agency in the composition, and perhaps the angel was even seen as dictating to Matthew. Virgil Solis (1514–1562) produced a similar arrangement, with the angel holding the book and more obviously speaking to Matthew, as the Holy Spirit appears overhead in the form of a dove and asserts even more clearly divine inspiration for the project (1560Soli/00004751; see below). Finally, Pierre Eskrich (ca. 1550—ca. 1590) shows Matthew reading one book with Greek script, another volume lies on the table, and an angel—with pen and inkwell in hand and his back to the apostle—looks toward the observer (1573BiblC/00008590), suggesting that the angel wrote or otherwise assisted Matthew in writing his gospel, and now Matthew admires the finished work.

In other illustrations, the Holy Spirit appears as a dove above Matthew in order to affirm inspiration. Though a book is not visible, the Wolrab illustrated edition of Luther's New Testament, printed at Leipzig in 1541 (1541BiblA1/00006709; cf. 1560Soli/00004751), despite Luther's protest, shows Matthew working at his desk with his writing tools nearby as well as other correspondence or documents. An angel stands at the table to further emphasize the divine nature of Matthew's composition. Also using the dove to represent the inspiration of the Holy Spirit is the woodcut by Hans Brosamer (his monogram and the date 1549 indicates the reuse of a much older block, (1562Bibl/00017315), which has a halo over both Matthew and the angel and shows several other books on the table before the Evangelist, who is hard at work writing. The setting for the scene is a patio and garden—such open air settings are not uncommon in depictions of the Evangelists (Hollstein n.d., 4: 231).

### *The evangelist Mark*

Mark sits at a writing desk in a study with his attribute the lion (both Mark and the lion have halos), and no other books or signs of inspiration are shown in this woodcut from the *September Testament* (1522Bibl1-2/00030251; similarly, though more crudely and without halo for the lion, is the woodcut in the third edition of Erasmus' Greek New Testament, (1522Bibl/00002051). The Zurich Bible shows other books on the shelves nearby (1536BiblV2/00000577), and the Dietenberger Bible portrays Mark similarly (though with the sun beaming as brightly outside as Mark's does inside) and what may be the figure Hercules lifting Antaeus off the ground to dominate him, engraved on the side of the desk (1534Bibl/00000471).

Other illustrations of Mark include additional books in his study. In the case of a Missal printed at Venice in 1521, Mark is shown with halo in his study with one additional book on the floor near his desk (1521CathA/00016230). The only hint of divine inspiration would be the halo. The book on the floor serves to characterize the Evangelist as a learned man, but its position suggests that Mark did not need a reference library to compose his gospel.

On occasion, there are clear indications of inspiration for Mark's work. In the Basel *December Testament*, for example, the Evangelist writes at a desk, and he draws for inspiration on a painting of the risen Christ (1522BiblC/00010608) but with no other books nearby, and in Wolrab's 1541 Leipzig edition of Luther's New Testament, Georg Lemberger shows the resurrected Christ with banner is in the clouds above, as Mark writes his gospel in the open air with a winged lion nearby (1541BiblA1/00005245). Finally, in several instances, the Holy Spirit appears in the form of a dove to assert the inspiration of the Evangelist. Michael Lotther's Low German edition of Luther's New Testament (Magdeburg, 1547) shows, for example, the dove outside the window of Mark's study and gives halo to neither the Evangelist nor his winged lion (1547BiblA/00000942).

### *The evangelist Luke*

Luke appears regularly with a book and often with additional volumes nearby (e.g., 1527BiblL/00014308; 1558BiblC/00011864; 1595Bibl/00009818). His attribute, the ox (sometimes winged), is always shown with him (1521CathA/00016174; 1591BiblA/00013979; 1570BiblD/00020275; cf. the open air setting, 1539Bibl/00006940), and on occasion he appears with an easel, indicating his role as the patron saint of the Guild of Saint Luke and of artists generally (1567BiblC/00016079). He is usually, though not always, shown with a halo, and on occasion his ox is given a halo as well. In terms of indications of inspiration, he is sometimes shown with a dove, a vision of the Madonna and Child, or the crucified Christ.

Luke appears in the *September Testament* and in the first edition of the Dietenberger Bible in a study, writing his gospel at a desk (1522Bibl1-2/00030252; 1534Bibl/00000470). The third edition of the Dietenberger Bible adds an easel with an image nearby (1550BiblA/00001383).

As for indications of inspiration, Virgil Solis shows Luke and his ox with halos and draws a vision of the crucified Christ out the window and the Holy Spirit as a dove, shedding light on the evangelist. Luke's easel and painting supplies are in the background (1560Soli/00004755). A similar image, but with the crucifixion scene, including Mary and John, occurs in the Basel *December Testament* (1522BiblC/00010606). A vision of the Madonna and Child, set in the clouds, serves a similar purpose in Wolrab's edition of Luther's New Testament, in which Luke works in his study (1541BiblA1/00005246).

*The evangelist John*

The Apostle John is usually shown writing a book and is cast as a young man with the eagle as his attribute. He typically wears a halo (often the eagle is given one, too) and is set in the open air, rather than in a study with additional books nearby. As is the case with the other Evangelists, the source of John's inspiration for his work varies. In two instances the eagle dictates what John writes (1522Bibl1-2/00030253; 1527BiblL/00014311), but in several others it is a vision of the Madonna and Child that guides him (1517Teus/00001621; *September Testament*, 1522Bibl1-2/00030257), perhaps resonating with the description of the sign of Revelation 12. On other occasions it is a vision of the Christ child (e.g., the Zurich Bible, 1536BiblV2/00000580) that inspires John, and in another the inspiration comes from the crucified Christ (1555Kete/00018025, where an attempt is made to summarize the Gospel). Often, though, it is the resurrected Christ who is shown with John: Adam Petri's *December Testament* (1522BiblC/00010609), Hans Brosamer's illustration for Lufft's 1562 Luther Bible (1562Bibl/00017318), and Virgil Solis' *Biblische Figuren* (1560Soli/00004764; cf. 1570BiblC/00002839). In the case of Solis' woodcut, even the eagle is shown with a halo, and John is shown at work with book and writing instruments. His posture of looking over his shoulder at the vision of Christ may suggest that his eyes did not even look at the page as he wrote.

*The apostle Peter*

The Apostle Peter, designated the first pope by the triple tiara that he wears, is shown with his most common attribute, the keys of the kingdom (cf. Matthew 16:19), and a book in his lap, as other clerics gather nearby with books as well (1531Eck/00009949). Seated at a table and writing, with writing instruments and other books on the table and a key on his belt, Peter appears in this detailed and beautifully executed woodcut (1541BiblA1/00005249). An illustration of Peter preaching to a congregation, with another saint standing behind him, was used to illustrate a third volume of sermons by John Eck (1531Eck/00009962).

*The apostle Paul*

The Apostle Paul is regularly shown with halo and sword, and sometimes with one or more books, as well (e.g., 1560Soli/00004767). Rarely is the Holy Spirit in the form of a dove with him (1530BiblC/00004953), and only one image shows the suffering Christ above him (1550BiblB/00008973).

There is particular interest in the process by which Paul composed and sent his letters. For example, he is often shown with halo and one or two swords (his attribute) and writing (1534Bibl/00000452) or reading (1549FlacA/00001012) at a desk. The Zurich Bible shows Paul in chains and dictating a letter to his amanuensis, and both men have books on their desks (1536BiblV2/00000581). A favorite scene, though, is Paul sending or receiving letters via messengers: perhaps receiving a letter from Phoebe (1528Mela/00003631), a letter for the church at Rome (1560Soli/00004767), and two scenes in which messengers first wait for Paul to complete his letter and then are dispatched with it (1567BiblC/00016085 and 1567BiblC/00016086; on this generally, see e.g., 1555Geor1-2/00015499 and Virgil Solis, 1560Soli/00004768).

When Paul is shown writing, he is typically at a table (without halo or sword; placement in this Bible suggests that it is a letter to Timothy: 1547BiblA/00000939), and it is not uncommon for other books to be on the table or floor. On occasion, Paul's writing is connected with his preaching: in the 1547 Froschauer printing of Erasmus' Latin translation of the Greek New Testament, a woodcut by Heinrich Vogtherr the Elder (1547BiblB/00007672) sets forth the sequence of Paul's work. First, Paul proclaimed the Christian faith to audiences, as he traveled from city to city (background; note that he uses no book for his preaching), but later he wrote them letters to confirm them in the faith (foreground). An image that would resonate more effectively with sixteenth-century audiences, though, shows Paul holding a book and gesturing, as he preached to a church from the pulpit (initial letter P, 1524Brun/00009199; cf. 1532Caje/00007885).

Paul is also shown with or engaging other notable figures, such as Peter (1521CathA/00016268) or the other apostles (1523Zwin/00003074).

*Miscellaneous figures*

A complex scene of vignettes from the life of King Solomon (1527BiblL/00014275) includes one of him writing in a book at a desk, with several more books on the shelf above, and another of Solomon asleep on his bed. While there are not the customary indications of divine inspiration, it may be that the woodcut alludes to the time that God came to Solomon in a dream at Gibeon (1 Kings 3:4–15), promising him wisdom and great wealth. Consequently, Scripture praises Solomon's wisdom and tradition credits him with the authorship of Proverbs, Ecclesiastes, and the Song of Songs.

The first edition of the Dietenberger Bible shows Amos delivering his prophecies to a gathering indoors, reading from a book (1534Bibl/00000447). The head-coverings are similar to those described for Jews from the Middle Ages (see Palomino 2011), and it may be that the scene is influenced by synagogue practices in Germany during the sixteenth century. Amos' use of the book may well have been understood as the proclamation of his own prophecies to the congregation, since these words became part of the Jewish and Christian scriptures. Books also appear with Zephaniah (1560Soli/00004742), James the Greater (the son of Zebedee; 1541BiblA1/00005250), and Saint Jude (1573BiblC/00008721).

### *Summary*

In portraits of biblical authors, books also appear as icons of authorship and learning (Amos, the Evangelists, Peter, and Paul) and part of a larger presentation of the claim to inspiration for the earliest Christian authors (especially, the Evangelists). In addition, the books serve to relate the figures with whom they appear to the practices of Jewish prophesy (Amos) or Christian preaching and teaching and with the nurture of Christian churches by means of epistles (Peter and Paul).

## Biblical texts or figures

The third section of this survey assembles illustrations of various stories from Scripture in which books are shown. In most cases, the book has some sort of iconic value. From the Hebrew Bible are taken one story about Job and two about Jeremiah, and from the New Testament are six episodes from the life of Jesus (in five sections, since Jesus' circumcision and presentation in the temple are both described in Luke 2), an examination of John the Baptist, and one story from the book of Acts. The illustrations of other biblical stories, in which a book is present only to show what the narrative describes, have been omitted.

### *Job intercedes for his friends*

Most sixteenth-century illustrations of the book of Job in the Digital Image Archive show either the patriarch's afflictions or his questioning by God. Lufft's 1562 folio Bible, though, offers an illustration by Hans Brosamer of Job 42, in which the Job appears with an open book at a desk (1562Bibl/00017286). His three friends—Eliphaz, Bildad, and Zophar—have obeyed God's command to offer sacrifices for not speaking the truth about God (vv. 7-9; background), and now they kneel before Job, who prays for their forgiveness. While the book before Job may illustrate his piety (Job 1:1), perhaps it suggests that Job recorded his experiences for posterity (see also Job 19:23).

### *Jeremiah's call*

With Jerusalem in the background, God calls Jeremiah to become a prophet to the people of Judah (1560Soli/00004726). The yoke on his neck and the chain on the ground before him may anticipate his conflict with the priest Passhur, who put him in stocks for a time (Jer. 20:1). The book on the ground before him, though, suggests his role as author of the book of Jeremiah (cf. Jer. 25:13; 30:2; 45:1; 51:60, 63).

### *The burning of Jeremiah's scroll*

Jeremiah 36:23 reports that as Jehudi read from the scroll of Jeremiah's words, King Jehoiakim cut strips of text from the scroll and threw them into the brazier nearby. A very different picture of this emerges from three woodcuts of the scene (the Dietenberger Bible, first edition, 1534Bibl/00000465; the Zurich Bible, 1536BiblV2/00000560; the Dietenberger Bible, third edition, 1550BiblA/00001372): (1) King Jehoiakim sits on his throne and presides over the destruction of Jeremiah's prophecies but does not destroy the text himself; (2) one of the king's servants holds the book (not a scroll) of Jeremiah's words (the Zurich Bible shows the servant with a knife); and (3) this servant throws another volume into the fire. So, while the basic point—King Jehoiakim destroyed the record of the Jeremiah's prophecies—was presented in all three illustrations, the details were mangled. The book does not primarily appear as an icon in these images but as part of a representation of an ancient narrative, updated for a sixteenth-century audience. (It may also well be that the artists could not envision the king himself doing the lowly work of destroying the pages and so transferred this task to the royal servants.) Nevertheless, in both text and image, the scroll/book represents the divine message, and so its destruction is symbolic of a larger evil: disregard for God.

### *The Annunciation*

With few exceptions, the illustrations of the Annunciation (Luke 1:26-38) show Mary with a halo and a book in hand (e.g., Virgil Solis' *Biblische Figuren*, 1560Soli/00004757) or on a reading desk before her (e.g., Lucas Cranach the Elder's illustration in the Lutheran version of an historic prayer book, *Hortulus animae*, 1550Hort/00001065; Hollstein n.d., 6:38). Her hands are often clasped in prayer, and she typically kneels before a reading table, apparently in her bedchamber in some of the images (1560Soli/00004757). The angel Gabriel approaches Mary, sometimes making the sign of blessing (1550Hort/00001065), occasionally carrying a scepter (e.g., the 1563 Low German translation of Luther's church postils, 1563LuthB/00001222) or a lily (1560Soli/00004757). Writing may be shown in the book, but it is not clear whether Mary is reading Scripture or a devotional work. Michael Helding's 1552 Catholic catechism shows other books in the lower shelf of the reading desk (1552Held/00007193), and the 1563 Low German edition of Luther's postils show them on a shelf above her. The figure of Mary engaged in such devotional reading surely connected well with a sixteenth-century audience accustomed to the image of a woman of high standing using a work such as the Book of Hours for daily devotions, which celebrated the virtues of Mary and her role in bearing Christ. The Holy Spirit is often shown in the images as a dove (e.g., 1560Soli/00004757), providing an obvious connection with v. 35, and, in one woodcut, God may be seen out the window, having sent the Spirit (1563LuthB/00001222). Therefore, Mary's devotional book seems to serve as an icon of piety, and the others in the room may attest the learning and social status of the household.

### *Jesus' circumcision and presentation in the temple*

Jesus' circumcision and presentation in the Jerusalem temple are both reported in Luke 2 and are favorite subjects for sixteenth-century Bible illustrators. The Digital Image Archive includes twenty-seven examples of the former and thirty of the latter.

Luke's description of Jesus' circumcision is brief, and the reader may be left to assume that it occurred in the town of his birth, Bethlehem (v. 21). The 1516 Basel *Plenarium* (1516Cath/00001524) depicts the circumcision with Mary and Joseph standing nearby (left) along with four other figures, one of whom is holding a large book, apparently in the role of a functionary. Often the circumcision is depicted in grand surroundings, perhaps suggesting that the rite occurred in the Jerusalem temple or in an ornate synagogue (1549LuthG/00017131), and in one instance another figure with a book in hand walks by (establishing the precincts as a place of learning or devotion) but is not part of the circumcision ceremony (1550LuthE1/00011164). The presence of a bowl for the circumcision ceremony in some illustrations (1531Eck/00009944; the child standing in the basin, 1559BrenA/00014809; the child being held over the basin, 1560Soli/00004759) offers a certain parallel to the Christian baptismal font, shown in many images of sixteenth-century Christian ritual (1560BiblA1/00015080). The Christian baptismal images often show the family of the newborn (father, godparents, and others) gathered about the baptismal font, with attendants standing nearby and holding the baptismal liturgy for the priest or pastor, who baptizes the child (1560BiblA1/00015080). Rendering the circumcision of Jesus in ways that brought to mind Christian baptism would have supported Christian theological efforts to explain the significance of baptism by means of the earlier Jewish rite of circumcision.

As for the presentation of the infant Jesus in the Jerusalem temple, fulfilling the requirement of Exodus 13:2 for the firstborn, the volume of Luther's sermons on the New Testament Epistles and Gospels, printed by M. Lotter at Wittenberg in 1540 (1540LuthF/00009918), shows the event with Mary kneeling with a cage containing two birds for her purification (Luke 2:22-24), the offering of the poor (Lev. 12:8), and Joseph standing behind her. The righteous Simeon holds the infant Jesus (left; v. 28) and the prophetess Anna stands nearby with her hands folded in a prayer of thanksgiving to God (vv. 36-38). Two attendants are also present, a woman with a torch (perhaps connecting with v. 32) and a man reading from a large book (similar renderings may be found in 1550LuthE1/00011135 and elsewhere). In other representations of the event, an attendant with a book is not always present, and sometimes only Mary, Joseph, and a priest are shown (cf., 1531Eck/00009948). Hence, it may well be that those woodcuts showing the presentation of Jesus at the temple, in which an attendant with a book is included, were also influenced by sixteenth-century Christian practices, especially that of infant baptism.

Therefore, does the book appear in these depictions of the circumcision of Jesus and his presentation in the temple because the artist assumed that a book of ritual would have been used, or have the artists simply composed the scenes on the basis of what they observed in a more accessible ritual, Christian baptism? In addition, does the artist intend a theological point: to relate the Christian's experience in baptism with Jesus' own experience and with the traditional Jewish practice of circumcision, thus inviting the Christian reader to consider the significance of such connections?

### *John the Baptist*

John the Baptist appears in stylized fashion in the *Plenarium* (1516 Cath/00001496), where he holds a book with his left hand on which rests the resurrection lamb with its banner, and with his right hand he points to the lamb, thus embodying John 1:29, 36, "Behold, the Lamb of God, who takes away the sin of the world! ... Behold, the Lamb of God!" This comprehensive image proclaims both the sacrifice and the resurrection victory.

In the Lutheran prayer book, *Hortulus animae*, printed by Georg Rhaw at Wittenberg (1550Hort/00001071), John also appears in stylized manner, but he is not pointing to the lamb (which is also not the resurrection lamb). Instead, he poses as one who presents the lamb, as to an audience. The role of the book in these two images (1516Cath/00001496 and 1550Hort/00001071) may derive from John's quotation of Scripture in support of his message, and the placement of the lamb on the book may assert a claim: the message of John—that Jesus is the Lamb of God, who takes away the sin of the world—is based on the witness of Scripture itself: Isa. 40:3; Mal. 3:1; cf. also Matt. 3:3; Mark 1:1-3; John 1:23.

Two images show John the Baptist baptizing Jesus in the Jordan River. The 1563 printing of Luther's postils 3 (1563LuthB/00001218) shows a book on the river bank beside John. Since John the Baptist is not credited with writing a book, and Scripture does not mention him using a book, it may be that the artist has placed it in the scene to underscore John's use of Scripture to validate his ministry and message (see above). The second image

(1550LuthE1/00011129) shows John baptizing those who responded to his call for repentance (John 1) and responding to priests and Levites, who were sent by "the Jews of Jerusalem" to question him about whether he was the Christ, Elijah (Mal. 4:5–6) or the prophet (Deut. 18:15–18). These questions suggest their own expectations, based on Scripture. Just as the religious authorities bring books with them, John himself has a book on the bank of the Jordan River. John's book symbolizes the authority of his message in Scripture—and the view that his message and the one he announced were the fulfillment of the prophecies of Isaiah and Malachi. The books brought out by the priests and Levites of Jerusalem (Pharisees and Sadducees, according to Matthew 3:7, which reports his condemnation of them but nothing of their challenges to him) indicate their roles as interpreters of the Jewish Law and religion.

Therefore, in these four images, the book affirms that John's message is rooted in the Jewish Scriptures and so lends him authority before his audiences, and it serves to identify his Jewish opponents as experts in the Jewish Law and representatives of the Jewish religious authorities.

*Jesus and the teachers of the law*

While the Gospel of Luke reports that Jesus listened to the teachers in the temple and asked them questions and that the teachers were astonished at his answers (Luke 2:46-47), the woodcuts typically place Jesus in a position where he is elevated above the Jewish teachers and is preaching to or lecturing them. These scenes of Jesus' dominant role in the exchange with the Jewish teachers anticipate "his future role as teacher of Israel" (Schreckenberg 1996, 21-22). Usually Jesus sits at a desk (1530Luth/00009766, 1540LuthF/00009920), perhaps on the basis of statements in Scripture about Jewish teaching in synagogue (Luke 4:20) or what was known from sixteenth-century Jewish practice. These images are often reminiscent of woodcuts that show Christian preaching or worship services (Catholic and Protestant), with some concession made to the sitting position of the Jewish teacher (e.g., 1543LuthD/00000891). Several of these woodcuts show Jesus in the role of the Christian preacher, standing behind a pulpit and instructing the congregation, which sat around him in dutiful fashion (1569Kirc/00009555; sitting behind a pulpit, 1543LuthD/00000870). On occasion, though, Jesus sits on a throne, reminiscent of ecclesial authority (1556Feru/00005497). Alternatively, the setting may be reminiscent of the university in which Jesus assumes the role of the professor (Schreckenberg 1996, 197-211).

Mary and Joseph typically are shown in the back or at the borders, entering the temple space, their hands sometimes in pious gesture (1530Luth/00009766). As for the Jewish teachers, they are often shown with their heads covered and wearing a variety of hats characteristic of Jews (sometimes wearing turbans, reminiscent of Maimonides; see 1569Kirc/00009555, 1591Bibl/00014370; and on occasion the headdress of a priest, cf. 1530Luth/00009766). The teachers are usually paying attention to Jesus, perhaps even making a sign of blessing toward him (1563LuthB/00001161), but often they are engaged in conversation with one another (e.g., 1563LuthB/00001161), taking notes or using a pointer/yad (1540LuthF/00009920), reading and turning the pages in their books—in one instance, a figure sits with his back to Jesus (1591Bibl/00014370).

Jesus is usually shown with a book (unmentioned in Luke), and usually one or more of the Jewish teachers have books. Sometimes the artist has attempted to show Hebrew script in the book (1563LuthB/00001161), and occasionally books are shown scattered around on the floor (1543LuthD/00000870), unlikely in synagogues of ancient or modern times. While this reflects ignorance of Jewish practice, the illustrator may have been merely intending to show the temple as a center for scholarship. When the Jewish teachers have their books closed, are we to interpret this as a sign of their opposition to Jesus (minds as closed as their books?) or does it show such fascination and admiration for Jesus that they are totally absorbed in his words?

### *Mary and Martha receive Jesus*

Illustrations of the story about Mary and Martha receiving Jesus into their home (Luke 10:38-42) typically show Mary sitting near Jesus but do not include a book. In Andreas Osiander's harmony of the Gospels (Antwerp: M. Crommium, 1540), though, Mary is shown sitting at Jesus' feet, her hands folded and a book on her lap, and listening to his teaching, while her sister Martha is busily serving guests (1540Osia/00000788). Here, the book seems to symbolize Mary's piety and devotion to Jesus' teaching and functions as a foil to the household instrument in her sister's hand.

### *Garden of Gethsemane*

One woodcut illustrating Jesus in the Garden of Gethsemane before his arrest (Matthew 26; Mark 14; Luke 22 [Mount of Olives]; John 18) includes a book (1573BiblC/00008617). Designed by Pierre Eskrich and used in the Louvaine Bible, it shows the apostle John fast asleep with his head on a book while Jesus prays. Jesus and Peter (with his sword; cf. John 18:10) are clearly identifiable. James, the son of Zebedee, and John are left, and so perhaps the book and the youthful face were to identify John. Nevertheless, the role of the book in the image remains uncertain.

### *Pentecost*

Early Christian iconography showed Mary present at Pentecost, and she came to be regarded as the teacher of the Apostles (cf. Acts 1:14; Herbermann, 1913). Consequently, many of the sixteenth-century woodcuts—Protestant (1543LuthD/00000887, 1544LuthI/00007119) and Catholic (1532EckB/00015472) alike—show the Apostles at Pentecost gathered around Mary, who sits before them with an open book in her lap (see also, Verdon

2005, 169.). This image has obvious connections with the way that Mary is portrayed in scenes of the Annunciation, where she has a book and the Holy Spirit in the form of a dove descends upon her.

The second edition of Luther's *Large Catechism* illustrates the preaching of the Apostles at Pentecost, showing the Holy Spirit in the form of a dove (Acts 2:2), flames of fire from the mouths of the Apostles (Acts 2:3), and two books in their hands (1531LuthE/00007309). The figure at left center with the open book is Peter (the other man with a book is unidentifiable), since Peter is the leading figure at the occasion (his sermon is reported in Acts 2:14-40). Therefore, it is possible that the artist achieved three things by including books in the image. First, he illustrated Peter's reliance on the Jewish Bible for his sermon (Acts 2:34–35 cites Ps. 110:1) by showing him with an open book in his hands. Second, the image resonates with what many German Protestant Christians would have seen and expected in preaching—the use of a book (whether it was a Bible or a volume of Luther's postils). Finally, the image conveys the value that German Lutherans placed on the Scriptures and their respect for its use in Christian preaching and teaching, something asserted in many ways in Luther's *Large Catechism*.

### *Summary*

In the case of images incorporating books that illustrate various biblical stories, the books appear to serve as icons of biblical authorship (Job and Jeremiah), learning and piety (Mary the mother of Jesus and Mary, the sister of Martha and Lazarus, and the Jewish doctors of the Law whom the youthful Jesus engaged in the temple; impiety in the case of Jehoiakim), reliance on Scripture for preaching and instruction (John the Baptist and Peter at Pentecost), as well as serving to contemporize the biblical stories (Jesus and Peter at Pentecost) and suggest a Christological interpretation of them (Jesus' circumcision and presentation in the temple as precursors or analogies to Christian baptism).

## Conclusions

A primary iconic function of books in sixteenth-century Bible illustration is to indicate authorship of biblical works. The artists place books in the hands of those whom tradition credited with writing the biblical books. Sometimes, the figures are actually shown writing in books, but on other occasions the men are simply shown holding the products of their labor. The books are drawn so that they reflect publishing and binding practices of the sixteenth century, rather than of antiquity when the works would have been written. The same artistic conventions are followed as are found in many other aspects of art from this period, whether with respect to dress, architecture, or other areas of human culture. The interest was not to engage in critical analysis of tradition (did Matthew or Job really write the works attributed to them?) or show things as they actually appeared a millennium and a half before, but to identify figures (just as attributes such as the Pauline sword, Petrine key, etc.) and honor them for their roles as conduits of divine revelation and instruction of the people of God. It is in this connection, as well, that the artists also made use of other elements (the Holy Spirit as a dove, visions of the Madonna and Child, visions of the resurrected Christ, etc.) to affirm that God through various means inspired the authors and so blessed their literary creations. In addition, those who designed the title-page borders used images of books iconically to assert the orthodoxy of the works that they introduced and affirm that these works were congruent with the historic Christian faith. On occasion, the artists went beyond this to suggest that the authors of the Bible and certain sixteenth-century books were part of the larger creative and redemptive plan of God and so served to instruct and enlighten all humanity.

A second and more general iconic function of books in these illustrations was to elevate those writers, saints, and other figures from antiquity, who were shown holding books or having them nearby, as people of learning, piety, and social standing. At a time when most people were illiterate, ill-informed on religious matters, and living in poverty, these figures from antiquity were shown as literate, devoted to learning and to the service of God, and as people of substance and standing among their peers. Even in the case of those who were cast as the opponents of John the Baptist or Jesus, books were placed in their hands to show them as learned men who led their religious institutions. Consequently, when King Jehoiachim is shown destroying the books produced by Jeremiah, he is shown as impious and resistant to the redemptive work of God.

A third iconic function that books served in these illustrations was to contend that the message and ministries of those drawn with them were based on Scripture. This was most notably the case with John the Baptist and with Peter at Pentecost. The Gospels and the book of Acts report that the preaching of both of these men drew on the Jewish scriptures, and in so doing John and Peter based their appeals on books inspired by God. Even more dramatically, the image of John the Baptist with the lamb resting on a book seems to assert that Christian claims about the identity of Jesus are founded upon the Jewish scriptures.

Finally, images of books serve to link antiquity with the Early Modern period. On some occasions, for example, books relate the figures with whom they appear to the religious practices of ancient Israel or the Christian church. In the case of Amos, the book suggests how a prophet discharged his office, and in the cases of Peter and Paul, the illustrations show how they preached, engaged in public teaching, composed their epistles, and communicated with churches far removed. Similarly, books are used to contemporize biblical stories and otherwise clothe ancient figures in the garb of the sixteenth century and so facilitate the effort to make them resonate with the experience of those who would view these woodcuts and engravings. Related to this is the way that books were used by illustrators as part of the effort to support Christian theology and a Christological interpretation of the Hebrew Bible. Jesus' circumcision and presentation in the temple were offered as precursors or analogies to Christian baptism and the entrance into the new covenant with God. All this, of course, is less iconic than illustrative.

## References


Bartrum, Giulia, 2006. *Virgil Solis, Book Illustrations, Part 1.* In *The New Hollstein. German Engravings, Etchings and Woodcuts, 1400–1700.* Compiled by Dieter Beaujean. Ouderkerk Aan den Ijssel: Sound & Vision.

Brown, Karin Brinkman. 1996. "Dietenberger, Johann." In *The Oxford Encyclopedia of the Reformation*, 1: 484–485. New York: Oxford University Press.

Cochlaeus, Johannes. 1529. *Septiceps Lutherus.* Leipzig: Valentin Schumann.

Cole, Richard G. 1984. "Reformation Printers: Unsung Heroes." *The Sixteenth Century Journal* 15: 337–339. http://dx.doi.org/10.2307/2540767

Cross, F. L. and Elizabeth A. Livingstone, eds. 2005. "Gregory I., St." In *The Oxford Dictionary of the Christian Church*, 3rd ed., rev., 710–711. Oxford: Oxford University Press.

Harthan, John P. 1981. *The History of the Illustrated Book: The Western Tradition.* New York: Thames and Hudson.

Hendrix, Scott. 2004. *Recultivating the Vineyard.* Louisville, KY: Westminster John Knox.

Herbermann, Charles George and Edward A. Pace, eds. 1913. "The Blessed Virgin Mary." In *Catholic Encyclopedia.* New York: Encyclopedia Press. http://www.newadvent.org/cathen/15464b.htm (accessed 7 February 2011).

Hieronymus, Frank. 1984. *Basler Buchillustration 1500-1545.* Universitätsbibliothek Basel, 31. Oberrheinische Buchillustration, 2. Basel: Universitätsbibliothek.

Hollstein, F. W. H. n.d. *German Engravings, Etchings and Woodcuts: 1400–1700*, vol. 6. Amsterdam: Menno Hertzberger.

———. 1988. *German Engravings, Etchings and Woodcuts: 1400–1700*, edited by Tilman Falk and compiled by Robert Zijlma, vols. 14–14A. Roosendaal: Koninklijke Van Poll.

Hornik, Heidi J. 2003. *The Infancy Narrative in Italian Renaissance Painting*, vol. 1 of *Illuminating Luke*, 3 volumes. Harrisburg, PA: Trinity Press International.

Iconic Book Symposium. 2010. http://jameswwatts.net/iconicbooks/IB%20About.htm (accessed 11 September 2010).

Keen, Ralph. 1996. "Cochlaeus, Johannes." In *Oxford Encyclopedia of the Reformation*, 1: 369–371. New York: Oxford University Press.

Landesmann, Peter. 2010. *Die Darstellung "der zwölfjährige Jesus unter den Schriftgelehrten" im Wandel der Zeiten.* Biblical Interpretation Series, 101. Boston, MA: Brill.

Marty, Martin. 2004. *Martin Luther.* Penguin Life. New York: Penguin.

Melanchthon, Philipp. 1528. *Underricht Philip Melanchthon Wider die here der Wiederteuffer*. Hagenau: Johann Setzer.

Melion, Walter S. 2009. "Bible Illustration in the Sixteenth-Century Low Countries." In *Scripture for the Eyes: Bible Illustration in Netherlandish Prints of the Sixteenth Century*, edited by James Clifton and Walter S. Melion, 14–106. New York: Museum of Biblical Art.

Moore, Walter L. 1996. "Eck, Johann." In *Oxford Encyclopedia of the Reformation*, 2: 17–19. York: Oxford University Press.

Palomino, Michael. 2011. *History in Chronology*. http://www.geschichteinchronologie.ch/MA/judentum-EncJud_judenfleck-u-judenhut-im-MA-ENGL.html (accessed 7 February 2011).

Raimundi, Giovanni Battista, ed. 1591. *Evangelium sanctum Domini Nostri Iesu Christi conscriptum a quatuor Evangelistis sanctis id est, Matthaeo, Marco, Luca, et Iohanne*. Rome: Typographia Medicea.

Schöner, Petra. 2006. "Visual Representations of Jews and Judaism in Sixteenth-Century Germany." In *Jews, Judaism, and the Reformation in Sixteenth-Century Germany*, Studies in Central European Histories 37, edited by Dean Phillip Bell and Stephen G. Burnett, 357–391. Leiden: Brill.

Schreckenberg, Heinz. 1996. *The Jews in Christian Art: An Illustrated History*, translated by John Bowden. London: SCM Press. Originally published as *Die Juden in der Kunst Europas: Ein Bildatlas*. Göttingen: Vandenhoeck & Ruprecht, 1996.

Solis, Virgil. 1560. *Biblische Figuren des Alten vnd Newen Testaments*. Franckfurt am Main: David Zephelium, Johan Raschen, and Sigmund Feyerabent.

Strand, Kenneth A. 1982. *Catholic German Bibles of the Reformation Era*. Naples, FL: Ann Arbor Publishers.

String, Tatiana C. 2000. "Politics and Polemics in English and German Bible Illustrations." In *The Bible as Book: The Reformation*, edited by Orlaith O'Sullivan, 137–143. London: The British Library; New Castle, DE: Oak Knoll Press.

Tribb, Jonathan D. 1994. *Baptism in the Theology of Martin Luther*, Studies in the History of Christian Thought 56. Leiden: Brill.

Verdon, Timothy. 2005. *Mary in Western Art*. New York: Hudson Mills Press.

Von Ubisch, E. 1889. *Virgil Solis und seine biblischen Illustrationen für den Holzschnitt*. Leipzig: Ramm & Seemann.

Wedewer, Hermann. 1988. *Johannes Dietenberger, 1475–1537: Sein Leben und Wirken*. Freiburg im Breisgau: Herdersch Verlagshandlung. First printed, Nieuwkoop: B. de Graaf, 1967.

Wendland, Henning. 1984. *Signete: Deutsche Drucker- und Verlegerzeichen, 1457–1600*. Hannover: Schlüterschen Verlagsanstalt.

# III

# Materials and Markets

# 10

# *Muṣḥaf* and the Material Boundaries of the Qur'an

Natalia K. Suit

Muṣḥaf *is what Muslims call the physical body of the Qur'an, its pages, binding, and print. Scholars traditionally focused on the textual analysis of the Qur'an as theological, political, historical or literary productions, favoring a semantic dimension of the text and detaching it from its materiality. In this paper, I propose to shift our attention from the understanding of the Qur'an exclusively as message to its material existence as* muṣḥaf *in the hands of its manufacturers and users in order to highlight the process through which the status of the Qur'an as a sacred message is negotiated.*

## Introduction

One day in 1997 when I was living in Cairo, Egypt, I went to a bookstore that had a richly decorated Qur'an on display in the shop window. I intended to take pictures of its front page as a representation of a particular style of Arabic calligraphy. The place was crammed with books. I wanted to photograph the page against a white background, so I laid a big white plastic case on the floor. On that case I placed the Qur'an. Three men and a woman, who were shopping, became interested in what I was doing and came closer to take a look. When they realized that it was the Qur'an that was lying on the case on the floor, they objected. The woman asked the shop assistant to lift the Qur'an off the floor and hold it up in his hands so that I could continue photographing its pages.

This paper is about the physical body of the Qur'an—the paper, binding, and print which the Muslims call the *muṣḥaf* (pronounced mus-haf with the "s" and "h" as two separate consonants). Drawing on my field notes from Cairo from 1996–2001, I will show what spheres of religious practice become visible when we do not separate the materiality of the text from its message. I will also demonstrate that textual materiality is important to the way Egyptian Muslims understand the Qur'an. This materiality is mostly overlooked in Western accounts of Islam. Scholars of Islam have traditionally focused on the textual analysis of the Qur'an as a theological, political, historical, or literary production, favoring a purely semantic definition of the text that detaches it from its materiality. But a shift of attention from the understanding of the Qur'an exclusively as message to its material existence as a *muṣḥaf* in the hands of its manufacturers and users will highlight the process through which the Qur'an as a message is constantly negotiated. In other words, the meaning of the Qur'an is not situated only in its inspired content but is inexorably generated by its materiality. Of course, foregrounding the *muṣḥaf* does not involve an elision of the Qur'an because the message is indivisible from its material form. My intention is to deepen understanding of the Qur'an by multiplying the dimensions in which its influence extends. What follows, then, is a preliminary account of some of the issues raised by the existence of the Qur'an not only as a text but also as a material object, or *muṣḥaf.*

## Discursive tradition

The reaction of my fellow shoppers in the ethnographic vignette above was not idiosyncratic, but rather was indicative of a wider concern shared by many Egyptian Muslims about how to treat the Qur'an as a material object. But the preoccupation with the ways in which a *muṣḥaf* should be handled is not unique to Muslims in Egypt. It is a part of an Islamic tradition that, as Talal Asad points out, "consists of discourses that seek to instruct practitioners regarding the correct form and purpose of a given practice" (1986, 14). Asad calls a given dialogue with a foundational text a "discursive tradition" and defines it as a relationship to a body of knowledge with which Muslims engage and through which they actively shape their present. The texts on which religious reasoning is based, apart from the Qur'an itself, include compilations of the words and deeds of the Prophet Muhammad (*ḥadīth*) assembled by Muslim scholars in order to direct the comportment of all members of the *ummah* (Muslim community). Collections of *aḥādīth* (plural of *ḥadīth*), such as *Ṣaḥīḥ al-Bukhārī* by the Persian Muhammad ibn Ismail al-Bukhari (810–870), *Ṣaḥīḥ Muslim* also by the Persian Muslim ibn al-Hajjaj (817–874), or more recently the work on Islamic law *Fiqh al-Sunnah* compiled by the Egyptian scholar Sayyid Sabiq (1915–2000), are continually consulted, interpreted, and debated in the process of evaluation and validation of contemporary practices and ideas. Among the numerous regulations of various aspects of daily life, they include instructions on the proper handling and protection of the holy text. Many of my friends referred to specific *aḥādīth* while commenting on particular uses of a copy of the Qur'an. Their palpable concern about the right handling of the object and common references to the written sources suggest a gap in Western understanding of the Qur'an: in Islam the Qur'anic text and its materiality have not been epistemologically separate. For many Muslims the materiality of the Qur'an is a matter of concern in daily practice, the most well known instance being the necessity to perform ablutions before touching a *muṣḥaf.*

The problem of the materiality of the holy word can be linked to some doctrinal debates in early Islam, so a brief summary of them is important for understanding the relationship between the text of the Qur'an and its carrier. Disputes over the theological status of the Qur'an have been a part of a long tradition of Islamic thought (Corbin 1993). The most consequential of these debates (lasting almost five hundred years), reaches back to the eighth century when members of the religious Mu'tazili school (with strongholds in Basra and Baghdad), in response to the Christian doctrine of the incarnate Word and out of an imperative to emphasize God's oneness, argued that the Qur'an was not coeternal with God. Instead, they claimed, it was created as a message to be revealed to humans. Their argument was eventually opposed by those who maintained that the Qur'an was uncreated and was one of God's eternal attributes, which suggested that God spoke in the very words of the Qur'an. This position, accepted nowadays in Sunni Islam, means that the text of the Qur'an is the literal word of God given to humanity in the form of a book. As a result, among Sunnis there is an ontological distinction between the word of God (the Qur'an) as the message that is to be read or recited and the medium through which the message is transmitted (the *muṣḥaf*). Etymologically, the word Qur'an comes from the root *qaraā'*, which means to read or recite. The difference between reading and reciting the Qur'an is rather blurred and points to its primarily aural character. The word *muṣḥaf* is related to the word *ṣuḥuf* and means pages that "contain" the Qur'an. This distinction between Qur'an and the *muṣḥaf* theoretically delineates the boundaries between the divinely originated message and the "earthiness" of the object that fixes it materially. Because of the doctrine of the Qur'an's eternal co-presence with God, however, this situation creates a practical dilemma: how should a Muslim treat the object in a way that would emphasize the uniqueness of what it contains without attributing to the object the divine status of its content?

This question became especially relevant with changes in the way *maṣāḥif* (plural of *muṣḥaf*) were produced. Over a century ago, the introduction of mechanical printing challenged the stable relationship between the inspired word, its graphical materiality, and the status of the artisan in its production. In 1833 the director of the Egyptian press which released the first printed parts of the Qur'an had to address the concerns of religious authorities. It was hoped that the emergent mass medium of print would make it easier to duplicate *maṣāḥif*, but scholars viewed the press as a dubious innovation. They disliked the use of metal letters to apply pressure in printing the name of God, and protested the industrial environment of the printing house as being far from a state of purity required in preparing the text (Albin 2001, 270). There were further concerns and questions regarding the materiality of the printing process, for example whether any elements of the production process made use of the skin of dogs (dogs appear as ritually unclean animals in several *aḥādīth*).

How should we interpret the apprehension of the religious authorities about the way in which the text of the Qur'an was produced? Historian Roger Chartier insists that the production, circulation, and use of texts are spaces in which the construction of their meaning takes place:

> The space between text and object, which is precisely the space in which meaning is constructed, has too often been forgotten, not only by the traditional sort of literary history that thinks of the work as an abstract text whose typographic forms are without importance, but also by the "aesthetic of reception" that, in spite of its desire to historicize the reader's experience, postulates a pure and unmediated relationship between the "signals" emitted by the text (which play with accepted literary conventions) and the "horizon of expectation," of the public to which those signals are addressed. (Chartier 1994, 10)

Chartier's comments remind us of several obvious facts that are rarely explored: that even a holy text, such as the Qur'an, has its manufacturers (copyists, print makers, or computer designers), its diverse interlocutors (readers at different levels of literacy), and its media (parchment, paper, or digital bytes).

## Traditional scholarship on the Qur'an

At this point it may be worth asking why the materiality of the *muṣḥaf* has not been addressed by ethnographers, given that it is so important to Muslims? The answer partially lies in the history of Western scholarship on the Qur'an, which arose within the broader milieu of nineteenth century Orientalist Studies. As Edward Said (1995) notes, a growing interest in scriptural archaeology, linguistics, and hermeneutics was intimately bound up with colonial agendas and relations of power. Tracing the history of the Qur'an from a revelation memorized by followers of the Prophet Muhammad to a message written on stones, bones, and parchment interested Western scholars of religion in the same way that tracing the history of the Bible did. Many of them discussed the text of the Qur'an in relation to Biblical themes and studied Qur'anic language as a form of Ur-Semitic that held answers to riddles in Biblical Hebrew and Aramaic (Reynolds 2008, 12). Such religious or theological studies focused on chronology and historical accuracy, typically offering naturalistic or scientific explanations for apparent miracles in these holy texts. For example, in his article on "The Koran" for the *Encyclopedia Britannica* (1891), the "father" of Western Qur'anic criticism, Theodor Nöldeke summarized Qur'anic revelation in this way: "It is plain that we have here a somewhat crude attempt of the Prophet to represent to himself the more or less unconscious process by which his ideas arose and gradually took shape in his mind" (Nöldeke 1998, 37). This academic tradition of searching for the naturalistic origins of the Qur'an still appears in contemporary Qur'anic studies in the West (Donner 2008). Other approaches now acceptable include studies of the Qur'an as a literary genre (Nouryeh 2008; Hoffmann 2007), as a commentary on social relations

(Stowasser 1994; Decasa 1999) or as an historical source (Watt 1988). The wide range of practices related to the *muṣḥaf*, however, has never been examined by scholars in religious or anthropological studies.

Interestingly, the occasional ethnographic discussion of practices focused on the *muṣḥaf* as an object have come not from religious scholars but from nineteenth century travelers such as Edward W. Lane or Stanley Lane-Pool. Through them the *muṣḥaf* becomes part of Western discourses on magic and superstitions, in the form of amulets, charms and objects associated with the "evil eye." W.J.T. Mitchell (2005, 162) names them the "bad objects of the Empire"—vexing embodiments of Western beliefs about the beliefs of others. As epistemologically murky things, they lingered in what Margaret Wiener (2003, 130) calls "the space between fraud and fear" in the imagination of modern Europeans, and participated in the complex relations of colonial governance and indigenous resistance. Colonial discourse on the magical qualities of certain objects persisted in anthropological narratives about the Middle East in the nineteenth and twentieth centuries, usually appearing in the margins of ethnographic monographs (Zwemer 1939; Ammar 1954; Blackman 1968; Critchfield 1978).

While later studies rejected the patronizing focus on the magical qualities of the *muṣḥaf*, there was no work that bridged the gap between the Qur'an as a text and the *muṣḥaf* as its "container." Studies of the Qur'an that did not give preference to the content of the text addressed the *muṣḥaf* only in relation to its potentially "positive" aesthetic quality as an example of the art of calligraphy. Contemporary Western museum exhibits display their *maṣāḥif* mostly to demonstrate the development of various calligraphic and ornamental styles. The *muṣḥaf* as an object of academic interest is thus commonly limited to the study of the *muṣḥaf* as an object of artistic beauty.

Recent anthropological interest in the materiality of objects, stimulated by a realization that "materiality is a precondition for the social circulation and temporal persistence of experiences and ideas" (Keane 2008, 230), has recovered the concept of texts as objects. Scholars who are used to conceiving of them as repositories of meaning have neglected their corporeality that surreptitiously shapes our responses to them. Texts have their mediators that involve forms, colors, textures, and matter. What happens when they change? Perhaps my experience from one of the libraries in Cairo can shed some light on this issue.

Going over my fieldwork notes from nine years ago in Cairo, I came across a comment I wrote after my visit to the Library of Dar al-Kutub, which possessed a large collection of old manuscripts. This collection was not available to the public but the materials could be accessed and used with special permission for academic research. Most of the rare books, including copies of the Qur'an, were stored on the library shelves. Some of the oldest and biggest *maṣāḥif*, however, were placed on tables because of the difficulty in storing them on regular bookshelves. Those *maṣāḥif* were covered in dust (a ubiquitous characteristic of Cairo), were scattered on the tables, and were not protected against the humidity coming through the open windows. Although I was aware of my culturally inherited concern for the institutional preservation of old objects, I nonetheless could not help expecting to see extraordinary regard given to these especially valuable *maṣāḥif*. I was wrong. One of the workers in charge of the collection, in order to show me the text of the Qur'an, would flip through a five hundred year old *muṣḥaf* with un-gloved hands, quickly soiling the pages with the dust covering the books and his fingers, leaving black marks on the parchment. He would also moisten his finger with saliva in order to turn the pages, staining them even more. Many of the workers in the archival section could not read the text of old *maṣāḥif* or had difficulty deciphering the old script. They did not seem to consider those manuscripts as something unique.

Today, this collection has been moved to the Islamic Art Museum and given the "proper" museum care accorded to "works of art." But in going back to my notes I noticed the propensity to aestheticize Oriental objects so entrenched in the Western imagination, visible in the way *maṣāḥif* are displayed in the West. Moreover, it made me alter the question I had pondered then, which was, why didn't the *maṣāḥif* in Dar al-Kutub seem to evoke any kind of awe? Now I wonder if it is the act of reading that gives the text a status different from that of a text that is not in use? Put another way, to what extent was the unreverential treatment of the *maṣāḥif* in the library caused by their physical "otherness"? Old manuscripts do not resemble contemporary *maṣāḥif* in Cairo. The landscape of their text is unfamiliar to most Egyptians: their calligraphy is different from the one in modern copies, their ornamentation much more opulent, the pages are much larger than contemporary editions, and the orientation of their pages is horizontal rather than vertical. So to what degree does familiarity with the visual landscape of the text make that text meaningful? The workers were referring to the copies of the Qur'an in the collection as *makhṭūṭāt* (manuscripts) rather than *maṣāḥif*. Was this sign of being distanced from the text because of its altered form?

## Before print as medium

In order to better understand the importance of the materiality of the *muṣḥaf* in print and to see how it mediates the message of the *muṣḥaf*, it is necessary to have a picture of the way in which the text of the Qur'an had been organized before print became its medium. I draw on examples from the collection I had a chance to see, because they were representative of some general characteristics of the visual landscape and material organization of the *muṣḥaf* in different periods in the past (although there were regional design "mannerisms" and color and calligraphy preferences). The oldest *maṣāḥif* written on parchment in *kūfī* angular calligraphic style appear "austere" in comparison to the script and ornamentation of copies from later centuries. There are no diacritical marks or signs for short vowels, nor are the verses numbered. Letters are big and not connected, having wide spaces between them, with a relatively small number of words on the page. They lack the ornamental text frames and lavish decorations that appear in later copies. The first page of the text may be lightly decorated with gold compared to the later illuminated *maṣāḥif* in the collection which are very heavy and bound mostly in leather. Although the increase in ornamentation over time is not always the case in other collections (Blair and Bloom 2001, 594), the more contemporary manuscripts that I saw displayed increasingly elaborate decorative elements. So, later copies have pages abundantly illuminated with richly colored geometrical and floral arabesques that are drawn according to the principles of repetition, rhythm, symmetry, and balance, formulated by copyists over time. Elements of this decoration have meaning and function of their own (Lings 2005).

The text of the Qur'an comprises 114 chapters (*sūrah*) and approximately 6200 verses. *Al-Fātiḥa* (the first chapter and the creed) typically outshines other pages of the text. In a few copies in the collection, adornment on the first pages considerably exceeded the space devoted to the text. The decoration of each *sūrah* that follows also abounded in different forms of ornamentation, but without the lavishness of the initial pages. The title of each *sūrah* was placed in decorative panels with a background (often blue) decorated with flowers in wide circular arabesques and an external ground of black, gold, or another color, decorated with floral or geometrical patterns. The size and calligraphic style of the title of each *sūrah* (written in *kūfī* or *thuluth* calligraphic styles) differed from the rest of the text, which was often written in other styles such as *naskh* or *ruq'a*. Like the title of each *sūrah*, verses of the text were fixed in a frame that visually encloses the Qur'an on the page. Margins were a space for additional signs, such as the numbers of the chapters, abbreviations guiding the manner in which the text should be recited, or signs dividing the text into the sevenths and thirtieths (to read the Qur'an over a week or a month) placed in small geometrical-floral panels. Resembling contemporary printed *maṣāḥif* on which a reader is not supposed to scribble, there were no extra notes on the margins of the manuscripts, although they did have cataloging numbers written in ink on the covers. *Ayāt* (individual verses) were separated from each other by geometrical or floral rosettes, stars, basic and modified palmettos, and solar roundels that, again separated from the rest of the text, may have included the numbers and prostration (*sajda*) or bowing of the head (*rukū'*) signs. All words that do not belong strictly to the text of the Qur'an were written in script different from the one in which the text is written. The color palette was considerable, but the light to medium golds and the medium to dark blues were preferred, perhaps since they were the most expensive pigments (Blair and Bloom 2001, 600), or perhaps because colors, like designs, evoked certain qualities, such as "wisdom" or "mercy" (Lings 2005, 27) with which contemporary readers are usually not familiar.

Production of such richly illuminated *maṣāḥif* was a joint task that might have taken the calligrapher and the illuminator many years of work and might have resulted in the Qur'an being divided into as many as thirty to sixty volumes (Blair and Bloom 2001, 599).

From this very brief description of the ornamental and calligraphic techniques in these old *maṣāḥif* it is clear that over time copyists and illustrators would introduce certain innovations. Sometimes those innovations were a direct response to changing materials, such as a shift from parchment to paper that allowed for different and more abundant decorating techniques (Blair and Bloom 2001, 594). Inevitably, innovations and changes must have evoked responses, debates, and sometimes protests, such as the one over the introduction of prostration markings into the text in the eleventh century which was contested by some Islamic scholars as irreverent additions (Blair and Bloom 2001, 596). What is most central in this discussion, however, is that whenever the Qur'an was materially fixed, its visual form was important, as is made evident by the number of works devoted to calligraphy and the illumination of *maṣāḥif* (Baker 2007, 43), the practice of separating the text from any additions, and the fact that copying the text of the Qur'an became an artistic discipline as well as a profitable occupation. In the midst of these aesthetic and theological deliberations over the visual form of the *muṣḥaf*, one issue always acutely bothered the copyist—how was he to secure the accuracy of the text in the process of transmission? The method chosen to address the problem was consistent with the principle used in verifying the accuracy of other texts: confirmation of the chain of copyists who had produced previous *maṣāḥif*. Selecting an authoritative copyist, however, meant at the same time making a choice between different schools of reading the Qur'an, all of them entailing certain differences in techniques of recitation.

Of course the hand-crafted *maṣāḥif* described above were very rare, and not as common a possession as the millions of printed ones available nowadays around the Muslim world. Nevertheless, and in spite of the fact that the Qur'an in its aural form is still more "accessible," assertions such as the following (whether in reference to the past or to the present) are quite surprising:

> Islam is [...] characterized by an almost entirely oral approach to its scripture. One finds no physical book at the center of Muslim worship; nothing at all reminiscent of the crowned Torah scroll or the embellished lectionary. On the contrary, the simple ritual and the recitation of the Qur'an that forms part of it are carried out from memory. Even the prodigious effort of memory required to have the entire sacred text by heart is not considered at all out of the ordinary for a Muslim. To have to consult a written copy to quote the Qur'an is thought a failure of piety. (Madigan 2001, 3)

First of all, one might wonder what Madigan means by worship? Is not holding a *muṣḥaf* in one's hands while reciting it with the eyes sometimes fixed on the text, sometimes forgetfully wandering off to the surroundings (a practice commonly seen on busses and subways in Cairo) a form of worship? And, how do we account for the sumptuously ornamented *maṣāḥif* available for purchase in upscale bookstores of the city and often displayed on a decorated *kursī* (lit. chair) in houses and mosques during worship? Secondly, the statistics showing high levels of illiteracy in the Middle East should not mislead us into simple conclusions about the use of *muṣḥaf* in worship. In his famous and widely quoted *Al-Tibyān fī ādāb Ḥamalāt al-Qur'an* [*Etiquette with the Qur'an*], which was based on the authority of *aḥādīth*, Syrian scholar Yahya ibn Sharaf al-Nawawi (1234–1278) argued that "Reciting the Qur'an from the *muṣḥaf* is better than reciting from memory since looking in the muṣḥaf is a kind of worship one seeks, for it combines recitation and looking. This is what some of our *Shāf'ī* companions, al-Qaḍi Ḥusayn, Abu Hamid al-Ghazali, and groups of Righteous Forebears have said" (al-Nawawi 2003, 52). The idea of not letting the day pass by without looking at a *muṣḥaf* came up in several conversations with modern Muslims in Cairo, referring to the continuing conviction that the ability to recite the Qur'an while holding the *muṣḥaf* is the most satisfying form of communing with its message.

Finally, the transition from parchment to paper and then to print would not have raised any concerns had the materiality of the *muṣḥaf* been of no significance to Muslim scholars. The contested transition to print not only highlights the complex relationship between the Qur'anic message and the *muṣḥaf*, but also raises interesting issues regarding authenticity, technological reproduction, and tradition.

## *Muṣḥaf* in print

Mechanical printing came to the Middle East in the nineteenth century. Historians suggest that the lack of earlier experiments with moveable type in the region had been partially caused by the technical difficulty of reproducing the complex designs of over a hundred Arabic letterforms, and partially by the opposition of scribes and calligraphers who saw mechanical printing as a threat to their occupation. But after lithography was invented in the late 1800s in Germany, it became the preferred technology in the Middle East. It was cheaper, more accommodating to the Arabic letters, and, as historian of Arabic print Ian Proudfoot says, "it permitted calligraphic preparation of the Qur'anic text to the point where a well designed and executed lithograph may be mistaken for a manuscript" (Albin 2001, 269). Initially (except for a few "royal" editions), the average lithographed copies were rather plain and did not use color as producers sought to make print copies affordable for everybody. The continued development of printing techniques eventually culminated in lavishly decorated computer printed *maṣāḥif* in the late twentieth century.

In Egypt, the first printed publication of parts of the Qur'an took place in 1833, for the purpose of supplying texts for pupils in government schools. This first edition had not received a thorough proofreading and was therefore withdrawn after a few years on the recommendation of Muslim scholars who found errors in it. The accuracy of editions that followed, printed by the Bulaq Press, were supervised by the newly established Department of Printing al-Muṣḥaf al-Sharīf.

For Roger Chartier, the most fascinating aspect of the study of texts and their users is the transformation of forms of sociability, the emergence of new modes of thought, and changes in people's relationship to power caused by the increasing circulation of printed matter (Chartier 1994, 3). In this case, mechanical printing demanded new forms of supervision of the production and distribution of *maṣāḥif* on a much larger scale than before. The 1920 King Fu'ād *muṣḥaf*—the most common edition in Egypt in the past and today and a model for editions in other countries—was prepared under the guidance of a special committee of scholars from al-Azhar University who approved the calligraphic styles, supervised printing conventions used in the edition, and included editorial notes at the end of the volume.

This particular publication of the *muṣḥaf* poses interesting questions. As a result of the transition to print, on the one hand readers received a less individualized and aesthetically refined object, but on the other, they received a text that seems even more fixed and "unalterable." A hand-made *muṣḥaf* may have been a product of artistic sensibilities and individual devotion, but King Fu'ād's *muṣḥaf* firmly positions the text in the sphere of tradition by giving it a standardized and "official" form. The relationship between the original and reproduction—usually thought of in terms of devaluation—is not as clear here either: what original do we mean here, the hand-made manuscripts or the uncreated Speech of God?

In his well-known essay, "The Work of Art in the Age of Its Technological Reproducibility," Walter Benjamin says:

> It might be stated as a general formula that the technology of reproduction detaches the reproduced object from the sphere of tradition. By replicating the work many times over, it substitutes a mass existence for a unique existence. And in permitting the reproduction to reach the recipient in his or her own situation, it actualizes that which is reproduced. (2002, 104)

So, from an aesthetic perspective, a mass reproduced *muṣḥaf* loses the aura of authenticity rooted in scholarship, calligraphy, and hand-production. But removing the same *muṣḥaf* from these aesthetic concerns enhances the Qur'an's authority with individual readers through multiplication.

In 1999, I visited Dar al-Sha'ab, a small publishing house which prints not only *maṣāḥif* but also other religious and lay publications. This visit provided me with some insight into the ways in which the authority of the Qur'an is mediated through the production of *maṣāḥif*. Mediation by print shows that a producer's desire to incorporate the styles of "traditional" *maṣāḥif* can be both thwarted *and* facilitated by the demands, limitation, and capacities of the equipment. The process of printing in this workshop was fully automated and most of the work took place on the screen of a computer. But, in order to achieve the greatest resemblance to hand-made manuscripts, in Dar al-Sha 'ab old *maṣāḥif* were scanned and retouched on a computer. The worker responsible for print design had the freedom to choose frames, colors, and backgrounds for new editions of the Qur'an. He did not have as much choice, however, when it came to selection of fonts. He told me that "colors can be changed, frames can be changed, but the words—never!"

His statement can be understood in two ways. First, the style of printing had to remain "manuscript-like." It had to visually resemble hand-made copies, so that the words in print looked like those in manuscripts. The prayer book, which one worker was editing when we spoke, includes verses from the Qur'an. The text of the prayer and a *ḥadīth* are printed in regular modern *naskhī* font (the font in which most books are printed) without signs for short vowels normally omitted in regular print, but the Qur'anic text itself was a scan of a handwritten manuscript to ensure that none of the vowels and reading marks were missing. Another assistant pointed out, "The computer doesn't imitate the beauty of the handwriting well enough. The old calligraphic styles are meant to preserve the beauty of the writing and bring pleasure to the eye." Beauty as a characteristic of writing designed for copying the text of the Qur'an often came up in conversations about Arabic script.

Indeed, certain calligraphic styles were developed and refined for the purpose of decorating the text of the Qur'an. Over time, the connection between those styles of writing and the text has become so close that what was meant to beautify the text of the *muṣḥaf* is now considered beautiful by virtue of being a part of the *muṣḥaf* itself. This connection is reinforced by the fact that the Department of al-Muṣḥaf al-Sharīf at the Islamic Research Academy at al-Azhar, the organization that oversees issues related to the publication of the Qur'an, does not accept *maṣāḥif* with fonts other than those traditionally used in manuscripts. *Tashkīl* (vocalization signs that are omitted in contemporary writing) and other reading signs cannot be modified either. At the print shop, I was shown examples of a computer printout with *tashkīl* over the letters that, depending on the kind of letter, were slightly shifted forward or backward from the center of the letter. These, the designer pointed out, would not be accepted by al-Azhar. The designer maintained that there had been efforts to create a computer program that would perfectly imitate not only the handwritten text but also the shape and position of the vowels and readings signs, but the programs that were available at the time we spoke (in 1999) contained the text of the Qur'an without the proper *tashkīl*, and some of the letter signs or signs for recitation were missing. Therefore, workers at Dar al-Sha'ab preferred to scan old manuscripts or older authorized print copies.

A second explanation for the worker's comment is that the text cannot be altered. Changing the text of the Qur'an is a punishable transgression. For every new edition of the Qur'an printed in Egypt, the Department of al-Muṣḥaf al-Sharīf at al-Azhar issues a special *taṣrīḥ* (permission or certificate) that is copied and included in every single *muṣḥaf* to attest to its accuracy. Such a *taṣrīḥ* usually includes a description of the new edition (its size and calligraphic styles) and warns that in the case of any inaccuracies, the copies will be confiscated and the publisher's permission to print will be withdrawn. Before a new *muṣḥaf* can be distributed for sale, the printing house has to submit samples of the new edition to the Department of al-Muṣḥaf al-Sharīf to be proofread for errors. Only then will a sales permit be issued to the publishing house. Frequent misprints often cause al-Azhar to reject *maṣāḥif* produced in India and Pakistan. Copies printed in those countries contain a larger number of errors, such as deleted letters or even words, which changes the meaning of the text.

As I suggested at the beginning of this essay, when the Qur'an is problematized in its material dimension as a *muṣḥaf*, the relationship between the object and its content becomes more visible. The easy reproducibility of the *muṣḥaf* today thus has a double effect: it more widely disseminates the Qur'an among believers but at the same time it more widely endangers the material text of the *maṣāḥif* in unexpected ways. For instance, the process of printing produces a lot of waste. Torn, stained, misprinted or unfinished pages containing the text cannot be recycled, as is the case with regular scrap paper. Because they contain the text of the Qur'an, they must be burnt, like the confiscated copies that contain mistakes.

Once it leaves the print shop, a *muṣḥaf* becomes a commodity. Most bookstores and many bookstalls have *maṣāḥif* for sale. Usually they are quite inexpensive, although the price depends on the quality of paper, the richness of decoration, and the material used for covers. More expensive *maṣāḥif* are typically more colorful, with ornaments in gold, embossed leather covers and velvet cases. Less expensive ones have the text and decorations printed in solid green or blue, on cheap paper, with synthetic hard covers, in a simple sheathe or even without any cover. The cheapest *maṣāḥif* are distributed or sold in the form of small paperbound booklets that contain only certain portions of the text and few decorations. They are small and handy for reading in a metro carriage or a bus, and are often sold in such locales by peddlers.

Undeniably, mechanical printing has been beneficial, making the Qur'an widely available to the public, while also increasing its visibility as a commodity and changing its methods of distribution and acquisition. It has stimulated new ways in which it can be read, displayed, protected, or given to someone as a gift. But what happens when a *muṣḥaf* becomes a commodity? In an article on religious commodities in Cairo following Appadurai's classic approach to the social life of things, Gregory Starrett, suggests that:

> As signifiers, religious commodities prior to the sale transaction signify differences in taste rather than differences in absolute worth. A *muṣḥaf* is comparable to a bouquet of flowers or a box of chocolate for some purposes. A papyrus bearing the "Fatiha," the opening chapter of the Qur'an, is comparable to a

> papyrus showing Pharaoh on his war chariot. It thus makes little sense for a merchant to take special precautions in the placement of religious commodities relative to other commodities. (Starrett 1995, 59)

But Starrett's last sentence does not reflect the reactions of people in the bookstore where I photographed *maṣāḥif* for sale by placing them on the floor. Their objections make me doubt that there is no difference between a *muṣḥaf* and other objects that share the status of commodity. Are *maṣāḥif* really "activated as religious objects only when taken out of the shop"? Or, perhaps in the whirlwind life of contemporary Cairo is it difficult to notice the precautions that are nevertheless taken by the sellers when trading the text of the Qur'an? From my perspective, even in the entourage of other commodities, the *muṣḥaf*'s exchangeability is not its only socially relevant feature. What sets it apart, in spite of its exchange value as a commodity, is its materiality, the fact that it is a book that contains a holy text written in a certain calligraphic style and set in an appropriate decorative format.

## Materiality, objects, things

In the *Handbook of Material Culture*, Webb Keane summarizes the anthropological interest in objects:

> Within the social or human sciences, material objects have rarely been a focus of attention simply in and of themselves. Rather, they have been of special interest primarily for the insights they may provide into human social and cultural worlds. Emerging as these sciences did out of Western philosophical and religious traditions, they commonly formulated the relations of humans and material things with reference to the broader conceptual opposition between subject and object. (Keane 2006, 198)

I earlier sketched the history of Western interest in the Qur'an, indicating that the trajectory of Oriental Studies that emerged from the philosophical and religious traditions, as mentioned by Keane, prevented Westerners from ever noticing the materiality of the *muṣḥaf*. That trajectory was not exceptional—as Keane points out, academics have a history of superficial and patronizing attitudes towards objects that were to serve human purposes. Yet *maṣāḥif* cannot easily be compartmentalized as mere objects. Thinking about *muṣḥaf* "requires disrupting habits of thought and writing in anthropology that are rooted in the Western philosophical tradition" (Ochoa 2007, 479). Notions of the passivity of objects belong to that tradition, but an ethnography of the *muṣḥaf* can hardly be fitted into such a theoretical framework. This is because in a very real sense, to a Muslim a *muṣḥaf* is recalcitrant and has authority over one's behavior, forcing one to act in a certain way. I observed a customer in a waiting room of one of the popular cellular phone companies in the upper-class al-Maʿādī neighborhood of Cairo who, before going to the bathroom, suddenly stopped, opened his briefcase, took out a *muṣḥaf*, and handed it to another man sitting close to him. Once he returned from the bathroom, the customer took it back and once again put it in his briefcase. On another occasion, I watched my friend Rehab trying to pull out something tangled in her hair. "What are you doing?" I asked. "Taking my *muṣḥaf* off," she murmured fighting with the hair knot, "I'm going to the bathroom." Rehab was trying to remove her golden pendant in the shape of a *muṣḥaf*, one of the most popular pendants among Egyptian Muslim women. (As an aside I should mention that some sheikhs resent the popularity of miniaturized *muṣḥaf* in the form of jewelry because of the risk of defiling or losing the pendant during daily activities, and also because in this form they cannot be read.)

One way to disrupt the habitual ways of thinking about objects might be to stop calling them objects, as Bill Brown suggests in his essay "Thing Theory" (2001). Brown ponders the consequences of a move from talking about objects to talking about things, bemoaning the fact that "[as they] circulate through our lives, we look through objects (to see what they disclose about history, society, nature, or culture--above all what they disclose about us), but we only catch a glimpse of things. We look through objects because there are codes by which our interpretive attention makes them meaningful, because there is a discourse of objectivity that allows us to use them as facts" (2001, 4). Things, on the other hand, demand attention and do not let themselves be looked through. Things are objects that assert themselves through a changed relation to the human subject. Things are objects that break (causing us to suspend what we have been doing), they make us trip, they spill on us, or stop us on our way to the bathroom. For Brown, things are not objects, but are embodiments of a particular subject-object relation that are disclosed through chance interruption of everyday life. Thus it may be useful to think about the *muṣḥaf* as a thing in a state of permanent assertion. It is this "thingness" that prevents a *muṣḥaf* from being just one of the very many other commodities on the street stands, objects on book shelves, in bathrooms, in kitchens and in other places. This "thingness" that Brown defines as that "which is excessive in objects, as what exceeds their mere materialization as objects or their mere utilization as objects—their force as a sensuous presence or as a metaphysical presence" (2001, 5) calls for attention, forces us to react, and interrupts the subject-object dichotomy. I was often reminded that the *muṣḥaf* was not a mere object when I worked at the library at the American University in Cairo where patrons would move the library copy of the Qur'an to the upper shelf although (according to its call number) its place was on one of the lower shelves. On another occasion, my friend Iman admitted that she got in trouble for accidentally treating the *muṣḥaf* as an ordinary book. She was carrying a pile of books in the library and put her keys on top of them. The top book happened to be a copy of the Qur'an. Another worker made her feel embarrassed by ostentatiously taking the keys away.

My notes brim with examples of situations when a *muṣḥaf* forces its user to be attentive to its tangible form. If a reader is in the habit of licking his fingers before turning the pages of a book, he cannot do it when reading a *muṣḥaf*. It should not be stained with saliva and if this happens, the saliva should be wiped off with a clean cloth slightly moistened with water. A *muṣḥaf* cannot be thrown on the floor, or tossed up in the air. It cannot be used as a pillow or leaned upon. Throwing a *muṣḥaf* in the dirt is a sure sign of atheism. But burning an old *muṣḥaf* or giving it away to a mosque is a mark of piety. I was made aware of how important it is to properly discard pieces of the Qur'anic text when I was printing pictures to illustrate an essay, and some of these photos were of the text of the Qur'an. A colleague, watching me printing the pictures remarked, "But you know that you should burn them after you use them?" I said that they would be a part of my paper. Although satisfied with my answer, he nevertheless added, "But remember to burn them if you don't need them. Or give them to me."

The emphasis on the appropriate handling of the *muṣḥaf* may seem to contradict the Egyptian practice of placing the Qur'an on the front dashboard of the car or suspending it from the rearview mirror--a habit very common in Cairo. And indeed, it is a subject of debate that was echoed in conversations with my friends. Some criticized this practice while others defended it with a variety of reasons. Reflecting on the nature on these often conflicting opinions, it will be helpful to remember the words of Webb Keane: "By virtue of their material autonomy from their original producers, externalizations of one set of ideas can enter into new combinations with material externalizations arising in quite different times and places, and from quite different purposes" (Keane 2006, 230–231). For instance, *barakah*, the spiritual blessing Muslims believe is present in the Qur'an, may be seen as emanating from the *muṣḥaf*. The availability of *maṣāḥif* in inexpensive printed forms makes a democracy of spiritual grace possible, which is beneficial for those who desire to experience the blessing but cannot afford a hand-made and expensive *muṣḥaf*. Another example can be seen in the contested practice of leaving an open Qur'an behind a shop window. Merchants often leave a *muṣḥaf* open to the "ayat al-Kursī" (the Throne verse, one of the more popular verses of the Qur'an) in a shop after working hours. In these cases, the *muṣḥaf* is usually placed on a chair or a table in front of the door to protect the shop from robbers. In one of the shops at the bazaar Khan al-Khalili there was an open copy of the Qur'an on display. I asked the owner about it, since dust and dirt could be seen on the pages. He said that he opened it only to a certain *sūrah* and that the *muṣḥaf* itself was cleaned every day. From its appearance, I doubted his claim but found his response significant--even if he did not actually dust the *muṣḥaf* every day, he felt that it should be done.

A sheikh with whom I was acquainted was very concerned about this practice. In his mind it was an invention that, although appearing harmless, was nevertheless not clearly a part of tradition and was, in his opinion, somewhat problematic. He said: "I think it is in the Qur'an that when you keep the Qur'an open there's an angel waiting for you on the book until you come back and start reading again. So why keep the angel waiting for me all of the time?" In the Rifa'ī Mosque, one of the most famous mosques in Cairo, however, the tomb of a descendant of Sheikh Rifa'ī is permanently surrounded by a wreath of open *maṣāḥif*. These two situations reflect the fact that it is often hard to draw a clear line between what is permissible and what is prohibited, and the point of agreement will depend on the particular historical configuration of power and intensity of public engagement in the debate over a particular practice. At the same time one ought not lose sight of the materiality of the thing that will participate in these debates by determining the range of possible practices. The interplay of discursive tradition and textual materiality creates a situation in which the *maṣāḥif* can partake in practices that, when juxtaposed, should exclude each other. For instance, a *muṣḥaf* both is and is not a source of *barakah* because the blessing is in the message of the Qur'an, but this message is fixed by the *muṣḥaf*. Is this a case of which Brown (2001, 5) says, "the thing seems to name the object just as it is even as it names some thing else"? Brown pays attention to the ambiguous nature of things and their latent capacity to become something else. But, unlike Bruno Latour, he does not elaborate on the effects of things participating in the course of action. For Latour, things may be mediators. They are actors that "transform, translate, distort, and modify the meaning or the elements they are supposed to carry" (2007, 39), transforming themselves in the process. A *muṣḥaf* translates the authority of the Qur'an through techniques of its appropriation as a thing. Yet, in the process, it shifts between different degrees of being a commodity, a source of blessing, and a container of the holy word, all the while asserting itself into the world.

As the container of the holy word, a *muṣḥaf* requires a state of *wuḍū'* (physical and spiritual cleanliness) if a person wants to hold it. Although scholars disagree about the meaning of the word "clean" and, depending on the school of law, tend to favor either a physical or a spiritual interpretation, they all agree that menstruation and ejaculation cause impurity. The latter always requires *wuḍū'* and the former prevents a woman from touching a *muṣḥaf*. As a result, during her monthly period Rehab would take two books, or any other things, and use them as holders whenever she wanted to move her *muṣḥaf*. The requirement of spiritual and physical purity finds its extension in the conviction that a non-Muslim should not touch the *muṣḥaf*. Not everyone agrees on this issue, however. Some of my friends thought that such a prohibition would prevent me from learning about Islam and becoming Muslim. A few others, like Rehab, preferred me not to take a *muṣḥaf* in my hands. She explicitly asked me not to touch her *muṣḥaf* because my hands were not "clean." Curious about her explanation, I prodded her by saying, "I've just washed them!" She laughed and then clarified that she meant *wuḍū'* and the fact that I was not a Muslim. No one, however, ever refused to sell me a *muṣḥaf*.

## Conclusions

Throughout this paper I have highlighted some of the ways in which the Qur'an's authority is mediated by its physical container—the *muṣḥaf.* I have pointed to some conceptual paths that could be further explored when one focuses on the materiality of the Qur'an. I have also introduced an Arabic word, *muṣḥaf*, that has so far been absent from the anthropological vocabulary. It redirects our attention away from an entirely textual approach to the Qur'an to its material and textual existence and contributes, like other papers in this volume, to the idea that books function not only as repositories of information but also as objects whose materiality (paper, size, font or color) certainly affect their meaning.

## References

Asad, Talal. 1996. "The Idea of an Anthropology of Islam." In *The Social Philosophy of Ernst Gellner. Poznan Studies in the Philosophy of the Sciences and the Humanities*, edited by John A. Hall and Ian Jarvie, 48: 381–403. Amsterdam: Rodopi.

Albin, Michael W. 2001. "Printing of the Qur'an." In *Encyclopaedia of the Qur'an*, edited by Jane Dammen McAuliffe. Leiden: Brill.

Al-Nawawī al-Imān al-Rabbānī Abū Zakariyyā Yaḥyā Ibn Sharaf. 2003. *Etiquette with the Qur'an: Al-Tibyan fi Adab Hamalat al-Qur'an*. Starlatch Press.

Ammar, Hamed. 1954. *Growing up in an Egyptian Village*. London: Routledge & Kegan Paul.

Baker, Colin F. 2007. *Qur'an Manuscripts: Calligraphy, Illumination, Design*. London: British Library.

Blackman, Winifred S. 1968. *Fellahin of Upper Egypt: Their Religious, Social and Industrial Life with Special Reference to Survivals from Ancient Times*. London: Frank Cass and Co.

Blair, Sheila S., and Jonathan M. Bloom. 2001. "Ornamentation." In *Encyclopaedia of the Qur'an*, edited by Jane Dammen McAuliffe. Leiden: Brill.

Brown, Bill. 2001. "Thing Theory." *Critical Inquiry* 28: 1–22. http://dx.doi.org/10.1086/449030

Chartier, Roger. 1994. *The Order of Books: Readers, Authors, and Libraries in Europe between the Fourteenth and Eighteenth Centuries*. Stanford, CA: Stanford University Press.

Corbin, Henry. 1993. *History of Islamic Philosophy*. London: Kegan Paul International.

Critchfield, Richard. 1978. *Shahhat, an Egyptian*. Syracuse, NY: Syracuse University Press.

Decasa, George C. 1999. *The Qur'anic Concept of Umma and Its Function in Philippine Muslim Society*. Rome: Pontificia Universita Gregoriana.

Donner, Fred M. 2008. The Qur'an in Its Historical Context. London: Routledge.

Hoffmann, Thomas. 2007. *The Poetic Qur'an: Studies on Quranic Poeticity*. Wiesbaden: Harrassowitz.

Keane, Webb. 2006. "Subjects and Objects." In *Handbook of Material Culture*, edited by Christopher Y. Tilley et al., 198–202. London: SAGE.

———. 2008. "On the Materiality of Religion." *Material Religion* 4: 230–231. http://dx.doi.org/10.2752/175183408X328343

Lane, Edward William. 1860. *An Account of the Manners and Customs of the Modern Egyptians: Written in Egypt During the Years 1833-, -34, and -35.* London: J. Murray.

Lane-Poole, Stanley. 1884. *Social Life in Egypt: A Description of the Country and Its People.* New York: Collier.

Latour, Bruno. 2004. *Politics of Nature: How to Bring the Sciences into Democracy.* Cambridge, MA: Harvard University Press.

Lings, Martin. 2005. *Splendours of Qur'an Calligraphy and Illumination.* Liechtenstein: Thesaurus Islamicus Foundation.

Madigan, Daniel A. 2001. *The Qur'an's Self Image: Writing and Authority in Islam's Scripture.* Princeton, NJ: Princeton University Press.

Mitchell, W. J. 2005. What Do Pictures Want? The Lives and Loves of Images. Chicago, IL: University of Chicago Press.

Nöldeke, Theodor. 1998. "The Koran." In *The Origins of the Koran: Classic Essays on Islamic Holy Book*, edited by Ibn Warraq. New York: Prometheus Books.

Nouryeh, Christopher. 2008. *The Art of Narrative in the Holy Qur'an: A Literary Appreciation of a Sacred Text.* Lewiston, NY: Edwin Mellen Press.

Ochoa, Todd Ramón. 2007. "Versions of the Dead: Kalunga, Cuban-Kongo Materiality, and Ethnography." *Cultural Anthropology* 22: 473–500. http://dx.doi.org/10.1525/can.2007.22.4.473

Reynolds, Gabriel Said. 2008. *The Qur'an in Its Historical Context.* London: Routledge.

Sabiq , Al-Sayyid. Nd. *Fiqh us-Sunnah*, translated by Muhammad Sa 'eed Dabas, Jamal al-Din M. Zarabozo and M.S. Kayani. Dar El Fateh for Arab Information. Part: at-Tahara and as-Salah.

Said, Edward. 1978. *Orientalism.* Harmondsworth: Penguin.

Starrett, Gregory. 1995. "The Political Economy of Religious Commodities in Cairo." *American Anthropologist* 97: 51–68. http://dx.doi.org/10.1525/aa.1995.97.1.02a00090

Stowasser, Barbara Freyer. 1994. *Women in the Qur'an, Traditions, and Interpretation.* New York: Oxford University Press.

Watt, W. Montgomery. 1988. *Muhammad's Mecca: History in the Qur'an.* Edinburgh: Edinburgh University Press.

Wiener Margaret. 2003. "Hidden Forces: Colonialism and the Politics of Magic in the Netherlands Indies." In *Magic and Modernity: Interfaces of Revelation and Concealment*, edited by Birgit Meyer and Peter Pels, 129–158. Stanford, CA: Stanford University Press.

Zwemer, Samuel M. 1939. *Studies in Popular Islam: A Collection of Papers Dealing with the Superstitions and Beliefs of the Common People.* London: The Sheldon Press.

# 11

# The End of the Word as We Know It: The Cultural Iconicity of the Bible in the Twilight of Print Culture

Timothy Beal

*This essay attends to a distinction that requires closer examination and theorization in our discourse on iconic books and other scriptures: the difference between iconic object and cultural icon. How do we conceive of relations between the particular, ritualized iconicities of particular scriptures in particular religious contexts and the cultural iconicities of scriptures in general, such as "the Bible" or "the Qur'an," whose visual and material objectivity is highly ambiguous? How if at all are the iconic cultural meanings of the ideas of such books related to the particular iconic textual objects that more or less instantiate them? These questions are explored through particular focus on the relationship between the particular iconicities of particular print Bibles, as iconic objects, and the general iconicity of the cultural icon of the Bible.*

It's the end of the Word as we know it. By which I mean it's the end of a certain idea of Christian Scripture that has accrued tremendous cultural value at the heart and soul of Western print culture since the late fifteenth century: Christian Scriptures as the Bible: The Book of books, the mass-reproducible, infinitely repeatable, literally authoritative, Word of God in a single bound volume from Genesis to Revelation.

I have recently argued that this end of the Word as we know it is the result of the convergence of two interrelated cultural forces. First is the decline of bibliographic culture, that is, the media regime in which the mass-produced book was the dominant medium of writing. People, especially younger people, are buying and reading fewer and fewer books as new electronic media occupy more and more attention. The bound, mass-reproduced, highly replicable volume of linear textual discourse is losing itself within an ever-expanding and constantly reconfiguring network of hypertextual flows. Book publishers are still selling billions of books, but their numbers drop every year as more and more of the market share goes to electronic media. As one of my editors told me, "flat is the new up." Of course, the decline of bibliographic culture does not spell the end or even the decline of writing. But it's different in the emerging digital network society. It's more fragmented, scattered, nonlinear, mosaic, dialogical, intertextual, transient, and harder to separate from reading.

The second force bringing about the end of the Word as we know it is the rise since the 1970s of what I call *evangelical capitalism*, a wedding of evangelicalism and capitalism that has given birth to a kind of supply-side Christianity in which it's hard to tell the difference between spreading the Word and moving product (Beal 2011, 71–83). Within this new evangelical market economy, the Bible is a form of what I call "sacred capital," to be packaged and repackaged in a wide array of consumer goods. Indeed, the Bible is not only the flagship of print culture, but also of evangelical capitalism. Together, these converging forces are leading to a revolution in the cultural history of the Bible that will be as radical as the invention of moveable type or the Protestant Reformation.

## Iconic Bibles and the cultural iconicity of the Bible

With this setting in mind, I want to draw attention to a distinction that requires closer examination and theorization in our discourse on iconic books and other scriptures: the difference between *iconic object* and *cultural icon*. How do we conceive of relations between the particular, ritualized iconicities of particular scriptures in particular religious contexts and the *cultural iconicities* of scriptures in general, such as "the Bible" or "the Qur'an," whose visual and material objectivity is highly ambiguous? How, if at all, are the iconic cultural meanings of the ideas of such books related to the particular iconic textual objects that more or less instantiate them?

My particular focus here is on the relationship between the particular iconicities of particular print Bibles, as iconic objects, and the general iconicity of the cultural icon of the Bible; or, to put it in dialogue with S. Brent Plate's essay in the present volume, the relation between *images of words* and *the image of the Word.*

A "cultural icon" is not the same as an icon *per se*. An icon is a particular material thing whose meaning cannot be separated from its religious ritual context. So it is with scriptural icons. As James W. Watts makes clear, the religious ritualization of a particular scripture's iconic dimension cannot be separated from the ritualization of its semantic and performative dimensions, that is, the interpretations and performances of its textual content (Watts, Chapter 1, this volume). All these ritualized dimensions work together to produce scripture in particular religious contexts. Dorina Miller Parmenter's analysis of images of Bible books in early Christian ritual contexts (Gospel processions and displays, ritual uses of scripture as a miracle-working object) provides an excellent example of how this ritualization process plays out vis-à-vis Christian scriptures. In that early Christian context, she defines a Christian biblical icon as both visual and material, a material image that mediates a transcendent reality "and thus is a portable locus of religious power" (Parmenter, Chapter 4, this volume). As such, the iconicity of a particular Bible depends on particular ritual performances that imbue and maintain its mediatory role between the material and spiritual realms.

A cultural icon, by contrast, does not, and indeed cannot, have a particular visual or material form. It is, rather, an immaterial, amorphous, inarticulate condensation of cultural meaning and value, a symbol whose outline is vague, impossible to pin down to a particular image or thing. The image of the closed black leather book, for example, is a common one for the cultural icon of the Bible, but the Bible's cultural iconicity is not inextricably tied to that image. It could be brown or red, zippered or clasped, indexed or plain, open or closed, and so on. Indeed, this visual-material vagueness is essential to a cultural icon's power. It gives it a flexibility that allows more people to identify with it; it allows it to stretch further before breaking—and, by the same token, to hold together and stabilize an otherwise unstably heterogeneous, potentially explosive population as a cultural group identity.

We need to distinguish between particular biblical icons, whose iconicities are tied to their particular material forms and are created and maintained by particular rituals, and the cultural icon of the Bible. To be sure, many particular iconic Bibles help create and maintain the Bible's cultural iconicity. Think, for example, of a monument to the Ten Commandments in a courthouse, of the Gutenberg Bible, Luther's Bible, and the Bible used at the swearing-in ceremony of Presidents Lincoln and Obama. Likewise, participation in and observation of particular semantic, performative, and iconic ritual practices vis-à-vis particular Bibles in particular communities can feed into the Bible's cultural iconicity. Scriptural anthropologist James S. Bielo's *Words upon the Word* offers some fascinating windows into this process within conservative evangelical small-group Bible studies. Bielo found that successful group facilitators were able to inculcate certain "textual practices" *with* the Bible and "textual ideologies" *about* the Bible that downplayed differences and fenced the table, so to speak, from those potential participants who could not conform. The strongest textual ideology was the concept of the Bible as the only absolute, infallible authority for faith and life. While studying Proverbs 11–12, for example, a participant in one group questioned the text's proclamations that the righteous always prosper while the wicked suffer—"when I see faithful people take it on the neck. How do you square that?" Without dismissing or directly challenging the question, the facilitator steered the discussion back to the group's agreed presupposition of biblical authority. "I don't have all the answers. All I'm saying is that this is a book of promises from beginning to end ... We have life, and a better life, by claiming all the promises in this book as ours" (Bielo 2009, 57). Although the man's experience may appear to contradict scriptural authority in that moment, the leader suggests, continuing to claim it as such will, in the long term, be a blessing—not only to the individual but to the group as a whole. Here and in other cases, Bielo reveals how the often subtle governing of "words upon the Word" within

Bible-study culture works to downplay hermeneutical and theological differences and tensions that could otherwise fragment not only the group but also the very Word that is believed to be its foundation.

Such particular ritual practices with particular visible, material scriptures, from pews on Sunday mornings to Denny's on Wednesday nights, do indeed pump up the cultural iconicity of the Bible for the participants but also, perhaps even especially, for non-participants who observe or hear about them. Yet the Bible as a cultural icon cannot be reduced to any one of these particular ritualized Bibles. The cultural icon of the Bible exists not in particular but in general. It is the "Bibleness" of particular Bibles.

One way to explicate the general iconicity of the Bible in mass culture is to consider the many hundreds of instruction books and manuals that are called Bibles, from *The Bartender's Bible*, to *The Curtain Bible*, to *The Small Game and Varmint Hunter's Bible*. What does it mean to call something "the Bible"? What does this title claim for a book? What does it promise? What is the cultural meaning of "the Bible" that a publisher claims when it publishes something like *The Hot Rodder's Bible*? What are the iconic cultural attributes of "the Bible" that these books claim? What does "the Bible" mean?

> It means authoritative. A book called "the Bible" is the ultimate authority. It is the alpha and omega, first and last Word on the subject.
>
> It means univocal. A book called "the Bible" speaks for itself in one, unified voice, without contradiction.
>
> It means practical. A book called "the Bible" promises to serve as a reference manual and a dependable guide for how to proceed along the path its reader has chosen.
>
> It means accessible. A book called "the Bible" promises to speak to anyone and everyone clearly and simply, without ambiguity, in terms "even I can understand."
>
> It means comprehensive. A book called "the Bible" claims to cover everything human beings may ever possibly need to know about its subject: past, present, and future.
>
> And it means exclusive. A book called "the Bible" admits no rivals, no alternative perspectives. It is complete unto itself, closed, and self-contained within a single book: A to Z, Alpha to Omega, Genesis to Revelation. Nothing may be added or taken away.

This is, in a nutshell, the iconic cultural meaning of the Bible. And it is this meaning that publishers claim for any book they call "the Bible." The Bible as cultural icon is the Book of books, the authoritative, authorial, univocal, comprehensive, final, graspable and readable Word of God. It is the perfect book by the perfect author, the ultimate image of divine authority and authoriality, and thus of religion as divinely authored:

black-and-white certainty, set and proofed, clean and free of errors. As such, it stands for faith as black-and-white certainty and religion as right-and-wrong morality. It's no accident that the most common visual image of the Bible is that of a closed black book (nor that the second most common image is an open but illegible one). The cultural icon of the Bible represents religious faith as what closes the book on questions about the meaning and purpose of life, putting them to rest in the name of God.

Nearly all Americans are familiar with this iconic meaning of the Bible, and most endorse it. According to the Pew Forum on Religion and Public Life, seventy-eight percent of all Americans say that the Bible is the "word of God," and almost half of those believe that, as such, "it is to be taken literally, word for word" (Pew Forum 2006). Polling data from the Barna Group indicate that nearly half of all Americans agree that "the Bible is totally accurate in all of its teachings" (eighty-eight percent of all "born-again" Christians believe the same), and the Gallup Poll finds that sixty-five percent of all Americans believe that the Bible "answers all or most of the basic questions of life" (Gallup and Simmons 2000). These statements are shorthand descriptions of the idea of the Bible as God's *magnum opus*: the first and last Word on who God is, who we are, why we're here, and where we go after this—depending, of course, on how well we follow The Book.

As *The Hot Rodders's Bible* and others suggest, moreover, this iconic Bibleness possesses sacred capital that sells. By "sacred capital," I mean the accrued cultural value of a thing, idea, or tradition as sacred: literally "set apart." Although this form of capital can and often does translate to financial capital, the two are not reducible. Indeed, the performative dimension of iconic books, as described by Watts (Chapter 1, this volume), often serves to maintain their set-apartness from consumer culture. Not so, however, with regard to sacred capital that circulates outside ritualized religious practices in the mainstreams of popular culture, where the ontological filter of money prevails: if it is not monetizable, it does not exist. Clearly, the sacred capital of the Bible, that is, its accumulated value as sacred, set apart, associated with divine authority and authoriality, sells. It is widely popular and desirable.

This idea of the Bible as a divine manual for finding happiness with God in this world and salvation in the next is so familiar to us today that we might as well assume it's been around forever, that it's as old as Christianity itself. It's not. In fact, its genesis was in nineteenth century Protestantism, where the Reformation ideal of *sola scriptura*, "Scripture alone," combined with a popular Protestant evangelistic movement, sometimes described as a new Puritanism because of its romantic idealization of that earlier, seemingly simpler form of Christianity, to promote the Bible as the key to solving all of industrial America's emerging problems. The Bible, it was believed, could integrate immigrant populations in the new big cities. It could heal factions among Protestant churches and denominations. It could keep husbands sober and hold nuclear families together, even under new stresses of urban poverty and isolation. Rooted in nostalgia for the mythical, romanticized image of sixteenth- and seventeenth-century Puritan piety, this movement believed that the Bible was the solution for all social, familial, and individual ills.

Writing in 1851, theologian and biblical scholar John W. Nevin described this movement's then-novel idea of the Bible this way:

> In this sacred volume, we are told, God has been pleased to place his word in full, by special inspiration, as a supernatural directory for the use of the world to the end of time; for the very purpose of providing a sufficient authority for faith, that might be independent of all human judgment and will ... The great matter accordingly is to place the bible in every man's hands, and to have him able to read it, that he may then follow it in his own way. The idea seems to be, that the bible was published in the first place as a sort of divine formulary or text book for the world to follow ... so that the dissemination of its printed text throughout the world, without note or comment, is the one thing specially needful and specially to be relied upon for the full victory of Christianity, from sea to sea and from the river to the ends of the earth. (Nevin 1851, 549)

Nevin's reference to "without note or comment" alludes to one of the movement's most important organizations, the American Bible Society. Founded in 1816 and modeled on its British sister organization, the British and Foreign Bible Society, its sole objective was "to encourage a wider circulation of the Holy Scriptures without note or comment." The Society's initial address "To the People of the United States" is indicative of the missionary zeal surrounding this new movement to "claim our place in the age of Bibles."

> This is no doubt of the Lord, and it is marvelous in our eyes. But what instrument has he thought fit chiefly to use? That which contributes, in all latitudes and climes, to make Christians feel their unity, to rebuke the spirit of strife, and to open upon them the day of brotherly accord—the Bible! the Bible!
>
> (American Bible Society, 1816)

Led primarily by Christian businessmen who made their money in the emerging fields of insurance and banking, the American Bible Society followed the latest industrial business models and was quick to adopt new innovations in the print industry, especially stereotype plates and steam power. Its highly efficient methods of management, production, and distribution led to tremendous success in fulfilling its mission to get the Word out, which its members fervently believed to be the only way to save American society.

The ABS's stipulation that Bibles be printed "without note or comment" was central. It was an expression of commitment to the Puritanic Biblicist ideal that the Bible was complete unto itself, spoke for itself, and required no supplemental explanations or interpretations. Indeed, the ABS's commitment to vigilant stewardship of this idea is evident in their early minutes, which record several instances in which the board refused to innovate their Bibles by adopting emerging popular media formats (e.g., printing biblical books as newspapers) or adding supplemental content.

## *The Way* forward

Joel A. Carpenter (1997) has provided the larger historical trajectory by means of which this Puritanic Biblicist idea of the Bible found its way from late nineteenth- and early twentieth-century Protestant fundamentalism into the neo-evangelicalism of the mid-twentieth century, marked by a renewed engagement with secular youth pop culture and the eager adoption of mass media technologies and modes from the secular entertainment industry, and from there into contemporary evangelical culture, and how it remains the core of the iconic meaning of the Bible in popular culture – even, as we have seen, among those who reject it as such. Along the way, however, the mission of the ABS and BFBS to deliver its "without note or comment" and their concomitant commitment to strict stewardship of its material form and contents, have fallen by the wayside.

The biblical flagship of the neo-evangelical movement's breakthrough into pop culture was *The Way: The Living Bible Illustrated.* First published in 1972, it was the result of an innovative collaboration between a new publisher, Tyndale House, and the editors of *Campus Life* magazine, a slick, popular publication of Youth for Christ. Combining innovative form and content in a way that appealed specifically to the popular youth culture of the early 1970s, it was a breakout Bible. The floppy dark green cover of *The Way* looked more like a Doobie Brothers album than the Holy Bible: big groovy capital letters filled with photos of hip stringy-haired teens smiling and hanging out. Only the subtitle, in a much smaller, standard font, let on that this was "the Bible." Inside were more images of young people, black and white, male and female, playing guitars, laughing, and talking. Other pictures illustrated contemporary issues: a homeless man curled up on a sidewalk vent, a razor-wire fence, a garbage dump. At the beginning of every biblical book was a short introductory essay that spoke to concerns shared by many youth: poverty and homelessness, war and peace, love and marriage, making a living versus making a life.

Its biblical text was that of *The Living Bible,* a hugely successful modern English paraphrase of the American Standard translation, done by Kenneth N. Taylor while he was working at Moody Bible Institute, a cornerstone school and publishing house of neo-evangelicalism in Chicago that gained prominence during fundamentalism's separatist decades. During Taylor's long commutes to and from work, he wrote what he called a "thought for thought" paraphrase of the New Testament Epistles. When Moody and several other publishers declined to publish them as a book, Taylor and his wife, Margaret, created their own press, Tyndale House, named after the sixteenth-century English Bible translator William Tyndale who was martyred for translating the Bible into common English. The Taylors did not share Tyndale's fate. Operating out of their dining room, they self-published *Living Letters* in 1962. A year later, the book won the enthusiastic endorsement of Billy Graham, who ordered more than half a million copies to offer to his television audiences. Taylor's *The Living Bible* (1971), encompassing the entire Christian Bible, was an even greater success. It was the *New York Times* nonfiction bestseller in both 1972 and 1973. In 1983, Taylor presented the 28 millionth copy to President Ronald Reagan in commemoration of the Year of the Bible. As of 1996, *The Living Bible* had sold over 40 million copies.

Throughout its history, evangelicalism has faced a fundamental dilemma in the publication of its gospel message: "getting the Word out" by whatever means necessary while still protecting and preserving the sanctity of its scriptural and liturgical traditions. Nowhere is this dilemma more apparent than in the production and circulation of the Bible. On the one hand, to what extent should the Bible be adapted and altered, in form or content, to make it more available and accessible? On the other hand, to what extent should its holiness be preserved and maintained, at the expense of easy availability? Taking as its motto the apostle Paul's declaration, "I have become all things to all people so that by all possible means I might save some," evangelicalism has tended toward the former, that is, popularization. Although we tend to think of American evangelical Christianity as a conservative movement, in fact it tends to be the most liberal of Christianities when it comes to adapting religious tradition to popular interests and consumer demands. This is, after all, the movement that brought us Oreo-and-milk Communion services and birthday cakes for Jesus on Christmas.

Nearly a half century ago, Marshall McLuhan famously declared that the "medium is the message," that there is no separating content from form or meaning from technology, and that the electronic age is bringing an end to the age of print (McLuhan, 1994, 7–21). Evangelicalism often seems to be pronouncing a counter-declaration to the McLuhanian one. The medium, it seems to be saying, is by no means the message; the message is entirely independent of the medium. Indeed, as the Word of God, it transcends whatever form is adopted to mediate it.

The collaboration between the editors of *Campus Life* magazine and Tyndale House that culminated in *The Way* leaned hard in the direction of popularization, staking its faith in getting the message out by whatever media means necessary. The magazine editors, whose offices were next door to Tyndale's, were especially ambitious in reaching to fit in with the popular youth culture of the 1960s and early 1970s. It was a time of cultural revolution, and any Bible trying to speak to that ethos would inevitably be pushing against traditional boundaries. They designed the layout, wrote all the introductory essays, and provided the images, but nothing went forward until it was approved by Tyndale House. In most cases, the two editorial teams were simpatico. Occasionally, however, Tyndale would ask for something a bit less edgy.

Given that this collaboration was between a Bible publisher and a magazine publisher, it was no accident that *The Way* turned out to be something of a hybrid of the two print formats. Its floppy cover, trendy fonts, varied layouts, contemporary photomontages, and upbeat, engaging introductory essays give it a magazine feel. At the same time, it's clear that Tyndale was concerned to preserve a sense of the publication as "the Bible" as well. This concern is most clear on the pages of the biblical text itself, which offer a strong visual contrast to the introductory parts. The biblical text is very plain, laid out in the traditional two-column style, with traditional fonts and no pictures.

*The Way* sold an unprecedented 6.4 million copies. Although no one made a dime on it (the *Campus Life* editors took it on as a creative outreach project, and Tyndale donated all profits from sales to Christian missions), its huge success, along with that of *The Living Bible,* drew attention to the tremendous profit potential for publishers interested in reinventing the Bible in new, value-added forms. In the decades since, as pop culture and consumerism have become synonymous and as Christianity has emerged as a mass culture industry, the Bible business has gone much further. Indeed, it has burgeoned into one of the biggest and fastest-growing fields of publishing, selling many thousands of different Bibles in every imaginable form for many hundreds of millions of dollars a year. The biggest Bible publishers in this highly competitive business guard their sales data closely, but reliable industry sources estimate that 2007 saw about twenty-five million Bibles sold, generating revenues of about $770 million in the United States alone. That was an increase of more than twenty-six percent since 2005, which saw U.S. sales of about $609 million. In fact, the Bible publishing business has been enjoying a healthy compounded growth rate of close to ten percent per year for several years. Even during the low point of economic crisis in late 2008, when other book sales were hurting badly, Bible sales continued to boom, with an estimated $823.5 million that year. Indeed, Bible publishing tends to thrive during times of war and financial disaster. Although it's too early to know for sure, it may well turn out that the latest economic bust will be another boom time for the Bible business.

Despite the little-publishing-house-on-the-prairie myths of origins promoted by most big Bible publishing companies, this is no mom-and-pop Christian cottage industry. In fact, the two biggest and most ambitious Bible publishers are owned by larger non-Christian media conglomerates. Thomas Nelson, which publishes more than three hundred different Bibles and controls about twenty percent of the Bible market share in the United States, was purchased in 2006 by the private equity firm Inter-Media Partners VII in a deal worth $473 million. Zondervan, which lists more than five hundred different Bibles in its online catalogue and controls about thirty-five percent of the Bible market, was purchased in 1988 by HarperCollins, which is part of News Corporation, Rupert Murdoch's media empire.

## Values added

In fact, no one needs to buy a Bible. Free ones abound. Ancient biblical texts have no copyright, and many translations, including the King James Version, are in the public domain, part of free culture. They are very cheap to produce in book form, and essentially free to publish online. Any church I know, moreover, would happily give a Bible to anyone who asks for one or even looks potentially interested. And just about every time you spend a night in a hotel, there's a Bible in your nightstand that you're free to take home, courtesy of the Gideons International. The Gideons say they place more than 63 million free Bibles and New Testaments in hotels and other human traffic lanes around the world every year. That's 120 free Bibles per minute. And they're not the only ones handing them out. Throw a rock and you're as likely as not to hit a free Bible or someone who wants to give you one. How do you monetize Bibles when so many are freely available? *The Way* pointed the way forward: keep reinventing the Bible in new got-to-have, value-added forms, all marketed as incarnations of the one and only iconic Bible, the Word made paper. Which is what Bible publishers are doing. In 2005 there were 6,134 different Bibles published, which was over 600 more than were published in 2004.

In some cases, of course, adding value is simply a matter of packaging. Although the fully armored *Metal Bible* from Tyndale House boasts "the hippest exterior ever!" for example, its insides are the same as one of its publishers' standard editions available in many other formats. Likewise is Tyndale's handbag/Bible combination (the bag has an outside pocket made to fit the Bible perfectly); also *The Waterproof Bible* (Bardin and Marsee) and *Immerse* (Thomas Nelson), popular with outdoor enthusiasts, troops overseas, and tub soakers; and Nelson's *Duct Tape Bible,* which offers that extremely well-read look (see Parmenter, Chapter 12, this volume). Like the fashion jeans industry, the fashion Bible industry understands that many customers prefer products that look like old favorites right off the shelf. And yes, of course, Bibles are available in a number of denim washes.

In most cases, however, adding value goes well beyond innovative packaging and physical format. Most value-added Bibles literally drown out the biblical text under a cacophony of loud and colorful added content, "extra," "supplemental" material that is very clearly meant to be the center of the reader's attention. In true magazine fashion, all this added content distracts from serious, sustained reading. It's the biblical text that becomes supplemental. Adding value to the Bible almost always means adding "biblical" *values* that are either missing or really hard to find in the Bible itself but that provide that feeling of Bibleness so many biblical consumers seek. What follows are a few examples.

### *Biblezines*

Biblezines are market-specific Bibles in magazine form published by Thomas Nelson, Inc. They were originally developed by Hayley Morgan, whom Nelson hired away from that ultimate branding machine, Nike, in 1998 to be its young-adult brand manager. Using market research techniques that she learned at

Nike, there are Biblezines for just about every consumer. *Becoming* targets college-age and young professional women. *Explore* is for preteen boys, and *Refuel* is for teenage boys. *Blossom* is for preteen girls, and *Revolve* is for teenage girls. *Magnify* is for the Nickelodeon Channel generation. *Align* is for young professional men, and *Redefine* is for baby boomers.

Each Biblezine is a market-specific combination of text boxes, short articles, graphic hooks, ads for other Nelson products, and selections of biblical literature. The cover of the first installment of *Refuel*, for example, is deep burnt orange with an edgy sketch of an ancient battle scene. Cover lines promise to reveal "How Unstoppable Warriors Got So Awesome," "70 Ways To Live Out Radical Faith," "How to Impress the Girls!," and "Tons More Random Cool Stuff Lists." The biblical selections included focus on ancient Israel's conquest of Canaan (Joshua and Judges), the story of Ruth (which comes after Judges in the Christian Bible), and the rise and fall of the Israelite and Judean monarchies (the books of Samuel, Kings, Chronicles, Ezra, and Nehemiah). As in other Biblezines, these scriptural texts within the magazine's pages are typeset in a much more traditional, old-style bookish font, which makes them look much more Bible-ish, if also more boring.

On every page, the plain biblical text is overwhelmed by bold and colorful callouts, special columns, and other extras laid out in catchy fonts and colors. Whereas most of the biblical literature is about real, bloody battles, including some of the most explicitly described violence in Scripture, these value-adding extras speak of metaphorical battles: how to "guard your heart" when dating, how to resist peer pressure to drink, use drugs, or have sex (and how to deal with embarrassment as a Christian who doesn't do those things), how to maintain eye contact with a girl when talking with her, how to do your own laundry and dishes, and how to promote a creationist viewpoint to your biology teacher and classmates.

In contrast to the colorful, jump-off-the-page text boxes about highly relevant topics of teenage life, the bland, colorless biblical text quickly recedes into the background. The content of those biblical books, moreover, isn't exactly easy reading. Much of it concerns territorial boundaries and monarchical chronologies. To be sure, there are some fascinating stories here, including some of the all-time greatest femmes fatales, like Jael, the non-Israelite woman who becomes an Israelite heroine after tucking the fugitive army commander Sisera into bed and then driving a peg through his head. But those stories are buried. There are no "Guard Your Heart" features anywhere near Jael.

### *Manga Bibles*

As the Biblezine phenomenon demonstrates, one successful way to reinvent the Bible and create new consumer markets is to graft it onto other, less-bookish media that are selling well. In that light, we should have seen *manga* Bibles coming. *Mangas* are Japanese graphic novels or comic-book-style serial publications (*man* = "involuntary" or "cartoon"; *ga* = "brushstroke" or "picture"). In Japan, about forty percent of all print publications are *mangas*, including a very wide range of styles and subjects. In recent years, the market for English-language *mangas* in the United States has grown rapidly, as it has in other world markets, especially among teens and young adults. Annual sales in the United States grew from about $60 million in 2002 to $220 million in 2007, with 1,468 titles published. Although sales dropped in 2008 along with most other kinds of books, the future of this market looks bright.

Several Christian publishers see Bibles and *mangas* as a match made in heaven and are scrambling to gain the high ground in this new market niche. Tyndale House, for example, has partnered with NEXT, a nonprofit evangelical company of Japanese *manga* artists and media-savvy professionals committed to creating high-quality, innovative Christian *mangas* for teens and young adults in many languages. Tyndale purchased exclusive English-language rights for all *mangas* produced by NEXT. Their *Manga Messiah* is a full-color graphic-novel version of the story of Jesus, based on particular passages selected from the four Gospels of the New Testament. Not surprisingly, the editorial selections streamline the narrative to encourage readers to accept Jesus Christ as their personal lord and savior who died for their sins. Note that this biblical *manga* is called *Manga Messiah,* not *Manga Bible,* and its back-cover blurb takes care to describe it as "adapted from the ancient texts" rather than as "the Bible."

Tyndale and NEXT's *Manga Bible,* by contrast, is far less of a Bible genre bender: it is basically comprised of Tyndale's complete Slimline Reference edition of its New Living Translation Bible with a modestly *manga*-ish cover and three thirty-two-page glossy inserts of *manga* illustrations of select biblical narratives. A *manga* offers far more than simple illustrations of literary texts. Its visuals are by no means supplementary to the word, but interactive with it and with one another. Its layout invites the eye to move back and forth between frames on the page in a nonlinear fashion. That is very different from the linear, left-to-right and top-to-bottom way we read the text of a typical Bible book. In its titles, Tyndale implicitly recognizes this difference, reserving the title of "Bible" for that which more closely resembles its traditional Bibles.

Zondervan has demonstrated less reserve. Its *Manga Bible* is a series of small graphic novel style booklets, each covering a selection of biblical narrative. Targeting young readers, they include very few words, and even fewer biblical quotations. Their simple black-and-white scenes are loaded with cute talking animals and childlike biblical characters. In the Genesis-Exodus volume (2007), Adam and Eve look like pre-teens, and there is plenty of lighthearted humor ("Excuse me!" interrupts a whale just after being created on day five, "Have you seen my son Nemo?"). Yet the stories often reinforce particular morally conservative and patriarchal "biblical values" far more powerfully than any reading of the biblical narratives themselves can easily sustain. In the story of Eve, the Serpent, and Adam, for example, Eve is reimagined as a cute but dangerous (at least when left to her own devices) young temptress who pouts and coaxes a protesting Adam into partaking of the fruit. As Adam reflects, "It is good, but God said not to ...," she smiles and winks at the reader and says, "Hee hee ... Girls can make guys do anything." The last scene of this story depicts the couple after their departure from Eden: Eve stands at the door of their little house and waves at Adam as he heads off to work with the sack lunch she made for him.

### *Niche Bibles*

There are the hundreds of new niche-marketed Bibles available to consumers every year. These Bibles tap into the iconic idea that the Bible speaks directly and personally to each and every reader, as though God wrote it for and dedicated it to her or him. Every niche Bible claims to understand its target reader's personal interests and questions and claims to address them in familiar terms. The niche may be sports-related: *The Golfer's Bible,* for example, includes meditative photos of golf courses and reflections on passages by golf tour chaplains. Or it may appeal to people preoccupied with a big upcoming event: *The Bride's Bible* includes notes and articles that relate biblical passages to issues of marriage and family. Or it may address readers associated with a particular group or program: *The Life Recovery Bible,* the *Celebrate Recovery Bible,* and *Serenity* are Bibles with notes and meditations that relate biblical passages to eight- or twelve-step programs. There are also Bibles for specific ethnic groups of women and men. Popular titles for African Americans include *Aspire: The New Women of Color Study Bible: For Strength and Inspiration* from Zondervan, and the *Men of Color Study Bible* and *The Strength and Honor Bible for Young Men of Color.* In fact, market research indicates that African Americans own more Bibles per household than the general population and read their Bibles more often.

Another winner for publishers is to combine Scripture with one of their celebrity Christian authors. Thomas Nelson has been particularly successful in these ventures, with titles like *Holy Bible, Woman Thou Art Loosed! Edition,* featuring the renowned African American author and preacher T. D. Jakes, and Max Lucado's *The Devotional Bible: Experiencing the Heart of Jesus.* This comes in a variety of sizes and formats, all including extensive notes, short articles, and devotional excerpts from Lucado, whose inspirational books have sold well over 40 million copies. Another from Nelson, favored by many conservatives and fundamentalists, is the *MacArthur Study Bible,* replete with detailed notes from the well-known conservative intellectual preacher, author, and AM radio celebrity John MacArthur. With each of these Christian celebrity Bibles, we see a compounding of value: the Bible adds value to the author even as the author adds value to the Bible.

Clearly, many Bible niches are gendered, suggesting that the Bible speaks differently to men than to women. *Every Man's Bible,* for example, which is the foundation piece for a series of bestselling books, boasts of having more than three hundred text boxes and one-page perspective essays on a range of manly topics: "hard-hitting instructions from the Bible on work, sex, competition, time management, and much more." For the man's man who doesn't have time to mess with gray areas (no pun intended), this Bible promises "real answers, real fast ... No more second guessing what God really means." Inserted at the beginning of each book of the Bible is a feature titled "What's the Point?" in which a short answer is given to satisfy every man's need to get to the point, fast. "What's the point of Leviticus? God pays attention to detail." Of the Song of Songs? "The love of a good woman is worth cultivating." Of Zephaniah? "Actions lead to consequences." Of the Gospel of Luke? "Jesus cares about the individual." Of Revelation? "In the end, the Great One wins."

*Necessary supplements*

The back cover of Tyndale's best-selling *Life Application Study Bible* captures the felt need of many potential Bible buyers and repeat buyers have for that iconic Bible: "How many times have you read your Bible and asked: 'How can this possibly apply to my life, my job, my friendships, my marriage, my neighborhood, my family, my country? ... Why can't I understand what God is saying to me through His Word?'" The Bible is supposed to be God's clear and unambiguous Word, offering practical guidance and solutions to every problem. Other Bibles have not come through. This Bible understands.

Indeed, what it mainly seems to understand is that the biblical text itself, rife as it is with tensions and ambiguities among other hermeneutical challenges, is a big part of the problem, perhaps the greatest obstacle to discovering the iconic Bible readers/consumer seek. About one-third of the text in the *Life Application Study Bible* is extrabiblical, "supplementary" content, including notes on verses, synopses, charts, diagrams, topical sidebars, and reflective essays. Its main competitor in the field of devotional study Bibles is Zondervan's *NIV Study Bible,* which boasts more than twenty thousand notes. Nearly half of this Bible is "supplemental." Some of this material offers to help readers delve deeper into the biblical text itself, providing information about historical contexts, or alternative translations of the original Greek or Hebrew. More often, however, the intention is not to encourage readers to interpret for themselves but to interpret *for* them, to control meaning, dispelling doubts and questions and directing readers toward specific conclusions.

The same may be argued about the growing market for new translations that promise a level of biblical readability that has been missing for most readers. Indeed, the most successful new translations are based on functional equivalency approaches—"thought for thought" type renderings of larger semantic units (sometimes even paragraphs), more or less informed by work with Hebrew, Aramaic, and Greek editions that we used to call paraphrases. These too speak to the felt need of Bible consumers for a Bible that can overcome the biblical text's own apparent refusal to conform to the iconic cultural meaning they expect it to deliver.

## In conclusion

Such is the landscape of biblical consumerism today: thousands of different things, varying widely in media and message, all being sold as "the Bible": magazines, graphic novels, full-metal-jacketed, furry, duct-taped, waterproof, not to mention digital media, on the Internet, CDs, DVDs, iPods, e-books, mediating dozens of different translations, the most successful ones being highly interpretive, often selecting, distilling, and resifting biblical passages into new orderings and layouts, and of course providing lots of value-adding and values-adding extras, especially in the form of disambiguating "helps" and "supplements."

"If you put chocolate coating on an Oreo, it's a different cookie, and you ought to be able to charge more," says Paul J. Caminiti, a vice president at Zondervan. "The packaging has to scream that this is something really new: First time! Fudge-dipped! Chocolate coated!" (in Simon, 2007). If I follow this metaphor correctly, the Bible is the Oreo, and the fudge dip is the extra stuff that the publisher adds. As we've seen, there's at least as much double-stuffing as there is fudge-dipping. In any case, as he himself says, "it's a different cookie." Is it still an Oreo?

One may argue, as I have (Beal, 2011, 70–83), that the Bible business is unwittingly deconstructing the cultural icon of the Bible on which it depends, producing a wider and wider range of material things and semantic contents as "the Bible," thereby diluting its meaning to the point of eventual worthlessness. This is coinciding, moreover, with the twilight of print culture, which will have its own deleterious effects on the iconicity of the Bible. While it may appear that the Bible business is flying in the face of the larger fate of the book market, it's not. What we're witnessing is not a bumper crop but a distress crop.

Yet this semiotic disconnect between the iconicity of Bibles and the general cultural iconicity of "the Bible" is not really new. Indeed, if there's anything that's clear from the cultural history of the Bible, from earliest Christian scriptural culture through print culture to today, it's that there never has been such a thing as "the Bible" in the singular. To be sure, the print revolution lent a sense of fixity, closure, and immutability to the idea of the book. As Walter J. Ong famously observed, the printed book "encloses thought in thousands of copies of a work of exactly the same visual and physical consistency" (1982, 129–132; see also Plate and Stam in this volume). What was true of books in general was especially true of the Book of books, that is, the Bible. Yet the reality of the Bible in the age of Gutenberg has been quite the opposite: it has led to the proliferation of more Bibles in more forms and translations than ever. In fact, in their historical catalogue of Bibles in the British Library, T. H. Darlowe and F. H. Moule (1903–1911) count at least one thousand different editions of the Bible in English alone published by 1800. Among them, moreover, one finds a stunning array of forms and contents all published as "the Bible": from highly condensed pocket and thumb Bibles (some only a few pages long) to huge, multivolume study Bibles comprised mostly of "supplementary" notes and comments, often by celebrity preachers and scholars; from complete reshufflings of biblical content into new thematic reorganizations to alternative canons; from paraphrases and translations (some from otherwise unknown "original" sources) to picture Bibles; appearing in every possible shape, size, format, texture, and color.

Indeed, all seeds of current Bible biz proliferation were there since the beginning of the print revolution: a wide variety of physical forms and formats, often promoting novelty over readability; voluminous value-adding "extras" attached to celebrity ministers and authors, often overpowering, even burying, the biblical text in a mass of "supplemental" notes and comments; new and alternative translations and paraphrases; and massive abridgments, reshufflings, and rearrangements.

Here we find a paradox in the history of the print Bible: it appears that the cultural iconicity of "the Bible," which projects a solid, bookish singularity, unity, oneness, and authority, emerges alongside an ever-increasing plurality of Bibles. Both the emergence of that singular cultural iconicity and the proliferation of Bibles, the oneness and the manyness, it seems to me, are effects of the print revolution. The iconicity—the image and idea of "the Bible" as the Book of books and singular, literal Word of God—has grown in tandem with its multiplication in material form and semantic content (textual and visual). The image of oneness and the reality of manyness have developed hand in hand, each simultaneously encouraging and challenging the other. Indeed, it appears to me that the cultural icon of the one and only Bible, the Book of books, has been fortified in the course of this centuries-long flooding of Bibles.

All this raises, once again, the loose, largely one-way relationship between, on the one hand, the cultural iconicity of the Bible and other scriptures and, on the other hand, the particular iconicities of particular Bibles and other scriptures as developed and maintained through religious ritual practice. The cultural icon of the Bible draws imagery and attendant feelings from religious contexts in which scriptural iconicity is ritually performed, and then attaches the sacred capital generated by such religious practices to a wide variety of scriptural objects, many of which would fall far outside the regulations, explicit or implicit, of the religious contexts from which that sacred capital has been divested.

How far can the cultural icon stretch before breaking? How much material, visual, and literary heterogeneity can it hold, and under what conditions, without deconstructing? How, moreover, will the continuing decline of print book culture relate to the Bible's cultural iconicity?

## References

American Bible Society. 1816. Constitution and address "To the People of the United States." May 8, 1816. Courtesy of the American Bible Society archives.

Beal, Timothy. 2011. *The Rise and Fall of the Bible: The Unexpected History of an Accidental Book*. New York: Houghton Mifflin Harcourt.

Bielo, James S. 2009. *Words upon the Word: An Ethnography of Evangelical Group Bible Study*. New York: New York University Press.

Bourdieu, Pierre. 1986. "The Forms of Capital." Translated by Richard Nice. In *Handbook of Theory and Research for the Sociology of Education*, edited by John G. Richardson, 241–258. Westport, CT: Greenwood Press.

Carpenter, Joel A. 1997. *Revive Us Again: The Reawakening of American Fundamentalism*. New York: Oxford University Press.

Crosby, Cindy. 2006. "Not Your Mother's Bible." *Publishers Weekly*. 30 October.

Darlowe, T. H. and F. H. Moule. 1903–1911. *Historical Catalogue of the Printed Editions of Holy Scripture in the Library of the British and Foreign Bible Society*. London: The Bible House.

Gallup. 2011. "Religion." http://www.gallup.com/poll/1690/Religion.aspx. Accessed 3 January, 2011.

Gallup, Alec and Wendy W. Simmons. 2000. "Six in Ten Americans Read Bible at Least Occasionally." http://www.gallup.com/poll/2416/Six-Ten-Americans-Read-Bible-Least-Occasionally.aspx. Accessed 3 January, 2011.

Malley, Brian. 2004. *How the Bible Works: An Anthropological Study of Evangelical Biblicism*. Walnut Creek, CA: AltaMira Press.

*Manga Bible: Names, Games, and the Long Road Trip* (Genesis–Exodus). 2007. Written by Young Shin Lee, created by Brett Burner, and illustrated by Jung Sun Hwang. Grand Rapids: Zondervan.

McLuhan, Marshall. 1994. *Understanding Media: The Extensions of Man*. Cambridge, MA: MIT Press.

Myers, Kenneth A. 1989. *All God's Children and Blue Suede Shoes: Christians and Popular Culture*. Westchester, IL: Crossway Books, 1989.

Nevin, John W. 1851. "Early Christianity." *Mercersburg Review* 3: 1–26; 220–238, 359–398, 461–490, 513–562.

Ong, Walter J. 1982. *Orality and Literacy: The Technologizing of the Word*. New York: Methuen. http://dx.doi.org/10.4324/9780203328064

Pew Forum. 2006. *Many Americans Uneasy with Mix of Religion and Politics*. http://pewforum.org/Politics-and-Elections/Many-Americans-Uneasy-with-Mix-of-Religion-and-Politics.aspx. Accessed 3 January, 2011.

*Refuel: Old Testament Epic War Battles*. 2005. Nashville: Thomas Nelson.

Reid, Calvin. 2007. "New Report Finds Manga Sales Up; Anime DVD Down in '07," *Publishers Weekly*, 7 December.

Simon, Stephanie. 2007. "Selling the Good Book by Its Cover." *Los Angeles Times*, 25 December.

Skidmore, Sarah. 2008. "Bible Publishers Go Niche in Hopes of Gaining Readers." *USA Today*, 7 October.

Thuesen, Peter J. 1999. *In Discordance with the Scriptures: American Protestant Battles over Translating the Bible*. New York: Oxford University Press.

*The Way: The Living Bible Illustrated*. 1972. Wheaton, IL: Tyndale House Publishers.

Wosh, Peter J. 1994. *Spreading the Word: The Bible Business in Nineteenth-Century America*. Ithaca, NY: Cornell University Press.

# 12

# Iconic Books from Below: The Christian Bible and the Discourse of Duct Tape

Dorina Miller Parmenter

*Investigating the Christian Bible as "America's Iconic Book" (following Marty 1982) reveals that this icon is generated and maintained not only through lofty theology and high church rituals, but also through mundane and often invisible biblical practices. By examining how people engage with their personal Bibles, scholars can better understand how status and authority is generated not only through semantic meaning, but also through material and embodied actions. This paper looks at one example of this in contemporary American Evangelical Christianity: the display of worn-out Bibles and the discourses that surround the phenomena of duct-taped Bibles.*

If you see a Bible that is falling apart, it probably belongs to someone who isn't!
(Havner 1986)

## The heavenly book

There can be little doubt that the traditional theologies and epistemologies that support Christianity as well other "religions of the book" that developed in the Near East (Judaism and Islam: see Qur'an 5:65, 29:46; Widengren 1955; Peters 2007) privilege ideas "from above" over things "from below." Following the basic structure established by the mythologies of the Tablet of Destinies from Mesopotamia (see Parmenter 2009, 300–302) and influenced by Hellenistic and Neoplatonic *logos* theology (see Boyarin 2004, 89–111; Wiles 1982, 13–23), Christians have built upon Jewish myths of scriptural origins to articulate their own views of God's revelation from on high. The foundational story of Hebrew Scripture is the Exodus narrative of how God's Book was revealed to humans when Moses went up to Mount Sinai to write the covenant dictated by God (Exod 24:4–7, 34:28; see *Baba Bathra* 15a), and when Moses received the Tablets of the Law written by God (Exod. 24:12, 32:16, 34:1). Regardless of the hand that generated the copy, God in heaven is imagined as the originator of the Torah that is handed down to humans (*Sanhedrin* 99a). Following the same pattern of the revelation of the heavenly Book, Christians imagined Jesus as the divine Word from above (John 3:31) made flesh in the world below (John 1:14, 8:23) and embodied in the Christian Scriptures (see Parmenter 2009, 302–309).

This mythological image of Christian scripture, lying behind what Barbara Holdrege has called the "ontological status of scripture" (1989, 181), is an important component for understanding the Bible as an iconic book. Martin Marty first described the Bible as an iconic book in his 1980 centennial address to the Society of Biblical Literature entitled "America's Iconic Book." Observing Americans' ignorance of modern biblical criticism, Marty claimed that Protestant-infused America treats the Bible as an icon. The Bible is a ubiquitous image that is taken for granted; it structures and organizes experiences based on its prominent visibility as it is carried in rituals, enshrined in homes, illustrated in and as religious art, encapsulated in monuments, lauded in miracle stories, and even read from time to time (Marty 1982, 5–7). According to Marty, "icon" is an apt designation for a book such as this, functionally equivalent to icons used in Orthodox Christianity—accessible, material objects perceived to evoke experiences of the sacred and allow for participation in that reality through myth and ritual (1982, 13–14, 16; Parmenter, Chapter 4, this volume, 64; Parmenter 2010, 55–56).

At first glance it would seem that calling the Bible an icon is just another reiteration of the prominent status given to the Book from above, for the Bible is undeniably an immediately recognizable symbol with connotations of admiration or veneration (Wharton 2003, 4). But if one looks beyond colloquial understandings of icons (see Parmenter, Chapter 4, this volume, 64; 2009, 298; Stam in this volume) to examine the history, theory, and use of icons in Orthodox Christianity more carefully, calling the Bible an "icon" turns out to be iconoclastic. Religious icons are not untouchable images; they are material objects that facilitate access to their transcendent prototypes through resemblance (Eastmond 2003, 74; Rice and Rice 1974, 10). As material mediators they make the divine, invisible world available to human sensory perception. Thus, in practice, icons blur the boundaries between above and below, invisible and visible, divine and human, immaterial and material. This liminality was precisely the reason why the use of icons was opposed by many ecclesiastical and political leaders during the iconoclastic controversies of the eighth and ninth centuries. For those who police the boundaries between above and below, icons smack of idolatry. Therefore, Byzantine iconodules had to walk a thin line between praise for the sensory material world through which God is revealed and the primacy of God. The Decree of the Second Council of Nicaea (787) is articulated carefully to defend icons against the iconoclasts' charges of idolatry: "the honour which is paid to the image [the icon] passes on to that which the image represents, and he who reveres the image reveres in it the subject represented" (*NPNF* ser. 2, vol.14, 550). The epistemology of signification and representation that maintains the hierarchy of God above and creation below always dominates Christian theoretical and theological perspectives.

But ritual practices that employ icons (including the Bible as an icon) reveal a different story—and it is the meaning generated through these ritual uses "from below" that I will emphasize in the remainder of this essay, after a brief excursus into modern biblical studies and the contemporary state of the study of religion.

## Seeing the invisible book

The Bible as a ritual and material object has been frequently overlooked in the academic study of religion, particularly in the study of Christianity. While ritual uses of the Bible have been noticed when it appeared that the Bible was being misused in some way—for example, as an amulet, for divination, or in unsavory rituals—the Protestant standard of *sola scriptura* lying behind *Religionswissenschaft* made the semantic uses of scripture, and its inherent anti-materialism and anti-ritualism, the invisible standards for "advanced" religion (see Parmenter, Chapter 4, this volume, 65). This attitude has created blind spots in scholarship toward the material and ritual contexts of many "normal" Christian practices, such as Bible ownership, display, and reading, and the social and economic modes of production that make these practices possible.

But in the past ten years or so, the tide has begun to turn in biblical studies. In his plenary address given to the Society of Biblical Literature in 2008, Jonathan Z. Smith reflected upon recent changes in the academic study of the Bible and called for a conscious redescription of biblical studies as part of the study of religion. As scholars take into account ways that various world religions are studied, Smith pointed out, one must apply the same approaches and concerns to studies of the Bible. He said that "alongside a focus on ritual, on performance, equal to that given to myth, to sacred text," there ought to be "an equivalent concern for sacred texts as embodied material objects commensurate with interests in those texts as documents of faith and history" (Smith 2009, 28). This shift has been taking place as the book of the Bible has been brought "low" into studies of popular, material, and visual culture (e.g., Beal 2011; McDannell 1995; Morgan 2005; Parmenter 2010), as well as in analyses of "biblicism" (Malley 2004; Bielo 2009b), a useful term that has emerged from recent studies in the anthropology of Christianity. My own interest in examining the Bible from below—as an object that "works" in ways that would be regarded as unorthodox when viewed from above—is to demonstrate the dialectic between the slippery poles of "high" and "low" and official and unofficial religion, among other dichotomies. The meaning and status of the Bible is not only generated by the authority of the text and the discourse surrounding the text, but also by the Bible as an image and object employed in diverse practices that generate meaning and authority in other ways besides semantic interpretation.

## The performance and discourse of duct taped Bibles

> At Leonard's [Book Restoration] we care about your Bible. We're a pastor and his family, and we recognize the value of the Bible. It's not just any old book! … NEVER use rubber cement or glue guns on a book, unless, of course, you don't like the book and wish to destroy it, in which case, I would also suggest cello tape, or even duct tape. (Haley 2010)

> I think the best Bibles have some sort of tape on the outside, and front or rear pages that are barely attached to the binding. Bibles get this way because people actually read them, carry them, write in them, pray and weep over them, spill coffee on them, clutch them, leave them on the car dashboard in error on hot summer days, and love the God whose words they hold. (Farley 2009)

My initial interest in uses of the Bible as an icon in contemporary American Protestantism derived from observing people's desire to treat the Bible with care. I have found that many Christians are reluctant to set a Bible on the floor, to set other books on top of it, and carry the Bible in a protective case (David B. 2008) because "it's not just any old book" (Haley 2010); it is the Word of God and should be treated with respect (see Parmenter 2010; Malley 2004, 45–48). But there are contemporary Bible rituals that demonstrate an opposing sentiment, as articulated by one Bible-user:

> I WANT my Bible to look well used. … I love knowing that my less-than-pristine cover and pages remind me that I take it with me everywhere. I bought it to use and mark and carry around—why should I spend extra time, money, and effort to make it look like that's not what I'm doing with it? (Jessica 2009)

The case that I would like to investigate as an example of "iconic books from below" involves the practice common in some American evangelical communities of conspicuously displaying a worn-out Bible, a phenomenon that frequently is distilled by exhibiting a Bible held together by duct tape. Versatile, utilitarian, and iconic in its own right, popular culture screams that everyone loves duct tape; it "has secured a place in American culture right along with Mom, baseball and apple pie" (Putnam 2010). Duct tape, as it is known today, was developed during World War II as a waterproof tape for sealing ammunition cases, but its strength and durability soon turned it into an all-purpose fix-it tape for military equipment. It was originally "army green" and perhaps called 'duck' tape because it was made with cotton duck fabric and shed water much like a duck's feathers would. After the war it was commonly used to seal duct work for heating and air conditioning and was henceforward silver-colored and called "duct" tape (Putnam 2010; Safire 2003). Duct tape has become known for its quick-fix abilities not only around the house but by NASA astronauts (Putnam 2010; NASA 2008), and has become the punch line for many political jokes since the United States Department of Homeland Security recommended in 2003 that households stock up on duct tape as a part of an emergency kit to have on hand in case of a terrorist attack (HSD 2003; James 2003).

Similar to the iconic jeweled Gospel-books or Bibles commonly associated with handwritten and illuminated manuscripts and often seen in the hands of Jesus, the apostles, and saints in portraiture (see Brown in this volume), duct-taped Bibles send a message about the piety of their users. But, unlike the Book as a repository of divine power, "an object of adoration and a jewel-box of mysteries, not to be used directly and thus closed" (Petrucci 1995, 29; see Parmenter, Chapter 4, this volume, 76), the implication of a duct-taped Bible is that the book is read and referenced as an "owners manual" (Misen 2008). It marks "a person who is sincere about his desire to have the Bible influence every part of his thinking" (Farley 2009).

The performances and discourses around duct tape Bibles are poignant examples of biblical iconicity because they are intentionally iconoclastic; that is, they arise out of Protestant-Reformed religious traditions that self-consciously reject practices from highly liturgical forms of Christianity (such as Roman Catholicism, Eastern Orthodoxy, and Anglicanism or Episcopalianism) that frequently process with and prominently display large and lavishly decorated Bibles. These "high church" rituals would be regarded as misplaced or even idolatrous to the evangelical Protestant communities whose religious practices and daily lives center instead upon the prominent use of personal Bibles. While there are some mainline Protestant denominations that are evangelical, many American evangelicals are also "non-denominational" Christians. Implied and often overtly displayed through the rejection of institutional structures and liturgical guidelines, the self-identity of non-denominational, evangelical Bible-believers involves anti-ritualism and anti-materialism with regard to their religious practices. For example, one online testimonial states,

> We didn't recognize [Bob's] Bible because his name was embossed in gold on the cover. It wasn't. We knew Bob's Bible by the duct tape that held it together. Bob brought the Bible to Sunday school, Bible study, and the Tuesday evening pastor's class. He read it at home. He used it. He used it so hard and so often that the cover began to fall off. So he bound it with duct tape. And he continued to use it until the tape itself began to wear and fray. (Carl 2006)

In cases like Bob's Bible, duct tape signifies the frequent physical manipulation of the Bible in the service of textual reference. One might argue that the tape is purely functional—it holds together a book that it is important for the individual to retain because it contains highlights, marginal notations, questions, and comments that contribute to the individual's understanding of the text. But the material and ritual performance of displaying a duct tape bible is inescapable:

> Bob's Bible—the Duct Tape Bible—became something of an icon at his memorial service earlier this year. We used it as our processional Bible. When we read the lessons from it, there seemed to be a message-within-the-message: "This is the word of God, which today we hear in a special way because it comes to us from the pages of a Bible that belonged to a person who was profoundly transformed

by the word." (Carl 2006; see also Watts, Chapter 1, this volume, 28–30, on the phenomenon of "relic books" and Stam in this volume on "association copies")

I would like to explain what I mean by the phrase "contemporary evangelical Protestant Christianity," since Christians who self-identify with the term "evangelical" are numerous and very diverse. Most, though certainly not all, evangelicals see themselves as being politically, socially, and theologically conservative, united by "their common adherence to the basic *authority* of Scripture as the *only* dependable guide for faith and practice" (Falwell 1981, 53, italics added). While many also describe their method of interpreting the Bible as "literal," most scholars of Christianity agree that in evangelical circles, "literal" is a metaphor for an authoritative attitude toward the text and a referential, rather than performative, view of language (Bielo 2009a, 49). A similar idea is meant by evangelicals' self-identification as "Bible-believers": they believe that the Bible is the authoritative W/word of God, the only guide for true Christian living, and is therefore an important reference point for all thought and action. Another important tenet of evangelicalism—and that which has distinguished evangelical Protestant Christians from more insular fundamentalist Protestant Christians since the 1920s—is the mission to engage with and witness to the world (Marsden 1970, 4; Weber 1982, 102; Malley 2004, 20), to demonstrate one's faith in all words and deeds, with the hope of inspiring others to convert to Bible-centered or Jesus-centered Christianity (see Prothero 2003, 79–82).

For these related purposes, it is necessary for evangelical Christians to have Bibles nearby for ritualized and impromptu textual reference as well as to act as an identity marker. The evangelical Bible market feeds this Bible-desire, creating a variety of mass-produced, inexpensive, and easily identifiable softcover "floppy" leather and paperback Bibles, as well as Bible-covers and other Bible accessories. With the Bible at the center of Protestant life, it is no surprise that there is an abundance of commercial Bibles available, both in terms of translations, and, more recently, in terms of "niche Bibles" or Bibles targeted at particular consumer groups (see Gutjahr 2008; Harding 2009; Beal 2011 and in this volume).

In many cases, using and displaying Bibles held together with tape is an intentional rebuff to the conspicuous consumption of "Bibles for every occasion" or quality "luxury Bibles" marketed by various evangelical publishing houses. A certain kind of Bible consumerism is being rejected with duct-tape practices such as these. This discourse values instead economy, functionality, nostalgia, sentimentality, and personal relevance. For example, I have found that a common internet genre associated with duct-taped bibles is a narration of one's life-journey with his or her book, illustrated through photographs that reveal the condition of that book. Many people write about the battered book as a metaphor for the trials and tribulations of their lives, and like the tape that holds this object together, the Bible held them together as well.

One woman writes:

> I have a confession to make: I've got a duct-taped Bible.... Maybe you have a Bible that proudly displays an NIV, KJV, NCV, RSV, or NKJV on the cover. Me? I've got a DTV. My Duct-Taped Version and I have traveled more than a few road miles together.... When the spiritual switch flipped on for me, that Bible—the one now soaked in nail polish remover—had been a life raft.
>
> Now it was ruined and it smelled funny, to boot. But I simply couldn't abandon it. Those that loved me attempted an intervention. Graduation, birthday and Christmas gifts became predictable: Bibles—shiny and new, one was even hand-painted by a gifted artist. I saw behind their subterfuge: my friends were embarrassed by the state of my Bible. I graciously accepted their gifts, slapped some duct-tape on ol'faithful, and kept on trucking.
>
> Once, many years later, my sweet husband bought me a tastefully crafted leather cover for the precious Book. I tried it for a while, but by that time, anything so pristine felt foreign in my hands. I had come to appreciate the tattered feel of my DTV. On a deeper level, I suspect that my Bible's rough and tumble appearance was a memorial of sorts—a visceral reminder of how God takes the broken shards of a life and creates something useful and good.
>
> The original pieces of duct tape are still there, holding together the Bible that represents the topography of my redemption. It strikes me that, in so very many ways, we're all a little like the duct-taped Bible: little frayed around the edges, beautifully marked by life, and held together by a God who never lets go.
>
> (Allen 2008)

This sentiment is captured in a popular evangelical slogan found on bumper stickers, church placards, and Christian home art: "a Bible that is falling apart usually belongs to someone who isn't" (modified from Havner 1986). While this phrase generally prompts the-poor-condition-of-my-Bible narratives like the one above, negative responses to the motto reveal a less edifying side of the display or worn-out or duct-taped Bibles. "I knew a person who bragged about how he read his bible so much, it now needed to be duct taped," writes one Christian blogger. "Isn't this similar to praying out loud in the streets to be heard?" (Yoo 2010). J. Mark Bertrand, who operates a blog about functional Bible design and quality binding, laments what he learned growing up, that

> there was an inverse relationship between the condition of your Bible and the condition of your soul. The nastier your Bible looked, the better your chance of eternity. We were saved by grace, but with a little help from patina.
>
> (Bertrand 2008)

Therefore, "artificial aging" techniques (like dipping Bibles in puddles or throwing them against a wall) were used to cover the shame of being a new Christian with a new Bible (Bertrand 2008; see also Anna 2008, Mike 2008; on the status of "young Christians," see Bielo 2009b, 39–40). Bertrand speculates that the sentiment, "a Bible that is falling apart usually belongs to someone who isn't," has contributed to consumer apathy about poor Bible manufacture:

> When a Bible does fall apart, the last thing you want to do is replace it. That thing is Pharisee Gold, the ultimate status symbol! Come to think of it, quality publishing might not be such a good thing. If occasional use was no longer tantamount to abuse, what would become of our pretenses?
>
> (Bertrand 2008)

Recognition of these "pretenses" about the apparent wear of one's Bible has elicited worry from those who feel judged for not using a nastier-looking Bible.

> I have purchased six or so new Bibles and read from all of them. Thus, each Bible I own only gets 8–15% of the wear it would get if it were the only one. What do people think when they see my forever new Bibles on Sundays?
>
> (McCullars 2008; see also David T 2008 and John 2008)

Similarly, one respondent questions where this attitude leaves those Christians who read their Bibles electronically (Mueller 2008).

The idea that biblical iconicity can come in many forms is captured in comments about worn-out Bibles as being "pharisaical":

> Jesus hounded the Pharisee's [sic.] for looking pristine on the outside but dirty on the inside. This worn Bible thing is just the opposite, looking for something dirty on the outside to indicate that something is clean on the inside…
>
> Somehow it seems shallow and superficial to desire a worn out falling apart Bible for the purpose of displaying piety. You know, in the OT, God put a premium on keeping the holy vessels in pristine condition and proper care of those items. I think it's a good thing to follow similar care for our Bibles and value their beautiful condition when they are new. And as they age, they begin to show the character of being an item that we use, but at some point, they will need to be replaced as all things in this world eventually rot and turn to dust. It's not a symbol of piety, it's the reality of our fallen world and the effect sin has on creation. One day, when creation is renewed by Jesus, all Bibles will look new. Thieves will not come in and neither will the moths or rust destroy.
>
> It's a twist in perspective to think, wear on our Bibles is the effect of sin on our Bibles. And to induce premature wear on your Bibles, is to artificially induce the effects of sin on our Bibles. Does that sound good!
>
> "What shall we say then? Are we to continue in sin that grace may abound? By no means!"
>
> Romans 6:1(Lombardi 2008; see also Bertrand 2008 and David B. 2008)

Looking at duct-tape Bibles as objects that signify through appearance and use is an effective example of how iconic books work because one could regard the use of duct tape as purely functional. The tape holds together the book that has come apart due to excessive use (or poor quality manufacture); how that tape looks to others could be merely a side-effect of its functionality. But the meaning generated by the use and appearance of a duct-tape Bible exceeds all practical purposes, particularly when duct-tape is applied to Bibles that are *not* in need of repair. Do you want to militarize or ruggedize your Bible (Kroencke 2008)? Need tips for how to turn your child's Bible into a personalized book that he or she can be proud of (Brett 2009)? How-to web websites and videos can guide you through the process of creating a "cheap and exciting" custom Bible with duct tape (Brett 2009; Abbygale1 2010; Luke 2009) that will serve as a reminder that God "heals the brokenhearted and binds up their wounds" (Psalm 147:3 in Weber 2007; see also Carl 2006). *The Gospel According to Duct Tape* webpage with audio sermon advocates duct tape as an apt metaphor for Christians, because as it is used one can see "in the physical world what the scripture teaches us in the spiritual world" (Simone 1997); that is, that Jesus "is the savior of all things broken" (Tim n.d.). Thus, duct tape is called "Jesus tape" in Finland ("*jeesusteippi*" 2009).

## Conclusion

It probably comes as no surprise that one of the most recent developments in the performance and discourse of duct tape Bibles is the production of a New Century Translation of the Bible from Thomas Nelson Publishers called *The Duct Tape Bible* (2006). One reviewer of the product succinctly described the marketing appeal of this book:

> With the hundreds of Bible choices available, what makes The Duct Tape Bible stand out is its appearance. Some might think having a paperback Bible wrapped in Duct Tape is nothing more than a money-making gimmick, but others might appreciate the visual metaphor that can be both a conversation starter and also a personal reminder that God's Word, even more than the ever-durable duct tape, never fails, is totally reliable, accomplishes its job, and lasts forever.
>
> Combining this visual object lesson with the readability of the thought-for-thought New Century Version (NCV) makes this a Bible especially suited for teenage boys or others who are not content to remain inside a cushy comfort zone, but are into "living it" or "keeping it real," or rolling up their sleeves and getting busy after leaving the Sunday morning pew.
>
> The silver duct tape version speaks to me more than the camouflage version, though I can see how those heavy into spiritual warfare might choose the camouflage version. (Encompassed Runner 2007)

Whether lavishly decorated or worn-out and held together with duct tape, the appearance of one's Bible and the engagement of that Bible in social performance creates more than a metaphor. Underlying the idea that the Bible operates as an icon—as a vehicle for an experience of the sacred—are ritual practices that treat the Book as if it were the divine presence itself. Throughout the history of the Bible, in both formal liturgical rites and in private use, Gospel-books and Bibles were objects that mediated the power and authority of Christ. Unconsciously intertwined with these rituals were shared cultural narratives, or myths, about where the Book came from. Like pictorial icons and like the incarnate Christ, the Bible was seen to mediate sacred power because of its divine origins. The slipperiness between the philosophical idea of the Word of God, words on a page that convey meaning, and the Word's/words' relationship to the Book continue to contribute to the complexity and the power of the image of the Bible (Parmenter 2009, 2010, and Chapter 4 this volume).

This examination of iconic books "from below" shows that rituals that engage the Bible as the Word can be subtle, and the narratives of a book's origins can be mundane. But nevertheless, how one engages a Bible signifies more than one's ability to read the text; the combination of material performances and discursive acts with a Bible send a "metatextual message—a message about the text" (Malley 2004, 71) as well as a message about the user of that text. One blogger wrote how he was encouraged by his wife's worn-out Bible:

> I was thankful and thrilled as I started thinking about all the days of reading, chewing, and thinking on the Scriptures that have led to this destruction. My wife's steady Bible work was, at that moment, very attractive. Think about the accumulative effect of the daily intake of the Word. God steadily and continually reforms and conforms the minds of his saints by his powerful Word so that we might think his thoughts after him. What a privilege it is to be confronted and consoled with the divine Word. (Erik 2009)

What I have attempted to demonstrate throughout this study is that in various uses of and attitudes toward the Bible, in discourses that are verbal, visual, and material, Christians have treated the Bible in ways that mirror their perceptions of Christ as a mediator of divine power and authority. While many of those same Christians might deny the efficacy of pictorial icons as they are used in Eastern Orthodox Christianity, their words and deeds treat the Bible as an icon embedded in a long history of complex yet taken-for-granted social practices that negotiate the relationship between embodied human experience and spiritual ideals.

## References

Abbygale1. 2010. "My AWESOME Bible!" *YouTube*. http://www.youtube.com/watch?v=uigYic4lH8A. Accessed 13 August 2010.

Allen, Allison Metcalf. 2008. "From One Woman of Faith to Another with Allison Allen." *Women of Faith Association*. 27 Februrary. http://www.allisonallen.net/February_27_2008.pdf. Accessed 13 August 2010.

Anna. 2008. Response to "Does a Trashed Bible Signal One's Piety?" *Bible Design Blog*. 14 November. http://www.bibledesignblog.com/2008/11/does-a-trashed-bible-signal-ones-piety.html. Accessed August 2010.

Barna Research. 2004. "Religion Activity Increasing in the West." *Barna Group*. 1 March. http://www.barna.org/barna-update/article/5-barna-update/136-religious-activity-increasing-in-the-west?q=bible+reading. Accessed 13 June 2008.

Beal, Timothy. 2011. *The Rise and Fall of the Bible: The Unexpected History of an Accidental Book*. New York: Houghton Mifflin Harcourt.

Bertrand, J. Mark. 2008. "Does a Trashed Bible Signal One's Piety?" *Bible Design Blog*. 13 November. http://www.bibledesignblog.com/2008/11/does-a-trashed-bible-signal-ones-piety.html. Accessed 15 August 2010.

Bielo, James S. 2009a. *The Social Life of Scriptures: Cross-cultural Perspectives on Biblicism*. New Brunswick: Rutgers University Press.

———. 2009b. *Words Upon the Word: An Ethnography of Evangelical Group Bible Study*. New York: New York University Press.

Boone, Kathleen C. 1989. *The Bible Tells them So: The Discourse of Protestant Fundamentalism.* Albany: State University of New York Press.

Boyarin, Daniel. 2004. *Border Lines: The Partition of Judaeo-Christianity.* Philadelphia: University of Pennsylvania Press.

Brett, 2009. "Bible Makeover #1 – My Son's Bible (Colorful to Camo)." *Pastor Brett.* 8 September. http://pastorbrett.wordpress.com/2009/09/08/bible-makeover-1-my-sons-bible-colorful-to-camo/. Accessed 5 September 2010.

Carl, Phil. 2006. "Bob's 'Duct Tape Bible': Its wear shows the power of the word." *The Lutheran.* October. http://www.thelutheran.org/article/article.cfm?article_id=6080. Accessed 13 August 2010.

David B. 2008. Response to "Does a Trashed Bible Signal One's Piety?" *Bible Design Blog.* 14 November. http://www.bibledesignblog.com/2008/11/does-a-trashed-bible-signal-ones-piety.html. Accessed 15 August 2010.

David T. 2008. Response to "Does a Trashed Bible Signal One's Piety?" *Bible Design Blog.* 14 November. http://www.bibledesignblog.com/2008/11/does-a-trashed-bible-signal-ones-piety.html. Accessed 15 August 2010.

*Decree of the Second Council of Nicaea* 1890-1900. In *Nicene and Post-Nicene Fathers*, Second Series, edited by Philip Schaff and Henry Wace, vol. 14, 549–554. Edinburgh: T & T Clark. [Reprint ed., Grand Rapids, MI: Eerdmans, 1991].

Eastmond, Antony. 2003. "Between Icon and Idol: The Uncertainty of Imperial Images," In *Icon and Word: The Power of Images in Byzantium*, edited by Antony Eastmond and Liz James, 73–85. Aldershot: Ashgate.

Encompassed Runner. 2007. "It's about the Metaphor..." (review). *Amazon.*7 January. http://www.amazon.com/Duct-Tape-Bible-Thomas-Nelson/dp/0718018249/ref=cm_cr_dp_orig_subj. Accessed 13 August 2010.

Erik. 2009. "Encouraged by my Wife's Torn Up Bible." *Irish Calvinist.* 29 April. http://www.irishcalvinist.com/?p=2820. Accessed 5 September 2010.

Falwell, Jerry, Ed Dobson, and Ed Hindson. 1981. *The Fundamentalist Phenomenon.* Garden City, NY: Galilee-Doubleday.

Farley, A. J. 2009. "That's a Funny Name," *Worn Out Bibles: Do you know the real Jesus, or the one you made up?*, 10 December. http://wornoutbibles.blogspot.com/2009/12/thats-funny-name.html. Accessed 15 August 2010.

Gallup, Alec and Wendy W. Simmons. 2000. "Six in Ten Americans Read the Bible at least Occasionally." *Gallup.* 20 October. http://www.gallup.com/poll/2416/Six-Ten-Americans-Read-Bible-Least-Occasionally.aspx. Accessed 17 December 2004.

Gutjahr, Paul C. 2008. "The Bible-zine *Revolve* and the Evolution of the Culturally Relevant Bible in America." In *Religion and the Culture of Print in Modern America*, edited by Charles L. Cohen and Paul S. Boyer, 326–348. Madison: University of Wisconsin Press.

Haley, Eric, J. 2010. "Bible Post-Op Instructions: How to Care For Your Bible." *Leonard's Book Restoration Station*. 29 July. http://www.leonardsbooks.com/what-we-can-do/bible-care-pages/bible-post-op-instructions/. Accessed 5 September 2010.

Harding, Susan. 2009. "*Revolve*: The Biblezine: A Transevangelical Text." In *The Social Life of Scriptures: Cross-cultural Perspectives on Biblicism*, edited by James S. Bielo, 176–193. New Brunswick, NJ: Rutgers University Press.

Havner, Vance. 1986. In *The Vance Havner Quote Book*, edited by Dennis J. Hester. Grand Rapids, Michigan: Baker Publishing. http://www.wordsearchbible.com/catalog/sample.php?prodid=1929. Accessed 25 December 2010.

Heen, Erik M. 2007. "Bible Reading in North American and Constructivist Learning." *Teaching Theology & Religion* 10: 175–177. http://dx.doi.org/10.1111/j.1467-9647.2007.00353.x

Holdrege, Barbara A. 1989. "The Bride of Israel: The Ontological Status of Scripture in the Rabbinic and Kabbalistic Traditions." In *Rethinking Scripture: Essays from a Comparative Perspective*, edited by Miriam Levering, 180–261. Albany: State University of New York Press.

Homeland Security Department. 2003. "Preparing Makes Sense: Get Ready Now." *U.S. Department of Homeland Security*. http://www.ready.gov/america/_downloads/Ready_Brochure_Screen_EN_20040129.pdf. Accessed 18 August 2010.

"*jeesusteippi*." 2009. *Wiktionary*. 19 October. http://en.wiktionary.org/wiki/jeesusteippi. Accessed 22 December 2010.

James, Frank. 2003. "Critics unglued by government's advice to buy duct tape." Chicago Tribune. 13 February. http://articles.chicagotribune.com/2003-02-13/news/0302130317_1_duct-tape-homeland-security-department-terrorist. Accessed 18 August 2010.

Jessica. 2009. Response to "How to Carry Your Bible." *Bible Design Blog*. 4 June. http://www.bibledesignblog.com/2009/06/how-to-carry-your-bible.html. Accessed 5 September 2010.

John. 2008. Response to "Does a Trashed Bible Signal One's Piety?" *Bible Design Blog*. 14 November. http://www.bibledesignblog.com/2008/11/does-a-trashed-bible-signal-ones-piety.html. Accessed 15 August 2010.

Kroencke, J. Kent. 2008. "Things you can put duct tape on...." *Fear and Trembling*. 10 October. http://fearandtrembling.spaces.live.com. Accessed 13 August 2010.

Lombardi, Robert. 2008. Response to "Does a Trashed Bible Signal One's Piety?" *Bible Design Blog*. 14 November. http://www.bibledesignblog.com/2008/11/does-a-trashed-bible-signal-ones-piety.html. Accessed 15 August 2010.

Luke. 2009. "How to make a 'Duct Tape Bible' (with my daughters)." *YouTube.* 22 August. http://www.facebook.com/l.php?u=http://www.youtube.com/watch?v=sW3yBFVwuIg&h=f307d&ref=nf. Accessed 11 August 2010.

Malley, Brian. 2004. *How the Bible Works: An Anthropological Study of Evangelical Biblicism.* Walnut Creek, CA: Alta Mira Press.

Marsden, George M. 1970. *Fundamentalism and American Culture: The Shaping of Twentieth-Century Evangelicalism, 1870-1925.* Chicago, IL: University of Chicago Press.

Marty, Martin. 1982. "America's Iconic Book." In *Humanizing America's Iconic Book: Society of Biblical Literature Centennial Addresses 1980,* edited by Gene M. Tucker and Douglas A. Knight, 1–23. Chico, CA: Scholars Press.

McCullars, Stan. 2008. Response to "Does a Trashed Bible Signal One's Piety?" *Bible Design Blog.* 14 November. http://www.bibledesignblog.com/2008/11/does-a-trashed-bible-signal-ones-piety.html. Accessed 15 August 2010.

McDannell, Colleen. 1995. *Material Christianity: Religion and Popular Culture in America.* New Haven, CT: Yale University Press.

Mike. 2008. Response to "Does a Trashed Bible Signal One's Piety?" *Bible Design Blog.* 14 November. http://www.bibledesignblog.com/2008/11/does-a-trashed-bible-signal-ones-piety.html. Accessed 15 August 2010.

Misen, Robert. 2010. Response to "How Old's Your Bible." *Soulpants.* 2 May. http://soulpants.wordpress.com/2008/04/03/how-olds-your-bible/. Accessed 13 August 2010.

Morgan, David. 2005. *The Sacred Gaze: Religious Visual Culture in Theory and Practice.* Berkeley: University of California Press.

Mueller, Eric S. 2008. Response to "Does a Trashed Bible Signal One's Piety?" *Bible Design Blog.* 14 November. http://www.bibledesignblog.com/2008/11/does-a-trashed-bible-signal-ones-piety.html. Accessed 15 August 2010.

NASA. "Moondust and Duct Tape." 2008. *NASA Science: Science News.* 21 April. http://science.nasa.gov/science-news/science-at-nasa/2008/21apr_duct-tape/. Accessed 18 August 2010.

Parmenter, Dorina Miller. 2009. "The Bible as Icon: Myths of the Divine Origins of Scripture." In *Jewish and Christian Scripture as Artifact and Canon,* edited by Craig A. Evans and Daniel Zacharias, 298–309. London and New York: T. & T. Clark.

———. 2010. "A Fitting Ceremony: Christian Concerns for Bible Disposal." In *The Death of Sacred Texts: Ritual Disposal and Renovation of Texts in World Religions,* edited by Kristina Myrvold, 55–70. Farnham: Ashgate.

Peters, F. E. 2007. *The Voice, the Word, the Books: The Sacred Scripture of the Jews, Christians, and Muslims.* Princeton, NJ: Princeton University Press.

Petrucci, Armando. 1995. "The Christian Conception of the Book in the Sixth and Seventh Centuries." In *Writers and Readers in Medieval Italy,* edited and translated by Charles M. Radding, 19–42. New Haven, CT: Yale University Press.

Prothero, Stephen. 2003. *American Jesus: How the Son of God Became a National Icon.* New York: Farrar, Straus, & Giroux.

———. 2007. *Religious Literacy: What Every American Needs to Know—And Doesn't.* New York: Harper Collins.

Putnam, Daryl. 2010. "Duct Tape in Popular Culture." *Factoidz.* http://factoidz.com/duct-tape-in-popular-culture/. Accessed 23 December 2010.

Rice, David and Rice, Tamara Talbot. 1974. *Icons and their History.* Woodstock: The Overlook Press.

Safire, William. 2003. "On Language: Why A Duck." *New York Times Magazine.* 2 March. http://www.nytimes.com/2003/03/02/magazine/the-way-we-live-now-3-02-03-on-language-why-a-duck.html. Accessed 18 August 2010.

Sal. 2009. Response to "Encouraged by my Wife's Torn Up Bible." *Irish Calvinist.* 30 April. http://www.irishcalvinist.com/?p=2820. Accessed 5 September 2010.

Simone, Mark A. 1997. "What I Like About Duct Tape" (Sermon at Federated Church, Chagrin Falls, Ohio). *The Gospel According to Duct Tape.* http://www.octanecreative.com/ducttape/Gospel/index.html. Accessed 21 August 2010.

Smith, Jonathan Z. 2009. "Religion and Bible." *Journal of Biblical Literature* 128: 5–27.

Tim, the Duct Tape Guy. n.d. *The Gospel According to Duct Tape.* http://www.octanecreative.com/ducttape/Gospel/index.html. Accessed 21 August 2010.

Weber, Timothy P. 1982. "The Two-Edged Sword: The Fundamentalist Use of the Bible." In *The Bible in America: Essays in Cultural History,* edited by Nathan O. Hatch and Mark A. Noll, 101–120. New York: Oxford University Press.

Wharton, Annabel. 2003. "Icon, Idol, Totem and Fetish." In *Icon and Word: The Power of Images in Byzantium*, edited by Antony Eastmond and Liz James, 3–11. Aldershot: Ashgate.

Widengren, Geo. 1955. *Muhammad, The Apostle of God, and His Ascension.* Uppsala: Almquist & Wiksells.

Wiles, Maurice. 1982. *The Christian Fathers.* New York: Oxford University Press.

Yoo, Joseph. 2010. "A Bible That is Falling Apart," *Step by Step*. 23 February. http://pressingtoward.wordpress.com/2010/02/23/a-bible-that-is-falling-apart/. Accessed 15 August 2010.

# 13

# Be-Witching Scripture: The Book of Shadows as Scripture within Wicca/Neopagan Witchcraft

Shawn Loner

*This essay describes the idea of the Book of Shadows (BoS) within both historical and contemporary Wicca/Neopagan Witchcraft, focusing specifically on how the BoS may be understood as "scripture." The concept of "scripture" within this work is defined as a tripartite matrix of textuality, performance, and iconicity. Through a descriptive investigation of the history of the religion and the BoS, its use as ritual text and as ritual object, its physical meaning and iconicity, and its invested authority, this essay shows that the BoS can be understood as a form of scripture, in a functional and analogous sense. In addition, the essay briefly discusses the effect of popular "how-to" books on scriptural or canonical authority and how these, along with the concept of the BoS, are serving to routinize and standardize a tradition that largely prides itself on being creative and spontaneous.*

In the realms of religion and the popular imagination, the term scripture almost immediately brings to mind the Western, largely Judeo-Christian-Islamic, idea of sacred text exemplified by the Tanakh, Bible, and Qur'an. While not disputing this understanding, I suggest that there is more to the notion of scripture/sacred text as a conceptual category than merely these collections. There is also more nuance to the categories of scripture and canon than these obvious examples may lead one to believe. William Graham observed that, "The extended use of 'scripture' for any particularly sacred text is now common in modern Western usage and widely current internationally... At times, even the word 'bible' has been used, albeit less often, in a similarly general sense to refer to any sacred scripture" (Graham 1987, 57). I expand this generic understanding of scripture as a religiously sacred text by applying it to the fluid text of a religion that is not usually conceived of as having a scripture or authoritative textual tradition at all. This religion is Wicca and/or Neopagan Witchcraft and its sacred book is most commonly named the *Book of Shadows* (*BoS*). A *BoS* (there are many) is generally conceived as a written, ritual text for a coven or individual practitioner. It is often a personal journal and guidebook for performing rituals and practicing a magical life. I will demonstrate through a largely descriptive investigation of the history of the religion and the *BoS*, its use as ritual text and as ritual object, its physical meaning and iconicity, and its invested authority, that the *BoS* can be understood as a form of scripture in a functional and analogous sense. In addition, I will briefly discuss popular "how-to" books which, along with the concept of the *BoS*, are routinizing and standardizing a tradition that prides itself on being creative and spontaneous. While there have been some excellent studies of ritual and community formation in Neopagan movements, there has been little scholarly work done on the relationship between textuality and Neopaganism. This subject deserves greater scrutiny, particularly because Neopagans and Neopaganism are often portrayed as being, in some sense, a-textual and ascriptural.

## What is Wicca?

Before discussing the history of Wicca and its texts, it might be helpful to begin with a discussion of Wicca itself and how it is conceived within scholarship. This brief discussion of Wicca cannot do justice to the complexity of the religion as a whole, but should suffice to provide a background for the history and textuality of the tradition. The question "*What is Wicca?*" has itself been the subject of many lengthy discussions, each important to the development of a Wiccan understanding, yet at times also at odds with each other. One must necessarily speak in generalities when discussing the religion, since there are many different traditions under the larger "umbrella" of Wicca and many claims about the religion contradict each other. These differing understandings of Wicca result from the general lack of dogma and explicit structure within the religion as a whole. Many of the beliefs and particulars of practice are highly plastic in nature. In addition, Wicca is largely geared toward personal transformation and thus individuals are free to pursue various paths in their own practice. There are several conceptual, orientational, and textual similarities, however, that allow one to speak of Wicca as a religious tradition. Some of these will be discussed at greater length below, particularly as they engage the category of scripture.

I use the terms "Wicca," "Wiccan," "Witch," and "Witchcraft" somewhat interchangeably. For the sake of clarity, I use "Wicca" to designate the religion, also known as the Craft (which has certain connotations toward magical practices), whereas "Wiccan" and "Witch" will designate either the practitioner or a line of belief or practice, as in a Wiccan practice. I do this mainly because the labels used within the religion are mutable; different designations are favored by different authors. "Witch" is also being used to refer to both females and males. There are some subtle differences between Wicca and Neopagan Witchcraft, depending on the author in question. Wicca is the designation for the Witchcraft religion that traces some association with Gerald Gardner and his conception of the Craft, while Neopagan Witchcraft is a form that does not stem from Gardner. That being said, however, with the increasing dissemination of information about the religion, the distinctions are at best blurry and Wicca is the generally accepted term for designating the religion as a whole.

Wicca falls under the general category of religious movements labeled modern paganism or Neopaganism. Neopagan is the general term given to "alternative," contemporary, non-mainstream religious movements that attempt to revive, recapture or reconstruct the indigenous, pre-Christian religions of Europe. Michael York observes that it is "essentially a sociological term—one against which even many practising pagans protest... Neopagan refers to a new religious movement, one which has re-appeared however much it is based on ancient practice and tradition. Neopagan indicates a religious orientation which has emerged in our times or in relatively recent times" (York 1996, 160). He distinguishes between pagan, Neopagan, and various polytheistic religious movements in the following way:

> [T]he contemporary Neo-pagan "family" may be said to include "genuine" pagans such as Asatru, Odinists, Vanirists, and certain Druids in Britain... The practices of Candomble, Santeria, Voodoo and some Native Americans conform to traditional expressions of paganism as well, though here the sociologist of religion is less likely to consider them as "Neo-pagan". On the other hand, though Neo-pagans may be distinguished from polytheistic paganism to various extents, as a loosely identifiable religious orientation, paganism as a whole may be said to include both traditional pagans and Neo-pagans. In other words, Neo-pagans *are* pagans though generally pagans of a different kind.
>
> (York 1996, 160–161)

These groups can be described as popular religious movements, developing from individuals and small like-minded groups without the benefit of a formal, overarching religious institution. Many practitioners approach these various traditions on an individualistic level, coming with their own unique perspectives and conceptions. This is especially easy or common in Neopagan religions, since there is usually little central authority or overarching organization.

Wicca, as with most forms of Neopaganism, is a highly ritualistic and magical religion that has no one set of unifying beliefs. The conception of divinity within Wicca is also highly plastic. There are atheist Wiccans who conceive of no personified power behind their magical practices, but understand their practices simply as the manipulation of energy; monists who understand the divine as a single unified, yet usually non-personified whole; duotheists who conceive of a divine pair, male and female; and polytheists who utilize and venerate a multitude of gods and goddesses from one or many pantheons. The individual practices and ritual performances of Witches are also highly fluid although there is a general structure or framework that most rituals follow, as Sabina Magliocco noted:

> Ritual is a form of practice that unites all the Neo-Pagan traditions... NeoPagans rely on a shared concept of the magical, interconnected universe as one determinant of community membership. Ritual is the practical expression of the magical worldview. The concept of the interconnected universe finds its most complete expression in the practice of ritual. It is ritual that creates common experiences that bind American Neo-Pagans together, linking them to the past, to each other, and to the larger cosmos, as well as expressing the community's hopes for the future... Ritual plays a central role in Neo-Paganism... [I]t is the movement's most important form of expression. (Magliocco 2004, 126)

While Magliocco is speaking of Neopaganism in general, her description is no less true of Wiccans. Ritual practice and the worldview expressed through practical experience and performance is what binds these disparate individuals and understandings into a religious collective or community. I will return to the topic of ritual later, particularly as it relates to scripture and the *BoS*.

## The formation of Wicca, Gerald Gardner, and the *Book of Shadows*

One cannot discuss the history or textuality of Wicca or the *BoS* specifically as a scripture/scriptural concept without discussing the supposed reviver, inventor, or popularizer of the movement, Gerald Gardner. There is a good deal of controversy surrounding the origins of Wicca as a modern religious movement as well as the origins of the *BoS*, particularly Gardner's role in their formation. I will address many of these issues, but it is not possible or profitable to try to resolve them since the questions are considered largely moot by modern practitioners. Still, Gardner's role is important for understanding the *BoS* as scripture in a functional and analogous sense. I will therefore discuss his principles, bracketing any truth claims concerning them and focusing instead on their status as rhetorical devices and functional analogies.

It should be noted that not all Wiccans claim to be Gardnerians, that is, followers of the Wicca as developed and presented by Gardner. As a contemporary movement, however, this is Wicca's generally accepted beginning. Gardner (1884–1964) was an English civil servant and colonial agricultural entrepreneur who reportedly made quite a sum of money from rubber plantations. He also fancied himself an amateur archaeologist, anthropologist, and folklorist. For most of his adult, professional life, he lived in "exotic" locales such as Ceylon and Malaysia. It was his work and life away from England that apparently sparked his interest in magic, ritual, and esoteric practice. He published a work on Malaysian ritual knives, particularly the wavy bladed dagger known as a *kris*. Not coincidentally, such blades became part of Gardner's ritual practice, commonly known as an *athame* in Wiccan practice.

Upon retiring from civil service in 1936, he returned to the New Forest region of England. While there, Gardner became associated with occultists, ceremonial magicians, and others who introduced him to the practice of the Craft. He became a member of the Fellowship of Crotona, a Masonic order founded by the daughter of theosophist Annie Besant. It was within this group that Gardner claimed to have made contact with a pre-existing coven of Witches, a coven into which he said he was initiated in 1939. This coven was headed by "Old Dorothy" (Dorothy Clutterbuck), a wealthy socialite and seemingly conservative Christian. "The coven into which Gardner was initiated was one of nine offshoots from one founded by George Pickingill (1816–1909) who traced his descent from Julian Brandon, a witch who died in 1071" (Orion 1995, 13).

Gardner also had extensive dealings with the occultist Aleister Crowley (1875–1947). Before his development of Wicca, Gardner was very much interested in reviving Crowley's Ordo Templi Orientis (OTO) society, which had become largely moribund in England at the time. Gardner was initiated into the OTO and there is some evidence that, had he not lost interest in the OTO in favor of creating or "reviving" pagan witchcraft, he would have taken over the leadership of the organization after Crowley's death (Hutton 1999, 216–21). What is of note is that Gardner subsequently excised from his own life story all references to his attempts to resurrect the OTO and his more than passing acquaintance with Crowley. Furthermore Gardner and others purged Crowley's language and some of his influence from Wicca and the later *BoS*. (There is a rumor circulating in Wicca that Gardner paid Crowley to write the original *BoS*. There is no verifiable evidence of such a transaction ever occurring, but the rumor persists.)

After the repeal of the last of England's anti-witchcraft laws in 1951, Gardner published *Witchcraft Today* in 1954 and *The Meaning of Witchcraft* in 1959. These books contain very little of actual Wiccan beliefs and even less concerning specific ritual practices. What is found in the works is a generalized emphasis on magical practice, a duotheism of fertility goddess and horned god, and more elaborately a "history" of Witchcraft in Europe and England specifically. Gardner provided a revisionist history of Witchcraft, tying it to pre-existing, historical cults and then even farther back to the supposed religiosity of paleolithic humanity. He also revised or recontextualized the myths and legends of faeries and the "little people" within English folklore, explaining them as a magic-practicing, pagan, pygmy race marginalized by invaders of the British Isles. As Magliocco (2004, 50) pointed out, Gardner drew heavily on the anthropology and folklore studies of the late nineteenth and early twentieth centuries, particularly the theories of James G. Frazer and Margaret Murray. Murray, in her 1921 work *The Witch-Cult in Western Europe*, argued that Witchcraft was the universal, organized, pre-Christian religion of Europe. This and similar ideas became the basis for what some call the Myth of Wicca. Margot Adler provides a convenient summary:

> It goes something like this: Witchcraft is a religion that dates back to paleolithic times, to the worship of the god of the hunt and the goddess of fertility. One can see remnants of it in cave paintings and in figurines of goddesses that are many

> thousands of years old. This early religion was universal. The names changed from place to place but the basic deities were the same. (Adler 1986, 45)

Murray based this supposition on "pagan" survivals in folklore and reports concerning witches and their craft made during the Inquisition (Adler 1986, 45–48). Drawing on ideas from Frazer's *Golden Bough*, Murray described the "old religion" as primarily a fertility cult centered on the goddess and her dying and rising consort, although the god is emphasized in her works that included *The God of the Witches* (1931). Based on Inquisition reports, she outlined Witchcraft's belief structure, ritual calendar and organization. Although many contemporary scholars and Neopagans view Murray's ideas with suspicion if not wholly disputing them, one cannot doubt her impact on the development of Wicca, since much of her Witchcraft became the foundation of Gardner's Wicca. Building on Murray's "history," Gardner described how Christianity and its persecution of heresy drove pagan witchcraft underground where it survived in various folkloric forms. He depicted the Wiccan religion that he claimed to have been initiated into as a survival of this religious tradition, one with an unbroken lineage to the past. He also attempted to deconstruct the dominant Christian understanding of Witchcraft as a cult of devil worshippers and of Witches as evil.

Gardner wrote these two books both to popularize his tradition among the spiritualist and esoteric remnants of mid-twentieth-century England and at least partly to "sanitize" Witchcraft in the popular imagination of the Christian majority. He also produced them to counter a perceived crisis within the Wiccan community. Doreen Valiente, a practitioner of Wicca initiated by Gardner in 1953, noted that some of Gardner's critics faulted him for generating undue and undignified publicity, "but, 'looking back,' she decided that Gardner was 'sincere.' Gardner's coven 'was mostly composed of elderly people' and he was afraid the Craft 'was in danger of dying out' " (Adler 1986, 62). Publishing his books was a way to guarantee that the tradition and its precepts would not be lost.

While these two books lay out a framework for understanding Wicca and its supposed origins, and while they were the first popularly disseminated books concerning the modern Craft, it is actually Gardner's unpublished works that are of larger import for the discussion of the scriptural nature or aspect of Wicca. Gardner's *Books of Shadows* (he seemed to have several over the span of his religious life) contain a great deal about the workings and procedures of ritual practice, including staging directions in certain earlier versions, chants, invocations and incantations, initiation procedures, the ritual calendar, ethical material, and descriptions of ritual tools. Loretta Orion notes that, "The Book of Shadows which contains the *liturgy* of Gardnerian witchcraft with the accompanying *grimoire* serve as guidebooks for religious practice and magical workings" (Orion 1995, 16, emphasis mine). The *BoS* serves as a ritual and magical text; in Gardnerian Wicca and many other traditions that branch off from it, it serves as the foundational text from which one draws ritual as well as legitimacy and authority for practice. This is, at its core, what the text is and the purpose it was meant to serve. Even non-Gardnerian Witches have a conception of a *BoS* that is utilized as ritual text and in a ritual context. Gardner's *BoS* was allegedly handed down to him from the coven into which he was initiated and was supposedly of sixteenth-century origin (Adler 1986, 64). Valiente, while discussing her apprehension about the "too modern" sounding phraseology and language of Aleister Crowley in Gardner's early *BoS*, relates that Gardner claimed that the *BoS* and, thus its rituals, were given to him in a fragmentary form and that he attempted to link them together with words and phrases that cast the right sound or atmosphere. For this he used many of Crowley's phrases, probably as a result of his own initial fascination with Crowley's OTO and its ceremonial and magical language and tradition. Gardner was also fearful of the possible extinction of the tradition and its rituals and thus pieced the *BoS* together the best he could. Valiente, working with Gardner, purged much of the Crowlian language from the *BoS* and increased the devotion to the Goddess within its rituals (Adler 1986, 63).

The documented history of Gardner's *BoS*, particularly the earliest extant version, *Ye Bok of ye Art Magical*, is as interesting and controversial as the man and the origins of the religion that he professed. While Gardner never published a full version of his *BoS*, he did publish

> several extracts from the Book, and pirated versions of the whole work were available in print from 1964 onward.... Between 1981 and 1984 Janet and Stewart Farrar, aided by Doreen Valiente, produced a critical edition of it which attempted to establish a standard text, identifying the differences between the successive early recensions and the sources for those of its contents which had been copied from or modeled on earlier pieces of literature or composed by known persons in the 1950s. Between them, they therefore managed to reconstruct an "original" text of 1953 and highlight a number of rituals with no known provenance. (Hutton 1999, 226–227)

Copies of Gardner's *BoS* are also now available of the internet, at such sites as Sacred-Texts.com. The initial document, *Ye Bok*, has been identified beyond a reasonable doubt as the precursor of the 1953 *BoS* and is thus the earliest known version of Wiccan liturgy (Hutton 1999, 227). Aidan Kelly, in his 1991 work *Crafting the Art of Magic*, conducted a textual analysis of *Ye Bok*, comparing it to other forms of the *BoS* and demonstrating that it is the precursor to Gardner's 1953 *BoS*. What makes this document even more interesting is the fact that it was lost and only discovered after Gardner's death behind a filing cabinet in Gardner's personal library (Magliocco 2004, 51). The manuscript itself has a distinctive look and feel, and

> [i]t appears that Gardner went to great pains to make the manuscript look like his idea of a medieval grimoire: he bound a number of sheets of paper into a leather cover taken from another book, the contents of which he removed. The

> writing on the leather cover and in parts of the book itself is done in careful calligraphy. Some words are misspelled, perhaps intentionally, to make them appear archaic. (Magliocco 2004, 52)

*Ye Bok* contained several blank pages interspersed within its contents for the addition of material at a later date. In this sense, *Ye Bok* was as much a notebook or personal journal of ritual/religious practice as it was an authoritative grimoire, much as some Witches conceive of their own personal *BoS* today.

> It [*Ye Bok*] was, however, much more than that, at least for a significant period; it was intended to be a grimoire in its own right… The latter [the contents of *Ye Bok*] were written in a number of different ornate scripts, with careful colouring and decoration of the letters; most of the volume is a work of art. The lettering is usually large enough to be easily read from a short distance, and those parts intended to be repeated by initiates (such as the initiation oath) are particularly plain and striking… [I]t seems a reasonable speculation that it was designed to function as the ritual book used by the group. (Hutton 1999, 227)

It would appear that *Ye Bok*, both in its contents and design, was intended as a ritual text of a particularly distinct status that was to be utilized within the ritual context.

*Ye Bok* was the foundation and first version of what would become Gardner's *BoS*. The material within the document was subsequently revised over the course of Gardner's religious career, each iteration of the text responding to a new context or situation. An example of this evolution of the text can be found in the development and inclusion of the ethical guidelines of Wiccan magical practice and social interaction within the *BoS*. "This was the case of the 'Craft Laws,' a set of rules and regulations that did not appear in the early Books of Shadows (although elements of them are scattered in some of Gardner's earlier writings), but which Gardner was able to produce almost overnight to resolve a dispute among coven members in the 1950s" (Magliocco 2004, 53). Regardless of the validity of the produced document and its seemingly instantaneous production, there are two points of note here. First, these general ethical guidelines were already part of the tradition through Gardner's early works and would be developed more fully over the course of his religious career and those of others. The ethical guidelines that were eventually entrenched within Gardner's *BoS* and are reiterated in practically every introductory "how-to" book and published *BoS* can be summed up as the Wiccan Rede and the Three-Fold Law. The Wiccan Rede, while often containing a great deal of poetic language, can be summed up as simply, "An' it harm none, do what ye will" (Guiley 1999, 359). The Three-Fold Rule can be understood as a sort of karma: if one does good they will be thrice blessed, if one does ill they will be thrice cursed. In essence, whatever energy or effort one actively puts forth into the world, it will return in kind three-fold. While Gardner's earliest *BoS* did not explicitly contain these precepts, thus leading to the dispute among coven members, they were integrated into subsequent editions and have become the ethical standard of Wiccan practice. The second point of note is the need for having the "Craft Laws" in a codified, textual form, one that could be added to the *BoS* or claimed to have been already present. The textual form provided a tangible authority which had the ability to resolve the dispute.

A great deal of controversy has developed in recent scholarship concerning Gardner's revival of Wicca as a pre-existing religion, including its rituals and thus the *BoS*. Witches and scholars debate the historicity of Gardner's claim of initiation and the existence of a pre-existing coven. Some maintain that there was such a hereditary coven, one among many, operating in England; others doubt Gardner's veracity, depicting his claim as either a rhetorical move or an outright fraud. Kelly (1991) used a textual analysis of the *BoS* and *Ye Bok* to justify his assertion that Gardner invented the tradition from whole cloth, having never been initiated into a pre-existing coven and pilfering the rituals from other sources. Ronald Hutton (1999) provides a more charitable reading of the tradition. He asserts that Wicca is a synthesized religion that has no paleolithic origins, but is one which does have deep roots in the esoteric and spiritualist movements of the past few centuries. Still others, such as Donald Frew (1998), cling to the veracity of Gardner's claims concerning the origin myth of Wicca and his role within its revival. Magliocco concludes:

> Ultimately, the question of whether Gardner invented revival Witchcraft, or merely discovered a group of English occult practitioners whose rituals he interpreted and publicized is moot. What is clear is that by the early 1950s Gardner has started a coven of his own; new versions of his Book of Shadows were being copied by initiates as early as 1953. Gardner's findings were already becoming a tradition; instead of disappearing as he had feared it would, Witchcraft was taking on a vibrant new life... (Magliocco 2004, 54)

Gardner's covens, his tradition, and most obviously his published works and his *BoS* were becoming the foundation of the modern Neo-Pagan Witchcraft movement and continue to be the over-arching framework for the larger movement. "All later changes and developments in revival Witchcraft have been based on his interpretations, or in reaction to them" (Magliocco 2004, 54).

## Other traditions of witchcraft and the *Book of Shadows* in ritual and as icon

As previously noted, not all Witches are Gardnerian in lineage or practice. Other traditions, meaning here orientations, styles of practice, and belief structures, have proliferated in the modern context, particularly in the United States. Because of the constraints of space, it is not possible to discuss even a small number of such traditions in any detail, but I will address a few of these alternative Witchcraft movements as they relate to the concept of the *BoS* and its role and import within the tradition. One such tradition is known as Alexandrian, named after its coven founder Alex Sanders and initially popularized by Stewart Farrar. Sanders claimed to be a hereditary Witch who was initiated into the Craft by his grandmother. The tradition itself is largely Gardnerian in form and structure, but excised certain portions of Gardner's tradition and added others particular to Sander's beliefs. What is of import for this discussion is the existence and proliferation of a *BoS* as a sacred, ritual text. Sanders claimed to have received his *BoS* from his grandmother, but later historical and textual criticism of the work "established beyond a reasonable doubt that the tradition taught by Alex Sanders was based upon the Gardnerian one and not inherited from his grandmother" (Hutton 1999, 339).

This knowledge, however, did not invalidate the tradition in any significant way. This history of borrowing and building upon other traditions and their *BoS* has become one of the characteristic features of modern Witchcraft. The movement as a whole, in its approach to ritual and text, has become more eclectic over time and more oriented toward communal and personal efficacy and legitimation. Rituals and their reproduction in and repetition from a *BoS* have become more of a personal affair: the text's contents are more fluid while the overarching framework initiated by Gardner still stands as a model or pattern of practice. Other traditions have been developed out of Gardner's own by such Wiccan luminaries as Doreen Valiente, Raymond Buckland, and Stewart and Maxine Farrar. These traditions often refer to Gardner's *BoS* as a "musty old book" (Adler 1986, 93), and turn to other sources of authority to legitimate their practices. Even this designation, however, reveals the foundational status that these traditions award Gardner's *BoS* and its framework. Gardner's *BoS* is barely fifty years old, yet it is "musty" and "old."

Another tradition that is more distant from Gardner's Wicca is the Reclaiming tradition founded by the popular author and Witch known as Starhawk (born Miriam Samos). In her incredibly successful work, *The Spiral Dance,* Starhawk outlines some of her own personal beliefs and practices and thus the core structure of her Reclaiming tradition. Reclaiming is a feminist and activist Witchcraft tradition that does not subscribe to the rigid hierarchical initiation structure for which Gardnerian Wicca is known. As different as Reclaiming is from Gardnerian Wicca in form and internal structure, however, it does follow its general model of ritual and the inclusion and use of a *BoS*. In her book, Starhawk excerpts some rituals and sections of her own *BoS*, providing a model of practice for the reader. Thus *The Spiral Dance*, as a work, is very similar to Gardner's own published books. It provides a revised history of Goddess worship, very much like Murray and Gardner's own, an introduction to the tradition's beliefs, and a "taste" of the rituals. While Reclaiming does not usually conceive of the *BoS* as a passed-down book in the way that most Gardnerian traditions do, there is still an emphasis on the transmission of ritual and magical practice through the *BoS* form. Starhawk wrote, "I suggest...the keeping of a magical diary, called a Book of Shadows. Traditionally, this was the 'recipe book' of rituals, spells, chants, and incantations, hand-copied by each Witch from her teacher. Today, although I blush to admit it, such information is general Xeroxed for coven distribution" (Starhawk 1999, 78–79). It is interesting that Starhawk would voice embarrassment at the mechanical copying of the ritual text, re-emphasizing the perception that a *BoS* should be constructed and look a certain way. She does go on to discuss one's personal *BoS* as part magical journal, much like Gardner's *Ye Bok*, which would necessarily be handwritten.

There are also those Witches who do not belong to a coven and operate within no one particular tradition. These individual Witches are known colloquially as Solitaries, as defined by Silver Ravenwolf:

> **Solitary Witch:** One who practices alone, regardless of Tradition, denomination, or sect. Solitaries come in various forms. Some were at one time initiated into a coven and eventually chose to extricate themselves from that environment and continue practicing a particular Tradition or sect by themselves. A solitary can be an individual who has no desire to practice with or learn from a coven structure, but still may adhere to a specific Tradition or sect through the teachings of another... And finally, a solitary Witch can be a person who has decided to tough it out on their own, learning from books, networking, and fellow Witches of different Traditions... More and more individuals are selecting the solitary path rather than group interaction. (Ravenwolf 1996, 14)

These Witches, especially those who have never participated in a coven, often turn to popular publications, "how-to" manuals and ritual almanacs, and published or otherwise disseminated *BoS* for knowledge and understanding of the religion and its practice. Two of the most widely read authors in this popular vein are the late Scott Cunningham and Silver Ravenwolf. They have become authorities within Solitary Practice for a number of reasons. Their works are published by Llewellyn Publications, a major Neopagan and New Age publishing house operating out of St. Paul, Minnesota. Since this house specializes in works of this genre, their books carry a reputation for quality and accuracy among practitioners and information seekers. Reading through the two authors' works, one is struck by their accessibility. The tone is pedagogical yet conversational. Any arcane or jargonized terms are explained. This ease of access certainly contributed to their sales and the tendency for others to use them as reference material, especially for those just entering the Craft. The authors also refer to each other in their works, both in the practices and interpretations illustrated, and in their suggested reading lists and resources. In essence, the authors validate each other's authority, as well as several other practitioners whom they reference. These books thus create a popular, published circle of elders or instructors who can introduce and guide the reader to an understanding of the religion and practice of Wicca. I assert that these popular authors are filling the role of coven leader or Priest/Priestess for those who have none. In Weberian terms, the authors have a sort of charisma that is transmitted through the texts they produce. They are transmitting their knowledge and interpretations as well as their beliefs and practices to the Solitary Practitioner, but in mediated, textual form. They carry the same authority, at least to the beginner, as a master does to an initiate within a coven.

The dissemination of information through works such as these, as well as the incredible growth of online chat rooms and forums devoted to Neopaganism, has begun to produce a routinization or standardization of Wiccan/Neopagan practice. Helen Berger (1995, 1999) describes the increasing routinization of practice within the Witchcraft movement. While her argument focuses on the role of administrative organization and the notion of paid clergy, she does comment on the role of "celebrity authors" and textuality in this standardization (Berger 1995, 3, 5, 9–10). As information concerning chants, rituals, and the like is disseminated and shared, religious practice becomes more and more uniform, and persons tend to express themselves in similar ways. She notes the influence of such authors as Gardner, Starhawk, Cunningham, and Ravenwolf on this phenomenon of routinization and the creation of a unifying tradition, not in a denominational sense but rather as a historical, meaningful, and repeated pattern.

Books such as Cunningham's and Ravenwolf's also popularize the idea of the *BoS*. These authors urge individual practitioners to create their own personal *BoS*, although Ravenwolf has actually gone so far to produce and publish a *Book of Shadows* specifically for the Solitary Witch. While the procedures of specific creation vary according to personal choice, there is a generalized conception of how one's own *BoS* should look, what it should contain, and how it should function. As with most other conceptions of the *BoS* that have been discussed, within the pages of these popular books the "Book of Shadows is a Wiccan workbook containing invocations, ritual patterns, spells, runes, rules governing magic, and so on" (Cunningham 1997, 34). Most books recommend that one ideally use a blank book, often with a leather or black cover. A *BoS* should be handwritten to invest effort and time into the work to make it personal, and allow it to be easily read by candlelight (Cunningham 1997, 34). In addition, "[c]opying the ritual(s) in your 'own hand of writ' helps to prepare you for the acceptance of the divine energies you will receive during the ceremony, especially if you plan to work as a solitary Witch" (Ravenwolf 2003, 94). In some sense, the act of creating and copying a *BoS* is a magical ritual in its own right. It is an activity that invests "sacrality" into the object. There is some discrepancy between Cunningham and Ravenwolf concerning the status of the *BoS*. Cunningham makes a point of stating that the *BoS* is not "holy writ" and there is no problem with adding or subtracting material from one's *BoS*. Ravenwolf, on the other hand, specifically describes a ceremonial ritual for empowering one's *BoS* (Ravenwolf 2003, 133–134). The ceremony as described includes needed supplies, ritual instructions, and an incantation/invocation. This would seem to point to her belief that the *BoS* is a text of some iconic status. One can read the divergent opinions of these two authors as less of a contradiction and more as a way of pointing out how Wicca, in its dealings with its own texts, is following the same path as ancient Judaism. That is, the iconicity of the text precedes the idea of its immutability, but perhaps encourages the development, over time, of a standardized, routinized, fixed text.

As has been discussed previously, the *BoS* is largely and at its core a ritual text. It is the depository of right practice and effective ceremonial expression. While the actual contents differ between Witches and traditions, the *BoS* is nevertheless almost always designated as housing ritual. "While different traditions may espouse slightly different belief systems, belief is not the most important distinguishing feature between them, as it is not considered necessary for membership or practice... Each tradition may have a sacred text or group of texts, usually known as a 'Book of Shadows'" (Magliocco 2004, 69–70). It is ritual practice, rather than belief, that is central in Witchcraft. A practitioner identifies him or herself as a Witch through ritual and magical practice and central to practice is the *BoS*.

While the text certainly acts as a repository of ritual knowledge, it is also often a living, performed text. One reads incantations, invocations, initiation oaths and other ritual pronouncements from the text itself. It is enacted and vocalized in the ritual context. Again, the actual words almost certainly differ between various versions of the *BoS*, but the performative use of the text crosses Witchcraft traditions. It is true that many popular works suggest that rituals and incantations should ideally be memorized, but the text is initially necessary for that to happen and provides a basis for repeatable and, in some sense, standardized performance. The designs of many *BoS* reinforce the performed nature of the text. The call for a handwritten text emphasizes ritual performance in the production of a *BoS*. Scripts of varying sizes allow for ease of reading aloud, particularly in low light or that of a flickering candle. Gardner's own *Ye Bok* was designed with the performance of the text in mind. The language of many of the *BoS* also speaks to the performative aspect of the text. The language of ritual and incantation often takes poetic form, demanding to be intoned and vocalized. Poetry is most effective when spoken and heard rather than silently read. The language is also often archaic, both to give the ritual or chant an air of history and also to sound appropriate for a presumably ancient Witch religion. One of the reasons Doreen Valiente wanted to purge the phraseology of Aleister Crowley from the *BoS* is that to her ear it sounded too modern for a Witch religion (Adler 1986, 63).

The *BoS* is often portrayed or described as ideally having a distinctive appearance; its physicality lends it authority and meaning within Witchcraft. *Ye Bok* and the subsequent *BoS* were intentionally patterned after Gardner's idea of what a medieval magician's grimoire looked and felt like. The cover was leather, covered with arcane symbols and elaborate calligraphy. The text itself was handwritten and words were often misspelled in such a way as to make the text appear archaic (Magliocco 2004, 52). The contents of *Ye Bok* also appear to have been copied from another source, presumably the fragmentary *BoS* of the coven into which Gardner claimed to have been initiated. The appearance of copied material, complete with errors, can be read as lending a veneer of authenticity to the work itself (Magliocco 2004, 52–53). The design and format of Gardner's *BoS* established the norm among most Witches and most popular works advocating the creation of a personal text. Ravenwolf's, *Solitary Witch: The Ultimate Book of Shadows for the New Generation*, has a distinctive appearance that mirrors the "traditional" *BoS*. While for publishing and price considerations the book's cover is paperback and not leather, it is mottled in such a way as to give the appearance of well-worn red leather. The cover also has a pentacle, the common symbol for Witchcraft, stamped upon it and the script adorning the face is archaic-looking calligraphy. The script inside is a combination of plain font type, italic font for the invocations, and a calligraphy font for the headings. The overall impression of the work is that of a "traditional" grimoire or *BoS*. Wiccan websites devoted to personal or traditional *BoS* also mimic the textual, book design. The web pages appear like leaves from a book or binder, rather than merely having a blank white background (*Magdalene's Online Book of Shadows* 1997; Darrell and Star Dancer 2003). The design of one's own *BoS* is often very time consuming and elaborate and much effort and intent is poured into its creation. The investment of effort endows one's *BoS* with a certain sense of authority as representative of the creator and one's identification with the tradition whose rituals are located within. The meaning or symbolism of such a *BoS* applies both to coven Witches, whether each has his or her own or access to a shared coven text, and to solitary practitioners. The physical text has a representative meaning beyond its contents. It serves as an icon for the religion itself that demonstrates the identity of its creator/bearer.

The distinctive symbolism of the *BoS* appears in representations of Wicca in popular culture. The television show *Charmed* is a drama featuring the adventures and exploits of three sisters who are the legendary "charmed ones," Witches of incredible power who fight for good. The relevance of the show, beyond the popular depictions of Wicca and Witches, is the central role played by the sisters' *BoS*. This *BoS* is a family text passed down through multiple generations. It is magically protected and supernaturally inspired. The *BoS* is the repository of the Witches' spells, rituals, and lore concerning their religion as well as their quest to vanquish evil. The *BoS*, while not the ultimate source of the sisters' power, is absolutely necessary to their mission and their identity as Witches. In those episodes when the *BoS* is stolen or otherwise "unavailable," the Witches lose their status as Witches, meaning they lose their supernatural powers. The *BoS* is designed along the same contours as Gardner's *Ye Bok* and the traditional Wiccan *BoS*. Thus the *BoS* in *Charmed* symbolically represents Witchcraft. Its physical form, more so than its contents, designates what is meaningful as a marker of belonging and identity. In the television program, the *BoS is* Wicca. Of course, the prominence of the *BoS* and its identification with the popular conception of Witchcraft in this show may have more to do with popular culture and the status of books/texts in American understandings of religion than with Wiccan practice per se. That being said, the show does mirror many of the aspects of Wicca as a religion, including the iconicity of the *BoS*.

A final aspect of the *BoS* links together its ritual, performative aspect, and its iconicity and materiality. The *BoS* itself often serves not only as a ritual repository and vocalized text; it also functions as a ritual object. The phrase "Bell, Book, Candle" demonstrates the objective nature of the book in ritual practice. The phrase itself comes from the Roman Catholic ritual of excommunication in which the holy book (the Bible) was closed, a bell sounded and a candle extinguished and thrown down. Rosemary Guilly explains that, "The phrase 'bell, book and candle' became associated with witches because the church believes them to be Devil-worshipers who should be excommunicated" (1999, 18). Modern Witches appropriated the phrase, changing its connotation but utilizing its identifying characteristics and worked it into their ritual practice. Bells, a sacred book (the *BoS* in most cases), and candles are utilized as ritual objects within Wiccan practice. The actual uses of the book in ritual are as plastic as the rituals themselves and so one cannot generalize about how the *BoS* is put to use. In *Solitary Witch*, Ravenwolf describes the *BoS* explicitly in her section covering ritual objects and tools. Also in this section, she has a sketch of a model altar on which the *BoS* is prominently situated (Ravenwolf 2003, 122–34). While this does not address all the ways the *BoS* is used, it does provide a clear and popular example of its nature as a ritual object.

## Ideas of scripture and the *Book of Shadows*

In light of the history of Wicca and the *BoS* and their relation to ritual and physical meaning, can the *BoS* be understood as a scripture? What aspects or nuances of the category of scripture are necessary for such an understanding? Much of my discussion thus far has been working toward an implicit analogy of the *BoS* with scripture, mirroring other Scriptures in description and function. The "generic" understanding of scripture is that of an authoritative, sacred or religious text as in the Jewish, Christian, and Muslim traditions. Several authors whose work I have discussed do describe the *BoS* as a sacred text. The *BoS* also functions as an authoritative text over ritual practice and ethical behavior for some practitioners, particularly those in or from traditions that are Gardnerian. Descriptive and functional theories of scripture and canonicity provide a useful framework for placing the *BoS* and related Wiccan texts within a comparative understanding of scripture.

Scripture as a category can be conceived of on a three-dimensional model that includes textuality, performance, and iconicity (see Watts, Chapter 1, this volume). These three dimensions work in greater or lesser degrees within "established" scriptures and can serve as a model for identifying scriptures outside the Western Judeo-Christian-Islamic context. An individual *BoS* is without a doubt a textual source; it is by name and definition a book. The specific contents of the *BoS* are fluid, but most follow a general pattern containing ritual procedures, incantations, and chants, as well as ethical precepts and personal information.

The *BoS* also has performative aspects. As a ritual text it is the repository for experiential practice. It also functions as a performed text, the contents being read aloud either from the text itself or from memory. William Graham describes the oral and aural aspects of Scripture: "Any concept of 'scripture' that is useful and meaningful for the study of religion must include recognition of its importance both as written and spoken word" (1987, 58). While Graham is addressing more than just performance, his focus on the spoken nature of scripture opens up the category and addresses specific practices both within the Judeo-Christian-Islamic context and beyond it. Wicca has just such a tradition of vocalization in its ritual practice stemming from or in conjunction with the written text of the *BoS*. Ritual performance, the poetry of incantation, and the often archaic speech are all aspects of this orality that is privileged within the religion and linked to its textual components.

The specific poetic and archaic language often utilized in the *BoS* is also analogous to the tradition of certain Christian churches that favor the King James Version of the Bible. In *How the Bible Works*, Brian Malley describes the relationship of Evangelical Christians with their scripture. Of particular interest for my work is Malley's discussion of the various versions of the Bible and the idealized sound of the text. "However much modern translations are used, the Bible is expected to sound stately, slightly archaic, with a nice prosody and maybe even some thee's and thou's... The Lord's Prayer as prayed is *least* like the Bible version most people actually read, the NIV... The King James Version, with its elegant if archaic language, continues to form the stereotype for the way the Bible sounds" (Malley 2004, 58). While this analogy does not explicitly define the *BoS* as scripture, it does provide an analogous example of the way many people believe that a scripture *should* sound when spoken aloud.

The final aspect of the tripartite model of scripture is that of iconicity: the materiality of a text and the meaning or referential nature of that text as object. In the ritual context, the *BoS* serves as a ritual object, complementing the bell and candle in the aforementioned designating phrase. The *BoS* as object is part of the altar set-up of many Witches and the use of the *BoS* as performed text also marks it as an object in ritual practice. This iconic aspect of scripture goes beyond merely the objective nature of ritual book. The text, because it has a distinctive appearance, can serve as a representative symbol for the religion as a whole. A Bible is designated as such because of its specific contents, but also by its appearance. One often recognizes a Bible just by looking at the leather-bound codex itself. In addition, the more a Bible fits the stereotypical physical pattern, the more representative the object becomes. The *BoS* has just such a stereotypical look and feel, one that is patterned on Gardner's conception of a medieval grimoire. As demonstrated by the look of published *BoS* and the one utilized in the television program *Charmed*, the stereotypical appearance authenticates and legitimates the work as well as becoming symbolic and representative of the religion that it espouses. An icon is loaded with meaning because it pictorially or physically refers to something else. The iconic dimension of sacred books refers to the religion and its theology, dogma, ritual, and the like. Possessing such an iconic book marks one as belonging to that religion. It becomes a representative symbol of identity.

Compared to the established scriptures of the Western monotheist traditions of Judaism, Christianity, and Islam, the *BoS* seems to be most analogous to the Jewish Torah, particularly certain early conceptions of it as ritual text. James Watts describes the idea of Torah as scripture and its authority as deriving initially from ritual contexts. His investigation deals with the question of how texts became authoritative scripture within Judaism. "In antiquity, claims for the authority of old texts were more frequently made for *ritual* texts than for others. Rather than law or diplomacy or bureaucracy or divination, the use of texts for and in ritual explains more plausibly the origins and development of book religion" (Watts 2005, 4). Watts discusses the relationship between text and ritual as validating each other in a circular fashion. Judaism, in its initial conception as a religion based on ritual practice, had to deal with issues of correct practice and the legitimate authority of ritual participants. Old texts, which would become the foundations of the ritual sections of the Torah, were used to address these issues, particularly in times of conflict or crisis. The proto-Deuteronomic text discovered in the Temple during the reign of King Josiah and "the book of the Law of Moses" utilized by Ezra after the Babylonian exile are examples of texts that addressed ritual practice and a crisis of communal identity. The texts also bridged temporal gaps in which "correct" practice had become moribund. In each case, the ritual practitioner or official "used ancient books to provide such reinforcement, because texts have the unique property of appearing to 'speak' from the distant past" (Watts 2005, 7). Through the use of text, the practice is legitimated and authority defined. In addition, the practice of ritual validates the authority and "authenticity" of the text, eventually leading to its extension beyond the ritual context.

As I read the history of Wicca, its origin myth, and the efforts of Gardner with his *BoS*, I see an analogous process to what Watts is describing in ancient Judaism. Wicca, as Gardner's ritualistic religion, initially had to deal with issues of legitimacy and the conception of right practice. The *BoS* serves the same function as the scriptural texts that Watts describes. Gardner's ritual practices draw on the *BoS* as a validating text and in turn the *BoS* is validated by the performance of its ritual. The Myth of Wicca as outlined by Gardner and his claims of initiation into a pre-existing coven provide historicity for the text and the ritual practice. The crises with which Gardner was dealing involved the possible extinction of the tradition, which necessitated the crafting of texts in order to establish community and to improve the perception of Witchcraft within the general Christian culture. The *BoS* as a textual concept and the "canon" of popular Wiccan books address the need for dissemination and communal formation. These texts, through linkage with a revised past, also address the negative conception of the religion within the larger culture. In a similar way to the role of the Torah (Watts 1999), the *BoS* and other related Wiccan works function rhetorically as a way to build a social, communal identity. The texts and thus the tradition become authorized by their ability to persuade and by the acceptance of the target audience. Even though the controversies surrounding Gardner and the founding of Wicca weaken these claims, the rhetoric of the tradition has done its work: a community has formed, the rituals continue to be practiced and the *BoS* still functions as a ritual text and framework.

The *Book of Shadows* and related popular works provide Witchcraft with something like an open canon of authoritative and informative texts, in the normative, formative, and exemplary senses defined by Halbertal (1997). The texts function in a normative, authoritative sense, by defining, delimiting, and providing examples of ethical behavior and right practice. The texts also function as a formative canon; many are taught, read, and transmitted but not followed in a normative sense. The *BoS* and popular texts also serve an exemplary function. The texts provide aesthetic models and selections worthy of emulation. Since the religion is so decentralized and geared toward personal choice and transformation, almost all of these texts can be viewed in various categories. One *BoS* or text might be considered normative by one practitioner and merely exemplary by another. Still, the *BoS* and many other such Wiccan texts do have some form of authority that one can consider canonical or scriptural.

Thus the *Book of Shadows* can be understood as a form of scripture. It is analogous to aspects of other established scriptures and it functions in certain scriptural ways. What is missing from this discussion of its scriptural status, however, is the voice of modern practitioners. Although it was beyond the scope of this essay, the question of the *BoS*'s scriptural status should include an ethnographic survey and the insights of those practicing within the tradition. While the question of whether the *BoS* is scripture cannot be fully resolved because of the ambiguities inherent in the use of the word "scripture", I believe that it functions in many scriptural ways by providing a textual claim to authoritative tradition, a basis for oral and ritual performance, and an icon of legitimacy for a tradition that is usually conceived of as spontaneous and a-scriptural.

## References

Adler, Margot. 1986. *Drawing Down the Moon: Witches, Druids, Goddess-Worshippers, and Other Pagans in America Today*. New York: Penguin Compass.

Berger, Helen A. 1995. "The Routinization of Spontaneity." *Sociology of Religion* 56: 49–61. doi: 10.2307/3712038.
———. 1999. *A Community of Witches: Contemporary Neo-Paganism and Witchcraft in the United States*. Columbia, SC: University of South Carolina Press.
*Charmed*. Prod. Aaron Spelling. Warner Brothers. 1998–2006.
Cunningham, Scott. 1997. *Wicca: A Guide for the Solitary Practitioner*. St. Paul, MN: Llewellyn Publications.
Darrell and Star Dancer. 2003. *Pages from Our Book*. Online Posting. September 17, 2003. *The Book of Shadows*. http://bookofshadows.info/main/pages.htm. Accessed May 2005.
Frew, D. H. 1998. "Methodological Flaws in Recent Studies of Historical and Modern Witchcraft." *Ethnologies* 1: 33–65.
Gardner, Gerald B. [1954] 2004. *Witchcraft Today*. New York: Citadel Press.
———. [1959] 2004. *The Meaning of Witchcraft*. Boston: Weiser Books.
Graham, William A. 1987. *Beyond the Written Word: Oral Aspects of Scripture in the History of Religion*. Cambridge: Cambridge University Press.
Guiley, Rosemary Ellen. 1999. *The Encyclopedia of Witches and Witchcraft*. New York: Facts on File.
Halbertal, Moshe. 1987. *People of the Book: Canon, Meaning, and Authority*. Cambridge, MA: Harvard University Press.
Hutton, Ronald. 1999. *Triumph of the Moon: A History of Modern Pagan Witchcraft*. Oxford: Oxford University Press.
Internet Sacred Text Archive. 2003. *The Gardnerian Book of Shadows*. www. sacred-texts.com/pag/gbos/index.htm. Accessed May 2005.
Kelly, Aidan. 1991. *Crafting the Art of Magic*. St. Paul, MN: Llewellyn.
Magliocco, Sabina. 2004. *Witching Culture: Folklore and Neo-paganism in America*. Philadelphia, PA: University of Pennsylvania Press.
Malley, Brian. 2004. *How the Bible Works: An Anthropological Study of Evangelical Biblicism*. New York: Altamira Press.
*Magdalene's Online Book of Shadows*. 1997. Michigan State University. www.msu.edu/~rohdemar/earth/BoS.html. Accessed May 2005.
Murray, Margaret. 1962. *The Witch-Cult in Western Europe*. London: Oxford University Press [1921].
———. [1931] 1970. *The God of the Witches*. London: Oxford University Press.
Orion, Loretta. 1995. *Never Again the Burning Times: Paganism Revived*. Prospect Heights, IL: Waveland Press, Inc.
Ravenwolf, Silver. 1996. *To Ride a Silver Broomstick: New Generation Witchcraft*. St. Paul, MN: Llewellyn Publications.
———. 2003. *Solitary Witch: The Ultimate Book of Shadows for the New Generation*. St. Paul, MN: Llewellyn Publications.
Starhawk. 1999. *The Spiral Dance: A Rebirth of the Ancient Religion of the Great Goddess*. San Francisco: Harper San Francisco.
Watts, James W. 1999. *Reading Law: The Rhetorical Shaping of the Pentateuch*. Sheffield:

Sheffield Academic Press.

———. 2005. "Ritual Legitimacy and Scriptural Authority." *Journal of Biblical Literature* 124: 401–17.

York, Michael. 1996. "New Age and Paganism." In *Pagan Pathways: A Guide to the Ancient Earth Traditions*, edited by Graham Harvey and Charlotte Hardman, 157–168. London: Thorsons.

# IV

# Book Rituals

# 14

# Engaging with the Guru: Sikh Beliefs and Practices of Guru Granth Sahib

Kristina Myrvold

*The Sikhs have perhaps taken the concept of a sacred scripture much further than any other religious community by treating the Guru Granth Sahib as a living guru. This essay analyzes various religious beliefs and practices by which contemporary Sikhs construct and maintain conceptions of their scripture as a guru with spiritual authority. A distinction is made between religious practices that serve to mediate and interpret the semantic content of the scripture, performative acts that are enacted to transform the social world, and rituals that aim to give the scripture a careful ministration and celebrate different stages of its worldly life. The various ritualized uses of Guru Granth Sahib can be approached as external strategies by which the Sikhs personify their scripture and make it socially alive as a living guru.*

In the spring of 2009, six men armed with daggers and a gun entered a Sikh temple in Vienna and started shooting at two visiting religious leaders of *Dera Sachkhand Ballan*, a religious center in Punjab (India) devoted to the fourteenth-century saint-poet Ravidas. The leaders were on tour through Europe and participated in a service together with Austrian Sikhs who venerate Ravidas because his hymns are included in the Sikh scripture, the Guru Granth Sahib. The ensuing bloodshed resulted in the death of one of the leaders while about thirty devotees were wounded. Hours after this event, the Punjab erupted in violence, a state curfew was imposed, and the army was called in to restore order. The motive of the suspects behind the Vienna attack, as presented by the prosecutor and the media, seem to have been their rage at the visiting leaders' "disrespect" (*beadbi*) of the Guru Granth Sahib.[1] Many followers of the Ravidas tradition, Sikhs as well as Hindus, regard such leaders as saints who sit at the same level as the Sikh scripture in temples and are bowed before. To mainstream Sikhs, these practices offend their belief that Guru Granth Sahib

1. In September 2010 the six men were sentenced to prison, one of them for murder, two for attempted murder, the other four for being accomplices in attempted murder and coercion (Groendahl 2010).

is the only "living" guru who was granted spiritual authority three hundred years ago. During the service in Vienna, the leaders of *Dera Sachkhand Ballan* supposedly challenged this authority by receiving acts of veneration. Thus the attack did not involve disputes over exegetical interpretations or the semantic content of the Guru Granth Sahib, but rather concerned the status and identity of the material book installed in a ritual space. In order to understand why the perceived desecration of their scripture would trigger some Sikhs to go to the length of using violence, it is not enough to analyze the text and its content. It is necessary to approach this question with a much broader cultural and anthropological understanding of the text and how it is perceived and used in ritual contexts.

Based on extensive fieldwork among the Sikhs in northern India, this paper introduces some of the religious beliefs and ritual practices surrounding Guru Granth Sahib in Sikhism today. How do contemporary Sikhs create and confirm religious beliefs about their scripture in and through their ritual practices? How can a mere book be perceived as "alive," even treated as a "person" of exalted status? A primary aim here is to describe emic understandings (i.e., understanding that religious Sikhs regard as legitimate) and strategies by which people construct and maintain conceptions of Guru Granth Sahib as a scripture that contains divine words and the teachings of historical human gurus and is simultaneously the present living guru with authority to provide spiritual guidance.

The scholarly study of Sikhism and the Guru Granth Sahib has long neglected the religious worship acts that Sikhs practice in public and private spheres to focus instead on historical, theological, and political aspects of the scripture. The Sikh scripture has primarily been approached from a textual viewpoint, as a canonized collection of the human gurus' written compositions. Contemporary scholars following this textual paradigm have done important research on the compilation history (e.g. Singh 2000; Mann 2001) and the poetic form of the scripture (e.g. Kaur 1995), as well as created and commented upon exegetical analyses (Kaur-Singh 1993; Singh 1998; Shackle 2008). Much fewer studies have focused on the ways in which the Sikhs in India and beyond conceptualize and use their sacred text in religious worship (e.g. Kaur-Singh 2008; Myrvold 2007; Mann 2008; Singh 2008), perhaps because modernist interpretations by Sikh apologists and other intellectuals often present Sikhism in terms of religious doctrines, history, and moral principles and emphasize that the tradition reacted against conventionalism, even suggesting it is "anti-ritualistic."[2] The focus of this paper, however, is on living practices among contemporary Sikhs who usually perceive their worship

2. See e.g. Kohli 2006. Arvind-Pal Singh (1995, 1996) has argued that Punjabi intellectual self-representations continue to bear the stamp of European modernist ideologies in the nineteenth century, because they translate indigenous phenomena culturally by using terminologies of European and Christian discourses. These discourses neutralize cultural differences in order to fit a homogenous and theologized representation of religion. Sikhism becomes a religion with

acts as the primary means for expressing devotion and a religious identity. Catherine Bell argues, regarding religious people in general, that religion "is not a coherent belief system but, first and foremost, a collection of practices" (Bell 1992, 185). It is primarily what the Sikhs do—their behaviors and acts—that gives substance to their religion and fosters their religious identities and beliefs. Ritual activities directed to Guru Granth Sahib can therefore be understood as strategies by which Sikhs actively invest the scripture with the status, authority, and identity of a living guru.

## Religious perceptions of Guru Granth Sahib

A unique feature of Sikhism, as the religion is lived and practiced today, is the supreme authority that Sikhs attribute to their scripture Guru Granth Sahib and the central role the scripture plays in their devotional and ritual life. The authoritative tradition of the broader community lays claim on an interpretation of the scripture as enshrining a historical and enduring agency of a personal Guru. Among lay Sikhs, perceptions and attitudes towards the Guru Granth Sahib can be placed along a continuum of stances. On the secularized end are Sikhs who claim that the scripture is a "holy book," comparable to the sacred texts of other world religions, which contains a teaching to study and translate into social action in everyday life. A more exclusive view at the other end asserts that Guru Granth Sahib is a manifestation of God and sometimes speaks of the text in terms of a deity. At the centre of the spectrum, however, is the most common view which acknowledges that the Guru Granth Sahib is the eternal guru of the Sikhs with authority to provide spiritual guidance and a scripture which enshrines words of an ontologically divine nature and the revelatory experiences and teaching of the historical human Gurus. Although the formless god should be the final target of devotion in the Sikh life, the object of worship is also the Guru Granth Sahib because its content—the words and the teaching—is the personal guru of the Sikhs, which mediates relationships between humans and God and shows the way to attain liberation. In spite of extensive migration and cultural influences from different parts of the world, the Sikhs continue to emphasize that their scripture is not an ordinary religious book for purchase and reading, but a "living" guru imbued with a divine light and spirit.[3]

A starting-point for understanding religious perceptions of Guru Granth Sahib is the web of relationships that constitutes the context of the scripture's role and status within communities at the present. First, there are the *onto-*

an authentic history, a venerated founder, a revealed scripture, holding a unique and rational ideology.

3. For instance, young Sikhs in India and in the diaspora have created several websites on the Internet and pages on Facebook to communicate knowledge of their scripture and gain members and "likes" for mottos, such as "Sri Guru Granth Sahib Ji our living Guru, not just a holy book", "Guru Granth Sahib – The True Living Guru" and "My Guru is the Respected Guru Granth Sahib" (see Facebook 2010a, 2010b, 2010c).

*theological relationships* that Sikhs believe existed between ten human gurus in history and the divine. Sikh historiography emphasizes the uniqueness of the founder Guru Nanak (1469–1539) and claims that he was a liberated bard entrusted by God to convey knowledge directly from a transcendence source. A popular narrative tradition asserts that Guru Nanak had a direct revelation and discourse through which the formless God in sound disclosed words and knowledge to him without any secondary means.[4] After this experience, the guru set out on extensive travels to refine and spread his message before he settled in Punjab and established a community of Sikhs (meaning "disciples"). Many contemporary Sikhs would emphasize that Guru Nanak did not have any personal guru himself, but exclusively reserved the term "guru" for *shabad*, the primordial word of God made manifest in the world through *gurbani*, the utterances and instructions of the human preceptor. When Sikhs say that the gurus' hymns included in Guru Granth Sahib are "words of God" (*dhur ki bani*), they thus appeal to a tradition which claims that divine words descended to mankind through the speech, writing and teaching of human messengers. The Guru Granth Sahib is believed to enshrine the economy and agency of the true *shabad*-guru, which is made accessible whenever the hymns of the texts are activated in reading practices and acts of devotion.

Second, one should take into account the *historical* and *spiritual relationships* between the human gurus and the Guru Granth Sahib in order to understand how the Sikhs view and treat their scripture as a personal guru. It is commonly held that Guru Nanak ensured the preservation of his teaching by committing his compositions to writing in the *Gurmukhi* script and by establishing a succession line of human gurus. A widely accepted interpretation stresses that all the ten Sikh gurus—from Guru Nanak to Guru Gobind Singh (1666–1708)—were preordained minstrels graced with power to hear and understand the voice of God and therefore displayed doctrinal agreement. Like ordinary humans, the physical body or "form" (*sarup*) of the guru was perishable, subjected to birth and death, and operated as a provisional "clothing" to conceal the divine illumination. When a nominee ascended to the guru-post, his body was mystically endowed with a "spirit" or "light" (*jot*) similar to his predecessor. The relationships that existed between the human gurus in the Sikh tradition consequently presume spiritual continuity and corporeal diversity: the same spirit inhabited all of them, while the bodily manifestations posited transformability as the spirit was passed on to ten different human shapes.[5] This belief also has implications for how the Sikhs conceptualize and behave towards the Guru Granth Sahib. The scripture was compiled

4. Narrators of the *Puratan Janam-sakhi* tradition took the notion of direct revelation seriously, embroidering the narrative scenery of how Guru Nanak in his twenties disappeared in the river Bein for three days and was gathered into a divine presence to hear the voice of God (see Bhai Vir Singh 1999 (1926), 43; and the analysis of Nikky Guninder Kaur Singh 1992).

5. The spiritual and mystical oneness of all the gurus is referred to in several historical Sikh sources, such as the writings (Var 24) of Bhai Gurdas (Singh 1998, 63 ff.), the Joat Bigas of Bhai

in 1604 by the fifth guru, Guru Arjan (1563–1606), who solemnly installed the manuscript in the newly constructed Harimandir Sahib at Amritsar. A century later, the canon was sealed after hymns of the ninth guru, Guru Tegh Bahadur (1621–1675), had been added to the text. The tradition stresses an early textual authority that reached its peak in 1708 when the tenth guru, Gobind Singh, declared the scripture to be the eternal guru of the Sikhs and commanded that devotional stances which disciples had taken up towards the human gurus should likewise apply to the scripture. As a consequence, the scripture was endowed with spiritual authority to guide the Sikhs and it is believed to encapsulate the total knowledge and "spirit" of all the ten preceptors. Moreover, similar modes of practices that presumably existed in the human culture surrounding the gurus were now valid for contexts in which the Sikhs interacted with the Guru Granth Sahib. Just like Sikh disciples in the past honored the physical manifestation of a living guru communicating a spiritual message, the corpus of the scripture should be venerated in a similar fashion. The importance of these historical events for contemporary Sikhs is that possible relationships between the Sikh guru and disciples did not end just because the line of human gurus was discontinued in the past. Quite the contrary: the agency and power of the guru lives on with Guru Granth Sahib and pious devotees can continually create relationships with the divine through the guru manifested in the form of a scripture.

Contemporary practices of Guru Granth Sahib suggest that Sikhs act and refer to the scripture in terms of having *social relationships* to their text that are shaped by human relations and continually maintained by devotional acts. Students of religion who have been fostered in secular Western traditions governed by an objectivist epistemology may at first find Sikh worship incomprehensible. In the daily liturgy of the gurdwara, literally the "house of the guru," the Sikhs install the scripture on a upraised throne and attend it like it is royalty granting audience: they present it with prayers, food, clothes, and offerings to be blessed; put it to sleep in a human bed at night; and recite and listen to its words as if the guru continued to give verbal instructions to disciples. It is easy to relegate these conducts to a symbolic field, but a greater challenge to understand the emic ontology underlying the treatment of the text. From the objectivist presupposition of what a book can or cannot be, the Sikh scripture remains a manmade silent "thing" made of paper and ink that serves to communicate a semantically comprehensible content and perhaps is sanctified because of the teaching it contains. Although Sikhs know very well that a book cannot be alive in any biological sense, unlike the human gurus of the past, quite another ethos seems to predominate in their religious culture. Through different ritualized acts they do not merely treat the Guru Granth Sahib as a seamless source of spiritual messages for humankind, but

Nand Lal (Bawa 2006, 387 ff.), and Bachitar Natak (section 5) in Dasam Granth which is attributed to Guru Gobind Singh (Kohli 2003, 126 ff.)

create and confirm religious ideas of the scripture as an entity with agency, endued with "personhood" and human-like habits, epithets and authorities.[6] Instead of objectifying the Guru Granth Sahib to a spiritless thing, their practices attempt to invest the text with the maximal social agency of a living guru dwelling in the form of a book. As the following sections of this chapter will show, many Sikh rituals create habits and routines of the Guru Granth Sahib within the framework of a social relationship that are patterned after human roles and relations. The on-going re-telling of historical accounts that elucidate the origin and ascendance of the scripture to the office of the guru are the discursive devices to legitimize the identity and status of a scriptural guru and current practices by evoking links to the human gurus and pious devotees in the past.

The Sikh religious life at present exhibits a rich tapestry of ritualized practices involving the scripture that is not easily put into simple words. On a general level, however, the emic distinction between the external "form" of the guru and the internal "spirit" within its pages can provide the base for a distinguishing between practices that primarily aim to engage devotees in the interior teaching of the text—the shabad guru—and practices that serve to venerate the identity and the manifested form of the worldly guru—the Guru Granth Sahib. The distinction between these two types of practices is quite significant for understanding the form and function of the careful ministrations that Sikhs are offering to their guru-scripture.

## Mediating and interpreting words

That Guru Granth Sahib is a text to be read and understood is evident from the rich oral traditions of rendering the sacred verses. Passages of the interior text are rendered daily in recitation (*path*) and devotional singing (*kirtan*), and explicated and interpreted in expositions (*katha*) in order to comprehend their subtler meanings and accommodate their teaching to contemporary human conditions. The ideal Sikh should read, listen, interpret, and continually dwell on the semantic dimensions of Guru Granth Sahib to develop understanding and insights of the guru's spiritual guidance.

Readings in congregational worship are usually performed in highly formalized ways and follow prescribed rules because the words rendered are not created from ordinary human discourses, but believed to be reproductions of utterances that stand far above and beyond the influence of contemporary temporal and spatial parameters. Historically, the words in Guru Granth Sahib

6. Perhaps the most illustrative case in point of the Sikh attribution of personhood to the Guru Granth Sahib is the longstandig tradition of recognizing the scripture as a "juridical person" with legal rights to receive donations presented by devotees and possess properties of land. In 2000, the legal right of the text gained national approval when the Supreme Court of India decreed that Guru Granth Sahib is a "juristic person" who can hold and use property that has been given in acts of charity (Myrvold 2007, 151).

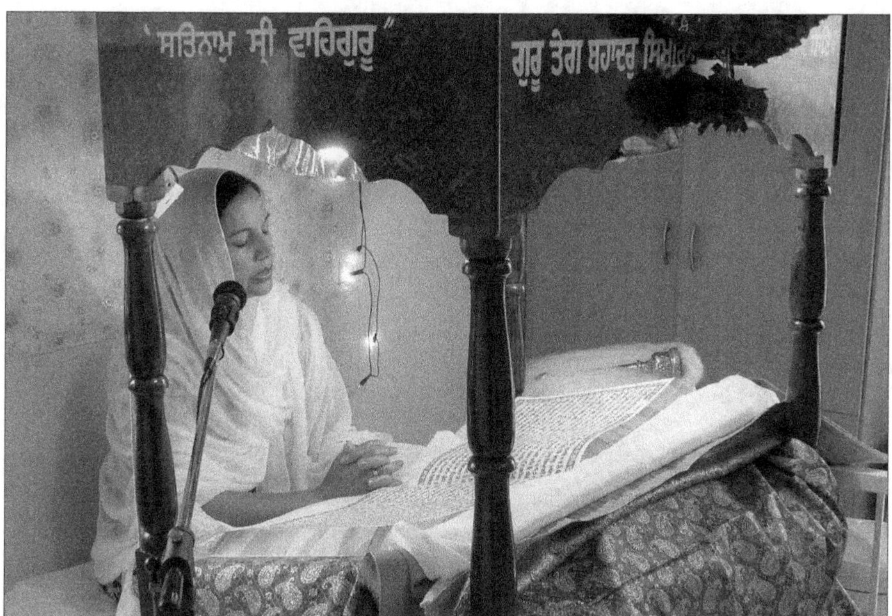


Figure 1. Sikh woman at Gurdwara Bibi Nanki Sahib in Upplands Väsby (Sweden) performs an open recitation (*khulla path*) of Guru Granth Sahib. Photo: Kristina Myrvold.

were revealed and "entexualized" by the human gurus,[7] and Sikh disciples today share the collective responsibility of bringing these sacred words out in performance. The sacred nature of the text forces a rendering in verbatim, a scrupulously re-citation or quotation during which the enunciation of each syllable should be correct and follow the fixed lines, word by word, according to the same syntagmatic order as given in the text. This stress on formal correctness can be viewed as a means to preserve the immaculate substance and form of the text and endow it with a clearly defined and object-like identity that is not created by the reciting person. In any rendition of Guru Granth Sahib, the Sikhs will attempt to suppress contextual variations and minimize the "intertextual gap" (Briggs and Bauman 1992, 150) between the utterances of the gurus and the contemporary discursive settings in which the continued transmission emerges by, for instance, embedding any recitation with linguistic markers and other types of speech acts that separate the quotation from the reciter and signal a special frame of interpretation.

Given these features, recitation is clearly separated from other types of readings, like analytical studies of secular books or "readings" of poetry. When

7. Bauman and Briggs define entexualization as the "process of rendering discourse extractable, of making a stretch of linguistic production into a unit—a text—that can be lifted out of its interactional setting. A text, then, from this vantage point, is discourse rendered decontextualizable" (Baumann and Briggs 1990, 73). It is a process that makes discourse detachable from its immediate context by transforming it into coherent and autonomous oral or written texts.

Sikhs wish to pursue knowledge of the scriptural content, they more often devote themselves to straightforward readings from *sanchi*, the Sikh scripture divided into two or more volumes that do not necessitate ritual installments, or they consult secondary literature. Especially the narrative tradition of live or recorded *katha*—"story-telling," or oral expositions conducted by professional exegetes (*kathavacak*)—is approached as an efficacious means to explore the semantic inner dimension of Guru Granth Sahib and cultivate devotion to the guru. Owing to the authoritative status of the text, anyone who is to undertake a "reading" from the Guru Granth Sahib should thus accept the formal conventions or otherwise not read at all. It is, for example, considered blasphemous to browse through the scriptural pages more wantonly or look up sentences and repeat words only for investigative purposes.

### Words to transform the world

As the supra-mundane words of the Guru Granth Sahib are manifest in recitations, they do not merely communicate a semantic content and shape discourses, but are believed to have strong performative powers to affect the spiritual and bio-moral conditions of humans, transform social categories, and act upon the human world in other ways. In fact, lay Sikhs are more often inclined to tell what they have gained or expect from devotional engagements in the verses of Guru Granth Sahib—a healthy child, a profitable business, a good partner, etc.—rather than occupying themselves with exegetical elaborations. These gains are not viewed as haphazard events but are recounted as casual histories about divine interventions through the power of the guru. As such, they are taken as evidence to prove that devotion to the guru will counteract problems in everyday life and generate good results for humans. From an analytical viewpoint, it would be possible to argue that these metapragmatic discourses reveal the existence of a "performativist" language ideology that does not only value words for their referential meanings but also views language as an effective means to present, constitute, and act upon the world (Rumsey 1990; Dusenbery 1992; Kang 2006). Drawing upon Austin's speech act theory, formalized enactments of the words in Guru Granth Sahib become "performative" acts that do not only signify something but have illocutionary force far beyond the text's confines and are capable of doing things in the social world depending on conventions, contexts, and/or the semantic components of the utterances (Austin 1969).

In Sikh worship, recitations of some specific hymns have gained conventional meanings and are associated with certain powers depending upon the form, content, and author of the compositions. For instance, Guru Arjan's beloved hymn *Sukhmani Sahib* is regarded as an endless source of peace and happiness, while Guru Nanak's *JapJi Sahib* is thought of as setting one on the path towards salvation, the recitation of which will grant spiritual merits and mark the beginning of a day, a human life and every new enterprise conducted therein. Illustrative examples of performative acts emerge in the context of healing and times of need. Many Sikhs believe that formal recitations of specific verses from the scripture may help them to overcome problems of illness, barrenness, financial shortage, conflicts with family members, and other dilemmas in life. A childless woman may daily, for forty days or more, recite a particular hymn by Guru Arjan which describes how a son is conceived and delivered from blessings granted by a divine agent (GGS, 396), believing that her devotional exercise will activate the power within the words and accomplish a real effect on her body. A prisoner can increase the chance of being released by reciting a verse that describes how mythological robbers and prostitutes were granted spiritual liberation (GGS, 830). A man suffering from bad health and suspected spirit affliction may similarly recite a verse about God's "medicine" of the divine name that cures all maladies and encloses the pious human within a circle (*ramkar*) that protects from all pains (GGS, 819).[8] Today, there exist numerous anthologies (e.g. different editions of *Sankat Mochan Shabad* and *Dukhbhanjani Sahib* ) with selected hymns drawn from the Guru Granth Sahib that instruct how hymns should be recited for particular desired ends in view.

Although there is usually a set of interrelated textual and contextual conditions that provide the infrastructure through which a speech act gains force as a particular type of action or is believed to have a special effect (Baumann and Briggs 1990), the illocutionary force of many Sikh recitations are often interlinked with the semantic elements of the texts. Metaphors, themes, parables or other semantic components of a particular hymn seem to generate indexical relationships to the effect anticipated from a recitation in a certain context, in the sense that the social, material, or biological effects of reciting the text becomes a part of the signifier within the text.[9] Thus, when the Sikh man wishes for good health and protection, he selects a hymn that has propositional meanings that draw upon similar themes. When the linguistic images within the text, such as the "protecting circle" and "medicine," are enacted in his performance they are believed to actually manifest divine protection and even cure him from spiritual and physical afflictions in a real life situation. From a religious viewpoint this is possible because the words of Guru Granth Sahib have causal powers to exert influences on humans and their social world in a number of ways. Propositional meanings extracted from the scripture are treated as meta-pragmatic directives of the guru who/which describes the results that can be accomplished by religious action.

On other occasions, it is the context that determines the illocutionary force of religious speech acts. When the complete Guru Granth Sahib is recited from the beginning to end without a break (*akhand path*) before a wedding ceremony, it is said to bring good luck to the bridal couple, while the same type of performance

8. For detailed descriptions and analyses of these practices, see Myrvold 2007.

9. See Rappaport's discussion on indexical relationships in rituals (Rappaport 1999, 57).

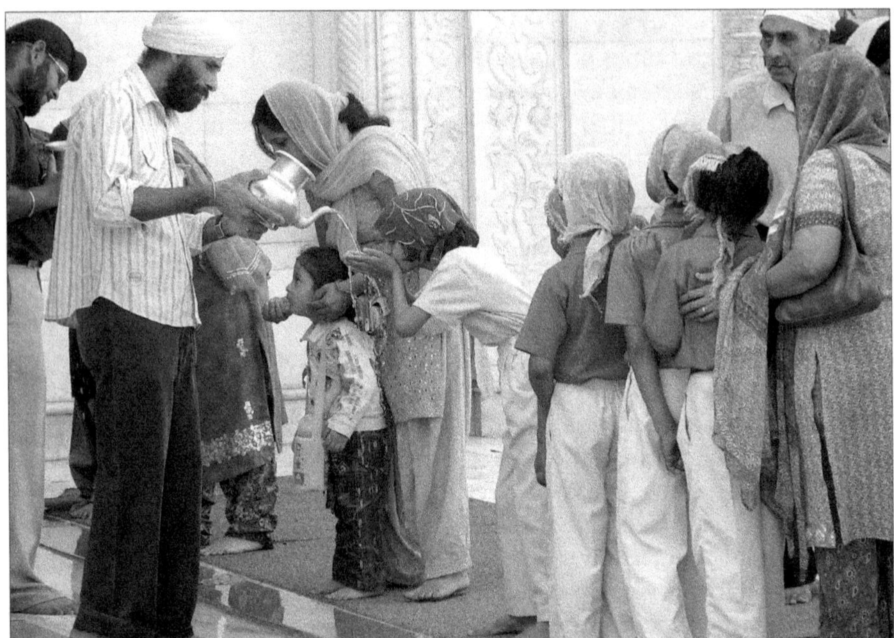

Figure 2. School children are given sanctified water (*amrit*) at Gurdwara Bangla Sahib in Delhi. Photo: Kristina Myrvold.

before a death aims to mitigate suffering and provide a good death for the dying. While some of the expected effects of this performance appear to be enduring conventions within the Sikh community, others are constantly changing and shifting depending upon the situational context. To engage in recitations of the total accumulation of knowledge in the scripture is believed to bring out the entirety of the guru dwelling within the pages. Many Sikhs will therefore attribute to this type of recitation a variety of results and capacities to alter human conditions (e.g. bring happiness to house or restore social order after a tragic event) as the complete guru is made present in temporal and spatial settings.

Another example of performative acts that deserves to be mentioned is the popular use of different *amrit*, that is, "nectar" (literally "immortal") made up by sweetened water that has been consecrated by recitations of hymns from the Guru Granth Sahib. Usually the term refers to the blessed nectar-water given to neophytes during the initiation ceremony of Khalsa, called "the ceremony of [taking] nectar" (*amrit sanskar*), when a person adopts a normative Sikh identity and consequently becomes a "bearer" or "holder" of *amrit* (*amrit-dhari*). The central act of this ceremony is to distribute sweetened water over which five hymns of the Sikh gurus have been recited while stirring it with a double-edged sword.[10] These two components—the recited texts and the

10. The five hymns constitute "the daily routine" (*nitnem*) of the Sikhs and consist of *JapJi Sahib* written by Guru Nanak, *Jap Sahib, Tav Prashad Savaiyye* and *Chaupai Sahib* ascribed to Guru Gobind Singh, *Anand Sahib* by Guru Amardas (see Myrvold 2007, 244).

sword—are believed to transform the water into a nectar substance that has the capacity to completely purify and distill the inner and outer composition of aspirants when they ingest and are sprinkled with it. On a popular level, the term *amrit* also implies taxonomies of additional consecrated waters that can be divided into subcategories depending upon the ways by which the water-nectar has been prepared and for which purposes. There are blessed waters prepared from recitations of selected stanzas of Guru Granth Sahib (*shabad amrit*), recitations of the whole scripture (*bhog amrit*), or just the name of God—*Vahiguru* (*gurmantra amrit*). Waters that have welled out of sacred locations and are associated with the wonders of the human gurus in the past are likewise labelled *amrit*. There is also *amrit* to be used as medication (*amrit dava*), or as a drinkable amulet for varying curative purposes. Even tap water from reservoirs is occasionally treated as purifying nectar if it has been properly prepared with verses from the scripture.

What all these categories have in common is that they are considered consecrated waters, imbued with positive substances and transformative powers of the guru dwelling in the scripture. The preparation of *amrit* presumes that the production of sacred texts in sound directly over the water materialize words as a hidden essence. The various types of *amrit* are also believed to produce different effects on people depending upon other forces and factors involved in the process of transforming ordinary water to nectar, such as the identity of the agent preparing the nectar, the space in which recitations take place, the ritual instruments utilized, and the dispositions of recipients. Moreover, the identity and transformative power ascribed to particular waters are intimately connected with semantic properties of the recited *gurbani* hymns or what these hymns have come to represent in the broader Sikh tradition. In healing contexts, for example, people will choose a verse from the Guru Granth Sahib which bears a semantic link to the purpose for which the *amrit* is prepared. The semantico-referential meaning of a text determines the expected material and spiritual benefits from drinking the nectar.

Thus, the Sikhs do not merely recite the Guru Granth Sahib for intellectual exercise and to comprehend its moral teachings, but they recognize both material and cognitive properties of language and articulated speech. Drinking texts is a widespread practice in the whole Sikh community that involves a "physiological engagement" (see Babb 1983; Dusenbery 1992) with God through the transformative power of the gurus' words. Even if a person does not understand the meaning of the words, the sacred verses recited and transformed into substances in water are ascribed performative powers to positively affect the human mind and body in numerous ways.

## Making the guru present

A primary illocution of many religious acts in Sikh worship is to evoke and manifest the presence of the guru in the here and now. Considering that the shabad-guru is believed to dwell in the words and teaching of Guru Granth Sahib, recitation of the text becomes a sacramental act to activate, reveal and make present the guru for enduring guidance. By reading, hearing, and learning the teaching, religious people will claim they are able to experience the guru. Particularly the unbroken cover-to-cover recitation of the Guru Granth Sahib (*akhand path*) is often said to be an act of "inviting the guru," not only by installing the book physically at the shop, the house, or wherever the recitation is to be conducted, but reciting the complete text is to disclose the interior of the book and manifests the true guru in the world—in the space of one's house, family, social life, and mind.

Even though a dominant ideal is to understand the teaching in the scripture, the body-form of the present worldly guru should also be revered, like the human gurus once were, for what it contains and mediates. In gurdwaras all over the world, contemporary Sikhs daily create a presence and authority of Guru Granth Sahib by means of arranging spaces and performing ritual acts. Any gathering in the gurdwara usually go by the idiom "royal court" (*darbar*) or "court of justice" (*divan*) to indicate the physical presence of a spiritual authority—Guru Granth Sahib—and the assembly of devotees gathered in attendance, that is, the *satsang* or "the congregation of virtuous people." Each morning begins with *prakash* or "the light," the opening ceremony when the scripture is installed on a majestic seat under a canopy and the "court" starts running. Throughout the day, devotees will attend the gurdwara as if to obtain audience in the court of a royal sovereign. In solemn acts they present prayers, offerings and pay homage to the upraised scripture by performing *matha tekhna*, the bodily act of going down on one's knees and bowing deeply until the forehead touches the ground.[11] Whenever the scripture is enthroned on the seat and not read from, it is covered with embroidered cushions and robes (*rumala*) that are adjusted to the season. During the summer, the throne will be dressed in cooler silk or nylon and in the winter coated with cotton or woolen robes to protect the scripture from the cold. Every day is concluded at nightfall with the ceremony of "the comfortable posture" (*sukhasan*), during which the Guru Granth Sahib assumes a closed position, is wrapped in robes, and carried in procession to a special bedroom (*sachkhand*) for nightly rest on a bedecked four-poster bed. During this nightly procession, all the assembled people create a pathway for the scripture by kneeling and touching the floor with their foreheads, while melodiously chanting the name of God (*satnam vahiguru*) in chorus. By these formalized acts performed daily in gurdwaras, Sikh devotees create a diurnal rhythm for the scripture and the framework for courtly sessions. The solemnized ceremonies of opening/revealing and

11. In social situations of everyday life, *matha tekna* usually refer to the symbolic act of touching the feet of an elder or other esteemed persons in order to salute and pay reverence. In the gurdwara, it is a humble act of submitting oneself by the letting the highest part the human body, the forehead, touch the ground before the guru-scripture.

closing/concealing the sacred book have the function of activating and deactivating the guru-scripture and regulating the routes of entry and access to its interior.

In other ritual contexts, the Guru Granth Sahib is also staged like a royal sovereign to be worshipped. In connection with *gurpurubs*,[12] festivals that commemorate the births (*prakash divas*) and deaths (*joti jot samae*) of all ten Sikh Gurus, their accession to the office of the guru (*gurgaddi*), and other major events of the religious calendar (*Nanakshahi samat*),[13] Sikh communities may draw together all groups of devotees and jointly create sometimes mile-long processions (*nagar kirtan*) in the city or village of residence to exhibit collective social and religious activities. The most essential feature of these processions is the presence of the Guru Granth Sahib, which temporarily leaves the abode of the gurdwara to conduct a tour for a day, attended and escorted by devotees. The scripture is often installed on a decorated palanquin mounted on a float that may be transported in various ways depending upon local resources and initiative—ranging from a simple motor-rickshaw to a large flamboyant trailer—in order to provide the scripture comfort and to display the sovereignty of the text. As the guru traverse the neighborhoods, the Sikhs may wash, perfume, and throw flowers before its way. Individual Sikh families with houses or shops along the way may illuminate their buildings with electric lights to celebrate the arrival of the guru-scripture in their neighborhood. Many Sikhs perceive the processions as a means to honor and celebrate a particular human guru in the past by taking the Guru Granth Sahib out in majestic splendor to grant blessings.

During other celebrations that index social transfers in an individual Sikh life, such as weddings and turban ceremonies, Sikh families arrange spaces for the physical scripture in their house and read and sing from the sacred texts as if the worldly guru is present to witness and bless the social occasion. Religious people may even argue that the scripture has capacities to see and foresee what is happening in its immediate spatial presence and the social life of devotees, such as being a witness (*sakhi*) in attendance, formally installed in the center of a wedding when a couple perform the acts which contract a marriage. The scripture is even believed to speak in the world and facilitate a real physical channel of communication with the divine. When Sikhs are seeking divine protection or assistance in a life situation they will present a formal petition (*ardas*) with their wishes and requests and make various types of promises in its immediate physical presence. The scripture is randomly opened and the first hymn appearing on the left page is taken to be a divine

12. In total there are thirty-four *gurpurubs* in the present Sikh calendar that annually attract large segments of the community into action.

13. *Nanakshahi samat* is the Sikh calendar based on a tropical solar year with the new year beginning on the first day of the month *Chet*, corresponding to March 14 in the Julian calendar. The new calendar was formally implemented by the SGPC in 2003.

order (*hukam*), the guru's guiding reply to the human appeal. Many perceive this as a dialogic and interactive event during which the invisible divine is directly communicating to humans through the mediating link of the guru, who is present and able to reciprocate. Thus, through different culturally-prescribed and learned acts conducted with the temporal and spatial dimensions of the Guru Granth Sahib, people both generate and integrate religious experiences and notions of a presence and supreme authority of a worldly guru manifested in the text.

## Rituals of Guru Granth Sahib

The most illustrative example of how the Sikhs venerate the Guru Granth Sahib in modern times appears in the context of ceremonies celebrating different stages and events in the worldly life of the scripture. When printing technology was introduced in the Punjab during the nineteenth century, the Sikhs did not believe that the process of committing their guru-scripture to print would eliminate its religious status, but quite the contrary welcomed the opportunity to once and for all fix the "completeness" of Guru Granth Sahib and remove the traces of human editors found in handwritten manuscripts.[14] Today, most Sikh communities use printed editions with a standard pagination (1,430 pages) of the text in a single volume. The autonomous Sikh organization *Shiromani Gurdwara Parbandhak Committee* (SGPC), which was established in 1925 and perceives of itself as a religious "government," set up its own printing press in Amritsar during the 1950s and has made serious attempts to control and monopolize the production and distribution of scriptures. The religious sentiments underlying this radical strategy presume that Guru Granth Sahib is not an ordinary book or consumer item and should not be merchandized for profit. Neither can a person purchase the scripture from the publisher but will give a "donation" in exchange for the book and a guarantee that he or she is able to follow its ritual requirements, that is, transport the scripture in solemnized ways and install it daily on a throne (see Myrvold 2007, 2008). The printing process must furthermore protect the sanctity of the scripture by complying with the Sikh *maryada*, or the code of conduct. In practice, this implies that the publisher should produce Guru Granth Sahib in accordance with its sanctioned content and form and give due respect to the book during the printing process. Workers at SGPC's printing house must, for instance, sign a pledge that they will remove shoes and cover their heads inside the printing house and abstain from intoxicants. During the printing procedures they are expected to chant the name of god and cover all printing matter with robes. To arrange the gurus' words in one single volume is believed to be a process by which the

14. To all appearances the first printed edition of the Guru Granth Sahib in *Gurmukhi* script was published in 1864 (Mann 2001, 125). Three decades later at least a dozen additional reprints of the Sikh scripture had come into existence and the number of printing presses in the Punjab exceeded more than one hundred (Oberoi 1995, Pashaura Singh 2000, 232 ff.).

eternal shabad-guru is embodied in the form of a written book which assumes the identity and status of Guru Granth Sahib.

When a new text is received in a gurdwara or a private house, it is customary to perform an installation ceremony that is usually called *prakash*. At the new abode, the text will be offered an honorable seat and then ceremonially opened in accordance with the routine of the morning liturgy. Characteristic of this event is the custom of reading either the whole or the first five stanzas of the composition *JapJi Sahib*, the opening hymn of Guru Granth Sahib, which creates the symbolic stage of the scripture's entrance and incorporation into a new social sphere of a community. The scripture is no longer a text to be used by any assembly of devotees but will be subject to ministration and devotion within the social spaces and activities of a particular community. When religious Sikhs imagine Guru Granth Sahib being invited to their house, they attribute to the scripture the identity of an honored guest who demands devout ministration and will be involved in the socio-religious life of the family. To provide the scripture proper respect, it is usually offered a separate room in the house which is kept pure and peaceful and sometimes richly embellished with flower bouquets, oil-lamps, incense holders, and other religious paraphernalia. Except for the daily installation ceremony and readings from the Guru Granth Sahib, the family may also give the scripture a portion of all their meals as a symbolic offering and placing a glass of milk or water beside the scripture at night just as a guest would be given drinkables in case of thirst.

In more recent years, the Guru Granth Sahib has gained its own festival days in the Sikh calendar which, just like important historical events in the lives of the human gurus, are called *gurpurubs*. The present almanac includes three historical events that legitimize the scripture's identity and authority. In the end of August, a festival called *Sampurnta divas Shri Guru Granth Sahib ji* commemorates the completion of the scripture in 1604, and two days later the first installation and opening of the text—*Shri Guru Granth Sahib ji Pahila Prakash*—in the Golden Temple at Amritsar the same year. In October, a third festival celebrates the day of coronation, *Gurgaddi divas Shri Guru Granth Sahib ji*, when the scripture ascended to the office of the guru in 1708. On these occasions, and especially in connection with anniversaries, Sikh congregations may take out the Guru Granth Sahib in lavish processions to honor the text as a worldly and living guru. During the tercentenary of the scripture's guruship in 2008, for instance, Sikhs worldwide celebrated with religious programs for weeks, including processions, non-stop readings of the complete texts, public distributions of food, seminars and a number of other activities.[15]

A physical book is bound to temporality and can only provide the guru an honorable garb for a limited time. When a printed edition of the Guru Granth

15. See for example the articles published on the website of World Sikh News, http://worldsikhnews.com/worldsikhnews/Tercentenary%20of%20Guruship%20to%20Guru%20Granth%20Sahib.htm. Accessed 31 August 2010.

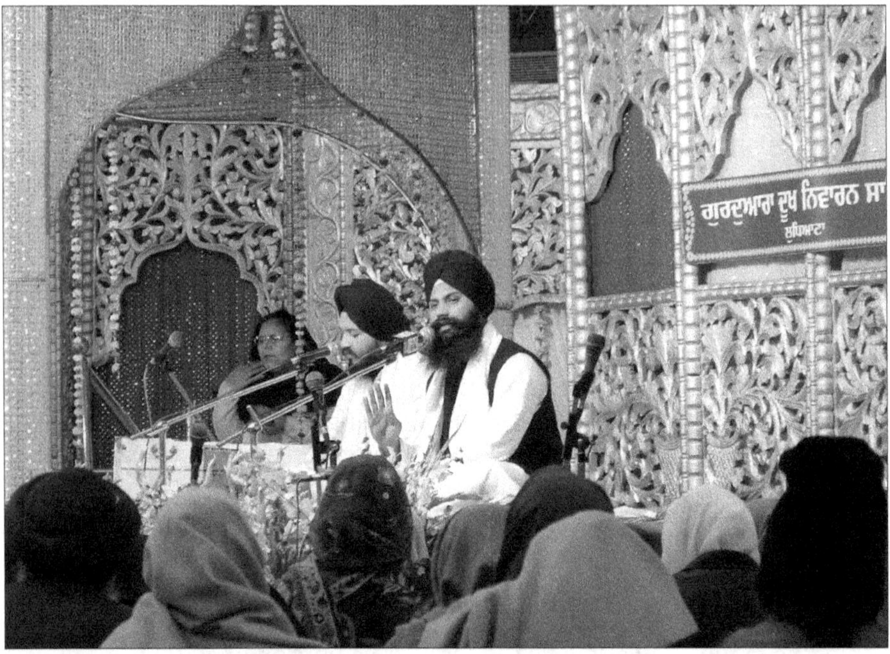


Figure 3. A professional exegete (*kathavacak*) delivers religious discourses (*katha*) on the Sikh scripture and history of Guru Gurdwara Dukh Niwaran Sahib in Ludhiana (Punjab). Photo: Kristina Myrvold.

Sahib is getting old and can no longer be used in worship and for reading practices, the book should be exchanged for a new volume. To simply dispose of the sacred pages or the whole scripture like secular books is however considered an extremely blasphemous act. Instead, worn-out scriptures are transported to any of several newly constructed cremation centers in India to be solemnly dissolved in the fire during a ceremony called "the rite of the fire sacrifice" (*agn bhet samskar*) (Myrvold 2007, 2009). What these ritual practices seem to underscore is the division between the interior "spirit" (*jot*) of Guru Granth Sahib and the form (*sarup*) of the worldly guru-scripture. Religious Sikhs would argue that the true guru is eternal and will never be extinct, but divine words were revealed and made manifest through the utterances of the human gurus and later embodied in the text. Because the temporal form of Guru Granth Sahib is subject to bodily change, the scripture seems to have its own life-cycle with ceremonial events that mark its entrance and departure from the community of disciples and existence in the world. Through the typographical process the scriptural guru assumes its stipulated form and identity, embodying the shabad-guru, to be incorporated into the religious life of the Sikhs. When its life-time is complete, its body is reverently disposed of in a cremation ritual that returns the divine words to their celestial origin.

## Providing meanings to ritual acts

When religious Sikhs explain their celebration and careful ministration of the Guru Granth Sahib, they may first recur to history and explain what the human gurus did in the past. Sikh historiography provides several accounts of how the gurus and their closest disciples early embedded the scriptures in courtly symbolism and stipulated models for handling the text.[16] For contemporary Sikhs these textual references legitimize the careful choreography of action in presence of the Guru Granth Sahib. Descriptions of what the gurus did in the past function as prescriptions for proper handling of the text in the present. Since the Guru Granth Sahib belongs to the same line of succession, the scripture should be subject to acts of reverence similar to those that presumably existed in the courtly culture of the human gurus. Just as the historical gurus sat on a cot (*manji*) and uttered hymns, the Sikhs should place the Guru Granth Sahib on a bed covered with robes whenever it is sung or recited from. A set of selected habits that aimed to confirm the supreme status of the human gurus have been perpetuated around the Guru Granth Sahib, albeit reshaped to the more invariant ritualized events necessary for performance by Sikh disciples. It is important to observe that emic explanations like these are discursive strategies to traditionalize and justify current practices, some of which have been constructed in modern times, and simultaneously bridge the temporal distance between the gurus' deeds of the past and the disciples' action in the present.

The careful ministrations to Guru Granth Sahib are categorized under the religious notion of *gurseva*, or selfless "service to the Guru." In concept and action, *gurseva* encompasses a wide range of individual and collective activities directed to the scripture, such as the daily ceremonies in the gurdwara, practical duties of keeping the spaces of the guru's house tidy and clean, ceremonial and comfortable transportations of the scripture, and so on. As the Guru Granth Sahib is the worldly guru with the authority and capacity to reveal divine knowledge and guidance to humanity, the scripture should be served and honored in the best possible. To be a humble servant of the guru and do altruistic work is considered a paradigmatic way of purifying the human's interior self and cultivating humility and virtue. Moreover, the idea and practice of *gurseva* articulate and invoke enduring relationships between Sikh disciples and the spiritual preceptor embodied in the text. The scripture should be venerated, not merely because the tradition prescribes it, but because the scripture continues to bestow transcendental knowledge and to mediate links between humans and the divine. From this perspective, rituals per-

16. For example, the oft-quoted *Sri Gurbilas Chhevin Patshahi* ("The splendour of the sixth master"), a nineteenth century text attributed to Sohan Kavi, describes the ceremonial installation of the Sikh scripture at Harimandir Sahib in 1604 when the newly appointed custodian of the scripture, Bhai Buddha, carried the text on his head to the temple and Guru Arjan walked behind waving a whisk over it. For an English review of this reference, see Fauja Singh 1990, 45–50.

formed to Guru Granth Sahib are not considered symbolic in the sense that they represent something else, but to believing Sikhs the ritual acts signify real services that permit actual physical interaction with the guru.

From a religious viewpoint, the ministrations to Guru Granth Sahib may appear as the type of action that best respond to the nature of the text, but one could also claim that these acts create and confirm perceptions of the scripture as a person and invest it with the spiritual authority and "social agency" of a guru acting in the world. In a practice-oriented approach, Bell suggests that the bodily acts and gestures of humans who are moving about within a specially constructed space actually project and define the cultural-specific qualities that order that space and simultaneously re-embody the same cultural values and schemes. People may experience sacrality and respond to the environment as if nonhuman forces had shaped it while they deploy and embody the schemes for creating this space through their bodily movements (Bell 1992). Following anthropological theories, Gell also argues that ritual activities can be viewed as strategies for making inanimate objects socially alive by establishing exchanges between humans and objects and creating spaces that emphasize the interior identity of the object. In his view, inanimate objects may indeed have a "personhood" and operate in the social world as mediators of "social agency," because such agency is not necessarily defined by biological qualities but rather by relational ones. It appears in the context of social relationships between people and objects. Gell exemplifies how people animate and impose a "soul" and agency on objects by, for instance, placing life-substances within the objects or wrapping them with clothes or various layers of "skins" and enmeshing the objects in daily routines and creating spaces that emphasize their interior identity (Gell 1998). Through ritual activities, the object will be thought and spoken of as if it inhabits a soul, possess capacities to communicate ideas, exchange gifts with humans, and in other ways express the underlying relationality that defines its position (De Castro 2004; Harvey 2006).

Applying these ideas to Sikh worship, many ritualized acts performed to the Guru Granth Sahib do not merely communicate messages or perceptions of a scripture but mould meanings and values and personify the scripture. In other words, they attribute to the text the social agency of a personal guru. Sikhs may a priori consider the Guru Granth Sahib a living guru, as the tradition advocates, but the different modes of speech and ritual behaviors set the book in a context of external relationships in which the scripture is presented as a "social other" or a "person" of exalted status who continues to speak and act in the world. The ritual ministrations and daily routines of the text can be approached as external strategies by which devotees effectively create the presence, authority, and agency of a guru. Looking at practices of addressing the text, for instance, the Sikhs utilize an honorific nomenclature that is used for male subjects in the surrounding society. In addition to the name Guru Granth Sahib, devotees may use epithets such as the "great king" (*maharaja*) or "respected holy man" (*baba ji*) and thereby cognitively classify the text with a living person of higher position and not as an inanimate object.[17] To simply use the personal pronoun "it," which is normally utilized for inanimate objects, would be considered derogatory to the scripture. The attribution of personhood and agency to Guru Granth Sahib through these and other acts is not complicated by the fact that it is a book, simply because agency is relational. This might be a significant analytical starting point if we are to understand Sikh religious beliefs and positions. The Guru Granth Sahib is not considered to be a symbol representing the guru or an icon like the guru, but rather an index that *is* something. To religious Sikhs the scripture is the present guru firmly embedded in a web of historical and contemporary relationships to humans. Ritualized acts of veneration and devotion are not perceived in any symbolic sense but are culturally and historically prescribed ways to provide the text a real ministration through which devotees construct and maintain devotional, didactical, and social relationships to the scripture and the teaching it enshrines.

Whether the motive of the defendants in the Vienna case was to violently protest against a perceived disrespect of Guru Granth Sahib or involved some other conflict, it still remains the case that any attempt to challenge the attributed authority and agency of the scripture, by for instance placing a human religious leader on the same level as the text, will be considered a provocation and blasphemous act by the majority of religious Sikhs. To them, history stands witness to a divine intervention when words and a teaching of a higher order were embodied in the gurus' utterances and later in the scriptural form of Guru Granth Sahib. To sustain a devotional relationship to the scriptural guru and continually engage in acts of reading, singing, and explicating the words as well as honoring the physical body of the text is to be a Sikh, a disciple of the guru.

## References

Austin, J. L. 1962. *How to Do Things with Words*. Cambridge, MA: Harvard University Press.

Babb, Lawrence A. 1983. "The Physiology of Redemption." *History of Religions* 22(4): 293–312. http://dx.doi.org/10.1086/462927

Bauman, Richard and Charles L. Briggs. 1990. "Poetics and Performance as Critical Perspectives on Language and Social Life." *Annual Review of Anthropology* 19: 59–88. http://dx.doi.org/10.1146/annurev.an.19.100190.000423

17. Harvey (2006, 33) observes that in some languages and patterns of speech, objects are even "grammatically animate rather than grammatically inanimate," that is, the language does not grammatically distinguish between people and objects but will use nouns in animated gender for a number of non-living things which "can be spoken of and to as persons—as they are spoken with." According to De Castro (2004), honorific titles are "relational pointers," that is, nouns that define something in terms of its relation to something else and are "two-place predicates". For instance, a sovereign of worldly power will only exist and be addressed by the term "king" in so far as there are other subjects who acknowledge his authority and whose king he is.

Bawa, Ujagar Singh. 2006. *Bhai Sahib Bhai Nand Lal Ji: Biography and Writings.* Delhi: Hemkunt Publishers.

Bell, Catherine. 1992. *Ritual Theory, Ritual Practice.* New York: Oxford University Press.

Briggs, Charles L. and Richard Bauman. 1992. "Genre, Intertextuality, and Social Power." *Journal of Linguistic Anthropology* 2(2): 131–172. http://dx.doi.org/10.1525/jlin.1992.2.2.131

De Castro, Eduardo Viveiros. 2004. "Exchanging Perspectives: The Transformation of Objects into Subjects in Amerindian Onthologies." *Common Knowledge* 10(3): 463–484. http://dx.doi.org/10.1215/0961754X-10-3-463

Dusenbery, Verne A. 1992. "The Word as Guru: Sikh Scripture and the Translation Controversy." *History of Religion* 31(4): 385–402. http://dx.doi.org/10.1086/463294

Facebook. 2010a. "Sri Guru Granth Sahib Ji our Living Guru – Not Just a Book", available at http://www.facebook.com/home.php?#!/group.php?gid=29961024825. Accessed 21 November 2010.

Facebook. 2010b. "Guru Granth Sahib – The True Living Guru." Available at http://www.facebook.com/pages/Guru-Granth-Sahib-The-True-Living-Guru/139778176040374. Accessed 21 November 2010._

Facebook. 2010c. "Mere Guru Dhan Dhan Sri Guru Granth Sahib ji Han"[My Guru is the Respected Guru Granth Sahib]. Available at http://www.facebook.com/home.php?#!/group.php?gid=148169765220237. Accessed 21 November 2010.

Gell, Alfred. 1998. *Art and Agency: An Anthropological Theory.* Oxford: Clarendon Press.

Groendahl, Boris. 2010. "Sikh Sikh Men Sent to Prison for Austria Temple Attack." *Reuters.* 28 September. Available at http://in.reuters.com/article/idINIndia-51784920100928. Accessed 21 November, 2010.

Harvey, Graham. 2006. *Animism: Respecting the Living World.* New York: Columbia University Press.

Kang, Yoonhee. 2006. "'Staged' Rituals and 'Veiled' Spells: Multiple Language Ideologies and Transformations in Petalangan Verbal Magic." *Journal of Linguistic Anthropology* 16: 1–22. http://dx.doi.org/10.1525/jlin.2006.16.1.001

Kaur, Guninder. 1995. *The Guru Granth Sahib: Its Physics and Metaphysics*. New Delhi: Manohar Publishers.

Kaur Singh, Nikky-Guninder. 1992. "The Myth of the Founder: The Janamsakhis and the Sikh Tradition." *History of Religious* 31(4): 329–343. http://dx.doi.org/10.1086/463291

———. 1993. *The Feminine Principle in the Sikh Vision of the Transcendent.* Cambridge: Cambridge University Press. http://dx.doi.org/10.1017/CBO9780511557415

———. 2008. "Guru Granth: The Quintessential Sikh Metaphor." *Postscripts* 4(2): 157–176.

Kohli, Surinder Singh. 2000. *Ritualism and Its Rejection in the Sikhism*. Amritsar: Singh Brothers.

———, trans. 2003. *Sri Dasam Granth Sahib (Vol. 1).* Birmingham: The Sikh National Heritage Trust.

Mann, Gurinder Singh. 2001. *The Making of the Sikh Scripture*. New York: Oxford University Press. http://dx.doi.org/10.1093/0195130243.001.0001

———. 2008. "Scriptures and the Nature of Authority: The Case of Guru Granth in Sikh Tradition." In *Theorizing Scriptures: New Critical Orientations to a Cultural Phenomenon*, edited by Vincent L. Wimbush, 41–54. New Brunswick, New Jersey, and London: Rutgers University Press.

Myrvold, Kristina, ed. 2010. *The Death of Sacred Texts: Ritual Disposal and Renovation of Texts in World Religions*. Farnham Surrey: Ashgate.

———. 2008. "Personifying the Sikh Scripture: Ritual Processions of the Guru Granth Sahib in India." In *South Asian Religions on Display: Religious Processions in South Asia and in the Diaspora*, edited by Knut A. Jacobsen, 140–156. London and New York: Routledge.

———. 2007. *Inside the Guru's Gate: Ritual Uses of Texts among the Sikhs in Varanasi*. Lund: Media-tryck.

Oberoi Harjot. 1995. *The Construction of Religious Boundaries: Culture, Identity, and Diversity in the Sikh Tradition*. Delhi: Oxford University Press.

Rappaport, Roy A. 1999. *Ritual and Religion in the Making of Humanity*. Cambridge: Cambridge University Press.

Rumsey, Alan. 1990. "Wording, Meaning, and Linguistic Ideology." *American Anthropologist* 92: 346–361. http://dx.doi.org/10.1525/aa.1990.92.2.02a00060

Shackle, Christopher. 2008. "Repacking the Ineffable: Changing Styles in Sikh Scriptural Commentary." *Bulletin of SOAS* 71(2): 255–277.

Singh, Arvind-Pal. 1995. "The Ambivalence of Tradition in the Representation of Sikh Culture *International Journal of Punjab Studies* 2(2): 217–238.

———. 1996. "Interrogating Identity: Cultural Translation, Writing, and Subaltern Politics." In *Punjabi Identity: Continuity and Change*, edited by Gurharpal Singh and Ian Talbot, 187–227. New Delhi: Manohar Publishers.

Singh, Bhai Vir, ed. 1999 (1926). *Puratan Janam Sakhi Sri Guru Nanak Dev Ji*. New Delhi: Bhai Vir Singh Sahitya Sadan.

Singh, Fauja, ed. 1990. *The City of Amritsar: An Introduction*. Patiala: Publication Bureau Punjabi University.

Singh, Gurnek. 1998. *Guru Granth Sahib: Interpretations, Meaning and Nature*. Delhi: National Book Shop.

Singh, Jodh. 1998. *Varan Bhai Gurdas: Text, Transliteration and Translation*. Patiala, New Delhi: Vision and Venture.

Singh, Pashuara. 2000. *The Guru Granth Sahib: Canon, Meaning and Authority*. New Delhi: Oxford University Press.

———. 2008. "Scripture as Guru in the Sikh Tradition." *Religion Compass* 2(4): 659–673. http://dx.doi.org/10.1111/j.1749-8171.2008.00080.x

World Sikh News, available at http://worldsikhnews.com/worldsikhnews/Tercentenary%20of%20Guruship%20to%20Guru%20Granth%20Sahib.htm. Accessed 31 August 2010.

# 15

# A Birthday Party for a Sacred Text: The Gita Jayanti and the Embodiment of God as the Book and the Book as God

Joanne Punzo Waghorne

*For over a decade, various Hindu organizations in Singapore have joined to celebrate an extraordinary series of events, called the Gita Jayanti. The term jayanti literally means "victory" or "victorious" but more usually indicates celebration of the birthday of a holy figure or a deity. Put simply, this is a birthday celebration for the Gita, a compact text that increasingly functions in the Hindu diaspora much like the Bible—a portable compendium of teachings, a deeply poetic source of individual comfort, a text to be memorized, chanted, studied. I know of no other Hindu text with such a birthday, nor had any of the people whom I interviewed about it encountered this celebration outside of Singapore. As part of the celebrations, the Gita undergoes a ritual that parallels the consecration of a deity for use in a temple. In this case the Gita takes on the body of Krishna who is understood to have spoken these holy words many centuries ago. In this sense the Bhagavad Gita, here treated as the Holy Book of contemporary Hinduism, is an iconic body of Krishna just as the bronze murti is also an iconic body—the ultimate iconicity.*

For over a decade, various Hindu organizations in Singapore have joined together to celebrate an extraordinary series of events called the Gita Jayanti. The term *jayanti* literally means "victory" or "victorious," but more often indicates a celebration of the birthday of a holy figure or a deity such as Gandhi Jayanti, a national holiday in India, or Krishna Jayanti. The Gita Jayanti, according to an invitational brochure, "celebrates the birth of the Song Celestial—'the Bhagavad Gita.' The Bhagavad Gita was song by Lord Krishna in the battlefield of Kurukshetra, in response to the despondency of Arjuna, and is widely regarded as one of the primal scripture of Hinduism." Put simply, this is a birthday celebration for the Gita, a compact text that increasingly functions in the Hindu diaspora much like the Bible—a portable compendium of teachings, a deeply poetic source of individual comfort, a text to be memorized, chanted, studied, and now used in law courts for oaths.[1] I know of no other Hindu text

1. In the United States, I have seen members of governing bodies of temples swear on it, and

with such a birthday, nor had any of the people whom I interviewed about it encountered this celebration outside of Singapore, although some claimed that the few guru-centered movements had brought the observance back to India.[2]

The Gita Jayanti, with a series of events extending over four months from late September to a culminating ritual in early February, celebrates the *birth* and not the *revelation* of a sacred text; the choice of words in this highly educated English-speaking city-state must be read seriously. The intense birth imagery in which a sacred text taking bodily form gives nearly literal expression to the term *iconic book* is played out, as I will show, in much of the celebration in 2007–2008. The term *birth,* however, does not easily translate in this Singaporean Hindu milieu as "incarnation." Rather, the singular Singaporean innovation of the Gita Jayanti came alive within particular Hindu religious sensibilities formed out of South Indian Hindu temple culture, particularly from the state of Tamilnadu, the ancestral home of the greater majority of Singaporean Indians. The Gita Havan, the "main event" as listed in the brochure for Gita Jayanti 2008, replicated the intricate Tamil-style rituals for the consecration of a divine image within a temple. The Bhagavad Gita, in the context of the Gita Havan, "took birth" as an icon, or more properly in Hindu temple terms, as a divine *mūrti* (body, form), more like the stone and bronze bodies of the Gods in temples than words made into flesh. Yet other events—chanting, essay and quiz contests, cultural dance performances, and an academic conference—preceded this long complex ritual event in February. The elegantly produced publication *Gita Vani 2008* distributed at the Gita Havan included essays like "Therapy and Realization—in the Bhagavad Gita," and yet presented this conglomerate of the "iconic, performative, and semantic dimensions" (Watts, Chapter 1, this volume) of the Gita as a seamless whole. Officials of the organizing committee honored the beaming young winners of the various essay, chanting and quiz contests at the end of the daylong havan. Indeed, both literally and metaphorically, at the end of the day the Gita Jayanti enlivened the Song of the Lord performatively, discursively, and finally, more literally than we have seen it elsewhere, as an *icon*. This point is both a peremptory conclusion as well as question for the comparative study of iconic books: how does a process whereby a holy book primarily expounded, chanted, and read increasingly by educated Hindus in urban India and in diaspora somehow meld its semantic use within a larger sense of embodiment—a metamorphosis of book into body engendered by a ritual process of consecration? Here, then, is yet another case, which eases—

there is currently an ACLU sponsored suit in North Carolina to allow multiple religious text to be used in court oaths asking that the phrase "Holy Scriptures" in the North Carolina state statute must be read to permit texts such as the Qur'an, the Hebrew Bible and the Bhagavad-Gita in addition to the Christian Bible (ACLU 2007).

2. I could not confirm these reports of the Gita Jayanti in India but several people did tell me that the public chanting of the Gita was increasingly popular in urban India, especially in Chennai. On the web, annual Gita Jayanti celebration in Malaysia gives credit to Singapore as the origin ("Gita Jayanti Malaysia" n.d.).

perhaps deliberately—the dichotomies between ritual-based and textual-based religions, between discursive thinking and ritual action, and *for us*, between ethnographic and textual studies. That Singaporean Hindus in particular imagined, constructed, and continue to refine this event is no accident. I say this after several years of research with Hindu-based movements and various Indian Hindu communities in this city-state that provides the context for this development.

Indian Hindus form a small but highly visible part of an urban collage of emigrant ethnic groups in Singapore, for two centuries settled here from southern China and southern India, brought together in the early nineteenth century by the enterprising Stanford Raffles, whose deal with a local Malay prince to acquire this tip of the peninsula caused much controversy rather than celebration within the East India Company. Raffles, unlike many other colonial progenitors, is celebrated and not reviled in Singapore, where his plan of massive labor recruitment from China and India set in motion the successful multiethnic enterprise that has become Singapore, Inc.[3] Few are native to this city, which hangs off the tip of Malaysia and yet counts only fourteen percent of the population as Malay. Indian Hindus are an even smaller minority, less than ten percent, while the greater majority of citizens share various Chinese heritages. Waves of immigration from India continue as many younger people settle in the city. They are now both men and women and are usually educated in management, the applied sciences, engineering, and computer technologies. While nineteenth-century immigrants and current laboring guest workers came from Tamilnadu, newer émigrés from the last decades come from a variety of urban centers in India. Many of the people that I met at Gita Jayanti events were from this latter group, but they shared with more established Indian Singaporeans sensibilities honed not from the natural world, but from manufacturing and trading—from constructing not tending. Such middle-class people value education as a pragmatic enterprise that provides tools for working. They emphasize practicality even in spiritual learning. New Hindu movements emphasize practice and pragmatic skills for daily life at work and at home, albeit with different discursive registers.

Although sensibilities are shared, divisions remain among Indians rooted in differing mother tongues, in some continuing caste differences that separate Brahman from non-Brahman, and in different ethnicities within India. The plethora of organizations among Indians in Singapore reflects such differences. In addition to a variety of guru-centered organizations, there are ethnolinguistic groups for those who speak Telegu (Andhra Pradesh), Marwari (Rajasthan), Kanada (Karnataka), Malayali (Kerala), all of whom have in turn taken the lead in organizing the Gita Jayanti over the last decade. In fact,

3. The Singapore History Gallery in the National Museum of Singapore (http://www.nationalmuseum.sg/) presents Raffles as a fearless founder who paid dearly for his insistence on establishing Singapore. The statue to Raffles in the heart of the downtown waterfront continues to be a popular place for iconic snapshots of the city.

the Gita Jayanti remains the only celebration that Singaporean Hindus—at least those that join together for this event—regard as transcending ethic and regional differences. The invitational brochure describes the Gita Jayanti as a "community celebration," using the singular for an otherwise divided Hindu conglomerate. The Gita Jayanti, then, ritually confirms an already common acceptance of the Bhagavad Gita as the *one* easily identifiable *Hindu* scripture—an important form of identification with other religious groups in this city-state where upper middle-class Hindus are acquainted with the Bible from their high school educations at Christian (mostly Roman Catholic) private schools, where conversions to Bible-centered evangelical Christianity continue among many Chinese, and where the Qur'an, in spite of the small percentage of Muslims, remains ever-present for this island nation bounded by a Southeast Asia Muslim world to the north in Malaysia and to the south in Indonesia. Singaporean Hindus are well aware of religious texts as singular *books*. This emphasis on the Gita as not only a singular religious text but as the unifying holy *book* will emerge below.

Many of the events associated with this celebration appeared to conform to the more usual academic and devotional uses of a sacred text: they ritualize its "semantic dimension." An International Gita Forum followed the pattern of an academic conference: a two-day series of lectures on the Gita ranging from the expected discussions of the text such as "Concept of Action in the Bhagavad Gita" to the interesting "Art of Leadership and Management: Gita Perspectives." Added for the first time in 2008 were several events for children and their proud parents, included a Gita Quiz, "Gita Chanting Competitions," "Oratorical Competition," and "Essay Competition." I attended many of these events which are important stories in themselves and to which I will return. However, on February 3, 2008, the "main event," the Gita Havan which is the focus of this paper, took place on the grounds of the Sri Perumal Temple under the auspices of the Hindu Endowments Board, which is also headquartered within this large temple compound.

When I arrived at the "Gita Havan 2008," eighteen fire pits called *havan* (also *vedi* or *homa kuṇḍam*) covered the side ground of one of the main outbuildings, a pillared pavilion often used for weddings or other functions. Returning to the oldest form of Hindu ritual, these fire pits were carefully constructed square brick hearths for offering ghee (clarified butter) into a sacred fire made according to ancient precedent from wooden twigs and other special substances. Offerings of ghee and grain ablaze in such *yagasala* (places of sacrifice) usually initiate rituals to consecrate a new temple, to sanctify a new home, to enliven a newly constructed divine *murti* (the image-body of a deity), or to renew an older divine image in need of re-empowerment. The *yagasala* (*yākacālai*),[4] a hall

4. The term literally means "the hall for sacrifice" in a temple but sometimes refers to the fire pit as the place of sacrifice. Because so many of these terms are used in Roman script both in Tamilnadu but especially in English-speaking Singapore, there is a colloquial understanding

or ground for sacrifice is a Tamil form of the Sanskrit word, *yajña*, an ancient term for the Vedic sacrifice; the alternate Sanskrit word for the fire altar *vedi* also echoes the most ancient form of Hindu practices. Although modified in modern times, the *yajña* nonetheless remains the emblem of Hindu orthodoxy.

Today, instead of the more usual *mantras*—phrases from the most ancient Hindu texts, the Vedas, used as potent invocations/enchantments—the words of from each chapter of the Bhagavad Gita would be chanted verse-by-verse at the *vedi*. The plan was to have the process repeated at each *vedi*, in a kind of Vedic round robin, as the chapter assigned to each pit was chanted. Each attending priest, who I later found were all Brahmans by birth although not priests by profession, took the a carved wooden spoon, an accoutrement described in very early ritual texts, dipped this into the ghee pot and poured a spoonful as he chanted each verse with those who sat with him at each pit. Those seated at the havan then offered grains into the fire. With my "Havan Ticket" in hand that I purchased from a friendly attendant, I found myself seated around one of the *vedi* next to my tall husband as he threw gains from a tray into the fire (Figure 1). Stunned to be in the ancient position that was once reserved for the virtuous wife of a Hindu man born into the upper castes, I beamed as a smiling official grappled our camera and took a photo. I spotted older women seated at the *vedi* alone, little children making offerings with their grandparents, and very bored teenagers—all of this at the ultimate seat of orthodoxy.

So this event both embraced and simultaneously defied orthodoxy. Shri Sunil, who served as chief priest for this event, is a learned Brahman, employed full time not at one of the traditional temples in Singapore but at the Amriteswari Society dedicated to Mata Amritanandamayi, the very popular "hugging saint" who also both incorporates and confronts orthodox Hindu practices. An interview with Vivek Kumra, who acted as the liaison with the Hindu Endowments Board and organized many details of the ritual, confirmed that Singaporean temples seldom use, invoke, or concern themselves with texts like the Bhagavad Gita. Instead, those expounding and recommending the Gita are the guru-centered societies—many of whom promote a contemporary form of practice that (at least in their rhetoric) excludes no one based on old caste boundaries or even ethnicities or religious identities. Their role was evident at the very back of the sacrificial grounds where an altar stood with a central image of Vishnu flanked by a tiered display of posters or photos of many gurus, acknowledged ancient teachers on the right and tiers of recently departed or currently living gurus on the left. The criteria for their selection was only that someone had a graphic image to contribute and that the master had recommended, chanted, or explicated the Gita.

and use that does not appear in dictionaries. Some terms are actually not used correctly or are confusing in their use. The *yagasala* is the correct term for the whole area. The fire pit is the *vedi* in Sanskrit. An alternate term is *kundam* (*kuṇṭam*) in Tamil.

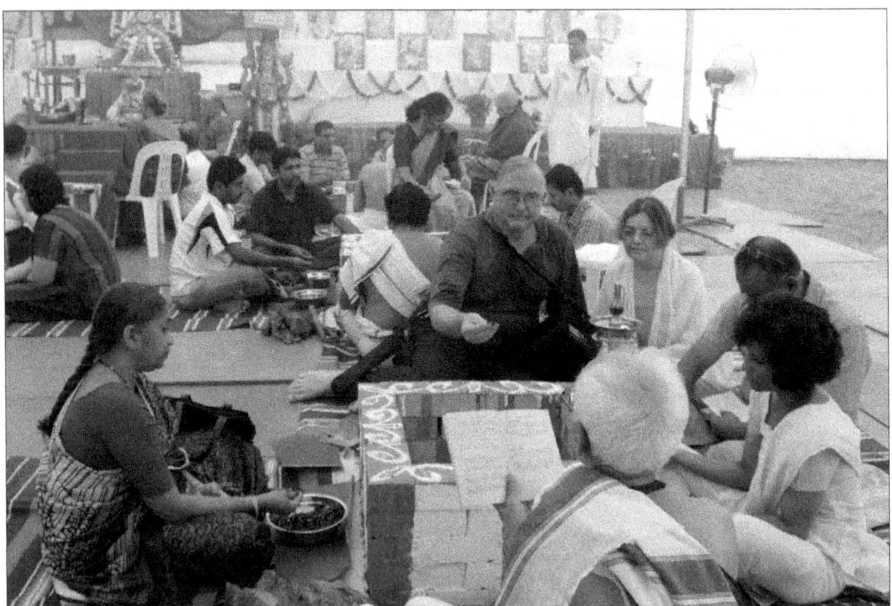

Figure 1. I sit next to my husband in the proper place of a wife as he offers grain into the fire.

The Gita Jayanti celebration began in 1997 when members of two old organizations associated with gurus, Krishna Our Guide and the Geeta Ashram, joined with the Hindu Center and began to pull together the many organizations within the larger Hindu community in Singapore. Krishna Our Guide was founded in Singapore in the 1960s to support the Ramakrishna Mission to fill the "the gap" because Hindu youth "could not find the answers from their visits to temples and from their elders, they turned to other belief systems for answers."[5] Another guru, Swami Hariharji Mahara, established the first Geeta Ashram in North India conterminously with India's independence in 1948 to focus on "spreading the message of Bhagvad Geeta [alternate transliteration] throughout the world." The organization's chapters now stretch from Malaysia to Minnesota, from San Francisco to Singapore. Members of Krishna Our Guide and the Gita Ashram have chanted and studied the Gita for many years in venues from homes to community halls. Unlike the general Indian population, many of the members in Singapore are Hindi speakers from North India, but they are now readily joined in the Gita Jayanti by South Indian ethnic organizations (the conveners for 2007 Gita Jayanti was the Singapore

5. From the website, Krishna Our Guide (2007). The organization was founded by Mr. A. Suppiah. The site also states that Krishna Our Guide believe that "it would be a good start to focus on one of the major scriptures, the Bhagavad Gita. The essence of the Upanishads and the way of life of a man of wisdom are contained in this holy scripture. This would be a good start for anyone who wants answers to questions like: What does it mean to be a Hindu? What are the teachings of Hinduism? Are rites, rituals and ceremonies the end to the means?"

Telegu Samajam and the 2008 was headed by the Kannada Sangha).[6] A guru-centered, not a traditional temple-centered or even a priestly-centered, ethos permeated the event.

Krishna Our Guide, the Geeta Ashram and the many gurus looking down on the proceedings from the tiers on the altar in the back all use the Gita as a text for chanting and for study, often as an alternative to what many consider an empty or under-explicated ritual. Many of the modern gurus have crafted their own temple architecture and developed their own rituals—Mata Amritanandamayi uses women priests—in contention with or as a counterpoint or a complement to more traditional temple forms and practices, which are often understood to leave the spiritual dimension of the devotee untouched. I frequently heard the usual participation in temple rituals and festivals described as "just social;" people are thought to be there only to make contacts or to be seen. In Singapore, many members of guru-centered organizations name the rote quality of rituals in the temples as an impetus for their search for alternate practices within a broad Hindu frame. Although not all organizations reject temple rituals, many consider ritual unsupplemented by textual knowledge to be insufficient. Krishna Our Guide, which does meet in the community hall at Krishna Temple, lists as one of their major questions, "Are rites, rituals, and ceremonies the end to the means?" So, the Gita Jayanti conjoined both orthodox Vedic sacrificial and common temple ritual idioms with the words of the Bhagavad Gita to create a rite—perhaps in the same mode and with the same energy as the gurus' reforged temple techniques—that re-formed words into the divine personage who gave birth to them. The word did not become flesh, but rather the enlivened bronze icon body of Lord Krishna. In some sense, the Gita Jayanti was literally the birthday of both Krishna and of his powerful words. But before I say too much about the ending, I need to return to those early hours in the *yagasala*.

When we arrived very early in the morning, one of the main conveners greeted us warmly yet warned me that the chanting of the full Bhagavad Gita would take almost four hours, "not like the Ten Commandments." And indeed the chanting continued all morning and into the early afternoon as the attention moved from fire pit to fire pit as each chapter was completed. The entire area, however, had multiple levels with continuing activities at each. On one level was this *yagasala* (Figure 2). A large altar stood at the back of the area with a carefully decorated image of Vishnu, in the unique form of Melukote in Karnataka who has Lakshmi, the Goddess of Wealth at his feet. The temple to Lord Cheluvaraya in Melukote in the state of Karnataka remains one of the most famous temples associated with Krishna. Kannada Sangha, who spon-

6. These organization represent other ethnic groups from South India: the Telegu, both a language and a people, derive from the current Indian state of Andhra Pradesh just north of Tamilnadu and Kannada-speakers are from Karnataka west of Tamilnadu. The Tamil people from Tamilnadu dominate the Hindu community and the Tamil language, not Hindi, is one of the four official languages of Singapore.

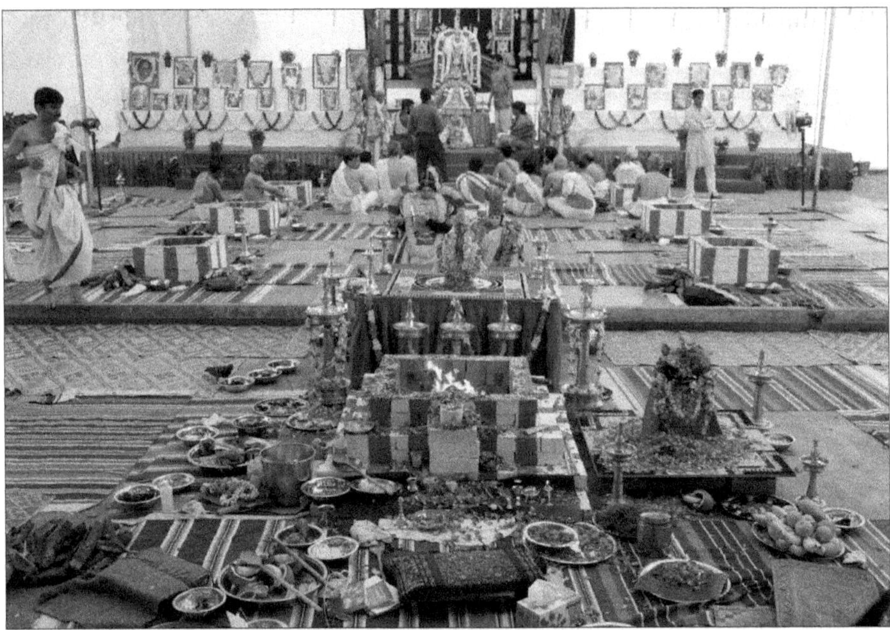

Figure 2. Those acting as priests for each fire pit offer prayers in front of the altar before beginning.

sored the event, considers Lord Cheluvaraya their patron deity, and hence his divine image graced the altar. At the very bottom of the altar stood a beautiful bronze murti of Krishna playing his flute (Figure 3). The back of the grounds evoked temple culture; the event began not with the havan, but with a brief obeisance to the deities at this altar. Implements derived from temple ritual appeared also at the central *vedi* where Shri Sunil presided with the chief guests in attendance. Within the pillared pavilion, however, the wordiness—or better the "bookness"—of the Gita was never lost. Holy book, Vedic ritual, temple ritual, and gurus all played within this venue.

While at each *vedi* the presiding priest always held the Gita in book form in his hands, in the very front of the pavilion raised on a platform two feet from the ground below, older women acted as cantors, chanting the verses over microphones from their books (Figure 4). Meanwhile, at the back of the pavilion, many devoted readers of the Gita followed along with their own books in hand; a projected PowerPoint text with the original Sanskrit and a Roman transliteration provided a place maker. They seemed intent on the book. I spotted a Muslim woman outside reading but ignoring the Hindu ritual element in the *yagasala*.

Hours later, when the chanting ended and the participants at the fire pits moved to the sides to become observers, the focus shifted to a now visible axis formed from the central vedi to the altar at the back. Suddenly, temple culture appeared in the form of the icon bodies in the rear and at the main vedi. These had been present from the beginning but I did not notice them until the priests and participants parted like a curtain revealing a new view. I suspect that others had the same change of perspective at this point. A table fronted the major fire pit with a decorated bronze pot (*kumbha*) placed atop a geometric design carefully created from colored grains, called a *yantra*.[7] Vivek later explained that this *yantra* was drawn "to invoke the blessings of Devi (the Goddess)" while the kumbha held the power of Krishna. He clarified the presence of a total of three holy pots:

> The kumbha placed on top of the yantra draws the divine energies towards it when mantras are chanted. There have been 3 kumbhas always. One is placed beside the main homa kunda [*vedi*], to the right. That is for Lord Ganesha. For all prayers to proceed successfully, it is very important to worship Lord Ganesha first. The second kumbha is placed on a peedham [*pīṭha*] (elevated pedestal) and connected to the main homa kunda. The divine energy of Lord Krishna is invoked into this. The third kumbha is placed on another peedham at the main altar. Again, Lord Krishna is invoked into this kumbha during the chanting of the 108 names of Lord Krishna before the commencement of the Gita homam. (Vivek 2010)

Presiding over the activities in this main vedi were wooden doll-like images of Krishna and his eternal lover Radha that Vivek confirmed were "borrowed from the temple for the event."[8] At the back, the altar became the focus of the priests as well as the observer-devotees now standing at the sides of the holy grounds. Anyone who has witnessed the concentration ceremony (*kumbhābhiṣeka*) to empower or re-empower a divine image would recognize these accoutrements. And soon a form of this temple ritual of consecration soon began.

Every empowerment ceremony, from the consecration of a new image to the re-consecration of an entire temple after renovations, includes a *yagasala* with a fire pit and a *kumbha* for each divine icon. The shape of the *vedi* reflects the deity; I have seen round as well as heart-shaped hearths. Normally priests do not use books for chanting—indeed in a ritual context, the Vedas never took book form until F. Max Müller published his edited edition from Oxford in 1891. I have heard the Vedic mantras described as drawing the powers of the elements of nature back into the fire and then transferred—sometimes literally through a string leading from the *vedi* to the kumbha—into the waters

7. Patterns made of flowers are call Pookkalam ("Metroplus Pookkalam contest" 2010). In Tamilnadu these likely are understood as form of Kolam. The *yantra* was formed much like the now better-known Tibetian sandpaintings but using grains of rice rather than ground gems and rock.

8. Such images are usually often made of wood and plaster and are actually called "dolls" in English to distinguish them from the bronze icons also decorated during festivals but fully enlivened and hence deities not dolls. According to Vivek in his email message said about the dolls, "the face is made with sandalwood powder and the detailed facial features are painted on them. The main body of the statues is made with cloth."

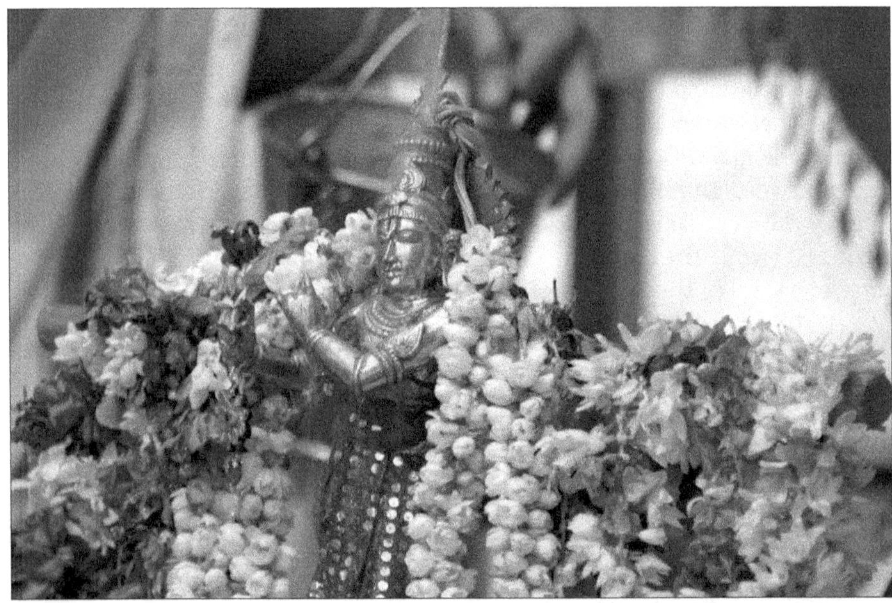

Figure 3. Jasmine flowers bedeck the beautiful bronze images of Krishna.

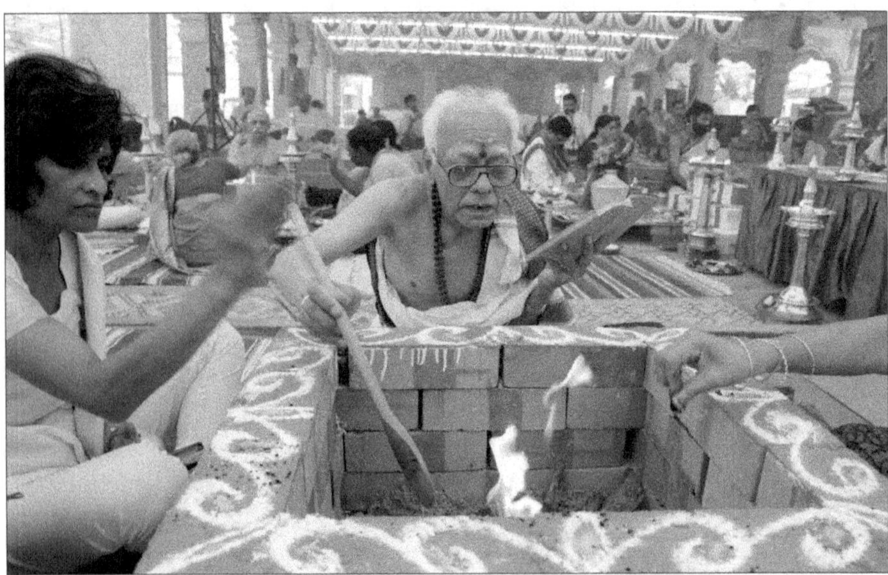

Figure 4. The officiating priest keeps his copy of the Gita but chants from memory as he offers ghee.

within the bronze pot. In this ritual process, words liquefy. Usually in a temple context, the powers of nature plus the innate human powers of all those who chant and even all those who attend the ritual are understood to re-assemble into the holy *kumbha*—according to some accounts in the Vedas the universe began as just such a watery totality. The pot filled with the cosmic power of the mantras, the sonic power of the Vedas, is poured over the still insert (in a temple, stone) body, giving it life. Chants, sounds, become divine flesh. However, something changed in the Gita Havan: the sounds were not Vedic mantras, but the words of the Bhagavad Gita read from the book. Neither the powers of nature nor of human bodies were collected; only the liquid words of the Gita, chanted with human devotion, filled those pots.

Soon a procession formed, led by the chief priest Shri Sunil. Three men had the honor of carrying the *kumbha* on their heads to the back altar. There the bronze image of Krishna received the *abhiṣeka,* the pouring of the waters, which had been transferred to multiple pots, some already partly filled with milk, honey, turmeric water, and other substances. His own words now enlivening him, the re-empowered Krishna was fit for worship. After the usual pause, a curtain fell over the altar while Sunil and other key officiates preformed the *alaṅkāra,* the dressing and adornment of the divine body. When the curtain opened with everyone assembled, Sunil completed the always-beautiful *ārati*, the waving of multiple oil lamps in front of the images revealing the faces and forms of the divine bodies of Krishna and Melukote Cheluvaraya in the undulating flames. Krishna was wholly empowered again, his words now melded into his body.

The full power of this ritual and its logic depended on a number of unspoken assumptions about the very permeable lines betweens words and substance, between words and embodied deities, and between Krishna's body and the production—the "birth"—of the Bhagavad Gita. As a text, the Bhagavad Gita is classified as *laukika*, that is "worldly," in contrast to *vaidika,* "Vedic," which is revealed eternal language without beginning or end. The Gita, usually treated as a separate text but found in the larger epic, the Mahabharata, begins with the prince Arjuna paralyzed with indecision and recriminations as he is about to lead the attack on a rival faction of his own family. His charioteer, Krishna, then turns to him, telling him to fight. Revealing his divine form, Krishna the charioteer becomes Krishna the divine lord. The Gita takes the form of a philosophical argument with complex but pithy teachings, precepts, and principles. Hence, contemporary Hindus view it as the Hindu Bible; its status tends to overshadow the four Vedas, which nonetheless remain the tutelary emblem of orthodoxy. This is the usual understanding of the form and status of the Gita that we tell students in the classroom. However, during an interview with Vivek as well as with others during all of the events of the Gita Jayanti, another more body-centered dimension of the Gita emerged.

As we sat at the end of a large table in the conference room of the Hindu Endowments Board, Vivek patiently explained to me that many Hindus consider the Gita to be the fifth Veda, because it is said that the four Vedas were created out of the air "that is exhaled from the nose of the Lord, so it is from the nose," but the Gita gains its superior purity because it came "from the mouth of the Lord himself." He explained that any thing that is exhaled is not as pure, but the Gita came from words of Krishna directly out of his mouth. "It is held with much higher respect than other books, because the Ramayana was written by Valmiki and so are the other Puranas, but the Gita is something the Lord himself narrated and it is a condensed version of all the Vedas, all the Upanishads." Embedded in Vivek's statement was another key element more deeply rooted in a Hindu world and closely associated with the Gita Jayanti—the birth-day of the text. Put another way, Vivek was saying that Krishna birthed the Gita out of his own body. The Gita Havan reunited his words with his body.

At another event, I heard yet another account of the superiority of the Gita: "It has the essence of all of our spiritual texts… You can very roughly say, it is the application of whatever text the spirituality takes, the Upanishads and all, it's an application." These statements taken together make the Bhagavad Gita a condensation of the major Hindu texts into a useful, applicable form for daily life—echoing its traditional *laukika* status—but also allowing easy production and publication in book form. And as a direct revelation of God, this holy "book" moves closer to the status of the Qur'an, the Ten Commandments, or the Gospels.

I heard these laudatory descriptions of the Gita as an ultimately practical compendium of Hindu scriptures during an intermission at the Gita Quiz competitions held in January of 2008 at one of the oldest Hindu organizations in the city, the Arya Samaj. In the early days of Indian migration to this colonial port city, this reform movement saw itself as the preserver of ancient Vedic culture that transcended later accretions of caste and priest craft. Just before the prizes were awarded, the current president of the Arya Samaj said that his heart was "crying with joy" to see these children know so much about Hinduism when in 1954, when he first arrived, no one knew anything about Hinduism. The nature of this knowledge, however, gradually became a serious question for me as I listened to the quiz program. Was this really a disjunctive event that returned the semantic dimension of the text to supremacy by catering to sentiments like those of the Arya Samaj and subtlety countered the deep materiality of the grand *ritual* finale?

The talented quizmaster—a young man, Anand, who came to Singapore in 2001 from Chennai to join a company that is based in Greensboro, North Carolina—put children, mostly ages seven to ten, though several different rounds of intense questioning. I came in at the "visual round" where an image flashed only for a minute on a screen and then Anand posed questions about the figure—very fun. The gender of the children seemed evenly split in both sessions. Once such learning was an exclusively male, often Brahman, task. I also recall the round where Anand asked the teams to pick a topic from a list of six—they could ask for an easy or a hard question. The easy question was worth ten points, the hard twenty, but they could loose points for getting it wrong. The scores went back and forth while the kids looked so proud when they knew the answer.

None of the questions, however, focused on the philosophical meaning of the Gita. Instead, they were similar to simple Bible-study questions: all asked for facts about which character did this or the different names of the characters or the meaning of Sanskrit terms. In a *Bhagavad Gita Quiz Book* published earlier as a study guide for these students, the book's forward explains that it, "should serve a very useful purpose to learn the text in a modern way. Even the elders would benefit greatly from knowing the various fine details of the Gita in a direct way." The "modern way" is obviously the textbook-and-answer style found in a typical secular classroom. The questions included in this sky blue book with Krishna on the cover include questions that directly relate to Krishna's moral teachings, but they are offered as data, for example:

> 189. All study, reflection, detachment and mediation practice at the intellectual level, whereby the mind experiences its own Infinitude are called _______.
> Ans: Jñāna Yoga (18.56) (37)

Certainly while memorizing the answer, a young student would in some sense encounter the philosophy embedded in the verse, however the purpose of the exercise is to master the text in all its fine details. The answer is in no way inflected by the voice of the youngster, but must be given in the exact words of the Gita, in Krishna's words. Here was another version of the Gita as *application,* a very direct form of *mastery* that does not aim for speculation or inner imagination or poetic reverie. During the quiz, and now reading the quiz book, I hear echoes of a phrase used by a yoga instructor during a weeklong course that I attended. When any person asked what a position meant or why we had to do a certain form of breathing, the instructor quickly silenced such questions, "Do not philosophize!"

This same emphasis on mastery became apparent a day later at the final rounds of the Gita Chanting Competitions held in the auditorium of a temple.[9] Here, about forty youngsters, seven or eight years old, competed in chanting the same verse from the Gita in the original Sanskrit. The same master of ceremonies, Anand, presided dressed in a white kurta (a long shirt reaching below the knees with the well-known Nehru collar). All of the little girls had on either a kurta or more ornate blouses and long skirts in a style that I remember from 1967 but do not see on the streets of Chennai now; the boys' dress varied. I saw some with the long kurtas in white or colors but I also saw fashionably faded jeans and even cargo pants. I moved to both sides of the auditorium. The children, who had completed their task, did not seem interested in listening to the others; they fidgeted and whispered. They went to the stage with folded hands but did not really seem to feel, at least in my opinion, that this was a sacred event. Their parents did the usual videotaping or photographing

9. January 27, 2008 in the Sri Muneeswaran Temple, No. 3 Commonwealth Drive, Singapore.

of their child while he or she performed. The children were all remarkably calm for a performance in such a large hall. The highlight was the little girl who kept reciting without even flinching as one of the rows of seats collapsed when a man fell to the floor; she just went on—very impressive.

I had a conversation with one of the fathers who told me that the kids did not know what the verses meant but that they memorized them with the help of the coaches and parents. I later saw Sunil, the chief priest for the Gita Havan who was also in charge of this event. He told me that the children were judged on pronunciation, presentation, and the accuracy of memorization, in that order. I asked him why this was useful and he said that it inculcates a spirit of competition in the children and that even though they did not know the meaning of the verses now, later in life, the verses would come back to them and they would then find meaning and understanding. This "spirit of competition" could well be the motto for Singapore. In this case, the mastery of unfamiliar Sanskrit words, as well as the details of the Gita, could become a prelude to semantic sophistication, or perhaps not. But this kind of mastery of a book could perhaps reveal a material dimension somewhere between semantic and iconic. In the process of memorization, the book retains its factuality. Its solidity never dematerializes into thoughts or speculations.

I return now to that interview with Vivek. Embedded in Vivek's statement on the production of the Gita from Krishna's divine mouth was another key element more deeply rooted in a Hindu world and closely associated with the Gita Jayanti—the *birthday* of Bhagavad Gita. Vivek was saying that Krishna birthed the Gita out of his own body. The Gita Havan reunited his words with his body. Adding yet another case of the embodiment of the Bhagavad Gita within an image-body, Vivek showed me a photograph of Geeta Mata, "Mother Gita"—the Bhagavad Gita embodied as a goddess. He cautioned me that devotees refer to the Bhagavad Gita as the divine mother, not a father. I was not surprised, because the embodiment of sacred words into goddesses has roots in the ancient Vedic hymns which invoke the Goddess Vak, symbolizing speech in divine female form. None of the ritual texts that followed the early Vedic period mention divine images, but the poetic imagery of the Vedic hymns created vivid verbal portraits of the gods that can be compared to the "verbal icons" of God in the Biblical psalms (Dick 1984). In the Hindu world, however, there has never been a sharp line between substance and sound and in the contemporary Tamil world, mantras more literally become icons: the ancient Gayatri mantra, a much-used powerful invocation that was once the exclusive property of the upper castes has recently emerged as the Goddess Gayatri. Vivek did acknowledge that Geeta Mata has not become popular and is installed only in the Geeta Ashram in Faridabad in Haryana. Nonetheless, the notion of a close connection between divine words and divine bodies remains.

In the larger context of South Indian religious culture, however, the embodiment of words never excludes the embodiment of words even more solidly into a book. Throughout all the ritual transformations in the Gita Jayanti, even in the quiz and the chanting, the Bhagavad Gita, for these urban Hindus, remained a *book*. Unlike the Maharashtra Brahman women that Laurie Patten describes, Tamil Hindus do not now nor ever have historically revered orality to the diminution of the book. The area of the current state of Tamilnadu supported a book culture—or better, a palm-leaf culture—well before European mercantile incursions. Indira Peterson relates the story told in a fourteenth-century text of the "canonization" of the great Tamil language, an anthology of passionate hymns to Shiva. Shiva's son, Ganesha, leads a poet, charged by the king to "reveal the hymns and lives of the saints to the world," to a secret sealed chamber of the great temple of Chidambaram where the manuscript of the Têvāram lay half-eaten by ants. She comments, "this story of the 'discovery' of the Tēvāram hymns in written form...suggests that prior to the eleventh century there may have been a break in the oral tradition though which the Têvāram hymns were transmitted" (Peterson 1989, 15–16). Whatever their exact historical genesis, a culture of the sacred "book" came early to Tamilnadu in combination with the centrality of temples, as this story also shows and the Gita Jayanti once again reveals.

The Gita Havan, the final event of the Gita Jayanti, an innovative modern ritual, transformed the chapters of the Bhagavad Gita as a book back into divine energy. Chanting the book, verse by verse, into the sacred fires turned words into sound and then into energy. These holy words, this sound, collected in the waters of the *kumbha*, poured over the bronze image of Krishna, re-enlivened and re-formed Krishna's icon body into a living divine presence. Krishna's verbal substance now returned to his body which was at the same time contained in all of those books in the hands of devotees at the Havan. This ultimately iconic quality of the Gita infused all aspects of the celebration, even the seemingly more semantic dimensions. When students held their copies of the Bhagavad Gita, the strong sense of mastery over the book materializes as facts or as chant but finally it was Krishna in their hands—for those who could read the final message in the Gita Havan. The Gita Jayanti did not revere an iconic book. In an act of transubstantiation, words of the *book* originating out of Krishna's once earthly body, offered into the fire through a ritual processes literally re-enlivened an icon, or in Hindu term a *murti*, a living bronze body of Krishna. In this sense the Bhagavad Gita, here treated as the Holy Book of contemporary Hinduism, is an iconic body of Krishna just as the bronze *murti* is also an iconic body—the ultimate iconicity.

## References

ACLU. 2007. "North Carolina Appeals Court Allows ACLU Lawsuit Over Court Swearing-in Practice to Go Forward." American Civil Liberties Union, January 16, 2007, at http://www.aclu.org/religion-belief/north-carolina-appeals-court-allows-aclu-lawsuit-over-court-swearing-practice-go-for (accessed September 26, 2010).

"Arya Samaj." N.d. http://aryasamajsingapore.org/aboutus.html (accessed January 7, 2011).

Dick, Michael. "Prophetic Poiesis and the Verbal Icon." *Catholic Biblical Quarterly* 46: 226–247.

"Geeta Ashram." N.d. http://www.geetaashram.net/default.aspx (accessed January 7, 2011).

"Gita Jayanti Malaysia." N.d. Wikipedia article, http://en.wikipedia.org/wiki/Gita_Jayanti_Malaysia (accessed April 13, 2011).

"Krishna Our Guide." 2007. http://www.krishnaourguide.org/ (accessed September 27, 2010).

"Metroplus Pookkalam contest." 2010. Slideshow in *The Hindu*, August 20. http://www.thehindu.com/arts/art/article584191.ece?sms_ss=email&at_xt=4ca5e2064ad22780,0 (accessed October 1, 2010).

Peterson, Indira Viswanathan. 1989. *Poems to Śiva: The Hymns of the Tamil Saints.* Princeton: Princeton University Press.

Kumra, Vivek. 2010. "Questions on the Gita Jayanti 2008." Personal email message to Joanne Waghorne sent Monday, September 6.

# 16

# Possession and Repetition: Ways in which Korean Lay Buddhists Appropriate Scriptures

Yohan Yoo

*This paper demonstrates the need for the iconic status and function of Buddhist scripture to receive more attention by illuminating how lay Korean Buddhists try to appropriate the power of sutras. The oral and aural aspects of scripture, explained by Wilfred Cantwell Smith, provide only a limited understanding of the characteristics of scripture. It should be noted that, before modern times, most lay people, not only in Buddhist cultures but also in Christian and other traditions, neither had the chance to recite scriptures nor to listen to their recitations regularly. Several clear examples demonstrate contemporary Korean Buddhists' acceptance of the iconic status of sutras and their attempt to appropriate the power and status of those sacred texts. In contemporary Korea, lay Buddhists try to claim the power of scriptures in their daily lives by repeating and possessing them. Twenty-first century lay believers who cannot read or recite in a traditional style have found new methods of repetition, such as internet programs for copying sacred texts and for playing recordings of their recitations. In addition, many Korean Buddhists consider the act of having sutras in one's possession to be an effective way of accessing the sacred status and power of these texts. Hence, various ways of possessing them have been developed in a wide range of products, from fancy gilded sutras to sneakers embroidered with mantras.*

## The iconic status and power of sutras in Buddhism

Just like scriptures of many other religions, a Buddhist sutra is itself a sacred object rather than just a written book. Buddhist scriptures enjoy a status equivalent to that of the Buddha as his representation. This is a well-known fact among Koreans and people from other cultures where Buddhism constitutes an essential part. Korean high school students learn in national history class that in the eleventh century, the Koyro Dynasty (918–1392) commissioned the engraving of the *Tripitaka* on wooden blocks and printed it in order to obtain the Buddha's protection against the Mongolian invasion, rather than to study or teach the contents of the scripture. Moreover, Koreans who have interest in cultural heritage know about the tradition of putting Buddhist sutras into the stupas of Korean temples. A stupa, originally a burial place for relics of the Buddha, has been equated with his body and revered as an object of worship. Sutras can replace the relics in stupas because many Buddhists identify the Buddha with his teaching, dharma, and believe that the book of his teaching is no different from his body.

The iconic status and power of written texts that represent the Buddha himself have been acknowledged by Korean Buddhists for a long time. This is manifest in the "Ka-gu-kyeong-hang (or Kyeong-hang)" ritual, which can be translated into English as "the parade of the sutra." It began in 1046 and continued until the following dynasty, Choseon, started to repress Buddhism. According to *The History of the Koryo Dynasty*, the Koryo court performed this ritual in the second month of the lunar calendar for the purpose of driving away disasters and diseases from the capital city Kae-sung. The main part of this ritual was the parade of Buddhist monks, government ministers, high officials, and many citizens marching around the capital. It was headed by a splendidly decorated, huge palanquin in which a copy of *Benign King Prajna Sutra* was placed just as if it was the Buddha himself. Monks recited the sutra when they paraded through the city. It is recorded that in 1106, a long spell of dry weather came to an end when many citizens of the capital performed Kyeong-hang. The king was pleased and praised the power of this ritual (Choi 1996, 29; "Kagukyeonghang" 1983, 37). This example demonstrates that the people of Koryo considered the sutra to be the embodiment of the Buddha and that people recognized and attempted to appropriate its power.

Despite the widely acknowledged iconic status and magical power of sutras in the history of Buddhism, most scholars of Buddhism and historians of religion have neglected these important aspects of sutras. An examination of six textbooks that are used for introduction courses to Buddhism at American colleges and universities reveals that none explain the status, function, or power of Buddhist scriptures. All six books deal mainly with the contents of scriptures and their process of canonization (Gethin 1998, 35–58; Mitchell 2002, 64–94; Harvey 1990, 73–120; Robinson and Johnson 1997, 51–55; Williams 2000, 1–40; Strong 2002, 88–175). Korean scholars of religion have also largely overlooked the function, status, and power of Buddhist scripture.

It is true that some scholars have shown an interest in how the Buddhist scriptures were accepted and appropriated by early Indian Mahayana Buddhists. Instead of studying the doctrines, teachings, or philosophy contained in sutras, they have focused on the ritual context in which sutras came to acquire the status of the Buddha and a magical power (Schopen 1991, 1–22).[1] In *Beyond the Written Word*, William Graham says the "cult of the book that may once have

1. Schopen points out that Western scholars have mainly relied on literary material and disregarded a large body of archaeological and epigraphical material because they have been influenced by the Protestant assumption which values the contents of textual sources.

existed in India alongside or even in competition with the more familiar relic cult in early Mahayana tradition" (Graham 1987, 61). Though he cites some studies on Japanese and Tibetan Buddhism, he does not point out that the so-called "cult of the book" can be found in almost every Buddhist culture, including that of Korea. Richard Gombrich argues that the rise of Mahayana was due to the emergence of written tradition and that the early Mahayana texts were only able to survive because they were written down. The beginning of Mahayana, one of the most significant events in the history of Buddhism, was caused by a change in the way of maintaining sutras rather than by controversies over doctrines (Gombrich 1990). Further developing Gombrich's argument, Will Tuladhar-Douglas claims that "the ritual conundrum of written texts was constitutive of Mahayana Buddhism" and that Mahayana sutras were reproduced because each book was recognized as a deity (Tuladhar-Douglas 2009, 250). Contemporary examples should be added to the historical ones that Shopen, Gombrich and Tuladhar-Douglas call attention to. In addition, theoretical explanations need to be developed for Buddhists' appropriation of the iconic status and sacred power of sutras.

This paper examines the ways in which Korean Buddhists attempt to appropriate the power of sutras in order to demonstrate the importance of the iconic status and the function of scriptures for contemporary Buddhists. The abundant examples available from Korean Buddhism will also help us suggest a theoretical explanation for this phenomenon. First, I will point out that while Wilfred Cantwell Smith and his followers, including William Graham, have rightly recognized the importance of the function and status of scriptures, they limited their analysis of the topic, for the most part, to the oral and aural aspects of scriptures. It should be noted that most lay persons, before modern times, not only in Buddhist cultures but also in Christendom and other places, did not have many chances to recite scriptures or even to hear recitations regularly. The oral and aural repetitions of sacred books were privileges enjoyed only by religious elites, mainly priests and monks, although the common people devised their own methods of repetition by reciting abbreviated versions of sutras, such as *dharani* and *mantra.*[2]

Next, I will provide several examples of contemporary Korean Buddhists' appreciation of the iconic aspect of sutras and appropriation of their power and status. Contemporary Korean Buddhists have developed various ways of

2. Dharani, which is translated into Korean as *Neung-ji* or *Chong-ji*, indicates a passage that summarizes the basic principles of a long sutra. Dharani is believed to have been originally made in order to help people remember the teaching of a sutra. The recitation of dharani creates the same meritorious effect as reading the entire original version. Thus dharani passages cannot be understood separately from the text of scriptures. In a broad sense, dharani includes mantra, which is translated into Korean as "*Jin-eon.*" In general, shorter passages (or even words or syllables) are called mantra and longer ones dharani. More strictly speaking though, mantra means Sanskrit passages or words that are phonetically read and used like a spell. Buddhists believe the recitation of mantra itself produces an effect even if the person reciting does not know the meaning of passage.

possessing scriptures in which neither reading nor reciting plays an essential role. On the basis of these examples, I will argue that repetition and possession have been two important ways in which people appropriate the sacred power of scriptures. Korean Buddhism in the twenty-first century provides lay persons who cannot read or recite sutras with new means for copying sacred texts and listening to recitations, often by means of the internet. It will also be shown that possessing sutras is considered an effective way of taking their power and sacred status for oneself.

## The theoretical problem of scriptures for those who cannot read or recite

In 1971, Wilfred Cantwell Smith pointed out that scholars of the Bible in liberal-arts departments of religion should consider the Bible as scripture and scripture as a generic phenomenon. Smith argued that they should treat scripture "as a religious form" and "a living force in the life of the Church." According to Smith, scholars should study the cultural significance of scripture and the roles that it plays in the life of religious people. We should also find out what gives scripture sacred status and what people do with the Bible now (Smith 1971). Smith is right. Adherents of religions do not limit their use of scripture to interpreting its contents alone. They accept their scripture as a sacred being or a representation of it, and attempt to utilize its power. As Smith has stated, it is the task of a scholar of comparative religion to suggest general explanations for the significance, status, roles, and functions of scripture in the life of religious people. The question that I address in this paper is a more specific version of Smith's question: What do Korean Buddhists who cannot read their scripture do in order to experience its power? I will describe various ways of appropriating sutras which have been developed for, or even by, Korean lay Buddhists who are not able to read the written text.

In another work, Smith criticized Western scholarship for neglecting the various forms, concepts, and roles of scripture. He also asserted that scripture should not only be understood as "a written sacred book" but should also be examined in the context of "oral/aural tradition" (Smith 1989, 30, 35–36). However, the focus of Smith and other scholars who agree with his assertion on oral/aural tradition cannot provide explanations for all the different roles that scriptures play in the religious life of believers and all the meanings accorded to these sacred texts.

In *Rethinking Scripture: Essays from a Comparative Perspective*, a group of scholars who had been influenced by Smith carried out an in-depth study on the significance and role of scripture as their mentor had suggested (Levering 1989). The contributors tried to apply Smith's comparative perspective to their research field. Graham, in a chapter of this book and his book *Beyond Written Words*, asserts that we must pay attention to scripture's function as text "in the oral and aural round of daily life" (Graham 1987, 156; Graham 1989). He also says, "The most important result of attention to the oral dimension of scripture is to make more vivid the intensely personal engagement of a community with its sacred text" (Graham 1987, 162). But the oral and aural dimensions of scripture cannot give a satisfactory answer to his own question: "How do we discern the ways in which scripture has penetrated into those sectors or religious life that lie outside the more or less elitist domains of the literati or intellectuals?" (Graham 1987, 163). It is obvious that the oral/aural aspect of scripture should necessarily be considered in order to understand forms and roles of religious scripture. However, as I mentioned above, in many traditional religious communities, members who could recite scripture or read it out loud were few in number. The number of people who could listen to the recitation of scripture regularly was also quite limited. The situation for some contemporary communities has not changed much. Therefore, if we pay attention only to the oral/aural aspects of scripture, we still miss many of the ways that lay believers view and use scripture.

I do not intend to diminish the importance of Graham's contribution to the study of religious text. Graham properly attempts to explain religious scriptures in relationship to "men and women of faith." He indicates that no text can be called "scripture" in and of itself and that a religious text acquires its ultimate and transcendent status, namely "scripturality," through interactions with religious people (Graham 1987, 5–6). I also think that his focus on the function of the oral dimension of the written scriptural text is important. By emphasizing this dimension, he successfully overcomes academia's conventional inclination towards studying the literary content of religious texts. He expects "the strong orality of scriptures" to reveal "the functional meaning of scriptural texts in religious life" and argues that this functional meaning is tied to "folk appropriation of such texts for divination, healing or the like" as well as to the literal and intellectual content (Graham 1987, 111). While explaining the process through which a text is accorded magical power, he demonstrates how people often believe written and spoken texts to have a magical quality that can be used "for purposes of divination or augury, sealing of oaths and contracts, or talismanic protection from evil or harm" (Graham 1987, 61, 58–62). Graham knows well that there is widespread reverence for physical copies of scripture among many religious communities, including Buddhist ones such as the Japanese Nichiren Sect (Graham 1987, 62–65).

Therefore, we need to examine more than the oral/aural dimension in order to understand the "folk appropriation of texts" that Graham emphasizes. Many religious communities in history had a very limited number of elites who could utilize the magical power of scriptures by reading and reciting them. Therefore, Graham's explanation ultimately sheds light only on the religious elites' way of using scriptures rather than "folk appropriation." Though it is true that adherents of religion often recite or read scriptures for magical purposes, we should not miss other various ways in which lay believers have been trying to use the power of scriptures.

In her article, "Scripture and Its Reception: A Buddhist Case" in *Rethinking Scripture*, Miriam Levering, another intellectual descendant of Cantwell Smith, shows how religious texts are appropriated in a contemporary Buddhist convent in Taiwan. From a comparative perspective, she suggests "four fundamental modes of reception" of scriptures that are found "wherever words and texts are scriptural": the first is the informative mode, which allows texts to shape one's understanding of the world; the second is the transactive mode, which enables people to experience the power of the ultimate by reading and reciting scripture; the third is the transformative mode, which uses the power of scripture in ritual to induce an encounter with a transcendental being or a transformation of oneself; the fourth is the symbolic mode, which accepts scripture itself as a symbol of the ultimate (Levering 1989, 60, 72–90). The third and fourth modes especially help Levering account for the status and power of scripture. As part of the explanation for the third mode, she demonstrates that sacred words including scriptures are believed to provide power and protection, create merits, bring benefits to people, and so on. She describes the sacred status of scripture as an object of worship when she expounds the fourth mode. Levering suggests concrete examples of how the power of scriptures is ritually assumed for Buddhist soteriology. For instance, in the convent that she observes, Buddhist nuns recite and copy sutras because they believe these actions can "eliminate past negative accumulations" (Levering 1989, 73).

Although Levering seeks to show "what essentially characterizes scripture by examining all of the ways in which individuals and communities receive these words and texts" (Levering 1989, 59), she ends up mainly emphasizing elite reception of sutras because she investigates a Taiwanese convent community. To observe Buddhists' appropriation of their scriptures in a wider context, we should pay attention to what lay persons outside the temple and convent think of and do with the texts.

In pre-modern Korea, only a few elite monks could read and copy Buddhist sutras. It was very difficult for common people to understand the early sutras, not only because they contained very specialized terms but also because they had been translated into classical Chinese from Pali and Sanskrit. Later sutras that originated in China were too difficult to be read by lay persons, most of whom were peasants. The opportunity to be educated in classical Chinese was rare, and these texts were full of philosophical, ethical, and cosmological discourses. After the invention and dissemination of easier Korean alphabets in the fifteenth century, certain people acquired translated versions of some sutras.[3] But still in ritual contexts, recitation and reading were performed only by Buddhist monks and only in the language that had first been introduced to Korea.

3. While Japanese Buddhists began to translate sutras written and recited in Chinese into Japanese since the early twentieth century, Koreans started their translation of some important texts into colloquial Korean in the fifteenth century.

The studies developed by Graham and Levering center upon literate religious elites. Therefore, they are not entirely successful in offering a balanced and extensive explanation of the status and roles of scriptures as Smith had suggested. Recent works by D. Max Moerman and Jacob Kinnard cover what Graham and Levering missed. In demonstrating Buddhist sutra burial rituals in early medieval Japan that were practiced in order to "forestall the decline of the Buddhist teachings and preserve the Dharma for a future age," Moerman points out that in this context "the texts were never to be recited, studied or taught." He rightly asserts "the power of sacred texts lies not only in their words and ideas but in their materiality and instrumentality as well" (Moerman 2010, 71, 87). Kinnard offers examples from medieval Indian Buddhism. He shows that a Mahayana Buddhist text "is not necessarily a book that needs to be read but can also simply be looked at and worshipped" (Kinnard 2002, 95, and in this volume). These two scholars successfully show that Buddhists do not necessarily have to read or recite their sutras in order to appropriate the sacred status and power of their sutras.

Examples from Korean Buddhism will make this point clearer. It is a matter of course that many Korean monks and nuns recite and copy sutras to appropriate their sacred power and status.[4] But other various ways of appropriating the power and status of sacred sutras, which do not involve reading, reciting, learning, or studying them, have been developed for Korean lay Buddhists.

## Obtaining the power and status of sutras through repetition and possession

Tuladhar-Douglas (2009) shows how Buddhists appropriate the power and sacred status of sutras by repeating and reproducing them. He further develops Gombrich's argument to demonstrate Mahayana Buddhists' extension of the ritual functions of sutras by reciting, copying, and printing sutras, and by spinning cylindrical devices into which a copy of a sutra is placed. These actions have nothing to do with the contents of the texts. Tuladhar-Douglas says that it was after the introduction of writing to Buddhism that the worship of the relics of the Buddha's physical body and of the body of his teachings in written form came to be regarded as the same thing. According to him, written texts themselves came to be recognized as the "materialized" dharma of the Buddha, exceeding the powers of any non-Buddhist deity, and they began to be ritually worshipped just like the body of the Buddha. In the case of the *Prajnaparamita* (Perfection of Wisdom) sutra, the text itself is the source of the ritual because it includes instructions on how the book should be ritually used. Most of all, this sutra asks people to recite and write out its contents so as to bring about rapid multiplication of the manuscript.

4. Korean monks and nuns use reciting and copying sutras to stimulate experiences of the supernatural. This is similar to the Taiwanese convent case observed by Levering in which nuns read and recite sutras not only to achieve a peaceful mind but also to make their bodies "wonderfully warm" (Levering 1989, 84).

Tuladhar-Douglas describes an example of ritual recitation of "the last remaining Sanskrit Buddhist Community" in the Kathmandu Valley. After a selected sutra is worshipped, it is torn into as many pieces as the number of priests present, and each person recites the part that is given to him. In this ritual, it is impossible for a listener to understand the content of the text because many different parts are read simultaneously, creating a tumultuous din. He argues that intelligibility and meaning should be distinguished from each other and that the meaning of repeated recitations of incomprehensible mantras and *dharanis* should be found in the act of reciting itself.

Tuladha-Douglas provides useful examples for understanding the appropriation of scripture by way of repetition. Since about 1,000 years ago, Tibetan Buddhists have been using prayer wheels, called *mani chos-khor* (Tuladhar-Douglas 2009, 265). There are similar devices, such as a rotating sutra case or library, that have been made in China, Korea, and Japan.[5] Tibetans put up prayer flags, *darchor* and *lungta*, in high places in order to have the wind blow the power of the text and send meritorious effects far away. Tuladhar-Douglas also mentions the Chinese and Japanese tradition of printing *dharani* or sutras in great numbers for the purpose of ritual repetition rather than education or wider readership. There is "an instance of Tibetan monks carefully pressing woodblocks into the running surface of a stream" in order to maximize the repetitive effect. He even introduces recently developed methods of ritual repetition for purifying negative karma and increasing good karma, such as installing computer recitation programs, posting animated prayer wheels on the web, and downloading mantras to a hard disk or CD-ROM to have it spin at a very high speed.

Tuladhar-Douglas's work is very valuable in that it not only traces historical contexts of the ritual repetition of sutras in Mahayana Buddhism, but it also offers examples, including recent ones. But I would like to point out one problem that his research does not solve. Although he says, at the beginning of his article, that Buddhist sutras have been worshipped just like the Buddha relics, he does not consider the power that the simple existence of sacred texts can exert. His work focuses on the ritual repetition that is only one way of ritually

5. To quote Tuladhar-Douglas's description (2009, 266), "These rotating libraries are always large. Guo, translating a Sung Dynasty handbook of 1103, gives the standard height as 6.4 meters, but some were much larger.... It is octagonal in shape, and the library has handles on the outside allowing it to be rotated." Tuladhar-Douglas provides Chinese and Japanese names of this device, *lun ts'ung* and *rinzo*, but seems to be unaware of the Korean version of it. In Korea, it is called *yun-chang-dae*. Though he says that the Tibetan prayer wheels and the Chinese rotating sutra case are "almost certainly genetically related," he does not indicate which was made first. He just says that Schopen locates the origin of rotating sutra cases in Indian, and Q. Guo gives a much earlier date for the first Chinese rotating sutra case. Considering that this device is mentioned by the poet Bai Ju Yi (白居易 in Chinese, 772–846), a Chinese writer of the Tang Dynasty, I think that the Chinese rotating sutra case precedes the Tibetan one. There is, however, no clear evidence when it began to be made in Korea. A construction record of a temple in Kyungbuk Province, which seems to date from 1840, reports the *yun-chang-dae* of that temple was made in the twelfth century.

appropriating the power of sutras.

Tuladhar-Douglas overemphasizes the ritual repetition of sutras and also suggests an incorrect example from Korean Buddhism. He says that a full set of *Tripitaka* blocks was completed in the early eleventh century for the purpose of ritual repetition, praying for the protection of the country against the Mongols. He argues that the court made the blocks because printing sutras was a successful way to perform ritual repetition. It is true that the Koryo Dynasty carved a *Tripitaka* of over 80,000 woodblocks in order to protect the country from the Mongols. However, in this case, printing was not the main reason for the production of the blocks. The power that Koreans intended to obtain was not expected to come from the ritual repetition of printing sutras. It was impossible to produce many copies of the full set of *Tripitaka* blocks due to its enormous quantity. The power was thought to come from its simple existence in Korea. The idea was to make the teachings of the Buddha into correct and inclusive woodblocks as perfectly as possible. The possession of the complete set of *Tripitaka* in Korea was believed to harness the power of the Buddha and to protect the country from the Mongolian invasion.

The act of possessing sutras is as important as their ritual repetition for understanding Buddhists' appropriation of the sacred status and power of a sutra. These two important practices of repetition and possession are clearly attested among contemporary Korean lay Buddhists.

## Korean lay Buddhists' appropriation of sutras by way of repetition

One of the easiest ways of appropriating the power of a sacred text is to recite its short versions, namely *dharani* or *mantra*. Just as Indian Buddhists who believe in the power of sacred words of Buddhas and Bodhisattvas recite *mantra* and *dharani* (Levering 1989, 64), Korean lay Buddhists often recite short versions of these sacred words. Also, as I mentioned above, Korean Buddhists have set up rotating sutra cases in temples. Spinning the sutra case is believed to create as much merit as reading all the sutras in the case. Rotating this device, as Tuladhar-Douglas says, is one of the easy ways for lay Buddhists to repeat sutras. As a matter of fact, monks also use similar means of repetition. They spin prayer wheels, recite mantras, and rotate sutra cases. For both lay Buddhists and monks, these rituals are easy and efficient. However, lay Buddhists who are unable to read or recite texts rely on these easy ways more heavily than monks do.

Nonetheless, these simple ways of creating positive merit and eliminating past negative accumulations by reciting short phrases or rotating sutra cases were apparently not enough to satisfy lay Buddhists. Some temples came up with a structure called "*Hae-in-do*" for illiterate lay Buddhists. *Hae-in-do* is a labyrinth-shaped pathway on which a summary of *Hua-yen Ching* (*Flower Ornament Sutra*) is written. It is said to have been invented by the founder of Korean *Hua-yen* (*Hwa-om* in Korean) school, *Uisang* (625–702). He designed a labyrinth-shaped pathway filled with words of the abbreviated version of *Hua-yen Ching* with the help of his mentor, Chih-yen (602–688, the second patriarch of the Chinese *Hua-yen* school). We can see the purpose of *Hae-in-do* from the notice board in the courtyard of *Hae-in-sa*, which is one of the "Three Jewel Temples" of Korea.

> ...Walking through the course of *Hae-in-do* is a journey of eliminating negative karma effects and awakening to the truth. If you write your wishes down on a piece of wish-paper and walk through *Hae-in-do*, they will be fulfilled. Furthermore, if you write down penitent confessions then walk through, there will be great merit for your afterlife. When a person who has walked through *Hae-in-do* many times while alive stands before the mirror of karma after death, *Hae-in-do* will be reflected on the mirror. Then sinful karma of the person will go through the labyrinth of *Hae-in-do*. During the process, each sinful act will vanish away while passing through letters of the summary of the *Flower Ornament Sutra*. The finishing spot after walking around the whole *Hae-indo* is the same point as you started. This is a place of the Perfection of Wisdom (*prajnaparamita*) where you will become free from evil passions. You will be born anew with sinful karmas removed through the mercy of all Buddhas and Bodhisattvas.

According to this board, walking through the course of *Hae-in-do* results in awakening to the truth, fulfillment of wishes, elimination of sinful karma, and being born anew. Considering that the letters of the abbreviated version of the sutra eliminate sinful acts, it is manifest that the purpose of this ritual walking is to appropriate the power of the sutra. The board also articulates the effect of repeating the sutra with the mention of the salvific power that can be created by walking through the pathway "many times."

Unlike the portable prayer wheels of Tibet, we cannot say that rotating sutra cases and *Hae-in-do* are closely connected to the daily lives of lay Buddhists, because they are available only at temples. But as Mircea Eliade argued more than sixty years ago, religious people's experiences of the sacred do not necessarily happen within temples or convents. "The dialectic of hierophany" is supposed to penetrate into the daily lives of religious persons (Eliade 1949, 446). As "*homo religious*" tends to put the sacred into his profane reality, sacred scriptures, or their abbreviated words that are revered and recited in temples, are naturally brought into the everyday lives of lay believers. Therefore, those who recognize sutras as sacred objects but are not capable of reading or reciting them must develop ways to appropriate their sacred power and status in their everyday lives.

In Korea, there is a tradition in which devoted Buddhists invite a monk from a nearby temple and ask him to recite specific sutras for important family events, such as rites of passage, moving, or house construction. Such recitations have been available only to wealthy lay Buddhists. But contemporary Korean lay Buddhists are enjoying a kind of democratization of recitation, thanks to the development of electronic devices and the internet. They can purchase a CD that contains recitations of sutras and play it whenever they feel a need for it. In fact, some Buddhists play CDs or tape recordings of sutras for purification of a new house or land. Recently, many internet websites have become popular among lay Buddhists who try to use free sutra recitations. They visit websites that are run not only by temples,[6] but also by private individuals. There are some sites that mainly supply Buddhist music and recitation of sutras.[7] Some other sites provide all kinds of information and contents related to Buddhism including educational materials, a Buddhist dictionary, an art gallery, cartoons, and children's stories, as well as recordings of sutras.[8]

One internet Buddhist community (internet café) has more than 16,000 members. The average number of daily visitors at this website is over 2,000 and about 500 new writings are posted every day.[9] Many Buddhists try to create positive merit by copying texts or mantras online. While one website offers its members the chance to write calligraphic letters of a passage from a sutra with a computer mouse,[10] most of the other internet sites let people type parts of sutras and post them on a board titled "copying sutras board."[11] Of course, people write or type passages of sutras that are translated or transliterated into Korean. Alhough there have been controversies among Korean Buddhists over the efficacy of these internet means, more and more lay Buddhists are accepting them as convenient tools for appropriating the power of sutras. In sum, the internet has made lay Buddhists' attempts to use the power of sutras by way of repetition much easier than before. The development of technology is extending "the dialectic of hierophany."

### Korean lay Buddhists' appropriation of sutras by way of possession

Levering mentions the important role that lay Buddhists play in the Indian Buddhist publishing industry. While chanting sutras remains the most common method of cultivating and transferring merits for monks and nuns, the Buddhist publishing industry is "largely supported by lay donors planting merit by sponsoring the copying and publication of sutras" (Levering 1989, 74). In Korea as well, financially underwriting the publication of sutras has been a very important way of assuming the power of sutras and creating positive merits for oneself. Many contemporary Korean Buddhists purchase complete collections

6. For example, Song-gwang-sa, one of the "*Three Jewel Temples*" of Korea runs www.songgwangsa.org and another "*Jewel Temple*," Tong-do-sa, runs www.tongdosa.or.kr. (accessed 24 July 2009).

7. For example, see www.sambori.com (accessed 10 August 2010).

8. For example, see www.buddhapia.com (accessed 10 August 2010).

9. I referred to http://cafe.daum.net/yumhwasil (accessed 10 August 2010).

10. I referred to www.sagyeong.net. The last time I accessed this site was November 2009, but this site was closed when I tried to access it in August 2010.

11. See http://cafe.daum.net/yumhwasil, http://cafe.daum.net/bohhyun, http://cafe.daum.net/BNet33, http://cafe.daum.net/gPdh (accessed 5 January 2010).

of sutras just for the sake of possessing them, not for reading or studying them. When Tan-huh (1913–1983), a revered Korean Buddhist priest of high virtue and a buddhologist, translated and published collections of sutras in the 1960s and 70s, even many illiterate Buddhists bought them for the purpose of having them. The act of possessing sutras has little to do with the actual reading and learning of their contents. Putting a nice collection of sutras on a bookshelf of one's house is believed to have the same meaning and effect as enshrining a Buddha statue in one's house. To borrow the words of Eliade again, Korean lay Buddhists' appropriation of sutras by way of possession is a good example of *homo religiosus'* attempt to realize the sacred in the profane world.

Buddhists often present a copy of sutras, especially the *Flower Ornament Sutra*, *Lotus Sutra*, *Diamond Sutra*, and *Heart Sutra*, to their cherished friends and family members. This custom is called *Bup-bo-si* (*dharma dana*), which means "giving alms of the sacred teaching." The givers think that they can plant merit by distributing the sacred words of the Buddha, and that it is an excellent gift because the receiver can have the blessing and power of the Buddha by possessing the sacred text.

Splendidly decorated or gilded bronze sutras, as well as traditional book type sutras, are popular among lay Buddhists. The "Golden Heart Sutra" is one of the best-selling products advertised in papers and on the internet. The internet advertisement does not directly state that good effects will be brought about by simply having the product in one's possession. Rather, it mentions the peace of mind that results from reading it. But it is clear that this gilded sutra is not made for reading at home. Very few lay Buddhists would be able to read it, because the content is not translated into Korean. The marketers try to avoid violating legal restrictions against misleading and exaggerated advertisements, but they still allude to the positive effects of possessing this product. For instance, by referring to it as "a household god that each Buddhist family should enshrine at home," the marketers assert that the gilded sutra has sacred power and status. The advertisement recommends this product, which is "infused with the high virtue of the Buddha" especially to persons "moving to a new house, beginning a new business, praying for success in business, supporting a child, preparing for an important examination, experiencing insomnia caused by wavelength from an underground water vein, suffering from misfortunes and disasters at home, or going through distress because of money problems."[12]

In addition to sutras in book form, other goods containing printed or engraved words from sutras also attract Korean lay Buddhists. Buddhist shops serve customers with almost every kind of thing for daily use, such as stationary, tableware, tea cup sets, towels, and more. In newspaper and online advertisements, I could find steadily selling products such as wristwatches with a passage from *Heart Sutra* engraved on them. Goods on which "Great Dharani" is

12. http://dabosa.co.kr/shop/shopdetail.html?brandcode=001001000001&search=&sort=brandname (accessed 10 August 2010).

printed are also very popular.[13] The text is printed on towels, tea-table cloths, wall clocks, mobile phone ornaments, purses, wallets, and many other goods. The catch phrase for advertising a "Dharani Purse" or a "Dharani Wallet" is "Miraculous Experience of Obtaining Your Fortune and Having All of Your Wishes Fulfilled." It attracts lay Buddhists by saying that "the possession of this purse (or wallet) helps the owner fulfill any wishes, avoid disasters" and "makes money flow in from all directions."[14] The possession of these products with printed words of sutras is believed to exert the power that the Buddha can offer.

In 2007, the product "*Seong-bul-wha*," which means "becoming Buddha sneakers," was released on the market. These shoes are embroidered with a mantra, "Om-Mani-Padme-Hum." Its newspaper advertisement emphasizes that the mantra on the shoes always leads people in auspicious ways and helps them avoid misfortunes.[15] It also says that by wearing these shoes "people can achieve peace of mind, have sound judgment, plant positive merit, and terminate three disasters [flood/fire/wind or war/pestilence/famine]." The owner does not have to recite the mantra. He or she has only to wear the shoes to experience the miraculous power of the sacred phrase.

The commercial motives of marketers who exploit the faith of Buddhists are obviously involved in the advertisements I cited above. On the other hand, the success of these advertisements in marketing such products proves that many Korean lay Buddhists try to appropriate the power of sutras or certain parts of their sacred words by possessing them. Korean lay Buddhists have developed various ways of possessing sutras in order to assume the sacred status and power of sutras.

## Conclusion

The power, status, and roles of religious scripture have not received due attention, in spite of their importance. Wilfred Cantwell Smith and his followers regard scripture as a type of sacred words and emphasize its oral and aural dimensions in order to overcome the tendency of Western scholarship to focus on the contents of written texts. They have successfully brought into relief the importance of orality that had previously been neglected. But if we focus only on the oral/aural dimensions, it is difficult to explain how lay persons, who lack the ability to read or recite sutras, appropriate religious texts. To uncover this unexplained aspect of scripture, we have to investigate various ways in which lay persons make use of scripture in their daily lives.

In this paper, by examining examples from Korean Buddhism, I suggested

13. "Great Dharani" is a part of *Thousand Hands Sutra* which originated in China.

14. From March 2008, advertisements have been on the internet and newspapers including Don-A Daily and *Kum-kang-sin-mun* (Diamond Newspaper). Both were published in Korean.

15. The first advertisement was on *Bul-gyo-sin-mun* (Buddhism Newspaper), 24 October 2007, which was published in Korean.

two important ways in which lay Buddhists appropriate the power and status of sutras: repetition and possession. As is well known, Buddhists have developed facile ways of efficiently repeating sutras and maximizing meritorious virtues. Such ways include reciting *dharani* and *mantra*, which are abbreviated versions of sutras, and spinning prayer wheels. Additionally, contemporary Korean lay Buddhists have come up with new means of repeatedly hearing recited sutras and copying passages of these texts on the internet. "*Bup-bo-si*," a tradition of giving sutras for the purpose of possession is also still practiced. Some lay Buddhists purchase fancy gilded sutras in order to do well on a college entrance examination or to increase their wealth with the help of the transcendent power of these sacred texts. Some wear shoes that are embroidered with words of a mantra to gain peace of mind and to avoid misfortunes. Korea, a country that boasts the most advanced internet technology in the world and where people advertise a purse printed with sacred words that allegedly draws money from all directions, provides excellent examples of ways for appropriating sutras.

## Acknowledgements

This paper is based on a paper that I published in the Korean language in *Religion and Culture* vol. 17, 2009, 113–131 (Seoul: Center for Religious Studies at SNU). This paper has benefited from the comments by Woncheol Yun, for which I am grateful.

## References

Choi, Keunyoung. 1996. "Kagukyeonghang." In *Pascal Dongsuh's Korea-World Encyclopedia* vol. 1, 29. Seoul: Dongsuhmunhwa publishing.

Eliade, Mircea. 1949. *Patterns in Comparative Religion*. Translated by Rosemary Sheed. New York: Sheed & Ward (reprinted 1958).

Gethin, Rupert. 1998. *The Foundations of Buddhism*. New York: Oxford University Press.

Gombrich, Richard. 1990. "How the Mahayana Began." In *The Buddhist Forum, Vol. 1: Seminar Papers 1987-1988*, edited by Tadeusz Skorupski, 21–30. London: School of Oriental and African Studies, University of London.

Graham, William A. 1987. *Beyond the Written Word: Oral Aspects of Scripture in the History of Religion*. Cambridge: Cambridge University Press.

———. 1989. "Scripture as Spoken Word." In *Rethinking Scripture: Essays from a Comparative Perspective*, edited by Miriam Levering, 129–169. Albany: State University of New York Press.

Harvey, B. Peter. 1990. *An Introduction to Buddhism: Teachings, History, and Practices*. New York: Cambridge University Press.

"Kagukyeonghang." 1983. *Donga World Encyclopedia*, vol. 1, 37. Seoul: Donga.

Kinnard, Jacob N. 2002. "On Buddhist 'Bibliolaters": Representing and Worshiping the Book in Medieval Indian Buddhism." *The Eastern Buddhist* 34: 94–116.

Levering, Miriam. 1989. "Scripture and Its Reception: A Buddhist Case." In *Rethinking Scripture: Essays from a Comparative Perspective*, edited by Miriam Levering, 58–101. Albany: State University of New York Press.

Mitchell, Donald W. 2002. *Buddhism: Introducing the Buddhist Experience*. Oxford: Oxford University Press.

Moerman, D. Max. 2010. "The Death of the Dharma: Buddhist Sutra Burials in Early Medieval Japan." In *The Death of Sacred Texts: Ritual Disposal and Renovations of Texts in World Religions*, edited by Kristina Myrvold, 71–90. Farnham: Ashgate.

Robinson, Richard H. and Johnson, Willard L. 1997. *The Buddhist Religion: A Historical Introduction*. 4th ed. Belmont: Wadsworth Publishing Company.

Schopen, Gregory. 1975. "The Phrase '*prthivipradesas caityabhuto bhavet*' in the *Vajracchedika*: Notes on the Cult of the Book in Mahayana." *Indo-Iranian Journal* 17: 147–181. http://dx.doi.org/10.1163/000000075790079574

———. 1991. *Bones, Stones, and Buddhist Monks: Collected Papers on the Archaeology, Epigraphy, and Texts of Monastic Buddhism in India*. Honolulu: University of Hawaii Press (reprinted 1997).

Smith, Wilfred Cantwell. 1971. "The Study of Religion and the Study of the Bible." *Journal of the American Academy of Religion* 39: 131–140. Reprinted 1989 in *Rethinking Scripture: Essays from a Comparative Perspective*, ed. Miriam Levering, 18-28. Albany: State University of New York Press.

———. 1989. "Scripture as Form and Concept: Their Emergence for the Western World." In *Rethinking Scripture: Essays from a Comparative Perspective*, edited by Miriam Levering, 20–57. Albany: State University of New York Press.

Strong, John S. 2002. *The Experience of Buddhism: Sources and Interpretation*. Belmont: Wadsworth/Thomson Learning.

Tuladhar-Douglas, Will. 2009. "Writing and the Rise of Mahayana Buddhism." In *Die Texutalisierung der Religion*, edited by Joachim Schaper, 250–272. Tübingen: Mohr Siebeck.

Williams, Paul. 2000. *Buddhist Thought*. New York: Routledge.

# 17

# The Bible in British Folklore

Brian Malley

*This essay surveys magical and mantic uses of the Bible as attested in British folklore reports, with an eye to developing a model of the Biblicist tradition as that tradition was received by the British laity. The evidence shows that (1) in contrast to the church's emphasis on the Bible's meaning, the laity exploited the Bible's textual and artifactual properties as supernatural means to practical ends; (2) charmers made use of particular biblical (or taken-for-biblical) texts, whereas the Bible generally was used in exorcisms, which seem to have remained the purview of clergy; (3) lay traditions about the Bible seem to have been focused on specific issues, though a general uncertainty about what powers Bibles might have is also indicated.*[1]

> Old Mrs. Wesby of N. Walsham used to give pills composed of paper on which texts of scripture were written, and on being remonstrated with by the Vicar ... defended her practice by saying that it was in the Bible, and on being pressed to give the locality, quoted,—"'The word of God is good for all things, for doctrine and for instruction in righteousness,'—now you give it for instruction in righteousness, and I give it for doctoring." (M. R. Taylor 1929, 132)

Practices like Mrs. Wesby's raise a broad problem for anyone interested in the ways Christians have received, understood, and manipulated scripture. Of course, the primary thing people do with Bibles, and have always done with Bibles, is to interpret them. But people have also pressed Bibles into service in other ways, ways that elude easy categorization beyond vague notions of "ritual," "magic," or "superstition." These Bible practices indicate that many lay Christians regarded the Bible as a text not only *meaningful*, but *efficacious*. Such an understanding is quite alien to us, the compulsively literate, and so such practices tend to be neglected in studies of the Bible's reception.

In this essay I survey Bible uses from British folklore—to my knowledge, the first time that these materials have been gathered together. In preparing

1. This essay has benefited from comments by James Bielo, Judy Malley, and Marianne Schleicher. Remaining errors and omissions are, of course, my responsibility alone.

this essay, I relied heavily on the work of the English Folklore Society, which has published collections and studies of folklore since 1878. I consulted as many other collections of English, Scottish, Welsh, and Irish folklore as possible, in the hope of providing, if not a comprehensive survey, then at least a broad one. But the purpose of this survey is not merely the cataloguing of exotic Bible practices—as helpful as such might be—but also the development of a model of the Biblicist tradition as that tradition was received by the laity in the British Isles.

Some limitations of the present study should be noted. Although I have grouped different practices based on similarity in the way they used the Bible, it is important to recognize that these traditions were not passed on as a single, coherent body of lore. There is no reason to think that any one person knew all of these charms and procedures: they had overlapping distributions, and some were much more widespread than others.

It is also important to recognize that these traditions were thoroughly intermingled with traditions that did not involve Bibles or biblical texts. In collecting this material, I tried to include all folklore that involved either the manipulation of Bibles as physical objects or invocation of what people understood to be biblical texts. Some apocryphal texts were thought to be from the Bible, and I have included these, because the purpose of this study is to explore the Bible's social and psychological reception. In a few places, I have, unhappily, had to guess whether people thought a given charm was from the Bible. I have included charms involving the actions of biblical figures—especially Christ—and charms very similar to charms that were clearly thought to be biblical. I have not included folklore that merely refers to people or places from the Bible, such as explanatory stories, magical formulae that invoke the evangelists' names, or the use of *Judas* as a verb, because these show only that biblical stories were part of British folk knowledge. Some such distinction between biblical and extra-biblical lore was necessary for the present study, but such a division bisects the folklore corpus unnaturally: I am nearly certain that British folk did not distinguish between biblical lore and ecclesiastic lore more generally, and even the boundary between ecclesiastical and general lore seems to have been more transgressed than observed. But I think I have cast the empirical net in a way that makes sense for the present study.

Other limitations had to do with the nature of the material collected. Most of the reports I found were not first-hand observations, but descriptions related second-hand, or based on earlier printed reports, the evidential basis for which is uncertain. The reports are fragmentary by ethnographic standards, and there is much more we would wish to know in all cases. Despite these serious limitations, I believe the basic facts are reasonably secure, and sufficient to ground my analysis.

## Magical acts

Given the length of time Christianity had been in Britain and the emphasis on the Bible in important strands of British Christianity, it is perhaps unsurprising that there are documented a number of "magical" uses of Bibles. The following practices are all magical acts, in the sense that they employ Bibles to achieve some effect, and practitioners regard the effect as an unmediated result of the procedures.[2]

### *Simple artifactual uses*

Probably the most widely known of the Bible's simple artifactual uses was in the trial of witches. King James instituted an evidentiary standard wherein an accused witch would be weighed against a church Bible or a family Bible.[3] If the woman weighed more than the Bible—a virtual certainty, as James intended—she was freed. Most uses, however, were not nearly so institutionalized.

Bibles were used as simple artifacts in a variety of protective practices. Possession of a Bible on one's person was said to offer protection from fairies, ghosts, and the devil.[4] When it was impractical, owing to age, childbearing, or death, to have a Bible on one's person, Bibles were touched or put in close proximity: a Bible was placed under the pillow of a woman in labor to protect her and her child from witches or fairies; a baby born on a Friday was set upon a Bible after having its head washed with rum; a Bible was opened next to an infant when the mother stepped away; Bibles were placed on coffins to keep away evil until the body could be buried.[5] The same principle of "protection through possession" was extended also to homes: in Wales some of "the bettermost farms" kept a Bible in a locked chest to protect the house from evil, and in England Bibles were to be among the first items carried into a new home.[6]

Bibles were also used in laying to rest ghosts, as the following procedure describes:

> The *modus operandi* of laying a ghost was to wait till it was on the prowl, and then a parson...got on the grave with a Bible and a lighted candle, thereby cutting off its retreat... If the laying is to be done regardless of expense, there should be seven or even more parsons, all with Bibles and lighted candles, for

2. On the category *magical acts*, see Barrett and Malley 2007.

3. *Church Bible*: Aspin 1832, 20; Banks 1943; Gurdon 1893, 175; Lean, Wood-ward, and Williams 1902, 2:442. *Family Bible*: Simpkins and Rorie 1914, 106–107.

4. *Fairies*: Briggs 1957, 276; Gregor 1883, 56. *Ghosts*: Ozanne and Carey 1915, 200; Tongue and Briggs 1965, 55. *The devil*: Owen 1896, 150–51; Underwood 1911, 330–331.

5. *Witches*: E. M. Wright 1913, 231. *Fairies*: Kirk and Lang 1893, 29–30; Opie and Tatem, *s.v.* "Bible Protects" (www.oxfordreference.com/views/ENTRY. html?subview=Main&entry=t72.e93, accessed February 2007). *Babies set on Bible*: Carrick 1929, 278. *Open Bible next to child*: Napier 1879, 40. *Bible on coffin*: Banks 1927, 399; Craigie 1898, 374.

6. *Bible in locked chest*: Owen 1896, 246. *Bible carried into new home*: Burne 1897, 91; Harland 1873, 236; Peacock 1889, 315; Winstanley and Rose 1926, 174.

> there is great virtue in the light... In laying a ghost, the great thing is to corner it, keep your candles burning, and pray like fury.
>
> (Moss 1898, quoted in Simpson 1976, 91)

Specific incidents of ghost laying were reported from Herefordshire and Fife (Leather 1912, 30–31; Simpkins and Rorie 1914, 42).

The Lord's Prayer was also used as a protective artifact: writing out the Lord's Prayer on a piece of paper, dissolving the ink in water, and drinking it was supposed to cure the effects of the evil eye, and one man kept on him a charm of the Lord's Prayer written backward in order to stave off the ghost of his "cantankerous" wife (M. R. Taylor 1929, 126, 132). Another man attached the thumb of a glove, with the Lord's prayer written on a paper inside, to the neck of his horse. The reporter said it was to prevent stumbling and to counter the evil eye (E. S. Taylor 1852, 480).

> Other Bible passages too were used as curative and protective artifacts. Mrs. Wesby, with whom this essay began, used scripture pills to treat various ills in humans. Unspecified texts from Old Testament genealogies were hung in a bag from a child's neck to protect a child from an outbreak of scarlet fever (Hayward 1938, 228). Another passage could be used to curse: a woman forsaken by her lover was said to be able to curse him by writing out a copy of Psalm 59 and sending it to him (Gregor 1881, 87). An amulet containing a paper on which were written the first three verses of John's Gospel was said to protect the wearer against sickness, and another amulet, in which appears John 1:1–14 and the Lord's Prayer in Greek, is in Oxford's Bodleian library.[7]

In Shropshire, for cure of an animal's bad knee joint, a charmer wrote an unspecified verse from the Bible on a paper and gave it to a man to put into the animal's manger to be eaten (Hayward 1938, 230). The passage is not specified, but it is possible that it was similar to the following charm widely used for sprains:

> Our Lord Jesus Christ rode over a bridge. His horse lighted [? limped] and he lighted. He said "Marrow to marrow, and bone to bone, and sinews to sinews, and blood to blood, and skin to skin" (and to the others). In the name of the Father, and of the Son, and of the Holy Ghost, I cast this sprain away. Amen. So be it.[8]

The story here is of course apocryphal, but a number of charms involved stories attributed to the Bible. A very widely reported cure for ague involved the following charm:

> When Jesus saw the Cross whereon he was to be crucified he trembled and shook, and the Jews asked him "art thou afraid, or has thou the ague?" Jesus

7. Black 1883, 92; Ettlinger 1943, 242; Wilde 1902, 211. See also Lean, Woodward, and Williams 1902, 2:460–61, where this is said to be a Catholic practice.

8. "Sixteenth Report" 1899, 113; see also "Thirteenth Report" 1895, 65; Baring-Gould 1925, 144; Black 1833, 78–79; Carmichael, Watson, and Watson 1928, ii. 14, 19, 21; "Charms from Devonshire" 1851, 258–259; Dyer 1880, 149; "Orkney Charms" 1854, 221; Tongue and Briggs 1965, 37. For a variant in which St. Agnes cures her own broken ankle with this charm, see Wilde 1890, 11.

> answered and said, "I am not afraid, neither have the evil ague; whoever wears this about them shall not be afraid nor have that evil ague."
>
> (Simpson 1976, 105)[9]

This charm had many variants. Owen Davies notes that in one variant the words "or witchcraft" were added after the final *ague* to adapt the charm to a different use (O. Davies 1998, 42, discussing "Sixteenth Report" 1899, 112).

Another widely used apocryphal text was the following charm for toothache:

> As Peter sat weeping on a marvel stone, Christ came by and said to him, Peter, wat hailest thou—Peter answered and said unto him, My Lord and my God, my tooth eaketh. Jesus said unto him, Arise, Peter, be thou hole; and not the only but all them that carry these lines for my sake, shall never have the tooth ake.
>
> (Latham 1878, 40)[10]

Usually this text was to be memorized, worn as an amulet around one's neck, carried on a paper in one's pocket, or sewn into one's clothes, but Charlotte Latham reported that "the belief is that the possession of a Bible or Prayer Book with this legend written in it is a charm against toothache."[11] In some reports, this charm was said to be found in the Bible.[12] An apparently well-known "conjurer," Nicholas Johnson, used an unspecified "Bible text" (probably this charm) or Bible reading to cure toothaches (T. A. Davies 1998, 46). Another charm for toothache involved Jesus and his brother:

> Christ pass'd by his brother's door,
> Saw His brother lying on the floor.
> What aileth three, brother?
> Pain in the teeth?
> Thy teeth shall pain thee no more.
> In the name [of the Father, the Son, and the Holy Ghost]
>
> (Black 1833, 77; Hunt 1871, 414)

For our purposes, the following charm for toothache is of particular interest:

> In the name of God, when juses saw the Croos on wich he was to be crucified all is bones began to Shisver. Peter standing by said Jesus Christ cure all Deseces. Jesues Christ cure thy tooth ake. (Jackson and Burne 1883, 182)

9. See also "Charm for Ague" 1852; Courtney 1887, 202; O. Davies 1996, 2223; 1998, 42; Dyer 1880, 158; Henderson 1879, 169; *The Physicians of Myddvai; Meddygon Myddfai* 1861, 455–456; Rushton 1980, 116; "Sixteenth Report" 1899, 112; Wilde 1890, 11; A. R. Wright 1912, 235. It is probably this charm that Gurdon 1893, 15 reports was "taken, it was believed, from the Gospel of St. John."

10. See also "Seventeenth Report" 1900, 91–92; Opie and Tatem, *s.v.* "Toothache, Charm For" (www.oxfordreference.com/views/ENTRY.html? subview=Main&entry=t72.e1471 [accessed June 2007]); Black 1833, 77–78; Bruce 1850; "Charms from Devonshire" 1851, 258–259; O. Davies 1996, 22; T. A. Davies 1937, 54; Denham 1892, 9–10; Dyer 1880, 156; Northall 1892, 134–136; "Orkney Charms" 1854, 221; Townend 1948; and E. M. Wright 1913, 249. For an account of a toothache charm being applied, see Hunt 1871, 417–418.

11. *Memorized*: T. A. Davies 1937, 54. *Worn as amulet*: "Charm for the Tooth-Ache" 1851, 20; Harland 1873, 226. *Carried in pocket*: Simpson 1976, 104. *Sewn into Clothes*: Simpson 1976, 196; Wilde 1902, 196. *Inscribed in Bible*: Latham 1878, 40.

12. "Charm for the Tooth-Ache" 1851, 20; Barclay 1894, 338; Jackson and Burne 1883, 183; *The Physicians of Myddvai; Meddygon Myddfai* 1861, 453–454.

Owen Davies notes that the text of the charm has been generalized ("all Deseces"), and may have been adapted to specific cases merely by changing the condition identified at the end (1996, 22).

Finally, a printed copy of a putative letter from Christ to Agbarus, King of Edessa, was carefully kept by an old woman as an amulet for protection from witchcraft and the evil eye, and in South Berkshire the same text was used as a charm for protection against illness and for protection in childbirth.[13]

I have called the foregoing simple artifactual uses because in them the text-artifacts—Bibles or written passages—are touched, kept, worn, or consumed, but not read or expounded. That is, their semantic properties serve as the background for these uses, but are not part of the practices themselves: the scriptures were regarded as efficacious objects. In contrast, the next group of practices involved the reading or recitation of some biblical text.

### *Simple performative uses*

The act of Bible reading afforded protection from ghosts and was part of exorcisms, usually involving religious specialists, especially clergy. An extravagant procedure reported from the Kennet Valley involved thirteen ministers reading simultaneously from the Bible—six reading forward and seven backward.[14] Bible reading was also used to exorcise the Devil and to remove witches' spells.[15]

Recitation of the Lord's Prayer was also regarded as efficacious to protect against the Devil and to remove spells, "fairy stroke," or other fairy mischief.[16] The inability of an accused witch to recite the Lord's Prayer accurately was taken as evidence of guilt.[17] The Lord's Prayer was also used in many curative charms: for a thrown arm or shoulder, for burns, for whooping cough, for a hernia, for hiccups, for a toothache, for bleeding or a hemorrhage, "or anything."[18]

Other texts were also used in curing. Psalm 8 was to be read seven times for three mornings over the patient for cure of a sore throat or thrush (E. M.

13. Latham 1878, 24; Salmon 1902, 424. Black 1833, 87, notes that it was regarded as a "genuine epistle of Christ".

14. *Ghosts*: Craigie 1898, 374. *Exorcisms*: Owen 1896, 215. *Religious specialists*: Courtney 1887, 27; Evans 1892, 274–276; Simpson 1976, 92–93. *Procedure*: Salmon 1902, 429.

15. Jackson and Burne 1883, 146–47; Owen 1896, 245; Spooner 1961, 325.

16. *Devil*: Read 1911, 314. *Spells*: Dempster 1888, 169, 223; Burrows 1939, cited in Maple 1965, 214; Napier 1879, 135, 157, 159; Wilde 1890, 17–18. *Fairy-stroke*: Wilde 1902, 233. *Fairy mischief*: Westropp 1910, 195–196.

17. Gurdon 1893, 175; Kingsbury 1950, 136, 143–144; Lean, Woodward, and Williams 1902, 2:442; Newman 1946, 23; see Tongue and Briggs 1965, 66, for lore about how witches would change the prayer so as to be able to recite it.

18. *Thrown arm*: Eyre 1905, 168. *Burns*: Eyre 1905, 168; Latham 1878, 36. *Whooping cough*: Leather 1912, 82. *Hernia*: Hartland 1913, 506–507. *Hiccups*: Tongue and Briggs 1965, 40. Courtney 1887, 202 and Lean, Woodward, and Williams 1902, 1:499 have it that the Lord's Prayer must be recited backward. *Toothache*: Wilde 1890, 12. *Bleeding or hemorrhage*: Tongue and Briggs 1965, 36, 40. *Anything*: Eyre 1905, 168.

Wright 1913, 240; "Sixteenth Report" 1899, 111). Charms to treat the bite of an adder involved quotation of Ps 67:1–2 or Ps 68:1–2.[19] (Curiously, charmers do not seem to have made use of the biblical encounter between St. Paul and a serpent, or Jesus' promise that his followers could handle serpents safely.) The following text, derived from Ezek 16:6 and 9, was used to stop bleeding:

> And when I passed by thee (here give the name of the person in full) and saw thee polluted in thine own blood, I said unto thee, when thou wast in thy blood, "Live; yea, I said unto thee when thou wast in thy blood, Live." Then washed I thee with water; yea, I thoroughly washed away thy blood from thee, and I anointed thee with oil. In the name of the Father and of the Son, and of the Holy Ghost. Amen ! Amen ! Amen ! ("Thirteenth Report" 1895, 68)[20]

Sometimes this charm seems to have been memorized, other times it was the reference that was passed on:

> The verse to stop nose-bleeding is the 6th verse of the 16th chapter of Ezekiel which must be repeated by one of the opposite sex of the patient.
> ("Seventeenth Report" 1900, 92)

Either way, this cure for bleeding occurred in many variants.[21] John 17:15 was recited in the treatment of burns ("Charms" 1933, 126–127). The recitation of an unspecified verse was used to treat ringworm, and another unspecified text could be said over the burial of a stillborn calf to prevent further stillbirths in the herd (Vickery 1978, 157; Napier 1879, 84–85).

Again, extracanonical texts were sometimes taken to be canonical and regarded as efficacious. The following three charms were used to stop bleeding:

> Jesus came to the River Jordan and said, Stand and it stood, and so I bid thee blood stand in the name of the Father, the Son, and the Holy Ghost.
> (Hockin 1882, 175)[22]

> Christ was born in Bethlehem, Baptised in the river Jordan; There He digg'd a well, And turned the water against the hill, So shall thy blood stand still. In the name [of the Father, the Son, and the Holy Ghost]. (Black 1833, 76)[23]

> Three wise men came from the East, Christ, Peter, and Paul— Christ bleeding crucified, Mary on her knees at the foot of the cross. And Christ drew a cross over the three women that were crossing the waters. One said, Stop, One said, Stand, One said, "I will stop the blood of [here name the person.] In the name

19. *Psalm 67*: O. Davies 1996, 26; E. M. Wright 1913, 240. *Psalm 68*: "Second Report" 1877, 97; Hunt 1871, 420.

20. See also "Manx Folk-Lore and Superstitions" 1891, 294; T. Brown 1970, 42; E. M. Wright 1913, 240.

21. "Manx Folk-Lore" 1891, 294; Baring-Gould 1925, 144; T. Brown 1961, 395; 1970, 42; Rhys 1901, 297; E. M. Wright 1913, 240.

22. See also O. Davies 1996, 20–21; "Seventeenth Report" 1900, 91; Gurdon 1893, 16.

23. See also "Charms" 1857; "Charms from Devonshire" 1851, 258–259; Henderson 1879, 169; Hunt 1871, 410, 414.

> [of the Father, the Son, and the Holy Ghost]." (Henderson, 1879, 170)[24]

The first charm was described as "a verse of the Psalms" and was used by an old woman as part of a charm to stop nose bleeds. The first two of these charms were in widespread use; the third is reported only from northern England.

Several apocryphal stories about Jesus were used in the removal of thorns.

> Our Blessed savour Came Down from heaven, was pricked with a thorne, his Blood went up to heaven again, his flesh Neither Kankered, Eaukled, nor fustured, Neither shall thine [insert client's name], in the name of father, &c., &c. Amen. ("Thirteenth Report" 1895, 65–66)

> Christ was of a virgin born,
> And he was prick'd by a thorn,
> And it did never bell nor swell,
> And I trust in Jesus this never will (Hunt 1871, 413).[25]
> Christ was crown'd with thorns:
> The thorns did bleed, but did not rot,
> No more shall thy finger.
> In the name of the Father, Son, and Holy Ghost.
> (Hunt 1871, 413; see also "Charms" 1857)

The following variant deserves particular mention because, as Owen Davies notes, it appears to be derived from John 19:5:

> To Drawe a thorn.—Then came Jesus forth whering the crown of thorns and the purpel robe and pilat said write [? unto] them behold the man Amen Amen Amen—to be said 9 times and the Lordes praier before and hafter hold your midil finger on the place and go round it each time and marck it thus ✚.
> (Morgan 1895, 203)[26]

It is quite possibly one of the preceding charms that was in view when L. Salmon reported that a "witch" gifted in removing thorns would "whisper some words out of the Bible backward"—there were many variants of the same charm.

The following apocryphal text was to be repeated three times, for three mornings, while kneeling before a cross, as a cure for measles:

> "The child has the measles," said John the Baptist. "The time is short till he is well," said the Son of God. "When?" said John the Baptist "Sunday morning, before sunrise," said the Son of God. (Wilde 1902, 190)

A number of charms for inflammation also involved apocryphal stories. One invoked a tender moment between Mary and one of Jesus' young brothers:

> As our Blessed Vergen Mary was walking over along leading her youngest son by the hand he hang down his head. "Why dew you hang youre hed so low my

24. I have found no other reports of this charm.

25. See also "Folklore of South Northamptonshire" 1850, 37; Henderson 1879, 171.

26. See also O. Davies 1996, 27–28; Dyer 1880, 173; Salmon 1902, 426; "Seventeenth Report" 1900, 91; "Thirteenth Report" 1895, 65–66.

> son"? "My hed doth ake and all my bones." "I fear some ill things you have. I will bless you for ill things" (red ill, wite ill, black or blew or all other) down to the ground in the name of our Lord Jesus Christ. I bless you (you must mention the name of the person) in the name of our Lord Jesus Christ, Amen—of the Father, the Son, and Holy Ghost. Amen. ("Sixteenth Report" 1899, 112–113)

This charm was to be followed by a motion of "the hand the same way as the sun goes, and pass it towards the ground." A second charm also involved Mary, this time treating Jesus:

> The Virgin Mary set the Babe on her lap, and there an Inflammation caught and a blister rose. She blew on it, and the Child also; and the Blister left. So shall it leave...in the Name of the Father, and of the Son, and of the Holy Ghost. (To be repeated thrice.) (Baring-Gould 1925, 144)

A third charm involved an apocryphal meeting between Jesus and Abraham:

> Our Lord Jesus Christ came from the Mount's foot (&) saw Abraham asleep on the cold ground—Our Lord spoke and said "What liest thou here for"? Abraham spoke and said "It is good to know what I lie here for. (I am) taken, without blow, acheing, burning that I know not what to do." Our Lord Jesus Christ said "Rise up Abraham, rise up Abraham from the cold ground—I will make thee safe (&) sound. In the name of the Father of the Son, and of the Holy Ghost. Amen." ("Sixteenth Report" 1899, 113)[27]

Stranger still is the following apocryphal encounter between Jesus and a queen:

> Our Saviour Christ blessing for an inflammation or any other evil thing or any like evil. (bless.) The Queen of parest is gone into a far country to kill and destroy both men women and children, and then her meet our blessed Lord and Saviour Jesus Christ. He said "Where art thou going thou Queen of parest?" "I am going into a far country to kill and destroy both men women and children." "Thou Queen of parest turn again : thy evil shall never do no harm, in the name of the father and of the Son, and of the Holy Ghost. Amen."
> ("Sixteenth Report" 1899, 111)

A final charm for inflammation involved an apparent mixture of biblical and apocryphal stories:

> Our dear Lord Saviour Jesus Christ hee sawe Joseph lying on the cold ground thy side-lese year.
> Joseph—I are stricken sordbolt, sordbolt, sordbolt, stricken stabing, pricking, aching; I know not what to do.
> Our dear Saviour—Take up thy Bed and walk.
> Our dear Lord saw Jesus Christ and pailet sit at the gate of Jerusalem weeping. Faith I hope the Lord will Bless it to thee wherever it is. In the name of the Father, and of the Son, and of the Holy Ghost.
> ("Thirteenth Report" 1895, 65).

27. For another apocryphal encounter between Jesus and Abraham, see Bonser 1963, 279.

It would appear that this charm has undergone some corruption in its transmission, suggesting that whatever role the sense of the text might have originally played, it was being transmitted as a formula by the time it was reported.

A charm for snake-bite involved an apocryphal story about Jesus and Mary:

> Our Blessed Vergen Mary sot and soad
> her Blessed Babe sot and Plead
> Their Ting Worm out of Eldern wood
> did Ting our Blessed Saviour by the foot
> his Blader Blud and never broke
> Thine shall Break [insert client's name]
> Ting Ting or Rye Ting in the Name
> of the Father Son and Holy Gost
> Amen, Pray God expell the Ting.[28]

Reading and recitation are ambiguous activities, not only because they might be carried out with various intentions, but also because their object may be the text in itself or the text as an avenue to meaning. The foregoing I have classified as simple performative uses because the practices involve reading or recitation of the text as text. In some cases the reading is clearly reading aloud; other reports are ambiguous in this regard. Evidence that it is the text itself, not the meaning, that was regarded as efficacious comes from practices in which the text was inverted. Backward Bible reading could be used to summon a witch and repeating the Lord's Prayer backward was part of procedures for raising the Devil, apparently learned by children, and also in divination.[29] The meaning of a text is inverted by negating its sentences: backward reading is a means of inverting the text. The practices just discussed involved performance of the text, the assumption being that the text itself, as performed, was efficacious.

### Mixed uses

Although most Bible use involved just one mode, a few practices involved using the Bible both as text and as artifact. According to one method for the removal of spells, a

> key should be laid on two crossed sticks, one of witty (mountain ash), and one of yew, both held potent against witchcraft. These are placed on the verses in the Bible beginning "put on the whole armour" (Ephesians vi., 13, 14, 15). These

28. "Seventeenth Report" 1900, 92. In the "First Report" 1876, 55, this charm, in combination with the Lord's Prayer said "afore and arter," is said to cure a "worm in a bullock's tongue." However, I suspect the folklore collector misunderstood the purpose of this charm. Traditionally, the stinging organ of a snake (one kind of "worm") was thought to be the tongue (OED), and I suspect that this cure was for a bull bitten by a snake. This makes the most sense of the cure's title, apparently given by the folklorist's informant: "cure for a ting bullock."

29. *Witch*: March 1899, 488. *Devil*: Fenwick 1879; Parker 1913, 84; Salmon 1902, 427; Tongue and Briggs 1965, 69. *Learned by children*: Leather 1912, 40; P. Opie 1963. *Divination*: Wilde 1890, 118.

> verses are to be read aloud nine times, and at each repetition a little tear is made in a piece of white paper. To break the spell, the paper is to be folded up, and sewn into the clothing of the person thought to be bewitched, without his or her knowledge. (Leather 1912, 66)

This practice involved using the text as a physical object upon which the key and sticks were placed, and also as a text to be read aloud nine times. In Devon, the Bible was used in the cure for croup—"Place a Bible on the child's head and recite 'Out of the mouths of babes and sucklings...' etc." (T. Brown 1961, 395)—and from Wales comes report of a method how to call up a ghost, which involved reading Psalm 70 from a Bible consecrated by sprinkling it with the performer's own blood and reciting the following:

> I do by the power of the holy names Aglaon, Eloi, Eloi, Sabbathon, Anepturaton, Jah, Again, Jah, Jehovah, Immanuel, Archon, Archonton, Sadai, Jeovaschap, etc., of this holy work, in the name of the Father, Son, and Holy Ghost. Amen.
> (J. C. Davies 1908, 328–29; see also 1911, 253–254)

In these uses the compounding of Bible modes seems intended to compound effects. A similar strategy seems to have motivated the use of several Bibles in exorcisms, but I found no report wherein several distinct charms were coordinated to achieve a cure.

## Analysis

Several important points emerge from the magical uses of the Bible just described. These have to do with the Bible's efficacy, the distinction between general and specific Bible traditions, the difference between the functions of whole Bibles and specific passages, and social mediation between text and artifact.

### *Efficacy*

The first point that emerges from this catalogue is that the Bible was considered efficacious as a text and as an artifact. This point might seem a truism to scholars of religion, but seldom has the required evidence been marshaled to demonstrate this unambiguously. As will be seen from Table 1, in the majority of practices described here, the Bible itself enabled ordinary folk to resist evil powers and to effect cures, without the aid of any kind of religious specialist.

Not included in Table 1 are a few practices that might have introduced redundancies that would skew the data: reciting an unspecified text to cure ringworm (no specialist required), whispering an unspecified passage backward to remove thorns (carried out by a charmer), and reading an unspecified passage to summon a witch (the report is ambiguous regarding the involvement of a religious specialist). Reports describing the practice of weighing a witch against the Bible do not specify that any kind of specialist was involved, but I suggest it is "probable" because it was a legal, evidentiary procedure. In

Table 1. Practices and whether religious specialists were required.

| Description | Specialist required? |
| --- | --- |
| Weigh witch against Bible | Probably |
| Have Bible on person | No |
| Put Bible in bed or under pillow | No |
| Set baby upon Bible | No |
| Place Bible on coffin | No |
| Bring Bible to new home or keep Bible in home | No |
| Read Bible as part of exorcism | Clergy |
| Drink dissolved ink from written copy of Lord's Prayer | No |
| Have Lord's Prayer on person | No |
| Eat copy of Lord's Prayer | Charmer |
| Write out and send Psalm 59 | No |
| Wear ague charm about neck | No |
| Wear toothache charm around neck, carry in pocket, etc. | No |
| Recite Lord's Prayer | Charmer in some |
| Recite Lord's Prayer backward | No |
| Recite Psalm 8 seven times a day for three days | No |
| Recite Ezek 16:6, 9 or charm derived therefrom | No |
| Recite Ps 67:1–2 | No |
| Recite apocryphal text to stop bleeding | Charmer |
| Repeat apocryphal text three times | No |

many cases the texts were charms, transmitted and sometimes administered by charmers. I have not categorized charmers as specialists, in this analysis, because reports indicate that it was the charm, not the charmer, that was regarded as efficacious:

> A retired farmer, still living, claimed to be able to charm ringworm in cattle, and a woman who claimed to be able to charm human ringworm lived in the parish for several years. Her remedy was to recite a certain verse from the Bible. She did not do this by herself, but would tell her patient which verse was used and leave him to find and recite it. (Vickery 1978, 157)

Another folklore collector commented:

> All these charms were regarded as holy, not as magical; sometimes they were passed down openly in families, as for instance by being written down in the family Bible, but more often they were taught in confidence, there being a great reluctance to reveal them unnecessarily, or to strangers. When used, they were generally muttered too low and too fast to be heard, or else they were written down on a piece of paper which the sufferer was given, but which he was told he must not unfold and read. Some said that in order to be effective they ought only to be used by a woman to cure a man, and by a man to cure a woman, but this rule was not always followed. Many of the "charmers" and "conjurors"...

> used them, but since their effectiveness lay in the sacred words and allusions themselves, they were believed to work even when applied by ordinary people; indeed, the toothache charm was often self-administered.
>
> (Simpson 1976, 104–105)

The role of charmers seems primarily to have lain in their *expertise*, that is, in their knowledge of charms, though Owen Davies (1998, 43–44) points out that there does seem to have been a minor tradition of regarding charmers as possessing a special gift. In most cases, however, it is clear that anyone who knew the charm might use it, the efficacy inhering in the charm itself—hence the oft-reported desire of charmers to keep their charms secret.

The Bible was not used by itself, however, for exorcisms. For exorcisms, clergy or other religious specialists (in one case, a Sunday school teacher) were required. An obvious interpretation of the need for a religious specialist for exorcisms is that the Bible was regarded as insufficiently powerful for this purpose. There is evidence to support this interpretation: possession of a Bible was not always sufficient to protect from malicious spirits; several Bibles were often used in exorcisms, as if more Bibles concentrated more power; and Bibles were used in combination with other religious implements, such as candles and crosses. On this interpretation, religious specialists were required to supplement the power of the Bible.

But this leaves unexplained the specific need for religious specialists: if religious specialists were just one more source of power, then they should be replaceable by any other efficacious person or object (of which, in British folklore, there were many). We should find occasional, but hardly exclusive, use of religious specialists, and at least some accounts should say what could be substituted for them. But this is not what we find.

What we find in the sources is simply the assumption that clergy will participate in exorcisms. I suggest that this results from the fact that exorcism was an official function of the church and from the folk belief that the church had all spiritual matters in its purview. If we look about the religious landscape of the British laity, we find the church offering itself as the agent of exorcisms, obviating the need, when an exorcism was required, for the laity to look elsewhere. The assumption that clergy will be involved in exorcisms is a result not of a folk theory about the limited efficacy of the Bible, but rather of the self-promotion of clergy for this purpose. To be sure, not all clergy were eager to perform exorcisms, and many were quite skeptical of folk belief in ghosts, but, at an institutional level, the church had for centuries promoted itself as the sole authority in matters spiritual, and, perhaps partly owing to its remunerative potential, many clergy seem to have been willing to satisfy the folk demand for exorcisms.[30]

In descriptions of how exorcisms should be performed, clergy are always the ones performing them. But in the story of one specific exorcism, it is

30. Remuneration implied in Moss 1898, as quoted in Simpson 1976, 91.

a Sunday school teacher who is involved (Evans 1892, 274–276). This story presents a problem because, according to church doctrine, Sunday school teachers, not having been ordained, were not supposed to be able to perform exorcisms. It may be significant that, in this story, the Sunday school teacher takes it upon himself to perform the exorcism—he is not asked— but the story is nonetheless an exception to the general rule.

An implication of this interpretation is that, for healing, people turned to charmers because clergy did not offer the required services. The church might have claimed for itself medical functions—as it has in various times and places—but by this period the division between mundane and heavenly realms had shaped both church doctrine and folk understandings. This division, in Britain and elsewhere, apparently went back at least to Anglo-Saxon times when, although monasteries reproduced medical texts such as the *Lacnunga* and even provided accommodations for a physician, the physicians themselves are depicted without tonsure (Grattan and Singer 1952, 12–17). But if the church left healing to others, physicians and charmers found a place in their practice for Christian names, prayers, and the Bible. Yet this adoption created a tension, to which we will return.

### *General and specific traditions*

Traditions about *specific* uses for the Bible were complemented by ideas about the Bible's *general* efficacy. Several lines of evidence point to beliefs that the Bible was generally efficacious, with uncertain powers. One line of evidence is the interchangeability of functions across procedures: it will be noted that Bibles were used in diverse procedures to achieve the same goal, and in the same procedures to achieve diverse goals. The following charm was designed to be used for a variety of injuries:

> "When our Lord Jesus Christ was upon earth, He pricked himself with a [*here name the cause of the injury*], and the blood sprang up to heaven. Yet His flesh did neither canker, mould, rot, nor corrupt; no more shall thine. I put my trust in God. In the name," & c.—say these words thrice, and the Lord's Prayer once. (Henderson 1879, 169)

Owen Davies has noted that other charms appear to have been adaptable to different conditions (1998, 42, discussing "Sixteenth Report" 1899, 112; see also Davies 1996, 22). It is very much as if, somewhere in a curative tradition's history of transmission, someone reasoned that if the Lord's Prayer was effective against ghosts, it might also work quite well against the evil eye—as if the ends for which it was efficacious were ill-defined.

A second line of evidence comes from statements about a charm's general efficacy, as when an old charmer told a young woman that a charm involving the Lord's Prayer could be used to treat a thrown arm or shoulder "and the same if it was scalds or burns or toothache, or anything" (Eyre 1905, 168; see also O. Davies 1996, 22).

A third line of evidence has to do with creative uses of the Bible, such as that of the London woman who placed a Bible over her baby's head following the visit of an "obeah woman"—obeah being a kind of folk sorcery from the West Indies, similar to Voodoo (Newall 1978, 41)—and the following anecdote about "Old Mr. Hodgson," after some boys had raised the devil:

> Mr. Hodgson knew that the only way to get rid of him would be to give him a task he could not perform, and that, if in three trials they could not hit upon such a task, the case would be hopeless.
>
> Mr. Hodgson first desired him to count the blades of grass in the Castle Croft. This task the Devil performed directly. He was next ordered to count the grains of sand on the School Brow. This gave him no more trouble than the former feat. Only one chance was left. A happy thought occurred to Mr. Hodgson. He commanded the Devil to count the letters in the large Bible in the Parish Church. In an instant the Devil descended to the lower regions...
>
> (Burne 1909, 205)[31]

These uses, while analogous to established practices, are innovative extensions of existing practices, and as such indicate a kind of faith in, or at least uncertainty about, what powers the Bible might have.

A final, fourth, line of evidence are miscellaneous stories, unconnected to practices, in which the Bible effects some unpredictable transformation: a hunchbacked stone was said to be a man who stole a church Bible and placing a Bible upon a particular disappearing island was said to cause it to remain above water.[32] Related to these uncertain consequences were beliefs that one should set nothing on top of a Bible, or that tearing or dropping a Bible would bring ill luck.[33]

British Bible folklore therefore includes traditions both about procedures employing Bibles to achieve specific effects and clues that the Bible was regarded as generally efficacious. In scholarly discussions, the former have tended to be aggregated to the latter, as if the specific uses were *derived from* general ideas about the Bible's efficacy. But this is to reverse the inference actually attested in the sources. The sources suggest, rather, that ideas about the Bible's general efficacy were secondary to traditions about specific cures: that specific curative procedures tended to be generalized, and served as the analogical source of innovations. Notions about the Bible's general efficacy are attested, but not so robustly as traditions about specific cures.

### *Contests and cures*

A third observation has to do with a distinction between the functions of Bibles as whole objects and as specific biblical texts. Table 2 compares the functions for which whole Bibles (or reading from the Bible, without respect

31. The reason the devil could not perform this task is unclear.
32. *Theft*: Grinsell 1937, 254; see also Grey 1977 [1934], 143–44. *Island*: Paton 1940, 288.
33. Opie and Tatem, *s.v.* "BIBLE, treatment of," (www.oxfordreference. com/views/ENTRY.html?subview=Main&entry=t72.e93 [accessed June 2007]).

to passage) and specific Bible texts were used.

Table 2. Comparison of Bible modes and functions.

| | Protect from a being | Exorcism | Protect from a disease | Cure |
|---|---|---|---|---|
| Whole Bible | × | × | | |
| Lord's Prayer | * | | | × |
| Other texts | * | | × | × |

As Table 2 reveals, there is a systematic difference between the uses of whole Bibles and those of specific passages. There is no evidence that either entire Bible artifacts or generic Bible text was used to protect from or cure diseases. Rather, the generic Bible was primarily used in contests between spiritual powers. When it came to curing diseases, specific biblical or taken-for-biblical texts were used instead.

The two asterisks in Table 2 designate two cases that constitute probable exceptions to this rule. The first has to do with the Lord's Prayer: in one report, "an old man of eighty...since his wife's death a few months ago, goes about with the Lord's Prayer written backwards as a charm against the return of that erstwhile cantankerous old lady" (M. R. Taylor 1929, 132). In another report, an elderly woman regarded daily recitation of the Lord's Prayer as a form of protection from the Devil. Both of these cases are reported as unique instances rather than as indicators of general practice, but they do employ the Lord's Prayer in spiritual contests. More ambiguous is recitation of the Lord's Prayer to remove spells and against "fairy stroke" and other "fairy mischief." In these cases the Lord's Prayer is used to treat the *effects* of witches and fairies—effects often identified with physical maladies. These uses should perhaps be classified as curative, but the evidence is too partial to allow certainty. It is better to allow that the Lord's Prayer is a specific biblical text that was used in contests with spiritual beings.

The second asterisk is warranted by two reports. The Letter of Agbarus was reportedly used by an old woman to protect her household from witchcraft and the evil eye. This letter is otherwise mentioned only once, as a charm against illness and for protection in childbirth. It may explain her exceptional usage that the old woman understood the Letter of Agbarus to be written by Jesus, and perhaps then as a kind of holy text in its own right. Certainty is precluded by the limited evidence. The second case is more ambiguous: one variant of the widely attested cure for ague has the added ending "or witchcraft." Again, this may be only a way of referring to miscellaneous ailments. Both of these cases are unusual, but at least the first constitutes an exception to the rule I propose.

Still, admitting these exceptions, the general pattern is that the Bible as a whole was used in contests with ghosts, witches, and fairies, and that specific Bible texts were used in curing.

### *Textual attribution*

A final point also has to do with the relation between Bible-as-artifact and Bible-as-text. In my earlier ethnographic work, I analyzed how meanings were attributed to the Bible by American evangelical Christians (Malley 2004, Chapter 3). There I argued that the relation between meanings and the text involves a cognitive process of *attribution*, and that interpretive traditions make heavy use of this process. Here a similar point emerges about the relation between the Bible as artifact and the Bible as text. As we have seen, charmers and other folk often attributed apocryphal texts to the Bible. The reports suggest that in part this was due to illiteracy, but this was not so in all cases. Consider the following conversation between a Dame Grey and a parson:

Parson: Well, Dame Gray, I hear you have a charm to cure the toothache. Come, just let me hear it; I should be so much pleased to know it.

Dame Grey: Oh, your reverence, it's not worth telling.

*(Here a long talk—Parson coaxing the Dame to tell him—old lady very shy, partly suspecting he is quizzing her, partly that no charms are proper things, partly willing to know what he thinks about it.) At last it ends by her saying—*

Dame Grey: Well, your reverence, you have been very kind to me, and I'll tell you: it's just a verse from Scripture as I says over those as have the toothache:—"And Jesus said unto Peter, What aileth thee? And Peter answered, Lord, I have a toothache. And the Lord healed him."

Parson: Well, but Dame Grey, I think I know my Bible, and I don't find any such verse in it.

Dame Grey: Yes, your reverence, that is just the charm. It's in the Bible, but you can't find it![1]

In this and other reports we see that literacy did not—could not—ensure a perfect mapping between the published Bible—the artifact—and the text, as that text was understood by readers. The attribution of an apocryphal text to the Bible, a kind of tradition about what the Bible said, had intervened. The existence of such traditions forces us not only to distinguish between the Bible as text and the Bible as artifact, but also to recognize that social processes may intervene in this relationship.

## Bible divination

The preceding practices are all magical acts, manipulations of Bibles or biblical texts to achieve some effect. Another common sort of practice, however, was Bible divination.

1. "Old Charms" 1850, 293. I have modified the quotation by consistently marking speakers. For another story involving the same charm, see Barclay 1894, 338.

### *Sortes Biblicae*

Very widespread was the consultation of a Bible at random to achieve some kind of foreknowledge. This practice was sometimes connected with New Year's Day, as in the following account:

> This superstitious practice is still in common use, and much credit is attached to it. It is usually set about with some little solemnity, on the morning of New Year's Day before breakfast, as the ceremony must be performed fasting. The bible is laid on the table unopened, and the parties who wish to consult it are then to open it in succession. They are not at liberty to choose any part of the book, but must open it at random... Wherever this may happen to be, the inquirer is to place his finger on any chapter contained in the two open pages, but without any previous perusal or examination. The chapter is then read aloud, and commented upon by the company assembled. It is believed that the good or ill fortune, the happiness or misery of the consulting party, during the ensuing year, will in some way or other be described and foreshewn by the contents of the chapter. (Forby 1830, ii. 400)

Another variant of this practice was less formal: it involved an individual taking a Bible to bed and opening it at random when first waking on New Year's Day (Gurdon 1893, 137–138; Lean, Woodward, and Williams 1902, 2:343; Tongue and Briggs 1965, 152). The practice was not restricted to New Year's Day, especially when important decisions were to be made.[2]

The historian of religion will recognize this practice as a form of what was, in the classical world, called *sortes Homericae* or *sortes Virgilinae* (using the works of Homer or Virgil) and is more commonly called *Bible dipping* today. Although a couple of folklorists suggested that this form of bibliomancy was a *continuation* of the ancient practice, the rate of reinvention is probably high enough that the mere fact of resemblance is not sufficient evidence of continuity (Malley 2004, 101–103).

The information thought to be yielded by this form of bibliomancy is sometimes said to be one's fortune and sometimes God's will, but it is not clear that the folklorists distinguished these interpretations—in fact, Simpkins, quoting an earlier writer, describes it both ways as if they are equivalent (Gurdon 1893, 137–38; Simpkins and Rorie 1914, 117). My hunch, based on ethnographic work among American evangelicals, is that the practitioners probably did not distinguish these interpretations either.

Another practice, also reported as an example of the *sortes Virgilinae*, is a kind of birth date divination (Lean, Woodward, and Williams 1902, 2: 343; Simpkins and Rorie 1914, 117). In this, Proverbs 31 was used, supposedly because it has 31 verses, and the relevant verse was selected according to the day of the month on which a person was born. For example, because I was born on September 7, Prov 31:7 would tell my fortune. (Unfortunately for me, Prov

2. Aubrey and Britten 1881, 115–116; Harland 1873, 237; Lean, Woodward, and Williams 1902, 2:344; Simpkins and Rorie 1914, 117.

31:7 reads, "Let him drink, and forget his poverty, and remember his misery no more.") A man could also use this form of divination with a potential spouse's birthday, to determine what kind of life he would lead with her (Gurdon 1893, 95; Hunt 1871, 428; Lean, Woodward, and Williams 1902, 2:343).

*Bible & key*

The second bibliomantic practice was so prevalent that it appeared in two novels: the curious practice called the Bible & key (Hardy 1997; Naipaul 1961). The following instance is reasonably typical:

> One Mrs. White, it seems, had lost some property, and agreed with the neighbours to resort to the Bible & key in discovery of the thief. They placed the street-door key on the fiftieth Psalm, closed the volume, and fastened it tightly with a string. The Bible & key were then suspended to a nail, and the name of Mrs. Blucher (the person on whom suspicion had fallen) was repeated three times by one of the women, while another recited these lines: "If it turn to thee / Thou art the thief, and we are all free." The key then turned, or was thought to do so, and Mrs. Blucher was proclaimed to be the thief.
>
> (Henderson 1879, 234–235)

Although this is a prototypical instance of the Bible & key, the practice is reported in many procedural variants: in fact, there were almost as many variants as there are reports.[3] But for our purposes the only variations that are important are those pertaining to the purpose of the ritual and the text on which the key was placed.

The primary purpose of the Bible & key was discovery, either of a person's future spouse or of the identity of a thief. Regarding marriage, there were many variants as to what precisely the Bible & key would reveal: whether a woman would marry, which of two people would be married first, which of two people would have a better marriage, whether a particular admirer would offer marriage, whether a woman would accept a suitor, whether a woman would be a good wife, whether a couple would marry, or whether the course of love for a prospective couple would be smooth.[4] Most commonly, the procedure was used to discover the initial letter or two of the future husband's or

3. Adams 1904, 515; Aubrey and Britten 1881, 31; Banks 1943; Billson 1895, 58; R. Brown 1884; T. Brown 1961, 395; Courtney 1886, 111; J. C. Davies 1911, 1314; Forby 1830, 398–399; Grey 1977 [1934], 150–152; Groome 1895, 118; Gutch and Peacock 1908, 138, 141; Hadow and Anderson 1924, 352; Henderson 1879, 233–236; Hone 1967, 254–255; Kilvert and Plomer 1960, 1: 300–301; Latham 1878, 31; Lean, Woodward, and Williams 1902, 2: 338–339; Leather 1912, 65; Napier 1879, 106–107; "Notes and Queries" 1883; "Notes and Queries" 1884; Owen 1896, 288–289; Parker 1913, 80; Salmon 1902, 422–423; Tongue and Briggs 1965, 152; "Twelfth Report" 1894, 82–83; Westropp 1911, 205.

4. *Whether a woman would marry*: Billson 1895, 58. *Married first*: Henderson 1879, 236; Latham 1878, 31. *Better marriage*: Aubrey and Britten 1881, 31. *Particular courter*: Courtney 1886, 111; Napier 1879, 106; Westropp 1911, 205. *Accept suitor*: Owen 1896, 288–289. *Good wife*: Gurdon 1893, 95. *Couple marry*: T. Brown 1961, 395. *Course of love smooth*: Gurdon 1893, 95.

wife's name.[5] Should the key not turn at all, lifelong celibacy was indicated.[6] The Bible & key was similarly used to identify a thief, the expectation being that the key would turn at mention of the guilty person's name.[7]

A few other uses appear in scattered reports. Related to its use in discovering a thief, the Bible & key could be used to discover the location of stolen or lost goods (Gutch and Peacock 1908, 138). There is also mention of the procedure being used to determine which of two "mesmerisers" had the strongest will and in the trial of a witch (Henderson 1879, 236; Groome 1895, 118). Reports from Gloucestershire and Shropshire describe a curative use of the Bible & key in healing a nose bleed, and a report from Norfolk says the Bible & key was used to effect the successful departure or arrival of a ship (Eyre 1905, 169–170; E. M. Wright 1913, 240–241; Gerish 1893).

The passages used show a small degree of variation. For marriage, the passages were Ruth 1:15–16 or Songs 8:6–7. The passage in Ruth 1 (KJV) reads:

> And she said, Behold, thy sister in law is gone back unto her people, and unto her gods: return thou after thy sister in law. 1:16 And Ruth said, Intreat me not to leave thee, or to return from following after thee: for whither thou goest, I will go; and where thou lodgest, I will lodge: thy people shall be my people, and thy God my God.

Songs 8:6–7 (KJV) reads:

> Set me as a seal upon thine heart, as a seal upon thine arm: for love is strong as death; jealousy is cruel as the grave: the coals thereof are coals of fire, which hath a most vehement flame. Many waters cannot quench love, neither can the floods drown it: if a man would give all the substance of his house for love, it would utterly be contemned.

Proverbs 31 was used for the identification of a good wife. For the discovery of a thief, the passage was Ps 50:18 (KJV), "When thou sawest a thief, then thou consentedst with him."

Like Bible dipping, the Bible & key is reported to be a variant of an earlier form of divination known as the sieve and shears, or what the ancient Greeks called *coskiomancy*, which was also an ongoing practice in Ireland (Henderson 1879, 233–234; Wilde 1902, 207). The resemblance between these different practices is so considerable, and the likelihood of independent invention so low, that it is probable we have a single, ancient tradition that has appeared in two major variants in addition to a host of minor ones.

It is important to note that, at least in some instances, the practitioners took the results of the Bible & key quite seriously: in one case the Bible &

5. Billson 1895, 58; J. C. Davies 1911, 14; Forby 1830, 399; Gutch and Peacock 1908, 141; Hadow and Anderson 1924, 352; Henderson 1879, 236; Leather 1912, 64; Parker 1913, 80.
6. Billson 1895, 58; J. C. Davies 1911, 13–14; Forby 1830, 399; Gutch and Peacock 1908, 141.
7. Banks 1943; T. Brown 1961, 395; R. Brown 1884, 156–157; Forby 1830, 398–399; Kilvert and Plomer 1960, 1: 300–301; "Notes and Queries" 1883; "Notes and Queries" 1884, 380–381; Salmon 1902, 422; E. M. Wright 1913, 264.

key was accepted as exonerating a female servant suspected of theft; in some cases the results were brought to the police.[8] Accused persons took it seriously too: one man accused of thievery consulted a lawyer in response, and an accused woman came and beat the person who initiated the ritual. In another case the man identified by the Bible & key as a thief was forced to relocate. The Bible & key thus seems to have been a mechanism affecting reputation and social status.

Two folklorists reported on the opprobrium with which the Bible & key was regarded, even by those who practiced it. Leather quotes one informant describing the Bible & key as "wicked work" (1912, 65). Another commented to her that "when you sees a thing like that, you feels there's a power on earth besides the power o' human beings," to which a second replied "Ay, ay, but some says as the power as does it is a bad power." James Napier too comments:

> This method of divining was not frequently practised, not through want of faith in its efficacy, but through superstitious terror, for the movement of the key was regarded as evidence that some unseen dread power was present, and so overpowering occasionally was the impression produced that the young woman who was chief actor in the scene fainted. The parties holding the key and Bible were generally old women, whose faith in the ordeal was perfect, and who, removed by their age from the intenser sympathies of youth, could therefore hold their hands with steadier nerve. (Napier 1879, 107)

Yet it was not always taken seriously: a report from Suffolk relates a man trying it at a Christmas party, though it left him "right scared" (Hadow and Anderson 1924, 352). It is interesting that, despite use of a Bible, people did not attribute the turning of the key to God—they seemed to have only vague ideas about a "bad" or "dread" power.

### *Other forms of bibliomancy*

Other forms of bibliomancy were also practiced. An amalgam of Bible dipping and the Bible & key had the inquirer "place a key at random in a Bible, and note the letter to which it points" (E. M. Wright 1913, 259). The Bible was also used in two procedures that promised to give the inquirer a vision of her future spouse:

> read the verse: "Lay down now, put me in a surety with thee; who is he that will strike hands with me?" *Job* xvii. 3, after supper, then wash up the supper dishes and go to bed without speaking a word, placing the Bible under your pillow with a pin stuck through the verse previously read.
> (E. M. Wright 1913, 262; see also Lean, Woodward, and Williams 1902, 2: 371)

Presumably, the variety of divinations related to courtship, usually practiced by young women, was related both to normal romantic interest and to young

8. Banks 1943; R. Brown 1884, 156–157; "Notes and Queries" 1883, 333; "Notes and Queries" 1884, 380–381.

women's social dependence on their husbands.

Bibles were sometimes integrated with other forms of divination. There is a report of a London woman accused of fortune-telling, in whose home was found "a Bible ... interleaved with extracts from a dream-book" ("Notes and Queries" 1887, 73–74). While this mixed book was clearly used for divination, the procedure is unspecified. A report of similar inscriptions—in German—in a Psalter comes from Liverpool ("Auguries" 1899). Another elaborate procedure combined the Lord's Prayer with a kind of moon divination.

> If you want to see whom you will marry, miss, you must go out of the house in the first quarter of the new moon (Hallows Eve is the best, but the moon must be in its first quarter, if not you will see nothing). And you must see it for the first time. When you get a sight of it kneel down, and with a *black-handled knife* lift a sod from under your right knee and from under the toe of your right foot, repeating:
>
> "New moon, true moon, Happy may I be; Whoever is my true love This night may I see."
>
> Then repeat the Lord's Prayer; lift a sod of earth, and with the earth you took from under your right knee and foot, hide it somewhere outside the house till you are ready to go to bed, then bring it inside. You must not speak a word to a living soul once the earth is brought into the house. Then put the earth into the right-foot stocking, and put that under your head. But be sure you speak to no one till morning. (Singleton 1904, 461)

Such practices again suggest that the Bible was thought an efficacious power in its own right.

## Analysis

Two major additional points emerge from this examination of bibliomantic practices, the first having to do with the creation of context, the second with the role of artifactual and textual properties.

### *Context creation*

At a glance, the *sortes Biblicae* might seem a variety of reading. After all, the Bible is a big book, and might a person not decide to start somewhere other than "In the beginning"? And do not many Bible readers expect the text to speak to their lives? Of course.

But a critical difference has to do with the construction of context. In normal reading, a passage is naturally understood as a part of a larger text, the larger text forming the context in which the passage has meaning. Were we, in reading a work of fiction, to interpret each sentence as an independent text, we would never enjoy the story—we might not even be aware that there *was* one. And we need context: seldom is an isolated sentence of much interest.

In the *sortes Biblicae*, the context within which a Bible passage is interpreted is not the larger literary work, but the life circumstances of the diviner. The

Bible is opened and the passage is read, but what is interpreted is the encounter between a specific diviner, in specific life circumstances, and this specific text. The mechanical manipulation of the text corresponds to a *cognitive* manipulation, a manipulation of the context within which the text is interpreted. Similarly, the Bible & key was occasioned by circumstances—mainly courtship questions or a theft—that set the context for interpreting the turn of the key as a signal.

What is essential in these practices is that the specific signal could not be predicted by those involved. This is not the same as saying that the signal was random: it was not, nor is there any indication that the users sought to make it so. But this interruption of discernible processes of causation, Pascal Boyer has suggested, seems to create the kind of cognitive context in which beliefs about supernatural agents are highly salient (Boyer 1990). This inferential gap theory fits well with the observation that people were uncertain about the agencies involved.

### *Artifact and text*

The bibliomantic practices described above occur at the intersection of divination and reading. The practices of *sortes Biblicae* and the Bible & key turn precisely on Bibles' (or other books') artifactual properties while also treating them as texts. One difference between bibliomancy and reading is the role that Bibles' artifactual properties play in the procedure: readers treat a physical book as a medium—preferably a transparent medium—for the text, and the text as a vehicle—again, preferably a transparent one—for meaning. In the *sortes Biblicae*, the physical book is manipulated to *disrupt* the text and the text's meaning, allowing the discovery of a different kind of signal and a different kind of meaning. In bibliomancy, the artifact is valued not for its transparency but for its opacity. Such opacity is necessary to create the inferential gap discussed above.

Whereas the *sortes Biblicae* manipulate the artifact to produce a text, the Bible & key uses the text to create a Bible-key artifact. The placement of the key is determined by the occasion, and the focus of the ritual moves from the Bible's textual to artifactual properties. It is noteworthy that the Bible & key involved a Bible, and that, at least when the concerns were romantic, involved biblical texts that were generally relevant to the occasion at hand. It would seem that in these cases, the fact that the text was biblical and topically relevant was important in setting the stage for a ritual that otherwise made no use of the book's textual properties at all. The text's semantic properties seem to have been important.

The discovery of a thief constitutes an exception to this generalization: Ps 50:18 is relevant only in that it includes the word "thief." But the Bible has many texts that deal with theft, and some would seem more relevant than the passing mention in Psalm 50. Why not Exod 20:15, "Thou shalt not steal"? Or 1 Pet 4:15, "Let none of you suffer...as a thief"? Here a historical factor may be at play: Ps 50:18 is the only place in the book of Psalms where the word *thief* appears. One report refers to the Bible & key as the "Psalm-book and key," and it is possible that the selection of passages was influenced by the existence of an alternate or perhaps earlier variant in which the Psalter was used instead of an entire Bible. Even so, the use of Psalm 50 for detection of a thief seems to have been widespread, and it does constitute an exception to the analysis offered above. The exceptional nature of this practice is strengthened by two reports, which hold that Ruth 1 was used in the detection of theft ("Notes and Queries" 1883; Henderson 1879, 235). This exception suggests that it may have been the text—in this case, the word *thief*—rather than the meaning of the passages that was important for the Bible & key. If so, then in the Bible & key as much as the *sortes Biblicae*, the Bible functioned as an artifact and as a text, quite apart from the semantics of the passages involved.

## Conclusion

The British laity seem to have exploited the Bible as text and artifact in rather different ways than ecclesiastical Christianity. Whereas ecclesiastical Christianity has generally emphasized the *message* of the Bible over its status as artifact and even its text, concern with the Bible's teaching is almost entirely absent from the folk practices described here. Indeed, even when the Bible is made to speak, as in the *sortes Biblicae,* it is made to speak in a very different way than either historians or theologians would have it.

One is tempted almost to see a complementarity between the folk and ecclesiastical emphases, but I think it is better to interpret this difference as the result of competitive exclusion: the church, owing to its superior organization as an institution, could claim for itself the Bible in its artifactual, textual, and semantic aspects. And, in various ways, it made use of all of these, but its emphasis was always on the Bible's semantic properties, the Bible's message. But as the church promoted the Bible, it was unable to monopolize it: charmers opportunistically adopted the Bible as a new tool in their arsenal of trinkets, texts, salves, and rituals; those wishing to gain hidden knowledge found it easy to substitute the Bible for other instruments. Charmers and layfolk developed a kind of practical Biblicism that the better-organized church could perhaps, had it been willing, have claimed for itself.

The relationship between ecclesiastical Christianity and the folk practices surveyed here was varied. Both advocates and opponents of these kinds of folk Biblicism could be found among the clergy. One woman was afraid that her parson would find out that she had not brought a Bible into her new house when first she entered (Winstanley and Rose 1926, 174). Others disapproved of such practices, and at least one charmer felt he had to give up his practice in order to be a Christian (Kilvert and Plomer 1960, 3:27374). This clash of institutions could be acrimonious and costly to those caught in the middle:

> Mr. Ashmole told me, that a Woman made use of a Spell to Cure an Ague, by the Advice of ______. A Minister came to her, and severely repremanded her, for making use of a Diabolical help, and told her, she was in danger of Damnation for it, and commanded her to burn it. She did so, and her Distemper returned severely; insomuch, that she was importunate with the Doctor to use the same again: She used it, and had ease. But the Parson hearing of it, came to her again, and thundred Hell and Damnation, and frighted her so, that she burnt it again. Whereupon she fell extremely Ill, and would have had it a Third time; but the Doctor refused, saying, That she had contemned and slighted the power and goodness of the Blessed Spirits (or Angels) and so she died.
>
> (*Miscellanies* 1721, 107–108)

## References


Adams, Maxwell. 1904. "Some Notes on the Church and Parish of Churston Ferrers." *Report and Transactions: The Devonshire Association for the Advancement of Science, Literature and Art* 36: 506–516.

Aspin, Jehoshaphat. 1832. *Ancient Customs, Sports, and Pastimes, of the English.* London: J. Harris.

Aubrey, John, and James Britten. 1881. *Remaines of Gentilisme and Judaisme.* London: Published for the Folklore Society by W. Satchell Peyton & Co.

"Auguries." 1899. *Folklore* 10: 115–16.

Banks, M. M. 1927. "Keys in Coffins," *Folklore* 38: 399.

———. 1943. "Gleanings from Magazines." *Folklore* 54: 309–310.

Barclay, Isabella. 1894. "Scraps of Folklore." *Folklore* 5: 336–338.

Baring-Gould, S. 1925. *Further Reminiscences, 1864–1894.* London: John Lane.

Barrett, Justin L., and Brian Malley. 2007. "A Cognitive Typology of Religious Actions." *Journal of Cognition & Culture* 7(3–4): 201–211.

Billson, Charles James. 1895. *Leicestershire & Rutland.* London: Published for the Folklore Society by D. Nutt.

Black, William G. 1883. *Folk-Medicine: A Chapter in the History of Culture.* London: Published for the Folklore Society by E. Stock.

Bonser, Wilfrid. 1963. *The Medical Background of Anglo-Saxon England: A Study in History, Psychology, and Folklore.* London: Wellcome Historical Medical Library.

Boyer, Pascal. 1990. *Tradition as Truth and Communication: A Cognitive Description of Traditional Discourse.* Cambridge: Cambridge University Press.

Briggs, K. M. 1957. "The English Fairies." *Folklore* 68: 270–287.

Brown, Robert. 1884. "Notes and Queries." *The Folk-Lore Journal* 2: 156–159.

Brown, Theo. 1961. "Some Examples of Post-Reformation Folklore in Devon." *Folklore* 72: 388–399.

———. 1970. "Charming in Devon." *Folklore* 81: 37–47.

Bruce, John. 1850. "Charm for the Toothache." *Notes and Queries* (Fifth Serial) 1(25): 397.

Burne, Charlotte S. 1897. "More Staffordshire Superstitions." *Folklore* 8: 91–92.

———. 1909. "Reminiscences of Lancashire and Cheshire when George IV Was King." *Folklore* 20: 203–207.
Burrows, J. A. 1939. "Medical Services in Our Countryside." *Transactions of the Southend-on-Sea Historical Society* 3.
Carmichael, Alexander, Elizabeth Catherine Watson, and James Carmichael Watson. 1928. *Carmina Gadelica: Hymns and Incantations with Illustrative Notes on Words, Rites, and Customs, Dying and Obsolete*. Edinburgh: Oliver & Boyd.
Carrick, T. W. 1929. "Scraps of English Folklore, XVIII. Cumberland." *Folklore* 40: 278–290.
"Charm for Ague." 1852. *Notes and Queries* 5(131): 413.
"Charm for the Tooth-ache." 1851. *Notes and Queries* (First Serial) 3(63): 20.
"Charms." 1857. *Notes and Queries* (Second Serial) 4(80): 25.
———. 1933. *Report and Transactions: The Devonshire Association for the Advancement of Science, Literature and Art* 55: 126–28. "Charms from Devonshire." 1851. *Notes and Queries* 3(75): 258–259.
Courtney, M. A. 1886. "Cornish Feasts and 'Feasten' Customs." *The Folk-Lore Journal* 4: 109–32.
———. 1887. "Cornish Folk-Lore." *The Folk-Lore Journal* 5: 14–61, 85–112, 177–220.
Craigie, W. A. 1898. "Some Highland Folklore." *Folklore* 9: 372–379.
Davies, Jonathan Ceredig. 1908. "Ghost-Raising in Wales." *Folklore* 19: 327–331.
———. 1911. *Folk-Lore of West and Mid-Wales*. Aberystwyth: Printed at the "Welsh Gazette" Offices.
Davies, Owen. 1996. "Healing Charms in Use in England and Wales 1700–1950." *Folklore* 107: 19–32.
———. 1998. "Charmers and Charming in England and Wales from the Eighteenth to the Twentieth Century." *Folklore* 109: 41–52.
Davies, T. A. 1937. "Folklore of Gwent: Monmouthshire Legends and Traditions." *Folklore* 48: 41–59.
Dempster. 1888. "The Folk-Lore of Sutherland-Shire." *The Folk-Lore Journal* 6: 14989, 215–252.
Denham, Michael Aislabie. 1892. *The Denham Tracts: A Collection of Folklore: Reprinted from the Original Tracts and Pamphlets Printed by Mr. Denham Between 1846 and 1859*. London: Published for the Folklore Society by D. Nutt.
Dyer, T. F. Thiselton. 1880. *English Folk-Lore*. 2nd ed. London: D. Bogue.
Ettlinger, Ellen. 1943. "Documents of British Superstition in Oxford." *Folklore* 54: 227–249.
Evans, Griff. 1892. "Exorcism in Wales." *Folklore* 3: 274–277.
Eyre, Margaret. 1905. "Folk-Lore of the Wye Valley." *Folklore* 16: 162–179.
Fenwick, J. G. 1879. "Note." *The Folk-Lore Record* 2: 205.
"First Report of the Committee on Devonshire Folk-lore." 1876. *Report and Transactions: The Devonshire Association for the Advancement of Science, Literature and Art* 9: 49–58.
"Folklore of South Northamptonshire." 1850. *Notes and Queries* 2(33): 36–37.

Forby, Robert. 1830. *The Vocabulary of East Anglia: An Attempt to Record the Vulgar Tongue of the Twin Sister Counties, Norfolk and Suffolk, as It Existed in the Last Twenty Years of the Eighteenth Century, and Still Exists; with Proof of Its Antiquity from Etymology and Authority*. London: Printed by and for J. B. Nichols & Son.
Gerish, W. B. 1893. "Key Magic." *Folklore* 4: 391–392.
Grattan, J. H. G., and Charles J. Singer. 1952. *Anglo-Saxon Magic and Medicine*. London: Oxford University Press.
Gregor, Walter. 1881. *Notes on the Folk-Lore of the North-East of Scotland*. London: Published for the Folklore Society by E. Stock.
———. 1883. "Stories of Fairies from Scotland." *The Folk-Lore Journal* 1(2): 55–58.
Grey, Edwin. 1977 [1934]. *Cottage Life in a Hertfordshire Village*. Harpenden and District Local History Society.
Grinsell, L. V. 1937. "Some Aspects of the Folklore of Prehistoric Monuments." *Folklore* 48: 245–259.
Groome, W. Wollaston. 1895. "Suffolk Leechcraft." *Folklore* 6: 117–129.
Gurdon, Eveline Camilla. 1893. *Suffolk*. [London]: Published for the Folklore Society by D. Nutt.
Gutch, Eliza, and Mabel Geraldine Woodruffe Peacock. 1908. *Examples of Printed Folk-Lore Concerning Lincolnshire*. London: Published for the Folklore Society by D. Nutt.
Hadow, Grace E., and Ruth Anderson. 1924. "Scraps of English Folklore, IX. (Suffolk)." *Folklore* 35: 346–360.
Hardy, Thomas. 1997. *Far from the Maddening Crowd*. Seattle: World Wide School.
Harland, John. 1873. *Lancashire Legends, Traditions, Pageants, Sports, etc., with an Appendix Containing a Rare Tract on the Lancashire Witches, &c. &c*. London: G. Routledge & Sons.
Hartland, M. E. 1913. "Breconshire Village Folklore." *Folklore* 24: 505–517.
Hayward, L. H. 1938. "Shropshire Folklore of Yesterday and To-Day." *Folklore* 49: 223–243.
Henderson, William. 1879. *Notes on the Folk-Lore of the Northern Counties of England and the Borders*. London: W. Stachell Peyton & Co.
Hockin, Frederick. 1882. "Notes." *The Folk-Lore Record* 5: 147–178.
Hone, William. 1967. *The Year Book of Daily Recreation and Information; Concerning Remarkable Men and Manners, Times and Seasons, Solemnities and Merry-Makings, Antiquities and Novelties, on the Plan of the Everyday Book and Table Book*. Detroit, MI: Gale Research Co.
Hunt, Robert. 1871. *Popular Romances of the West of England: or, The Drolls, Traditions, and Superstitions of Old Cornwall*. 2nd ed. London: J. C. Hotten.
Jackson, Georgina F., and Charlotte S. Burne. 1883. *Shropshire Folk-Lore: A Sheaf of Gleanings*. London: Trübner & Co.
Kilvert, Robert Francis, and William Plomer. 1960. *Kilvert's Diary, 1870–1879; Selections from the Diary of the Rev. Francis Kilvert, 1 January, 1870–1819 August, 1871*. 3 vols. London: Cape.

Kingsbury, J. B. 1950. "The Last Witch of England." *Folklore* 61: 134–145.
Kirk, Robert, and Andrew Lang. 1893. *The Secret Commonwealth of Elves, Fauns & Fairies. A Study in Folk-lore & Psychical Research*. London: D. Nutt.
Latham, Charlotte. 1878. "Some West Sussex Superstitions Lingering in 1868." *Folklore Record* 1: 1–67.
Lean, Vincent Stuckey, Julia Lucy Woodward, and T. W. Williams. 1902. *Lean's Collectanea*. 2 vols. Bristol: J. W. Arrowsmith.
Leather, Ella Mary. 1912. *The Folk-Lore of Herefordshire*. Hereford: Jakeman & Carver.
Malley, Brian. 2004. *How the Bible Works: An Anthropological Study of Evangelical Biblicism*. Walnut Creek, CA: AltaMira Press.
"Manx Folk-Lore and Superstitions." 1891. *Folklore* 2: 284–313.
Maple, Eric. 1965. "Witchcraft and Magic in the Rochford Hundred." *Folklore* 76: 213–224.
March, H. Colley. 1899. "Dorset Folklore Collected in 1897." *Folklore* 10: 478–489.
*Miscellanies, Upon the Following Subjects. I. Day-Fatality. II. Local-Fatality. ... XXII. The Discovery of Two Murders by an Apparition. Collected by John Aubrey*. 1721. 2nd ed. with large additions. London: Printed for A. Bettesworth and J. Battley J. Pemberton and E. Curll.
Morgan, W. E. T. 1895. "Charms." *Folklore* 6: 202–204.
Moss, Fletcher. 1898. *Folk-Lore, Old Customs and Tales of My Neighbours*. Published by the author from his home the Old parsonage, Didsbury; and from his room in the Spread Eagle hotel, Hanging Ditch.
Naipaul, V. S. 1961. *A House for Mr. Biswas*. London: A. Deutsch.
Napier, James. 1879. *Folklore, or, Superstitious Beliefs in the West of Scotland Within This Century*. Paisely: Alex Gardner.
Newall, Venetia. 1978. "Some Examples of the Practice of Obeah by West Indian Immigrants in London." *Folklore* 89: 29–51.
Newman, L. F. 1946. "Some Notes on the History and Practice of Witchcraft in the Eastern Counties." *Folklore* 57: 12–33.
Northall, G. F. 1892. *English Folk-Rhymes: A Collection of Traditional Verses Relating to Places and Persons, Customs, Superstitions, etc*. London: K. Paul, Trench, Trübner.
"Notes and Queries." 1883. *The Folk-Lore Journal* 1: 330–335.
———. 1884. *The Folk-Lore Journal* 2: 377–382.
———. 1887. *The Folk-Lore Journal* 5: 71–75.
"Old Charms." 1850. *Notes and Queries* (first serial) 1: 293–294.
Opie, Iona Archibald, and Moira Tatem, eds. 1989. A Dictionary of Superstitions. New York: Oxford University Press. Available through Oxford Reference Online, Oxford University Press: www.oxfordreference.com/views/BOOK%5FSEARCH.html?book=t72&subject=s17.
———. 1963. "The Tentacles of Tradition." *Folklore* 74: 507–526.
"Orkney Charms." 1854. *Notes and Queries* 10(255): 220–221.
Owen, Elias. 1896. *Welsh Folk-Lore: A Collection of the Folk-Tales and Legends of North*

*Wales; Being the Prize Essay of the National Eisteddfod, 1887*. Oswestry and Wrexham: Woodall.

Ozanne, Christine, and F. Carey. 1915. "Notes on Guernsey Folklore." *Folklore* 26: 195–202.

Parker, Angelina. 1913. "Oxfordshire Village Folklore (1840–1900)." *Folklore* 24: 74–91.

Paton, C. I. 1940. "Manx Calendar Customs." *Folklore* 51: 43–63, 90–96, 179–94, 277–294.

———. 1941. "Manx Calendar Customs." *Folklore* 52: 35–69, 120–35, 184–97, 254–271.

Peacock, Edward. 1889. "Notes and Queries." *The Folk-Lore Journal* 7: 313–322.

*The Physicians of Myddvai; Meddygon Myddfai*. 1861. Llandovery: D. J. Roderic.

Read, D. H. Moutray. 1911. "Hampshire Folklore." *Folklore* 22: 292–329.

Rhys, John. 1901. *Celtic Folklore, Welsh and Manx*. Oxford: Clarendon Press.

Rushton, Peter. 1980. "A Note on the Survival of Popular Christian Magic." *Folklore* 91(1): 115–118.

Salmon, L. 1902. "Folklore in the Kennet Valley." *Folklore* 13: 418–429.

"Second Report of the Committee on Devonshire Folk-lore." 1877. *Report and Transactions: The Devonshire Association for the Advancement of Science, Literature and Art* 9: 88–102.

"Seventeenth Report of the Committee on Devonshire Folk-Lore." 1900. *Report and Transactions: The Devonshire Association for the Advancement of Science, Literature and Art* 32: 83–92.

Simpkins, John Ewart, and David Rorie. 1914. *Examples of Printed Folk-Lore Concerning Fife*. London: Published for the Folklore Society by Sidgwick & Jackson.

Simpson, Jacqueline. 1976. *The Folklore of the Welsh Border*. London: B. T. Batsford.

Singleton, A. H. 1904. "Dairy Folklore, and Other Notes from Meath and Tipperary." *Folklore* 15: 457–462.

"Sixteenth Report of the Committee on Devonshire Folk-Lore." 1899. *Report and Transactions: The Devonshire Association for the Advancement of Science, Literature and Art* 31: 110–119.

Spooner, B. C. 1961. "Cloud Ships over Cornwall." *Folklore* 72: 323–229.

Taylor, E. S. 1852. "East Norfolk Folk Lore." *Notes and Queries* 6(133): 480.

Taylor, Mark R. 1929. "Norfolk Folklore." *Folklore* 40: 113–133.

"Thirteenth Report of the Committee on Devonshire Folk-Lore." 1895. *Report and Transactions: The Devonshire Association for the Advancement of Science, Literature and Art* 27: 61–74.

Tongue, Ruth L., and Katharine Mary Briggs. 1965. *Somerset Folklore*. London: Folklore Society.

Townend, B. R. 1948. "The Narrative Charm with Special Reference to the Cure of Toothache." *British Dental Journal* 85: 29–34.

"Twelfth Report of the Committee on Devonshire Folk-lore." 1894. *Report and Transactions: The Devonshire Association for the Advancement of Science, Literature and Art* 26: 79–85.

Underwood, Mary Grace. 1911. "Courted by the Devil: A Perthshire Folk-Tale." *Folklore* 22: 330–331.

Vickery, A. Roy. 1978. "West Dorset Folklore Notes." *Folklore* 89: 154–159.

Westropp, Thomas J. 1910. "A Folklore Survey of County Clare." *Folklore* 21: 180–199.

———. 1911. "A Folklore Survey of County Clare." *Folklore* 22: 203–213.

Wilde, Lady. 1890. *Ancient Cures, Charms, & Usages of Ireland*. London: Ward & Downey.

———. 1902. *Ancient Legends, Mystic Charms & Superstitions of Ireland, with Sketches of the Irish Past*. London: Chatto & Windus.

Winstanley, L., and H. J. Rose. 1926. "Scraps of Welsh Folklore, I. Cardiganshire; Pembrokeshire." *Folklore* 37: 154–174.

Wright, A. R. 1912. "Seventeenth Century Cures and Charms." *Folklore* 23: 230–236.

Wright, Elizabeth Mary. 1913. *Rustic Speech and Folk-lore*. London: H. Milford.

# V

# Power and Scholarship

# 18

# The Pride and Prejudice of the Western World: Canonic Memory, Great Books and *Archive Fever*

Karl Ivan Solibakke

*This paper examines controversies arising from the perception of the instruments of cultural memory and the logic of their transmissibility. On the one hand, we have a carefully selected, temporally and geographically orchestrated body of texts, the Great Books, which are an enduring testament to the authority of Western intellectual artifacts. On the other hand, Jacques Derrida's* Archive Fever *locates a furtive transformation of collective memory in the informal practices exemplified by oral narrative and public discourse. Not only do both models rely on archives as a functional instrument of collective identity, but they also value them as institutions circumscribing social and cultural conventions. However, when synchronizing the traces embedded in oral discourse and written documents, the repositories are frequently subject to manipulation by interpretive communities. Recognizing the processes underlying archives and artifacts is essential to comprehending how canons and canonic practices impact Western cultural memory.*

> These books are the means of understanding our society and ourselves. They contain the great ideas that dominate us without our knowing it. There is no comparable repository of our tradition.
>
> Robert M. Hutchins, *Great Books of the Western World*

## Theories of archives and textual repositories

For the past 4,000 years, written archives have regulated the politics of cultural memory, since such repositories contain the textual capital to transmit collective wisdom and social norms from one generation to the next. Endowing cultural orders with common identities and mnemonic markers, a collection of texts also serves as the basis for tracing the processes of cultural memory and conjecturing how mnemonics mold collective desire. Because of their mobility, written artifacts are also the starting point for investigations into the transmissibility of collective meanings as signifiers that either work to consolidate the mnemonic objectives inscribed into the texts or induce transformations of cultural traditions. Specifically, commentary and exegesis substantiate the spatial and temporal dispersion of literate traditions, which, while they do not contest the difference between thought and language, words and things, verbal language and active response, they expose these as adaptable effects of historical approaches to collective knowledge.

Although confidence in literate memory as a stabilizing agent seems justified, textual memory does not always keep up with the proliferation of media in the age of global communication. Rather, the mobility of textual archives seems to be neutralized by the sheer velocity of new media, which infuses objects and events with a temporal immediacy belying the apposition of past and present. Because they demand instant disclosure, new media usurp the time lag attributed to written artifacts, given that these depend upon being deciphered and interpreted before their meaning becomes apparent and the remnants undertake an active role in defining collective memory spaces. More specifically, if one focuses on texts that have the invariable attributes of canons, suggesting that the semiotic markers have been fixed in an immobile memory mode, these may still be intelligible, but they also become inaccessible to future signifiers. As iconic repositories, canonic archives encapsulate a discrete mnemonic practice that stimulates performative and ritualistic approaches to cultural memory. Accordingly, they are blind to the exigencies of the dissemination process and the multiplicity of discourses in a global society undergoing perpetual transformations.

In connection with the challenges of the post-war era, Robert M. Hutchins' portrayal of the Great Conversation in the introductory volume of Encyclopedia Britannica's *Great Books of the Western World* is emblematic of an iconic repository, since his encomium accentuates the importance of the canon of the Western World for intellectual paradigms based on European traditions. Although the famous educator appeals to the need for dialogue, his plea is couched in logocentric and moral terms, accentuating an ideology that lionizes Western heritage and dissociates itself from non-Western cultural traditions.

> The tradition of the West is embodied in the Great Conversation that began in the dawn of history and that continues to the present day. Whatever the merits of other civilizations in other respects, no civilization is like that of the West in this respect. No other civilization can claim that its defining characteristic is a dialogue of this sort. No dialogue in any other civilization can compare with that of the West in the number of great works of the mind that have contributed to this dialogue. … The spirit of Western civilization is the spirit of inquiry. Its dominant element is the Logos. … The exchange of ideas is held to be the path to the realization of the potentialities of the race. (Hutchins 1952)

The archive models discussed in the following essay (see also Larson in this volume) articulate controversies with regard to the perception of the instruments of cultural memory and the logic of their transmissibility. On the one hand, we have a carefully chosen, temporally and geographically orchestrated body of texts, the Great Books, an enduring testament to the legitimacy of Western cultural traditions. On the other hand, there is the clandestine, surreptitious transformation of collective memory that Jacques Derrida locates in the "archival problems of oral narrative and public property, of mnesic traces, of archaic and transgenerational heritage, of everything that can happen to an 'impression' in these at once 'topic' and 'genetic' processes" (1996, 34). Not only do both models identify archives as a functional part of collective traditions, but they also praise them as social institutions circumscribing socio-cultural conventions that can be manipulated by interpretive communities or modified by redefining the memory traces embedded in oral discourse and written documents. Even within this mnemonic context, though, dogged devotion to a finite collection of signifying artifacts ignores a primary disposition of textual storage spaces (Assmann 1987, 21): in contrast to theological or legal canons, intellectual texts represent a system of norms that facilitate didactic and political objectives. According to the cultural memory experts, Jan and Aleida Assmann, the function of canonic texts is coupled with social integration, and anything that counteracts that objective must be regarded with suspicion. With this mediating quality of the canon in mind, the perseverance of the Great Books reveals itself as a transatlantic transfer that resists the porosity of transcultural currents in today's global network. Provocations, such as the dissemination of new meanings, the acceleration of transcultural exchange, and the reciprocity of regional epistemologies, do not take place. Perceived through the lense of Derrida's Freudian approach to collective repositories in *Archive Fever*, misgivings arise as to the subconscious appropriation of a European intellectual tradition that guards against alien ideas and manipulates texts to comply with parochial or even liturgical doctrines of memory.

### St. John's College: The *Great Books* program

Triggered by a national crisis in the educational sector following the First World War as well as the economic crisis in Europe and the USA, several American universities investigated the viability of compiling a European archive and transforming it into a four-year undergraduate curriculum. Two reasons were cited as the driving force behind the project. The first reacted to a perceived intellectual corrosion instigated by the system of electives at American institutions of higher learning, which a canonic syllabus devoid of superfluous courses would offset with a comprehensive curriculur strategy. The second motivation was spurred by Fascism in Italy and Germany and the destructive impact that totalitarian orders had on the artifacts of Western civilization. The most promising projects were launched by Alexander Meiklejohn at the University of Wisconsin, John Erskine with the assistance of Mark Van Doren and Mortimer Adler at Columbia, and Robert M. Hutchins at the University of Chicago (Nelson 2001, 3–63), all of which adapted models that had been developed for adult educational programs on both sides of the Atlantic.

In 1936, two unknowns in American academia, the philosopher Scott Buchanan und the historian Stringfellow Barr, who had compiled a comprehensive Great Books reading list at the University of Virginia, were given the opportunity to test the merits of their canon at a small college in Annapolis, Maryland. Although the New Program, as the Great Books curriculum was designated, was highly controversial from the start and the program did not gain national recognition until after the Second World War, St. John's College has since become the flagship of *Great Books* institutions the world over. Internationally acclaimed, the college maintains two campuses on the American continent; in the early 1960s, the Annapolis campus was augmented by a satellite in Santa Fe, which has in turn encouraged its graduate academy to open up the canon of texts to artifacts stemming from Eastern, as well as Western, cultural traditions.

The core of the four year undergraduate curriculum in Annapolis and Santa Fe is comprised of works considered indispensible to the Western European intellectual canon, from Homer to Joyce, Plato to Heidegger, Euclid to Einstein, and Palestrina to Stravinsky. In addition to philosophical and literary documents, the reading list also focuses on mathematical, scientific, and musical texts which were chosen in compliance with the seven liberal arts fundamental to scholastic traditions. From the beginning of the new program at St. John's, one of its ambitions was to integrate the natural sciences into what was seen as a revival of a traditional liberal arts education, of a *studia liberalia*, as it was designated in the Middle Ages. As Scott Buchanan elucidates in his study *The Doctrine of Signatures*, in which he endeavors to bridge the rift between the humanities and modern medicine, the trivium and quadrivium form the basis for a structural and semiotic approach to cultural memory.

> The trivium deals with the gross distinctions in the modes of signification that are to be found in the use of symbols. The quadrivium deals with those finer distinctions which are necessary for the special use of symbols that we have in mathematics. The distinction, the making of the trivium and quadrivium, is the feature in medieval thought that is often referred to by modern writers as logic-chopping and endless argumentation. Both these epithets are just, but neither logic-chopping nor endless argument should be objected to by moderns who become unintentionally tangled in their own symbols in simple conventional discourse. (Buchanan 1991, 6)

Not unexpectedly, the first statement of the St. John's program impugns modern science for the departure of undergraduate colleges from their mission to provide a liberal education founded on the canonic texts of the Western world. Accordingly, the great books that focus on an understanding of nature, ancient as well as modern, are read in seminar, while labratory activities are organized as practical introductions to scientific investigation and experimentation. The ambition to include the sciences within the liberal arts is mirrored in the seal of the new program, which features seven books depicting the late Classical and medieval enumeration of the liberal arts. The seven books encircle a scale as an allegory for how the arts should embrace the experimental methods characteristic of modern science, balancing out the discord between the disciplines that was generated by Cartesian duality. What becomes manifest here is that, thanks to a unity of purpose, the Great Books represent an extreme case of a literate cultural tradition, since the texts derive their value from their privileged status within the interpretative community. The acculturation they endorse is *kat exochen*, implying that it is at odds with transcultural theories of socio-cultural interaction. Expressions of alterity and otherness, including numerous artifacts and branches of learning beyond the canon, as well as the allpervasiveness of today's visual culture, are subject to censure. This elitist approach to the mnemonic repository is a significant factor, since canon and censure are usually manifest in societies in which a selective return to the past and the recovery of traditions both stimulate and are instigated by didactic aspirations.

Another origin for the kind of iconicity that St. John's propagates harks back to one of the nation's founding fathers and its third president, Thomas Jefferson, who compiled a Greco-Roman canon for the University of Virginia. Couching the liberal arts tradition that Jefferson tried to codify for a nascent nation in purely apolitical terms, one of the college's eminent scholars contends that the canon at St. John's includes "neither the old customs nor the recent routines, neither the sedimentary wisdom nor the petrified habits of communities. I mean [simply] a collection of books" (Brann 1989, 64). On the one hand, the Greco-Roman canon forms the intellectual sediment for an enduring curriculum at St. John's College; on the other, the hermetic handling of the material is fortified by an instructional method that shuns critical annotations or historical analyses of the institutional, socio-cultural, and rational contexts in which the documents were written. Speaking for themselves, the texts are expected to resonate with each other as the readings progress from Homer to Heidegger. Carefully safeguarded from external influences, they limn the ideas and the motivation for a cultural paradigm that is mimetically anchored to Western European intellectual memory.

In order to initiate the Great Books curriculum and accomplish their program goals, Barr and Buchanan became highly proficient administrators, instituting a state of exception within which they were not only able to enforce their curricular reforms, but also to circumvent the restrictions imposed on them by the college's Board of Visitors and Governors. Their strategy was at once radical and paradoxical, especially if one calls to mind that a primary motivation for the canonic curriculum was the emancipation of Western thought from fascist manipulation and the state of exception was the primary political tool of Nazi Germany. After Barr and Buchanan turned their backs on the college in 1947 (apparently they were no longer able to advocate for the new program after a decade of conflict), responsibility for the canon was delegated to the German-Jewish philosopher and mathematician Jacob Klein. A student of Martin Heidegger at the Universität Marburg and a long-standing friend and colleague of Leo Strauss, Klein corresponded extensively with some of the world's most prominent intellects, among them Gadamer and Strauss. The latter's assessments of the canon during its nascent years are enlightening and he spent his final years in Annapolis. The Klein-Strauss correspondence confirms how painstakingly the philosophers pondered the canonic texts, many of which were not at all or only partially available in English translations at the time. The letters also provide practical insights into the philological concerns behind a compilation of great texts. They detail the transformations of the curriculum during the years in which McCarthy attempted to purge American intellectual circles from foreign influence.

While canonic repositories are not only advantageous for developing cultural literacy, they are also effective mechanisms for improving text immanent methods of interpretation and for inculcating written and oral competency. Acquiring these skills is reminiscent of the value canons had in Classical antiquity (Casement 1996, 1–39), during which the archived material was used to instill moral, social, and political maxims serving the collective identity of the group. Skilled readers, as the champions of the Great Books assert, have every chance of becoming civilized men and effective citizens, although the underlying dominance of the patriarchy is irrefutable and the role of women readers nebulous. In keeping with the subordinate role of women within the social fabric of the Classical polis, women writers, with the exception of Jane Austen, have not been incorporated into the reading list. As disconcerting as that lapse may be, the greatest paradox is that the canonic project appropriates European texts for a cultural framework that has been rededicated and promoted as intrinsically American. Feeding into the exclusivity of the Great Books supporters, the transcultural trajectory of the documents is abandoned, especially when the iconic attributes of the texts and the didactic handling of the material precludes transatlantic or, at the very least, cosmopolitan exchanges of ideas. Since the impetus for this American-European epistemology can be also traced back to the prominent emigrants, among these Klein and Strauss, who brought Husserl's and Heideggers's phenomenological methods to bear on the configuration of the canon, three questions with regard to the iconicity of the Great Books project come to mind: the first focuses on the degree to which liberal mnemonic cultures are also premeditated systems of knowledge; the second queries the discrepancy between meanings that have become entrenched and the prospects for differences of opinion, that is, the relationship between canon and censure; and the third scrutinizes the application of canonical instruments to mold national cultural memory goals. With these three questions in mind, the following section sheds light on the inception of the *Great Books of the Western World*, one of the most ambitious publication projects with an overt canonical trajectory.

## Hutchins and Encyclopedia Britannica's *Great Books of the Western World*

On November 30, 1943, Robert M. Hutchins invited Stringfellow Barr, Scott Buchanan, Mortimer Adler, and other proponents of the Great Books movement to attend an Editorial Advisory Board Meeting at the corporate offices of Encyclopedia Britannica in Chicago. Scheduled for mid December, the meeting followed a series of memos regarding the contents of the multi-volume *Great Books* project that Encyclopedia Britannica was to release nearly a decade later. Initiated by the University of Chicago, where university president Hutchins had joined with Adler to develop a curriculum originally aimed at educating businessmen, the series was designed to close intellectual gaps and familiarize a lay readership with the great ideas of the past three millennia. Among the program's first students was William Benton, the future Senator and later CEO of Encyclopedia Britannica. Benton proposed drawing the greatest books of the canon together, complete and unabridged, as a compendium of Western thought and suggested that Hutchins and Adler edit the series for distribution to a national readership. Hutchins responded disapprovingly at first, fearing that the series would be sold by subscription and suffer the indifference that is the common to many reference works and lexicons. His greatest concern, however, was a devaluation of the formative influence that the great texts had exercised on Western culture and the transmissibility of a body of incomparable ideas to a mass audience. After many debates about what to include as well as how to present the material to an American public, the project was completed in 1951. Introduced at a gala in New York on April 15, 1952, Hutchins reinforced the iconic quality of the compendium, claiming that the collection was more than a set of books and an instrument for a liberal education, but an act of piety. Here, he asserted, were the sources of the Western World; indeed, this was the Western archive in its purest form as well as a reflection of its heritage and significance, compiled for all to scrutinize. In their own way, the sixty volumes that comprise the *Great Books of the Western World* have taken on the status of iconic books in a post-war secular society lacking a true awareness of its textual heritage.

The five premises postulated at the beginning of the highly competitive selection process were codified in Hutchins' invitation to the members of the selection committee. Beyond providing methodological assumptions to steer the efforts of the search committee, the criteria shed light on the derivation of an intrinsically iconic approach to the canon of Western thought.

1. Each book must be important in itself and without reference to any other; that is, it must be seminal and radical in its treatment of basic ideas or problems.
2. Each book must obviously belong to the tradition in that it is made

more intelligible by other great books, as well as increasing their intelligibility.
3. Each book must have an immediate intelligibility for the ordinary reader even though this may be superficial.
4. Each book must have many levels of intelligibility for diverse grades of readers or for a single reader re-reading it many times.
5. Each book must be indefinitely re-readable; that is, it should not be the sort of book that can never ever be finally mastered or finished by any reader.

As spelled out by Hutchins, these criteria not only summarize the project's guiding principles, but also provide evidence of the iconicity of the books as an instrument of cultural memory. Broadly, the five points endorse the ideological and performative features of the repository by emphasizing: 1. the uniqueness of the material selected; 2. the close interplay between documents that resonate with one another; 3. the 'auratic' effects that the texts have on an unitiated readership; 4. the plurality of interpretative positions that could and should be applied to a culturally iconic text; and, 5. paradoxically, the intellectual and spiritual nucleus of the texts that precludes their exhaustive interpretation. Pinpointing these mystical attributes of the canon, Hutchins exposes the epistemological gap between a collection of textual artifacts and a space of transmissibility, between an empirical body of signs and a transcendental approach to their substance. In the spirit of pasts and presents that belie codification and preclude closure, he appeals to an eschatological and messianic reception of the canonic texts. Although the approach may be one of shared meanings and mutual articulation, the books ultimately remain elusive to everyone except the arbiters who have selected and assembled the canonic artifacts. Hence, the liminal space in which the archive arises is peculiarly reminiscent of Walter Benjamin's appraisal of Franz Kafka's enigmatic work, "its widely spaced focal points are defined, on the one hand, by mystical experience (which is, above all, the experience of tradition) and, on the other hand, the experience of the modern city-dweller" (2005, 325). Indicative of the debris that natural or man-made catastrophes leave behind, Kafka's texts aspire to index the signs of a modern era that, as Benjamin is careful to point out, has lost all consistency of integrity and intellectual rigor. Writing a decade later, Hutchins expresses analogous sentiments at the outset of the post-war era, emphasizing that the Great Books had salvaged, preserved, and transmitted the tradition on many occasions similar to the challenges posed by the reconstruction of the Western World after 1945. This approach to a literate enculturation reflects the distinctiveness of a community of readers as well as the need to reinforce truths by recuperating textual traditions from the past. Mobilizing celebrated textual artifacts and promoting lofty conversation, Hutchins aspires to a practice of cultural memory that unites uncommon communities under the baldachin of Western European intellectual supremacy.

By the time the Advisory Board met on October 19 and 20, 1944, it found itself immersed in discussions about the choice of specific texts to be included in the compendium. Their deliberations exist in the form of minutes that reveal how scrupulous the committee was in shaping the canon for an unseen and uninitiated readership in need of interpretative stewardship. "Mr. Hutchins felt there should be extended essays in the various large sections. The use of minimal aids to the reader was cautiously agreed upon." Dwelling on edifying tools that would assist the reader in deciphering the texts, the Advisory Board raised questions about whether the members of the selection committee were in a position to measure the greatness of the documents they endorse, "whether the choice of books may be supposed to represent the experience, to date, of the committee of selection. If so, is the educative value of the books proved—or is this a sign that those who have taught the great books have been imperfect users? If the sign is confirmed, might that not call in question the entire validity of the list?"

The concerns expressed have credence within the iconic approach to the texts that the Advisory Board selected and archived, one that purports to authenticate how texts recount the collective memory of the Western world. In essence, the mnemonic artifacts are a reminder of an endeavor to unite a community of readers spread across the American continent, pointing subliminally to the synthesis of a diasporic collective. The suggestion is that the Great Books could have succeeded in keeping Western civilization intact, had real attempts been undertaken to prevent the corrosion of scriptural traditions. Accordingly, the economic strategy behind the Encyclopedia Britannica project requires marketing the canonic texts to remote regions of the nation where individual readers could close the gaps in their intellectual background. Superimposing historical and existing realities, European pasts and American presents, Hutchins mourns the state of Western culture after the Second World War, maintaining that the autonomy of the canon should redeem mankind from its folly.

Essentially, the canon is the directive of an interpretative community struggling to remain objective as it wields an unbridled authority over the reader. With regard to the many questions about cultural beliefs and secular objectives, inner strength and exterior security, and individual and collective memory that canonic archives kindle, the belief in interpretative empowerment remains controversial. Since the texts aspire to go beyond the issue of a collective that rallies around a specific admiration for Western civilization, they also become an allegory for the many flaws characterizing modernity. At once profane and sacred, Hutchins' stance is mixed in unholy confusion with the primeval, given that the technological advancements of the Western World counteract a cultural origin that has long been forgotten. Hence, the proponents of the Great Books search for the constellation between the present moment and obscured fragments from the past that are torn out of their original contexts; these, then, represent the hidden source of textual authenticity within the profane mnemonics of a post-modern global society that commands a broad ensemble of media opportunities. Once again, this dialectic between old and new is reminiscent of Kafka's legacy to a world confronted by the loss of authority, given that "like the haggadic parts of the Talmud, these books, too, are stories; they are a Haggadah that constantly pauses, luxuriating in the most detailed descriptions, in the simultaneous hope and fear that it might encounter the halachic order, the doctrine itself, en route" (Benjamin 2001, 496). For Benjamin and Hutchins, the space in which form and content, literature and dogma converge can only be the revelation of a messianic truth that emboldens Western cultural traditions.

### *Archive Fever* and Derrida's archive beyond the archive

In contradiction to the mnemonic autonomy that is inscribed in Hutchins' *Great Books of the Western World*, Derrida expresses misgivings about the mnemotechnical conclusiveness of the archive as an agent of cultural memory, arguing in *Archive Fever* that the texts "will never be either memory or anamnesis as spontaneous, alive and internal experience. On the contrary: the archive takes place at the place of the originary and structural breakdown" (Derrida 1996, 11) of the commemorative process. A latent force working from some remote venue, the genuine archive or the fever that launches the visible repository becomes a subconscious longing for memorization, repetition, reproduction, and re-impression. As Derrida teaches us, the term is derived from the Greek *arkheion* and means house, dwelling, or address. Moreover, it was used to denote the residence of the higher magistrates, the archons, who were not only entrusted with the physical security of the documents deposited in their homes, but were also accorded the privilege of consulting and interpreting them. Situated in a liminal space between the private and public sector, archontic power incorporates the "functions of unification, of identification, of classification" and reveals the human infatuation with consignation. On the one hand, a form of written proof, on the other, something presupposing a hermeneutic authority, consignation is often misunderstood as "a system or a synchrony in which all the elements articulate the unity of an ideal configuration" (Derrida 1996, 3).

Although the act of consignation involves gathering objects together, these are usually nothing more than signs, since almost any object can be transformed into a signifier if it represents something other than itself. A collection of signs implies that the material elements of the archive are correlated to arbitrary meanings. Formally, this characteristic of the archive is receptive enough that what might or might not be included in the repository can be adapted to new meanings. However, the consequence is that the configuration of signs is by no means a synchrony, an ordered storage area, but a myth, since the signs are often lodged in an interstitial, indeterminate space that is as fertile as it is inchoate. "Institutive and conservative," the dialectic of consignation becomes "revolutionary and traditional. An *eco-nomic* archive in this double sense: it keeps, it puts in reserve, it saves, but in an unnatural fashion, that is to say in making the law (*nomos*) or in making people respect the law" (Derrida 1996, 7). Included in these explanations of archival space are political, social, and economic deliberations, as well as the misconception that the logos has a direct impact on how the signs in the repository are collected, salvaged, and interpreted.

The archive's sole obligation is to leave a trace, one that is decipherable for future generations, but this obligation also requires that the traces take part in a never-ending process of displacement and suppression. By the same token, both displacement and suppression embolden the prolongation of the act of writing, since generating signs "inflects archive desire or fever" as well as the tendency of the signs to liberate the future, "their dependency with respect to what will come, in short, all that ties knowledge and memory to promise" (Derrida 1996, 30). According to Derrida, an unrelenting drive to derive artifacts and new meanings from the repository of signs taps into an invisible archive behind or underlying the archives perceptible to the collective. This demonstrates that the inexorable inscriptions of the sign collector do not serve the purpose of launching a "concept," but rather an "impression through the unstable feeling of a shifting figure, of a schema, or of an in-finite or indefinite process" (Derrida 1996, 29). The promise with regard to what will come, then, is the point at which Derrida's understanding of the textual artifact takes on messianic qualities. Counter to Hutchins' canon, Derrida's archive targets a constitutive plurality, mnemonically capable of sustaining a centrifugal movement of styles, expressions, and instruments with which the memory process distances itself from exclusive monocultures: ontologically bridging pasts with a surplus of meanings and presents lacking a vocabulary for recollection, and aesthetically attuned to an endless variety of semantic and syntactic options. The archive reveals itself as a liminal space that is not a diagonal between two points, but a zone of unlimited dissemination, which impresses its public as a theater of ideas. The zone is imbued with a theatrical, performative and iconic quality, because it invites the audience to cross the threshold into a memory space integrating pasts and presents, what has been told and what the future might hold in store. Based upon an iconicity that exploits mankind's desire to play with the ingredients of memory, Derrida's plurality of archival meanings stands in opposition to the remoteness of the Great Books project. Intentionally opaque, the canonic trajectory safeguards the texts from clashing with unsolicited signifiers and confronting the erosion of memory in the global perspective. Braced to withstand transatlantic challenges, Hutchins' books become monuments that abrogate any responsibility to acknowledge how volatile cultures of memory can be. From a Derridean standpoint the aporia is that canonic traditions, which, in their archival form, should be the most supple, self-referential, and unrepressed medium of cultural recollection, are subject to authoritarian treatment. Attempting to counteract the loss of cultural memory by stipulating which meanings are valid and which are not, this rigid practice only succeeds in jeopardizing the mnemonic vitality of the archive.

## Conclusion

The dialectics underlying Hutchins' closed canon and Derrida's open archive are also central to Pierre Nora's cultural theories. They are based on a criticism of the acceleration of historical thought in modern societies, in which the narrative of the individual has become indistinct and living memory has been usurped by history. Acceleration "confronts us with the brutal realization of the difference between real memory—social and unviolated, exemplified in but also retained as the secret of so-called primitive or archaic societies—and history, which is how our hopelessly forgetful modern societies, propelled by change, organize the past" (Nora 1994). Brought about by an increase in temporal velocity, the provocations find themselves subsumed in the formation of a social order that the doctrine of progress has subjected to a loss of tradition. Nora's sites of memory, the central figure around which his theory is constructed, form an exception to this trend, since they entail a material, a functional, and a symbolic dimension. In their polyvalent materialization as texts, buildings, rituals, and museums, they compensate for the mnemonic deficiencies besetting global societies today and for the demise of memory in modernity. Moroever, *lieux de mémoire* acquiesce to this loss in a dual sense of the word by commemorating the temporality of a particular object and by memorializing the collapse of collective memory itself. Nora himself likens the spatiotemporal overdetermination of sites of memory to a kaleidoscope of objects that have been given the task of forging political identities. Hence, the interaction between history and memory in Nora's *lieux de mémoire* takes on significance only when the mnemonic factors—object and meaning on a phenomenological level, forgetting and remembering on an epistemological level—begin to resonate with one another.

Consistent with Nora, canonic archives are stimulated by an eschatologic drive that envisions death and forgetting as something that can be eradicated and laid to rest. However, since the death drive evokes aggression and destruction, "it not only incites forgetfulness, amnesia, the annihilation of memory, as *mnēme* or *anamnēsis*, but also commands the radical effacement, in truth the eradication, of that which can never be reduced to *mnēme* or to *anamnēsis*, that is, the archive, consignation, the documentary or monumental *hypomnēma*, mnemotechnical supplement or representative, auxiliary or memorandum" (Derrida 1996, 11). Although archives motivate a loss of memory through eradication, effacement, and censure, they also control the memory process, and every act of control which reinforces canonic autonomy is an act of suppression. If importance is placed on a liberal arts program as a mnemonic practice that both reifies a storage area for collective memory and regulates latent subcultures resisting mnemonic governance, then the real question is: what happens to the excess or clandestine signs that arise in the process of reading and writing? Reconfiguring the mnemonic repository insinuates that the signs circulate in new constellations, and their signifying potential either necessitates adaptation to the pride and prejudice inherent in prevailing traditions or triggers open resistance to the instruments of memory, be they canons, archives, *lieux de mémoire,* or iconic books.

## References

Assmann, Jan und Aleida. 1987. Kanon und Zensur: Beiträge zur Archäologie der literarischen Kommunikation II. München: Fink Verlag.

Benjamin, Walter. 2002. *Selected Writings. Volume 2, Part 2: 1931–1934.* Ed. Michael Jennings, Howard Eiland, and Gary Smith. Cambridge, MA: The Belknap Press of Harvard University Press.

———. 2005. *Selected Writings. Volume 3: 1935–1938.* Edited by Howard Eiland and Michael Jennings. Cambridge, MA: The Belknap Press of Harvard University Press.

Brann, Eva T. 1989. *Paradoxes of Education in a Republic.* Chicago, IL: University of Chicago Press.

Buchanan, Scott. 1991. *A Defence of Theory in Medicine.* Champaign: University of Illinois Press.

Casement, William. 1996. *The Great Canon Controversy.* New Brunswick/London: Transaction Publishers.

Derrida, Jacques. 1996. *Archive Fever: A Freudian Impression.* Chicago, IL: University of Chicago Press.

Hutchins, Robert M. 1952. *The Great Conversation: The Substance of a Liberal Education,* vol. I, *The Great Books of the Western World.* Chicago, IL: Encyclopedia Britannica, Inc. Internet edition. http://www.thegreatideas.org/libeducation.html. Accessed 11 November 2010.

Nelson, Charles A. 2001. *Radical Visions. Stringfellow Barr, Scott Buchanan, and Their Efforts on behalf of Education and Politics in the Twentieth Century.* Westport CN: Praeger.

Nora, Pierre. 1994. "Between Memory and History: Les Lieux de Mémoire." In *History und Memory in African-American Culture,* edited by Geneviève Fabre and Robert O'Meally, 284–300. New York/Oxford: Oxford University Press.

# 19

# Indigenous "Texts" of Inhabiting the Land: George Washington's Wampum Belt and the Canandaigua Treaty

Philip P. Arnold

*Wampum is symbolic, or iconic, of a long and enduring lineage of immigrant and indigenous relationships in North America throughout the colonial and into the American period. Wampum almost always represented co-habitation agreements for how diametrically different human communities—colonial and indigenous peoples—could live together on the same lands. A vivid example is the George Washington Wampum Belt created by the U.S. government to commemorate the Canandaigua Treaty of 1794. Vitally important for understanding this agreement is that wampum is a sacred and ceremonial material that has been utilized by the Haudenosaunee since time immemorial until the present day.*

President George Washington commissioned the creation of a wampum belt to commemorate the signing of one of the most important, yet little known, documents in United States history. It has been alternatively referred to as the Treaty at Canandaigua, or Canandaigua Treaty, or the Pickering Treaty signed in Canandaigua, New York on November 11, 1794 (Jemison and Schine). This treaty was the result of about five years of constant negotiation between the Six Nations Iroquois, whose own name is *Haudenosaunee*, meaning "People of the Longhouse," and the newly formed Federal Government of the United States. The treaty was negotiated by Timothy Pickering, President Washington's Secretary of War. Most remarkable, however, is that Washington elected to utilize the medium of wampum as a diplomatic devise to commemorate this occasion and cement the deal with the Haudenosaunee.

Wampum is symbolic, or iconic, of a long and enduring lineage of immigrant and indigenous relationships in North America through the colonial and into the American periods. Uses of wampum on these inter-cultural occasions were almost always co-habitation agreements having to do with how diametrically different human communities—colonial and indigenous peoples—could live together on the same lands. Vitally important for understanding these agreements is the fact that wampum is a sacred and ceremonial material that has been utilized by the Haudenosaunee since time immemorial until the present day.

Below is a photo of the original George Washington Wampum Belt. It has been duplicated many times to commemorate the Canandaigua Treaty. Every year on November 11th, there is a parade to commemorate this treaty through Canandaigua, New York. During the parade, the wampum belt is used in the procession. So before describing the significance of the Canandaigua Treaty, I must discuss the ceremonial significance of wampum for the Haudenosaunee and its significance in American economic history.

## The significance of wampum

Wampum is a worked shell bead that was manufactured along the Eastern Seaboard. Its purple (black) and white colors had, and still have, cosmological significance for the Haudenosaunee. Purple is associated with earth, night, and the mischievous forces of creation, and white is associated with sky, day, and the benign forces of creation. Their account of creation includes stories of the creator twins who embody these opposing forces. Wampum is also featured in the story of the founding of the Great Law of Peace, which is the beginning of the Confederacy of the Iroquois, or the Haudenosaunee, which is composed of the Seneca, Tuscarora, Cayuga, Onondaga, Oneida, and Mohawk. One of the principle formulators of the Great Law of Peace was Hiawantha. While trying to promote the Great Law of Peace, he was stricken by a sorcerer who killed his family. His grief caused him to wander aimlessly throughout the Central New York region. It was the words of the Peacemaker (a sacred being who came to the Haudenosaunee with a message for creating a society based on principles of peace), who used wampum strings, which finally resolved Hiawantha's grief. It is said that through this condolence, Hiawantha's eyes were wiped of tears so he could see; his ears were swept clean of the dust so he could hear; and his

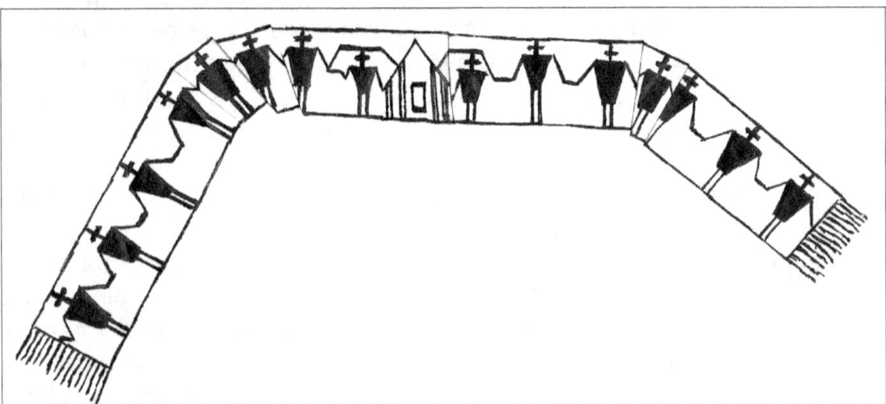

Figure 1. Drawing of the George Washington, or Canandaigua Treaty Wampum Belt. By Sandy Bigtree and the author.

throat was cleared of the lump so he could speak. Together, the Peacemaker and Hiawantha enlisted the help of a powerful being called the Tadadaho to form the Great Law of Peace. On the shores of Onondaga Lake, which is now surrounded by the city of Syracuse, these three planted the Great Tree of Peace. This was the beginning of the Longhouse tradition.

The Hiawantha or Confederacy Belt represents the relationship of the Haudenosaunee 5 Nations; from right to left Mohawk, Oneida, Onondaga (represented by the Central Tree), Cayuga and Seneca. The wampum belt is also represents the geography across what is now upstate New York and Canada. There is an intimate connection between the founding of the Longhouse and the peace of the land.

Today, clan chiefs who are raised into office through the Longhouse tradition are referred to as being condoled—as was Hiawantha—in Condolence Ceremonies. This makes leaders far sighted and good listeners and speakers on behalf of their clans and communities. In addition to raising chiefs, however, wampum is used in many Longhouse ceremonial contexts. It has many meanings particular to the way it is fashioned and the reason it was fashioned. Wampum is sometimes strung together into belts or into strings. Several of these items were exchanged between various groups, including Europeans, to substantiate verbal agreements. From the Haudenosaunee perspective, the cosmological meanings that wampum retained in ceremonial usage were the reason why wampum was used in intercultural exchanges.

Barbara Mann's description of the meaning of wampum integrates a number of historical, material, and cosmological attributes of the Haudenosaunee

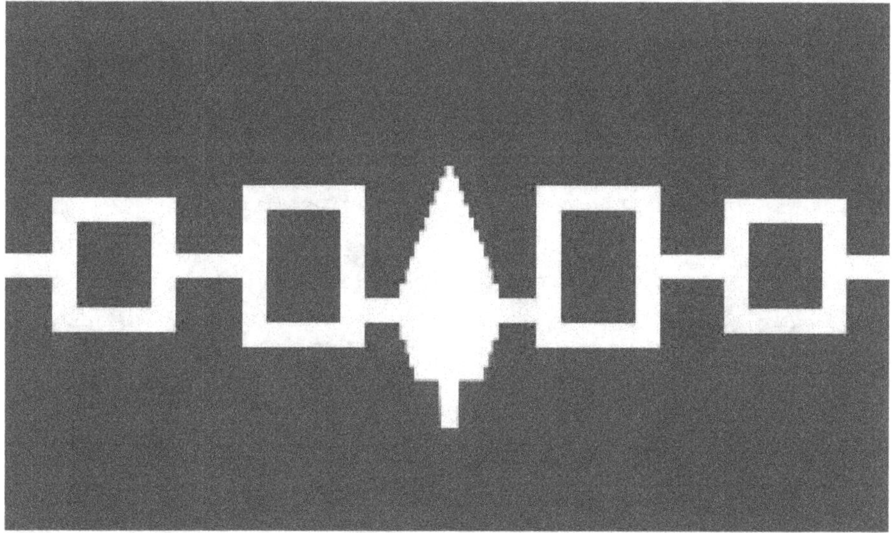

Figure 2. Hiawantha or Confederacy Wampum Belt (http://en.wikipedia.org/wiki/File:Flag_of_the_Iroquois_Confederacy.svg).

(Mann). Wampum is worked into a tubular shape bead from shell. The two colors of wampum, white and black (which is actually a deep purple), symbolize the integration of the sky (white) and earth (black). When strung together to form either strings or belts, wampum symbolizes the integration of the cosmos. In this way, wampum embodies the creation made possible by the interaction of celestial and earthly beings. Therefore, wampum allows the Longhouse people to directly participate in the processes of creation (Eliade).

Central to creation stories are the activities of the Twins, known most commonly in English as Sapling and Flint. Sapling's creative acts, described as benevolent, were followed by Flint's jealous creative impulses which made life harder. For example, when Sapling created a lush forest, Flint would follow up by creating thorns and briars. Early interpretations by missionaries, however, tended to transform these qualities into elements of absolute good (i.e. Sapling) and evil (i.e. Flint) which adhere closer with modern Christian understandings. According to Mann, this evaluation is distant from Haudenosaunee understandings. The activities of the Twins more closely describes an interaction of forces involved with creation, as an ongoing process, which move back-and-forth between ascending and descending forces in sky and earth (Mohawk). In the interplay of these tendencies, which are part of every living being, creativity (or participating in creation) is possible. The use of wampum in ceremonial contexts like the Midwinter Ceremony, articulates the ongo-

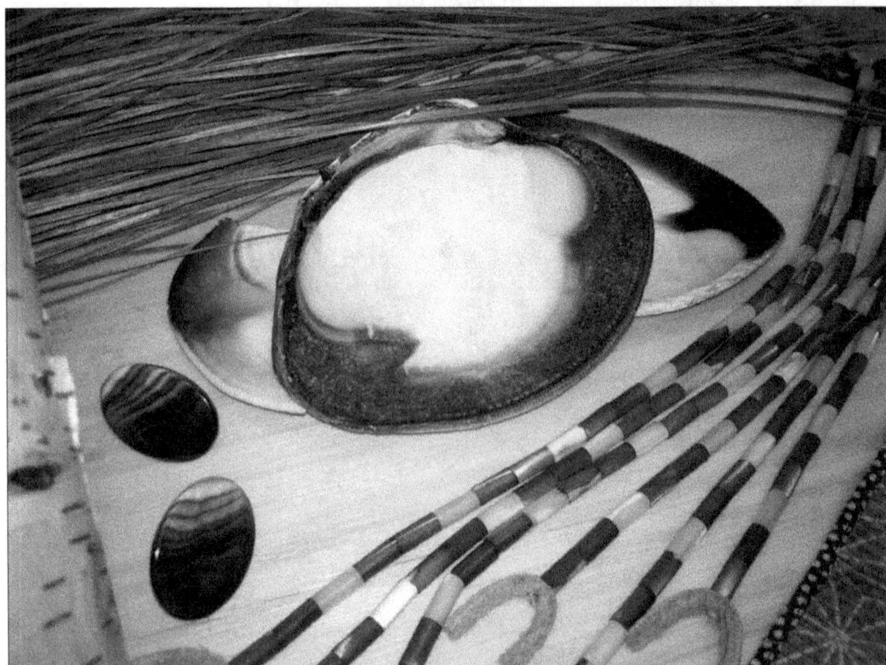

Figure 3. Quahog shell with wampum jewelry.

ing interaction of these twin forces, thus tying human creativity to creation.

The elder twin, Sapling, has associations with white and the sky, particularly the dawn, because saplings shoot up, or reach for the sky. This earns him nicknames "He Who Grasps for the Sky" and "Sky Holder." Conversely, the younger twin, Flint, has associations with black and the earth and is thus associated with medicine, herbs, tobacco, storms, climatic disturbances, and Medicine Societies. The activity of the creator twins is embodied by Wampum and strung designs of examples, cited by Mann, seem to adhere loosely to these meanings: a wampum belt made to commemorate a peace agreement whereby discrete nations of people could live side-by-side contrasts with a wampum design of a war ax made of black beads explicitly associating it with the twin Flint.

The use of wampum in Haudenosaunee ceremonies highlights its cosmological significance. Holding wampum at once enables one to speak and allows the speaker to speak *into* wampum. This seems to be an extension of their understanding of *orenda*, which, according to J.N.B. Hewitt is "'The force, principle, or magic power' assumed by the Iroquois 'to be inherent in everybody and being of nature and every personified attribute, property, or activity belonging to each of these and conceived to be the active cause, force, or dynamic energy, involved in every operation or phenomenon of nature, in any manner affecting or controlling the welfare of man'" (Tooker 1979, 15). In this light, wampum embodies not only the force of a living cosmos and natural landscape, but also the activities of human beings responsive to the conditions of creation.

Various accounts of the formation of the Haudenosaunee clearly articulate a formal relationship between wampum and the abolition of grief. Central to this story is Hiawantha who, with the Peacemaker, brought the Great Law of Peace to the Haudenosaunee. Hiawatha's grief began when his daughters were killed by witchcraft. Being a man dedicated to peace and therefore unable to seek revenge, which would continue the cycle of violence in which his people were embroiled, Hiawantha was overcome by grief. He wandered aimlessly trying to resolve his deep sense of loss. A cloud covered his mind. Rushes grew at one of his camping places. He made three strings from a joined rush plant. As he strung them together, he also put words together, saying, "If I found or met anyone burdened with grief as I am, I would console them. I would lift the words of condolence with these strands of beads, and these beads would become words with which I would address them" (*Traditional Teachings*, 24).

He continued his journey to a lake—now understood to be Tully Lake, thirty miles south of Syracuse, New York—where ducks floating in the water flew up so quickly that they lifted the water with them. Hiawantha walked across the dry bottom and noticed layers of shells of fresh water clams—some were white and some were purple—and he placed them in his deerskin pouch. The next day, he erected two poles and hung on them three shell strings of wampum, saying, "[t]hese strings would become words that would lift away the darkness which they [the grieving] are covered" (*Traditional Teachings*, 25). He was then invited into an Oneida village but remained at the village edge with strings of wampum hung over a horizontal pole and reciting his words of condolence. He sat in council with the Oneida leaders but did not speak.

When Hiawantha met the Peacemaker, he found someone who would listen to his sorrow and suffering. As he addressed Hiawantha, the Peacemaker strung additional wampum, making fifteen strings in all. After his ceremonial address, the Peacemaker said, "[m]y younger brother, now that your mind is clear and you are competent to judge, we shall make our laws, and when we have finished, we shall call the organization we formed THE GREAT PEACE" (*Traditional Teachings*, 27).

The formal structure of The Great Law of Peace is a series of wampums that outline the law's features for the Haudenosaunee. Fashioned by Hiawantha and the Peacemaker, these wampums are material manifestations of the familial relationships established, through a process of abolishing grief, between the original Five Nations. Wampum defines a landscape of peaceful relations between people who once were embroiled in cycles of violence.

## Wampum in American economic history

Formal moments of contact between the Haudenosaunee and Europeans and European Americans were often commemorated with wampum belts and treaties. Wampum and treaties, however, represent distinctive understandings of the responsibilities attendant to relationships between human beings. As we have seen, wampum embodies and expresses one's duties and responsibilities to a living cosmos. One of its primary uses extends familial relationships to other groups of people through condolence, or the abolition of grief, in order to establish peace. Likewise, treaties formally express responsibilities between human groups. Conversely, treaties have been interpreted—and systematically violated by the United States—in specific ways because their form

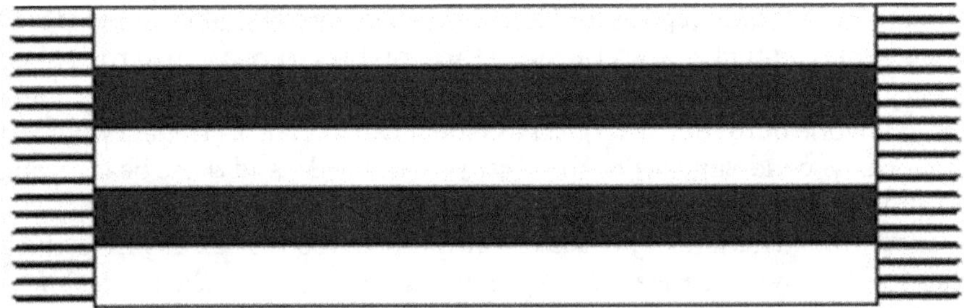

Figure 4. Representation of the Two Row Wampum, or Guswentha, from a 1613 agreement between the Dutch and Haudenosaunee (http://en.wikipedia.org/wiki/File:Tworowwampum.jpg ).

does not directly embody the responsibilities of human beings who occupy a living cosmos. From an indigenous Haudenosaunee perspective, treaties, unlike wampum, are self-referential—created by and for human beings independent from creation.

It is helpful to examine some features of European American interpretations of wampum to clarify the meaning of written documents such as treaties. Like the early missionary's understanding of black and white wampum as absolute good and evil, the commonly accepted, but mistaken, association between wampum and money says more about European concepts of value and freedom than it says about those of the Haudenosaunee. While wampum is clearly not money in a modern sense, the reason for the confusion of the two systems of value is worth pursuing.

Early French and English explorers noted the importance of wampum for the Haudenosaunee and continually compared it to jewels like pearls and diamonds and precious metal like gold and silver. But for Europeans, wampum was little more than costume jewelry and its high status among Native people puzzled them. They assumed that its value must be high due to the scarcity of shells used in its manufacture. Unlike the French and English who brought glass beads from Europe, Dutch settlers in Manhattan began manufacturing wampum commercially in the early seventeenth century. The Dutch would trade an authentic looking wampum, in strands of either 23 inches of white or 12 inches of black, for beaver pelts. So successful were the Dutch that wampum became the basic unit of exchange from New England to the Carolinas. With more European traders came an overabundance and devaluation of wampum. The result was inflation and instability of exchange rates and the wide-spread depletion of forests and game. In an attempt to stabilize the wampum--currency relationship, exchange rates were set at three black and six white beads for one British penny. This formally established the old Dutch ratio of 2:1 of white to black wampum. In 1770 the Thirteen Colonies, while moving toward independence, created a wampum mint, and it wasn't until 1899 that the last wampum factory closed down (Mann 41).

The extractive economy of the colonial period created individual fortunes at the expense of the natural world. Early modern notions of freedom were directly tied to creating and defending property, with the effect for Native people of extending their grief. In the European system of value, wampum "stood for" some good which enhanced ones prestige, or value, among other Europeans. The value of wampum extended only as far as it was able to determine the relative worth of a world of things fit for human consumption. In contrast, the Haudenosaunee understand wampum as an embodiment of an ongoing creative process. Its prestige arises from its ability to reveal and substantiate human relationships with the natural world.

A growing number of native and non-native scholars have recently been describing the long relationship between the Haudenosaunee and European

American people (Grinde, Johansen, Mohawk, Schaaf). This relationship is called the Covenant Chain, and its material expression is found in the Two Row Wampum, which dates to 1613. The Two Row Wampum at once documents a meeting between Dutch merchants and the Haudenosaunee, and clearly symbolizes the conditions by which both groups can peacefully occupy the land together. Each of the two rows represents a nation whose path is parallel to but does not intersect or interfere with the other. The first Dutch written account of this event resurfaced in 1968. In it, however, a constant emphasis is placed on gaining access to furs. It thus determines the future relationship between the nations strictly in terms of European economic concerns. While wampum and written treaties commemorate a single event, the significance for each group of people is markedly distinct (Hill).

Closer to home, however, is recent work on the influence of the Haudenosaunee on the development of Democracy in the United States. Haudenosaunee Chiefs were present and active participants at meetings in Lancaster, Pennsylvania (1744) and in Albany (1755), New York, which were important for determining the structure of the United States. Benjamin Franklin had witnessed a Condolence Ceremony in which men were raised to chiefs. In the 1750s, he served as secretary to a British commission that was negotiating with the Haudenosaunee. He also read Cadwallader Colden's *History of the Five Nations* and often talked about the native confederation of nations both here and abroad as a potential model for "civilized" government. Both John Adams and Thomas Jefferson were drawn to the Haudenosaunee model due to their suspicion, and outright hostility, toward European institutions and ideas.

In addition to intellectual inspirations, more common expressions of freedom were often symbolized by Native Americans, and Mohawks in particular. Before the Revolution, the word "American" was synonymous with the word "Indian." On a visit to England, the "Four Mohawk Kings," as they came to be known, created a great stir. When the "sons of liberty" dumped tea into the Boston harbor, they were dressed as Mohawks, not just to disguise their identities, but also to express their Americanness (Venables).

During the 1776 Philadelphia Convention, the Haudenosaunee presence was not an accidental occurrence, but an expression that European American identity and survival was contingent on Native American support. Both William Penn and Franklin acknowledged this. Other historical and material forces, however, finally determined the character of American freedom diametrically opposed to indigenous understandings by emphasizing the centrality of individual rights to private property.

After 1787, the character of U.S. and Native American relations changed dramatically from co-existence—a common understanding that European American existence was completely intermingled with Native American existence—to an emphasis on the subjugation of Indian people. The deep relationships between the Haudenosaunee and European people expressed themselves at specific moments as wampum belts and peace treaties. Yet, in spite of these ties, American freedom became inalienably associated with private property. Predictably, the mythic origins for democracy shifted away from indigenous influences to classical Greece and Rome. According to Robert Venables, as the U.S. entered the nineteenth century, European descendants chose to be Romans—in other words, their European oppressors. U.S. citizens could not simultaneously honor the original inhabitants of the Americas as vital to their own survival and self definition, and at the same time systematically destroy Native American communities and violate treaty obligations in the pursuit of land which defined their freedom. It is telling that today the US Federal Government does not recognize the Haudenosaunee, but does recognize each of the six nations individually that comprise the Confederacy. Ironically, during a meeting at the White House to which hundreds of Native American leaders were invited, President Clinton acknowledged the Haudenosaunee influence on American democracy.

This ambiguity in U.S. attitudes towards indigenous peoples has been problematic right from the beginning of the United States. For example, in 1776, a treaty was struck with the Haudenosaunee at Fort Pitt to keep the Six Nations neutral during the Revolutionary War. John Hancock commissioned a wampum belt for this occasion that symbolized the "13 fires" of the newly formed United States. The neutrality of the Haudenosaunee was a theme in the Treaty of Paris (1784) and the Peace Treaty at Fort Stanwix (1784). During the Revolutionary War, between 1776 and 1784, there occurred the infamous "Sullivan Clinton Campaign" against the Haudenosaunee in 1779 (see below). George Washington had reason to worry about Native American military power; his armies would later be defeated in battles with the Miami and Shawnee in the Ohio Valley area (Oren Lyons personal communication). The schizophrenia exhibited toward Native Americans, and particularly toward the Haudenosaunee by Washington and the United States until today, is a product of unsettled relationships. On the one hand, we admire and respect Native Americans and, on the other hand, we consider them to be a deterrent and an obstacle to building the United States.

## Canandaigua treaty-making

When making what is now called the "George Washington Belt," the young United States was participating in an ancient ceremonial and symbolic practice that was indigenous to the American continent. Of course, President Washington was doing this out of a sense of political urgency and was most likely uninterested or ignorant of the significance of wampum and of the importance of the Haudenosaunee for U.S. Democracy. As mentioned, just before the treaty at Canandaigua he had been much more invested on the wholesale destruction of the Haudenosaunee.

In spite of the Oneida having saved him and his troops from starvation at Valley Forge in 1779, General George Washington ordered the forced removal and/or destruction of the Haudenosaunee. According to both written and oral records, Washington ordered Major General John Sullivan to lead the Continental Army on a mission to destroy the power of the Iroquois, whether they were allies, enemies or neutral to the American Revolution. At that time, the Haudenosaunee were living in what is now New York State (founded in 1788) and had direct influence as far north as the Ottawa River, into Vermont, Massachusetts, Maine, and west into Pennsylvania. In December, General Washington recommended that the campaign be planned for 1779. Congress approved Washingtons plan on February 25, 1779, "directing him to take all measures necessary to protect the settlers and to punish the Indians." The other threat was seen as the Haudenosaunee supplying food to the British army. Washington knew the potential value of virgin lands in western New York, Pennsylvania, and other areas to the south and west, which were directly under the control of the Haudenosaunee. Washington wrote to Sullivan on May 31, 1779, "...The immediate objects are total destruction and devastation of their [i.e., the hostile tribes of the Haudenosaunee] settlements and the capture of as many prisoners of every sex and age as possible. It will be essential to ruin their crops in the ground and prevent their planting more."

Journals of the officers involved with the campaign report in some detail the extent of the destruction. Writing to Washington, one said, "The officers and men had been much impressed by the prosperity of the Indians and the extent of their villages. The greatest part of the Indian houses were larger than common [houses]" (Cook).

The campaign ended on about September 30th. Sullivan reported to the Continental Congress that 160,000 bushels of corn, as well as other fruit and vegetables, were destroyed. Forty Indian settlements had been burned to the ground. People recall that the winter of 1779–1780 was severe and most of the Haudenosaunee territory was under five feet of snow. Deer and other game were very scarce. It was presumed that many Haudenosaunee died from cold and starvation. According to the oral stories that have survived, many Haudenosaunee returned to their villages in the spring of 1780 to rebuild their homes and replant their crops. At Onondaga, people were in dire straits because their homeland had been particularly hard-hit. Those people who survived the attack were starving and there was little food to support them in the early season.

The Haudenosaunee refer to the office of the President of the United States as Honnahdahguyuss, which translates as "He Who Destroys Villages" or "Burner of Villages." It is directly linked to the Sullivan campaign and their broader history of relationships with the U.S. For example, when the Tadadaho of the Haudenosaunee, Sid Hill, wrote a letter of condolence to the President of the United States for the September 11, 2001 attacks on New York and Washington, DC, to George W. Bush, he referred to him as Honnahdahguyuss.

By 1790, Washington realized he had to make peace with the Haudenosaunee because military action had not worked. In 1790, he signed and ratified the "Indian non-Intercourse Act." This effectively required that all treaties with Native American nations had to be negotiated with the Federal Government and not with individual state govenments. This legal move ensured that the United States, and not individual States like New York, would have control of the land. It also required that negotiations between the US and Native American nations must be regarded as international treaties. In fact, Native American law rests on these treaties and is the model for International Law between the US and other countries.

The Treaty of Canandaigua of 1794, therefore, is a significant legal and cultural event in the history of the U.S. and the Haudenosaunee. It is regarded now, however, quite differently by each group. The religious import of the event is often overlooked. The fact that George Washington would make a wampum belt to commemorate an international peace agreement with the Haudenosaunee is a remarkable piece of American history that is little known today, in spite of its significance.

## References

Cook, Frederick, New York Secretary of State, editor. 1887. *Journals of the Military Expedition of Major General John Sullivan against the Six Nations of the Indians in 1779 with Records of Centennial Celebrations*. Prepared Pursuant to Chapter 361, Laws of the State of New York, of 1885. Auburn, NY: Knapp, Peck & Thompson.

Eliade, Mircea. 1954. *The Myth of the Eternal Return, or Cosmos and History*, Bollingen Series XLVI, translated by Willard R. Trask. Princeton, NJ: Princeton University Press (original French: 1949. *Le Mythe de l'éternel retour: archétypes et répétition*, Paris: Librairie Gallimard).

Gibson, John Arthur. 1992. *Concerning the League, The Iroquois League Tradition as Dictated in Onondaga by John Arthur Gibson*, newly elicited, edited and translated by Hanni Woodbury in collaboration with Reg Henry and Harry Webster on the basis of A.A. Goldenweiser's manuscript (dated 1912). Winnipeg, Manitoba: Algonquian and Iroquoian Linguistics, Memoir 9.

Grinde, Donald A., Jr. 1992. "Iroquoian Political Concept and the Genesis of American Government." In *Indian Roots of American Democracy*, edited by José Barreiro, 47–66. Ithaca, NY: Akwe:kon Press.

Hill, Richard. 1992. "Oral Memory of the Haudenosaunee: Views of Two Row Wampum." In *Indian Roots of American Democracy*, edited by José Barreiro, 149–159. Ithaca, NY: Akwe:kon Press.

Jemison, G. Peter and Anna M. Schein, co-editors. 2000. *Treaty of Canandaigua 1794: 200 Years of Treaty Relations Between the Iroquois Confederacy and the United*

*States*. Santa Fe, NM: Clear Light Publishers.

Johansen, Bruce E. 1982. *Forgotten Founders: Benjamin Franklin, the Iroquois, and the Rationale for the American Revolution.* Ipswich, MA: Gambit Publishing.

Mann, Barbara A. 1995. "The Fire at Onondaga: Wampum as Proto-Writing." *Akwesasne Notes: A Journal of Native and Natural Peoples, 26th Anniversary Issue* 1 (1): 40–48.

Mohawk, John C. 1987. "Cultural Encounters: Europe Meets the Indian Mind." *Northeast Indian Quarterly* 4 (1–2): 10–17.

———. 1992. "Indians and Democracy: No One Ever Told Us." In *Exiled in the Land of the Free: Democracy, Indian Nations, and the U.S. Constitution*, edited by Oren R. Lyons and John C. Mohawk, 43–72. Santa Fe, NM: Clear Light Publishers.

Schaaf, Gregory. 1990. *Wampum Belts & Peace Trees: George Morgan, Native Americans, and Revolutionary Diplomacy*. Golden, CO: Fulcrum Publishing.

Tooker, Elisabeth, ed. 1979. *Native North American Spirituality of the Eastern Woodlands: Sacred Myths, Dreams, Visions, Speeches, Healing Formulas, Rituals and Ceremonials*. New York: Paulist Press.

*Traditional Teachings*. 1984. Cornwall Island, Ontario: North American Indian Travelling College.

Venables, Robert W. 1992. "The Founding Fathers: Choosing to be the Romans." In *Indian Roots of American Democracy*, edited by José Barreiro, 67–107. Ithaca, NY: Akwe:kon Press.

Wallace, Paul A. W. 1994. *White Roots of Peace, The Iroquois Book of Life*, illustrated by John Kahionhes Fadden, foreword by Chief Leon Shenandoah, epilogue by John Mohawk. Santa Fe: Clear Light Publishers. (Originally published by University of Pennsylvania Press, 1946).

# 20

# THE GOSPELS AS IMPERIALIZED SITES OF MEMORY IN LATE ANCIENT CHRISTIANITY

JASON T. LARSON

*This paper considers the intersection of Christian and imperial memory in the physical Gospel book. Besides describing the function of gospel books in the post-Constantine Roman Empire, it examines the connection between the Roman construction and production of sites of memory that established Roman imperium in the Mediterranean and the development of the Christian Gospel codex as a site of memory within Christianity. It also explores the related issues of imperial and divine power as manifest through material things, the rhetoric of seeing and iconicity, and the invented tradition of Christian orthodoxy. The paper shows that the Christian Gospels and Roman sites of memory, despite a vast difference in their intended functions and original uses, both established imperium. It maintains that the creation of the Gospels' imperial iconicity was not based on their function as texts of spiritual enlightenment in late ancient Christianity, but on the fact that the production of Gospels as material cultural objects depended on Roman cultural exemplars and ideological rhetoric.*

When Emperor Constantine wrote to Eusebius, the chief librarian and scholar-in-residence at Caesarea sometime around 322 instructing him to produce fifty copies of the Christian Scriptures for use in the new imperial churches in Constantinople (Eusebius, *VC* 4.36), he fused Roman and Christian technologies of memory with conventional book production to create a new image of imperial power. Constantine's Bible was more than a pew Bible in the ancient churches of Constantinople. It was the prototype for the monumental Bibles that signified both the presence of Christ and the power of Roman *imperium* in late ancient orthodox Christianity. Gospel books were used as gifts to and from emperors (Gregory of Tours, *Gloria Confessorum*; *Liber pontificalis* 54.5); they filled the empty throne of Christ as surrogates for the absent Christ during imperial trials and ecclesiastical councils (Humfress 2007, 141–158; Rapp 2007, 196–197); and they indicated that "the Lord himself is present" when the Gospels were ritually opened during church services (Isidore of Pelusium, *Epistle* 1.136).

Christian and imperial corporate memory intersected at the site of the physical Gospel book. Roman production of sites of memory that established Roman *imperium* in the Mediterranean after Constantine incorporated the development of the Christian Gospel codex as a site of memory within Christianity. Therefore, the creation of the Gospels' imperial iconicity was not based on their function as texts of spiritual enlightenment in late ancient Christianity, but on the fact that the production of Gospels as material cultural objects was dependent on Roman cultural exemplars and ideological rhetoric.

## Christian Gospels and sites of memory

Memories are embedded in the social frameworks constructed by communities. They establish linguistic, communicative, and actuary contexts in which events, emotions, feelings, persons, and so on are remembered and given meaning (Halbwachs 1992). Without such settings, memories cannot survive (Hutton 1993, 78). They need continuous support from the materiality of specific frameworks (Connerton 1989, 37). Memories also depend on repetition and retelling through various representations and expressions, such as liturgies, narratives, and other kinds of performances (Castelli 2004, 11–12). Memories are thus a critical component of ritual, and both ritual and memory share the possibility (and even necessity) of becoming fixed in iconography and discourse, even to the point of acquiring stasis (Assmann 2000, 8).

Because of the cultural location of memories in social contexts, they are collective manifestations that belong to particular groups. They may "be remembered, forgotten, silenced, contested, or revised" (Climo and Cattell 2002, 10). At all times, memories depend on "cultural vehicles for expression" (Lambek and Antze 1996, 10). The French historian Pierre Nora called these cultural vehicles *lieux de mémoire*, "sites of memory." He argued that sites of memory can consist of just about anything so long as they are material things, have some significant functional purpose, and carry symbolic import (Nora 1994, 295). Nora's primary example is a modern archive: it inhabits material space, serves a functional purpose, and conveys symbolic power to whoever uses, controls, or destroys it.

Nora also showed that sites of memory are most apt to be concentrated around historical turning points in a society, "where consciousness of a break with the past is bound up with the sense that memory has been torn," such as the transition between the Republican age of Rome and the imperial age of Augustus and the emperors. When these perceived breaks in traditions occur, "an immense and intimate fund of memory disappears, surviving only as a reconstituted object beneath the gaze of critical history" (Nora 1994, 284, 288). These "reconstituted objects" are then used as icons of power relations between groups who promote a new memory and contest old mnemonic connotations. Sites of memory can thus become ideological battlegrounds out of which new narratives and traditions may be invented.

While there is no necessary connection between texts or other written documents and sites of memory, modern historiography has obviously privileged the "document" as the primary form of evidence and the archive as its most acceptable housing (Hutton 1993, 150). While it is the semantic content of such sites of memory that evokes reminiscence, it is still the *physical* document, the document's *materiality*, that shapes the way the past is to be remembered and recalled. Changes in the physical housing of the document often reflect a corresponding change in how the text is perceived and apprehended in the community's collective memory.

It is not much of a step from the privileged importance of the document and the archive to a corresponding recognition of the *book*. The book is a primary example of the communicative nature of memory as it is transmitted through a cultural medium that is defined by a particular social group. Any book is potentially a site of memory. Since sites of memory are important to truth claims and identity as well as for social and cultural continuity (Climo and Cattell 2002, 19), books that become *lieux de mémoire* are candidates to become contested sites. Indeed, few other kinds of sites have been subjected to more contests over identity and truth than books. Books are also subject to the vicissitudes of technologies of communication, information storage, and retrieval. In the process, they can serve as signposts to shifts in a group's perception of its foundational memories and narratives.

To be sure, not every book is a site of memory. But most world scriptures demonstrate the three-fold criteria of sites of memory, and some, such as the Adi Granth, Qur'an, Torah, and Bible fit exceptionally well. I am interested in how ancient Gospels gradually acquired these traits.

It has often been said that the Gospels, and the canon of the Bible in general, can be best understood as a library (for example, Beal 2011, 147–149). Though there are some similarities between a library and the Bible, in my judgment the metaphor is not appropriate. Libraries are typically "open," in that they contain within them a conglomeration of texts that may or may not reflect precisely the ideals, memories, and other essential information that preserves a community's sense of who it is and where it came from. In addition, it is entirely possible to "update" a library by weeding out those books that are no longer useful and by adding new texts. To be sure, there is a certain "scope" that both community libraries and modern institutional ones use to guide such decisions, but there is no necessary connection between the contents of the collection and the group that maintains, uses, and updates it.

The canon of scripture is different. The Bible is much more like the modern archive. Archivists generally understand their task to be to preserve the memory of the world in general and of the particular institution or social group they serve (Cook 1997; Hedstrom 2002). Archives are "houses of memory," and archivists keep "the keys to the collective memory" of nations, social groups, and institutions and to the protection of all the rights, privileges, and power of them (Wallot 1991, 282). The archivist's *ethos* is to preserve and provide access to the social memory of the collective and thereby encourage continuity with the past, with the group's or institution's sense of its roots, and corporate identity (Cook 1997, 2). The archivist knows, moreover, that institutional and collective memory preserved in such "houses of memory" is neither accidental nor haphazard, and is not preserved without controversy (or, at least, the *potential* for controversy). The archivist's major task is to survey all potential information and records that stream into his or her departments in order make determinations on what is worthy of institutional remembrance. The rest are consigned to collective amnesia, usually by destruction. However "open" the collection of New Testament documents may have been before Irenaeus' denouncement of other Christian texts posing as Gospels in the late second century CE, by the middle of the fourth century the matter of what documents were in the Christian New Testament was largely, though not completely, settled in imperial orthodoxy (Eusebius, *EH* 8; Athanasius, *Festal Letter* 39). As with a modern archive, the contents of the New Testament were deemed to be essential to the identity of imperial Christianity and was largely the product of a decision making process undertaken by imperially-sponsored intellectuals and bishops. This is the way archives work; they preserve those documents that conform to the ideological identity and self-understanding that an institution's or community's leadership has established, and in most cases the archive is maintained by a professional who is trained to keep the self-proclaimed memory and identity of the larger body intact. This process always involves the selection of documents and other materials that are approved by those in power, and often entails the disposal of unnecessary or even contrary material. Institutional archives are often symbolically charged and are considered the "final authority" when questions regarding the institutional or community memory manifest themselves (O'Toole 2002). That is to say, the physical existence of the archive, as well as the archive's contents, represents the official memory and authority of the community and has the power of the community's leadership behind it.

Initially, Gospel texts were bound together into leaf-books, or codices, that were scarcely more than notebooks. The codex was a new technology in the first century and had a specific function. Orators, such as Quintilian, used codex books as *aides de mémoire* for their speeches and for taking notes that might be useful in the future (*Institutes* 10.3.31–32). Even before Quintilian, codices were apparently used to archive letters and other documents of state, including military reports (Suetonius, *Julius Caesar* 56.6). Seneca assumed general knowledge of codices in *de Brevitae Vitae*, and the satirist Martial encouraged prospective readers to buy his own works (as well as those of other classical writers) in the new format because codices, being much less cumbersome than scrolls, were easier to travel with and handle (*Epigrams* 14.184–192). To the Romans, codices were portable archives that assisted the user in remembering what was deemed worthy of remembrance now or might be considered worthy and necessary in the future. The actual medium itself was little valued as a material object. It was the archival content of codices that was significant, the semantic message or data they contained that had to be captured and preserved, at least until they could be transferred to a more permanent or appropriate medium.

From the beginning, Christians adopted the codex as their preferred medium for preserving, storing, and retrieving messages that they regarded as central to the survival of their communities. Gospels proliferated between 70 and 180 CE as early Christian communities codified their memories, stories, and identities into written form. They used them as mnemonic and teaching aids for the enculturation of their communities, and they evidently shared the Roman view that codices were better suited than scrolls for this task. Certainly they shared Livy's perception that writing is the guarantor of memory ("*Litterae ... una custodia fidelis memoriae rerun gestarum,*" 6.1.2). As Christianity spread, and as new gospels were composed, competing memories of Jesus complicated the picture of what exactly counted as critical knowledge of Jesus. Some of the Christian literati, such as Irenaeus, suspected that many of these collections were responsible for the explosion of *haireiseis*, "heresies," throughout the Empire, and began to adopt only certain texts as their official "memoirs of the Apostles" (Justin, *Apology* 1.66.3, 1.67.3; *Dialogue* 100–107).

Written gospels were important because they encapsulated the words and acts of Jesus himself. Archivists speak of encapsulation to refer to a preservation technique that permits rearranging or re-preserving the contents of an archive on occasion without damaging the material. It is a flexible technique where items can be removed or added. The contents are preserved, while the old preservation medium is discarded or destroyed with no concern for its sanctity and no fear that the contents they contain will be lost or destroyed. Written texts worked similarly in the Greco-Roman world. Students, teachers, and preachers would appeal to the semantic content of something preserved in writing and not to the actual physical document itself. In other words, teachers and preachers did not spend their time discussing ligature, orthography, ink-quality, or cover design with their students in order to determine whether Aristotle's (or Jesus') teachings were worthy of discussion. So long as teachers and students or preachers and disciples knew the contents of what was written, what they were written on was of secondary importance.

The earliest gospels were therefore "places where memories are kept," but they were not yet sites of memory. To be sure, gospel books were material, functional, and semantic, but they possessed no symbolic or signifying importance. By the early third century, however, memories preserved in books and texts were augmented by memories preserved and transmitted by the ritualization of early Christian books (Parmenter, Chapter 4, this volume).

## Ritual and memory

In several recent studies, James Watts has shown that the authority of the Jewish Torah derived from its function as the regulative ritual law of the Jerusalem temple, with the result that the physical scroll itself became a symbol of Jewish identity and practice (Watts 2005). Drawing from the work of J. Z. Smith, Watts argues that the act of reading and interpreting any text, whether Torah or Gospel or Sibylline books, can be ritualized (Watts, Chapter 1, this volume). As Smith (1982, 63) noted, "Ritual relies for its power on the fact that it is concerned with quite ordinary activities placed within an extraordinary setting, that what it describes and displays is, in principle, possible for every occurrence of these acts." By any account, a book is an ordinary object and the act of reading it is an ordinary activity, as is the act of interpreting and understanding it. By drawing attention to their "ordinariness" in sacred or extraordinary settings, both the book and what is done with it or to it become ritualized.

Various gospels of the Christian churches were being ritualized by the beginning of the third century, if not sooner. Gospels validated and authenticated the rites of reading and interpretation, which transformed many of them into "scripture" and authoritative sites of memory. While at first this ritualization was limited to the texts' semantic element, by the end of the third century it was clear to both Romans and to Christians that the books themselves were charged with symbolic power that could be wielded in the face of adversity.

What this means is that the iconic gospel cannot be extricated from its ritualized context without negating the rites of which they were a part. For Christians such as Irenaeus, Tatian, Hippolytus, Origen, and many others, it simply was not possible for a Christian service to include the *Gospel of Truth* or *Judas* or any other "gospel-falsely-so-called" as part of the liturgy instead of Matthew, Mark, Luke, and John. Watts' example of the ritual origins of the Torah suggests a parallel with the canonical gospels. Parmenter's argument that the Bible's iconic dimension depends on its ritualized contexts indicates where to find the transition of gospels from archives to material sites of memory.

As Christian liturgy became more formalized and regulated through various authorities, books and reading were ritualized right along with the memories of Jesus of Nazareth that they contained. That actual books were already used by early Christian congregations is clear from sources as early as 1 Timothy 4:13, Revelation 1:3, and possibly even 1 Corinthians 11. In the second century, Justin describes in detail the Sunday assembly, where "the memoirs of the apostles or the writings of the prophets are read for as long as time permits," after which "the reader ceases, and the president speaks, admonishing and exhorting us to imitate these excellent examples" (*Apology* 1.67). By the middle of the second century, it is likely that the public liturgical reading of these "memoirs" and prophets was an "established and universal Christian liturgical custom" (Gamble 1995, 205–206). Twenty years after Justin, Irenaeus insisted that only the four gospels of Matthew, Mark, Luke, and John could be used in worship (*Against Heresies* 3.8–9). By the end of the second century, many churches had dedicated liturgical readers; Tertullian, for example, complains about how "the heretics" have no structure in their churches and anyone can hold the office of reader (*Against the Heretics*, 41). Hippolytus notes that the "reader is ordained when the bishop gives him the book" (*Apostolic Tradition* 1.12). In the *Apostolic Constitutions*, the reader is explicitly described as being a new "Ezra" who reads the Law to the people (*Apostolic Constitutions* 8.22). In the third century, Cyprian commented that it is the privilege of the reader to read the Gospel, for "nothing is more suitable for the voice which has confessed the Lord in a glorious utterance, than to sound Him forth in the solemn repetition of the divine lessons" before returning the Gospel "to the desk under the scaffold so as to be conspicuous to the multitude of the Gentiles and be beheld by the brothers" (Cyprian *Letters* 38.2; 39.4). Here, the Gospel is clearly positioned to be *seen* as much as heard. By the end of the fourth century, however, the privilege of reading the Gospel was evidently reserved for deacons and presbyters, while the *lector* or *anagnostes* was limited to lections from the Old Testament or the Epistles (*Apostolic Constitutions* 2.57.5; Jerome, *Epistles* 147.6; *Canons of Basil* 97; cf. Gamble 1995, 223).

The importance of this liturgy of the word lies in its direction of development. By the middle of the third century, the ritual's purpose was to impart the saving knowledge of God, for which there were two main guides: the teacher, such as Origen and other bishops, and the *logos*, the Christ/Word as mediated through the ritualized text. As Bernhard Lang puts it, "When listening to the biblical text as read and preached in church, Christians are somehow *taught by Christ himself*" (Lang 1997, 159, emphasis mine).

## The monumental Gospel and the book of empire

When Christians adopted the Roman codex as their preferred medium, the codex was still a utilitarian object that shared practical associations with ancient notebooks. Only rarely were codices used to publish literary works, although this was not completely unknown, and still less were they used for copying and publishing sacred texts or scriptures. With few exceptions, early Christian texts were produced for local use, not for mass consumption. These books were nondescript in appearance, written in pedestrian orthographic hands, and probably covered in basic leather covers, if in fact they were covered at all (Lowden 2007). As they were incorporated into Christian liturgy and ritual, small collections of "gospels" and "apostles" began to disseminate to other churches from their original places of publication. While the Apostolic Fathers knew of a number of Paul's letters, it is unclear whether these letters were kept as individual manuscripts or whether they were already being bound together. In the second century, however, Marcion possessed a collection of ten letters of Paul, and this may have been based on an earlier collection (Gamble 2006, 28). The earliest material evidence for such collection that has survived is a bound edition of Paul's letters from the early third century, the Chester Beatty Papyrus 46 (P 46), which was arranged with the letters in a sequence of decreasing length. Material evidence of Gospel codices begins to trickle in from the beginning of the third century, although it must be noted that even the most fragmentary single-page manuscripts of the Gospels were also originally part of codices. Literary evidence for collections of four Gospels containing Matthew, Mark, Luke, and John is found as early as Irenaeus in 180 (*Against Heretics* 3.11.8–9), and the earliest material evidence is the third-century Chester Beatty Papyrus 45, containing Matthew, Mark, Luke, John, and the Acts of the Apostles. Irenaeus' contemporary Tatian cut and pasted the four canonical gospels, as well as some additional gospel material, to create his *Diatesseron*, a single Gospel narrative used by the Syrian churches.

Thus by the third century, the "Apostle" and the "Gospel" were being bound in two codices, perhaps to indicate that each of these collections should not be added to or subtracted from. As I described above, their function was for liturgical teaching and reading. That is to say, the functional dimension of sites of memory was ritualized in the Gospel books of the third-century churches. The symbolic element began to manifest itself with Irenaeus' limitation of acceptable Gospels to Matthew, Mark, Luke, and John, and especially in his creative and inventive application of "four-fold" symbolism found in the Hebrew Bible and the book of Revelation. It was encapsulated by the technological practice of binding acceptable Gospels together for use in the Church. However, increasing ritualization of the Gospel books' physical dimension also owed much to Christianity's interactions with the Roman empire.

In the late second-century *Acts of the Scillitan Martyrs* (ca. 180), the proconsul in charge of prosecuting some Christians inquired as to the contents of the group's *capsa*, or "book bucket." They answered that the *capsa* contained "books and letters of Paul, a just man." While the *Acts* do not record the fate of these books, it is significant that this small Christian library was brought to the judgment hall. Whether they were brought by the prisoners who could not bear to be parted from them or whether they were hauled in by the magistrates as evidence is impossible to say. The books were understood to be valuable and important enough to warrant having them physically present at the trial. Here, the "books and letters of Paul" no longer served a purely functional purpose. The books in the *capsa* were now symbolic objects as much as they were functional ones.

Eusebius of Caesarea records another incident during the reign of Gallienus (253–268), when a certain Marinus came up for promotion as a centurion. However, he was a Christian, which evidently disqualified him from the honor of the office. The local bishop Theotecnus presented Marinus with a stark choice:

> And standing with him within, in the sanctuary, he raised his cloak a little, and pointed to the sword that hung by his side; and at the same time he placed before him the Scripture of the divine Gospels, and told him to choose which of the two he wished. And without hesitation he reached forth his right hand, and took the divine Scripture. (Eusebius, *EH* 7.15.4)

This symbolic gesture was not lost on either Theotecnus or Marinus. Eusebius records that Marinus went "before the tribunal, and manifesting greater zeal for the faith, immediately, as he was, he was led away and finished his course by death."

Second and third century sources do not permit us to assert with any confidence that Rome believed the physical books of the Gospels (or any Christian books) warranted systematic destruction or desecration during periods of persecution. Iconically speaking, there was nothing self-evidently dangerous about Christian books. The same cannot be said about their semantic or functional element, however, for it was well-known that Christianity was "constitutionally oriented to texts" from the beginning (Gamble 1995, 141). Other teachers and philosophers, such as Celsus and Porphyry, attacked the teachings of Christianity by critiquing the contents of their documents. In a similar vein, the satirist Lucian of Samosata ridiculed the Christians for virtually deifying a certain Peregrinus for his ability to interpret, explain, read, and even write Christian texts (*De morte Peregrinus* 11). The solution to the "Christian problem" did not yet entail actively seeking out and destroying the books used by the Christians, but it did involve discrediting them by exposing the texts as unworthy of serious teaching.

Roman officials, however, were already in the habit of ritually destroying books to target seditious groups that they thought threatened the established order of the state (Tacitus, *Annals* 4.35; see Sarefield 2007, 159). Their targets included the books of astrologers, diviners, magicians, and sorcerers, as well as religious and philosophical groups such as Manichaeans and, eventually, Christians (Sarefield 2007, 156–164). Book burning was symbolic and rhetorical as much as it was practical. By publicly destroying books, Rome demonstrated its rejection of "the beliefs contained and represented in these books" (Sarefield 2007, 161), and could even be understood as burning the author himself (Lucian of Samosata, *Alexander* 47).

While official censorship, confiscation, and destruction of books was common, it does not appear that emperors personally authorized the burning of texts on religious grounds until the fourth century (Sarefield 2007, 162). Bucking official precedent, Diocletian issued his first edict against the Christians in 303 and specifically targeted Christian books and churches for confiscation and destruction, rather than arresting individual Christians (Eusebius, *EH* 8.2.4). Local authorities soon followed suit in other cities and searched for Christian books to condemn. Eusebius records that he witnessed "the Divine and Sacred Scriptures committed to the flames in the midst of the market-places" (Eusebius, *EH* 8.2.1). The participation of bishops was mixed; some complied, while others resisted, and still others attempted (successfully, it seems) to fool the imperial agents into accepting either heretical works or non-religious works altogether (Augustine, *Breviculus collationis com Donatistis* 3.13.25 [*CSEL* 53.73-75]).

Other "Acts of Martyrs" describe similar incidents. The "Martyrdom of St. Felix" describes the saint meeting his fate because he refused to yield all of his books and parchments to the magistrate. In the "Acts of Euplus," the hero stormed into the council chambers to proclaim his faith, carrying his books as proof of his conviction. When asked why he kept these writings, since the emperor had made it a capital offense to keep them, Euplus responded: "Because I am a Christian and it [is] forbidden to give them up ... Whoever gives them up loses eternal life." Euplus was executed with his iconic Gospel hanging around his neck (Musurillo 1972, 311–315).

Euplus' story demonstrates that by around 304, the Gospel book was understood to be "scripture" by the Roman authorities and by Christians. The Gospel book functioned at a symbolic level for both the Romans and the Christians. For both groups, Euplus' possession of the book(s) was proof that he was a Christian, and the herald's description of him as "Euplus, the Christian, an enemy of our emperors and our gods" suggests that whoever possesses a copy of this book is an enemy of the State. Euplus, in other words, possessed an icon of defiance to Rome. He even identified his Gospel books with Christ. Although Euplus no doubt believed that eternal life was found in no one else, he also clung to his Gospel as a kind of talisman that kept the presence of Christ with him. It would be unthinkable to him to surrender the books without also denying Christ, which indeed is precisely what the Romans wanted. By condemning and destroying both Euplus and his Gospel, the Romans signaled their agreement with Euplus's book symbolism.

After Constantine's Edict of Milan in 313 and his gifts and interventions to and with the Christian churches, Rome began to adopt and co-opt the memories, traditions, rituals, and institutions of the Churches. But it is equally true that Christianity began conforming its outward institutions to the practices and processes of the Empire. Pre-Constantinian church traditions, customs, rituals, calendar, houses of worship, sites of memory, and uses of ritualized Gospel books were subsumed by the traditions, customs, rituals, and calendars of the state. Far from preserving and conserving the sites of memory and the iconicity of the ritualized Gospel book within the Church, Constantine's intervention imperializing Christianity. It invented a completely new tradition within Christianity by co-opting and deploying its most important memories and symbols into the service of the new imperial orthodoxy.

The new imperial Christian attitude toward books is an instructive example of this. Constantine did not merely rescind Diocletian's edicts; after the Council of Nicaea in 325, he reversed them with an Edict Against the Heretics that required all Christians to conform to the Catholic Church. Eusebius commented:

> Thus were the lurking-places of the heretics broken up by the emperor's command and the savage beasts they harbored. ... For the law directed that search should be made for their books [which they had to give up].

As for the authorized Gospels, Constantine recognized that they were essential for the growth and livelihood of the new churches that were created after the "conversion" of thousands of new orthodox, imperial Christians in Constantinople. Believing it to be prudent that the books be produced by the best, most "empire worthy" institution, Constantine asked Eusebius to provide the Empire with "fifty volumes with ornamental leather bindings, easily legible and convenient for portable use, to be copied by skilled calligraphists well trained in the art, copies that is of the Divine Scriptures, the provision and use of which you well know to be necessary for reading in church" (Eusebius, *Life of Constantine* 4.36).

Under Constantine, Gospels were transformed from small, practical, and functional codices into artifacts more befitting a king. Doron Mendels argues that the Church adopted and then transformed standard forms of Roman "media," which included statues, festivals, coins, public monuments and architecture, and especially books and public records, in order to "shape what people should know and decide what they should forget" (Mendels 1999, 3). This was very much the Augustan and imperial program of memory controlled throughout the empire; what was new under Constantine was the application of this to books, and in particular to the Gospel books. Christianity, with an assist from the Empire, adopted the Roman media of monuments as a form of memory creation and perpetuation and applied it to the Christian codex, with profound and long-lasting implications.

We can assess the impact that these new, monumental, and iconic Gospel books had on their viewers and users by using Mendels' (1999, 2) concept of a medium as "any means, agency, or instrument that stands between information and the public" that represents a constructed reality through the production of "works of communication." The ancient Romans employed a variety of rhetorical strategies to convey meaning and construct reality, but it was the visual spectacle of monuments that Romans deemed particularly effective for ideological communication in the empire at large. What mattered was what was viewed and its relationship to the viewer and the response the object evoked as part of the communicative process. As Christopher Frilingos (2004, 16) puts it, "Rome was a public society in which everything, everyone was at all times on display." Through an interactive experience of viewing the physical symbols of Rome, citizens could "ground themselves in the Roman world" (Frilingos 2004, 27).

Constantine's monumental Gospel books now became imperial icons that, through word and text, communicated the memory of Jesus *and* of the new understanding of the Kingdom of God. They functioned just as the *Res Gestae* and other dedicatory inscriptions had throughout the empire (Larson 2012). However, this was not all. The monumental Gospel now stood next to monumental statues of Constantine and other emperors, conferring sacred and salvific benefits on those who viewed them. The Gospel book after Constantine was part of the imperial spectator culture, where "showing, performance, and affirmation became as important as argument" (Cameron 1991, 79). Now, the Gospel book itself was shown, performed, and affirmed not merely for its role in the formation and preservation of Christian identity, but of the Roman Empire as well.

This was the beginning of the age of the production of the great codices, and there is a noticeable physical change in the surviving texts. Gospels became much larger and were produced with higher quality parchment and in more professional orthographic hands. Perhaps more significantly, it was also during this period that we begin to find physical evidence of decorated book covers. John Lowden catalogued the evidence of book covers from the late third to the sixth century. The most elaborate examples come from the end of this period: the painted wooden covers of the Freer Gospels ("Codex Washingtoniensis" or simply "W", possibly seventh century) depicting the four evangelists functioned as a protective box whose sole purpose was to *signify* the contents inside, rather than encourage readers to actually open, read, or otherwise use the text (Lowden 2007, 23). What is more, each of the evangelists depicted on the covers of Codex W bear their own gold and jeweled Gospel books, an additional indication of the iconic significance of Gospel books.

In fact, there is much earlier literary evidence for exactly the kinds of Gospel books depicted on the Freer covers. At the end of the fourth century, Jerome made a caustic criticism of books written in gold on purple parchment and studded with jewels and gems (Jerome, *Ep.* 22.32). In the *Apophthegmata Patrum*, there are numerous sayings of the Desert Fathers that demonstrate the presence of "many fine books" in the desert, as well as a deep ambivalence about them. By the fifth century, Emperors were already gifting and receiving brilliantly adorned Gospel books. Gregory of Tours, in the *Gloria Confessorum*, describes how a dishonest goldsmith attempted to swap fake silver hinges for the original gold ones on a Bible of the emperor Leo (457–474), which had a "cover for enclosing the holy Gospels, a paten, and a chalice made from pure gold and precious gems." In the *Liber Pontificalis*, we read of a papal "Gospels with gold covers and precious jewels, weighing fifteen pounds" that was a gift of the Emperor Justin in the early sixth century (both cited in Lowden 2007, 32). These texts are roughly contemporary, with the only surviving gold and jeweled binding known from the fifth to early seventh centuries, the Gospel book of the Lombard queen Theodelinda, which bears a strong resemblance to the gold and jeweled book depicted on the famous *Christus Imperator* icon of St. Catherine's Monastery on Mount Sinai (Lowden 2007, 33–34). Concerning the evidence for these early monumental, "imperial" gospels, Lowden concludes that most of them were primarily intended to be seen, not actually (or not only) read. The iconicity of these monumental books "offered a message too, perhaps even more forceful than that imparted by the texts themselves" (Rousseau 2007, 2).

## Conclusion

The postcolonial theorist Homi Bhabha noted that, in the context of British imperialism in India, "the holiest of books—the Bible—*having both the standard of the cross and the standard of the empire* finds itself strangely dismembered" (Bhabha 2004, 131). In assessing the evidence of the Gospel's change in iconic status from the fourth through the sixth centuries, it is apparent to me that the surplus meaning of Gospel books was determined in no small measure by the world of Constantinian imperialism inscribing itself on the icons, symbols, and even mythologies and narratives of the various forms of Christianity throughout the Mediterranean. The transformation of the Gospel book from an archive of preaching and teaching aids to a persecuted thing consigned to *damnatio memoriae* by Diocletian and then to its lofty status as the iconic book of the Empire captures in a microcosm, not the inexorable movement from "paganism" to "Christianity," but rather a discourse of identity over how Christianity would locate itself in its larger imperial context. The imperial Gospel was not merely a prop in the invented tradition of Orthodox Christianity in the Constantinian Age; in the hands of the Emperor, it was the icon that led the procession.

The Gospels did indeed bear the standards of both the cross and the empire, as Bhabha observed about the British colonial King James Bible. In the process, a new site of memory was created where Christian identity would be established and contested for the next sixteen hundred years. What for Bhabha was an icon that was "strangely dismembered" in the nineteenth century was, in the early days of the Christian Roman Empire, an iconic site of memory that was strangely "dis-remembered" when the imperial Book replaced the memoirs of the Apostles.

## References

Assmann, Jan. 2006. *Religion and Cultural Memory: Ten Studies*. Stanford, CA: Stanford University Press.

Beal, Timothy. 2011. *The Rise and Fall of the Bible: The Unexpected History of an Accidental Book*. Boston, MA: Houghton Mifflin Harcourt.

Beard, Mary. 1991. "Writing and Religion: Ancient Literacy and the Function of the Written Word in Roman Religion." In *Literacy in the Roman World, Journal of Roman Archaeology* Supplement 31, edited by J. H. Humphrey, 35–58. Ann Arbor: University of Michigan Press.

Bhabha, Homi K. 2004. *The Location of Culture*. New York: Routledge.
Brunt, P. A. and J. M. Moore. 1967. *Res gestae divi Augusti: The Achievements of the Divine Augustus.* Oxford: Oxford University Press.
Burton-Christie, Douglas.1993. *The Word in the Desert: Scripture and the Quest for Holiness in Early Christian Monasticism*. Oxford: Oxford University Press.
Cameron, Averil. 1991. *Christianity and the Rhetoric of Empire*. Berkeley: University of California Press.
Casey, Edward. 2000. *Remembering: A Phenomenological Study*. 2nd ed. Bloomington: Indiana University Press.
Castelli, Elizabeth A. 2004. *Martyrdom and Memory: Early Christian Culture Making.* New York: Columbia University Press.
Climo, Jacob and Maria Cattell. 2002. *Social Memory and History*. Walnut Creek, CA: AltaMira Press.
Connerton, Paul. 1989. *How Societies Remember*. Cambridge: Cambridge University Press. http://dx.doi.org/10.1017/CBO9780511628061
Cook, Terry. 1997. "What is Past is Prologue: A History of Archival Ideas since 1898, and the Future Paradigm Shift." *Archivaria* 43. Retrieved April 8, 2011, from http://www.mybestdocs.com/cook-t-pastprologue-ar43fnl.htm
Elsner, Jaś. 1991. "Cult and Sculpture: Sacrifice in the Ara Pacis Augustae." *Journal of Roman Studies* 81: 50–61.
———. 1996. "Inventing Imperium: Texts and the Propaganda of Monuments in Augustan Rome." In *Art and Text in Roman Culture,* edited by Jaś Elsner, 32–53. Cambridge: Cambridge University Press. http://dx.doi.org/10.2307/300488
Flower, Harriet I. 1998. "Rethinking Damnatio Memoriae." *Classical Antiquity* 17(2): 155–187.
Frilingos, Christopher. 2004. *Spectacles of Empire: Monsters, Martyrs, and the Book of Revelation.* Philadelphia: University of Pennsylvania Press.
Gamble, Harry Y. 1995. *Books and Readers in the Early Church.* New Haven, CT: Yale University Press.
———. 2006. "Bible and Book." In *In the Beginning: Bibles Before the Year 1000*, edited by Michelle Brown, 15–35. Washington, DC: Smithsonian Institution.
Gowing, Alain. 2005. *Empire and Memory: The Representation of the Roman Republic in Imperial Culture*. Cambridge: Cambridge University Press. http://dx.doi.org/10.1017/CBO9780511610592
Gūven, Suna. 1998. "Displaying the *Res Gestae* of Augustus: A Monument of Imperial Image for All." *Journal of the Society of Architectural Historians* 57(1): 30–45.
Halbwachs, Maurice. 1992. *On Collective Memory*. Chicago, IL: University of Chicago Press.
Hedrick, Charles. 2000. *History and Silence: Purge and Rehabilitation of Memory in Late Antiquity*. Austin: University of Texas.
Hedstrom, Margaret. 2002. "Archives, Memory, and Interfaces with the Past." *Archival Science* 2: 21–43. http://dx.doi.org/10.1007/BF02435629
Humfress, Caroline. 2007. "Judging By the Book: Christian Codices and Late Antique

Legal Culture." In *The Early Christian Book*, edited by William Klingshirn and Linda Safran, 141–158. Washington, DC: Catholic University Press.

Hutton, Patrick. 1993. *History as an Art of Memory*. Hanover, NH: University Press of New England.

Keightley, Georgia. 2005. "Christian Collective Memory and Paul's Knowledge of Jesus." In *Memory, Tradition, and Text: Uses of the Past in Early Christianity*, edited by Alan Kirk and Tom Thatcher, 129–150. Atlanta: SBL Press.

Krencker, Daniel M. and Martin Schede. 1936. *Der Tempel in Ankara*. Berlin: DeGruyter.

Lambek, Michael and Paul Antze. 1996. *Tense Pasts: Cultural Essays in Trauma and Memory*. New York: Routledge.

Lang, Bernhard. 1997. *Sacred Games: A History of Christian Worship*. New Haven, CT: Yale University Press.

Larson, Jason T. 2012. *The Gospels as Ritualized Sites of Memory in Late Antiquity: Books, Memoirs, Monuments*. Ph.D. dissertation, Syracuse University.

Lowden, John. 2007. "The Word Made Visible: The Exterior of the Early Christian Book as Visual Argument." In *The Early Christian Book*, edited by William Klingshirn and Linda Safran, 13–47. Washington, DC: Catholic University Press.

Mendels, Doron. 1999. *The Media Revolution of Early Christianity: An Essay on Eusebius' Eccleisastical History*. Grand Rapids, MI: Eerdmans.

Musurillo, Herbert. 1972. *The Acts of the Christian Martyrs*. Oxford: Clarendon Press.

Nicolet, Claude. 1994. *Space, Geography and Politics in the Early Roman Empire*. Ann Arbor: University of Michigan Press.

Nora, Pierre. 1994. "Between Memory and History: Les Lieux de Mémoire." In *History and Memory in African-American Culture*, edited by Genevieve Fabre and Robert O'Malley, 284–300. New York: Oxford University Press.

O'Toole, James M. 2002. "Cortes's Notary: The Symbolic Power of Records." *Archival Science* 2: 45–61. http://dx.doi.org/10.1007/BF02435630

Rapp, Claudia. 2007. "Holy Texts, Holy Men, Holy Scribes: Aspects of Scriptural Holiness in Late Antiquity." In *The Early Christian Book*, edited by William Klingshirn and Linda Safran, 194–224. Washington, DC: Catholic University Press.

Rousseau, Philip. 2007. "Introduction." In *The Early Christian Book*, edited by William Klingshirn and Linda Safran, 1–11. Washington, DC: Catholic University Press.

Sarefield, Daniel. 2007. "The Symbolics of Book Burning: The Establishment of a Christian Ritual of Persecution." In *The Early Christian Book*, edited by William Klingshirn and Linda Safran, 159–175. Washington, DC: Catholic University Press.

Smith, Jonathan Z. 1982. *Imagining Religion: From Babylon to Jonestown*. Chicago, IL: University of Chicago Press, 1982.

Wallot, Jean-Pierre. 1991. "Building a Living Memory for the History of Our

Present: Perspectives on Archival Appraisal," *Journal of the Canadian Historical Association* 2: 263–282.

Watts, James W. 2005. "Ritual Legitimacy and Scriptural Authority." *Journal of Biblical Literature* 124: 401–417. http://dx.doi.org/10.2307/30041032

Zanker, Paul. 1990. *The Power of Images in the Age of Augustus*. Ann Arbor: University of Michigan Press.

# 21

# Possessing the Iconic Book: Ben Sira as Case Study

Claudia V. Camp

*I propose that the notion of possession adds an important ideological nuance to the analyses of iconic books set forth by Martin Marty (1980) and, more recently, by James Watts (Chapter 1, this volume). Using the early second century BCE book of Sirach as a case study, I tease out some of the symbolic dynamics through which the Bible achieved iconic status in the first place, that is, the conditions in which significance was attached to its material, finite shape. For Ben Sira, this symbolism was deeply tied to his honor-shame ethos in which women posed a threat to the honor of his eternal name, a threat resolved through his possession of Torah figured as the Woman Wisdom. What my analysis suggests is that the conflicted perceptions of gender in Ben Sira's text is fundamental to his appropriation of, and attempt to produce, authoritative religious literature, and thus essential for understanding his relationship to this emerging canon. Torah, conceived as female, was the core of this canon, but Ben Sira adds his own literary production to this female "body" (or feminized corpus, if you will), becoming the voice of both through the experience of perfect possession.*

My entry point into the topic of iconic books is a book in the Old Testament Apocrypha, variously known as Ecclesiasticus, Sirach, or the Wisdom of Ben Sira.[1] Though little known by many Bible readers today, Sirach is the subject of a continual stream of scholarly research, especially by Catholics, whose tradition upgrades the book's status from the dismissive Protestant label "Apocrypha" and rates it rather "Deuterocanonical." I shall turn in a moment to why Sirach is relevant for our discussion but, before trying to capture your interest in the esoteric, let me frame my work here in terms of some larger questions and concerns that might help make sense of the particulars.

Thinking of the Bible as an "iconic book" has long been part of the intellectual repertoire I bring to studying this material. It is entirely possible that

1. For convenience, I follow a common convention in referring to the book itself as Sirach and its author as Ben Sira.

the term latently entered my deep mental recesses through a now forgotten encounter with the iconic Martin Marty's iconic article about America's iconic book (Marty 1980). But it was my experience teaching students in the Bible Belt that brought the notion of iconicity powerfully to mind as a way of understanding the oxymoronic phenomenon of self-proclaimed biblical literalists who were so little concerned with most of what the Bible actually says. Polling data has consistently shown the discrepancy between the devotion Americans profess to the Bible and amount they actually read it. For example, the average of Gallup polls in 2005, 2006, and 2007 indicates that 31% of Americans believe that the Bible is the actual word of God, to be taken literally,[2] with another 47% regarding it as inspired by the word of God. Despite this level of proclaimed reverence, 2000 polling showed that 41% read the Bible rarely or never and another 10% read it less than monthly, while 37% read it at least once a week.[3] But I would suggest that such figures still mask the extent of the disjunction, insofar as they measure only *how often* people read the Bible, but not *how much* of it they typically *skip*. In other words, of the 37% who do say they read at least once a week, how many are re-reading beloved portions rather than reading widely?

Marty's essay analyzes the reasons why critical approaches to the Bible are almost doomed to failure in this "iconolotrous" environment, focusing on the Bible's role in the "carapace" of images that constitute the U.S. American ideology of identity. Such a carapace "is necessary in order for individuals and society to function cognitively or morally" (10): a collective carapace gives meaning, indeed, prevents madness (6). Noting President Grover Cleveland's rejection of "notes or criticisms or explanations about authorship or origin or even cross-references" in favor of "just the good old book under which I was brought up," Marty (2) suggests that "what is going on here is a reference to an aspect of the American *consensus juris*, the minimal basis of consensus on which civil life is ordered," powerful no matter how minimal that consensus may actually be. Invoking the notion of icon helps "lead beyond merely rational analysis to the root emotions of people in a culture. Only then can we assess the power situation, which has little to do with the *content* of ancient scriptures but much to do with the *form* of modern American life" (4). Marty thus argues that "the main reason for ignoring or resisting critical scholarship has been the iconic regard for the Bible as an object in the national shrine, whether read or not, whether observed or not: it is seen as being basic to

2. This represents a drop from 38% in the years just before and after Marty wrote, though consistent on average since 1991.

3. The relevance of the Bible to Americans was also measured in the 2000 poll, with 65% of Americans agreeing that the Bible "answers all or most of the basic questions of life," but 28% of those reading it rarely or never (though, to be fair, half of that group read it at least weekly). Relevance was also measured in Gallup's 2003 poll: 49% said they believed that the Bible "has decisive authority over everything I say and do," while only 28% said they "regularly study the Bible to find direction for my life." The Pew survey on religion in 2010 showed that 37% of Americans read the Bible at least once a week, the same as Gallup found in 2000.

national and religious communities' existence. They hold it in awe and give *latreia* [sacred service] to it" (21).

Though I was never inclined to preach or pastor, my own life and early teaching experience tracked Marty's exact description of those biblical scholars (whom he assumed to be typical in 1980 and I suspect are not much less so now) who "fused critical scholarship and faith, and wonder why others are not allowed to share their enthusiasm" (17). To personalize Marty's poignant encapsulation of the experience: having come through the passages of faith and life inspired by childhood experience of the Bible as icon in mind, home, church, and culture, [and] having had the critical sense enliven my adult life, I was often mystified about why so many of my students did not make my passage (20–21). Further experience, though, eventually led me inductively to the realization Marty again explicates so perspicaciously: that the "iconic sense" so many of my students bring to the classroom produces in them the intuition "that there will be less, not more, Bible as well as less, not more, faith, once one enters the mental furnished apartment in which the critic has no choice but to live" (17).

I would, though, like to add a couple of thirty-years-on footnotes to Marty's still-pertinent analysis. The first has to do with the change in critical methods that have emerged during this time. When Marty wrote in 1980, the dominant forms of critical scholarship were historically based, efforts either at historical reconstruction of events related to or in the Bible or at reconstruction of the development of biblical religion based on hypotheses about the dating and authorship of different parts of the literature. Teaching such critical approaches meant asking students to judge the truth of what is written in the Bible by external and, self-proclaimedly, human criteria—either the sources and standards of evidence used by historians, or scholarly constructions like the documentary hypothesis. "Don't believe the Bible," says the professor, in effect. "Believe me!" No wonder students worried about having less, not more, of the Bible or faith as a result.

In ensuing years, though, both my own changing philosophy of teaching and the growth of literary methods of biblical interpretation have significantly reoriented my approach to teaching critical biblical study. Forget JED and P! Let's just read Genesis 1 and 2, with their demonstrably different stories of creation, and see what comes up. How could self-proclaimed biblical literalists object to just *reading what the Bible says* and thinking about the issues of interpretation that that reading itself presents? Fairly easily, I found. And here is where I'd make my first small addendum to Marty's analysis. It's not just that the iconic nature of the book can make reading it irrelevant, it's that there seems to exist in certain sectors of U.S. Christianity a set of beliefs that subjects what the Bible says, prima facie, to the most tortured of hermeneutics in order to *make* it say what someone has predetermined it *should* say. The tenets of (a certain kind of) Christian doctrine control what the Bible is allowed to say, while convoluted twists and turns of evidence and logic ensure that it does so. Iconicity in this case does not simply ignore biblical content, but subjects content to its service. Thus, for example, despite the "appearance" of two creation stories in Genesis, some students come prepared with (or at least have no problem finding with a little web surfing) seemingly reasonable but actually specious refutations of the two story "theory" (Jackson 1991). I will not be the first to observe the degree to which these intellectual contortions are, paradoxically, driven by the implicit need to have a Bible whose truth can be measured by the same standards of scientific and historical credibility, however misconstrued, that caused the problems in the first place. *Die Aufklärung über alles.*

I find reason for concern in this development, and here is my second footnote to Marty. Whereas he anticipated the increasing de-centering of the Bible in the midst of the increasing number of icons in our secular-pluralist culture, my experience in Texas over the last thirty years suggests, whether instead of or despite that de-centering, that the anti-critical spirit is becoming increasingly rigid. Marty notes the wishful thinking of William Rainey Harper's 1892 declaration that "the cry of our times is for the application of scientific methods to the study of the Bible," suggesting that Harper "heard the cries of University of Chicago students and the lay elite, while Grover Cleveland probably spoke for louder cries when he wanted an uncommented-upon Book" (18). One might have thought that the commonplaces of critical biblical scholarship had failed to take hold in the national consciousness in the late nineteenth century because few lay Bible readers had had the opportunity to encounter such insiders' information, that their tendency to hold the Bible as an icon was founded in an ignorance that could be, as Marty puts it, *exploited by others* to anti-critical ends (17). But no such overt control is needed, it seems, for some of my students—on their way to becoming the twenty-first century "lay elite"—who, when offered the opportunity and sympathetic guidance to think critically, simply self-censor. The problem, in other words, is not a conscious refusal to accept the best of what scholarship has to offer, but rather the self-protective impulse to *stop thinking* when one's beliefs and identity are at stake.

I have a hypothesis about this situation that I am not sure how to test. But let me propose it nonetheless: such students are evidence of a change in the attitude or affect at work in the iconizing relationship between believer and Bible. Whereas Marty spoke of people holding the Bible in awe and rendering it sacred service, what I think I see is an attitude of possession that makes the Bible the servant of its wielder. As James Watts (Chapter 1, this volume) has pointed out, there is a natural circle of authorization that moves between the authorization *of* scriptures through ritual manipulation and the authorization provided *by* scriptures to the persons and institutions so engaged. What happens, though, in an individualistic culture like our own, where Bible-believers often shun the church as institution and its collectively authorizing public rituals in favor of contexts and practices that reinforce the individual's personal salvation and, concomitantly, their personal authority to interpret the Bible to suit themselves?[4] The iconic book is important in this situation because it is something they *have*, something that ostensibly controls their lives but, *as thing*, is also a possession *they control* (compare Yoo in this volume). While on one level reading the Bible critically might seem to reinforce its status as possession, through exerting one's intellectual control over it, the effect is paradoxically the opposite. For in order to be possessed, the book's "thinginess"—indicative of its canonically definitional comprehensiveness and completeness[5]—must be all the more reinforced. Only an integral "It" can be possessed, not a complex "Other" with twists and turns that may surprise or provoke its possessor to change. The carapace at stake is not that of national identity but of individual identity, and opening its biblical component may be hazardous to one's faith. In place of the collective consensus that allowed the freedom of mystical reverence, and in a context where the diffusion of icons calls the true value of any into doubt, the "Bible believer" is forced to defend the icon as much as worship it, in effect reversing the position of relative strength between the two.

If only understanding a problem would allow it to be solved! In my case, at least, all I can say is that it has inspired another set of questions about the other end of the process, that cultural point, or phase, in which the iconic potential of the Bible first emerged. The question of when and why the diverse materials that constitute the Bible were written and gradually assembled into the compilation we now have—what we might call the question of canon formation—has long lurked in the background of biblical scholarship and in the last ten to fifteen years has increasingly come to the fore in its own right, engendering both new consensus (about the work of scribes, for example) and a whole new range of debate on dates and circumstances (see, e.g. Davies 1998, Schniedewind 2004, Carr 2005, and van der Toorn 2007).

One issue is definitional: to what are we referring with the term "canon"? A common and seemingly commonsense approach within biblical studies identifies two phases of development. The earlier phase, for which the term "scripture" is sometimes preferred, involves a possibly open-ended body of writings considered authoritative or even sacred by a given community. "Canon," in this case, is reserved for the later phase when one finds a closed or virtually closed list of standardized texts. The line between the two is fuzzy, though, and there have been various efforts to theorize the concept more precisely.[6] As the

4. This is, at least, the subjective experience involved. There are in fact, of course, institutional authorities lurking in the shadows, but they function by masking rather than declaring themselves. Individualism, that is to say, is as socially constructed a value as any other.

5. Beal (2002 and in this volume) argues that a comprehensive, A–Z, quality is one of five definitive traits of books called "bibles," which must also be authoritative, exclusive, practical, and devotion-inspiring.

6. Graham (1987, 142) speaks of a diffuse process that begins already in a "perceived unicity of scripture" that often "leads to a felt need for an authoritative 'canon' … or 'list'" and is

ensuing discussion will make clear, I find that Watts (Chapter 1, this volume) brings helpful precision to this question with his three-dimensional model of the functions of what he calls "scriptures." Watts speaks of the semantic dimension (the meaning of what is written, including all matters of interpretation and commentary); the performative dimension (including public and private reading of scriptural words as well as dramatization and artistic rendition of scriptural content); and the iconic dimension (the physical form of scriptures which is often decorated, manipulated, and prominently displayed or hidden). The iconic dimension will be of particular importance to my own argument, though all overlap to some degree. Watts' model is synchronic, however, and I would like to add some diachronic sensibility to it with my study of biblical scriptures in a time of transition.

To provide some background for the uninitiated with respect to the Bible: most scholars would agree that some sense of authoritative writing, connected to some of the material now in its first six books, had developed by the late monarchic period (late seventh century BCE); or, alternatively, was pushed to an unexpected level of cultural prominence by the events of that period, events that ultimately led to the political demise of the nation of Judah at the hands of the Babylonians. And there is likewise widespread agreement that the creation and promulgation of authoritative writings increased during the ensuing exile in Babylon of the leadership class and, later, in the attempts of this class to reassert their authority and control when they returned to Judah under the Persians during the fifth century. But this was still only the beginning of the process of the formation of the Hebrew canon, which was still not finished at the turn of the Common Era.

In those 400 years in between, we have little direct data regarding this religio-literary process, so there are many debates about how and why the different writings reached the form they finally did. I'm going to ignore most of those because my interest lies in a different problem, namely, how and why the notion of the materials' *reaching a form*—becoming, in other words, *a thing*, which is to say, potentially *an icon*—ever became an issue at all. This is no doubt an even thornier problem, about which we have even less data.

The question of when the body of erstwhile authoritative writings became a canon, in the sense of a closed list of standardized texts, is not irrelevant here, even if not ultimately decidable. One must, on the one hand, heed Folkert's cau-

often dependent "upon the pressure of defining one 'orthodoxy' against one or more competing interpretations of faith." Sanders (1992, 1:839) distinguishes between two meanings of "canon": as "the shape of a limited body of sacred literature" and its (antecedent) "function"; while Sheppard (1987, 3:65, 66) distinguishes between Canon 1 (canon as "rule, standard, ideal, or norm") and Canon 2 ("a list, chronology, catalog, fixed collection, and/or standardized text"). But compare the different use of these labels by Folkert (1989, 173), for whom Canon I and Canon II are distinguished by their "vectoring," "the means or mode by which something is carried." Canon I is vectored by "some other form of religious activity," while Canon II, closed and complete, is its own vector, a carrier of religious authority in its own right. This formulation leads Folkert to the conclusion that there is no Canon II until the Reformation.

tion (1989, 173) that a full closure of the (one should rather say *a*) biblical canon only occurred with the Protestant Reformation and, further, Beal's more radical observation that, given the variation of versions and translations, the notion of a "standardized text" is an illusion (2002 and in this volume). And yet, both Jews and Christians have long persisted in treating this illusion as reality. The five books of Moses became "the Torah" even while they were still written on multiple scrolls, and the Written Torah was (and still is) regarded as different from the Oral Torah even after the Oral Torah got written down (in the Talmuds). More colloquially, as we like to say in Texas: if King James English was good enough for Jesus, it's good enough for me. The notion of scriptures as icon, in other words, requires some sense of closure. In Watts' three-dimensional model of scriptures, the ritualization of the iconic dimension of scriptures entails the public decoration, manipulation, dressing, and so on, of such texts (Chapter 1, this volume). For such activities to occur, though, there must be some finite, containable thing upon which to perform them. When and how, then, did this counterfactual yet iconicity-generating thinginess of the Bible take hold?

The question brings me finally to the Wisdom of Ben Sira, which may need a bit of introduction.[7] Sirach is the work of an early second-century BCE Jerusalem scribe[8] and one of the few sources contemporaneous with early biblical formation that offers a glimpse into the development of biblical thinginess—what we might call "canon-consciousness" (cf. Sheppard 1980, 109)—by which I mean the emerging sense that there is a list of authoritative writings, and that this list may be finite and moving towards closure. Alon Goshen-Gottstein (2002), for example, argues, based on a reading of Ben Sira's hymns of praise to the fathers (chs. 44–49) and to the high priest Simeon (ch. 50), that the sage knew not only a fully formed Torah, but also the books of the Former and Latter Prophets in essentially their current shape and order; in other words, that these books had also achieved a closed, canonical status. This argument can also be read against itself, however: insofar as Ben Sira clearly distinguishes between a singular Torah and multi-volume Prophets, and struggles with their relationship, one could as well infer a polemic on his part to validate the latter. My own reading of the book of Sirach as a whole inclines me to see such tensions as significant for understanding this work, both in itself and as a dark glass into the canonizing/iconizing process.

Whatever the precise state of affairs, the possibility that some books might make an authoritative list while others do not, and that the list may be finite

7. The perspective I offer here is based on a larger project, centered on the connection between Sirach's gender ideology and imagery to its view of scripture (Camp forthcoming).

8. The book was widely read by Jews, and later Christians, and was translated into Greek in Alexandria by the author's grandson, who also supplied a Preface to the work. There are several Hebrew versions extant, none complete, thus translators must often rely on the Greek, which not infrequently varies from the Hebrew that we do know. The translations here are my own, though often heavily reliant on the text-critical work and felicitous phrasing of Skehan and Di Lella (1987).

rather than infinite, was certainly not fully realized in Ben Sira's day. Yet important features of his work, several of which I shall discuss below, suggest at least an implicit awareness of such a canonizing process. At the same time, his claim to inspiration and his self-identification as author of his own original work suggest his hope that it would be included in the roster of an emerging, a.k.a. closing, canon. It may be too much to call Ben Sira a causative agent in this process. I see him rather as a hinge figure, representative of a hard bend in that larger cultural road (in that sense, perhaps, something of an icon himself!). I shall focus here on the symbolic moves he makes that I think ultimately help turn the Bible into an iconic book, a thing he—and eventually my students—can possess.

This fifty-one chapter book by Ben Sira is a late representation of what scholars call the biblical wisdom tradition, whose flagship is the canonical book of Proverbs, a writing clearly known (if perhaps not in its final form) by Ben Sira. Like Proverbs, Ben Sira writes instructional poems, usually in the two or three line parallelism typical of Hebrew poetry, that teach young men a class ethic of social responsibility, piety, and self-preservation. The teacher-sage, often self-styled as a "father" speaking to "sons," advocates a search for "wisdom" that was not merely an intellectual pursuit, but a striving for enough understanding of both human society and divine workings to be able to live successfully. Respect for authority, self-control, hard work, and restrained but efficacious speaking are major social values, reinforced by a piety centered on "fear of the Lord," usually understood less as the *mysterium tremendum et fascinans* than as an attitude of submission to divine will.

There are some changes that appear in Sirach compared to the earlier book of Proverbs, though, and a couple of these are relevant to my interest in the emerging sense of canon. First is a difference in the use of the Hebrew term *torah* in the two books. *Torah* means instruction or direction, sometimes law, either human or divine. Of the thirteen occurrences of *torah* in Proverbs, the teacher three times uses the singular possessive ("my *torah*" 31:1, 4:2; 7:2) and six times refers to it as the *torah* of the mother or of the wise, or places it in such a context (1:8; 6:20, 23; 13:14; 31:26). All these instances clearly indicate human instruction in wisdom. Four verses speak of "forsaking" (*'zb;* 28:4), "keeping" (*shmr*; 28:4; 29:18), or heeding (*shm'/ntsr*; 28:7; 28:9) *torah*, terminology reminiscent of the covenantal language of obedience to Yahweh's law (Torah, capital T, so to speak), but such an allusion is implicit at best and the specifics fit well within standard wisdom teachings.[9] Ben Sira, however, regularly specifies *torah* (Gk: *nomos*) as "the law of the Most High/the Lord" (9:15; 19:15, 24; 21:11; 23:23; 24:23; 39:1, 8; 41:8; 42:2; 44:20; 46:14: 49:4), connects it

9. Proverbs 28:7–9 comes closest in content to the covenantal Torah. Verse 7 inveighs against shaming one's parents by association with gluttons, a concern also found in Deut 21:20, which also uses the rare root *zll*; the following verse condemns wealth gained by charging interest (*nshk*; also in Deut 23:20 and other laws); and v 9 provides an inclusio by again using torah.

with fear of or belief in the Lord (2:16; 15:1; 19:20; 32:24), or refers to God's giving of it (17:11; 45:5, 17; cf. 46:14).

Ben Sira is, moreover, among the first to use something like the terminology that later came to signify the three major parts of the more fully consolidated Hebrew Bible, also known by the acronym TaNaK: the Law (Torah), the Prophets (Nebi'im), and the Writings (Ketubim). Reveling in the vocation of the scribe, Ben Sira says that "He devotes himself . . . to the study of the Law of the Most High/ He studies the wisdom of all the ancients/and occupies himself with prophecies" (38:24–39:1). "Law" here seems to indicate a known corpus, while "prophecies" is used more loosely, and "the wisdom of all the ancients" is more open-ended yet. Just sixty or so years later, though, Ben Sira's grandson will translate this book into Greek and provide it with a Prologue that twice refers to "the law and the prophets and the later authors (or: the rest of the books)" and, specifically, to his grandfather's reading of "the law and the prophets and other books of our fathers." In addition to Ben Sira's primary authoritative corpus, the Torah, another has been added to it, the Prophets. More additions ("other books of our fathers") seem possible and the list remains somewhat open-ended, but it is notable that, for the grandson, the authoritative form is now designated "books." The biblical canon is still open but increasingly defined by category and by the thinginess of books. The canon *concept* has made a major advance in Ben Sira's wake.[10]

But Ben Sira himself has made an important contribution to this development through his own use of "book," and we come here to another significant way in which this scribe both uses and transforms his heritage from the book of Proverbs. While Proverbs often represents an exercise in conventional mores and piety, it also offers a strikingly innovative move in personifying its defining concept, wisdom, as a woman. "She" is variously portrayed in a series of poems in chapters 1–9 as a prophet, wife, lover, meal-preparer, and housebuilder. The young man who responds to her public call for followers, embracing her and loving her, will be saved from the dastardly strange woman who leads to death. In one poem, Woman Wisdom is strikingly exalted. Speaking in praise of herself, Wisdom reveals that she existed with Yahweh before the beginning of creation and that, having watched or perhaps participated in the formation of the world and its human inhabitants, she has come from delighting and rejoicing before Yahweh down to earth to delight and rejoice in human beings (8:22–31). This heavenly origin lends credence to her claim to be both the source of right governance on earth and of life itself for those who love her (8:15–16, 35–36).

The central poem of Ben Sira's book (chapter 24) also comprises a self-praise of Woman Wisdom that reiterates her claim to a heavenly origin and participation in creation, followed by a descent to her home on earth. Whereas

10. The Maccabean war (167–164 BCE), which led to one hundred years of Jewish self-rule in Judah, took place in between the generations of Ben Sira and his grandson. The nationalistic fervor of this era was undoubtedly a major factor in consolidating the sense of an iconic scripture as a symbol of identity.

in Proverbs, however, Wisdom dwells among all humans, Ben Sira places her in Israel, where she "finds rest" specifically in its political and religious center, Jerusalem.

> Then the Creator of all gave me a command,
> and he who created me chose the place for my tent.
> He said, in Jacob make your dwelling,
> and in Israel receive your inheritance.
> Before the ages, from the first, he created me,
> and for all the ages I shall not cease to be.
> In the holy Tent I ministered before him;
> and thus in Zion I was established.
> In the beloved city likewise he gave me rest,
> in Jerusalem is my domain.
> I took root among the honored people,
> in the portion of the Lord, his inheritance. (24:8–12)

Wisdom goes on to compare herself, in sensual terms, to a variety of desirable plants, culminating in her invitation to partake of her and live.

> Come to me, you who desire me,
> and with my fruits be filled.
> For my memorial is sweeter than honey,
> and my inheritance than the honeycomb.
> Those who eat of me will hunger still,
> and those who drink of me will thirst for more.
> He who obeys me will not be put to shame,
> and those who work with me will not fail.[11] (24:19–22)

The punch line, though, is yet to come, as the sage returns to his own voice in the next verse:

> All this is the book of the covenant of the most high God,
> the law that Moses commanded us,
> an inheritance for the congregation of Jacob. (24:23)

But Ben Sira is not finished yet. Having equated the book of the covenant of the most high God, the Torah, with the female embodiment of his own tradition of wisdom teaching and speculation, he goes on to imagine himself in a unique bond of prophetic intimacy with Woman Wisdom.

> The first man did not know her fully,
> nor will the last succeed in fathoming her.
> Deeper than the sea are her thoughts,
> her counsel than the great abyss.
> Yet I, like a stream from her river,
> like a canal, I went forth into a garden.
> I said, I will water my plot,
> and I will drench my flower bed;

11. The translation "fail" is with Skehan and Di Lella (1987, 328, 336). The Greek word (and its reconstructed Hebrew original), however, more typically means "sin," which is well within the semantic purview of the verse.

Yet suddenly my stream became a river,
    and my river became a sea.
Again I will make instruction shine forth like the dawn,
    and I will show it forth afar off.
Again I will pour out instruction like prophecy,
    and bequeath it to generations yet to come. (24:28–33)

I have already noted some evidence for the "thinginess" of the Torah in Ben Sira's hands, namely, his use of the term as, in effect, a title for a known and unified corpus of literature. For all his obvious reverence of the Law of the most high God, however, the sage spends almost no time in his own book actually citing, much less interpreting, any specifics from it.[12] This fact calls to mind Marty's reflections on the function of iconic books, whose role in a cultural carapace does not require actual reading, and I think we can imagine Ben Sira's relationship to the Torah as an example of this phenomenon.

This omission does not mean that Ben Sira did not ever do such interpretation. In fact, he often admonishes his students to keep, not transgress, "the commandments" (plural) as a synonym for "the (singular) Law," which assumes they knew and understood those specifics. The nearly complete absence of the content of the Torah *in Ben Sira's own book*, however, is noteworthy.[13] The grandson's Prologue refers to the law, the prophets and (some version of) the "other books" three times, emphasizing not only Ben Sira's close study of them, but also his grandfather's (as well as his own) intent in writing his own book to help people live "according to the law" (Prologue). What Ben Sira seems to assume, then, is that people will learn to follow the law by reading *his own* teachings. What Watts would call his ritualization of the semantic dimension—generally understood as the practice of commentary and preaching (Watts Chapter 1, this volume, 22)—takes place in this case through the creation of *new* authoritative literature rather than through direct interpretive extrapolation from the core text.

To this degree, Ben Sira somewhat paradoxically produces the desired effect of knowing and communicating the truths contained in the law—a semantic dimension enterprise—by handling the law as icon, or more precisely, since there is no actual material object involved, by inscribing the law as icon. I suggest that this second order, scribal iconization—a "meta-iconic" dimension, or thinking and writing about the text as an object—may contribute to the validation and use of a functioning iconic text. Of course, Ben Sira's own book

12. One exception to this generalization is Ben Sira's instruction about honoring one's parents in 3:1–15, which seems related to laws on this topic (Nickelsburg 2003), though the topos is equally at home in the wisdom tradition (cf. n. 9 above). The passage may be a kind of homily (Nickelsburg's interpretation) or might simply be an oft-repeated riff on a favorite passage rather than an act of intentional citation and interpretation.

13. Though there may be reasons for Ben Sira's lack of direct engagement with the Torah—Nickelsburg (2003 and cf. Nickelsburg 2001) argues by comparison with 1 Enoch that "Moses is not the only show in town" and that these writers prefer sapiential forms for moral instruction—such explanations do not account for the authority Ben Sira seems to seek for his writing vis-à-vis what for him is the quintessentially authoritative Torah.

would itself then get taken up in the cycle of mutual validation, moving (he hopes!) to its own iconization. Indeed, Ben Sira shamelessly promotes himself as a divinely inspired author, writing, "I will again pour out teaching like prophecy and leave it to all future generations" (24:33). Even more strikingly, for the first time I am aware of in the larger biblical tradition, he breaks with the cultural habit of anonymity or pseudonymity and even names himself as the author of his own work.

> Training in wise conduct, and smooth-running proverbs
> were inscribed in this book
> by Yeshua, son of Eleazar, son of Sira[14]
> who poured them out from his understanding heart.
> Happy is the one who reflects on these,
> wise will he be who takes them to heart!
> If he carries them out he will be strong in all things,
> for the fear of the Lord will give him depth. (50:27–29)

Ben Sira, in other words, seeks not simply to interpret the scriptures he has at hand but to gain scriptural status for his own self-identified work as well. He makes yet another key adaptation of Proverbs to accomplish this end by aligning the striking figure of Woman Wisdom with the book of the Law. Let me return to part of Watts' analysis of the three dimensions of scriptures to elucidate the point. Watts uses the terms of classical rhetorical theory—*logos*, *pathos*, and *ethos*—to address the different ways in which scriptures exert persuasive influence (Chapter 1, this volume, 24). "Though scriptures are not public speakers, ritualizing each of the three dimensions of scriptures enhances their persuasiveness in one of these three rhetorical modes as well" (Chapter 1, this volume, 24). *Logos* (in the semantic dimension) refers to the persuasiveness of the argument, enhanced by a long history of rituals of interpretation. Persuasiveness is also created through feelings, or *pathos*—in the case of scriptures, the feeling of inspiration induced by the performative dimension, which promotes the idea, and eventually the doctrine "that scriptures not only inspire but are themselves the product of uniquely divine kinds of inspiration" (Chapter 1, this volume, 25). *Ethos*, in the model of classical rhetoric, is concerned with the credibility of the speaker: in the first place the text itself as speaker and then, also, those who bring it to speech. "Ritualizing the iconic dimension of scriptures through decoration, ritual manipulation, and display demonstrates visibly their *ethos* as scripture. … Thus scriptures' iconic status enhances their own *ethos* and by association grants legitimacy to those in contact with them" (Chapter 1, this volume, 25).

14. The third-person construction in the Septuagint (Hebrew lacks v 27b) is similar to the colophons of Egyptian instructions, which are usually taken to have been composed by the writers themselves or, at least, to reflect their own purported claims to authorship. Skehan and Di Lella point out that most Greek and Latin manuscripts change the verb to the first person ("I inscribed in this book"), and concur that this change captures the likely reality that Ben Sira wrote the words himself (1987, 559). I have followed their translation (1987, 556) for this whole passage.

Notably for our purposes, Watts stresses the way in which

> ritual emphasis on the *logos*, *pathos*, and *ethos* of scriptures has the effect of giving them personas more like people than like books.... The feeling of being persuaded by the scriptures has generated the sense that they are more than just texts. Their ritualization produces personal effects that lead to their identification with human prophets or supernatural personalities. (page 25 above)

At the same time, they share their "ritualized enhancements" with the interpreters, leaders, and other performers who are associated with them. The biblical tradition, writ large, evidences one aspect of this pattern, associating major literary components of what became scriptures with authoritative leaders from the past—the law with Moses, the Psalms with David, Proverbs and other wisdom literature with Solomon, and, outside the current canon, the Enoch literature with that ancient figure. This impulse reaches a new level in Ben Sira's identification of the Torah with Woman Wisdom. Here, the larger dynamic of the rhetorical *ethos*, the mutual authorization between the icon and its handler, is more apparent, and the experience of *pathos* induced as well.

We have no evidence regarding what, if any, public ritual manipulation of the Torah was occurring in Ben Sira's day, but he does engage in what we might think of as a literary form of ritual decoration of the icon, clothing "the book of the covenant" in the sensual dress of Woman Wisdom. But Woman Wisdom is no casual ornament, for she represents a body of tradition herself. It is less circumscribed and thus (so far!) less iconic than the Torah in a literal, physical sense, but no less culturally important for a sage and scribe like Ben Sira. As a figural embodiment of her tradition, moreover, Woman Wisdom introduces a new iconic potential, including her own capacity for authorization: she, unlike the Torah, appears as a speaking subject in an oral culture. Identified by Ben Sira with the Torah, she in effect *becomes* the iconic text, in person. I would suggest, then, that Watts' notion that the persuasiveness of books functions akin to that of persons goes further than mere analogy, at least in the experience of a writer making the earliest moves toward the textualization of religious authority. Ben Sira seems unable to imagine textual authority in any other way than as that of a person.

We could go on to explore other ways in which Ben Sira exemplifies a kind of literary manifestation of Watts' phenomenological/functional analysis of the three dimensions of scriptures, and my larger project takes up the issue of the new alignment between orally and textually based authority that I think this book represents. That discussion is not my main agenda in this paper; however, since I do want to address the culturally-formed class consciousness (and thus personal unconsciousness) Ben Sira brings to his work, let me note briefly something of the social, and social-psychological, location of the scribal class to which he belongs, a group caught between their own self-validating rhetoric and the dangers of their necessary employment by men of power.

Ben Sira's text reveals an author who is a product of a culture deeply infused with an ideology of honor and shame (4:20–26; 5:13–6:1; 20:22–26; 22:1–5; 26:7–9, 24–27; 41:16–42:14; and passim; Camp 1991). In such a cultural system, a man's name is his most valuable possession (cf. Sanders 1979). Ben Sira's poem in praise of the scribal profession (his own, of course!) concludes:

> Many will praise his understanding;
> never will it be effaced.
> Unfading will be his memory;
> his name will live through all the generations.
> The nations will speak of his wisdom,
> and the assembly will declare his praise.
> While he lives he is one out of a thousand,
> and when he dies he leaves a good name. (39:9–11)

Yet Ben Sira's professional self-exaltation takes place in a social context where his authority and status are less secure than his idealized vision. Like all scribes, Ben Sira serves an earthly authority, in his case the priests of the Jerusalem temple, who govern Judah under the aegis of the Hellenist colonizers. His reverence for his cultic masters is apparent in his paean to his near-contemporary, the high priest Simeon (50:1–24), glorious as "the sun shining on the temple of the King, as the rainbow gleaming in the clouds" (50:7).

But Ben Sira is not simply a shill for the cult. As we have seen, he identifies himself, by name, as the author of divinely inspired literature, complementary to but not dependent on his already scripturalized core text. But here again is a rub: like the scribes, writing itself was in a culturally betwixt-and-between state. The evidence from the Dead Sea Scrolls, for example, shows that even the Torah itself, while arguably iconic to Ben Sira and his cohort, was not as highly reverenced by all.[15] Literacy, not to mention access to written texts, was the preserve of a very few, and it is far from clear what revelatory status such texts held for most of the population. Indeed, writing in an oral culture is often regarded as less authoritative than oral communication.

Ben Sira's deployment of the personified Wisdom figure in relation to both the Torah and his own inspired writing becomes important in this regard, especially in light of Watts' observations about the persuasive power of texts as persons. What I want to do here, though, is to open up a bit further some issues that arise when we focus on Ben Sira's iconizing embodiment of Wisdom-cum-Torah not simply as a person but as a *woman*. While this figuration might seem at first a thing of joy to a feminist, it has a poisonous undercurrent, for Ben Sira is not an ideologically innocent thinker where gender is concerned. He is, in fact, a misogynist—perhaps one of only two true misogynists (sharing the honors with Ezekiel) in the whole patriarchal tradition that is the Bible.

15. The Dead Sea Scrolls show that significant portions of what would become the biblical canon, especially the five books of the Law, or Torah, were held in high enough esteem by some groups to be copied repeatedly, but that this revelation through Moses had significant competition from revelations purportedly from Enoch. Generally, the range of writings found at Qumran shows little interest in the closing of a canon.

As is often the case, though, hatred derives from fear, and Ben Sira's attitude toward real women rests on a pervasive anxiety that is connected to his seemingly incongruous exaltation of Wisdom/Torah as female.

Male honor in Ben Sira's culture depends on the public recognition of one's good name (cf. 6:1; 15:6; 37:26; 39:9, 11; 40:19; 41:11, 12, 13; 44:3, 8, 14; 46:12). This sage, though, wants recognition extending beyond his own earthly span of days. As the quotation above demonstrates, he seeks the glory of an *eternal* name, his memory unfading, praised through the generations in the congregation and beyond. His hope for eternal honor lies in his writing, lending both poignancy and a sense of anxious overreaching to his claims to divine inspiration and intimacy with Woman Wisdom and to his remarkable act of signature.

Ironically, though, while Ben Sira seeks through his own writing the glory of an eternal name, this writing repeatedly reveals deep-seated anxiety about aspects of his life that he may be unable to control and that will bring him shame and dishonor instead. Chief among these is his fear of women's shame—their infective, often sexual, immodesty and self-will—that threatens the honor of men (23:22–27; 25:13–26; 26:5–12; 42:9–14). Ben Sira is the first to "blame Eve" for the human condition: "From a woman sin had its beginning, and because of her we all die" (25:24). But a man's wife and daughters present the greatest threat: "A bad wife is a chafing yoke; taking (or marrying) her is like grasping a scorpion," (26:7), and a headstrong wife or daughter may sin against her male keeper: "she will sit in front of every tent peg and open her quiver to the arrow" (26:12). Not to put too fine a point on it:

> A daughter is a hidden treasure causing a wakeful father,
> and worry over her drives away sleep:
> lest in her youth she be rejected;
> or, when she is married, lest she be hated[16]:
> In her virginity, lest she be defiled
> and become pregnant in her father's house;
> or, having a husband, lest she be unfaithful;
> and when she is married, lest she be barren.
> My son, keep a close watch over your daughter,
> lest she make you the sport of your enemies,
> a byword in the city and the assembly of the people,
> an object of derision in public gatherings.
> See that there is no lattice in her room,
> no spot that overlooks the approaches to the house.
> Let her not reveal her beauty to any male,
> or spend her time among married women.
> For just as moths come from garments,
> so a woman's wickedness comes from a woman.

16. Or, "forgotten." The Hebrew text is fragmentary, with an existing final h suggesting *tshnh* (forgotten), though the Greek reads *misēthē* (hated). See 13:10 for a case where the Greek translator read the Hebrew *tsn'* (hated) as *tshnh* (forgotten). Either meaning reads better in parallel to "rejected" than Skehan and Di Lella's "childless," a concern that appears appropriately in the next verse.

Better a man's wickedness that a woman's goodness... (42:9-14a[17])

This, then, is Ben Sira's gender dilemma: a woman (Wisdom) can admit him to eternity but his own women can keep him out. His anxiety over his honor before God and men is enfolded and expressed in the anxious contradiction between his culturally deformed experience of women and his appropriation of the female symbol of his vocation.

But this very symbol also provides him a way through his anxiety, precisely because "she" is a woman. On the one hand, Woman Wisdom is a hard taskmistress, a veritable dominatrix: she torments with her discipline (4:17); she must be yearned for and wrestled with (51:19); and to follow her is to put one's feet in her fetters and one's neck under her chain or yoke (6:24; 51:26). The end result, though, is this Woman's perfect service to her man. She will return to comfort the one she tormented (4:18); her fetters will become his defense and her chains a robe of glory (6:29); indeed, she herself will be a robe of honor and a crown of joy that he will put on (6:31). Woman Wisdom will, in sum, become his possession (4:16; 51:21).

To move from the metaphorical to the literal, what makes this perfect possession possible is that Woman Wisdom has become a book, a containable thing that can be held, manipulated, and controlled. This possession is emotionally satisfying, though, precisely because of its metaphorical femininity and the release "she" provides from the nagging threat of shame from all the real women Ben Sira might not be able to control. There is, though, a dangerous paradox involved: to claim possession of Woman Wisdom now means, as a result of Ben Sira's own iconizing rhetoric, to claim control of the Torah, the book of the covenant of the most high God. As is still true of my students and their own firmly grasped icon, the balance of power shifts in a way that may go consciously unremarked but is de-stabilizing nonetheless.

In sum, Ben Sira's work is marked by representations of women and uses of female imagery that are interwoven with the way he expresses both his self-identity as a sage and scribe and his relationship to the texts that materially embody this identity. The scribe must depend for his glory on the endurance of the texts he transmits and the texts he creates, but by Ben Sira's day eternal glory may require that he enter the canonical roster with his own book. And in 180 BCE, the cultural window of opportunity is narrowing—the canon is taking shape—and uncertainty remains as to whether such a self-promoting product of the scribal school could take its place alongside the Torah and the Prophets. What I think my analysis suggests is that the conflicted perceptions of gen-

17. The Hebrew of v 14b, though now apparently corrupt, is quite different from the Greek. The latter reads "and it is woman (or, a wife) who brings shame unto reproach." Skehan and Di Lella, following Cross' emendation of the Hebrew, read "but better a religious [lit: dreading] daughter than a shameless son." The misogyny of the Greek seems to fit better with the sense of the larger passage, but the translator is either reading a different Hebrew or making his own sense where there was none. A less sanguine translation of the extant Hebrew might be "but a daughter who lives in fear [of God, or her father?] is better than any disgrace."

der in Ben Sira's texts are fundamental to his appropriation of, *and attempt to produce*, authoritative religious literature, and thus essential for understanding his relationship to this emerging canon. Torah, conceived as female, was the core of this canon, but Ben Sira adds his own literary production to this female "body" (or feminized corpus, if you will); he thereby becomes the voice of both through the experience of perfect possession.

To frame these considerations more generally, this case study of Ben Sira opens up the question of how a given individual appropriates, internalizes, and contributes to such a significant cultural shift as that of an emerging canon-consciousness. And it exposes in the process the implicit ideological agendas at stake in the case of the Bible. If Ben Sira can be considered representative of his scribal class and context, his work may also provide a window into aspects of the larger cultural process of iconization, including the question of whether we would have a biblical canon—or have the canon we have—if the men in that particular patriarchal culture had not coded it in the gendered terms that Ben Sira did.

## References

Beal, Timothy K. 2002. "Bibles du Jour." *The Chronicle of Higher Education*, July 26, B5.

Camp, Claudia V. 1991. "Understanding a Patriarchy: Women in Second Century Jerusalem Through the Eyes of Ben Sira." In *Women Like This: New Perspectives on Jewish Women in the Greco-Roman World*, edited by Amy-Jill Levine, 1–39. Atlanta, GA: Scholars Press.

———. (forthcoming). *Gender and the Rise of Canon-Consciousness: Ben Sira and the Men Who Handle Books*. Sheffield: Sheffield Phoenix Press.

Carr, David M. 2005. *Writing on the Tablet of the Heart: Origins of Scripture and Literature*. New York: Oxford University Press.

Davies, Philip R. 1998. *Scribes and Schools: The Canonization of the Hebrew Scriptures*, Library of Ancient Israel. Louisville, KY: Westminster John Knox.

Folkert, Kendall A. 1989. "The 'Canons' of 'Scripture'." In *Rethinking Scripture: Essays from a Comparative Perspective*, edited by Miriam Levering, 170–179. Albany: State University of New York Press.

Gallup, George H. Jr. 2003. "How Are American Christians Living Their Faith?" *Gallup*. 19 August. http://www.gallup.com/poll/9088/how-american-christians-living-their-faith.aspx. Accessed 11 January 2011.

Gallup, Alec and Wendy W. Simmons. 2000. "Six in Ten Americans Read Bible at Least Occasionally." *Gallup*. 20 October. http://www.gallup.com/poll/2416/six-ten-americans-read-bible-least-occasionally.aspx. Accessed 11 January 2011.

Goshen-Gottstein, Alon. 2002. "Ben Sira's Praise of the Fathers: A Canon-Conscious Reading." In *Ben Sira's God: Proceedings of the International Ben Sira Conference (Durham, 2001)*, edited by Renate Egger-Wenzel, Beihefte zur Zeitschrift für die alttestamentliche Wissenschaft 321, 235–267. Berlin/New York: de Gruyter.

Graham, William A. 1987. "Scripture." In *The Encyclopedia of Religion,* edited by Mircea Eliade, 13: 133–145. New York: MacMillan.

Jackson, Wayne. 1991. "Are There Two Creation Accounts in Genesis?" *ApologeticsPress.org.* http://www.apologeticspress.com/articles/2194. Accessed 6 January 2011.

Marty, Martin. 1982. "America's Iconic Book." In *Humanizing America's Iconic Book: Society of Biblical Literature Centennial Addresses,* edited by Gene Tucker and Douglas Knight, Society of Biblical Literature – Biblical Scholarship in North America 6, 1–23. Chico, CA: Scholars.

Newport, Frank. 2007. "One-Third of Americans Believe the Bible is Literally True." *Gallup.* 25 May. http://www.gallup.com/poll/27682/onethird-americans-believe-bible-literally-true.aspx. Accessed 11 January 2011.

Nickelsburg, George W. E. 2001. *1 Enoch: a Commentary on the Book of 1 Enoch.* Hermeneia. Minneapolis, MN: Fortress.

———. 2003. "Response to Claudia Camp, 'Orality, Literacy, and Textual Authority in the Work of Ben Sira." Wisdom and Apocalypticism Section, SBL, November 23.

Pew Research Center. 2010. "U.S. Religious Knowledge Survey." *The Pew Forum on Religion and Public Life.* 28 September. http://pewforum.org/other-beliefs-and-practices/u-s-religious-knowledge-survey.aspx. Assessed on 11 January 2011.

Sanders, Jack T. 1979. "Ben Sira's Ethics of Caution." *Hebrew Union College Annual* 50: 73–106.

Sanders, James A. 1992. "Canon." In *The Anchor Bible Dictionary,* edited by David Noel Freedman, 1: 837–52. Doubleday: New York.

Schniedewind, William M. 2004. *How the Bible Became a Book: the Textualization of Ancient Israel.* New York: Cambridge University Press. http://dx.doi.org/10.1017/CBO9780511499135

Sheppard, Gerald T. 1980. *Wisdom as a Hermeneutical Construct: A Study in the Sapientializing of the Old Testament,* Beihefte zur Zeitschrift für die alttestamentliche Wissenschaft 151, Berlin/New York: de Gruyter.

———. 1987. "Canon." In *The Encyclopedia of Religion,* edited by Mircea Eliade, 3: 62–69. New York: MacMillan.

Skehan, Patrick W. and Alexander A. Di Lella. 1987. *The Wisdom of Ben Sira: A New Translation with Notes,* The Anchor Bible 39. New York: Doubleday.

van der Toorn, Karel. 2007. *Scribal Culture and the Making of the Hebrew Bible.* Cambridge: Harvard University Press.

# 22

# Ancient Iconic Texts and Scholarly Expertise

James W. Watts

*This paper probes the origins of iconic textuality in the ancient Near East, informed by post-colonial perspectives on iconic texts. The surviving art and texts from ancient Egypt and Mesopotamia exhibit at least four forms of iconic textuality: monumental inscriptions, portraits of scribes, displays and manipulations of ritual texts, and beliefs in heavenly texts. The spread of literacy did not displace the social prestige of scribal expertise that was established in antiquity. The every-growing number and complexity of texts account for the continuing cultural authority of scholarly expertise. The tension between expert and non-specialist uses of texts, however, explains scholarship's avoidance of the subject of iconic books and texts while drawing constant attention to texts' semantic interpretation instead.*

Contemporary cultures provide many examples of iconic books and texts. For five years, the *Iconic Books Blog* has chronicled their appearances in news media and other internet sources. Its entries show that iconic textuality takes diverse forms and serves to legitimize political, religious, educational, and various other cultural institutions, as well as individuals. That observation is confirmed by evidence from comparative scriptures studies, cultural anthropology, and book history that has stimulated several recent explorations of the typical functions of iconic books in comparison with other uses of texts (Myrvold 2010; and in this volume: Watts, Chapter 1; Graham, Chapter 2; Stam, Chapter 3; Parmenter, Chapter 4).

In contrast to this rich lode of iconic textuality available from contemporary cultures, historical investigations of the subject must struggle with gaps in the evidence that grow larger the further back one looks. They also risk imposing anachronistic models of textuality, or iconicity, on people and practices for which they are inappropriate. However, historical analysis can provide explanations for cultural features and functions that an examination of contemporary practices may miss. Historical distance can provide perspective to better understand the overall phenomenon of iconic books and texts.

A historical survey provides a promising avenue for explaining, first, the persistence of certain forms of iconic textuality and, second, the refusal of traditional scholarship to recognize and study it. A historical perspective not only draws attention to this long-standing lacuna in scholarship, but also finds its motivation in the commitment of humanistic scholarship to the semantic dimension of texts. This essay traces these issues back to the first cultures to adopt writing on a large scale, the civilizations of the ancient Near East. I describe four kinds of ancient iconic textuality and then consider the social power that they convey, in order to lay the basis for explaining why historians have usually ignored the significance and influence of iconic texts.

## Iconic textuality in the Ancient Near East

The surviving artifacts and texts from ancient Egypt and Mesopotamia exhibit at least four forms of iconic textuality. The most obvious is the monumental royal inscription. Throughout the Near East, rulers commemorated their victories and donations on stone, often of monumental size and expense. In Egypt, kings covered almost every temple wall with texts, most of which were brightly painted in chromatic colors. In these ancient cultures where the vast majority of people were illiterate, including most of the kings and aristocrats themselves, the primary purpose of monumental texts was not communication. Though scribes no doubt made themselves readily available in temples and courts to read the walls and stelae to interested parties for a fee, the politics motivating the massive expense of producing texts in this form and on this scale required no translation by experts: the look of the texts as much as their contents equated textual knowledge with power and wealth. Their production and display claimed political legitimacy for the king and his regime (Liverani 1995).

A second obvious form of iconic textuality can be found in ancient art depicting scribes plying their trade. Such scenes appear fairly often in tableaus of agricultural or military life. Egyptian funerary art also contains many prominent portraits of scribes, or at least the deceased portrayed as scribes. Here we find already a phenomenon common in later cultures: portraiture depicting people holding texts or surrounded by texts in order to characterize their educational achievements and their authority in transmitting and interpreting the literary tradition. The images of texts in their hands claim scholarly legitimacy for them, just as do displays of faculty books in universities today (see Kinnard's footnote 1, p 152 in this volume). When ancient kings could not plausibly claim scribal skills themselves, they could show themselves in the company of the scribes in their employ to lay claim to the same traditions of textual authority and legitimacy.

These two forms of iconic textuality are not limited to the ancient Near East or to cultures that have developed from it. For example, artifacts from the classical Maya of Central America also prominently feature monumental texts celebrating royal achievements and memorial sculptures of scribes plying their trade. Iconic ritualizations of texts in these unrelated agricultural societies probably fulfilled similar social and political functions.

Literary references to two more forms of iconic textuality have been preserved in ancient Near Eastern texts. Kings and priests frequently displayed and manipulated ritual texts to legitimize how rituals were performed (Watts 2005). Royal and temple commemorative inscriptions mention such practices while recording compliance with the instructions found in old texts. When restoring temples, texts were often found buried in their foundations to preserve the "original" designs of the gods. In Egypt, responsibility for ensuring compliance with ritual texts was delegated to specialists, the priests "who hold the ritual." Ceremonial art regularly depicts them holding high the scroll in which the ritual instructions were written. They kept these ritual texts in a temple library or archive, called by Egyptians the "house of life," and strictly limited access to them. Later centuries increasingly credited authorship of such ritual and omen texts to gods of wisdom—Ea in Mesopotamia and Thoth in Egypt (Rothberg-Halton 1984; Schott 1972). Egyptian scribal portraits sometimes depict their subjects writing at the inspiration of Thoth. Thus in ritual and in art, texts were displayed and manipulated to legitimize rituals and the priests who presided over them.

Ancient myths showed a particular interest in a fourth kind of iconic text, namely heavenly texts written by gods. Mesopotamian traditions conceived of the gods assembling annually on New Years Day to determine the fates for the coming year (Paul 1973). The scribal goddess (Nisaba) or god (Nabu) recorded their decisions with a silver stylus on tablets of blue lapis lazuli. In other words, they wrote with the stars of the sky (Parmenter 2009a). The huge corpus of Mesopotamian omen literature sprang from this conception of the stars and all of nature as a book in which the gods write their decisions regarding human fate (Dalley 1999, 166). The omen series occupied the peak of the educational curriculum, mastered only by the best and most privileged scribes. From omen texts they learned to *read nature like a text.* This conception of nature as text motivated the Mesopotamian's exhaustive records of the omens they observed. Subsequent cultures have continued to view nature as a text to be read, a metaphor that inspires much of modern empirical science (see e.g. Kosso 1992, 5–7). It provides mythic legitimation for the interpretive enterprise that underlies all scholarly disciplines.

But not all divine texts could or should be shared with humans. Several prominent myths depict the record of the gods' decisions, not just in the sky or in nature, but as a material text, though of course of a heavenly kind. It consists of tablets, often called "the Tablets of Destinies," whose possession grants supreme power and kingship among the gods. The Babylonian creation epic, *Enuma Elish*, features the tablets as a minor element in its plot (Foster 2005, 436–486). The primordial mother goddess, Tiamat, bestows them on her choice to be king of the gods, but after defeating her, Marduk takes them away. His victory makes him king of the gods, with obvious political implications for Babylon, the city that he patronized. In the *Anzu* epic, the tablets play a more central role in the plot (Foster 555–578). Here, the traditional high god, Enlil, who usually wears the tablets on a string, is tricked into taking them off in order to bathe. The supernatural bird Anzu steals them and thereby gains power to thwart every attempt by any god to get them back. Ultimately, the young deity Ninurta kills Anzu by trickery, but then refuses to return the tablets to Enlil. He claims them and kingship for himself.

Though many cylinder seals depict scenes from these myths, the Tablets of Destiny appear nowhere in extant Mesopotamian art. On reflection, that is not very surprising. The Tablets are heavenly texts, never meant for human eyes. They are therefore the paradigmatic occult texts. To reproduce them in art would be to infringe on that supreme divine prerogative. (In fact, one thing that distinguishes images of texts from other kinds of images is that while an image of a person produces only a likeness, a realistically detailed image of a text reproduces at least part of the text itself.)

So these stories depict the Tablets of Destiny as magical devices that give their owners power over heaven and earth. This brings me to my second major point, about the social power of iconic texts. It is tempting to characterize the function of these stories as serving to mystify omen texts, as perpetuating a misunderstanding of a text's nature. Omen texts *really* functioned as sources of information to the scribes who read them and who used that information to try to interpret the course of events around them. Though we may find their reasoning and conclusions flawed, we recognize the work of ancient scholars as similar to our own: they interpreted the semantic meaning of texts in search of information that they could use, just as we do. *We think* that reading alone transmits the text's influence and authority. Stories of magic tablets simply obscure the fact that limiting access to literacy and education reinforces social stratification.

That is of course true, so far as it goes. But Philip Arnold (1995, 2002) and Vincent Wimbush (2012) point out that indigenous and colonized peoples recognize the iconic power of colonizing texts in ways that the conquerors who wield them often do not. I want to apply that observation to ancient ideas about heavenly texts. What cultural reality in the experiences of non-scholars did these myths address? Where in the experience of ancient Near Eastern peoples did texts ever function in the way that the Tablets of Destiny do in *Enuma Elish* and *Anzu*?

As it turns out, texts were frequently the prizes and/or victims of military conflict in the Ancient Near East, just as they are in these myths. Conquerors erased or usurped the commemorative inscriptions of their enemies, captured and employed their scribes, and stole their libraries to augment their own. The latter practice is particularly interesting for illuminating the mythic theme.

Its outstanding practitioner in antiquity was the Assyrian king, Ashurbanipal.

During Ashurbanipal's reign in the mid-seventh century BCE, the Assyrian empire was at its height, ruling most of the Near East including Egypt. The Assyrians have a well-deserved reputation for brutality, reinforced by the fact that they decorated their palaces with reliefs depicting their military victories in violent detail. Even a domestic scene of the king reclining at dinner shows the head of an enemy hanging from a nearby tree. But Ashurbanipal also had a literary side. He boasted that he could read and write well (apparently not a wide-spread skill among royals at the time). He ordered his scribes and his armies to collect texts for him wherever they went. Their number and contents are enumerated in booty lists totaling the yield of personnel and goods from his military campaigns. In his capital at Ninevah, he built libraries in his palace and in the temple of Nabu where texts were catalogued, collated and reproduced (Lieberman 1990, 318). These collections were discovered by archeologists and are the source of many of our best texts from ancient Mesopotamia, including the *Enuma Elish* epic summarized above.

Given these kinds of political and military experiences, the myths about the Tablets of Destiny appear less mystifying. The idea that gods battled for control of powerful texts to establish supremacy simply projects the textual politics of earth onto heaven. It may be that for the very elite scribes/scholars who mastered the Mesopotamian omen series or the Egyptian ritual texts, a text's power lay in its semantic referents. For them, the gods wrote their decrees in nature and written texts only taught scribes what to look for or what to do. But to the less literate and illiterate royal elites as well as commoners, texts were more obviously used by kings and temples to manifest power, wealth, and authority. They were clearly prizes in wars that legitimized the winner's right to rule. The notion that possession of such texts conveyed supremacy would seem obvious enough.

Indeed, it still seems obvious. Libraries and rare books and texts continue to be used as the spoils of war to establish or buttress claims of national identity and international supremacy. For those who study the cultures and religions of the ancient Near East, as I do, the best place to go to see ancient texts and artifacts is not in the Middle East, but in London. The British Museum and the British Library seem to house fully half of all the manuscripts and artifacts that I and others in my field study on a regular basis. They include much of Ashurbanipal's library, which was excavated by British explorers and archeologists in the nineteenth century when the British Empire was at its height. Lawsuits by various countries to reclaim some materials from European and American museums underscore the fact that these objects continue to convey political legitimacy and cultural prestige. Thus texts, art, and other cultural artifacts remain prizes of war, just as they were three millennia ago. That is just as true for texts like the Rosetta Stone as for art objects like Nefertiti's Bust. Scholars protest that the needs of researchers, focusing on the semantic dimension of texts, should take priority over politics, represented most forcefully by the iconic dimension. But these texts still function as icons of cultural and political legitimacy whether we like it or not.

The motives behind ancient and modern textual politics are not very different, despite the wide cultural gap between the stated goals of ancient and modern librarians and collectors. A colophon to some of the texts in Ashurbanipal's Nabu temple archive testifies:

> I, Assurbanipal, king of the universe, king of Assyria, on whom Nabu and Tashmetu have bestowed vast intelligence, who acquired penetrating acumen for the most recondite details of scholarly erudition, no predecessors of whom among kings having any comprehension of such matters, I wrote down on tablets Nabu's wisdom, the impressing of each and every cuneiform sign, and I checked and collated them. I placed them for the future in the library of the temple of my lord Nabu, the great lord, at Nineveh, for my life and for the well-being of my soul, to avoid disease, and to sustain the foundation of my royal throne. O Nabu, look joyfully and bless my kingship forever! Help me whenever I call upon you! As I traverse your house, keep constant watch over my footsteps. When this work is deposited in your house and placed in your presence, look upon it and remember me with favor! (tr. Foster 2005, 831)

Here, Ashurbanipal boasts of his literacy as a mark of piety to gain personal favor with the gods, but also to gain political advantage from his reputation for wisdom and learning. However, the literate king also found it useful to be able to arbitrate the advice of his omen-reading advisers by scanning their texts himself. This is attested by colophons of texts in his palace library that list their purpose "for my review in perusing" and "for my examining" (Lieberman 1990, 318–320, 326–328). His mastery of the semantic dimension of texts gave him advantages over literate subordinates and illiterate rivals. King Ashurbanipal therefore collected and controlled texts (especially the omen series) in order to extend and maintain his power. He had reason to think that controlling the semantic and iconic dimensions of texts in his possession grants power on earth as well as in heaven.

Iconic textuality, however, was also a potent defensive weapon against cultural imperialism. In the face of the onslaught of Hellenistic culture in the last few centuries BCE, Egyptian, Babylonian, and Jewish temples became bastions of traditional culture and scribal training. Egyptians regarded a temple as the earthly realization of a heavenly book, both in its architectural plan and its inscriptions. The temple's design proclaimed the distinction between inner holiness and outer desecration (Assmann 1997, 179–185). The same can be said of Jerusalem's temple and its purity regulations in the same period. Within temple walls, priests learned to read and write in the native languages, in deliberate resistance to the Hellenizing political and social forces outside (Carr 2005, 177–214). Out of these circumstances developed the practice of ritualizing the iconic, performative and semantic dimensions of the Jewish Torah to produce the first scripture in Western religious traditions (Watts 2011). In the following centuries, Christians consolidated their identity over against the Roman Empire by wielding their Gospel books until Christian emperors transformed Gospels into monuments of the imperium itself, thus producing the second Western scripture (Larson in this volume). Iconic textuality, whether in monumental or manuscript form, represented visually in each of these situations the reconstruction and preservation of a culture and its values that was also furthered by the oral performance and semantic interpretation of texts (on these three dimensions, see Watts, Chapter 1, this volume).

## Iconic books, literacy, and expertise

One might expect that the spread of literacy would gradually shift the cultural emphasis from the iconic to the semantic dimensions of texts. As more people learn to read, textual contents would presumably take on greater importance than their visual forms. That is the way the story is usually told of, for example, the development of ancient Judaism. In the fifth and fourth centuries BCE, priests authorized by the iconic ritual texts of the Torah wielded supreme authority in Jerusalem. A thousand years later, however, rabbinic scholars had displaced priests as the religious and, sometimes, secular leaders of the Jews (see e.g. Hengel 1974, 1: 78–83; Cohen 1987, 75, 101–102, 160–162; Schaper 2004, 144; Assmann 2006, 122–138). Jack Goody (1986, 4) concluded that, as a result, "alphabetic religions spread literacy and ... literacy spread these religions."

This claim reflects a rhetoric of popularized textuality that is a distinctive feature of Judaism, Christianity, and Islam in contrast to the religions of the ancient Near East and Mediterranean. The temples of Babylon, Egypt, and Rome kept their most sacred texts for priests, or even the gods, alone. In contrast to such esoteric religions, Judaism, Christianity, and Islam published their texts openly. The scriptures themselves require religious leaders to make every effort to publish their contents:

> Every seventh year, ... you shall read this law before all Israel in their hearing. Assemble the people—men, women, and children, as well as the aliens residing in your towns—so that they may hear and learn to fear the Lord your God and to observe diligently all the words of this law.
>
> (Deuteronomy 31:10–12 NRSV; cf. 6:6–7)

> Go therefore and make disciples of all nations, ... teaching them to obey everything that I have commanded you.
>
> (Matthew 28:19–20 NRSV; cf. John 20:31)

> O Messenger! proclaim the (message) which hath been sent to thee from thy Lord. If thou didst not, thou wouldst not have fulfilled and proclaimed His mission. (Surah 5:67, Yusufali translation)

Many historians find here a major water-shed in religious and cultural development, what Assmann (2006, 128) calls "the transition from cult religion to book religion." However, such characterizations allow the *ideal* of universal access to scripture and scriptural interpretation espoused by these religions to obscure the social *reality* of how they actually organized their rituals, institutions, and surrounding communities. In fact, the increasing ritualization of Torah in all three dimensions (iconic, performative, and semantic) seems to have accompanied the rise to power of the Jewish priests who also monopolized temple rituals (Watts 2011). It played at least a supporting role in giving them unprecedented political as well as religious authority in the mid- and later Second Temple period.

Elsewhere too—and still today—the spread of popular literacy has not displaced learned elites, but rather strengthened and empowered them. Goody (1986, 18) observed that religious institutions have usually dominated scribal and scholarly education in most cultures, despite some prominent exceptions: "the kind of separation between the priest and the teacher, between the religious orders and written accomplishment that occurred in Greece, and to a lesser extent in China, has been a rare feature of literate civilizations." As cultures became more literate, iconic texts continued to play important roles both in religion (e.g. the Torah, Bible, Qur'an) and in politics (e.g. the Twelve Tables, the Magna Carta, the U.S. Constitution). Modern mass literacy turns out to be compatible with both the expertise of scholars and the ritualization of iconic texts.

Why does rising literacy and increasing popular access to texts empower scholarly elites? Because in literate societies, scholarship exemplifies a universal ideal that is nevertheless unattainable except for a small minority. That was certainly true when Deuteronomy first espoused this ideal (Schaper 2004, 109). As literacy spreads, the skills necessary to earn the status of expert scholars ironically increase as well. The multiplication and accumulation of texts creates the need for summaries, commentaries, and synopses, in other words, for the products of rabbinic and scholastic learning that only very few people will ever have the time or resources to master, much less produce (Goody 1983, 162). Thus while literacy spreads and produces more texts, expertise remains concentrated in relatively few people. Literate religious groups often try to expand the circle of textual participation by allocating performance (reading, recitation, memorization) to a wider, but still privileged circle (Watts, Chapter 1, this volume; Yoo 2006). But in these groups, the authority of the lector, the cantor, and the hafiz usually remains subordinate to that of the scholar.

Why does iconic textuality persist despite increasing literacy and access to texts? Because, it provides non-experts control over texts and whatever social and religious power they may possess. Unlike semantic interpretation and public performance for which one should defer to the inner circles of expert scholars and often also to the wider circles of trained readers, physical texts can be owned and manipulated by non-specialists whether literate or not (see Yoo in this volume). Venerating a material text lies entirely within the control of the individual worshiper. In antiquity and still today, textual amulets are common and widespread (Malley, Chapter 17, this volume). Already by the last two centuries BCE, Jews were placing phylacteries (*tifillin*) containing excerpts from the Torah on their foreheads and forearms during prayers and affixing similar containers (*mezuzot*) on their doorposts. Many ancient Christians carried scrolls that mixed scriptural texts, especially the words of Jesus, with magical formulas. In a seventh-century battle at Siffin between Muslim armies, one side displayed Qur'anic verses on spears to pressure the other side to agree to arbitration on the basis of the scriptures. Still today, people of various ethnic and religious backgrounds revere Arabic Qur'anic texts as powerful amulets.

Many scholars view such practices as a stage on an evolutionary spectrum between illiteracy and full literacy: Schaper (2004, 112), for example, comments that in ancient Judah, "writing is still a numinous act." But for very many people alive today, including cultural elites who take oaths on scriptures and stockpile books in expensive libraries, "writing is still a numinous act." Every one of the forms of iconic textuality in the ancient Near East continues to be reproduced in modernity, though in different proportions. If monumental inscriptions do not cover every inch of our public buildings, they still appear especially on government buildings and libraries to point to the huge collections of books and other documents inside. Books remain a prominent feature of portraiture, especially of civic, academic, and religious portraiture, though they also show up frequently in other kinds of art and illustration. Processions with books held high continue to be a standard feature of many Jewish, Christian, Sikh, and Buddhist rituals, while protestors waving scriptures have been prominent in recent political news from America, the Middle East, and Asia. And, while myths of supernatural books appear commonly only in fantasy novels, art, and movies, the divine nature of scriptures remains a potent point of theological contention between sects and denominations (Parmenter 2009b). Differences in emphasis and practice do not reflect different levels of cultural development, but rather the ideological stakes that different social groups have in books and other written texts.

Nineteenth and twentieth-century scholarship belittled such iconic book practices as folkloric or superstitious (on scholarship on Buddhism and Islam, see Kinnard and Suit in this volume), but that attitude was not new. In the fourth century, the ascetic Bible translator, Jerome (*Ep.* 22.32), was already criticizing Christians who valued Gospel books for their pretty appearance rather than reading them, and that critique has been maintained by preachers and professors ever since. Public manipulation of iconic books in political and judicial oath ceremonies and public monuments receives less criticism, since in these cases those manipulating the socially sanctioned textual icon tend to be powerful or rich. Even here, scholars treat the iconic dimension as second- or third-best, something that must be accommodated because of cultural traditions but should not be privileged (Watts 2009). Scholars' socially mandated focus is on the more prestigious semantic dimension. More than anyone else, it is scholars who look down on iconic manipulation of texts as folk custom or superstition.

As William Graham (1987, 164) has argued, historians have "seriously shortchanged both ourselves and our field of study by ignoring or minimizing the 'sensual' aspects of religious life." Though much has changed on that score in the study of religion since he wrote those words, the study of scriptures has not. This near-universal dismissal of iconic textuality is unexamined at best and prejudicial at worst.

Two recent political manipulations of iconic texts in American culture show that this blindness to the iconic function of texts is restricted to academic scholars. Politicians have frequently proven adept at manipulating the iconic dimensions of books and texts for political purposes. Their practices range from the conventional manipulation of sacred books while taking an oath of office to extraordinary staging, as these examples show.

On January 3, 2007, Keith Ellison took the oath of office on a Qur'an once owned by Thomas Jefferson. Ellison was the first Muslim elected to the U.S. Congress. His intention to take the oath on a Qur'an aroused a storm of controversy in a country accustomed to seeing only Bibles in this role. Ellison responded by using Thomas Jefferson's Qur'an for this purpose. This textual relic is valued for its association with an American founding father which places a nationalistic stamp on these particular volumes of Muslim scripture.

On May 21, 2009, U.S. President Barack Obama went to the Rotunda of the National Archives to give a speech about his plans to close the detention center at Guantanamo Bay, Cuba. The setting allowed him to use the relic manuscript of the U.S. Constitution as a backdrop while he addressed a television audience on the topic of constitutional law and terrorism. His picture standing in front of the Constitution conveyed visually his claim of defending the rights guaranteed by that document.

In both of these instances, politicians and their advisers manipulated national and religious texts intelligently and expertly to persuade their audience in their favor. They received no help from academic theories of iconic texts, which are rare and not widely known. These political examples show, however, that only scholars suffer from this blind spot about iconic books and texts. It is not produced by levels of literacy, social development, or intelligence.

Why has this lacuna in scholarship persisted for so long? As scholars of humanistic texts, we do not like to admit our own dependence on political and economic forces and their influence on our scholarship, even though nations try to leverage their investment in universities into greater economic productivity and competitive advantages in the so-called "information economy." We especially do not like to admit that the status and appeal of our favorite texts may depend as much or even more on such factors than on their semantic meaning (see further Carr 2005, 294–297, and Solibakke in this volume). Hence, scholarly ignorance about iconic texts: it allows us to be in denial of the social conditions of our own livelihood. We insist that a text's real meaning lies in its semantic interpretation that we are the experts at elucidating. But many of our texts mediate power and legitimacy in ways that semantic and even performative interpretation cannot understand or control.

The study of iconic books and texts will not change the power relationships mediated by texts. However, comparative and historical study of the functions of books and texts in the iconic dimension, as well as in the dimensions of semantic interpretation and performance, will enable us to describe those forces more clearly and understand better our own role as scholars in ritualizing books and texts. They will hopefully provide analytical tools that will help us employ all three textual dimensions more wisely and constructively in the future.

## References

Arnold, Philip P. 1995. "Paper Ties to Land: Indigenous and Colonial Material Orientations to the Valley of Mexico." *History of Religions* 35: 27–60. http://dx.doi.org/10.1086/463406

———. 2002. "Paper Rituals and the Mexican Landscape." In *Representing Aztec Ritual: Performance, Text, and Image in the Work of Sahagún*, edited by Eloise Quiñones Keber, 227–250. Boulder: University Press of Colorado.

Assmann, Jan. 1997. *Das kulturelle Gedächtnis: Schrift, Erinnerung und politische Identität in frühen Hochkulturen.* Munich: Beck.

———. 2006. *Religion and Cultural Memory*, translated by R. Livingstone. Stanford, CA: Stanford University Press.

Carr, David M. 2005. *Writing on the Tablet of the Heart: Origins of Scripture and Literature.* Oxford: Oxford University Press.

Cohen, Shaye J. D. 1987. *From the Maccabees to the Mishnah.* Philadelphia, PA: Westminster.

Dalley, Stephanie. 1998. *The Legacy of Mesopotamia.* Oxford: Oxford University Press.

Foster, Benjamin R. 2005. *Before the Muses: An Anthology of Akkadian Literature*, 3rd ed. Bethesda, MD: CDL.

Goody, Jack. 1986. *The Logic of Writing and the Organization of Society.* Cambridge: Cambridge University Press.

Graham, William A. 1987. *Beyond the Written Word: Oral Aspects of Scripture in the History of Religion.* Cambridge: Cambridge University Press.

Hengel, Martin. 1974. *Judaism and Hellenism.* Philadelphia: Fortress.

Iconic Books Blog. http://iconicbooks.blogspot.com/. Accessed April 5, 2011.

Kosso, Peter. 1992. *Reading the Book of Nature: An Introduction to the Philosophy of Science.* Cambridge: Cambridge University Press.

Lieberman, Stephen J. 1990. "Canonical and Official Cuneiform Texts: Towards an Understanding of Assurbanipal's Personal Tablet Collection." In *Lingering Over Words: Studies ... in Honor of William J. Moran*, Harvard Semitic Monographs 37, edited by Tzvi Abusch et al., 305–336. Atlanta, GA: Scholars Press.

Liverani, Mario. 1995. "The Deeds of Ancient Mesopotamian Kings." In *Civilizations of the Ancient Near East*, edited by J. M. Sasson, 2353–2365. New York: Scribners.

Myrvold, Kristina, ed. 2010. *The Death of Sacred Texts: Ritual Disposal and Renovation of Texts in the World Religions*. Farnham: Ashgate.

Parmenter, Dorina Miller. 2009a. "The Bible as Icon: Myths of the Divine Origins of Scripture," In *Jewish and Christian Scripture as Artifact and Canon*, edited by Craig A. Evans and H. Daniel Zacharias, 298–310. London: T. & T. Clark.

———. 2009b. *The Iconic Book: The Image of the Christian Bible in Myth and Ritual*. Ph.D. Dissertation, Syracuse University, 2009.

Paul, Shalom. 1973. "Heavenly Tablets and Books of Life." *Journal of the Ancient Near Eastern Society* 5: 343–353.

Rothberg-Halton, Francesca. 1984. "Canonicity in Cuneiform Texts." *Journal of Cuneiform Studies* 36: 127–144. http://dx.doi.org/10.2307/1360053

Schaper, Joachim. 2004. "The Theology of Writing: The Oral and the Written, God as Scribe, and the Book of Deuteronomy." In *Anthropology and Biblical Studies: Avenues of Approach*, edited by Louise J. Lawrence and Mario I. Aguilar, 97–119. London: T. & T. Clark.

———. 2005. "Exilic and Post-Exilic Prophecy and the Orality/Literacy Problem." *Vetus Testamentum* 55: 324–342. http://dx.doi.org/10.1163/1568533054359850

Schott, Siegfried. 1972. "Thoth als Verfasser heiliger Schriften." *Zeitschrift für Ägyptische Sprache und Altertumsurkunde* 99: 20–25.

Watts, James W. 2005. "Ritual Legitimacy and Scriptural Authority." *Journal of Biblical Literature* 124(3): 401–417 = "The Rhetoric of Scripture," *Ritual and Rhetoric in Leviticus*, 193–217. Cambridge: Cambridge University Press, 2007.

———. 2009. "Desecrating Scriptures," a case study for the Luce Project in Religion, Media and International Relations at Syracuse University. http://sites.maxwell.syr.edu/luce/jameswatts.html. Accessed April 11, 2011.

———. 2011. "Using Ezra's Time as a Methodological Pivot for Understanding the Rhetoric and Functions of the Pentateuch." In *The Pentateuch*, edited by Thomas Dozeman, Konrad Schmid, and Baruch Schwartz, 489–506. Tübingen: Mohr Siebeck.

Wimbush, Vincent L. 2012. *White Men's Magic: Scripturalization as Slavery*. New York: Oxford University Press.

Yoo, Yohan. 2006. "Public Scripture Reading Rituals in Early Korean Protestantism: A Comparative Perspective." *Postscripts* 2: 226–240.

# Acknowledgements

"The Three Dimensions of Scriptures" by James W. Watts was originally published in *Postscripts* 2(2–3): 135–159.

"'Winged Words': Scriptures and Classics as Iconic Texts" by William A. Graham was originally published in *Postscripts* 6(1–3): 7–22.

"Talking about 'Iconic Books' in the Terminology of Book History" by Deirdre C. Stam was originally published in *Postscripts* 6(1–3): 23–38.

"The Iconic Book: The Image of the Bible in Early Christian Rituals" by Dorina Miller Parmenter was originally published in *Postscripts* 2(2–3): 160–189.

"Images to be Read and Words to be Seen: The Iconic Role of the Early Medieval Book" by Michelle P. Brown was originally published in *Postscripts* 6(1–3): 39–66.

"Looking at Words: The Iconicity of the Page" by S. Brent Plate was originally published in *Postscripts* 6(1–3): 67–82.

"Between the Textual and the Visual: Borderlines of Late Antique Book Iconicity" by Zeev Elitzur was originally published in *Postscripts* 6(1–3): 83–99.

"It Is What It Is (Or Is It?): Further Reflections on the Buddhist Representation of Manuscripts" by Jacob Kinnard was originally published in *Postscripts* 6(1–3): 101–116.

"The Tell-Tale Iconic Book" by M. Patrick Graham was originally published in *Postscripts* 6(1–3): 117–141.

"*Muṣḥaf* and the Material Boundaries of the Qur'an" by Natalia K. Suit was originally published in *Postscripts* 6(1–3): 141–163.

"The End of the Word as We Know It: The Cultural Iconicity of the Bible in the Twilight of Print Culture" by Timothy Beal was originally published in *Postscripts* 6(1–3): 165–184.

"Iconic Books from Below: The Christian Bible and the Discourse of Duct Tape" by Dorina Miller Parmenter was originally published in *Postscripts* 6(1–3): 185–200.

"Be-Witching Scripture: The Book of Shadows as Scripture within Wicca/ Neopagan Witchcraft" by Shawn Loner was originally published in *Postscripts* 2(2–3): 273–292.

"Engaging with the Guru: Sikh Beliefs and Practices of Guru Granth Sahib" by Kristina Myrvold was originally published in *Postscripts* 6(1–3): 201–224.

"A Birthday Party for a Sacred Text: The Gita Jayanti and the Embodiment of God as the Book and the Book as God" by Joanne Punzo Waghorne was originally published in *Postscripts* 6(1–3): 225–242.

"Possession and Repetition: Ways in which Korean Lay Buddhists Appropriate Scriptures" by Yohan Yoo was originally published in *Postscripts* 6(1–3): 243–259.

"The Bible in British Folklore" by Brian Malley was originally published in *Postscripts* 2(2–3): 241–272.

"The Pride and Prejudice of the Western World: Canonic Memory, Great Books and Archive Fever" by Karl Ivan Solibakke was originally published in *Postscripts* 6(1–3): 261–275.

"Indigenous 'Texts' of Inhabiting the Land: George Washington's Wampum Belt and the Canandaigua Treaty" by Philip P. Arnold was originally published in *Postscripts* 6(1–3): 277–289.

"The Gospels as Imperialized Sites of Memory in Late Ancient Christianity" by Jason T. Larson was originally published in *Postscripts* 6(1–3): 291–307.

"Possessing the Iconic Book: Ben Sira as Case Study" by Claudia V. Camp was originally published in *Postscripts* 6(1–3): 309–329.

"Ancient Iconic Texts and Scholarly Expertise" by James W. Watts was originally published in *Postscripts* 6(1–3): 331–344.

# Author Index


Abend, Lisa: 128, 131
Adams, Maxwell: 333, 339
Adler, Margot: 243-244, 245, 248, 251, 256
Ahearn, Allen: 49, 58
Ainalov, D. V.: 72, 87
Albin, Michael W.: 191, 197, 205
Al-Dārimī: 45
Alexander, Jonathan J. G.: 94, 103, 115
Ali, Wijdan: 123, 131
Allen, Allison Metcalf: 231, 234
Ammar, Hamed: 193, 205
Anderson, Ruth: 333, 334, 335, 341
Antze, Paul: 374, 387
Appadurai, Arjun: 161, 163, 200,
Argan, Giulio Carlo: 153, 163
Arnold, Philip P.: v, 4, 5, 361, 410, 417, 420,
Asad, Talal: 190, 205
Aspin, Jehoshaphat: 317, 339
Assmann, Aleida: 349, 359
Assmann, Jan: 349, 359, 374, 385, 412, 413, 414, 417
Aubrey, John: 332, 333, 339, 342,
Austin, J. L.: 268, 279
Avrin, Leila: 95, 115
Ayerst, David: 101, 103, 115

Babb, Lawrence A.: 271, 279
Backhouse, Janet M.: 102, 118
Bagchi, Sitansusekhar S.: 152, 163
Baker, Colin F.: 196, 205
Baker, Nicholson.: 128, 132
Bal, Mieke: 120, 132
Banks, M. M.: 317, 333, 334, 335, 339
Baranov, B.: 74, 86, 87
Barclay, Isabella: 319, 331, 339
Barker, Nicholas: 58
Barnett, Paul W.: 143, 144, 145, 148
Barrett, Justin L.: 317, 339
Bartrum, Giulia: 185
Bauman, Richard: 267, 269, 279, 280
Bawa, Ujagar Singh: 265, 280
Beal, Timothy: v, 4, 5, 56, 207, 208, 221, 223, 227, 230, 234, 375, 385, 393, 395, 405, 419
Beard, Mary: 385
Becker, Marion Rombauer: 60
Bell, Catherine: 18, 30, 263, 278, 280
Belting, Hans: 77, 87
Benjamin, Walter: 198, 354, 356, 359
Berger, Helen A.: 250, 257
Bertrand, J. Mark: 131, 231, 232, 235
Betz, Hans Dieter: 79, 87
Bhabha, Homi K.: 385, 386
Bianchi, Ugo: 65, 87
Bidderman, Shlomo: 27, 30
Bielo, James S.: 209, 223, 227, 230, 231, 235, 236, 315
Billson, Charles James: 333, 334, 339
Black, William G.: 318, 319, 320, 321, 339
Blackman, Winifred S.: 193, 205
Blair, Sheila S.: 195, 196, 205
Bloom, Jonathan M.: 195, 196, 205
Bogdanović, Jelena: 70, 87
Bonser, Wilfrid: 323, 339
Boone, Kathleen C.: 235
Bourdieu, Pierre: 223
Bowers, Fredson: 57, 58
Boyarin, Daniel: 225, 235
Boyer, Pascal: 337, 339

Brandon, S. G. F.: 75, 88
Brann, Eva T.: 351, 359
Braude, William G.: 140, 148
Briggs, Charles L.: 267, 269, 279, 280
Briggs, K. M.: 317, 318, 320, 324, 332, 333, 339, 343
Bringhurst, Robert: 126, 132
Britten, James: 332, 333, 339
Broek, R. van den: 69, 77, 88
Brooks, E. W.: 85, 88
Brown, Bill: 157, 161, 163, 202, 204, 205
Brown, Karin Brinkman: 172, 185
Brown, Michelle: v, 3, 5, 12, 30, 49, 51, 52, 58, 81-83, 88, 93, 96-99, 101-105, 110-113, 115-116, 229, 386, 419
Brown, Peter: 67, 76-77
Brown, Robert: 333, 334, 335, 339
Brown, Theo: 321, 325, 333, 334, 339
Brown, T. Julian: 116
Brubaker, Leslie: 113, 116
Bruce, John: 319, 339
Brunt, P. A.: 386
Bryson, Norman: 120, 132
Buchanan, Scott: 350, 351, 353, 359
Buckton, David: 100, 116
Burne, Charlotte S.: 317, 319, 320, 329, 339, 341
Burner, Brett: 223
Burton-Christie, Douglas: 386

Cameron, Averil: 384, 386
Camp, Claudia V.: v, 4, 5, 389, 395, 402, 405, 406, 420
Carey, F.: 317, 343
Carl, Phil: 229-230, 233, 235
Carmichael, Alexander: 318, 340
Carpenter, Joel A.: 213, 223
Carr, David M.: 393, 405
Carrick, T. W.: 317, 340
Carter, John: 49, 58
Casement, William: 352, 359
Casey, Edward: 386
Castelli, Elizabeth A.: 5, 374, 386
Cattell, Maria: 374, 375, 386,
Chartier, Roger: 129, 130, 132, 192, 198, 205
Chazelle, Celia: 103, 116
Choi, Keunyoung: 300, 312
Climo, Jacob: 374, 375, 386
Coburn, Thomas: 40, 45
Cohen, Boaz: 146, 148
Cohen, Shaye J. D.: 413, 417
Cole, Richard G.: 168, 185
Colgrave, Bertram: 102, 116
Conley, Tom: 137, 148
Connerton, Paul: 374, 386
Conze, Edward: 153, 163
Cook, Frederick: 370, 371
Cook, Terry: 375, 376, 386
Corbin, Henry: 191, 205
Courtney, M. A.: 319, 320, 333, 340
Covino, William A.: 78-79, 88
Craigie, W. A.: 317, 320, 340
Cróinín, Dáibhí Ó.: 105, 118
Crosby, Cindy: 223
Cross, F. L.: 167, 185
Cunningham, Scott: 249, 250, 257
Cutler, Norman: 154, 164

Dalley, Stephanie: 409, 417
Darnton, Robert: 57, 59
Davies, Jonathan Ceredig: 325, 333, 334, 340
Davies, Owen: 319, 320, 321, 322, 327-328, 340
Davies, Philip R.: 393, 405
Davies, T. A.: 319, 340
De Castro, Eduardo Viveiros: 278, 279, 280
de Hamel, Christopher: 94, 116, 120, 132
Decasa, George C.: 193, 205
Denham, Michael Aislabie: 319, 340
Derrida, Jacques: 157, 163, 347, 349, 356-359
Deshman, Robert: 103, 116
Di Lella, Alexander A.: 395, 398, 400, 403, 404, 406
Dick, Michael: 296, 298
Diebold, William: 103, 116
Dilasser, Maurice: 69, 71, 88
Dix, Gregory: 69, 88
Dobson, Ed.: 235
Donaldson, James: 91
Donner, Fred M.: 192, 205
Drewes, David: 152, 153, 163
Drogin, Marc: 78- 80, 83-86, 88
Drucker, Johanna: 122, 132
Dunn, James D. G.: 143, 144, 148
Dusenbery, Verne A.: 268, 271, 280
Dutton, Paul: 103, 116

Eastmond, Antony: 226, 235, 238
Eck, Diana: 154, 163
Eckel, Malcolm David. 43, 45

Eliade, Mircea: 44, 45, 87, 90, 308, 310, 312, 364, 371, 406
Eliot, John: 53, 59
Elitzur, Zeev: v, 3, 5, 135, 419
Elkins, James: 120, 132
Elsner, Jaś: 386
Ettlinger, Ellen: 318, 340
Evans, Craig F.: 145, 148
Evans, Griff: 320, 328, 340
Eyre, Margaret: 320, 328, 334, 340

Falwell, Jerry: 230, 235
Farley, A. J.: 228, 229, 235
Fenwick, J. G.: 324, 340
Fischer, Steven Roger: 121, 132
Fisher, A. S. T.: 101, 103, 115
Flower, Harriet I.: 386
Folkert, Kendall A.: 394, 405
Forby, Robert: 332, 333, 334, 341
Foster, Benjamin R.: 409, 410, 412, 417
Foucault, Michel: 120, 132
Foucher, Alfred: 155, 163
Fowler, J. T., ed.: 83, 84, 87, 88
Freedberg, David: 154, 163
Frew, D. H.: 247, 257
Frilingos, Christopher: 383, 386

Gabra, Gawdat: 95, 113, 116
Gadamer, Hans-Georg: 160, 164, 352
Gaehde, Joachim: 103, 117
Gallup, Alec: 211, 223, 235
Gallup, George H., Jr.: 390, 405
Gamble, Harry Y.: 68, 79, 88, 379, 380, 381, 386
Gameson, Richard G.: 105, 116
Gardner, Gerald B.: 240-253, 255-256, 257
Gaskell, Philip: 57, 59
Geertz, Clifford: 42, 45
Gell, Alfred: 278, 280
Gerish, W. B.: 334, 341
Gethin, Rupert: 300, 312
Gibson, John Arthur: 371
Gingerich, Owen: 57, 59
Gitelman, Lisa: 5
Gombrich, Richard: 301, 305, 312
Gomez, Michael A.: 28, 30
Goody, Jack: 28, 31, 79, 89, 413, 414, 417
Goshen-Gottstein, Alon: 395, 405
Gowing, Alain: 386
Grabar, André: 74, 89
Grabar, Oleg: 122, 132
Graffin, Pierre: 63, 89
Grafton, Anthony: 57, 59
Graham, William A.: v, 3, 5, 10-14,16, 17, 19, 20, 26, 31, 33, 37, 39, 45, 137, 148, 239, 254, 257, 300-305, 312, 393, 406, 416, 417, 419,
Graham, M. Patrick: v, 4, 5, 165, 419
Grattan, J. H. G.: 328, 341
Greg, W. W.: 57, 59
Gregor, Walter: 317, 318, 341
Grey, Edwin: 329, 333, 341
Griffiths, Paul J.: 26, 27, 31, 41, 45
Grinde, Donald A., Jr.: 368, 371
Grinsell, L. V.: 329, 341
Groendahl, Boris: 261, 280
Groome, W. Wollaston: 333, 334, 341
Guiley, Rosemary Ellen: 246, 257
Gurdon, Eveline Camilla: 317, 319, 320, 321, 332-333, 341
Gutch, Eliza: 333, 334, 341
Gutjahr, Paul C.: 230, 236
Gūven, Suna: 386

Hadow, Grace E.: 333, 334, 335, 341
Haines-Eitzen, Kim: 81, 89
Halbertal, Moshe: 256, 257
Halbwachs, Maurice: 374, 386
Haley, Eric, J.: 228, 236
Hamel, Christopher de: 94, 116, 120, 132, 135, 148
Harding, Susan: 230, 236
Hardy, Thomas: 333, 341
Harland, John: 317, 319, 332, 341
Harthan, John P.: 185
Hartland, M. E.: 317, 319, 332, 341
Harvey, B. Peter.: 300, 312
Harvey, Graham: 258, 278, 279, 280
Havner, Vance: 225, 231, 236
Hayward, L. H.: 318, 341
Hedrick, Charles: 386
Hedstrom, Margaret: 375, 386
Heen, Erik M.: 236
Henderson, William: 319, 321, 322, 328, 333, 334, 338, 341
Hendrix, Scott: 185
Hengel, Martin: 413, 417
Herbermann, Charles George: 182, 185
Heyman, George: 25, 31
Hieronymus, Frank: 167, 168, 185

Hill, Richard: 368, 370, 371
Hindson, Ed: 235
Hirsch, E.: 42, 45
Hitler, Adolph: 48, 59
Hobbs, Vanessa: 48, 59
Hockin, Frederick: 321, 341
Hoffmann, Thomas: 192, 205
Hofmann, Ginnie: 60
Holdrege, Barbara A.: 10, 20, 31, 41, 45, 226, 236
Hollstein, F. W. H.: 167, 168, 170, 174, 178, 185
Hone, William: 333, 341
Hornik, Heidi J.: 185
Horowitz, Haim S.: 139, 148
Humfress, Caroline: 68, 71, 72, 89, 146, 148, 373, 386
Hunt, Robert: 319, 321, 322, 333, 341
Huntington, Susan L.: 154, 164
Hurst, David: 104, 116
Hurwitz, Leon: 43, 46
Hustwit, Gary: 126, 129, 132
Hutchins, Robert M.: 347, 348-349, 353-358, 359
Hutton, Patrick:
Hutton, Ronald: 243, 245- 248, 257
Hwang, Jung Sun: 223

Idel, Moshe: 142, 147, 148

Jackson, Georgina F.: 319, 320, 341
Jackson, Wayne: 392, 406
James, Frank: 236
Jemison, G. Peter: 361, 371
Jennings, Howard Eiland: 359
Johansen, Bruce E.: 368, 372
Johnson, Willard L.: 300, 313

Kaminishi, Ikumi: 120, 132
Kang, Yoonhee: 268, 280
Kapstein, Israel J.: 140, 148
Kassam, Tazim: 5
Kaur Singh, Nikky-Guninder: 262, 264, 280
Kaur, Guninder: 262, 280
Keane, Webb: 199, 201, 203, 206
Keen, Ralph: 185
Keightley, Georgia: 387
Kelly, Aidan: 245, 247, 257
Kelly, Eamonn P.: 111, 115, 116
Kelly, Susan: 97, 116
Kern, H.: 43, 46
Kessler, Edward: 15, 31
Kessler, Herbert: 74-75, 89, 103, 116
Kilvert, Robert Francis: 333, 334, 338, 341
Kingsbury, J. B.: 320, 342
Kinnard, Jacob N.: v, 4, 5, 11, 25, 26, 31, 151, 153, 154, 158, 159, 164, 305, 312, 408, 415, 419
Kirk, Robert: 317, 342
Kitzinger, Ernest: 145, 149
Kitzinger, Ernst: 100, 117
Klingshirn, William E.: 89, 90, 148, 149, 387
Kohli, Surinder Singh: 262, 265, 280
Kort, Wesley: 27, 31
Kosso, Peter: 409, 417
Krencker, Daniel M.: 387
Kroencke, J. Kent: 232, 236
Kumra, Vivek: 287, 298

Lambek, Michael. 374, 387
Landesmann, Peter. 185
Lane, Edward William. 193, 206
Lane, Eugene: 68, 90
Lane-Poole, Stanley: 193, 206
Lang, Andrew: 317, 342
Lang, Bernhard: 379, 387
Langer, Ruth: 146, 149
Lanhamp, Richard A.:137, 149
Larson, Jason T.: v, 4, 5, 52, 146, 348, 373, 384, 413, 420
Latham, Charlotte: 319, 320, 333, 342
Latour, Bruno: 204, 206
Lauterbach, Jacob Z.: 139, 149
Layton, Bentley: 74, 89
Lean, Vincent Stuckey: 317, 318, 320, 332, 333, 335, 342
Leather, Ella Mary: 318, 320, 324, 325, 333, 334, 335, 342
Lee, Young Shin: 223
Leipold, Johannes: 36, 46
Lesko, Leonard H.: 78, 90
Levering, Miriam: 32, 45, 236, 302, 304, 305, 307, 309, 312, 313, 405
Lewis, Todd: 161, 164
Liddell, Henry George: 66, 90
Lieberman, Stephen J.: 411, 412, 418
Lings, Martin: 123, 132, 195, 206
Liverani, Mario: 408, 418
Livingstone, Elizabeth A.: 185, 417
Lombardi, Robert: 232, 236
Loner, Shawn: v, 4, 239, 420
Long, Burke: 11, 31

Louw, J. P.: 130, 133
Love, Velma: 28, 31
Lowden, John: 68, 70, 90, 100, 117, 379, 384, 385, 387
Lupker, Stephen J.: 137, 149

MacMullen, Ramsay: 68, 85, 90
Madigan, Daniel A.: 20, 31, 196, 206
Magliocco, Sabina: 241, 242, 243, 245, 246, 247, 251, 252, 257
Malinine, M.: 74, 90,
Malley, Brian: v, 4, 5, 85, 90, 223, 227, 228, 230, 234, 237, 254, 257, 315, 317, 331, 332, 339, 342, 415, 420
Maltomini, F.: 80-81, 90
Manguel, Alberto: 85, 90
Mann, Barbara A.: 363, 364, 365, 367, 372
Mann, Gurinder Singh: 5, 262, 274, 281
Mansi, J. D.: 71, 76, 88, 90
Maple, Eric: 320, 342
March, H. Colley: 324, 342
Marion, Jean Luc: 154, 164
Marner, Dominic: 112, 113, 117
Marsden, George M.: 230, 237
Marty, Martin: 1, 6, 11, 31, 63, 64, 90, 168, 185, 225, 226, 237, 389, 390, 391, 392, 399, 406
Mathews, Thomas: 70, 71, 72, 90
McCullars, Stan: 232, 237
McDannell, Colleen: 227, 237
McDermott, James P.: 41, 46
McKenzie, Donald: 57, 59
McKerrow, Ronald B.: 57, 59
McLuhan, Marshall: 58, 214, 223
McMahan, David: 152, 164
Meades, Jonathan: 48, 59
Melanchthon, Monica Jyotsna: 15, 31
Melion, Walter S.: 186
Mellors, John: 105, 117
Mendels, Doron: 383, 387
Meyer, Stephanie: 48, 59
Migne, J. P.: 88-92, 104, 113, 116, 117
Miller, David L.: 67, 90, 120, 132
Miller, Harry: 82, 83, 90
Miller, Patricia Cox: 78, 79, 90
Mioni, Elpidio: 85, 90,
Misen, Robert: 229, 237
Mitchell, Donald W.: 300, 313
Mitchell, Marshall: 28
Mitchell, W. J. T.: 120, 132, 151, 160, 161, 162, 163, 164, 193, 206,
Moerman, D. Max: 305, 313
Mohawk, John C.: 364, 368, 372
Moore, J. M.: 386
Moore, Walter L.: 186
Morenz, Siegfried: 36, 46
Morgan, David: 5, 120, 132, 227, 237
Morgan, W. E. T.: 322, 342
Moss, Fletcher: 318, 327, 342
Mueller, Eric S.: 232, 237
Murray, Margaret: 243, 244, 248, 257
Musurillo, Herbert: 382, 387
Mütherich, Florentine: 103, 117
Myers, Kenneth A.: 223
Mynors, Roger A. B.: 102, 116
Myrvold, Kristina: v, 4, 5, 149, 237, 261, 262, 266, 269, 270, 274, 276, 281, 313, 407, 418, 420

Naeh, Shlomo: 138, 149
Naipaul, V. S.: 333, 342
Napier, James: 333, 335
Narayana, Vasudha: 154, 164
Nelson, Charles A.: 349, 359
Nersessian, Vrej: 95, 117
Neusner, Jacob: 141, 142, 149
Nevin, John W.: 212, 223
Newall, Venetia: 329, 342
Newman, L. F.: 320, 342
Newport, Frank: 406
Nickelsburg, George W. E.: 399, 406
Nöldeke, Theodor: 192, 206
Nora, Pierre: 358, 359, 374, 387
Nordenfalk, Carl: 94, 117
Northall, G. F.: 319, 342
Nouryeh, Christopher: 192, 206

Ó Floinn, Raghnall: 111, 117
O'Reilly, Jennifer: 84, 91, 101, 104, 105, 117
O'Toole, James M.: 376, 387
Oberoi, Harjot: 274, 281
Ochoa, Todd Ramón: 201, 206
Olmert, Michael: 131, 132
Ong, Walter J.: 96, 117
Opie, Iona Archibald: 317, 319, 324, 329, 342
Orion, Loretta: 243, 244, 257
Owen, Elias: 317, 320, 333, 340
Ozanne, Christine: 317, 343

Pace, Edward A.: 185
Pächt, Otto: 94, 117
Page, Ray I.: 96, 117
Palmer, Stephen E.: 137, 149
Parker, Angelina: 324, 333, 334, 343
Parker, George F.: 64, 91
Parkes, Malcolm B.: 96, 97, 117
Parmenter, Dorina Miller: v, 1, 2, 3, 4, 5, 12, 63, 143, 145, 146, 147, 149, 208, 216, 225-229, 234, 237, 377, 348, 407, 409, 415, 418, 419
Parsons, Ann: 105, 117
Pasulka, Diana Walsh: 27, 31
Paton, C. I.: 329, 343
Patton, Laurie: 5
Paul, Shalom: 409, 418
Peacock, Edward: 317, 343
Peacock, Mabel Geraldine Woodruffe: 333, 334, 341
Pelikan, Jaroslav: 75, 91
Peters, F. E.: 225, 237
Peterson, Indira Viswanathan: 297, 298
Petrucci, Armando: 69, 71, 76, 91
Pickstock, Catherine: 27, 31
Pietz, William: 66, 91
Plate, S. Brent: vi, 3, 5, 119, 120, 132, 136, 208, 221, 418
Plomer, William: 333, 334, 338, 341
Prothero, Stephen: 230, 238
Putnam, Daryl: 228, 238

Rabin, Yisrael A.: 139, 148
Raftery, Joseph: 83, 91
Raguin, Virginia Chieffo: 120, 133
Raimundi, Giovanni Battista: 186
Rapp, Claudia: 5, 63, 69, 71, 80, 84, 85, 91, 145, 146, 147, 149, 373, 387
Rappaport, Roy A.: 23, 31, 269, 281
Ravenwolf, Silver: 249, 250, 253, 257
Rawsthorn, Alice: 128, 133
Reeves, William: 83, 84, 87, 91
Reid, Calvin: 223
Reynolds, Gabriel Said: 206
Rhys, John: 321, 343
Rice, David: 226, 238
Rice, Tamara Talbot: 226, 238
Ricoeur, Paul: 160, 161, 164
Roberts, Alexander: 91
Roberts, Colin H.: 94, 117
Robinson, Richard H.: 300, 313
Rombauer, Irma von Starkloff: 60
Rorie, David: 317, 318, 332, 343
Rose, H. J.: 317, 338, 344
Rothberg-Halton, Francesca: 409, 418
Rousseau, Philip: 385, 387
Rückert, H.: 42, 45
Rumsey, Alan: 268, 381
Rushton, Peter: 319, 343
Ryan, Michael: 112, 117

Saenger, Paul: 121, 124, 129, 133
Safire, William: 151, 164, 228, 238
Safran, Linda: 89, 90, 91, 100, 117, 148, 149, 387
Said, Edward: 192, 206
Salmon, L.: 320, 322, 324, 333, 334, 343
Sanders, Jack T.: 402, 406
Sanders, James A.: 394, 406
Sarefield, Daniel: 381, 387
Sarma, Deepak: 5
Saussure, Ferdinand de: 137, 149
Schaaf, Gregory: 368, 372
Schaper, Joachim: 413, 414, 415, 418
Schede, Martin: 387
Schedel, Hartmann: 53
Schein, Anna M.: 371
Schleicher, Marianne: 142, 149, 315
Schniedewind, William M.: 393, 406
Schöner, Petra: 186
Schopen, Gregory: 1, 6, 152, 153, 164, 300, 306, 313
Schott, Siegfried: 409, 418
Schreckenberg, Heinz: 181, 186
Schroeder, H. J.: 76, 91
Schüssler Fiorenza, Elisabeth: 26, 31
Scott, Robert: 66, 90
Sebeok, Thomas A.: 136, 149
Shaw, George Bernard: 135, 136, 147, 149
Sheppard, Gerald T.: 394, 395, 406
Shlain, Leonard: 120, 133
Shopshire, James M.: 12, 31
Simmons, Wendy W.: 211, 223, 235, 405
Simon, Maurice: 148, 149
Simon, Stephanie: 221, 223
Simone, Mark A.: 233, 238
Simpkins, John Ewart: 317, 318, 332, 343
Simpson, Jacqueline: 318, 319, 320, 327, 343
Singer, Charles J.: 328, 341
Singer-Vine, Jeremy: 133
Singh, Arvind-Pal: 262, 281

Singh, Bhai Vir: 264, 281
Singh, Fauja: 277, 281
Singh, Gurnek: 262, 281
Singh, Jodh: 264, 281
Singh, Pashuara: 262, 274, 281
Singleton, A. H.: 336, 343
Skeat, T. C.: 94, 117
Skehan, Patrick W.: 395, 398, 400, 403, 404, 406
Skidmore, Sarah: 224
Smith, Jonathan Z.: 18, 26, 28, 32, 67, 92, 157, 164, 227, 238, 378, 387
Smith, Wilfred Cantwell: 9, 10-11, 13, 20, 26, 32, 143, 150, 299, 301-303, 305, 311, 313
Solibakke, Karl Ivan. vi, 4, 5, 37, 347, 417, 420
Spooner, B. C.: 320, 343
St. Clair, Archer: 70, 92
Stam, Deirdre C.: vi, 3, 5, 47, 221, 226, 230, 407, 418
Stansbury, Mark: 104, 117
Starhawk: 248-250, 257
Starrett, Gregory: 200, 201, 206
Stephens, Mitchell: 120, 133
Stokes, Margaret: 83, 92
Stowasser, Barbara Freyer: 193, 206
Strand, Kenneth A.: 186
String, Tatiana C.: 186
Strong, John S.: 300, 313
Stuart, John: 65, 67, 92
Suit, Natalia K.: vi, 4, 5, 122, 189, 415, 419
Suleman, Fahmida: 122, 133
Sun, Jung: 223

Tatem, MoiraL: 317, 319, 329, 342
Taylor, E. S.: 318, 343
Taylor, Mark R.: 315, 318, 330, 343
Thuesen, Peter J.: 224
Tongue, Ruth L.: 317, 318, 320, 332, 333, 343
Tooker, Elisabeth: 365, 372
Toorn, Karel van der: 1, 6, 11, 32, 66, 92, 393, 406
Townend, B. R.: 319, 343
Tribb, Jonathan D.: 186
Tucci, G.: 43, 46
Tudor, Victoria: 112, 117
Tuladhar-Douglas, Will: 301, 305, 306, 307, 313
Turgut, Ayse: 123, 133

Underwood, Mary Grace: 317, 344
Updike, John: 60
van Regemorter, Berthe: 111, 118

Venables, Robert W.: 368, 369, 372
Verdon, Timothy: 182, 186
Vickery, A. Roy: 321, 326, 344
Von Ubisch, E.: 186

Waghorne, Joanne: vi, 4, 5, 154, 164, 283, 420
Wallace, David Foster: 119, 133
Wallace, Paul A. W.: 372
Wallot, Jean-Pierre: 378, 387
Walsh, Maura: 105, 118,
Walter, Christopher: 71, 72, 74, 92
Ward, Benedicta: 85, 92
Ware, Timothy: 147, 150
Watson, Elizabeth Catherine: 318, 340
Watson, James Carmichael: 318, 340
Watt, W. Montgomery: 193, 206
Watts, James W.: vi, 1, 5, 9, 19, 32, 36, 49, 131, 136, 137, 140, 208, 211, 230, 253, 255, 256, 257, 284, 378, 388, 389, 392, 394, 395, 399-402, 407, 409, 413, 414, 416, 418, 419-420
Weber, Timothy P.: 230, 233, 238
Webster, Leslie: 102, 118
Wedewer, Hermann: 172, 186
Weitzmann, Kurt: 94, 118
Wendland, Ernst R.: 130, 133
Wendland, Henning: 186
Westropp, Thomas J.: 320, 333, 344
Wharton, Annabel: 64, 92, 226, 238
Whitelock, Dorothy: 102, 118
Widengren, Geo: 225, 238
Wiener Margaret: 193, 206
Wiles, Maurice: 225, 238
Williams, Paul: 300, 313
Williams, T. W.: 317, 318, 320, 332, 333, 335, 342
Wimbush, Vincent L.: 2, 5, 26, 31, 32, 281, 412, 418
Winstanley, L.: 317, 338, 344
Woodward, Julia Lucy: 318, 320, 332, 333, 335, 342
Wosh, Peter J.: 224
Wright, A. R.: 319, 344
Wright, E. M.: 317, 319, 321, 334, 335, 344
Wright, David H.: 94, 103, 118
Yoo, Joseph: 231, 238
Yoo, Yohan: vi, 4, 5, 299, 393, 414, 415, 418, 420
York, Michael: 241, 258
Zachariae, Theodor: 42, 46
Zanker, Paul: 387
Zwemer, Samuel M.: 193, 206

# Subject Index

1 John: 120, 123
ABC for Book Collectors: 49, 58
*Abhidharma*: 40, 43
Abraham of Harmonthis: 111
Adamnan: 83-84, 87
*Adhyāshaya-samcodana*: 40
Adi Granth (see Guru Granth)
Adler, Mortimer: 349, 353
Aeneid: 34, 35, 37
aesthetic: 49, 126, 167, 192, 193, 194, 196, 198, 256, 357,
Aethelwulf: 113, 115
African Americans: 10, 12, 32, 219
Agbar, Letter of: 80, 320, 330
*akhand path* : 269, 272
Alexandrinus, Codex: 94,
Al-Ghazali: 34, 197
Algonquin: 53
Al-Nawawī, Yaḥyā Ibn Sharaf: 197
Ambrose: 167, 168, 170
American Bible Society (ABS): 212, 223
Amiatinus, Codex: 104, 106
*amrit:* 270
amulets, talismans: 27, 28, 80, 81, 113, 193, 227, 271, 318-320, 415
aniconic: 11, 21, 64, 65, 108, 122, 155
Annunciation : 178-79, 183
Anthony (saint): 85, 95, 97:
Antigone: 35
antiquarian book trade: 49, 54-57
Anzu: 410
Arabic: 34, 123-24, 125, 189, 197, 199, 415
archive, archivists: 347-349, 352-359, 374-378, 385, 409, 412
Aristotle: 24, 377
Arjan, Guru: 265, 268, 269, 277
Armagh, Book of: 112
art: 2, 4, 11, 14, 15, 16, 25, 44, 51, 63, 96, 100, 102, 104, 107, 109, 123, 124, 151, 153, 154, 157, 160, 162, 165-185, 193, 194, 198, 226, 231, 246, 308, 408, 409, 410, 411, 415
Ashurbanipal: 411-412
association copy: 54
Assyrian: 411
*Aṣṭasāhasrikāprajñāpāramitā*: 153, 157, 163
Athanasius: 376
Augustine of Hippo: 34, 80, 85, 87, 104, 113, 167, 168, 170, 382,
Augustine of Canterbury: 102
Aureus, Codex: 95, 111
authority: 17, 20-24, 26, 29, 34, 36, 39, 40, 41, 66, 67, 71, 101, 102, 115, 151, 170, 181, 198, 201, 204, 205, 209, 210-212, 222, 225, 227, 230, 233, 234, 240, 241, 245, 247-252, 255, 256, 262, 263, 265, 272, 274, 275, 277-279, 327, 356, 376, 378, 390, 393, 394, 396, 399, 401, 402, 408, 410, 411, 413, 414

Babylon, Babylonians: 11, 12, 140, 255, 394, 409, 410, 412, 413
Basho: 35, 45
Basil: 97, 379
Baskerville type: 124-127
Bede: 81, 97, 99, 102, 103, 104, 108, 113
Ben Sira: 4, 389-406,
Besa: 71, 87
Besant, Annie: 243
Bhagavad Gita: 4, 35, 36, 37, 45, 283-298

Bible (see also Hebrew Bible) : 2, 10, 11, 12, 16, 17, 25-29, 35, 37, 41, 42, 44, 45, 50, 53, 54, 56, 63-92, 93, 97, 98, 104, 105, 115, 125, 126, 127, 130, 131, 139, 140, 147, 165-186, 192, 207-224, 225-238, 239, 253, 254, 283, 284, 286, 293, 302, 315-344, 373, 375, 384, 385, 389-395, 402, 405, 414
Bible dipping: 231, 332, 334, 335,
Biblezines: 216-217
Biblical scholarship: 26, 392, 393
biblicism: 227
bibliographic : 95, 207
Bibliomancy: 85, 332, 335, 336, 337
bindings: 52, 53, 70, 111, 114, 131, 183, 189, 228, 231, 380, 384
*Black Elk Speaks:* 35
Black Hebrew Israelites: 28
blessing: 14, 69, 123, 131, 173, 178, 182, 203, 204, 209, 310, 323
body: 43, 66, 67, 83, 86, 104, 111, 112, 114, 121, 123, 154, 189, 264, 269, 271, 272, 276, 279, 283, 284, 286, 289, 293, 294, 297, 300, 305, 317, 405
Boniface: 102
book history: 3, 47-60, 407
book of nature: 409, 411
book shrine: 82, 83, 111, 114, 115
*Brothers Karamazov:* 35
buddhavacana: 40, 41, 151
Buddhism: 12, 21, 151-164, 299-313, 415
Byzantine: 2, 66, 67, 70, 71, 94, 95, 100, 101, 108-111, 138, 143, 146, 226

calligraphy: 3, 15, 16, 20, 22, 23, 95, 96, 100, 120, 122-124, 125, 126, 189, 193-201, 246, 251, 252, 308, 309, 383
Canandaigua Treaty: 361, 362, 369-371
canon, canonical, canonization: 1, 10, 23, 40, 43, 95, 151, 159, 222, 239, 253, 256, 262, 265, 297, 300, 321, 347-359, 375, 393-397, 401, 402, 404, 405
*capsa*, book bucket: 380,
Cassiodorus: 84, 104, 116,
Cathach Reliquary: 83, 111
Catholic (see Roman Catholics)
Celsus: 381,
Ceolfrith: 104, 106
Chalcedon, Council of: 107
charm (see amulet and spell)
Chester Beatty Papyrus: 380
China: 122, 285, 304, 306, 311, 414
*chi-rho:* 99, 101
Christ: 21, 25, 41, 42, 69-77, 79, 85, 86, 96, 98, 99, 101, 103, 107-109, 111, 113, 143-148, 154, 172, 174-176, 178, 179, 181, 184, 218, 233, 234, 316, 318-323, 328, 373, 378, 379, 382
Christians: 4, 11, 12, 21, 25, 42, 52, 63-118, 138, 143, 145-148, 165-186, 207-238, 243, 244, 253, 256, 286, 315-344, 364, 373-388, 391, 395, 413, 415
Chrysostom, John: 80, 81, 89
Church of the Holy Sepulchre: 69
cinema (see movie):
classics: 3, 33-46
Cleveland, Grover : 64, 390, 392
codex: 3, 17, 20, 50-52, 68, 70, 79, 93-118, 254, 374, 376, 377, 379, 383
colonialism: 13, 65, 192, 193, 242, 285, 361-372, 385, 407
Columba, Saint: 77, 81, 83, 84, 95, 96, 105, 107, 111, 112, 113
Confucius: 35
Constantine: 69, 77, 94, 99, 101, 108, 373, 374, 382, 383
Constantinople, Councils of: 72, 76, 107
Copts, Coptic: 95, 98, 107, 109, 111, 113
Cranach the Elder, Lucas: 178
Crowley, Aleister: 243, 245, 251
Crux Gemmata: 101
Cuthbert: 28, 81, 101, 106, 107, 111-114
Cyprian: 379

Dante: 34, 45:
Daoist (see Taoist)
Dead Sea Scrolls: 29, 402
December Testament: 168, 171, 173, 174, 175,
desecrated scriptures: 9, 11, 16, 20, 262, 381, 418
*dharani:* 301, 306, 307, 310, 311, 312
Dharma: 39, 42, 43, 155, 156, 300, 305, 310
Diamond Sutra: 310
Digital Image Archive: 165-186
Dignāgā: 43, 46:
Diocletian: 381, 382, 385
diptych: 70, 101, 109
divination: 15, 27, 227, 255, 303, 324, 331-339
divinity: 25, 108, 241
Dogen: 34,

*Don Quixote*: 34, 35
drama, dramatization: 10, 11, 14, 15, 18-22, 24, 25, 57, 252, 394
*Dukhbhanjani Sahib:* 269:
Durham Gospels: 95
Durrow, Book of: 84

Eck, John: 170, 176
Edict of Milan: 382
editions: 28, 49, 50, 52, 53, 54, 56, 104, 172, 197-200, 216-221,
Egeria: 69
Ellison, Keith : 416
empire, imperialism: 94, 96, 97, 100, 110, 193, 373-385, 411, 412, 413
Enoch: 399, 401, 402
Enuma Elish: 35, 409, 410, 411
Ephesus, Council : 71
epics: 11, 19, 20, 34, 37, 293, 409, 410, 411
Erasmus: 167, 174, 176,
ethos of texts: 24-26, 400, 401
*etoki*: 120, 132
Eucharist: 41, 71, 77
Euplus, Acts of: 382
Eusebius of Caesaria : 94, 108, 373, 376, 380-383
evangelicals: 208, 209, 213, 214, 218, 225-238, 254, 286, 331
evil eye: 193, 318, 320, 328, 330
exorcism: 326-328, 330
Ezekiel: 143, 321, 326, 402

Fellowship of Crotona: 242
feminist: 248, 402
fetish: 2, 52, 161
films (see movies)
*Fiqh al-Sunnah*: 190, 206
*Flower Ornament Sutra*: 308, 310
folklore: 4, 243, 244, 315-344
font type: 121, 128, 129, 131, 199, 205, 213, 217, 252
Frankfurt Book Fairs: 54
Freer Gospels: 111, 384

Gallup poll: 211, 223, 235, 390, 405, 406
gender: 4, 219, 294, 389-406
Genesis: 15, 75, 94, 139, 140, 141, 142, 218, 223, 391, 392
*Genesis Rabbah*: 141, 142, 149,
Geneva Bible: 131
genizahs: 142
Germain of Paris: 71, 88
Germanus of Constantinople: 70, 75, 89
Ghazali, Abu Hamid al-: 34, 197
Gideons Bible: 56, 216
Gilgamesh: 35
Gita (see Bhagavad Gita)
Gobind Singh, Guru: 264, 265, 270
Goethe: 34, 45
Golden Canon Tables: 95
Golden Light Sutra: 159
Gospel of Truth: 74, 90, 378
Gospels: 3, 4, 16, 20, 22, 28, 63, 68-82, 85-87, 96-115, 129, 147, 167, 168, 170, 172-175, 179, 182, 184, 208, 218, 229, 233, 294, 373-388, 413, 415
Gotham: 121, 127, 128
Gothic Type: 125, 131
Great Books of the Western World: 347-359
Greek tragedies: 34
Gregory the Great: 96, 97, 99, 103, 108, 113, 167, 170
Gregory Nazianus: 72
Gregory of Tours: 373, 384
grimoire: 244-246, 251, 252, 255
*gurbani*: 264, 271
gurdwara: 265, 272, 273, 275, 277
*Gurmukhi* script: 264, 274,
guru : 4, 40, 261-281, 284, 285, 287-290
Guru Granth Sahib: 35, 41, 261-281
Gutenberg Bible: 28, 29, 54, 57, 93, 209, 221

hadith: 36, 40, 190, 191, 197, 199
halakha: 142
Halevi, Judah: 34
Haudenosaunee: 361-372
havan: 284, 286, 287, 290, 293, 294, 296, 297
Heart Sutra: 310
heavenly texts: 12, 72, 75, 77, 142, 225, 397-398, 409, 410, 412
Hebrew Bible: 26, 29, 98, 135-150, 177, 185, 225, 284, 380, 394, 397
Helvetica: 126, 129, 132
Hermes: 78
Hiawantha: 362, 363, 365, 366
hierophany: 44, 308, 309
Hindu: 2, 4, 10, 19, 20, 40, 41, 42, 154, 159, 261, 283-298

Hippolytus: 68, 89, 378, 379
Holbein: 167, 168, 170
Homer: 34, 44, 45, 85, 94, 332, 350, 351
*Hortulus animae*: 178, 180
Hours, Books of: 120, 135, 179

iconic books (selected): 2, 11-13, 35-36, 47-50, 63-92, 136, 142, 146, 208, 225-238, 284, 297, 389-390, 393, 396, 407-417
Iconic Books Blog: 49, 59, 407, 417
iconic dimension: 2, 3, 4, 14-30, 36, 129, 131, 135-150, 208, 253, 255, 284, 296, 297, 378, 394, 395, 399, 400, 412, 413, 414, 415-416, 417
iconoclasm: 2, 63-66, 75-77, 80, 86, 93, 99, 100, 108-110, 143, 145, 146, 226, 229
identity: 21, 72, 95, 97-99, 110, 209, 229, 230, 252, 255, 256, 263, 266, 270, 275, 276, 278, 332, 352, 368, 375, 376, 378, 384, 385, 390, 392, 393, 397, 404, 411, 413
ideology: 4, 129-131, 157, 159, 209, 268, 348, 390, 395, 402,
idol, idolatry: 2, 64, 65, 80, 95, 99, 100, 103, 109, 155, 161, 162, 226, 229
Ikea: 128
illiterate (see literacy)
illuminations: 16, 49, 72, 74, 81, 82, 95, 98, 100, 104, 109, 113, 114, 124, 135, 136, 195, 196, 229
image, imagery: 1, 3-4, 11, 12, 23, 165-186, 208-210, 222, 226, 227, 234, 283-298, 404, 408, 410
imperialism (see empire)
index, indexical: 23, 269, 273, 279, 354:
inscriptions: 15, 123, 384, 408-410, 412, 415
inspiration: 11, 22-26, 29, 48, 49, 97, 99, 104, 108, 109, 113, 172-177, 184, 190, 191, 212, 252, 390, 396, 400, 402, 403, 409
Irenaeus: 376, 377, 378, 379, 380
Irene (Empress): 100, 101
Isaiah: 29, 167, 180, 181
Isidore of Pelusium: 68, 373
Isidore of Seville: 97
Islam, Muslim: 1, 2, 3, 9, 12, 13, 20, 28, 34, 35, 40, 41, 42, 72, 95, 99, 100, 120, 122, 123, 124, 143, 154, 189-206, 225, 239, 253, 254, 255, 286, 290, 413, 415, 416
Brixianus Codex: 95
Jefferson, Thomas: 48, 49, 126, 351, 368, 416
Jeremiah: 104, 143, 177, 178, 183, 184,
Jerome: 69, 89, 167, 170, 379, 384, 415
Jesus (see Christ)
Job: 177, 183, 335
John (evangelist and apostle): 108, 113, 167, 170, 175, 184
John, Gospel of: 25, 73, 75, 99, 112, 181, 182, 226, 318, 319, 321, 322, 378, 379, 380, 413
John of Damascus: 75, 86, 87, 89, 100, 146, 147, 149, 162
John of Ephesus: 85
John of Salisbury: 112
John the Baptist: 69, 172, 177, 180-181, 183, 184,
*Joy of Cooking*: 48
Jewish, Jews, Judaism: 1, 2, 3, 9, 10, 11, 12, 13, 15, 17, 20, 26, 29, 35, 39, 40, 42, 69, 72, 79, 95, 100, 108, 114, 135-150, 166, 177, 179-184, 225, 251, 253, 255, 352, 378, 395, 397, 412, 413, 414, 415
Judas: 316
Judas, Gospel of: 378
Justin (emperor): 384
Justin Martyr: 68, 89, 377, 378, 379
Justinian: 70, 101
Justinian Code: 72, 88

Ka-gu-kyeong-hang (Kyeong-hang) Ritual: 300
Kalidasa: 34
*katha, kathavacak*: 266, 268, 276
Kells, Book of: 51, 95, 107, 116, 122
King James Version: 37, 44, 125, 130, 215, 254, 385, 395,
King Fu'ād *muṣḥaf: 198*
*kirtan*: 266, 273
*Kojiki*: 34
Koran (see Qur'an)
Krishna: 283-313

labyrinth: 307, 308
Laodicea, Synod of: 81
Laozi: 36, 45
law: 1, 40, 57, 72, 96, 97, 102, 104, 146, 181, 190, 204, 225, 246, 255, 283, 357, 362, 363, 365, 366, 371, 378, 379, 383, 396-402, 413, 416
lector (see reader)
legitimacy, legitimation: 4, 10, 15, 16, 22-23, 25-27, 29, 30, 66, 67, 69, 72, 79, 85, 87, 146,

151, 152, 157, 158, 160, 245, 248, 255, 256, 266, 275, 277, 349, 400, 407, 408, 409, 411, 412, 417
Leo the Isaurian: 101
Leo X, Pope: 168
libraries: 1, 2, 48, 53, 57, 82, 93, 95, 99, 104, 105, 115, 165, 193-194, 202, 221, 245, 306, 373, 375, 380, 409-412, 415
Lindau Gospels: 111
Lindisfarne Gospels: 28, 82, 96, 98, 99, 100, 101, 105, 106, 108, 111, 113
Lisbon Bible: 98
literacy: 78, 79, 85, 94, 96, 103, 104, 120, 123, 124, 130, 136, 184, 192, 197, 305, 307, 310, 315, 331, 348, 351, 352, 354, 402, 408, 410-415
liturgies (see also ritual): 23, 26, 36, 52, 65, 69-71, 75, 77, 81, 82, 87, 102, 107, 109, 113, 114, 147, 179, 214, 229, 233, 244, 245, 265, 275, 374, 378-380
Living Bible (*The Way*): 213-215
logos: 24-26, 41, 42, 75, 99, 101, 107, 110, 225, 348, 357, 379, 400, 401
Longhouse: 361, 363, 364
Lotus Sutra: 35, 40, 43, 45, 153, 310
Lough Kinale: 83, 111, 114, 115
Louvaine Bible: 182
Luke (Gospel and evangelist): 69, 100, 103, 108, 109, 167, 170, 174-175, 177, 178, 179, 181, 182, 220, 378, 379, 380
Luther, Martin: 42, 131, 167-170, 173, 178, 179, 180, 183
Luther Bible: 37, 44, 170, 171, 173, 174, 175, 209

magic: 13, 17, 65, 78, 79, 81, 122, 193, 239-258, 300, 303, 315-344, 365, 381, 410, 415
Magna Carta: 414
Mahabharata: 34, 35, 37, 293
Maimonides: 34, 181
manga : 217-219
Manichaeans: 381
mantra: 287, 291, 293, 296, 301, 306, 307, 309, 311, 312
Marcion: 379
Mark (Gospel and evangelist): 108, 167, 170, 172, 174, 180, 182, 378, 379, 380
Martyrdom of St. Felix: 382
Martyrs, Acts of: 380, 382
Mary, Virgin: 107, 175, 178-183, 321-324
Matthew (Gospel and evangelist): 85, 108, 167, 170, 172-174, 175, 182, 183, 378-380, 413
Maya: 408
Melanchthon, Philipp: 186
Melania the Younger, Life of: 84
Melville, Herman: 45
memory: 19, 20, 78, 96, 104, 115, 124, 146, 196, 197, 254, 292, 347-359, 373-388, 403, 404
Mengzi: 34:
Mesopotamia: 72, 225, 408-413
mezuzah: 415
midrash: 20, 39, 138-142, 144, 145
Milton, John: 34
Mishna: 36, 39
mnemonic (see memory)
Monophysite: 107
Montaigne: 45
monuments: 9, 11, 15, 20, 23, 30, 96, 209, 226, 357, 373, 379-385, 408, 413, 415
Moody Bible Institute: 213
Mormon, Book of: 13
Moschus, John: 85
Moses, Prophet: 25, 40, 108, 138, 139, 144, 145, 147, 225, 255, 398, 399, 401, 402,
movies, cinema, films: 10, 11, 15, 21, 26, 48, 56, 93, 126, 415
Muhammad, Prophet: 40, 98, 190, 192
museums: 28, 82, 358, 411
*muṣḥaf* : 189-206
Muslim (see Islam)
Mu‘tazili: 191
myth: 12, 20, 28, 64, 65, 68, 72, 73, 75, 77, 78, 86, 87, 120, 122, 161, 225, 226, 227, 233, 243, 247, 255, 269, 356-357, 369, 385, 409-411, 415

Nanak, Guru: 264, 268, 270
*naskhī* font: 199
neopagan 239-258
Nicaea, Councils of : 71, 72, 75, 100, 101, 103, 226, 382
Nicephorus of Constantinople: 75, 91
*Nihon Shoki*: 34
*Niṣpannayogāvalī*: 155, 164
*nomina sacra:* 99

oath: 16, 23, 72, 85, 96, 146, 246, 251, 283, 284, 303, 415, 416
Obama, Barack: 48, 121, 127, 128, 209, 416
occult texts: 239-258, 410
ogam: 96

omens: 409
oral, orality: 11, 16, 19, 20, 39, 40, 50, 96, 102, 122, 123, 129, 196, 254, 256, 266-268, 297, 301-303, 311, 349, 352, 370, 395, 401, 402, 413
Oral Torah: 39-40, 395
Origen: 104, 378, 379
Ovid: 35

Pachomius: 97
pathos: 24-26, 400, 401
Paul (apostle): 68, 108, 109, 143-146, 148, 167, 168, 170, 172, 176, 177, 184, 214, 321, 379, 380
Paul the Silentiary: 70
Perfection of Wisdom (see *Prajnaparamita*)
performance: 1, 9, 10, 11, 15, 17-23, 26, 27, 82, 93, 129, 208, 227, 228-234, 239, 241, 242, 251, 253-256, 267, 269, 270, 277, 283-298, 324, 374, 384, 413, 414, 417
performative dimension: 2, 3, 14-30, 36, 131, 137, 208, 211, 253, 284, 302, 303, 394, 395, 400, 413, 414, 417
persuasion: 15, 22, 23-26, 45, 84, 256, 400, 401, 402, 416
Peter (apostle): 108, 110, 167, 168, 170, 172, 175, 176, 177, 182, 183, 183, 319, 321, 331
Petri, Adam: 167-172, 175
phylacteries: 112, 415
Pickering Treaty: 361
Peirce, C. S.: 48, 136
Plato, platonic: 67, 78, 225, 350
Pliny: 68,
politics, politicians: 3, 9, 16, 20, 23, 26, 30, 44, 65, 122, 189, 226, 228, 230, 262, 347, 349, 351, 352, 357, 358, 369, 398, 407, 408-412, 414-416
Porphyry: 381
portraits: 21, 76, 103, 166, 172-177, 296, 408-409
*prajña* : 25, 157, 159, 161, 300
*Prajñāpāramitā*: 25, 26, 43, 153, 155-163, 305, 308
*prakash*: 272, 275
prayer book: 20, 129, 178, 180, 199, 319
prayer flags: 306
prayer wheels: 306, 307, 308, 312
preaching: 15, 18, 21, 22, 24, 28, 79, 81, 97, 98, 183, 184, 385, 399
print, printing: 1, 3, 4, 17, 49, 50, 51, 52-53, 54, 55, 57, 94, 115, 119-121, 124-133, 165-186, 189, 191, 192, 197-201, 203, 207-224, 274, 275, 299, 305-307, 310-312, 320
processions: 16, 22, 65, 68-71, 77, 79, 84, 87, 109, 110, 146, 147, 161, 208, 229, 272, 273, 275, 293, 362, 385, 415
prophets: 26, 52, 68, 378, 395, 397, 399, 401, 404
Protestants: 11, 21, 27, 39, 44, 64, 65, 87, 152, 155, 168, 181, 183, 208, 211, 212, 225-238, 300, 389, 395
provenance: 53, 54, 84
Proverbs: 142, 147, 177, 209, 332, 334, 396-398, 400, 401
Psalms, Psalter: 69, 83, 86, 96, 102, 104, 111, 113, 148, 183, 233, 296, 318, 320, 321, 322, 325, 326, 333, 334, 336, 337, 338, 401
Puranas: 37, 42, 294
purity, purification: 179, 191, 204, 271, 277, 294, 306, 309, 412,

Quintilian: 376
Qur'an: 4, 9, 11, 12, 13, 16, 20, 23, 25, 28, 35, 40, 41, 42, 45, 78, 98, 122-124, 189-206, 208, 225, 239, 384, 286, 294, 375, 414, 415, 416

rabbinic: 40, 138-143, 145, 148, 413, 414
Rabbula Gospels: 94, 95, 110
Ramayana: 20, 34, 45, 294
Ramanuja: 34
Rare Book Schools: 49, 60:
Ravenna: 70, 101
reader, lector: 14, 23, 39, 68, 84, 121, 125, 129, 130, 145, 195, 202, 219, 248, 249, 354, 355, 379, 414
reading: 10, 11, 15, 17, 18, 20, 21, 27, 35, 39, 57, 65, 68, 69, 71, 76, 80, 85, 93, 97, 103, 120, 121, 124, 128, 129, 130, 136, 137, 145, 148, 161, 163, 165, 170, 173, 178, 180, 191, 194, 199, 200, 203, 207, 208, 216, 227, 234, 251, 264, 266-268, 272, 275, 279, 290, 301, 303-305, 307, 308, 310, 319, 320, 324, 325, 329, 336, 337, 351, 354, 359, 378, 379, 380, 383, 390, 391, 393, 394, 399, 404, 410, 412, 414, 415
reception: 1, 11, 36, 51, 57, 96, 192, 304, 315, 316, 354
recitation: 10, 11, 15, 17, 19, 20, 21, 22, 24, 25, 41, 98, 122, 129, 196, 197, 199, 266-272, 301-304, 306, 308, 309, 320, 321, 324, 330, 414

Reformation: 67, 186, 208, 211, 394, 395
relic: 28-30, 68, 70, 76, 77, 78, 81-84, 111-113, 136, 152, 153, 155, 159, 164, 230, 300, 301, 305, 306, 416
*Res Gestae*: 384, 386
Revelation of John: 73-75, 175, 207, 210, 220, 378, 380
rhetoric: 15, 24, 44, 97, 153, 157, 158, 162, 256, 374, 400, 404, 413,
*Riding the Written*: 124, 125
ritual, ritualization: 4, 9-32, 36, 63-92, 114, 146, 152, 154, 159-162, 196, 208-211, 222, 225-344, 348, 358, 373, 374, 378-385, 399, 401, 409, 412-417
Roman Catholics: 104, 110, 168, 172, 178, 181, 182, 229, 253, 286, 318, 383, 389
Roman Empire: 94, 96, 373-388, 413
Rosetta Stone: 411
Rotunda of the U.S. National Archives: 416
Rumi: 34
runes: 96, 102, 122, 250

Sabiq, Al-Sayyid: 190, 206
*Ṣaḥīḥ al-Bukhārī*: 190
*Ṣaḥīḥ Muslim* : 190
Saint Catherine's Monastery: 94, 95, 98, 110, 384
Saint Augustine Gospels: 96
*sanchi*: 268
Sanders, Alex : 247, 248
Sankat Mochan Shabad: 269,
Sanskrit: 16, 20, 34, 290, 295, 296, 301, 304, 306,
scholarship: 1, 10, 11, 13, 14, 18, 21, 26, 192-194, 227, 302, 311, 347-360, 389-420
science: 285, 350, 351, 409
scribes: 4, 81-82, 95, 103-107, 113, 141, 142, 197, 397, 401, 404, 408-411
script: 95, 96, 104, 122-124, 129, 194, 195, 199, 252, 264, 274, 286
scriptorium: 95, 105
scroll: 11, 16, 17, 20, 48, 49, 50, 52, 73, 74, 114, 142, 145-148, 178, 196, 376-378, 409, 415
semantic dimension: 2, 3, 5, 14-30, 36, 131, 137, 208, 253, 266, 268, 284, 286, 294, 296, 297, 394, 395, 399, 400, 408, 411-412, 413, 414, 416, 417
September Testament: 131, 168, 174, 175,
*shabad:* 264, 266, 272, 275, 276,
Shadows, Book of: 4, 239-258
Shakespeare, William: 28, 34, 45
Shiromani Gurdwara Parbandhak Committee (SGPC): 273, 274
Shrine of the Book: 29
Sikh: 2, 4, 13, 16, 21, 41, 261-281, 415
silent reading: 14, 97, 129, 251,
Sinaiticus, Codex: 94
Sirach: 388-406
Solis, Virgil: 173, 175, 176, 178, 185, 186
Soka Gakkai: 12
Sophocles: 35
*sortes:* 85, 332-333, 336-338
spell (see also amulet) : 78, 80, 81, 301, 316, 320-325, 328, 330, 331, 339
St. Chad Gospels: 99, 114
Sta. Maria Maggiore: 74, 101
Starhawk: 248-249, 250
Stockholm Codex Aureus
Stoneyhurst Gospel: 28, 111, 116
stupa : 152, 153, 300
*Sukhmani Sahib*: 268
Sunnah: 40
sutras: 21, 40, 153, 299, 300, 305-307, 309, 310
sutra case: 306, 307, 308
symbols, symbolism: 1, 9, 11, 12, 16, 18, 19, 21, 23, 27, 34, 35, 47, 48, 64-66, 69, 74, 75, 79, 93, 95, 97-103, 108, 136, 144, 154, 158-162, 167-185, 209, 226, 232, 251, 254, 255, 265, 275, 277-279, 296, 304, 350, 358, 361, 364, 368, 369, 374, 376, 378, 380-383, 385, 396, 404

Taittiriya Brahmana: 42
Tale of the Genji: 34
talisman (see amulet)
Talmud: 20, 39, 138, 140-142, 356, 395
Tanakh (see Hebrew Bible)
Taoist, Daoist: 35, 39, 44
Tāra *:* 154, 156, 162
*tashkīl*: 199
*taṣrīḥ*: 200
Tatian: 378, 380
Taylor, Elizabeth: 93
Taylor, Kenneth: 213, 214
Tegh Bahadur, Guru: 265
temple: 106, 177, 179, 181, 182, 255, 261, 275, 277, 284, 286, 289-293, 295, 297, 304, 306, 378, 402, 408, 409, 411-412, 414

Ten Commandments: 9, 11, 23, 170, 209, 289, 294
Teresa of Ávila: 34
Tertullian: 379
textuality: 4, 143, 240, 242, 250, 253, 407-417
Theodore the Studite: 86, 92
thing theory: 168, 202, 205
Thomas Nelson, Inc.: 215, 216, 219, 233
Thoth: 78, 409
Three-Fold Law: 246
Torah: 11, 12, 16, 17, 20, 25, 35, 39-40, 41, 42, 69, 78, 142, 143, 145, 146, 147, 196, 225, 255, 256, 375, 378, 395-399, 401-405, 413-415
Tripitaka: 40, 299, 307
Trullo, Council of (Quinisext Council): 81,
Twelve Tables: 414
Two Row Wampum: 366, 368
Tyndale House: 213, 214, 216, 218, 220
Tyndale, William: 213
type, typography: 17, 48, 51, 52, 53, 54, 121, 124-131
Upanishads: 35, 37, 288, 294
U.S. Constitution: 28, 414, 416
U.S. Declaration of Independence: 28 :
Valmiki: 34, 294
Vaticanus, Codex: 94
Vedas: 20, 35, 37, 41, 42, 287, 291, 293, 294
vernacular: 20, 23, 34, 97, 98, 113
Vienna Genesis: 94
Vishnu: 287, 289
Vulgate: 37, 104, 167

wampum: 4, 361-372
Washington Bible: 54
Washington, George: 361, 362, 369, 370, 371
Washingtoniensis, Codex: 384
Wicca: 4, 239-258
William Rainey Harper 392
witchcraft 240, 243-256
word of God: 17, 25, 40, 41, 42, 75, 85, 102, 106, 122, 123, 191, 207, 210, 211, 214, 222, 228-230, 234, 264, 390
*wuḍū'* : 204

*Ye Bok of Ye Art Magical* (*Ye Bok*): 245-247, 249, 251, 252

*Zhuangzi*: 35, 36
Zondervan: 130, 131, 215, 218-221
Zurich Bible: 174, 175, 176, 178

www.ingramcontent.com/pod-product-compliance
Lightning Source LLC
LaVergne TN
LVHW010530100826
845148LV00001B/137

* 9 7 8 1 7 8 1 7 9 2 5 4 4 *